Prudence Crandall's Legacy

152
172
141
45
157
168
209
215
225
236
242
271
274
277
289
296
300

Prudence Crandall's
Legacy

The Fight for Equality

in the 1830s, *Dred Scott*, and

Brown v. Board of Education

DONALD E. WILLIAMS JR.

WESLEYAN

UNIVERSITY

PRESS

Middletown,

Connecticut

Wesleyan University Press
Middletown, CT 06459
www.wesleyan.edu/wespress
© 2014 Donald E. Williams Jr.

Manufactured in the United States of America
Designed by Richard Hendel
Typeset in Galliard and Klavika by Tseng Information Systems, Inc.

Wesleyan University Press is a member of the Green Press
Initiative. The paper used in this book meets theirminimum
requirement for recycled paper.

The Driftless Connecticut Series is funded by the Beatrice Fox Auerbach
Foundation Fund at the Hartford Foundation for Public Giving.

Library of Congress Cataloging-in-Publication Data
Williams, Donald E.
Prudence Crandall's legacy: the fight for equality in the 1930s,
Dred Scott, and *Brown v. Board of Education* / Donald E. Williams Jr.
    pages cm — (A Driftless Connecticut series book)
Includes bibliographical references and index.
ISBN 978-0-8195-7470-1 (cloth: alk. paper) —
ISBN 978-0-8195-7471-8 (ebook)
1. Crandall, Prudence, 1803–1890. 2. Women teachers —
Connecticut — Biography. 3. Women teachers — Illinois — Biography.
4. Discrimination in education — Law and legislation — Connecticut.
5. School integration — Connecticut — History. I. Title.
LA2317.C73W55 2014
371.100922 — dc23
[B]   2013046113

5 4 3 2 1

To three women

who inspire and

make a difference:

my wife, Laura,

my daughter, Nina,

and my mother,

Donna

CONTENTS

Illustrations follow pages 112, 208, and 320.

PREFACE

Since the founding of our country, many Americans have engaged in the legal and societal struggle to free the United States from the legacy of slavery, segregation, and racial prejudice. *Prudence Crandall's Legacy* views that struggle from the perspective of a nineteenth-century Connecticut schoolteacher and her allies. Prudence Crandall's story of creating a school for black women in the 1830s, while well known in its day, is often neglected compared with the efforts of other advocates and political leaders of both sexes and all races who have contributed greatly to the fight for equality.

Crandall's activism had an enduring impact. Of particular importance is the legal case of *Crandall v. State*, the first full-throated civil rights case in U.S. history. This book includes a detailed accounting and review of three separate legal proceedings directed against Prudence Crandall as a result of the discriminatory "Black Law" passed by the Connecticut legislature in reaction to Crandall's school, culminating in an appeal to the Connecticut State Supreme Court in 1834. Indeed, the *Crandall* case helped influence the outcome of two of the most fateful U.S. Supreme Court decisions: *Dred Scott v. Sandford* in 1857 and, nearly a century later, *Brown v. Board of Education* in 1954. Crandall's legal legacy also includes the prosecution of her brother, Reuben Crandall, for sedition and the judicial history of the *Amistad* case, presided over by Federal District Court Judge Andrew Judson, who earlier was Crandall's chief antagonist and prosecutor.

The intent here is not to magnify Crandall's contributions beyond their significance, but rather to place her achievements into proper context regarding the fight for equality generally and educational equality specifically. In order to better understand Crandall's work and influence,

I have presented her establishment of a working school for black women and subsequent legal battles within the context of her life story and the experiences of key allies, in particular, William Lloyd Garrison. I have included not only facts related to their public efforts, but also details regarding their families and personal lives in an effort to understand more fully their accomplishments and humanity. In following the trajectory of Crandall's influence on civil rights law through *Dred Scott* and *Brown v. Board of Education*, I have included the details of Crandall's life after the closure of her school as well as those who directly aided her; all of those who worked with Crandall continued in activist roles throughout their lives.

Of necessity, some of the ground that is covered here has been documented elsewhere. In that regard, Susan Strane's *A Whole Souled Woman* provides an excellent overview of Crandall's life. William Lloyd Garrison's life story has been well told beginning with the four-volume biography written by his sons and more recently in Henry Mayer's *All on Fire*. When describing the better-known aspects of the lives of Crandall and those who assisted her, I include new details or perspectives wherever possible. The story of her school and the controversy that ensued is informed by a thorough review of documents, letters, and news accounts in an effort to establish a definitive timeline of events and to separate fact from the speculation and fiction that was promoted by Crandall's opponents (and often passed in error into historical accounts).

Crandall's effort toward the end of her life to secure compensation from the State of Connecticut for the loss of her school is told for the first time with attention to the considerable legislative obstacles and opposition. The relationship between the *Crandall* case and the NAACP Legal Defense Fund's argument in *Brown v. Board of Education*, particularly in how the plaintiffs framed their interpretation of the Fourteenth Amendment, is discussed for the first time in significant detail. The arguments in *Crandall v. State* presaged the passage of the Fourteenth Amendment and inspired historian Howard Jay Graham's view of a "living constitution."

It is my hope that *Prudence Crandall's Legacy* will assist in understanding the work and life of Prudence Crandall and her unique role and influence in the fight for equality in America.

I would like to thank Kazimiera Kozlowski, the curator of the Prudence Crandall Museum in Canterbury, for bringing the Prudence Crandall story to my attention many years ago. In addition to helping to preserve Crandall's schoolhouse for future generations, she has played a critical role in documenting Crandall's life, and she and her staff have provided me with great assistance in navigating the resources of the museum. Thank you to the Friends of the Prudence Crandall Museum for their work in organizing events and publicizing the programs of the museum. Peter Hinks, author of *To Awaken My Afflicted Brethren: David Walker and the Problem of Antebellum Slave Resistance*, provided important encouragement; his work regarding David Walker is an inspiration. Mel E. Smith and the staff of the Connecticut State Library were especially helpful in locating original letters, legislative records, and the court proceedings in the *Crandall* case. I am grateful to Laurie M. Deredita and the staff of the Charles E. Shain Library at Connecticut College for access to the Prudence Crandall Collection in the library archives. Thank you to Eisha Neely at the Division of Rare and Manuscript Collections at the Carl A. Kroch Library at Cornell University, Rebekah-Anne Gebler at the U.S. Supreme Court, Christine Pittsley at the Connecticut State Library, Steve Fry in Elk Falls, Kansas, and Betsy M. Barrett, city clerk for Norwich, Connecticut, for their help in securing photos and images for the book. For assistance in tracking down key law review articles by Howard Jay Graham concerning the Fourteenth Amendment, I thank Lee Sims, head of reference services at the University of Connecticut School of Law Library. Matthew Warshauer, author of *Connecticut in the American Civil War: Slavery, Sacrifice, and Survival*, provided important advice. In Hopkinton, Rhode Island, thank you to Hope Greene Andrews, Scott Bill Hirst, Richard Prescott, and the Hopkinton Historical Association, and to Emery Mako, who in 2011 allowed me to tour the privately owned Hezekiah Carpenter House, where Prudence Crandall was born. In Elk Falls, Kansas, I am indebted to the knowledge and hospitality of Margery Cunningham. When my wife and I visited historic Elk Falls in 2013, many residents turned out to greet us; thank you to all who shared stories and to Gloria Jones-Wolf for documenting our visit in the *Prairie Star*. With Margery's assistance and the persistence of Steve and Jane Fry, we found the spot where Prudence Crandall's three-room farmhouse stood before it was destroyed by a tornado in 1916—a cellar hole in the middle of a vast and stony farm field.

Thank you to my staff at the Connecticut State Senate for heeding my plea not to promote the idea that I was writing a book so as to avoid the recurring question, "Is it finished yet?"

A special thank-you to Suzanna Tamminen, director and editor-in-chief of Wesleyan University Press, and her staff for their excellent suggestions and help in framing Crandall's legacy and to their external readers, who assisted through their insights and recommendations.

Finally, and most important, *Prudence Crandall's Legacy* could not have been written without the encouragement and understanding of my wife, Laura. This has been a journey we have traveled together. Thank you for your patience and inspiration.

Prudence Crandall's Legacy

1 : **Fire in the Night Sky**

Throughout her life, Prudence Crandall wanted to teach. Education offered the potential for opportunity, self-sufficiency, even freedom, especially for women, blacks, and the poor. Crandall discovered, however, that educating the oppressed involved risk and clashed with deep-rooted traditions in American society.

In 1833 Crandall's school for black women in Canterbury, Connecticut, attracted hostility and national attention. Newspapers throughout the country reported on the opposition to Crandall's school and the danger of emancipating blacks. On the evening of November 12, 1833, as Crandall's twenty black female students went to sleep, a natural phenomenon—some thought it was the end of the world—briefly overshadowed the controversy surrounding Crandall's school.

In the slave quarters of the Brodess farm in Bucktown, Maryland, thirteen-year-old Harriet Tubman slept soundly. Tubman was still recovering from a severe head injury that nearly had killed her; a slave owner had thrown an iron weight that hit her in the head after she had refused to restrain a fellow slave.[1] That November evening, her brother Robert stood guard watching for the white men known as the "slave patrol," who often harassed the slaves. Robert saw numerous bursts of light and shouted for Harriet to come outside. She watched silently as hundreds of stars broke free from their anchors and poured down from the sky.[2]

On the same November night, twenty-four-year-old Abraham Lincoln returned to a tavern in New Salem, Illinois, where he boarded. Lincoln, a struggling merchant who managed a general store and surveyed land, read the law books he had borrowed from a friend in the hope of becoming a lawyer and went to bed.[3] "I was roused from my sleep by a rap at the door, and I heard the deacon's voice exclaiming, 'Arise, Abraham, the day of judgment has come!'"[4] Through the glare of light streaming through his window Lincoln saw the sky ablaze with a thousand fireballs.

In the early morning hours of November 13, 1833, a meteor shower of extraordinary brilliance and intensity—"one of the most terrorizing spectacles" ever witnessed by Americans—turned night into day throughout North America.[5] One man compared it to a gigantic volcano exploding and filling the horizon with flying molten glass.[6] In many communities, including Natchez, Mississippi, and Baltimore, Maryland, residents believed that their cities were engulfed in flames, and sounded alarms. Tourists at Niagara Falls directed their attention to the flashes of light that descended "in fiery torrents" over the dark and roaring water.[7]

Yale Professor Denison Olmstead said no other celestial phenomenon in history had created such widespread fear and amazement. He calculated that he had seen hundreds of thousands of meteors in New Haven for many hours that night. It was "the greatest display of celestial fireworks that has ever been seen since the beginning of the world," Olmstead wrote.[8]

Some saw the meteors as a sign of hope. "I witnessed this gorgeous spectacle and was awe struck," said Frederick Douglass, who was fifteen years old and a slave in Maryland. "I was not without the suggestion, at the moment, that it might be the harbinger of the coming of the Son of Man; and in my then state of mind I was prepared to hail Him as my friend and deliverer."[9]

Others were certain that the meteors foreshadowed a time of great conflict. A minister in Winchester, Kentucky, opened his church in the middle of the night to accommodate frightened parishioners who feared they were witnessing the end of the world.[10] A columnist in Maine at the *Portland Evening Advertiser* concluded that the meteors signaled the beginning of the "latter days" and the end of civilization.[11] Another observer in Fredericksburg, Virginia, said the country could expect the rise of widespread violence and war. "The whole starry host of heaven seemed to be in a state of practical secession and revolt . . . which finds parallel only in the affairs of earth."[12]

■ During the 1830s racial tensions in the United States exploded. Nat Turner, a slave in Virginia, believed God had chosen him to lead other slaves in a violent overthrow of slavery throughout the South. After witnessing a solar eclipse in 1831 that Turner took as a divine signal, he commenced a bloody revolt that left sixty whites and more than one hundred blacks murdered in 1831.[13] Turner's attack triggered the fear of a broader slave uprising and terrified many in the South and the North. Southern newspapers claimed that the words of Boston publisher William Lloyd Garrison and black author David Walker—encouraging immediate emancipation of the slaves—had spurred Turner to violence. Many southern states passed laws prohibiting the distribution of Garrison's newspaper and antislavery materials and urged northern states to do the same.[14] Later in the 1830s race riots led to violence, destruction, and mob rule in New York City, Boston, Philadelphia, and other northern cities.

After Prudence Crandall opened her school for black women in April 1833 in Canterbury, Connecticut, a local attorney predicted no less than the surrender of the country to the black race and the end of America.[15] Andrew T. Judson said that Crandall's school was "a scheme, cunningly devised, to destroy the rich inheritance left by your fathers."[16] He claimed that Crandall and her supporters had disturbed "the tranquility of this whole nation" and "commenced the work of dissolving the Union."[17] Crandall's worst offense, Judson said, was to "have the African race placed on the footing of perfect equality with the Americans."[18]

Others weighed in with predictions of apocalypse and catastrophe as a result of Crandall's efforts. Her opponents said she planned to use her school for black women to promote intermarriage between the races and destroy the country. The fact that Crandall persisted in teaching black women was not "in itself so alarming a matter," one journalist noted. It was Crandall's support for an immediate end to slavery that created a larger threat. Her opponents said that immediate emancipation of the slaves would undermine the southern economy, cripple northern trade and commerce, and result in blacks "cutting the throats of all the white men throughout the south" and committing "horrible indignities upon all the white women."[19]

Legislators in Connecticut passed a law designed to criminalize and close Crandall's school. The Canterbury sheriff arrested Prudence Crandall for the crime of educating black women. Crandall noted that those who fought for equality between the races could expect "to be branded with all the marks of disgrace that can be heaped upon them by their enemies."[20] William Lloyd Garrison, who published an antislavery newspaper in Boston and helped Crandall launch her school, acknowledged he "had the worst possible reputation as a madman and fanatic" because he promoted immediate emancipation of the slaves and equal rights between the races.[21] Garrison's fierce opposition to slavery resulted in death threats; Garrison feared southern plantation owners would pay for his abduction and murder.[22]

Against a rising tide of violence toward those who opposed slavery and discrimination, Prudence Crandall—through the example of her school for black women—helped lead those who supported racial equality. In the first half of the nineteenth century, the abolitionist movement built a small but growing foundation of public support for equality in America, culminating in Abraham Lincoln's Emancipation Proclamation in 1862 and the passage of the Fourteenth and Fifteenth Amendments.[23] A century later the work of Crandall, Garrison, and their allies influenced the outcome of the pivotal 1954 decision by the U.S. Supreme Court in *Brown v. Board of Education*, striking down segregation.

In the 1830s and for many years thereafter, however, most Americans did not side with the abolitionists. Newspaper editors throughout the country attacked Crandall and Garrison as disturbers of the peace and opponents of the Union. In the 1830s Prudence Crandall and William Lloyd Garrison were national public figures—if not national public enemies.

Prudence Crandall's pursuit of equality may have originated in her Quaker faith, which associated slavery and prejudice with sin.[24] As early as 1688 the Quakers believed that "we should do to all men like as we will be done ourselves, making no difference of what descent or colour they are."[25] The Quakers were not alone in their quest for equality and respect for human dignity. The new world of America inspired dreams of equality long before Thomas Jefferson wrote "all men are created equal" in the Declaration of Independence.

"We must be knit together in this work, as one man," John Winthrop told the Puritans as they left England for America in 1630. "We must delight in each other, make others' conditions our own. . . . For we must consider that we shall be as a city upon a hill. The eyes of all people are upon us."[26] In 1765 John Adams wrote in his diary, "I always consider the settlement of America with reverence and wonder, as the opening of a grand scene and design in Providence for the illumination of the ignorant, and the emancipation of the slavish part of mankind all over the earth."[27]

The early history of America also included the introduction of slavery. Christopher Columbus reportedly had African slaves on his ships; on encountering the Native Americans of the New World, he wrote, "from here we can send as many slaves as can be sold."[28] Spaniards brought slaves to St. Augustine, Florida, as early as 1565, and Dutch traders sold African slaves in Jamestown, Virginia, in 1619.[29] Slavery represented the opposite of what John Adams had envisioned for America. "Every measure of prudence, therefore, ought to be assumed for the eventual total extirpation of slavery from the United States," Adams said. "I have, throughout my whole life, held the practice of slavery in . . . abhorrence."[30]

Many of America's founding fathers professed opposition to slavery. "There is not a man living who wishes more sincerely than I do, to see a plan adopted for the abolition of it," said George Washington in 1786.[31] In an address to the Pennsylvania Society for Promoting the Abolition of Slavery, Benjamin Franklin described slavery as "an atrocious debasement of human nature."[32] John Jay, the first chief justice of the U.S. Supreme Court said, "It is much to be wished that slavery may be abolished. . . . To contend for our own liberty, and to deny that blessing to others, involves an inconsistency not to be excused."[33] At the Virginia State Convention of 1788, concerning the adoption of the federal Constitution, Patrick Henry described the conflicts slavery presented: "Slavery is detested. We feel its fatal effects—we deplore it with all the pity of humanity. . . . But is it practicable, by any human means, to liberate (the slaves) without producing the most dreadful and ruinous consequences?"[34]

The founding fathers failed to outlaw the practice of slavery in their midst. Jefferson, Washington, Franklin, Jay, and Henry all owned slaves, as did most of the other founders. (John Adams did not; he and his wife Abigail consciously hired only free, white employees as servants.)[35] Throughout his life Jefferson remained uncertain about how and when to end slavery, and he could not envision different races living together as equals.[36]

"Deep rooted prejudices entertained by whites; ten thousand recollections, by the blacks, of the injuries they have sustained; new provocations; the real distinction which nature has made; and many other circumstances will divide us into parties," Jefferson wrote, "and produce convulsions, which will probably never end but in the extermination of one or the other race."[37] In *Notes On the State of Virginia*, Jefferson speculated that the intellectual capabilities of blacks were "much inferior" to whites and that blacks did not possess the same foresight, imagination, or empathy.[38] "Their griefs are transient," Jefferson wrote.[39] "This unfortunate difference of color, and perhaps of faculty, is a powerful obstacle to the emancipation of these people."[40] Jefferson later modified his view of emancipation: "I tremble for my country when I reflect that God is just: that his justice cannot sleep forever. . . . I think a change already perceptible, since the origin of the present revolution . . . preparing, under the auspices of heaven, for total emancipation."[41]

Jefferson wrote his last words on slavery—predicting its demise—in a private letter in 1826, the year he died. "The revolution in public opinion which this cause requires, is not to be expected in a day, or perhaps an age; but time, which outlives all things, will outlive this evil also."[42] Jefferson did not want to make public his prediction of even a gradual end to slavery; he asked his correspondent to keep the contents of his letter confidential.

In 1829 black writer and Boston activist David Walker, the son of a slave father and free black mother, challenged Jefferson and the founders. Walker contrasted Jefferson's pronouncement "that all men are created equal" with the "cruelties and murders inflicted by your cruel and unmerciful fathers and yourselves on our fathers and on us."[43] Walker asked whether England's oppression of American colonists was "one hundredth part as cruel and tyrannical as you have rendered ours under you."[44] Walker's words opened a controversial dialogue about the use of force to cast off the chains of slavery.

Slavery in America expanded significantly in the early 1800s. Alabama's slave population more than doubled in ten years, increasing to 117,000 by 1830. There were more than 200,000 slaves in Georgia and North Carolina, and South Carolina had more slaves than whites—315,000 slaves to 258,000 whites. Virginia had more slaves than any other state in 1830—nearly 470,000 or 43 percent of its population.[45] Slavery provided labor for planting and harvesting crops, transporting goods, and transforming wilderness into civilization. Skilled slave labor built many homes, businesses, churches, roads, and bridges. Southern families measured their wealth by the number of slaves they possessed. One official in Wilmington, North Carolina, noted that when a father married off his daughter, her dowry was measured in her share of the family slaves.[46]

South Carolina Senator John C. Calhoun, who had graduated from Yale and studied law in Connecticut, said slavery "was an inevitable law of society" where both slaves and masters "appeared to thrive under the practical operation of this institution."[47] Many agreed with Frederick Augustus Ross, who argued that the Bible sanctioned slavery.[48] Ross, a Presbyterian minister in Huntsville, Alabama, said that slavery in the United States provided a greater good for the slave. "The Southern slave, though degraded compared with his master, is elevated and ennobled compared with his brethren in Africa."[49]

The North had its own legacy of slavery. As one commentator noted, "the North found its profits in the traffic and transportation of the slave, the South in his labor."[50] Economic development in New England depended in significant part on slave labor, with textile mills and factories profiting from the cotton and raw materials produced by slaves. Throughout the 1700s and into the early 1800s, northern businessmen made fortunes importing and selling slaves. The northern slave trade involved distilling rum in New England, transporting the rum to Africa where it was traded for slaves, and delivering the slaves—shackled together in irons on crowded slave ships—to ports along the East Coast of the United States and plantations in Cuba.[51] Northern banks, blacksmiths, distillers, ship builders, sailors, merchants, and mill owners all profited from the slave trade.[52]

Stories about the mistreatment of slaves commonly were told and repeated among opponents of slavery. "I witnessed a heart-rending spectacle, the sale of a negro family under a sheriff's hammer," wrote Elkanah Watson of Massachusetts, a veteran of the Revolutionary War who later lived in North Carolina. "They were driven in from the country like swine for market," Watson said. "A poor wench clung to a little daughter, and implored, with the most agonizing supplication, that they might not be separated. But alas . . . they were sold to different purchasers."[53] White slave owners targeted black women for rape and sexual exploitation; by 1860 mulattos made up more than 70 percent of the free black population in North Carolina.[54]

David Walker wrote in graphic terms about the brutality toward slaves he witnessed: a son forced to whip his mother, a pregnant woman beaten until she lost her child, runaway slaves caught and murdered. "The whites have always been an unjust, jealous, unmerciful, avaricious and blood-thirsty set of beings, always seeking after power and authority. . . . We see them acting more like devils than accountable men."[55] Walker's writings in the late 1820s influenced a small group of activists, including William Lloyd Garrison and Prudence Crandall.

Prudence Crandall's unusual and privileged childhood began when she was born in the village of Carpenter's Mills, Rhode Island, near Hopkinton, on September 3, 1803. Carpenter's Mills was named for her maternal grandfather and grew as a result of his initiative as an early industrialist.[56] In 1770 Hezekiah Carpenter built a dam across the Wood River and created a series of small mills and factories that became known as Carpenter's Mills.[57] A community of workers and shopkeepers developed from the factories, and Hezekiah built a two-story home near the center of town. Prudence's parents, Pardon and Esther, lived with Esther's parents in their home.

Pardon Crandall and Esther Carpenter were married in Carpenter's Mills in December 1799; Pardon was twenty-one and Esther was fifteen on their wedding day. Esther wore a black satin, empire-style wedding dress—black was a popular wedding-dress color at the time—with a red broadcloth jacket and a red bonnet.[58] Four years later Esther gave birth to Prudence in the Carpenter family home—the second child for Esther and Pardon Crandall. Prudence had three siblings: an older brother, Hezekiah, a younger brother, Reuben, and a younger sister, Almira.[59]

Prudence Crandall spent her early childhood years near relatives and extended family members. Carpenter's Mills was located seven miles north of Westerly, Rhode Island, where her father's parents and many other Crandalls lived. Shortly after Prudence's birth, her parents moved into another home owned by Hezekiah Carpenter on nearby Mechanic Street—still within walking distance to Prudence's maternal grandparents and directly across the street from the mills. Pardon Crandall disliked living in a village dominated by his father-in-law. To further complicate matters, Pardon convinced Esther to leave the Baptist church—the church of the Carpenter family—and affiliate with the Quakers. Their conversion was not well received by the Carpenters.[60]

Pardon Crandall's unhappiness occasionally resulted in harsh behavior with his wife and family. During one summer Esther asked Pardon to take her to the Rhode Island shore, where she planned to meet friends for a picnic on the beach. After many pleas by Esther, Pardon reluctantly agreed. They traveled in silence for the hour-long trip. When in view of Esther's friends on the beach, Pardon turned the wagon around without stopping and returned home. "You wanted to go to the clam-bake," Pardon said. "I took ye, didn't I?"[61] Prudence Crandall's niece Rena Keith Clisby, who had heard the story repeated by Crandall relatives, noted that "men were stern in those days, showing little tenderness or concern for wives."[62] On another occasion years later, Pardon struck the family Bible, threw it to the floor, and shouted, "It's a damned lie!"[63] Esther rescued the Bible, and Pardon provided no explanation for his outburst.

Despite Pardon Crandall's occasional eccentricities, he wanted all of his children including his daughters to have access to education and opportunity. Pardon learned of other Quaker families who lived in Plainfield and Canterbury, Connecticut, and decided to move his family away from Carpenter's Mills. In 1813 Pardon purchased a farm in Canterbury, Connecticut, with the proceeds of a generous inheritance from Hezekiah Carpenter, who died in 1809.[64]

Pardon Crandall did not follow his father-in-law into the field of manufacturing. He concentrated instead on his farm and worked the land during the spring, summer, and fall months and taught school in the winter.[65] He bought additional land with money he earned from the sale of crops and timber. Pardon was not afraid to take risks; with his earnings from farming he took the unusual step of investing in a merchant schooner, the *Hope*, which sailed from Norwich, Connecticut, and frequented ports along the East Coast and the West Indies.[66] Pardon intended to sell his crops and livestock to distant markets and import foreign goods. The investment relationship concluded after only one year with Pardon presumably not reaping significant financial rewards. On balance, however, the Crandall family enjoyed financial security from the profit of their Canterbury farm and the inheritance from Hezekiah Carpenter.

Both Prudence and her brother Reuben attended the local Quaker school in the Black Hill section of Plainfield, a few minutes east from Canterbury on horseback.[67] Pardon Crandall considered the private school a necessary supplement to the local public district school, which offered little more than primitive instruction in reading and writing. "Reading, writing, geography, arithmetic, history, grammar, and all the branches of an English education were most successfully taught," one student at the Quaker school recalled.[68]

After classes the students often walked west across a red bridge that spanned the Quinebaug River to the shops in the Canterbury town center. They bought raisins at Stephen Coit's general store and "milk punch" at Chauncey Bacon's Tavern.[69] On arrival back at the school, "rye-biscuits, rye-dough-nuts, rye-bread (and) rye-coffee" kept the students in a "healthful condition."[70] Rowland Greene was the headmaster of the Black Hill Quaker School when Prudence was a student. Greene opposed slavery and later wrote an essay for William Lloyd Garrison's newspaper discussing the importance of education for black children.[71]

Many of the free blacks Prudence Crandall saw in northeastern Connecticut were former slaves. Farmers in her hometown of Canterbury owned slaves through the end of the 1700s. Throughout the eighteenth century, slave ships regularly brought captured blacks from Africa to harbors in the Northeast, including ports in Connecticut and Newport, Rhode Island.[72] Newport was one of the busiest slave-trading ports in America during the 1700s; slaves were held in pens on the Newport waterfront until they could be sold and transported throughout New England.[73] There were 951 slaves in Connecticut according to the national census of 1800.[74] By the time Prudence Crandall began her teaching career in 1830, the number had dropped to twenty-five as a result of antislavery sentiment and legislation that slowly phased out slavery in Connecticut.[75]

Prudence Crandall lived at a time of unprecedented social and economic upheaval; towns throughout Connecticut and New England experienced rapid growth and the dawn of the industrial age. "The manufacturing furor raged with great violence," one historian wrote.[76] "Everybody was hard at work, building, digging, planting, carting, weaving, spinning, picking cotton, making harnesses, dipping candles, and attending to the thousands of wants of the hour."[77] Men increasingly left their farms to work in mills, and a small but growing number of women left their households to work in factories or teach in the classrooms. The gentle landscape of open fields, stone walls, and family farms increasingly gave way to cotton factories, grain mills, clothier works, tanneries, brickyards, and sawmills. Prudence's brother Hezekiah decided to leave the family farm when he turned twenty-one; with his father's help he built a cotton mill next to Rowland's Brook in Canterbury that made yarn and rope.[78]

Hezekiah Crandall likely built his mill in response to speculation that a canal would provide easy transit for his cotton products. Plans called for a canal to connect all of eastern Connecticut with Massachusetts to the north and New London and the Atlantic Ocean to the south, and to link with Hezekiah's mill on Rowland's Creek. Before construction began, however, public opinion turned against it. A local newspaper ridiculed the canal idea as hopelessly outdated and embraced the new technology of railroads. In 1832 plans for a canal were abandoned in favor of the incorporation of the Boston, Norwich and New London Railroad Company.[79] The rail line did not pass near Hezekiah Crandall's factory in Canterbury.

The swift expansion of the local economy exposed the region's inadequate road system, which consisted primarily of poorly constructed cart paths. Businessmen pressured towns to raise taxes and invest in new roads and bridges. A few years earlier, residents of the nearby town of Killingly defeated a proposed turnpike to the Rhode Island border; taxpayers said they would "never submit to such invasion."[80] Despite pockets of opposition and the occasional defeat, most towns moved aggressively to build the roads and bridges that linked their businesses to the rest of New England. The Brooklyn and Windham Turnpike—an important passageway to Hartford to the west and Providence and Boston to the east—was completed in 1826.

Long days of work on the Crandall farm in Canterbury and in Hezekiah's cotton mill required hearty meals. Breakfast in New England was "no evanescent thing," Samuel Goodrich observed in 1832.[81] It often included boiled potatoes, beef, ham, sausages, pies, bread, butter, cider, and coffee.[82] The common bread of the rural towns was made from rye and Indian corn.[83] Pardon Crandall and other farmers set aside space in their homes to cure pumpkins, dry peaches and store apples, potatoes, and carrots.[84] Dinner included seasonal fruits and vegetables, meats, salted cod, and white beans baked with salt pork until the beans were thoroughly saturated with fat.[85]

Most New Englanders consumed modest amounts of alcoholic cider each day. "In the country, it is hardly considered reputable among farmers to omit to offer cider to any casual visitor or traveler," a traveler noted. "It is usually drawn in a mug or bowl."[86]

Local taverns provided food and drink.[87] Beer, wine, brandy, and gin all were popular. One of the most consumed and abused drinks in New

England was rum distilled from molasses instead of sugar cane. A day's wages purchased three gallons.[88] Those who drank at the tavern often were the first to hear the latest stories and controversies from surrounding communities. Private carriages and public coaches dropped off mail, newspapers, and passengers who brought news from Hartford, Providence, Boston, New York, and beyond.

Prudence Crandall enrolled in a prominent Quaker boarding school in Providence, Rhode Island, when she was twenty-two years old. The New England Yearly Meeting School, or the Friend's School as it was known, was located on land donated by Moses Brown, a Providence businessman.[89] After Prudence's first full year at the school beginning in the fall of 1825 and ending in the spring of 1826, she came home to Canterbury to help her parents at the Crandall farm. She did not go back to school in 1826. In the fall of 1827, however, she returned to the Friend's School and studied there for the next three years, graduating in the spring of 1830.[90]

The school's founder, Moses Brown, was eighty-seven years old when Crandall began her studies in 1825. At the beginning of each school year Brown met with students and faculty.[91] The Friend's School existed as a result of Brown's financial assistance and his desire to create a school that would teach young men and women "obedience to that principle of light and truth."[92] The Friend's School was unique in its progressive philosophy and attention to both male and female students.

Moses Brown converted to the Quaker faith when he was thirty-six years old, the same year he freed the slaves he owned and became a fierce abolitionist. He assisted runaway slaves on the Underground Railroad as they fled from the South to New England and Canada.[93] In 1784 Brown championed the first emancipation law in Rhode Island, granting freedom to all children of slaves on reaching adulthood.[94] He also introduced Samuel Slater, the English cotton yarn pioneer and industrialist, to Rhode Island and in turn helped establish New England as the center for the textile industry. Brown was personally acquainted with each U.S. president from George Washington to Andrew Jackson.

When Prudence Crandall arrived at Brown's school, she saw a large, brick school building, open fields and lawns, stands of oak and chestnut trees, and in the distance forests of maple and hemlock trees. Prudence likely joined with other students and climbed to the top of the school building's cupola where they looked across the state toward Narragansett Bay.[95]

Crandall's dormitory room was small and unadorned; Quaker traditions frowned on decorations of any kind.[96] Prudence and her fellow female students did not curl their hair or wear lace, ruffles, bright colors, or jewelry. Chores included sweeping, chamber work, carrying wood from the cellar for the stoves and fireplaces, and on occasion making the beds of the male students, which fellow student Elizabeth Buffum noted "in our narrow circle of amusements, was considered a privilege."[97] The boys followed similar rules; they helped with outdoor maintenance of the school and adhered to simple traditions in appearance and manners. "Plain language was in use and plain apparel, with nothing for show in form or color . . . no rolling collars or extra buttons for ornament on coats being allowed," one male student recalled.[98]

Classes began before sunrise and continued throughout the day.[99] Tin oil lamps provided light on each desk.[100] Faculty taught lessons in reading, spelling, and grammar in large classes with students reciting together. Other subjects, however, were taught on an individual basis. One of Prudence Crandall's classmates remembered "each student being independent and going as slowly or rapidly as his brain-power and ambition prescribed."[101] In addition to classes in Latin, natural and intellectual philosophy, political economy, history, and religion, Prudence and the other female students learned knitting, spinning, and other needlework considered essential for young women.[102] The entire school of 120 male and female students gathered together in the main room for Quaker meetings twice a week.

Crandall experienced firsthand Moses Brown's progressive educational philosophy. The Friend's School treated all students as equals. "All distinctions," Brown said, "are to be avoided as much as possible."[103] The students came from a variety of family and financial backgrounds, with scholarships provided to those in need. "They are all to be considered as children of one family, under the care of that body which interests itself deeply in the welfare of them all," Brown said. "The riches, the poverty, the good or bad conduct of their connections, must here have no other regard paid them."[104]

Living in Providence surrounded by students from throughout New

England exposed Crandall to a world with diverse perspectives and ideas. At the Friend's School, teachers valued the intellect of all students, including women. Prudence Crandall's academic and life lessons at the Friend's School influenced her decision to become a teacher and provided her with the confidence to open a school of her own.

When Crandall returned to eastern Connecticut in 1830, she began her teaching career. Connecticut's fledgling public schools lacked books and adequate funding. "There is no State of the Union today in a more desperate plight in respect to popular education than Connecticut in 1830," a commentator noted.[105] The "reactionary" repeal of the state school tax a few years earlier plunged the public schools—known as "district" or "common" schools—into steep decline.[106] "In addition to a lack of books, equipment was scarce and outmoded, facilities were poor, and teachers were underpaid and badly trained," one historian wrote. "Small wonder that teaching was neither a desired nor respected profession."[107]

Educators in the 1830s faced additional challenges. "The coming in of a foreign-born population at the call of the rising manufacturing interest" brought new languages and cultures into the classroom.[108] Connecticut had no child labor laws, and mill owners encouraged young children to leave school and work in their factories (the state did not address child labor in any way until 1841, when the legislature required that children under the age of fifteen work no more than ten hours a day).[109] Teachers taught obedience through liberal use of corporal punishment—the rod was a constant presence in the classroom. "If I was not whipped more than three times a week, I considered myself for the time peculiarly fortunate," remembered Eliphalet Nott, a student at the district school in Ashford, Connecticut.[110]

Connecticut native Noah Webster—the man who created the famous dictionary—spoke at a convention of educators in Hartford and pleaded for reform. Teachers could barely survive on their wages; male teachers were paid between twelve and sixteen dollars per month and female teachers received four to five dollars per month and were expected to "board round."[111] Reverend Samuel Joseph May, who moved from Boston to Brooklyn, Connecticut, in the 1820s and became a close friend of Prudence Crandall, "was astonished to find that the public schools were even inferior to those of Massachusetts."[112]

Prudence Crandall's first teaching job was in town of Lisbon, Connecticut, and shortly thereafter she taught at a small school in Plainfield. Plainfield was known for its numerous cotton and woolen mills and its excellent private school, the Plainfield Academy. Plainfield Academy attracted students from throughout New England and was "one of the most important, if not at the time the most important academy in the state."[113] Crandall did not teach at the Academy. The contrast between Plainfield Academy and every other school in northeastern Connecticut was not lost on Crandall. The families of most local children could not afford the tuition of a private academy. Amory Dwight Mayo wrote, "Naturally, the wealthy and educated class, as in all similar conditions of public opinion and policy, provided for themselves through the multiplication of private and academical schools."[114] Crandall taught at a more humble school where the conditions were similar to those found by Jehiel Chester Hart, a teacher at a district school in Connecticut. Hart described his school as an unsightly structure covered with poorly matched boards and an interior that was rough and tumbled down. "The seats were made from slabs from the neighboring saw mill . . . it was no uncommon thing to have them tip over and leave a lot of urchins sprawling on the floor."[115]

While teaching in the shadow of the Plainfield Academy, Crandall learned that the Academy provided a different model for educating young men and women, similar to what Crandall had experienced at the Friend's School in Providence. There was no corporal punishment. Instead, the Academy achieved results through "the use of moral suasion, and other kindred and kindly influences, in place of the rod."[116] At the Plainfield Academy, both men and women received lessons together in the same classroom.[117] Crandall sought to emulate many of the methods and practices enjoyed by those fortunate enough to attend Plainfield Academy.

Both parents and students recognized Crandall's superior teaching ability.[118] One year later, with the encouragement of local citizens in Canterbury, she made plans to open her own school and bought the former Luther Paine home. The house became the Canterbury Female Seminary, located in the center of town next to the home of Andrew Harris, a doctor, and across the street from Andrew T. Judson, an attorney and aspiring politician. Both men agreed to assist and promote her school for young women as members of the school's "Board of Visitors." Crandall bought the Luther Paine home for two thousand dollars; she paid five hundred dollars from her family's funds and borrowed the rest from

Samuel Hough, who owned a local factory that made axes. Hough also agreed to serve on the school's Board of Visitors.[119]

The community happily embraced Prudence Crandall's school for a variety of reasons. Public high schools or their equivalent did not exist in Connecticut. Parents who wanted an education for their daughters beyond the inadequate local district schools had few choices. Colleges were exclusively for men; Yale, Princeton, Columbia, and Harvard were all closed to women. Finishing schools taught women social graces and domestic skills but lacked academic rigor. Crandall's school provided a local solution for parents who wanted to truly educate their daughters. In addition, the town fathers believed Crandall's school would bring prestige and commerce to the small town by attracting young women from prominent families throughout the region and introducing them to the shops of the village.

As a show of support, eighteen local men, including three attorneys, a doctor, a minister, and local merchants, offered to provide assistance and guidance to Crandall and her school. Led by Andrew Judson, they sent her a formal note of encouragement on October 3, 1831. "Take this method to signify our entire approbation of the proposed undertaking, and our strong desire in its accomplishment," Judson wrote. "Permit us to offer you our efficient aid, and our cordial support."[120]

Crandall's school served the white daughters of well-established families in Windham County. There was no reason to foresee controversy for Crandall's school regarding the education of black women. The Canterbury Female Seminary was a private school. The tuition, while not exorbitant, was a barrier to some and would have been regarded—if anyone had thought about it—as impossible for the few black families in the region.

When Crandall moved into the schoolhouse in October 1831, newspaper advertisements promoted the new Canterbury Female Seminary: "The Board of Visitors recommend to the public patronage of Miss Crandall's school and cheerfully add that she has already acquired a high reputation as an instructress, and the assiduity and attention which she devotes to the health and morals of her pupils renders her school a suitable place for education."[121] Twenty-seven-year-old Prudence Crandall launched her school.

Crandall's experience working as a teacher in the neighboring town of Plainfield did not fully prepare her for the challenges involved in establishing an academy for girls. The idea of a woman creating a school, purchasing the necessary real estate, and serving as the school's director and head teacher conflicted with fundamental conventions of the day. When Crandall joined the Canterbury Temperance Society to fight alcohol abuse, protocol prohibited Crandall and other women from speaking at the society's public meetings—that privilege was reserved for men.[122] In the 1830s women could not speak or vote at town meetings. Ironically, the fact that Crandall was not married provided her with a crucial advantage; under common law married women did not have the right to own real estate, control their finances, or conduct business through contracts.[123] As a single woman, Crandall could control and manage the business affairs of her school.

The school operated continuously throughout the year, and students entered on a rolling basis. In the fall of 1831, more than twenty young women enrolled in the school. Most students came from Canterbury, but a few traveled from other towns and boarded at the school, including the daughter of State Senator Philip Pearl, who lived in the nearby town of Hampton.[124] Crandall expanded the course offerings to include art, piano, and French.[125] Her efforts impressed the Board of Visitors when they toured the Canterbury Female Seminary in January 1832.

Religion was always a central part of Crandall's life; she adopted the Quaker beliefs of her parents and attended Quaker schools. Crandall believed moral affronts such as slavery, however, demanded active opposition, which was not always the Quaker way.[126] At this pivotal moment in her life a religious movement took hold in much of the United States—a movement that drew her away from her Quaker roots.[127]

In the late 1820s and 1830s religious revivalism swept though the Northeast. After experiencing significant change in their social and economic lives, many Americans hungered for meaning and purpose beyond profit and materialism. Urbanization challenged agricultural traditions. Improved transportation created new markets and sources of goods, increased competition, and facilitated migrations of population.[128] These changes brought higher standards of living for some, but also hastened the end of a diverse and local village economy. Industrialization and the expanding scale of manufacturing threatened the livelihoods of individual craftsmen and artisans and caused many to question whether the economic changes benefited their communities.[129] As economic and social changes threatened older, familiar traditions, a new religious revival movement was born: the Second Great Awakening.[130]

Ministers such as Lyman Beecher preached evangelicalism as the religion of the common man.[131] "Men are free agents, in the possession of such faculties, and placed in such circumstances, as render it practicable for them to do whatever God requires," Beecher said.[132] Beecher was wary of too much activism, however, especially regarding slavery and emancipation. He opposed the immediate abolition of slavery and favored the plan of gradual repatriation of blacks to Africa as advocated by the American Colonization Society.[133] The religious awakening, however, soon promoted activism in all matters of reform, including abolitionism.

The religious movement became a crusade that challenged existing churches and denominations. Traveling ministers toured the New England countryside and held services in tents and open farm fields. Staid and predictable religious ceremonies were abandoned in favor of spontaneous revivals with emphatic and thrilling sermons. The charismatic preachers rejected complicated doctrine and spoke plainly and directly to parishioners. The outdoor revivals typically lasted three or four days and pushed all who attended to the brink of their endurance. In spite of exhaustion or perhaps as a result of it, those who participated were often filled with a sense of revelation and connection to the spiritual world.

The evangelical churches that focused on revivalism and reform included the Methodists, the Presbyterians, the Congregationalists, and the Baptists. Charles G. Finney, a Presbyterian minister who led revivals throughout the Northeast, was born in Connecticut, raised in upstate New York, and believed in religious self-determination. "Religion is the work of man," Finney said. "It is something for man to do."[134] Finney believed that true Christians followed the word of God and actively worked to eradicate sin. Finney expected the revival movement to achieve nothing less than the universal reformation of the world.[135] Finney preached against slavery on moral grounds, and other clergy and denominations in the Northeast followed suit.[136] The New England Baptists broke away from their southern colleagues on the issue of slavery and adopted a pro-abolition stance.[137]

Plainfield mill owner Daniel Packer—soon to be an important friend of Prudence Crandall—financed the construction of a new Packerville Baptist Church during this time on the town line between Canterbury and

Plainfield. For Packer, the church represented an opportunity to bring civility to a community he believed had deteriorated. Packer wanted to rid the region of newly developed "bad elements," including drinking, horse racing, loose morals, and general vice that wreaked havoc with his workforce.[138] A search for a minister resulted in the selection of Reverend Levi Kneeland, a graduate of the Hamilton Literary and Theological Institution in Hamilton, New York.[139] Kneeland became the church's first full-time minister in 1828. During the first eight months of Kneeland's ministry at Packerville, church membership quadrupled.[140] Kneeland baptized three hundred people during his six years at the Packerville Baptist Church.[141]

Prudence Crandall attended a number of Baptist revivals and started worshipping regularly at the Packerville church. On July 3, 1830, Crandall and a group of parishioners traveled by wagon to the banks of the Quinebaug River. Rev. Kneeland, Crandall, and a few of the church elders waded into the cool water. The current of the river was not strong in July, and they proceeded into the river until they were all waist deep. Holding Crandall's arm with one hand and placing his other hand on her head, Rev. Kneeland baptized Crandall as she plunged underwater—fully immersed in the river—three times in acknowledgment of the Holy Trinity.[142]

Prudence's interest in revivals and the "dunkers" as the Baptists were sometimes called, worried her younger brother Reuben, who practiced medicine in Peekskill, New York. Reuben believed her religious activity and attendance at revivals interfered with her responsibilities at the school. In the summer of 1831 he advised her in a letter to stop wasting time at revival meetings.[143] "Do you, all hands, run off three to four days to meeting?" Reuben asked. "If you, the principal, or your assistants do, I shall have a very poor opinion of the principal or her assistants."[144] This became an ongoing source of disagreement between brother and sister. "I said enough when I was home, and I presume you think by this time I have said enough on any of these subjects," Reuben wrote.[145] Prudence did not let the opinion of her younger brother change her course. Her faith played a significant role in her decisions regarding the school, and Levi Kneeland served Crandall as a spiritual leader and friend.

Another reform movement—the temperance cause—gained great popularity throughout New England. The ravages of alcohol abuse destroyed families and lessened productivity. During the 1820s and 1830s, community leaders and businessmen formed temperance societies in nearly every city and town with the goal of eradicating alcohol use.

"Every neighborhood had its death-roll of victims," historian Ellen Larned wrote, "its shocking casualties—drunken men and women frozen and burnt to death; children starved, women beaten and murdered, promising young men brutalized and lost."[146] In the late 1820s William Fisher, a foreman at a factory in Killingly, Connecticut, became alarmed when his three young sons did not return home after their last day of school. He did not know that teachers and students celebrated the end of the school year with generous toasts of alcoholic beverages—even the youngest students were expected to drink up. Fisher found his sons at the school, intoxicated; his youngest son was unconscious.[147]

The temperance movement swept through eastern Connecticut; the first temperance society was organized on August 25, 1828, in Canterbury.[148] Those who joined pledged to abstain fully from the use of "ardent spirits" as well as refrain from providing drink to friends or employees. Prudence Crandall joined the Canterbury Temperance Society and supported the temperance cause for the rest of her life.

The spring and summer of 1832 brought continued success for the Canterbury Female Seminary. Prudence Crandall had what most women of her time could never have—a professional career in a position of leadership, financial independence, and a life increasingly filled with the promise of security and stature. Crandall's family supported her work, and her sister Almira worked full time at the school teaching and managing its affairs. The community continued to embrace the school and assisted in its growing enrollment.

At the end of the school's busy first year the daughter of a local black farmer approached Prudence Crandall. The young woman knew one of the hired girls at the school and often visited during classes. She asked Crandall if she could enroll as a student; her father earned enough from his farm to pay for her tuition. This simple request likely triggered conflicting thoughts and considerations for Crandall. State law did not require segregation in schools or elsewhere, but social custom assumed separation of the races at most gatherings and functions. Many in the North opposed slavery, but few believed in true equality for blacks.

Crandall understood that if she granted the young woman's request she might offend her neighbors and supporters. She knew the admission of a black student could threaten the future of her school. Answering the woman's question required Crandall to reconcile her desire to meet the expectations of her community with the principles she had learned from her family, her faith, and the Friend's School. As Crandall met the gaze of the anxious, young black woman, she did not have an answer.

2 : **Liberators**

In the fall of 1831 a young writer sought out William Lloyd Garrison at his Boston office of the *Liberator*. Maria W. Stewart sat patiently as Garrison read her essays. The first concerned religious faith and "devotional thoughts and aspirations."[1] Garrison's interest grew as he read other essays by Stewart that called for an end to slavery and revealed the "intelligence and excellence of character" of an exceptional writer.[2] Garrison told Stewart he would print some of her essays in the *Liberator*—and publish the entire collection of her work as a short book.

Maria Stewart's book likely was the first political manifesto written by a black woman in America.[3] "Ye daughters of Africa, awake!" Stewart wrote. "No longer sleep nor slumber, but distinguish yourselves. Show forth to the world that ye are endowed with noble and exalted faculties."[4] Garrison published *Religion and the Pure Principles of Morality: The Sure Foundation on Which We Must Build* in 1831, and promoted Stewart's book in the *Liberator*. "The production is most praiseworthy," Garrison wrote, "and confers great credit on the talents and piety of its author."[5]

Stewart found a unique collaborator in Garrison, a white man willing to publish the opinions of a black woman at a time when the views of women of any color, on any serious subject, were not considered worthy of space in a newspaper.[6] Even the progressive Garrison, however, had difficulty in 1831 considering women as journalistic equals. He printed Stewart's essays in a separate "Ladies Department" section of the *Liberator*.[7]

Stewart wrote a brief biography of her life in the introduction to her book. Born in 1803 in Hartford, Connecticut, Maria Miller became an orphan at the age of five and lived with a minister's family. She helped with household chores and learned scripture, but longed for a more formal education.[8] At fifteen, she left the minister's family and supported herself through various domestic servant jobs. "How long shall the fair daughters of Africa be compelled to bury their minds and talents beneath a load of iron pots and kettles," Maria wrote.[9] During those years she attended church schools and developed an advanced ability to read and write.

She traveled to Boston and met James W. Stewart.[10] James was forty-four when he married twenty-three-year-old Maria Miller on August 10, 1826. James served in the War of 1812 and ran a lucrative business of "fitting out," or finishing, the interior quarters of newly constructed whaling and fishing vessels.[11] As a measure of the couple's standing in the community, Reverend Thomas Paul performed James and Maria's wedding.[12] Paul helped create the first independent black Baptist churches in the United States. His congregation met at the African Meeting House in the Beacon Hill section of Boston—the center of activity for the black community and the abolitionist movement. James and Maria Stewart's wedding likely took place at the African Meeting House.

At the beginning of December 1829, three years after they married, James Stewart became seriously ill and drafted his will. He died on December 17, 1829.[13] Maria and James had no children, and James left a considerable inheritance to Maria. When Maria brought an action in probate court to settle her husband's affairs, however, four white businessmen filed a separate action featuring a fraudulent Mrs. James Stewart. They succeeded in stealing James Stewart's estate and left nothing of value for Maria Stewart.[14] A friend described Stewart's experience: "I found her husband had been a gentleman of wealth, and left her amply provided for; but the executors literally robbed and cheated her out of every cent."[15] This was not an unusual fate for the widows of black men. Black businessman and activist David Walker wrote about such cases in Boston: "When a man of colour dies, if he owned any real estate it most generally falls into the hands of some white person. . . . The wife and children of the deceased may weep and lament if they please, but the estate will be kept snug enough by its white possessor."[16]

The meager opportunities available to black women frustrated Stewart: "How long shall a mean set of men flatter us with their smiles, and enrich themselves with our hard earnings?"[17] For Stewart, the discussion of ending prejudice and discrimination too often focused on the rights of men. "Look at many of the most worthy and most interesting of us doomed to spend our lives in gentlemen's kitchens," Stewart wrote."[18] "Have you prayed the legislature for mercy's sake to grant you all the rights and privileges of free citizens, that your daughters may rise to that degree of respectability which true merit deserves?"[19]

Beginning in 1832 Stewart delivered speeches on the issues of slavery and prejudice, often before mixed gatherings of both black men and women. This earned her both admiration and contempt; some in her own community did not appreciate receiving a call to action from a woman.[20] Women were expected to refrain from public speaking and avoid controversial issues.

William Lloyd Garrison's decision to print her speeches in a booklet and in the *Liberator* bolstered Stewart's efforts to challenge her community on a broad scale. A network of volunteer agents distributed the *Liberator* throughout New England.[21] These included many black individuals and families who promoted the newspaper and solicited subscriptions.[22] By 1832 several thousand subscribers received the weekly *Liberator*.[23] The number of readers was significantly greater, as subscribers passed along copies to family and friends. Stewart's call for equality for blacks and women commanded attention from many thousands of readers, both black and white.

Sarah Harris, a young black woman who lived in Canterbury, Connecticut, may have read Stewart's essays in the booklet printed by Garrison, as well as the other articles concerning emancipation and equal rights in Garrison's *Liberator*. The local agent and distributor for the *Liberator* in northeastern Connecticut was William Harris, Sarah's father. William Harris traveled from the West Indies to the United States and settled in Norwich, Connecticut. He married Sally Prentice in 1810; together they raised twelve children and moved to Canterbury, where William made his living as a farmer.[24]

The Harris family was part of a growing network of literate and informed black families who aspired to more than what the prejudices of the day permitted. Academies for blacks did not exist in Canterbury or anywhere else in Connecticut. William Harris was frustrated by what he saw as deliberate barriers to opportunities for blacks.

"The free blacks are prevented by prejudice and legal restraints from resorting to innumerable modes of supporting themselves and their families by honest industry," a commentator in Connecticut noted. "Our colleges and seminaries exclude them; the professions are sealed against them . . . they are prohibited, if not by law, yet in fact, from pursuing anything but menial occupation."[25] Reading the *Liberator* helped Harris imagine a country with equality for all. Harris thought so much of the *Liberator* and Garrison that he named one of his sons William Lloyd Garrison Harris.[26]

Maria Stewart's promotion of education and self-improvement would have resonated with William Harris and his daughter Sarah. "Many bright and intelligent ones are in the midst of us; but because they are not calculated to display a classical education, they hide their talents behind a napkin."[27] Stewart wrote that there were "no chains so galling as those that bind the soul," and encouraged her readers to claim their rights.[28] "Possess the spirit of independence," Stewart said. "Possess the spirit of men, bold and enterprising, fearless and undaunted."[29]

Mariah Davis, a close friend of Sarah Harris, worked at Prudence Crandall's school as a servant, or as Crandall referred to her, a family assistant.[30] Mariah was engaged to Sarah's brother, Charles Harris, and shared the Harris family's interest in education for black men and women. When Mariah finished her daily chores at the school, she occasionally sat in on classes with the white girls.[31] She read the *Liberator* and once gave a copy to Prudence Crandall; thereafter, Crandall faithfully read Garrison's newspaper.[32]

Sarah Harris dreamed of becoming a teacher.[33] On a visit to Crandall's school to see Mariah in September 1832, Sarah summoned the courage to ask Prudence Crandall if she could enroll as a student and attend class full-time.[34] Sarah said she did not need to board as she could walk each day from her father's farm. Her father could afford to pay the tuition. Sarah told Crandall about her desire "to get a little more learning, if possible enough to teach colored children."[35] Sarah also understood the magnitude of the request. "If you think it will be the means of injuring you, I will not insist on the favor," Sarah told Crandall.[36]

Crandall knew that no one objected when Mariah Davis sat in on classes after she finished her work. Mariah, however, was a school employee, not a student. The distinction was obvious and important. Crandall listened carefully to Sarah's request but did not give an answer. She told Sarah she needed time to think it over.[37]

Prudence Crandall considered the potential reaction of her family, the town fathers, the school's Board of Visitors, and her students and their parents. Crandall depended on the success of her school in a number of ways. Her family had invested in the school, and a significant mortgage on the schoolhouse was still outstanding. She employed her sister Almira at the school. The school provided Crandall with the opportunity for leadership and a career path with the potential for long-term financial security.

Crandall's first inclination was to deny Sarah's request. She later confided her doubts to Rev. Samuel May, who became a staunch supporter and teacher at her school. "Miss Crandall confesses that at first she shrunk from the proposal," May wrote, "with the feeling that of course she could not accede to it."[38] Crandall had succeeded against all odds as a single woman in establishing a well-respected school. "I am, sir, through the blessing of Divine Providence, permitted to be the Principal of the Canterbury Female Boarding School," she once wrote. "Since I commenced I have met with all the encouragement I ever anticipated, and now have a flourishing school."[39] Weeks passed and Crandall continued to ignore Sarah Harris's request. Despite all of the expedient reasons to be clear with Sarah and simply refuse her request, Crandall remained silent, conflicted, perhaps hoping that Sarah would not persist.

Mariah Davis continued to share copies of the *Liberator* with Prudence Crandall. In the summer and fall of 1832, articles appeared regarding the rights of women. William Lloyd Garrison wrote that advocates of immediate emancipation often overlooked the ability of women to assist in the cause. Garrison wrote that the cause of humanity is "the cause of woman," and women "undervalue their own power."[40] Without the assistance and hard work of women, Garrison wrote, social progress would be "slow, difficult, imperfect."[41]

An essay by Maria Stewart in the *Liberator* encouraged activism that combined religious faith with the fight against prejudice and discrimination. "It is that holy religion, which is held in derision and contempt by many, whose precepts will raise and elevate us above our present condition . . . and become the final means of bursting the bands of oppression."[42] Stewart noted that black men and women lacked the opportunity to receive an education, and called for change. "It is high time for us to promote ourselves by some meritorious acts," Stewart said. "And would to God that the advocates of freedom might perceive a trait in each one of us, that would encourage their hearts and strengthen their hands."[43]

In September, Maria Stewart delivered a lecture at a meeting of the

New England Anti-Slavery Society, at Franklin Hall in Boston. Garrison published her speech in the *Liberator*. Stewart said that black women lacked opportunity because employers feared "they would be in danger of losing the public patronage" if they hired blacks. "Such is the powerful force of prejudice. Let our girls possess whatever amiable qualities of soul they may; let their characters be fair and spotless as innocence itself; let their natural taste and ingenuity be what they may; it is impossible for scarce an individual of them to rise above the condition of servants. . . . Owing to the disadvantages under which we labor, there are many flowers among us that are 'born to bloom unseen, and waste their fragrance on the desert air.'"[44] Mariah Davis and Sarah Harris read the *Liberator* throughout the summer and fall of 1832, as did Prudence Crandall.[45]

Sarah did not let the matter drop. After she waited for what she considered a reasonable amount of time without receiving an answer, she made "a second and more earnest application" to Prudence.[46] This time, Crandall gave her a definitive answer. "Her repeated solicitations were more than my feelings could resist," Crandall said. "I told her if I was injured on her account I would bear it—she might enter as one of my students."[47]

Prudence Crandall's decision to admit a black student to her school was part of a growing and uncertain transformation in America. Black writers such as David Walker and Maria Stewart demanded an end to slavery and championed civil rights and citizenship for all free blacks. The first national antislavery convention of those who favored immediate emancipation was held in Philadelphia in December 1833. William Lloyd Garrison wrote that blacks were entitled to the same rights and privileges as whites and deserved equality in American society. Those views were far outside the mainstream of public opinion in the 1830s, but a perceptible shift was under way.

At the end of 1829, David Walker published a book that created a fierce debate about the role of blacks in the effort to end slavery. Walker's *Appeal to the Coloured Citizens of the World* created great interest in the black community and a firestorm of protest elsewhere; it also influenced those who worked with Prudence Crandall, including William Lloyd Garrison. What caught the public imagination was Walker's sensational call to arms; he said slaves should take up weapons and fight for their freedom just as American colonists fought for their independence from Great Britain. "Kill or be killed," Walker said.[48] One Boston newspaper noted the popularity of the *Appeal* in the black neighborhoods of Boston. "They glory in its principles as if it were a star in the east, guiding them to freedom and emancipation."[49] The editors of the *Boston Daily Evening Transcript* did not believe that a black man wrote the *Appeal* and speculated that the author was "some fanatical white man."[50] The *Niles Register* summarized Walker's book as "fanaticism, tending to disgust all persons of common humanity."[51] The *Richmond Enquirer* called it "the most wicked and inflammatory production that ever issued from the press."[52]

In the *Appeal*, Walker attacked a movement that had gained widespread popularity in the 1820s and purported to solve the problems of slavery and discrimination. Many of Prudence Crandall's supporters, including William Lloyd Garrison, initially supported the American Colonization Society (ACS) and its goals. The ACS was formed by a group of white citizens in 1817, including Senator Henry Clay, Reverend Robert Findley, and Francis Scott Key. The ACS sought to slowly liberate and "colonize" blacks in the United States by sending them back to Africa to the newly created country of Liberia. The ACS proposed a gradual end to slavery with an undetermined end date in order to placate the South and preserve the union of the states. Colonization gained significant support throughout the 1820s and 1830s.[53]

The ACS won supporters in both the North and South. Slave owners understood that removing the *free* black population would strengthen the institution of slavery by eliminating a competing source of cheap labor, thereby increasing the value of slaves. Slave owners successfully shifted the focus of colonization from ending slavery to sending free blacks back to Africa. They helped transform a movement that began as a means to free slaves into an enterprise that suited the needs of both slavery opponents and slave owners.[54]

The fierce opposition to colonization by David Walker and other black leaders, however, gave William Lloyd Garrison and other abolitionists reason to question the ACS. Walker equated colonization with banishment and surrender to the idea that those of a different race could never expect equality in America. "Will any of us leave our homes and go to Africa? I hope not," Walker wrote. "Let no man of us budge one step, and let slave-holders come to beat us from our country."[55] Walker's direct influence on Prudence Crandall is uncertain. She had access to some of his writings through the *Liberator*, but she most likely would have disagreed with Walker's willingness to embrace violence. Crandall's views, however, mirrored Walker's regarding the pursuit of equality through education. "For coloured people to acquire learning in this country makes tyrants quake and tremble on their sandy foundation," Walker wrote. "The bare name of educating the coloured people scares our cruel oppressors almost to death."[56]

Crandall drew on her Quaker roots and her new Baptist fervor to do God's will when she agreed to enroll Sarah Harris as a student. She considered whether Christians should "treat one with unkindness and contempt, merely to gratify the prejudices of the rest."[57] The articles and essays in Garrison's *Liberator* helped refine and stimulate Crandall's sense of right and wrong pertaining to racial prejudice.[58] Crandall acknowledged that the *Liberator* strongly influenced her decision to admit Sarah. She specifically noted how it exposed the "deceit" of the American Colonization Society's plan to return blacks to Africa, and convinced her of the wisdom of immediate emancipation of the slaves.[59] Crandall concluded, "Education was to be one of the chief instruments by which the condition of our colored population is to be improved."[60]

Maria Stewart likely influenced Crandall in her decision to admit Sarah Harris. "Shall it any longer be said of the daughters of Africa, they have no ambition, they have no force? By no means," Stewart wrote. "Let every female heart become united, and let us raise a fund ourselves; and at the end of one year and a half, we might be able to lay the corner stone for a building of a High School, that the higher branches of knowledge might be enjoyed by us; and God would raise us up . . ."[61]

In addition to the considerations of faith and equality, Crandall truly liked Sarah Harris as a person. Crandall wrote that Sarah was "correct in her deportment . . . pleasing in her personal appearance and manners."[62] Crandall was moved by Sarah's desire to become a teacher.

At first, there was no significant change at the school. Sarah enrolled and joined the other students in class. The students knew Sarah not only through her visits to the school, but also through her family's membership in the local Congregational Church at Westminster, where "racial background seems to have offered no barrier to Sarah's acceptance as a member of the predominantly white congregation."[63] No one objected when young black children attended the local district school, in part because of the young age of the children and the small number of black students.[64]

The white women at Crandall's school accepted Sarah as a fellow student without incident or complaint.[65]

It did not take long for word of the school's new black student to spread among the adult population of Canterbury. Crandall expected some criticism, but thought it "quite as likely that they would acquiesce, if nothing was said to them on the subject, as most of them were acquainted with the character of the girl."[66] The parents of the other students did not react favorably. Some approached Prudence's father and said they would remove their daughters from the school.[67] Crandall's older brother, Hezekiah, told Prudence that business at his cotton mill had declined because of her decision to admit Sarah Harris.[68] The patrons of the school told Crandall that, unless she dismissed Sarah Harris, the school would lose many students.[69] "By this act," Crandall conceded, "I gave great offence."[70]

As townspeople increased pressure on Crandall to reverse her decision, she responded with greater determination to keep Sarah as a student. The wife of an Episcopal minister told Crandall that she must dismiss her black student or else her school would fail. Crandall replied, "that it might sink, then, for I should not turn her out!"[71] Crandall presented herself with firmness and certainty when publicly challenged, but privately she had grave doubts about the survival of her school. "I very soon found that some of my school would leave not to return if the colored girl was retained," Crandall wrote.[72]

Only twelve months had passed since the citizens of Canterbury had embraced Prudence Crandall's school with enthusiasm. Now Crandall faced limited and troubling options. She could dismiss Sarah Harris or wait for the parents to withdraw their daughters and close her school. Under mounting pressure she thought of an alternative. She would not dismiss Sarah Harris. "Under the circumstances," Crandall said, "I made up my mind that, if it were possible, I would teach colored girls exclusively."[73]

The decision to remake the school and teach only black women was made by Prudence Crandall alone. She did not seek input from her family, friends, or the school's patrons.[74] She knew, however, that she could not pursue this change by herself. Crandall needed help recruiting black students from throughout New England. Her plan demanded great effort and courage, and she did not have much time.

Crandall reached out to a person she had never met but who had influenced her greatly. On January 18, 1833, she wrote to William Lloyd Garrison, "I am to you, sir, I presume, an entire stranger, and you are indeed so to me save through the medium of the public print."[75] She explained that she served as principal of the Canterbury Female Boarding School, and asked Garrison what he thought of her idea of "changing white scholars for colored ones."[76] She did not mention her decision to admit a black woman, Sarah Harris, as a student, and the adverse reaction in the community. Crandall provided no other clue as to why she was considering such a dramatic change in the mission of her school other than to say, "I have for some months past determined if possible during the remaining part of my life to benefit the people of color."[77] She described the necessary number of students and the amount of tuition they needed to pay in order to meet the expenses of the school, and she also laid out a strategy to recruit students from Boston and cities throughout the Northeast.

Months and years later, opponents of her school claimed the idea for Crandall's school for black women came from Garrison and that Crandall was merely a pawn of radical abolitionists. There is, however, no evidence that anyone other than Crandall originated the idea of transforming her school. When Crandall thought of the idea in response to the outcry after she admitted Sarah Harris, she broached the idea with Garrison in order to enlist his assistance—he did not know her or contact her; she reached out to him.[78]

"Will you be so kind as to write by the next mail, and give me your opinion on the subject," Crandall asked Garrison. "If you consider it possible to obtain twenty or twenty-five young ladies of color to enter the school for the term of one year at the rate of $25 per quarter, including board, washing, and tuition, I will come to Boston in a few days and make some arrangements about it. I do not suppose that number can be obtained in Boston alone; but from all the large cities in the several States I thought that perhaps they might be gathered."[79]

Crandall realized the *Liberator* had the potential to link allies together, facilitate a network of financial support, and provide the means for achieving specific goals. Crandall's letter impressed Garrison, and he agreed to a meeting in Boston. Crandall discovered a unique ally in Garrison.

William Lloyd Garrison lived a life filled with uncertainty and risk. Born in Newburyport, Massachusetts, on December 12, 1805, Garrison had an older brother and sister, James and Caroline, and a younger sister, Maria Elizabeth. His parents, Abijah and Maria Garrison, had moved from Nova Scotia to Newburyport before Garrison was born. Abijah was a sailor, and the economy in Nova Scotia had collapsed. "The scarcity of bread and all kinds of vegetables was too well known in this part of Nova Scotia," Abijah wrote.[80] He could not find work. Newburyport, a seaside town with a busy harbor, had a thriving economy. In Massachusetts, Abijah found work sailing as far south as Guadeloupe to pick up shipments of sugar, oranges, and other tropical cargo.[81]

By the time Garrison was three years old, Portland, Maine, surpassed Newburyport as the center for shipping and shipbuilding. In 1807 a federal embargo forbidding the export of American cargo, combined with declining prices for fish, quickly wrecked the economy of Newburyport.[82] Garrison's father could not find work, and the family struggled to survive. Garrison and his siblings often were desperate with hunger. Garrison's five-year-old sister Caroline ate a poisonous plant, and the family watched helplessly as she convulsed and died. Shortly thereafter Abijah left and never returned.[83] Garrison's family survived on income his mother Maria earned caring for infants of families connected with the Baptist church they attended. The two boys, James and William Lloyd, known to his family as Lloyd, sold homemade candy on the street, and the family ate leftover food from relief kitchens.[84] With help from friends and the church, they stayed together as a family.

On the evening of May 13, 1811, a fire began in a stable near the Newburyport harbor. Winds quickly carried it to the commercial buildings, docks, and wharves of Newburyport. As residents fled, they carried their belongings to buildings they thought were safe, such as the Baptist meetinghouse. A shift in the wind, however, put the entire town at risk. For the rest of his life, Garrison remembered when as a five-year-old boy he heard the roar of the fire sweep through the city and was held aloft in the night to see flames shooting out of windows and through the roofs of nearby homes. Garrison and his family joined those in the streets who had lost everything; they tried to make their way to safety in the midst of "the incessant crash of falling buildings, the roaring of chimneys like distant thunder, the flames ascending in curling volumes from a vast extent of ruins," and air filled with a shower of fire and ash.[85] It was a horrifying disaster that devastated Newburyport and the Garrison family. In all, the fire destroyed 250 buildings, including all of the structures along the harbor, the Baptist church, and all homes in the sixteen-acre heart of the town. Hundreds of residents, including Garrison's family, were homeless.[86]

Without a roof over their heads and without the support from the Baptist church, Garrison's mother left Newburyport with her son James to live with friends in Lynn, Massachusetts. Lloyd and his younger sister Elizabeth stayed in Newburyport in the care of a neighbor. Mrs. Garrison promised to send money to help support Lloyd and his sister, but the money was never sent, even after his mother secured a job. This arrangement continued until Garrison's eighth birthday, when an elderly couple, Ezekiel and Salome Bartlett, agreed to provide for the boy.[87] The Bartletts were poor; caring for Garrison was an act of Christian charity that placed additional stress on their already meager family budget. Garrison attended school in the fall of 1814 when he was nine, but soon left to take whatever odd jobs he could find to help them all survive.[88] He ran away once, traveling twenty miles on foot until a mailman picked him up and returned him home by wagon.[89]

His mother invited Lloyd to come live near her in Lynn with the family of Gamaliel Oliver, a shoemaker.[90] Lloyd's brother, James—who was only four years older than Lloyd—lived on his own and spent what little money he earned on alcohol. In the next four years Lloyd moved south to Baltimore and then back to Newburyport. He was shipped off to a cabinetmaker in Haverhill. All the moving around took a toll on Garrison. At thirteen years old, he ran away from the cabinetmaker and returned to Newburyport without a plan for his future.[91]

The *Newburyport Herald* had a sign in the office window, "Boy Wanted," and Garrison walked through the door. In the fall of 1818 he began a career in publishing that lasted the rest of his life. It did not begin well. He was hired for the position of "printer's devil." The primitive technology of the time required printers to light a fire underneath a pot of varnish and lampblack until it became a boiling, sticky cauldron of black ink. The printer's devil then applied the ink by hand to the metal type with sheepskin made pliable by soaking it in pails of urine. It was Garrison's job to make the ink and soak the sheepskin.[92] He thought of running away yet again, but stayed on hoping to advance from this bottom level of the newspaper business.

Garrison focused on learning his job and doing it well, and his superiors rewarded him for his hard work. He quickly advanced through the ranks of newspaper production and became an expert typesetter. He impressed the publisher of the *Newburyport Herald*, Ephraim Allen, with his talent and work ethic. Allen saw in Garrison some of the same ambition and determination that Allen possessed when he began his own career. Allen had purchased the *Herald* in 1801 when he was twenty-two years old; the newspaper went to press two days per week and had a small circulation. Allen served as the printer, editor, reporter, and carrier of the paper.[93] Allen's news-gathering technique consisted of traveling by stagecoach to Boston, purchasing all the newspapers he could find, and copying articles from other newspapers.[94] Twenty years later the *Herald* was the leading newspaper in Newburyport with dozens of employees.

Allen promoted Garrison to the position of apprentice and invited him to board at Allen's home. Ephraim Allen had six children, including a boy Garrison's age. Garrison discovered a world beyond the reach of poverty. Parents and children all lived together. No one went hungry. Garrison took advantage of the family's library and began an intense effort to educate himself; he read Shakespeare, Milton, and contemporary literature.[95]

By the beginning of 1823, Garrison supervised the production of the *Herald*. In 1826 he pursued an opportunity to purchase the *Northern Chronicler*, a rival newspaper in Newburyport. Ephraim Allen loaned Garrison the money needed for the purchase. Garrison was twenty years old. Allen and the staff of the *Herald* gave Garrison a congratulatory send-off on March 17, 1826. Garrison renamed his newspaper the *Free Press* and immediately plunged into local politics.[96]

The race for the region's congressional seat generated a fierce battle of editorials. Garrison backed the Federalist incumbent, while Ephraim Allen supported Caleb Cushing, a former *Herald* employee. Garrison and Allen had disagreed on other issues in their respective newspapers; however, this time the sparring became personal and consequences ensued. On September 21, 1826, with no warning, Garrison sold the *Free Press* to a newspaperman who quickly aligned it with the editorial point of view of the *Herald*. Garrison said he sold his newspaper for personal reasons, but one historian concluded that "it seems inescapable" that Ephraim Allen ran out of patience with his not so deferential protégé and called in his loan.[97] Garrison learned a bitter lesson in the ways of business and politics. After only six months he lost his newspaper. As a small consolation, Caleb Cushing lost the race for U.S. Congress.[98]

Garrison left Newburyport for Boston and took up residence in a boardinghouse owned by William Collier, a Baptist minister who published religious newspapers. Collier's newspapers promoted two popular social movements: the temperance campaign to curb alcohol consumption and the new religious revivalism. Collier asked Garrison to manage the *National Philanthropist*, a temperance newspaper with the slogan, "Moderate drinking is the downhill road to intemperance and drunkenness."[99] While editing the *National Philanthropist*, Garrison met Benjamin Lundy, a friend of Collier.[100]

Lundy needed wealthy patrons to help finance his antislavery newspaper, the *Genius of Universal Emancipation*. Lundy found little support even among progressive businessmen and clergy. Many reformers preferred to concentrate on less-contentious issues such as ridding society of public drunkenness.

Prior to meeting Benjamin Lundy, Garrison considered slavery as one of many issues worthy of reform. Garrison described himself as a friend to the poor, "a lover of morality, and an enemy to vice," and supported the temperance movement, antigambling efforts, and reform in local politics.[101] He had a high opinion of his own potential. "My name shall one day be known to the world," Garrison wrote in a letter to the *Boston Courier* in 1827. "This, I know, will be deemed excessive vanity—but time shall prove it prophetic."[102] Lundy's accounts of the evils of slavery helped Garrison conclude that slavery was the single most important problem in the United States, a moral outrage that demanded opposition and justice.

Garrison impulsively quit his job at the *National Philanthropist*, hoping to join Lundy in Baltimore. Lundy, however, could not afford to take on a partner, and Garrison scrambled to find another job. He traveled to Bennington, Vermont, to edit the *Journal of the Times*, a political newspaper created for the sole purpose of supporting John Quincy Adams in his 1828 reelection bid for president. While Garrison was essentially a hired political operative, he did find ways to write about slavery. Garrison attacked Adams's opponent, Andrew Jackson, and worked slavery into the story line, reminding readers that Jackson owned slaves.[103] The rival and well-established *Vermont Gazette*, which supported Andrew Jackson, accused Garrison of being a paid mouthpiece for the Adams campaign and said the *Journal* was nothing more than a broadsheet for John Quincy Adams, which was all true. Garrison denied the charges. "The blockheads who have had the desperate temerity to propagate this falsehood have yet to learn our character," he wrote.[104] The *Gazette* also claimed that Garrison and the *Journal* supported ending slavery through immediate emancipation, which the *Gazette* said would ruin the South and the nation. Garrison denied that charge as well. Immediate emancipation was "out of the question," Garrison wrote.[105] On election day, John Quincy Adams won Vermont and all of the New England states, but the South and the Midwest solidly supported Jackson, and Andrew Jackson was elected president. Garrison, still hoping to work with Benjamin Lundy, left the *Journal* and returned to Boston.

Surviving on a variety of temporary printing jobs, Garrison won an invitation from the Boston Society of Congregational Churches to deliver an address on Independence Day 1829 at the Park Street Church. The American Colonization Society sponsored the event and received donations collected at the service.[106] "The American Colonization Society has effected much good," Garrison wrote, "and deserves unlimited encouragement."[107] Garrison acknowledged, however, that colonization alone could not bring about the end of slavery.

Garrison wanted to utilize the speech to make a name for himself in Boston. He spent weeks working on the text and laying out the evils of slavery. A few days before the address he predicted his speech "will offend some, though not reasonably."[108] His dire financial circumstances provided extra motivation. "I am somewhat in a hobble, in a pecuniary point of view, and must work like a tiger," he wrote.[109] If the speech did not help him find employment in Boston, he told a friend he would return to Newburyport and plead with his former mentor, *Herald* publisher Ephraim Allen, for a job.[110]

The Park Street Church, which had seating for more than one thousand parishioners, was nearly full when Garrison delivered his address on the afternoon of July 4, 1829. Garrison startled his audience by demanding not only an end to slavery, but also full citizenship and equal rights for slaves and free blacks. "A very large proportion of our colored population were born on our soil, and are therefore entitled to all the privileges of American citizens," Garrison said. "Their children possess the same inherent and unalienable rights as ours."[111] He challenged the audience to consider the humanity of the slaves. "Suppose that . . . the slaves should suddenly become white. Would you shut your eyes upon their sufferings and calmly talk of constitutional limitations?"[112]

The only significant response to his speech appeared in the *American Traveler*, a Boston newspaper that summarized Garrison's speech as a combination of anti-American sentiment and procolonization advocacy. Garrison seemed destined to return to Newburyport. At this low point, Garrison received a letter from Benjamin Lundy. Lundy asked Garrison to join him in Baltimore to help publish his antislavery newspaper. On September 2, 1829, Garrison joined Lundy as the editorial assistant for the *Genius of Universal Emancipation*.

The differences between the two men were apparent from the outset of their partnership. At twenty-three, Garrison was seventeen years younger than Lundy, yet he had more practical experience in the newspaper trade. He had mastered the mechanics of typesetting and publishing at the *Herald* and served as the principal writer and editor for the *National Philanthropist*. While at the *Free Press*, Garrison drafted most of the articles and editorials without writing them out in advance; he acquired the mental discipline necessary to compose his stories as he set the type. In 1828 Garrison wrote in a more abrasive and fearless style compared to Lundy. Lundy once embraced slashing attacks on slavery and slaveholders, and paid a severe price. In December 1826, Lundy published an article that referred to a Baltimore slave trader as a "demon" and a "monster in human-shape."[113] Shortly thereafter, the man attacked Lundy—he choked him and repeatedly kicked Lundy in the head.[114] "I was assaulted and nearly killed," Lundy said.[115] Lundy's assailant was charged with assault, and the jury returned a verdict of guilty; the judge imposed a fine of one dollar. After defending slavery and noting its importance to Maryland's economy, the judge told Lundy, "If abusive language could ever be a justification for battery, this was that case."[116] Lundy realized those who challenged slavery had few protections; from that point forward he tempered his antislavery commentaries.

The two editors did agree that ending slavery would take time; Garrison, Lundy, and nearly all opponents of slavery supported a gradual approach and colonization. Even that point of agreement, however, soon changed. While in Baltimore, Garrison discovered Lundy's extensive library of antislavery literature. Garrison read *The Book and Slavery Irrec-*

oncilable, written by George Bourne in 1816. Bourne's book, together with David Walker's *Appeal* and a pamphlet written in 1824 by British abolitionist Elizabeth Heyrick, dramatically changed Garrison's thinking about slavery.

George Bourne is regarded by some as the first man in America to call for the immediate emancipation of the slaves.[117] In *The Book and Slavery Irreconcilable*, the "book" was the Bible, and Bourne equated slavery with sin. "A gradual emancipation is a virtual recognition of the right, and establishes the rectitude of the practice," Bourne wrote. "If it be just for one moment, it is hallowed for ever; and if it be inequitable, not a day should it be tolerated."[118]

In 1824 British writer Elizabeth Heyrick reached the same conclusion as Bourne, summed up in the title of her booklet, *Immediate, Not Gradual Abolition*. Heyrick wrote that delaying the end of slavery affirmed the institution and was the equivalent of doing nothing.[119] "An immediate emancipation then, is the object to be aimed at," Heyrick wrote. "It is more wise and rational, more politic and safe, as well as more just and humane, than gradual emancipation."[120] Benjamin Lundy promoted Heyrick's pamphlet in his newspaper.[121]

In his *Appeal to the Coloured Citizens of the World* in 1829, David Walker called for the immediate end of slavery. Lundy condemned Walker's book because of Walker's willingness to embrace violence as a means of destroying slavery. Garrison, however, was less critical. "It is not for the American people, as a nation, to denounce it as bloody or monstrous," Garrison said. Garrison reminded readers that colonists violently took up arms to shoot and kill the British and win a war of freedom. "Mr. Walker but pays them in their own coin, but follows their own creed, but adopts their own language. . . . If any people were ever justified in throwing off the yoke of their tyrants, the slaves are that people."[122] After reading Bourne, Heyrick, and Walker, Garrison embraced immediate emancipation and rejected the idea of colonization—sending free blacks and slaves back to Africa—as dangerous and wrong.

Garrison's partnership with Lundy concluded after six months. In that time, the *Genius of Universal Emancipation* suffered serious financial losses as the result of a libel suit filed against Garrison. Garrison accused merchant Francis Todd of Newburyport of transporting slaves on ships that Todd owned. During the course of the trial, Garrison proved that Todd in fact transported slaves. It made no difference. In the slave state of Maryland, the jury quickly returned a verdict of guilty. The judge fined Garrison fifty dollars plus costs, bringing the total fine to seventy dollars, and sentenced him to six months in the Baltimore jail beginning on April 17, 1830.[123] Lundy published Garrison's report of his trial and imprisonment, and he visited Garrison at the jail every day.[124]

Garrison received many visitors, sent many letters, and wrote protests on the prison walls. "The tyranny of the court has triumphed over every principle of justice, and even over the law—and here I am in limbo," Garrison said.[125] He spoke with escaped slaves who were held at the jail and befriended the warden, who allowed him to dine with his family. "True it is, I am in prison, as snug as a robin in his cage; but I sing as often, and quite as well, as I did before my wings were clipped," Garrison wrote.[126]

For Benjamin Lundy, Garrison's imprisonment meant the end of the *Genius of Universal Emancipation* as a weekly newspaper. As a result of "scanty patronage" and threats of more lawsuits, Lundy announced plans to scale back to a monthly publication.[127] Shortly thereafter, Lundy received a letter from New York businessman Arthur Tappan. "I have read the sketch of the trial of Mr. Garrison with that deep feeling of abhorrence of slavery," Tappan wrote. "If one hundred dollars will give him his liberty, you are hereby authorized to draw on me for that sum, and I will gladly make a donation of the same amount to aid you and Mr. Garrison in re-establishing the *Genius of Universal Emancipation*."[128] With Tappan's gift, Lundy paid Garrison's fine, and the sympathetic warden assisted in his early release from prison. On June 5, 1830, Garrison walked out of the Baltimore Jail after serving forty-nine days of his six-month sentence.[129]

Despite Arthur Tappan's hope that Lundy and Garrison would continue their partnership, their differences in style and approach convinced them to go separate ways. In a farewell to their readers, Lundy praised Garrison's "strict integrity, amiable deportment, and virtuous conduct." Garrison added, "We shall ever remain one in spirit and purpose."[130] Garrison had no regrets. "In all my writings I have used strong, indignant, vehement language, and direct, pointed, scorching reproof," Garrison said. "I have nothing to recall."[131]

While in jail, Garrison resolved to dedicate his life to the eradication of slavery. "Everyone who comes into the world should do something to repair its moral desolation, and to restore its pristine loveliness," Garrison wrote. "He who does not assist, but slumbers away his life in idleness, defeats one great purpose of his creation."[132] On his release, Garrison began a lecture tour to raise money for a new newspaper.

City officials and leaders in Boston did not rejoice when Garrison returned to the city in 1830. He tried to reserve a hall in Boston for a speech, but everyone he contacted refused his request. As a last resort, he announced plans for a speech on the Boston Common. The prospect of a large and unruly gathering on the Common changed the minds of city leaders. They quickly issued an invitation for the free use of Julien Hall, and Garrison accepted.[133]

Boston's abolitionist community turned out to hear Garrison on October 15, 1830. The audience included John Tappan, brother of Arthur Tappan; Moses Grant, a prominent local merchant in the paper business who was active in the temperance movement; attorney Samuel E. Sewall; and a number of ministers, including Lyman Beecher and Samuel Joseph May, a Unitarian minister from Brooklyn, Connecticut. Garrison discussed the "sinfulness of slave-holding" and "the duplicity of the Colonization Society." He also said, "Immediate, unconditional emancipation is the right of every slave and the duty of every master."[134]

Garrison's speech had a powerful effect. "That is a providential man; he is a prophet; he will shake our nation to its center, but he will shake slavery out of it," May said. "We ought to know him, we ought to help him."[135] May came from a prominent Boston family and had graduated from the Harvard Divinity School. He assisted at churches in Boston and New York City before accepting a call to a church in Brooklyn, Connecticut. Garrison, May, Amos Alcott, and Samuel Sewall gathered at Alcott's home after the speech. "Mr. Garrison, I am not sure that I can indorse all you have said this evening," May said. "Much of it requires careful consideration. But I am prepared to embrace *you*. I am sure you are called to a great work, and I mean to help you."[136]

May recalled an incident from the summer of 1821, when he and his sister traveled from Washington, D.C., to Baltimore to visit friends and relatives. While riding in a public stagecoach, they saw a row of black men chained together in handcuffs walking behind a wagon, and young children in another wagon, lying on straw. "My first thought was that they were prisoners," May said. "Scarcely had I uttered the words, when the truth flashed . . . They are slaves."[137] May recalled that another passenger, a southerner, noticed May's reaction: "It is bad. It is shameful. But it was entailed upon us. What can we do?"[138]

May had agreed to preach at the Summer Street Church in Boston as a favor to a minister who was away and decided to change the focus of his sermon to slavery. "It is our prejudice against the color of these poor people that makes us consent to the tremendous wrongs they are suffering," May said.[139] He concluded with a dramatic call to either end slavery or break up the United States. "Tell me not that we are forbidden by the Constitution of our country to interfere in behalf of the enslaved. . . . If need be, the very foundations of our Republic must be broken up . . . It cannot stand, it ought not to stand, it will not stand, on the necks of millions of men. For God is just, and his justice will not sleep forever."[140]

The congregation reacted with bewilderment and outrage that rippled through the rows of parishioners. May acknowledged the response at the end of the service, but did not apologize. "Everyone present must be conscious that the closing remarks of my sermon have caused an unusual emotion throughout the church," May said. "I am glad. Would to God that a deeper emotion could be sent throughout our land."[141] A woman who approached May after the service told him, "Mr. May, I thank you. What a shame it is that I, who have been a constant attendant from my childhood in this or some other Christian church, am obliged to confess that today, for the first time, I have heard from the pulpit a plea for the oppressed, the enslaved millions in our land."[142]

Not everyone who heard Garrison's speech had the same positive reaction as Samuel May. Moses Grant, the paper merchant, rejected Garrison's call for immediate emancipation and declined to help.[143] John Tappan strongly supported colonization and told his brother Arthur it was a shame he had bailed Garrison out of jail.[144]

Gradually, Garrison enlisted the help of other friends and supporters. Isaac Knapp, a boyhood friend and the original owner of the *Free Press*, offered typesetting assistance. Stephen Foster, a colleague at one of the religious papers, the *Christian Watchman*, volunteered to print Garrison's newspaper until he could afford a press of his own.[145] With the publishing arrangements in place, the newspaper needed a memorable name. Samuel Sewall suggested the *Safety Lamp*.[146] Garrison initially proposed to call it the *Public Liberator and Journal of the Times*.[147] This became the *Public Liberator*, and finally, the *Liberator*. The *Liberator* became the most famous, influential, and longest running of any abolitionist newspaper.

In the fall of 1830, Garrison reached out to the black population of Boston for support and subscriptions. Many knew of Garrison's brief partnership with Benjamin Lundy, his imprisonment in Baltimore, and his Independence Day speech regarding slavery. In the fall of 1830, the black community in Boston needed advocates. The black newspaper *Freedom's Journal* had ceased publication in 1829. Black leader David Walker had died, most likely as a result of tuberculosis, although some believed he was poisoned and murdered. The lanky twenty-four-year-old Garrison begged the question—how could this young, white man know of the trials and needs of the black community? Garrison persisted, and in November and December of 1830, he received support at black churches and in meetings with black leaders. As one commentator later wrote, "It is no wonder that, after launching his operation without a single subscriber or a penny in reserve, with borrowed type and paper obtained on the shakiest of credit, he quickly picked up 450 subscribers, of whom 400 were Negroes."[148]

Garrison published volume one, number one of the *Liberator* in Boston on New Year's Day 1831. In the time since his Independence Day speech in 1829, he had witnessed slave auctions in the markets and streets of Baltimore. He had supported and then rejected colonization and its goal of returning blacks to Africa, an idea "full of timidity, injustice and absurdity."[149] Garrison took aim at both the slave owners in the South and slavery apologists in the North. Comparing his time in Baltimore with his years in Massachusetts, Garrison concluded that prejudice in the North was as bad and often worse than in the South. "I found contempt more bitter, opposition more active, detraction more relentless, prejudice more stubborn, and apathy more frozen, than among slave owners themselves," Garrison said.[150] "I determined, at every hazard, to lift up the standard of emancipation in the eyes of the nation, within the sight of Bunker Hill and in the birthplace of liberty."[151]

While Garrison did not embrace violence, he aligned himself with the activist philosophy of David Walker. "Let all the enemies of the persecuted blacks tremble," Garrison wrote in his passionate statement of purpose. "I *will be* as harsh as truth, and as uncompromising as justice. . . .

I will not equivocate—I will not excuse—I will not retreat a single inch—AND I WILL BE HEARD."[152]

Garrison's launch of the *Liberator* in January 1831, when he was twenty-five years old, was an act of faith. From a business point of view the entire enterprise, held together with borrowed assets and romantic notions, seemed doomed to failure. The cause of the newspaper—the immediate abolition of slavery—severely limited his base of subscribers and advertisers. This did not deter Garrison. "The curse of our age is, men love popularity better than truth, and expediency better than justice," he wrote.[153] The modest success he had achieved did not make him cautious. Instead, Garrison vowed to risk everything, his newspaper, what little money he had earned, his safety, his own freedom—everything—in a cause he knew was right.

3 : Education for All

Prudence Crandall told no one in Canterbury about her plans to teach black women at her school; she confided only in William Lloyd Garrison. "I do not dare tell any one of my neighbors anything about the contemplated change in my school," she wrote to Garrison, "and I beg of you, sir, that you will not expose it to anyone; for if it was known, I have no reason to expect but it would ruin my present school."[1] To emphasize the point she ended her letter by saying, "I must once more beg you not to expose this matter until we see how the case will be determined."[2]

There is no evidence that Crandall seriously considered reversing her decision to admit Sarah Harris; however, she clearly did not want to lose her school. Crandall decided to travel to Boston to meet Garrison and discuss the feasibility of recruiting black students. She told local supporters, including her pastor, Levi Kneeland, that she planned to visit schools and purchase supplies, and she asked for letters of introduction to those who could assist her in Boston. She told no one of her meeting with Garrison or her idea to change the mission of her school. Eleven days later on January 29, 1833, she took the stagecoach from Canterbury to Boston.

The coach arrived at the Marlboro Hotel, a four-story building that served as the depot for many stagecoach routes.[3] The Marlboro was the oldest hotel in Boston; Lafayette stayed there, as did John Quincy Adams and Daniel Webster.[4] James Barker, the manager of the hotel, received Prudence Crandall when she arrived. She gave Barker a note that he promptly delivered to Garrison: "The lady that wrote you a short time since would inform you that she is now in town, and should be very thankful if you would call at Mr. Barker's Hotel and see her a few moments this evening at six o'clock."[5] Garrison was familiar with the Marlboro's large hall for speeches and its several drawing rooms for smaller meetings.

Garrison did not wish to see Crandall's idea of a school for black women meet the same fate as a recently defeated proposal for a black college in New Haven, Connecticut. In June 1831, Simeon S. Jocelyn—a white minister of a black church—told Garrison of his plans to create a black college. Arthur Tappan agreed to purchase the land and raise funds for the new school. Garrison visited New Haven and wrote that the laws of the city were "salutary and protecting to all, without regard to complexion."[6] Garrison made those observations before the Nat Turner insurrection in August, when Turner led the slave uprising that resulted in the deaths of hundreds of blacks and whites. One month later, with fears of black rebellion and violence fanning northward, city residents at a town meeting voted overwhelmingly against the creation of a black college in New Haven, much to the discouragement of Garrison.[7]

Prudence Crandall met with Garrison in one of the drawing rooms at the Marlboro that wintry Tuesday evening. Each was likely a surprise to the other. Garrison, the emphatic abolitionist in print, was reserved and polite in person. Crandall, who had come to Boston to explain why she wanted to risk her financial future for the benefit of black women, was an educator, not a political activist. They both were passionate about their work. Crandall described her plans for the new school. Garrison conveyed his concerns based on the events in New Haven. Garrison also came prepared to answer Crandall's specific questions about recruiting students from cities in the Northeast. He said he could solicit support from those he knew in Boston, including Arnold Buffum, a Quaker abolitionist and one of the founders of the New England Anti-Slavery Society. Garrison also said he could provide information about black families in New York, New Haven, and Providence. Crandall offered to travel directly from Boston to Providence to meet with those whom Garrison knew in the black community and said she would pursue the other contacts as quickly as possible.

Crandall told Garrison that when she returned to Canterbury she would seek out local supporters, including Daniel Packer, the mill owner and person responsible for the creation of the Packerville Baptist Church. They agreed that if the initial meetings and student recruitment efforts went well, Garrison would place an ad for her school in the *Liberator* and extensively promote her school. At the end of this extraordinary meeting, any lingering doubts on the part of Crandall or Garrison were replaced with determination. They agreed to work together to make the idea of a school for black women a reality.[8]

With introductions to those in the black community in hand, Prudence Crandall took the stagecoach from Boston to Providence. She arrived on Friday night and sought out Elizabeth Hammond, a black woman whose husband had purchased a boarding house in the 1820s. After her husband died in 1826, Hammond managed the boarding house and the family's financial affairs. Crandall visited Hammond at her home, where she met Hammond's daughter, Ann Eliza. Mrs. Hammond invited some of her black friends and two white gentlemen, George W. Benson, a Providence wool merchant, and his younger brother, Henry E. Benson, the Providence agent for the *Liberator*, to meet with Crandall. Coincidentally, the Benson brothers were originally from Brooklyn, Connecticut, a town adjacent to Canterbury and a short horse ride from Prudence's school. Crandall described the Bensons as "awake to the cause of humanity." They promised to help her with her school.[9]

The following morning Crandall returned to see Mrs. Hammond, who took Crandall to meet three colored families. The meetings went well, and Crandall told Garrison, "They seemed to feel much for the education of their children, and I think I shall be able to obtain six scholars from Providence."[10] Henry Benson gave Garrison a positive report concerning Crandall's visit. "The lady who was at your office last week to see about a school for colored females, passed through here Friday," Benson wrote. "She is, I should think, exactly the one for that purpose, and I hope she may meet with perfect success."[11]

Crandall returned to Canterbury late in the evening on Saturday, February 9, 1833. On Monday she met with Daniel Packer. She told Packer about her trip to Boston and how she intended to transform her school — to change the "white scholars for colored ones." If Packer had doubts about the wisdom of creating a school for black women, he did not say so directly. He called her idea "praiseworthy," but also said it likely would ruin her financially. "He is fearful that I cannot be supplied with scholars at the close of one year," Crandall wrote to Garrison, "and therefore he thinks I shall injure myself in the undertaking."[12]

Crandall believed the parents of her students would soon start withdrawing their daughters from her school. She prepared to travel once again, to New York City. Garrison promised to write to his friends in New York and prepare them for her visit. As of February 12, she had not received word from Garrison and wrote to remind him, "If you have not yet sent on to New York the information you intend, I would thank you if you would do it immediately, for I am expecting to take the next boat for New York, and shall be in the city early on Friday morning."[13]

Crandall spurred Garrison into action as she worked tirelessly to assemble the student enrollment necessary for success. She expected to make the final decision about her new school after her trip to New York City. "When I return from N.Y., I think I shall be able to lay the subject before the public," she told Garrison.[14] She arrived in New York on Friday, February 15, and met with a number of black ministers who supported Garrison, including Peter Williams, the pastor of the St. Phillips Episcopal Church in Harlem and the first black Episcopal minister in the United States.[15] Williams spoke out often against slavery and discrimination. "We are natives of this country; we ask only to be treated as well as foreigners," Williams said. "Not a few of our fathers suffered and bled to purchase its independence; we ask only to be treated as well as those who fought against it. We have toiled to cultivate it, and to raise it to its present prosperous condition; we ask only to share equal privileges with those who come from distant lands to enjoy the fruits of our labor."[16]

Crandall met other ministers who supported Garrison. They included Samuel C. Cornish, who established the First Colored Presbyterian Church in 1822 and was "one of the leading Negro journalists of the period."[17] Cornish helped create *Freedom's Journal*, the first black newspaper.[18] Theodore Wright, the pastor who succeeded Cornish at the First Colored Presbyterian Church, James Hayborn, pastor of the Abyssinian Baptist Church,[19] Theodore Raymond, and George Bourne, the white minister credited with being the first to call for immediate emancipation,[20] all lived in New York City and knew Garrison. These ministers helped Crandall schedule introductions with potential students and their families; they all agreed to provide references for Crandall and have their names appear in advertisements as supporters of Crandall's school.[21]

Garrison also provided Crandall with a letter of introduction to Arthur Tappan. Tappan was well known as one of the wealthiest merchants in

America. An early supporter of William Lloyd Garrison—he paid his libel fines and bailed him out of jail in Baltimore—Tappan committed his time and fortune to the cause of abolition. Tappan's brother Lewis described Arthur as the first man in the United States to "make use of money in large sums for benevolent objects. . . . the great lesson of his life was courage to do right whatever the consequences."[22] When asked by business associates to refrain from abolitionist activities so as not to offend customers, Tappan replied, "You demand that I shall cease my anti-slavery labors, give up my connection with the Anti-Slavery Society, or make some apology or recantation—I will be hung first!"[23] Prudence Crandall received encouragement from Tappan; he agreed to join the black ministers in support of her school. He also told her he hoped to accompany the black students from New York to her school in Canterbury.[24]

The trip to New York reassured Crandall. She received help from key leaders of the black community and was confident of enrolling many students. She also believed that Arthur Tappan's endorsement would alleviate the fears of her friends and neighbors in Canterbury. After meeting with Crandall, Tappan escorted her on a steamboat ride between New York and Crandall's next stop, New Haven.

The failure of the proposed college for black men in New Haven had occurred one year and six months earlier, and it was fresh in the mind of Simeon S. Jocelyn when he and his wife met Prudence Crandall in New Haven in February 1833. Jocelyn, a founding member of New Haven's Third Church, became the first pastor of a black church, known as the Temple Street Church, in 1829.[25] Jocelyn's white skin did not prevent the black congregation from accepting him as their minister. Religion and social reform were his passions but not his full-time profession. Jocelyn and his brother Nathaniel were partners in a printing and engraving business between 1818 and 1843.[26] Simeon converted his brother's oil paintings into engravings. When Nathaniel painted the portrait of William Lloyd Garrison in April 1833, Garrison wrote, "I think he has succeeded in making a very tolerable likeness."[27] As to Simeon's engraving of the portrait, Garrison said, "All who have seen it agree with me in the opinion that it is a total failure."[28]

The press reported extensively on Simeon S. Jocelyn's unsuccessful attempt to create a black college in New Haven. Jocelyn told Crandall about the obstacles he encountered but did not discourage her. Instead, he pledged support and agreed to serve as a reference for her school. His optimism impressed Crandall, and she later turned to him for advice and help.

When Crandall returned to Canterbury on Friday, February 22, she knew she owed her family and friends an explanation about her extended travels. She had traveled to Boston supposedly for the purpose of observing other schools and buying supplies. Her subsequent journeys to three other cities—all at a time when controversy raged in Canterbury—demanded further explanation. The time had come for Prudence to reveal her bold ideas.

"I called my family together and laid before them the object of my journey and endeavored to convince them of the propriety of the pursuit," Prudence later wrote. She told her family she intended to create a new school for black women. She hoped to make the change in the near future, perhaps as early as April. Her trip to Boston had been for the purpose of meeting with William Lloyd Garrison, publisher of the *Liberator*, to enlist his help in securing contacts in the black communities of the Northeast. In order to recruit students for her new school, she had made subsequent trips to Providence, New York, and New Haven.

Prudence's family knew she had to make a decision regarding her school and the controversy surrounding Sarah Harris. Nevertheless, Crandall's announcement that she intended to dismiss her white students and replace them with black students must have come as a shock to her family. When Prudence finished presenting her vision for the new school, she received a cautiously supportive response. "My views by them were pretty cordially received," Crandall wrote.[29]

Crandall decided to visit her neighbors the next day and tell them directly about her plans for the school: "Saturday morning I called on several of the neighbors and to my astonishment they exhibited but little opposition."[30] On Monday, February 25, 1833, buoyed by the lack of hostility if not support from her family and neighbors, Crandall gathered her students together at the Canterbury Female Boarding School. Her pupils were well aware of the controversy regarding Sarah Harris; nonetheless, they were stunned when Crandall announced the closure of her school. The school was as busy as ever; parents had not yet begun to withdraw their daughters from the school, and it was full to capacity with twenty-four students.[31] In subsequent accounts, writers often claimed that many or all of the white students had withdrawn from Crandall's school. In 1833, however, Samuel May wrote that Prudence "informed her pupils, then twenty-four in number, that, at the commencement of the next term, her school would be open for the reception of colored girls; and that twenty had engaged to come to her at that time. This annunciation caused a great excitement."[32] Crandall's announcement was met with confusion and sadness. Most if not all of the white students never objected to Sarah Harris joining their ranks. They could not continue as students at Crandall's school because adults—in some cases their own parents—opposed the idea of a black student attending their classes.

As the students relayed the news to their families, the reality of Crandall's plan took hold. The indifferent reaction she initially received when she told a few neighbors changed dramatically. One citizen of Canterbury called her idea to educate black women "reprehensible" and described the thought of young black women living in the center of town as "utterly intolerable."[33] Another said her decision showed a reckless, "stiff necked" and stubborn streak.[34] Others viewed Crandall as ungrateful and vengeful. As one local historian later said, "The people of Canterbury saw to their supreme horror and consternation that this popular school in which they had taken so much pride, was to be superseded by something so anomalous and phenomenal that it could hardly be comprehended."[35]

Critics doubted the "philanthropy" of her decision and attributed it to financial self-interest.[36] Some claimed she stood to profit more from a school for black women. That assertion ignored the obvious fact that Crandall's school was already thriving; dismissing Sarah Harris would have preserved a surer path to continued financial success. William Jay wrote, "Whatever may have been her motives, and pecuniary ones would not have been unlawful, she had a perfect right to open a school for pupils of any color whatever."[37] Crandall summed up her decision with a question: "Shall I be inactive and permit prejudice . . . or shall I venture to enlist in the ranks of those who with the Sword of Truth dare hold combat with prevailing iniquity?"[38]

On Monday night, February 25, 1833, a group of men who had supported Crandall's original school gathered to discuss the new developments. The following morning, the day after Crandall told the white students of their dismissal, "four of the most powerful men of the town" called on Crandall at nine o'clock in the morning.[39] Attorney and justice of the peace Rufus Adams, attorney Daniel Frost Jr., Dr. Andrew Harris, and merchant Richard Fenner agreed to the task of "persuading her, if possible, to give up the project."[40] One of Crandall's opponents later wrote that the men made their case for Miss Crandall to reconsider her actions with great respect and decorum.[41]

Crandall did not view the men and their treatment of her as either respectful or polite. Immediately after they left her home, she wrote that they had focused on "what shall be done to destroy the school."[42] They told Crandall they would make sure her school failed if she did not reverse her decision.[43] She rejected their threats and brought the meeting to a close. Crandall managed to conceal her anxiety; the men conceded that their threats failed to "produce any visible effect."[44] As they left, however, Crandall realized she faced powerful opponents. Her initial prediction from the previous week—that any opposition to her school would quickly fade away—now changed dramatically.

As soon as the men left, Crandall wrote to Garrison. She asked him to come quickly to Canterbury and bring Arnold Buffum to support her. She then wrote to Simeon Jocelyn and told him about the threats the men had made. They will "do everything in their power to destroy my undertaking," Crandall said.[45] She asked Jocelyn to intercede with Arthur Tappan and persuade him to come to Canterbury. Tappan's presence "would alleviate the feelings of many," Crandall said.[46] She closed by asking Jocelyn for help and advice, and twice asked him to write to her "IMMEDIATELY."[47]

The following day, Wednesday, February 27, 1833, word of Crandall's plan for her school and the opposition of local town fathers reached Samuel May in Brooklyn, Connecticut. "Although a stranger, I addressed a letter to her, assuring her of my sympathy," May said, "and of my readiness to help her all in my power."[48] May noted that the prominent location of her schoolhouse—in the center of the town at the intersection of two main roads—likely contributed to the controversy.

"Perhaps your removal to some more retired situation would at once allay the violence of your opponents," May wrote, "and be more favorable to your pupils, who would not be so exposed to insult as they might be where you now are."[49] He told Crandall that Canterbury officials had scheduled a town meeting regarding the school, and if she wished, he would attend on her behalf.[50] May's offer was significant—as a woman Crandall could not speak at a town meeting or vote on any motions. May's unsolicited letter encouraged Crandall, and she sent a quick response begging him to come to Canterbury.[51]

As Crandall worked furiously to assemble those who could defend her, William Lloyd Garrison prepared to leave on a trip to England in April. He had high expectations and hoped "the enterprise will give dignity to the abolition cause in this country . . . and secure the patronage and applause of abolitionists in Great Britain."[52] Garrison expected his journey to last for at least six months and inquired among his friends for someone to serve as guest editor for the *Liberator*.

In Boston, Maria Stewart continued writing and speaking out. On the evening of February 27, 1833, she delivered a "Lecture on African Rights and Liberty" to an audience of men and women at the African Masonic Hall in Boston. "Talk, without effort, is nothing," Stewart said. "We have performed the labor, they have received the profits; we have planted the vines, they have eaten the fruits . . . They say that we are not capable of becoming like white men, and that we can never rise to respectability in this country. They would drive us to a strange land. But before I go, the bayonet shall pierce me through. African rights and liberty is a subject that ought to fire the breast of every free man of color in these United States. . . ."[53]

Stewart asked black men and women, but especially black men, to fight harder for their rights. "Show me our fearless and brave, our noble and gallant ones," she said. "You are abundantly capable, gentlemen, of making yourselves men of distinction; and this gross neglect, on your part, causes my blood to boil within me."[54] Years later, William Cooper Nell remembered the obstacles she faced: "Maria W. Stewart—fired with a holy zeal to speak her sentiments on the improvement of colored Americans, encountered an opposition even from her Boston circle of friends, that would have dampened the ardor of most women."[55]

As the month of February ended, Prudence Crandall anxiously waited to hear from William Lloyd Garrison, Simeon S. Jocelyn, and Samuel May. She also wanted Arnold Buffum and Arthur Tappan to help defend her school. When the committee of town fathers decided to pay Crandall a second visit, however, she again faced her opponents alone.

On Friday, March 1, 1833, Rufus Adams, Daniel Frost, Dr. Andrew Harris, and Richard Fenner returned to Crandall's schoolhouse. At this meeting, attorney Frost led the discussion with Crandall, and "every argumentative effort was made to convince her of the impropriety and injustice of her proposed measure."[56] Frost tried new tactics to pressure her to abandon the proposed school for black women. He ignored Crandall's statements regarding the importance of education and her desire to "benefit the people of color." Instead, Frost stressed "the danger of the leveling principles."[57] What Frost meant by "leveling principles" was not the idea of providing equal opportunity for blacks in education. Frost told Crandall that he meant to use a more sensational argument. "The danger" he meant to emphasize was "intermarriage between whites and blacks."[58]

The four men, who later recalled the "kind and affecting manner" in which Frost addressed Crandall, made it clear that they intended to argue to the public that her school promoted "the amalgamation of the whites and blacks."[59] Crandall allegedly responded to Frost's assertion by pointing out that "Moses had a black wife."[60] The source of the "Moses" quote may well have been Crandall herself, but during the controversy it was cited only in accounts that were hostile to her and for the purpose of changing the subject from equality in education to "amalgamation" and interracial marriage. Many years later, historian Ellen D. Larned included the "Moses" quote in her account of Crandall's school, after she had corresponded with Crandall.

Crandall likely delivered the thoughtful "Moses" retort—she never denied it—and Frost and his committee made sure it was widely publicized as it helped them in their goal of discrediting the school. Fanning the flames of racial fear and prejudice by promoting the specter of "amalgamation" and interracial marriage promised to transform an already divisive issue into a broader panic. As a local publication soon confirmed, the inference that Crandall's opponents promoted through repeating the "Moses had a black wife" quote was irresistible for local newspapers.

"Her reply to the committee seems to have been made in justification of the course she adopted," one published account noted. "The public must decide whether the amalgamation of the whites and blacks is a profitable or safe doctrine."[61] Another reference to the "Moses" quote appeared in the *Norwich Republican*, submitted by Andrew T. Judson. "When she justified her proceedings and principles on the ground that Moses married a 'colored woman,' it was suggested that she might as well advocate polygamy now, because it was lawful in the days of antiquity."[62] The controversy escalated to a point where Crandall replied publicly to deny that her school promoted interracial marriage.[63]

After their second meeting, Frost and his companions left Crandall's school believing they had made progress toward changing her mind and acknowledged that "she had gone on with a firmness of design, and a decision of action, worthy the holiest cause."[64] Crandall did not, however, yield to the committee's request that she abandon her idea of an academy for black women. On the next day, March 2nd, an issue of the *Liberator* appeared containing both an article and an advertisement promoting Crandall's "High School for Young Colored Ladies and Misses."[65] The advertisement contained Crandall's thanks to those who had previously patronized her school and announced that the school would reopen for "young ladies and Misses of color" on Monday, April 1, 1833. Many courses would be offered, including reading, writing, arithmetic, geography, history, philosophy, chemistry, astronomy, art, piano, and French.

References for Crandall's school no longer included the local Board of Visitors, Canterbury men of good standing. Instead, her new list of supporters consisted of leading abolitionists from Boston, New York City, Providence, and Philadelphia. They included Arthur Tappan; George Bourne; Samuel Cornish and the other ministers she met in New York;[66] Joseph Cassey, a black banker from Philadelphia who was "the architect of his own fortune";[67] James Forten, a black businessman who owned a sail-making factory in Philadelphia;[68] George W. Benson of Providence; Arnold Buffum of Boston; and William Lloyd Garrison. There were three men from Connecticut: Simeon S. Jocelyn; Jehiel C. Beman, a black minister of the Cross Street AME Zion Church in Middletown and an agent for the *Liberator*;[69] and Prudence's new friend and ally, Samuel May of Brooklyn. The references included no one from Canterbury. Crandall submitted the advertisement on February 25, 1833, the same day she informed her students of their dismissal.

Garrison wrote a separate article about Prudence Crandall's new school in the same issue of the *Liberator*. He told his readers that she "richly deserves the patronage and confidence of the people of color" and promoted her diverse curriculum and schoolhouse—"she has a large and commodious house." Tuition was affordable, Garrison said, and "her terms are very low."[70] He recommended the village of Canterbury as a "central and pleasant" location for a school.

Garrison acknowledged that Crandall's new school faced challenges and opposition. "In making the alteration in her school, Miss C. runs a great risk; but let her manifest inflexible courage and perseverance, and she will be sustained triumphantly. Reproach and persecution may assail her at the commencement, but they will soon expire."[71] The *Liberator* carried the news to leading advocates of emancipation, both black and white, throughout the northeastern states and beyond. With Garrison's promotion in the *Liberator*, Prudence Crandall's school became a cause for the national abolitionist movement. The town fathers of Canterbury were stunned.

Andrew T. Judson was one of Prudence Crandall's earliest supporters, a member of the school's Board of Visitors, and her neighbor—he lived directly across the street from her schoolhouse. He was an early and strong supporter of the American Colonization Society, a well-known local attorney and public servant, and a director of both the Windham County Bank and the Windham County Mutual Fire Insurance Company.[72] He also served as the state's attorney for Windham County and had done so since 1819, prosecuting criminal cases on behalf of the state.

Judson had worked hard to become a leading citizen of Canterbury. He was born in the nearby town of Ashford on November 29, 1784. His father, also named Andrew, graduated from Dartmouth College in 1775—only the fifth graduating class for that institution—and served as a Congregational minister of a small church in Eastford, Connecticut. His father's college degree and religious calling did not provide a guarantee of a comfortable life. When Andrew was only six weeks old his mother Elizabeth died, leaving Andrew, his father, and two older brothers. His father remarried and had four additional children, a girl and three boys. The family struggled through financial hard times and personal tragedy. One Judson child died in infancy, and a son, John, was described as an "invalid."[73] Perhaps as a result of the personal and financial stress, Judson's father was "afflicted with a hypochondriac melancholy that at times incapacitated him for public service."[74]

Andrew T. Judson received his education at the local Eastford Common School that met a few months per year and provided only the basics. Judson knew this minimal schooling would "limit in a great degree my prospects and hopes for the future."[75] In 1802, when Judson was eighteen years old, his father's Dartmouth connections helped put him on a life-changing path. He met attorney Sylvester Gilbert of Hebron—a Dartmouth classmate of his father's—and Gilbert agreed to take Andrew under his wing and tutor him in the law. In addition to his law practice, Gilbert served as a state representative in the Connecticut Legislature and as the state's attorney for Tolland County. Gilbert later served in the U.S. Congress, the Connecticut State Senate, and as a judge.[76]

After four years of study and apprenticeship, Andrew Judson qualified to practice law in 1806.[77] His father did not live to see his son become a lawyer; he died one year earlier. Through his father's Dartmouth connection, however, Judson's life changed. In his career in politics and the law, Andrew Judson almost precisely followed in the footsteps of Sylvester Gilbert, including election to both houses in the state legislature and to the U.S. Congress. In addition to serving as a state's attorney, Judson also became a judge. Judson, however, faced the challenges of different times that more than once placed him in the center of great controversy.

Initially, Judson declined to pursue a legal career in Connecticut and left his native state "to seek a new home, and a field for business."[78] He went to Vermont to live among Judson family relatives and stayed for about one year; he returned to Connecticut "homesick and discontented."[79] He decided to settle in Canterbury to begin a law practice and start a political career. He aligned himself with the Federalist Party, the dominant political party in Connecticut.

When the United States went to war with Great Britain in the War of 1812, Andrew Judson and the Federalists strongly opposed the war. The New England economy depended on trade with Great Britain, and the war threatened local jobs. Governors from New England withheld state militia support; some in the Federalist Party even discussed the possibility of secession from the Union.[80] Many Federalists believed the war would destroy the country. Instead, it destroyed the Federalists.[81] In 1813, as U.S. ships attempted to leave the Connecticut harbor of New London in an effort to break through a British blockade, someone on shore reportedly alerted the British warships by signaling with blue lanterns. The American ships were forced to turn around and remain in the harbor. The press blamed the Federalists, and the phrase "blue light Federalist" was born, equating Federalists with treachery and treason.[82] An investigation raised many questions as to whether a British or American spy gave the "blue light" signal, or whether there was any signal at all. The Republican Party, however, succeeded in portraying the Federalists—who opposed the war—as unpatriotic and responsible for "the blackest treason."[83]

Andrew Judson never served his country in the War of 1812. In hindsight he viewed his failure to enlist as a terrible mistake even though the Federalists opposed the war and many refused to serve. Public support for the war increased as it progressed. Judson later claimed that he tried to enlist and was rejected because he was not a political friend of the officials who processed new recruits.[84] His explanation did not make sense, however, as recruits were hard to come by and the national goal of fifty thousand volunteers was never met.[85] Judson realized he had miscalculated badly by siding with the Federalists in their opposition to the war. He found himself on the wrong side of public opinion and resolved not to make that mistake again.

With a newfound appreciation for the unpredictable nature of politics, Judson ran for office and won election to the State House of Representatives in 1813. The tradition in the House at that time, Judson wrote, was for new members to be seen and not heard. Judson behaved accordingly. "I made no speeches," Judson wrote. "Once or twice an opportunity offered, but the idea alone gave me the palpitation to such a degree, that it was well my seat was retained."[86]

There were two significant changes in Judson's life in 1816. On March 20, when he was thirty-one years old, he married Rebecca W. Warren of Windham. He said they "trudged along together, harmonizing in our views, and mode of life, as well and perhaps better than most others."[87] Judson also changed political parties and no longer associated with the "blue light Federalists." He joined the new Toleration Party.[88] The Toleration Party replaced the Federalist Party as the dominant force in Connecticut politics, and Judson's switch came at an opportune time. The Toleration candidates for governor and lieutenant governor won the election of 1816, and the new party took control of the general assembly in 1817.[89]

As a more seasoned politician, Judson became involved in the creation of the state constitution in 1818. He regarded drafting the Connecticut Constitution as the most important achievement of the Toleration Party. At the end of 1819, the state's attorney for Windham County, William Perkins, died, and Judson secured the plum patronage position. "There is perhaps no point in my life to which I can turn with more propriety, and say this is the most important," Judson later said.[90] The office of state's attorney became an elected office with a two-year term in 1821; Judson served a total of twenty-five years in that post.

Andrew Judson had great political ambitions and sought numerous offices during the next two decades. While serving in the legislature in 1829, he competed with State Representative Thomas S. Williams for an appointment to a judgeship. "The Hon. Thomas S. Williams and myself were opposing candidates for a seat on the bench . . . and he was successful, which I did not much regret," Judson later wrote, "and this session closed all in good humor."[91] Judson won election to the state senate in 1830 and lost in a bid for reelection in 1831. He expressed interest in the U.S. Senate seat in 1832—at that time senators were elected by a vote of the state legislature instead of the public. After three ballots, Judson—who had changed parties again and was affiliated with supporters of Andrew Jackson in the Jackson Party—lost to Republican Nathan Smith.[92] Judson returned to the state legislature as a member of the house in 1833.[93]

Andrew Judson and his wife Rebecca did not have any children. In 1822, however, they took in Charles Ames, a ten-year-old boy whose mother recently had died and whose sea captain father, Isaac, either was deceased or was forced to give up his son because of time away on merchant ships. Andrew and Rebecca cared for Charles until he turned eighteen in 1830, just one year before Prudence Crandall started her school across the street from Judson's home. When Charles left Canterbury for New York and life on his own, Judson provided him with a "certificate of good moral character," documenting his good behavior and fitness as a young man.[94] Charles Ames loved Andrew and Rebecca Judson and was grateful for their care. Ames married in 1837; when he celebrated the birth of his first child in 1838, he named his son Andrew Judson Ames.

As the controversy concerning Prudence Crandall's school for "young ladies and Misses of color" intensified, Andrew Judson organized the opposition. Judson saw Crandall's plan as an attack on all he and others had done to improve Canterbury and Windham County. Crandall had benefited from Judson's good will and the help of other town leaders when she launched her school; now she turned away from her original supporters and embraced the abolitionists from Boston and New York. Judson called the abolitionists "dictators" and was offended by their opposition to the Colonization Society.[95] Judson believed Crandall's new antislavery friends cared nothing for Canterbury.

The two meetings between town leaders and Prudence Crandall failed to resolve the controversy, so Judson called for a formal town meeting. Word quickly circulated concerning a meeting at the Congregational Church, and George W. Benson read the news in the *Liberator* while in Providence. On Saturday, March 2, 1833, Benson decided to travel to Canterbury to offer his help. He arrived at Crandall's schoolhouse on Sunday morning and found her "calm and undaunted" in the face of increasing opposition.[96] Crandall told him about the meetings with the town fathers.[97] Later that Sunday morning, and just before the start of services at the Congregational Church, Benson watched as Andrew Judson walked from the church to the town signpost across the street where official notices were displayed. As Judson posted a notice for the March 9 town meeting for the purpose of denouncing Crandall's school, Benson thought it was hypocritical for Judson to take this official action on the Sabbath.[98]

The letters that Prudence Crandall wrote at the end of February, pleading for help, were delivered in early March. On receiving Crandall's letter, Samuel May contacted his friend George Benson, who was visiting his family in Brooklyn. When May learned that Benson had already met with Crandall the previous day, he convinced Benson to go with him to Canterbury again that afternoon so that he could meet Crandall and offer his help.[99] Arnold Buffum learned that Crandall had requested his help. Buffum told Garrison he could not go to Canterbury given the increasingly volatile situation. "I am informed that the excitement is so great that it would not be safe for me to appear there," Buffum wrote.[100]

On arriving in Canterbury, townspeople warned May and Benson that if they proceeded to Crandall's school they might face physical attack because of the "furious" opposition to Crandall's school.[101] May and Benson learned that Crandall's decision to teach black women surprised everyone in town, including her friends and supporters. A man who otherwise thought the town reaction to Crandall's decision was a "dreadful outrage" said she had not acted "judiciously" in her decision to admit Sarah Harris.[102] James Monroe, a Canterbury resident who years later taught political science at Oberlin College, complained about the "suddenness" of Crandall's action.[103] Despite the warnings, May and Benson proceeded to the schoolhouse and met with Crandall. They found her "resolved and tranquil" in the midst of controversy.[104] Their discussion focused on the town meeting and Crandall's dilemma—as a woman, she could not go to the meeting and speak for herself. Crandall turned to Samuel May, a man she had just met, and asked him to serve as her representative and defender at the town meeting. "Certainly, come what will," May replied.[105]

Crandall told May that he should explain why she chose to change her school. She did not wish to dismiss her white students, but did so only after parents threatened to withdraw their daughters. Crandall wanted May to explain that she could not expel Sarah Harris and deeply wound "the feelings of an excellent girl" and add "to the mountain load of injuries and insults already heaped upon the colored people."[106] Crandall knew, however, that those explanations would not end the controversy. At May's suggestion, Crandall agreed to offer to move the school to another location in Canterbury. As May recalled, "She seemed determined only upon this point—to maintain her right to teach colored pupils. . . . She claimed that she had a right to do this, on her own premises, in Canterbury."[107] Crandall told May she did not wish to offend her neighbors and "was perfectly willing to accede to any fair proposals for a removal to some more retired situation."[108] She told May he could extend this offer at the town meeting.[109]

As the week progressed, Crandall learned that Arnold Buffum planned to deliver a lecture twenty miles south in Norwich, Connecticut. She left her sister Almira in charge of the school and traveled to meet Buffum and implore him to come to the Canterbury town meeting.[110] George Benson invited his brother, Henry Benson, to attend the meeting and wrote to Garrison to inform him of the new developments. Garrison said Crandall's school "must be sustained at all hazards."[111] Keeping in mind the earlier failure to create a school for black men in New Haven, Garrison told Benson that Crandall's school must succeed. "If we suffer the school to be put down in Canterbury, other places will partake of the panic, and also prevent its introduction in their vicinity," Garrison wrote. "The New Haven excitement has furnished a bad precedent—a second must not be given, or I know not what we can do to raise up the colored population in a manner which their intellectual and moral necessities demand."[112]

Garrison knew that Benson's trip to Canterbury to see Prudence Crandall on March 3 was physically costly to Benson; Benson suffered frostbite on all of his fingertips on both hands, causing him great pain and discomfort.[113] "Ours is truly a great and arduous cause, my brother; but it is also a holy and benevolent cause, and it is one day to be a popular and triumphant cause," Garrison wrote. "Be not downcast; glory in the name of an abolitionist; speak always confidently of success; remember that the heavier the cross, the brighter the crown. . . . A spirit like yours cannot droop."[114] Garrison reminded Benson of the importance of Crandall's school to the abolitionist movement throughout New England. "In Boston," Garrison wrote, "we are all excited at the Canterbury affair."[115]

On Saturday, March 9, just hours prior to the town meeting, Samuel May and George Benson arrived at Prudence Crandall's school in Canterbury. Garrison sent words of encouragement to May. "Our brother May deserves much credit," Garrison wrote. "If anyone can make them ashamed of their conduct, he is the man."[116] May was apprehensive. Benson intended to stay with Crandall at the schoolhouse during the town meeting, leaving May to face a hostile crowd alone.[117] When May and Benson arrived at the schoolhouse, they were surprised to find Arnold Buffum, the agent for the New England Anti-Slavery Society, already strategizing with Crandall and planning for the evening's meeting.[118] Crandall's trip to Norwich to appeal to Buffum had succeeded. Together May and Buffum would defend Crandall's school at the meeting.

Crandall prepared letters of introduction for May and Buffum, specifying that she authorized them to speak for her at the town meeting. She also entrusted them to negotiate on her behalf and agreed to be "bound by any agreement" they made regarding her school.[119] Crandall told May that since her house was "one of the most conspicuous in the village, and not wholly paid for, if her opponents would take it off her hands, repaying what she had given for it, cease from molesting her, and allow her time to procure another house for her school, it would be better that she should move to some more retired part of the town or neighborhood."[120] May believed this proposal would resolve the controversy.

The town meeting took place at the Congregational Church located just off the town center. The church was built in 1805 in a New England style, with balconies on three sides and room above and below for hundreds of people.[121] May and Buffum made the short walk from Crandall's home to the church as others arrived and took their seats. As they entered, they were struck at the turnout; the church was "nearly filled to its utmost capacity."[122] All the seats in the high-backed pews were taken, and many men stood in the aisles. May and Buffum squeezed their way down the side aisle and sat in a wall pew near the front of the church.[123]

Henry Benson, from Providence, entered the church just as the meeting started and kept notes for an article he planned to write for the *Liberator*. Benson was relieved to see Samuel May and Arnold Buffum.[124] Townspeople quickly approved a motion for Asahel Bacon to serve as moderator of the meeting; Bacon was a friend of Andrew Judson and an opponent of Crandall's school. Attorney Rufus Adams introduced a series of resolutions regarding the school, and Judson, as town clerk, read each one, including a statement which predicted that Crandall's school would attract "large numbers of persons from other states whose characters and habits might be various and unknown." The result, Judson said, would be to render "insecure the persons, property, and reputations of our own citizens."[125]

Rufus Adams rose to speak. He recounted how Crandall started her school with the support of the town and how she ungratefully disregarded those who helped her. He questioned why she dismissed students from local families in order to give her school over to abolitionists. Adams "threw out several mean and low insinuations against the motives of those who were encouraging her enterprise," Samuel May later wrote.[126] When Adams finished, Andrew Judson spoke. He predicted the destruction of the town if Crandall's school for colored children succeeded. The school would attract criminals and townspeople would fear to leave their homes, Judson said. Judson cited the example of New Haven, where citizens at a town meeting successfully blocked a proposed college for black men. "Shall it be said," Judson asked, "that we cannot, that we dare not resist?"[127]

Judson either had heard of the proposed compromise to move the school or he anticipated it, because he said he "was not willing, for the *honor* and welfare of the town, that even one corner of it should be appropriated to such a purpose."[128] Judson could not stand the idea of a school for black women across the street from his home or anywhere in town. "He twanged every chord that could stir the coarser passions of the human heart," Samuel May said, "and with such sad success that his hearers seemed to be filled with the apprehension that a dire calamity was impending over them, that Miss Crandall was the author or instrument of it, that there were powerful conspirators engaged with her in the plot, and that the people of Canterbury should be roused, by every consideration of self-preservation."[129]

Judson knew that Prudence Crandall had authorized Samuel May and Arnold Buffum to represent her at the meeting. He called attention to Crandall's new abolitionist friends and her claim that she had the support of Arthur Tappan. "Are we to be frightened because Arthur Tappan of New York and some others are worth a few millions of dollars, and are going to use it in oppressing us? No, I know you will answer, *No*."[130] Judson concluded by referencing an old vagrancy law that prohibited out-of-town persons from becoming a burden and saying that it prohibited Crandall from providing room and board to black women from other states.

Other speakers followed Judson; they all denounced the proposed school and raised questions about the character and motives of Prudence Crandall and her supporters. Henry Benson wrote that Crandall's school was "basely misrepresented."[131] There was one speaker, however, who did not follow the script that Andrew Judson had crafted for the town meeting. George S. White unexpectedly challenged most of what Judson and others said about Prudence Crandall.[132] White was no stranger to controversy. He had served as the Episcopal minister for the Trinity Church in Brooklyn, Connecticut, beginning in 1818, but did not stay long. Initially very popular, White encountered difficulties that included feuding with influential members of his parish, including Daniel Putnam, son of Revolutionary War hero Israel Putnam. After two years his tenure "ended in alienation and detriment."[133] White moved to Canterbury, where he bought a house near the center of town and frequently performed the Episcopal service for the St. Thomas Parish.

The fate of Canterbury was *not* at stake in the Crandall school controversy, White told those at the town meeting. White specifically took issue with Andrew Judson's claim that black children at Crandall's school would ruin Canterbury, and he disagreed with Judson's opinion that an old vagrancy statute prevented out-of-state students from coming to Canterbury. The law did not concern students attending a school, White said.[134]

As White spoke, others tried to shout him down. Solomon Paine, an attorney and justice of the peace, appealed to the moderator to rule White out of order and cut off his comments, which Asahel Bacon did.[135] In the midst of the uproar, Arnold Buffum and Samuel May approached Bacon and presented their letters of introduction. They requested to speak on behalf of Prudence Crandall. Bacon handed the letters to Andrew Judson. May wrote that Judson "instantly broke forth with greater violence than before."[136] Judson accused May and Buffum of insulting the town by interfering with its local concerns.[137] Since they were not residents of Canterbury, Judson noted, they had no right to speak. "Other gentlemen sprang to their feet in hot displeasure," May said, "poured out their tirades upon Miss Crandall and her accomplices, and, with fists doubled in our faces, roughly admonished us that if we opened our lips there, they would inflict upon us the utmost penalty of the law, if not a more immediate vengeance."[138]

Given the increasing hostility at the town meeting, May and Buffum said nothing. No one spoke on behalf of Prudence Crandall. Henry Benson noted, "One thing was allowed—one thing was admitted—that the lady had borne an irreproachable character up to the time she first contemplated a school for colored females. Her unpardonable sin lay altogether in her wish to elevate the moral and intellectual condition of the blacks."[139]

The resolutions passed unanimously, and Asahel Bacon proclaimed the meeting adjourned.[140] Judson approached May and told him he should go home and stay out of the matter. Instead, May shouted to those still in the church to stay so that they might hear Miss Crandall's point of view.[141] Since the meeting had ended, anyone from any town could speak.

"Men of Canterbury, I have a word for you!" May said. "Hear me!"[142] About one-third of those who attended the meeting stayed to listen. May quickly answered the false charges against Crandall and her school and defended the character of black students. When Arnold Buffum began to speak, six trustees of the church came forward and demanded that May and Buffum cease their discussion and leave the church immediately.[143]

Outside on the church lawn, May continued to answer questions for the few who remained. When May returned home to Brooklyn, he wondered what would come of "the day's uproar."[144] Henry Benson was appalled. "Such disgraceful proceedings I never witnessed before."[145]

Benson speculated that the views of Crandall's opponents, while popular at the moment, would not stand the test of time. "The present generation may hail them as just, but the very next will execrate them," Benson wrote, three days after the town meeting. "The names of those who have been the most active in attempting the suppression of this school may be honored now, but future ages will consign them to ignominy and shame."[146]

4 : **A Mountain of Prejudice**

Andrew Judson immediately launched a campaign to publicize the outcome of the Canterbury town meeting and to attack Crandall's school. In letters to the local newspapers he praised the civility of Crandall's opponents and criticized Crandall's "foreign" supporters, who Judson said tried to intimidate the citizens of Canterbury. By Judson's own count there were just five supporters of Prudence Crandall at the Canterbury meeting.[1] While there were many hundreds of citizens in attendance—and no one voted against the resolutions—Judson wrote that Crandall's five supporters presented "an array of foreign power, bringing with it boasted foreign influence."[2] Their presence was "imposing" according to Judson, and they "took conspicuous posts" within the church.[3] "Their talking, language, and note-taking became offensive, and necessarily disturbed the progress of the meeting."[4]

Judson promoted the idea that outsiders had disrupted the town meeting. Another account, signed "A Friend of the Colonization Cause" and likely written by Judson, noted that foreigners, having "thrust themselves into (the) assembly of the freemen of Canterbury . . . soon began to disturb the meeting by whispering, laughing, and . . . taking notes, etc."[5] The odd objection to "taking notes" caught the attention of Samuel May, who replied in a published letter addressed to Judson. "Permit me to say sir, if you or some of your coadjutors had adopted the precaution of 'taking notes' at the time (for which precaution you seem to be offended at one of the Providence young men) you probably would have given as correct an account of the meeting as he has done in the *Liberator*, and not committed so many mistakes in your communications to the Norwich papers . . ."[6]

Judson also criticized the brief speeches by May and Buffum following the meeting. "Their language was so highly charged with threats," Judson said, and their "conduct so reprehensible" that the trustees of the church had no choice but to demand that they cease and desist.[7] Local newspapers printed Judson's false characterization of the meeting and its aftermath.

On Monday, March 11, 1833, two days after the town meeting, Judson traveled to Brooklyn to see Samuel May. Judson told May he did not have any personal dislike for him and apologized for "certain epithets" Judson delivered in "the excitement of the public indignation of his neighbors."[8] May later wrote an extensive and verbatim account of his exchange with Judson.

May told Judson that that he was "ready, with Miss Crandall's consent, to settle the difficulty" with Judson and the people of Canterbury peaceably.[9] May said that Crandall would agree to move her school to another location in Canterbury if she could recover what she paid for the house. Judson rejected any such compromise.

"Mr. May, we are not merely opposed to the establishment of that school in Canterbury," Judson said. "We mean there shall not be such a school set up anywhere in our state. The colored people never can rise from their menial condition in our country . . . They are an inferior race of beings, and never can or ought to be recognized as the equals of the whites. Africa is the place for them. . . . The sooner you Abolitionists abandon your project the better for our country, for the niggers, and yourselves."[10]

May told Judson that the United States must recognize the rights God gave to all men. "Education is one of the primal, fundamental rights of all the children of men," May said. "If you and your neighbors in Canterbury had quietly consented that Sarah Harris, whom you knew to be a bright, good girl, should enjoy the privilege she so eagerly sought, this momentous conflict would not have arisen in your village."[11]

They continued their private debate. Judson said if the old vagrancy law was insufficient to block students from coming into the town, "then we will get a law passed by our Legislature, now in session, forbidding the institution of such a school as Miss Crandall proposes, in any part of Connecticut."[12] May said Crandall's supporters would challenge such a law "up to the highest court of the United States."[13]

Judson's visit with May did not result in a reconciling of their respective views. "Mr. Judson left me in high displeasure," May wrote. "I never met him afterwards but as an opponent."[14] Three days later on Thursday, March 14, 1833, eleven men arrived at Prudence Crandall's home to present her with the resolutions passed at the town meeting. This time, Crandall did not face the committee alone—her father Pardon and sister Almira were with her when the men arrived.[15] Samuel Hough, the owner of an axe factory and the man who had loaned Crandall some of the money she needed to purchase the schoolhouse, read the resolutions to Crandall and her family.[16] The visit was an anticlimax to the hostility at the town meeting. The resolutions stated what was already well known; many in town were fearful of the proposed school and hoped Crandall would abandon her plan. There was no requirement for her to do or refrain from doing anything. Crandall resumed preparing the schoolhouse for the new students.

The war of words continued. The next issue of the *Liberator* appeared on March 16 and included Henry Benson's account of the Canterbury town meeting. William Lloyd Garrison set the names of five prominent opponents to Crandall's school—Andrew Judson, Rufus Adams, Solomon Paine, Richard Fenner, and Andrew Harris—in large, bold letters below the banner headline, "Heathenism Outdone." Garrison called them "shameless enemies of their species" and said their disgraceful behavior "will attach to them as long as there exists any recollection of the wrongs of the colored race."[17] Six days later, on Friday, March 22, Judson and his supporters released a lengthy attack on Crandall's school titled "Appeal to the American Colonization Society." Excerpts from Judson's letter were printed in a number of publications, including the *Norwich Republican*. "In their wild career of reform," Judson said, referring to Garrison and the abolitionists, "those gentlemen would justify intermarriages with the white people!!"[18]

Judson submitted a longer draft of his letter to the *North American Magazine* and took additional jabs at Garrison and his quest for emancipation. "What right has William Lloyd Garrison to tell us that we are slumbering in moral death, and that he and his immediate associates first made the attempt to arouse us?" Judson asked. "Before Garrison was born, there existed in the public mind as deep an abhorrence of slavery, as he can excite with his tongue or his pen. But New England well knows, that by the Constitutional terms of our national compact, she has no more right to interfere with the internal domestic policy of the Southern states, than with the concerns of a foreign power. . . . Talk of immediate abolition! You might as safely open the gates of a menagerie, and permit its savage tenants to roam among the haunts of men, as at once to emancipate the slaves. Talk of forcing the South to abolish slavery! You might as well think of uprooting the Allegheny Mountains from their deep foundations."[19]

Many in the North viewed slavery as a necessary evil permitted by the Constitution and required to support the economy of the South. Judson shared Thomas Jefferson's views regarding slavery in some respects; Judson believed that slavery would disappear at some ill-defined point in the future, perhaps through colonization and sending blacks back to Africa. "Southern prejudice in relation to slavery, is like the oak," said Judson. "But by calm rational effort, I doubt not, but that the axe may be laid at the root in due time, and this towering tree will come to the ground."[20]

As Judson intensified his campaign in favor of colonization and against Crandall's school, Arthur and Lewis Tappan moved to cut their last ties to the colonization movement. When the American Colonization Society became popular in the 1820s, the Tappan brothers had supported the effort to send blacks to Liberia. Lewis Tappan helped organize the Massachusetts Colonization Society in 1822.[21] Arthur Tappan joined the American Colonization Society in 1827, and he served as vice president of the African Education Society, a subcommittee of the Colonization Society.[22] Arthur and Lewis Tappan also had a financial interest in the colonization movement; the Tappans secured potentially lucrative contracts for exports and shipping between Liberia and the United States.[23]

The Tappan brothers left the Colonization Society in 1831. The shipping business that the Tappans expected from Liberia never materialized, and their business contact in Liberia died of fever.[24] Arthur Tappan did not criticize the colonization movement publicly at that time, as many of his friends and customers continued to support colonization. Two years later, however, Tappan decided to publicly denounce colonization when the Anti-Slavery Society of Andover, Massachusetts, asked him whether colonization "is worthy of the patronage of the Christian public?"[25] In his letter of March 26, 1833, he admitted he was once one of colonization's warmest friends, but now believed that colonization would "deepen the prejudice against the free colored people" and strengthen slavery.[26]

"It had its origin in the single motive to get rid of the free colored people, that the slaves may be held in greater safety," Tappan wrote. "Good men have been drawn into it under the delusive idea that it would break the chains of slavery and evangelize Africa; but the day is not far distant, I believe, when the society will be regarded in its true character, and be deserted by everyone who wishes to see a speedy end put to slavery in this land of boasted freedom."[27] Garrison published Tappan's letter in the *Liberator* on April 6, 1833.

Tappan's shift away from colonization represented an important turning point for antislavery activists in New York City and elsewhere. Tappan held many progressive views, but most regarded him as a moderate compared to abolitionists such as William Lloyd Garrison. Tappan helped promote Garrison's call for immediate emancipation to a broader audience. Throughout the 1830s, many opponents of slavery followed the example of the Tappan brothers and withdrew their support for colonization.[28]

Prudence Crandall prepared for the opening of her school for black women, scheduled for Monday, April 1, 1833. George Benson stopped by the school to assist Crandall. "I have just returned from Canterbury and Brooklyn, where all is commotion," Benson reported to William Lloyd Garrison. "The cause of the oppressed will be maintained, the school will go into operation next week, and I trust will be nobly supported."[29]

Andrew Judson and his allies realized the resolutions they had passed at the March 9 town meeting had accomplished nothing. Judson scheduled another town meeting specifically to call on the state legislature to close Crandall's school. On the evening of April 1, townspeople gathered at the Congregational Church to vote on a new resolution. The meeting had none of the tension and drama of the first town meeting. The rhetoric of the resolution, however, was more pointed and alarmist. It claimed the school was in fact not a school at all, but rather a theater from which the abolitionists would "promulgate their disgusting doctrines of amalgamation and their pernicious sentiments of subverting the Union."[30] The resolution stated that Crandall's school, under the false pretense of educating black women, would instead "scatter firebrands, arrows and death among brethren of their own blood."[31] After some discussion the townspeople "voted that a petition in behalf of the town of Canterbury to the next General Assembly be drawn up in suitable language, deprecating the evil consequences of bringing from *other towns* and other states people of color for *any* purpose. . . ."[32] Judson also attempted to outlaw criticism of the colonization movement. The resolution called on the legislature to prohibit schools from "disseminating the principles and doctrines opposed to the Benevolent Colonization System."[33] Finally, the resolution requested that the legislature enact such laws as necessary to put an end to the "evil" of Crandall's school.[34] The resolution once again established a committee, which included Andrew Judson, for the purpose drafting a petition to the general assembly and encouraging other towns to send similar petitions to the legislature.

The town meeting vote provided Andrew Judson, who served in the state legislature, with a directive to craft legislation to close Crandall's school. In addition, since the resolution encouraged other towns to petition the legislature for similar relief, Judson began the work of building a coalition of support in the legislature. He knew his legislation stood a better chance of passage if other towns supported and promoted the same cause. Judson organized petition drives throughout the state.

The debate in the press concerning colonization and Prudence Crandall's school continued to escalate. Samuel May published two lengthy responses to Judson's comments. In reply to Judson's statement that ending slavery was akin to uprooting the Allegheny Mountains, May said he would rather tear down the mountains than transport 2.5 million blacks to "the wilds of Africa" as the supporters of colonization had proposed.[35] May said he renounced colonization because it perpetuated the "degradation of our colored brethren" and was not committed to equality or emancipation.[36] May said both he and Prudence Crandall favored immediate emancipation: "We do so from the deep conviction that few if any sins can be more heinous than holding fellow men in bondage and degradation."[37]

May also addressed the more sensational charge that Crandall's school promoted marriage and "amalgamation" between blacks and whites. He noted the allegations regularly were "repeated in the Norwich papers" and "harped upon at the town meeting by the opposers of Miss Crandall."[38] May said Judson's claim was false and simply a tactic to "shock the prejudices of the people, and dupe their judgment."[39]

While May wrote that the purpose of Crandall's school was wholly unrelated to interracial marriage, he did not recoil from the idea, even in his public response to Judson. "Of course we do not believe there are any barriers established by God between the two races," May wrote. "Whether marriages shall or shall not take place between those of different colors is a matter which time must be left to decide. . . . We only say that such connections would be incomparably more honorable to the whites as well as more consistent with the laws of God and the virtue of our nation than the illicit intercourse which is now common especially at the south."[40] May published his letters in the local newspapers and paid a print shop to assemble them into a pamphlet and distribute it throughout the region.

Prudence Crandall heard rumors that Andrew Judson had prepared a libel lawsuit against William Lloyd Garrison for statements Garrison made in the *Liberator*, specifically in his article "Heathenism Outdone."[41] Garrison cared little about whether his comments offended anyone. The harshness of some of Garrison's articles, however, surprised Crandall, and she asked Garrison to restrain his attacks. "Handle the prejudices of the people of Canterbury with all the mildness possible," she wrote to Garrison, "as everything severe tends merely to heighten the flame of malignity amongst them."[42] While Samuel May respected and loved Garrison's "fervent devotion to the cause of the oppressed," he wrote that "no one can disapprove, more than I do, the harshness of his epithets, and the bitterness of his invectives."[43]

The pleas of May and Crandall may have resulted in a moment of reflection for Garrison, but in the end he refused to moderate his attacks on those who supported or tolerated slavery and prejudice. "It is a waste of politeness to be courteous to the devil, and to think of beating down his strongholds with straws is sheer insanity," Garrison wrote in the *Liberator*. "The language of reform is always severe, unavoidably severe."[44] Garrison had faced lawsuits, death threats, and time in jail. The rumor of Andrew Judson's libel suit did not intimidate him, at least not initially.

Garrison's inflammatory language had a more direct and personal consequence for Crandall and her supporters in Canterbury. Garrison could level his charges and print his attacks from the relative safety of his office in Boston. He had the support of a larger abolitionist community, both black and white. Crandall greatly appreciated Garrison's strong support and moral clarity, but she faced the daily anger of the Canterbury townspeople he criticized. When consequences ensued from Garrison's attacks in the *Liberator*, they fell on Crandall, her students, and her school.

It did not take long for Crandall's opponents to launch their next offensive. At an informal meeting at the Canterbury Masonic Hall on Friday, April 5, 1833, town leaders and businessmen agreed to cut off Prudence

Crandall and her family from the Canterbury community to the greatest extent possible. Merchants agreed not to sell her anything or assist her in any way.[45] At least one merchant refused to go along with the planned embargo. Stephen Coit opposed Crandall's school for black women but said he intended to sell his goods to anyone who wished to buy them, including Crandall.[46] Coit's daughters, Frances and Sarah, had attended Crandall's school prior to Sarah Harris's enrollment.[47]

The organized embargo—a tactic associated with war—sent a message to townspeople that they need not behave in a civilized manner toward Crandall or her supporters. The campaign succeeded in ostracizing Crandall and worsened relations with her neighbors. Taunts, threats, and vandalism directed against Crandall increased and went unpunished. In a letter written at the beginning of April to her friend in New Haven, Simeon S. Jocelyn, Crandall said she was "surrounded by those whose enmity and bitterness of feeling can hardly be contemplated."[48]

The official opening of her new school, a "high school for young colored ladies and misses," occurred as planned on April 1, 1833. Crandall hoped to have fifteen to twenty students. Instead, only two students, Eliza Glasko from Griswold and Sarah Harris, arrived on the first day.[49] Crandall remained concerned about Judson's efforts to close her school; however, she knew that an inability to enroll enough students to meet her basic expenses was the surest path to failure. "I have but one boarder yet and one day scholar," she wrote to Jocelyn. "I wish you to encourage those who are coming to come immediately."[50]

The Canterbury controversy did not prevent Garrison from proceeding with his plans to travel to England. While in England, he intended to raise money for the *Liberator* and speak out against colonization. "There, I shall breathe freely—there my sentiments and language on the subject of slavery will receive the acclamations of the people—there my spirit will be elevated and strengthened," Garrison said.[51] In March he asked George Bourne to serve as guest editor of the *Liberator* while he was away.[52]

Garrison met Bourne on a trip to New York a few years earlier, and they became colleagues and collaborators.[53] Bourne's historic antislavery tract, *The Book and Slavery Irreconcilable*, provided intellectual guidance for Garrison when he launched the *Liberator*.[54] Garrison enlisted Bourne to serve as a reference for Prudence Crandall's school, and Bourne's name appeared as one of the supporters of the school in the advertisements for the school in the *Liberator*. Bourne agreed to edit the newspaper each week in New York City while Garrison was away and write the strident, antislavery articles that Garrison's readers expected. In addition, Bourne agreed to write a weekly, anonymous column called "The Firebrand," write one or two other articles of his choosing, and contribute a full-length editorial each week. Bourne specifically told Garrison that he did not want an announcement that he was filling Garrison's shoes in any capacity.[55] Isaac Knapp, Garrison's assistant, and Oliver Johnson, a frequent guest editor and fellow abolitionist, agreed to assemble and print the newspaper in Boston.

Garrison traveled to Haverhill, Massachusetts, on Saturday, March 30, to meet with writer and poet John Greenleaf Whittier; Garrison was the first to publish Whittier's poetry in the *Newburyport Free Press* in 1826. Garrison hoped to convince Whittier to write for the abolitionist cause. In addition, he wanted to meet three young women who called themselves the "Inquirers after Truth." Harriet Minot and two female classmates wrote to him in support of his work in the *Liberator* and asked what, if anything, they could do to help end slavery. Harriet Minot was eighteen years old, Harriot Plummer was twenty, and Elizabeth Parrott was sixteen. Their letters intrigued Garrison.

"A thought has just occurred to me," Garrison wrote to Minot in March. "Suppose I should visit Haverhill previous to my departure for England: is it probable that I could obtain a meeting-house in which to address the inhabitants on the subject of slavery? . . . If I can be *sure* of a house, I will try to come Sabbath after next."[56] Garrison told Minot he also wanted to visit John Greenleaf Whittier. A week later, however, Garrison had not secured a hall for his speech nor had he contacted Whittier to arrange a meeting. He wrote to Minot, "I shall visit your beautiful village on Saturday next even should no arrangements be made for the delivery of an address."[57]

As his sons later wrote in Garrison's biography, the letters from Minot and her friends likely kindled romantic notions.[58] His sons even speculated that when Garrison wrote, "We declare that our heart is neither affected by, nor pledged to, any lady, black or white, bond or free," in the March 16 issue of the *Liberator*, he intended to send a message to these young female correspondents as to his own eligibility.[59] Although Garrison was usually shy in matters of romance, on a number of occasions he did send thinly veiled love notes to young women through the newspaper when he worked in Newburyport and Bennington.[60]

While in Haverhill, Garrison did contact and meet with John Greenleaf Whittier, who agreed to join the abolitionist cause. Garrison also met the three "Inquirers after Truth" and was captivated by Harriet Minot. He wrote promptly to her after his visit and told her how much he enjoyed Haverhill, where "my spirit was as elastic as the breeze, and like the lark, soared steadily upward to the gate of heaven."[61] Garrison told her that Haverhill "has almost stolen my heart. Already do I sigh at the separation, like a faithful lover absent from the mistress of his affections. Must months elapse ere I again behold it? The thought is grievous."[62] Garrison's not so thinly veiled interest in Minot resulted in friendship rather than romance, however. Garrison and Harriet Minot remained correspondents and friends throughout Garrison's lifetime.

After visiting Haverhill, Garrison embarked on a speaking tour of various cities in the Northeast to raise money for his trip to England. He gave a farewell address before a black audience in Boston on Tuesday, April 2, and traveled to Providence for a similar address on Friday. At the Providence event the local Female Literary Society and the Mutual Relief Society raised fifty-five dollars for Garrison.[63]

The Benson family attended Garrison's Providence speech. George Benson and his brother Henry lived in Providence, while the rest of the family—mother Sarah, father George, and sisters Mary, Sarah, Anna, and Helen—traveled from Brooklyn, Connecticut. They witnessed a passionate performance by Garrison and a fervent response by the crowd that took even Garrison by surprise. Many in the black congregation wept and surged around him at the conclusion of his remarks, and they reached out to touch him and shake his hand.[64] After the Providence speech Garrison wrote, "The separation of friends, especially if it is to be a long and hazardous one, is a painful event indeed."[65]

Garrison and the Bensons stayed overnight in Providence. The following morning, Garrison went to George Benson's Providence store, where he met briefly with George and his sister Helen. George talked Garrison into traveling to Brooklyn, Connecticut, that afternoon and invited him to stay at the Benson home they called "Friendship Valley." Once in Brooklyn, Samuel May—who lived across the street—came by to visit and provided Garrison with the latest news regarding Crandall's school. May also invited Garrison to address his congregation at the Unitarian Meeting House the following day on Sunday, April 7, 1833.[66] Garrison hesitated. He had not planned on speaking in Brooklyn. Garrison suspected that as a supporter of Prudence Crandall and editor of the *Liberator*, the Brooklyn parishioners would regard him as "a terrible monster."[67] Garrison rarely turned down speaking engagements, however, and he did not disappoint Samuel May.

Word reached Prudence Crandall that Garrison planned to speak on Sunday, and she and her sister Almira traveled to the meetinghouse to hear Garrison's promotion of immediate emancipation.[68] When the service began, Crandall noticed that every seat in the church was filled. Nothing Garrison said shocked or startled the congregation; Rev. May had discussed many of Garrison's ideas in his own sermons. When Garrison finished his speech, the parishioners did not weep as they had in Providence, nor did they rush the podium to shake his hand. Crandall and her sister noted, rather, that the congregation seemed supportive of his remarks. Garrison later said, "As far as I could learn, the address made a salutary impression."[69] In a letter to his brother Henry, George Benson optimistically concluded that Garrison's speech "removed a mountain of prejudice."[70]

After the service, Prudence and Almira spent the evening with Garrison at the Benson's home. Crandall and Garrison caught up on all of the news of the school, including details about the efforts of her opponents and how only two black women students had enrolled. Garrison assured her he would do all he could to boost enrollment.

"She is a wonderful woman, as undaunted as if she had the whole world on her side," Garrison wrote to his partner at the *Liberator*, Isaac Knapp. "She has opened her school, and is resolved to persevere. I wish brother Johnson (Oliver Johnson) to state this fact, particularly, in the next *Liberator*, and urge all those who intend to send their children thither, to do so without delay."[71]

Crandall's evening with Garrison left her renewed and optimistic. "Indeed it was a source of great joy," she wrote to Simeon S. Jocelyn.[72] She stayed that night at the Benson home in Brooklyn and was able to see Garrison off to his next stop in Hartford. His departure did not occur as planned. The stagecoach for Hartford passed by the Benson home without stopping. Nearly an hour elapsed before the Bensons realized no other stagecoach for Hartford would travel through Brooklyn that day. Rather than have Garrison spend another evening in Brooklyn and miss his appointments in Hartford, George Benson decided to drive Garrison in his own wagon. Traveling in a severe rainstorm, Benson and Garrison eventually caught up to the stagecoach, but not before both were soaked and covered with mud. Garrison arrived in Hartford late Monday evening and addressed a congregation at a black church on Tuesday.[73]

Thirty minutes after Garrison left the Benson home in the pouring rain, a sheriff from Canterbury arrived at Friendship Valley looking for Garrison. He meant to serve Garrison with papers concerning Andrew Judson's lawsuit for libel and require that Garrison appear in court. The Bensons said they did not know of Garrison's whereabouts; the sheriff rode westward on horseback in an unsuccessful attempt to catch Garrison. Crandall believed the sheriff wanted to arrest Garrison and take him into custody. "It was also hinted that they wished to carry him to the South," Crandall said. "This indeed was the occasion of much sorrow."[74]

After speaking in Hartford, Garrison traveled by stagecoach to New Haven on Wednesday, April 10. When the coach stopped in Middletown, he met with Jehiel Beman, a minister in the abolitionist movement and one of Prudence Crandall's supporters. "It was with as much difficulty as reluctance I tore myself from their company," Garrison said of his visit with Beman and his black parishioners.[75] On arriving in New Haven, Garrison was disappointed to find that his friend Simeon S. Jocelyn was away in New York City. Garrison allowed Simeon's brother Nathaniel to paint an oil portrait of him; the Jocelyn brothers wanted a likeness suitable for engraving and reproducing in the abolitionist press while Garrison was away in England. On Friday, Garrison traveled to New York to meet Simeon S. Jocelyn, who told Garrison of his close escape from the Canterbury sheriff.[76] "I was immediately told that the enemies of the abolition cause had formed a conspiracy to seize my body by legal writs on some false pretenses, with the sole intention to convey me south, and deliver me up to the authorities of Georgia—or in other words, to abduct and destroy me," Garrison said.[77] "No doubt the colonization party will resort to some base measures to prevent, if possible, my departure for England."[78]

In a letter to Harriet Minot, Garrison described the "murderous design" of those who were trying to abduct him, the diversionary tactics necessary to avoid them, and his friends who were "full of apprehension and disquietude" on his behalf.[79] "But I *cannot* know fear," he told Minot. "I feel that it is impossible for danger to awe me. I tremble at nothing but my own delinquencies."[80] While Garrison enjoyed describing if not exaggerating the danger he faced for Minot's benefit, Garrison had real reason for concern. Andrew Judson was not his only pursuer. Joshua N. Danforth, the New England agent for the American Colonization Society, noted in a speech in February that a person from one of the southern states had offered Danforth ten thousand dollars for the capture and delivery of Garrison.[81] Danforth did not accept the offer, but he acknowledged on March 28, 1833, that Garrison "is, in fact, this moment, in danger of being surrendered to the civil authorities of someone of the southern states."[82]

On the same day that Garrison met Simeon S. Jocelyn in New York City—Friday, April 12, 1833—Prudence Crandall received a third student at her school, Ann Eliza Hammond. Ann was from Rhode Island, and she joined Crandall as a boarding student. Crandall had met Hammond and her mother in February when she traveled to Providence.

Ann Eliza Hammond's enrollment as the first black student from another state spurred Crandall's opponents to quickly test the old vagrancy law. The law allowed town leaders to declare that a person from another state was a burden to the town and order the person to leave or risk paying a fine. Upon failure to pay the fine within ten days, the person would face either immediate expulsion or severe punishment—"he or she should be whipped on the naked body."[83]

On Saturday evening, one day after Hammond arrived, Canterbury officials notified Prudence Crandall that they regarded Miss Hammond as a burden to the town. On Sunday, Crandall traveled to Brooklyn to tell Samuel May that she expected the town to serve a writ upon her as the guardian of Miss Hammond and require that she pay the fines.[84] "I presume I shall be subjected to that penalty next Friday," Crandall said. "I think it is best to pay the first fine when demanded. . . ."[85] May told the treasurer of Canterbury that he and the Benson family were willing to post a bond in the amount of ten thousand dollars to protect the town from the cost of any vagrancy on account of students from other states.[86]

"A written offer of bonds has been presented to the selectmen by Mr. May to secure the town against any damage that shall be done by any of my pupils," Crandall wrote to Simeon S. Jocelyn. "I presume the bonds will not be accepted by them—this is a day of trial."[87] The unexpectedly small enrollment combined with the ongoing opposition to her school depressed Crandall. "Disappointment seems yet to be my lot," she wrote on April 17.[88] "Very true, I thought many of the high-minded worldly men would oppose the plan, but that Christians would act so unwisely and conduct in a manner so outrageously was a thought distant from my view," Crandall said. "If this school is crushed by inhuman laws, another I suppose cannot be obtained, certainly one for white scholars can never be taught by me."[89]

On Saturday, April 20, Crandall discussed the vagrancy issue with Rev. May, who told her she should not pay any fine. Instead, May said she should take the matter to court. Crandall favored paying the fine and avoiding a legal confrontation, but she told May she would consider challenging the ordinance in court. May also told Crandall he received a letter from a friend in Reading, Massachusetts, inviting Crandall to move her school for black women to their town. Crandall wrote to Simeon S. Jocelyn and asked what he thought of moving her school to Reading, but stressed, "Do not mention this to anyone until we get further information from that town."[90] Crandall was willing to relocate her school but did not want to be misled. She thought Jocelyn would understand and have good advice; he had once believed the people of New Haven would embrace a college for black men.

The sheriff of Windham County served a legal writ upon Ann Eliza Hammond at Crandall's school on Monday, April 22, 1833. The writ demanded that Hammond appear before attorney George Middleton, a justice of the peace, at the home of Chauncey Bacon on Thursday, May 2, at one o'clock in the afternoon, to answer charges brought by the town. Middleton could order Hammond to pay a fine of $1.67 for the previous week and command her to leave the town or face further fines. The writ also clearly stated that if Hammond refused to pay the fine and refused to leave, she would be "whipped on the naked body not exceeding ten stripes."[91] Word of the sheriff's visit to the school traveled quickly to Brooklyn and Samuel May.

"I feared they would be intimidated by the actual appearance of the constable, and the imposition of a writ," May said. "So, on hearing of the above transaction, I went down to Canterbury to explain the matter if necessary; to assure Miss Hammond that the persecutors would hardly dare proceed to such an extremity."[92] May told both Hammond and Crandall that they must not give in to the authorities, that no fines should be paid, and that Hammond must not leave Canterbury. He said that while the possibility of the town carrying out the ultimate punishment in the ordinance—a public whipping—was remote, May advised Hammond to submit to that fate "if they should in their madness inflict it."[93] Sixteen-year-old Ann Eliza Hammond had arrived in Canterbury only a week earlier to enroll in Prudence Crandall's school. Now a minister from Brooklyn asked Hammond "to bear meekly the punishment" of a public whipping in order to expose their opponents as barbarians. "Every blow they should strike her would resound throughout the land, if not over the whole civilized world," May said.[94] May saw the controversy not only in terms of personal suffering, but also as part of a larger campaign to advance the cause of emancipation. Hammond accepted May's challenge. "I found her ready for the emergency," May said, "animated by the spirit of a martyr."[95]

Andrew Judson traveled to New York City at the end of April. The purpose of his trip was likely to assist in efforts to capture Garrison. The colonization movement was very popular in New York, and Judson knew he could depend on assistance from those who were offended by Garrison's attacks on colonization. There were at least two options if Judson succeeded in capturing Garrison: return Garrison to Canterbury to face libel charges, or hand him over to those from the South who hated Garrison and the *Liberator*. Crandall and her sister Almira worried about Garrison's safety. "I hope that our friend Garrison will be enabled to escape the fury of his pursuers," Almira Crandall wrote to Henry Benson. "Our anxieties for him were very great at the time Judson went to New York, as we expected his business was to take Mr. Garrison."[96]

Eager to escape to England, Garrison left New York for Philadelphia hoping to board a boat bound for Liverpool, but he arrived too late—the ship had already set sail. Arthur Tappan persuaded Garrison to allow Tappan's friend Robert Purvis to drive him by horse-drawn carriage to Trenton, New Jersey. While traveling along the Delaware River, Garrison barely escaped a fatal accident.[97] A passing steamboat caught Garrison's attention, and he wanted to see it from a point closer than the road. Purvis accordingly steered the carriage off the road and toward the river. After nearing the edge of a cliff, Purvis turned the carriage back toward the road and stopped. For a few minutes Garrison had an unobstructed view of the steamboat. After the boat passed by, Purvis took the reins and signaled for the horse to pull forward toward the road. Instead, the horse began to back up, moving the carriage closer to the cliff with each step. Realizing the danger and unable to stop the horse, Purvis jumped out of the carriage, expecting Garrison to do the same. Garrison did not move. Purvis shouted, "Sir, if you do not get out instantly, you will be killed." Garrison finally jumped out the door, just as the horse abruptly stopped with the rear wheel of the carriage precariously balanced on the edge of the cliff.[98]

From Trenton, Garrison returned to New York City and traveled on to New Haven, where he continued to elude his enemies. He spent a few days with Nathaniel Jocelyn, who finished Garrison's portrait. Nathaniel's concern for Garrison's safety was so great that he painted Garrison not in his studio, but in a room next to the studio and near a side exit, in case Garrison needed to flee.[99] As for the portrait, Garrison deemed it a success and called it "a good likeness of the madman Garrison."[100]

Garrison traveled once more to New York City, hoping to evade his potential kidnappers and depart for Great Britain. "I was watched and hunted, day after day in that city, in order that the writ might be served upon me," Garrison said. "My old friend Arthur Tappan took me into an upper chamber in the house of a friend, where I was safely kept under lock and key, until the vessel sailed which conveyed me to England."[101]

On the morning of May 1, Garrison made his way to the harbor and the ship *Hibernia*, bound for Liverpool. No one recognized or stopped him as he entered the boarding ramp. While the ship was still at anchor in the Port of New York, Garrison wrote again to Harriet Minot. "I have been journeying from place to place, rather for the purpose of defeating my enemies than from choice," Garrison said. "I do not now regret the detention, as it enabled the artist at New Haven to complete my portrait . . . To be sure, those who imagine that I am a monster on seeing it will doubt or deny its accuracy, seeing no horns about the head."[102]

Two and a half hours after the *Hibernia* sailed out of New York, someone representing a law office in Canterbury, Connecticut, made an inquiry about Garrison along the docks of the New York harbor.[103] It was too late. Garrison was finally safe and away on his trip to England.

5 : The Black Law

As the month of April ended, Prudence Crandall had only three black students at her school. In addition to local opposition, Crandall now battled a dire fiscal situation and realized she could not rely on advertisements in the *Liberator* to increase enrollment. When she received a letter from Arthur Tappan encouraging her to keep her school open, Crandall saw an opportunity.[1] She traveled to Norwich on Monday, April 22, 1833, and boarded a ferry for New York City.

Crandall also made a decision concerning Ann Eliza Hammond and the vagrancy charge. While she appreciated the advice of Rev. May to stand firm and persuade Miss Hammond to submit to a whipping if necessary, Crandall did not agree. Crandall could not allow a child in her care to face even the remote possibility of brutal punishment at the hands of the town. With the deadline of the May 2 hearing fast approaching, Crandall paid the fine and ended the matter for the time being.[2]

The bitter opposition to the school took a toll on Crandall's family, particularly her father. Pardon Crandall did not enjoy public attention and wanted to see the controversy brought to an end. "I have advised her often to give up her school and sell her property, and relieve Canterbury from their imagined destruction," Pardon wrote. "Not that I thought she had committed a crime or had done anything which she had not a perfect right to do. But I wanted peace and quietness."[3]

While Pardon privately encouraged his daughter to abandon her plans to educate black women, he stood by her when others criticized her school. Andrew Judson's attacks in the press moved Pardon to respond. He sent a letter to Judson and Chester Lyon; Lyon was the assessor, sheriff, and judge of probate for Canterbury.[4] Pardon included his letter in a pamphlet titled *Fruits of Colonization*, which combined letters and editorials critical of Judson and other opponents of Crandall's school.

"The spirit of a father that waketh for the daughter is roused," Pardon wrote. "I know the consequence. I now come forward to oppose tyranny with my property at stake, my life in my hand."[5] Pardon described how a gang of men came to his house and threatened to destroy his daughter's schoolhouse unless she closed her school. The men also threatened to attack Pardon's farm and demanded that he leave Canterbury. "It will be easy to raise a mob and tear down your house," they said.[6]

The following day Pardon visited Andrew Judson and accused him of leading the "ungenerous and unrighteous conduct that has been pursued towards my daughter Prudence Crandall."[7] Judson responded with the threat of a lawsuit. "I had rather sue you than to sue her," Judson told Pardon.[8] Pardon said that a lawsuit seemed unnecessary given Judson's plans to "pass a law that will destroy the school without a series of litigations."[9]

Crandall's impulsive trip to New York City, where she implored Arthur Tappan and the black ministers who supported her school to immediately secure students, resulted in success. By early May 1833, six students arrived from New York City. Shortly thereafter, enrollment swelled from nine to thirteen and then to twenty-two, with students from New York, Philadelphia, Providence, and Boston. Within Connecticut, students came from Canterbury, Griswold, and New Haven.[10] Crandall finally had the income she needed to meet her basic expenses. Students filled the schoolhouse, and Crandall immersed herself in the job of teacher and headmistress of a school for black women. "In the midst of this affliction I am as happy as at any moment of my life—I never saw the time when I was the least apprehensive that adversity would harm me," Prudence wrote. "I have put my hand to the plough and I will never, no never look back—I trust God will help me keep this resolution."[11]

Crandall's work mirrored the ongoing efforts of black leaders and ministers in New York City, who operated schools for members of their congregations with guidance in "morals, literature, and mechanical arts."[12] In the spring of 1833, Reverend Samuel Cornish, Theodore Wright, Peter Williams, and Christopher Rush founded the Phoenix Society. They successfully opened a high school for young black men, and later opened a school for black women.[13] Both Arthur Tappan and his brother Lewis helped in the effort—Arthur served as treasurer, and Lewis taught at a Sabbath school sponsored by the Society.[14] Rev. Cornish wrote that the schools served as "seed sown in good ground," leading to better lives for people of color.[15] Cornish appealed to the community for donations of books, maps, and supplies for the education of black students. The Phoenix Society received many donations as a result of Cornish's appeal.[16]

Prudence Crandall could only dream of such a scenario.[17] In Canterbury, no one solicited contributions for her school. Instead, local officials lobbied the legislature to pass laws to close it. Andrew Judson and nine other men circulated petitions calling for an end to "the evil consequences of bringing from other States and other towns people of color for any purpose."[18] Sixteen Connecticut cities and towns sent petitions to the legislature supporting the law proposed by Judson. The petitions contained the same language: "We consider the introduction of the people of color into the state . . . as an evil of great magnitude, as a calamity," and the resulting "burdens of pauperism . . . (will) render less secure the person and property of our own fellow citizens."[19]

The legislature also received a letter from Prudence Crandall's father. Pardon expressed his disappointment with local officials, who sought to destroy his daughter's school rather than encourage the education of black women. "I entreat the members of the General Assembly, when acting on this petition, to remember those self-evident truths, that all mankind are created free and equal, that they are endued with inalienable rights, of which no man nor set of men have a right to deprive them. And my request is, that you will not . . . pass any act that will curtail or destroy any of the rights of the free people of this State or other States, whether they are white or black."[20]

State Senator Philip Pearl chaired the committee considering Judson's proposal. Pearl lived in Hampton, and his daughter had attended Prudence Crandall's school until she was dismissed with the other white students. The committee reviewed the petitions and quickly drafted a report.[21] In a preface to its findings, the committee discussed the evils of slavery but noted, "Our obligations as a State, acting in its sovereign capacity are limited to the people of our own territory."[22] Senator Pearl concluded that the Constitution denied blacks the basic rights of citizenship.

"It is not contemplated for the Legislature to judge the wisdom of that provision of the Constitution which denies the franchise to the people of color; but your committee are not advised that it has ever been a subject of complaint," Senator Pearl wrote.[23] The report said the legislature "ought not to impede" the education of blacks who lived in Connecticut, but concluded that the state had no duty to educate blacks from other states. "Here our duties terminate," Senator Pearl said.[24] "We are under no obligations, moral or political, to incur the incalculable evils of bringing into our own state colored emigrants from abroad. . . . The immense evils which such a mass of colored population would gather within this state . . . would impose on our own people burdens which would admit no future remedy, and can be avoided only by timely prevention."[25]

As the Connecticut legislature considered the law proposed by Andrew Judson, an article in the *Liberator* titled "More Barbarism" attacked those in Canterbury who charged Ann Eliza Hammond with violating the vagrancy law. William Lloyd Garrison was on a lengthy voyage to England at this time; George Bourne or Oliver Johnson wrote the forceful Garrison-style prose. "Georgia men-stealers have never been guilty of a more flagrant and heaven-daring transgression of the laws of humanity . . . Andrew T. Judson and his malignant associates bid fair to eclipse the infamy of Nero and Benedict Arnold!! . . . Shame to the Persecutors! Burning shame to the *gallant and noble Inflictors of stripes upon innocent and studious Females!"*[26]

After reviewing the petitions in support of Andrew Judson's legislation, Senator Pearl and his committee decided that black migration from other states into Connecticut posed a serious threat to the state's safety. "The dangers to which we are exposed . . . evince the necessity in the present crisis of effecting legislative interposition," Pearl concluded.[27] Pearl's committee submitted its report together with Judson's draft of a bill for the legislature to consider. The cumbersome title of the bill, "An Act in Addition to an Act Entitled 'An Act for the Admission and Settlement of Inhabitants of Towns,'" led others to refer to it simply as the "Black Law." It repealed the provisions of the old vagrancy law that permitted public whipping on the naked body—legislators agreed this corporeal punishment did not enhance the image of the state—and added new language that empowered towns to ban and prosecute those who assisted in teaching any "colored persons who are not inhabitants of this state."[28] Any person wishing to teach blacks from other states could do so only after securing permission, in writing, from the local town officials. The law also included a series of substantial fines for anyone who violated the new law: one hundred dollars for the first offense, two hundred dollars for the second offense, and doubled accordingly for succeeding offenses (for perspective, the typical wages of the day for mill workers and tradesmen in New England ranged from $.90 to $1.50 per day).[29] Even a wealthy patron such as Arthur Tappan would find it difficult if not impossible to pay multiple and continuous fines, always doubling in their amounts.

The law imposed the same escalating fines on anyone who aided or assisted the school.[30] Andrew Judson added this language—whereby the state could prosecute any merchant who sold items to Crandall for "aiding and assisting" the illegal school—to help enforce the informal embargo against Prudence Crandall. Judson also claimed this provision prohibited Prudence Crandall's mother and father from delivering food or clothing to the school and her sister Almira from teaching at the school.

No doubt as a result of Judson's considerable experience as a prosecutor, the legislation also made it easier to obtain testimony from witnesses for use as evidence at trial. The bill stated that any black student from another state "shall be an admissible witness in all prosecutions . . . and may be compelled to give testimony."[31] In the event that Prudence Crandall continued to operate her school in violation of the law, Judson wanted to ensure that the prosecution had the means necessary to obtain evidence and testimony from the students.

During the month of May, the legislature accepted and reviewed public input concerning the proposed statute, including Pardon Crandall's letter. Senator Pearl then submitted his committee's final report to the legislature, together with the legislation drafted by Andrew Judson. One commentator wrote, "Prudence's opponents in Canterbury represented no particular villainy of that community but an aspect of human nature at large . . . 'We should not want a nigger school on our common,' was said by many persons in other Connecticut towns."[32] House Speaker Samuel Ingham certified passage of the law on May 24, 1833, and it passed the Senate with Lieutenant Governor Ebenezer Stoddard presiding. Shortly thereafter, Governor Henry W. Edwards officially signed it into law. The "Black Law," designed to close Prudence Crandall's school and keep blacks from other states out of Connecticut schools, was officially the law of the state.

In Canterbury "joy and exultation ran wild."[33] The bell of the Congregational Church rang throughout the day. As Samuel May recalled,

"All the inhabitants for miles around were informed of the triumph."[34] Jubilant townspeople fired a cannon near the town center and gathered at Andrew Judson's home. "His success in obtaining from the legislature the enactment of the infamous 'Black Law' showed too plainly that the majority of the people of the State were on the side of the oppressor," May wrote. "But I felt sure that God and good men would be our helpers in the contest to which we were committed."[35]

The events at the state capital and the subsequent celebration of the "Black Law" did not go unnoticed by the students at Prudence Crandall's school. On the day that Judson's legislation became law, the students sought support and reassurance from the teachers and staff. Would Prudence Crandall send the out-of-state girls home? Would the school close? A few students took the time to write about what they saw and experienced at the school. "Last evening the news reached us that the new law had passed," one student wrote in a letter to the *Liberator*. "The bell rang, and a cannon was fired for half an hour. Where is justice? In the midst of all this, Miss Crandall is unmoved. When we walk out, horns are blown and pistols fired."[36]

After the initial celebration of the Black Law, townspeople increased their harassment of Prudence Crandall and her students. "The Canterburians are *savage*—they will not sell to Miss Crandall an article at their shops," a student wrote. "My ride from Hartford to Brooklyn was very unpleasant, being made up of blackguards" (*blackguard* was a term used to describe scoundrels or thugs).[37] After the stagecoach dropped the student off in Brooklyn, she could not find anyone willing to drive her to Crandall's school in Canterbury. "I came on foot here from Brooklyn. But the happiness I enjoy here pays me for all. The place is delightful; all that is wanting to complete the scene is *civilized men*."[38]

Prudence Crandall and her supporters continued operating the school as if nothing had happened at the state capital. Crandall told her students the school would remain open. Despite taunts and threats from townspeople, the students stayed on at Crandall's school and continued their lessons.

The sight of Liverpool, England, delighted an otherwise fatigued William Lloyd Garrison. His passage from New York took twenty-one days and was "inexpressibly wearisome both to my flesh and spirit."[39] Because of the "all disturbing influences of wind and water," Garrison became seasick while the New York harbor was still in sight. "There is some dignity in falling after a host of stout bodies," Garrison said, "but to be cast down when delicate females and bird-like children bear up bravely against the enemy is weak indeed!"[40]

On his arrival in England, Garrison saw the same sights and contrasts that Charles Dickens reported in the early 1830s. Garrison noted that "in England, there is much wealth, but also much suffering and poverty."[41] Liverpool was one of the busiest harbors in the world in 1833. Once called the "metropolis of slavery," Liverpool was the primary entry port for Europe's slave trade until England abolished the importation of slaves in 1807.[42] Garrison did not see the city as conducive to residential life. "Let this suffice—it is bustling, prosperous and great. I would not, however, choose it as a place of residence. It wears a strictly commercial aspect," Garrison wrote. "My instinct and taste prefer hills and valleys, and trees and flowers, to bales and boxes of merchandise."[43]

Garrison may have recalled the landscape of Friendship Valley, the home of the Benson family in Brooklyn, Connecticut, or perhaps Haverhill, Massachusetts, home of Harriet Minot, where "sweet is the song of birds, but sweeter the voices of those we love," as he wrote to her at the beginning of April.[44] Garrison traveled on to London and began his intended work in England; he sought out potential donors to the abolitionist cause, promoted immediate emancipation, and challenged colonization supporters to debate.

The passage of the Black Law provoked a new battle in the newspapers regarding Prudence Crandall's school. In a letter to the *Emancipator*, a New York-based abolitionist newspaper, a writer identified only as "Justice" attacked those who "violate their trust, infringe the rights of citizens and overlap the boundaries of the constitution."[45] Passage of the law was disgraceful, unconstitutional, and unjust, according to the writer. "I ask, has not enough been shown to stamp the deep brand of foul disgrace on all who have aided in the passage of this law or joined in its clamorous celebration?" The writer speculated that allowing blacks access to education "might seriously endanger that superiority in intellectual attainments which the whites at present boast, and also a more immediate consequence might mortify the pride of A. T. Judson, candidate for Congress and Captain Richard Fenner, rum retailer on the Canterbury Green."[46]

A letter appeared in the *Hartford Courant* on June 24, signed "Canterbury," that sarcastically condemned the new law. "The law does not prohibit colored people coming into the state—this you know would be against the Constitution of the United States—but it declares they should not be instructed. And why should they be? They are not white and it is doubtful if they have souls or will exist in a future state."[47] Connecticut had "taken her stand" against the "wicked and romantic act of putting down slavery," the writer mockingly said, and had defended the planters of the South who were the true lovers of liberty.[48] "I have long been convinced that nothing is more false than the specious statement in the Declaration of our Independence 'that all men are created equal; that they are endowed by their creator with certain inalienable rights . . . that none are entitled to exclusive privileges from the community,' this is all flummery. Let us rejoice that the time has come when our political leaders have dared to abrogate these heretical and pestilential notions."[49] The author said the law was "an enduring monument of glory," and "the inspiration of a distinguished statesman from Canterbury."[50]

During this same time, notices sincerely praising Andrew Judson and the Black Law also appeared. The directors of the Windham County Colonization Society appointed Andrew Judson as the agent and orator of the Society and said he "was the man they delighted to honor."[51] The pages of the *New York Commercial Advertiser* were "loaded with criminations of Miss Crandall, and vindications of the Black Act."[52] The *Advertiser* said of Judson, "a warmer heart than his throbs in few bosoms, and the *African race* has no firmer friend than him."[53] Most newspapers supported the Black Law. "The inhabitants of Canterbury . . . [are] as quiet, peaceable, humane and inoffensive people as can be named in the United States," said the editors of the *Advertiser*. They said the New York State Legislature should consider a law similar to Connecticut's Black Law "to prevent our charitable institutions from being filled to overflowing with black paupers from the South, and white paupers from Europe."[54]

Two weeks after passage of the Black Law, Andrew Judson paid a visit to Pardon Crandall and his wife, Esther. Judson wanted to discuss Pardon's letter to legislators and the severity of the sanctions in the new law. "Mr. Crandall, when you sent your printed paper to the General Assembly, you did not injure us, it helped very much in getting the bill through," Judson told Pardon. "When they received it every man clinched his fist, and the chairman of the committee sat down and doubled the penalty.

Members of the legislature said to me, 'If this law does not answer your purpose, let us know, and next year we will make you one that will.'"[55]

Judson told Pardon the new law would bankrupt those who assisted Prudence's school. "Mr. Crandall, if you go to your daughter's you are to be fined $100 for the first offence, $200 for the second, and double it every time," Judson said. "Mrs. Crandall, if you go there, you will be fined and your daughter Almira will be fined, and Mr. May and those gentlemen from Providence, if they come there will be fined at the same rate."[56]

Judson said he intended to use the full force of the law to arrest Prudence Crandall and close her school. "Your daughter, the one that established the school for colored females, will be taken up the same way as for stealing a horse, or for burglary," Judson said. "Her property will not be taken but she will be put in jail, not having the liberty of the yard. There is no mercy to be shown about it!"[57]

Samuel May and George W. Benson traveled from Brooklyn to Canterbury to visit Crandall and discuss the future of her school.[58] If Crandall dismissed the out-of-state students in order to comply with the Black Law, the school would not survive financially; there were not enough local black students whose families could afford the tuition. Neither Crandall nor her supporters wished to capitulate to the new law. They settled on a course of civil disobedience and wasted no time in preparation for her likely arrest and trial.[59]

May urged Crandall to challenge her opponents, "to show to the world how base they were, and how atrocious was the law they had induced the legislature to enact—a law by the force of which a woman might be fined and imprisoned as a felon in the State of Connecticut, for giving instruction to colored girls."[60] May previously had encouraged Crandall to allow Ann Eliza Hammond to risk a public whipping for violation of a vagrancy law in order to reveal the despicable nature of their opponents. Crandall had declined and paid a fine because she wanted to protect her students. Under the new law, however, those who risked prosecution were not the students, but rather the teachers and supporters of the school. Without hesitation Crandall agreed to challenge Judson and his allies and risk arrest, fines, and jail pursuant to the Black Law.[61]

With Crandall's knowledge and consent, May and Benson reached out to those who were sympathetic to Crandall and her school and asked for restraint in the event of her arrest. "Mr. Benson and I therefore went diligently around to all whom we knew were friendly to Miss Crandall and her school, and counseled them by no means to give bonds to keep her from imprisonment," May wrote. "Nothing would expose so fully to the public the egregious wickedness of the law, and the virulence of her persecutors, as the fact that they had thrust her into jail."[62]

Prudence's younger sister Almira turned twenty years old on June 27, 1833. The school for black women had existed for nearly three months, and Almira played a critical role. She worked and taught there every day; when Prudence Crandall traveled to Providence, Norwich, Boston, New York, or elsewhere, Almira managed the school. Rev. May, who also taught at the school, gave Almira great credit for the school's survival. "Miss Almira Crandall, though she did not plan the enterprise, has given it from the beginning her unremitted co-operation," May wrote. "Let her praise therefore be ever coupled with that, which is her sister's due. Having partaken largely in the labor, anxiety, and suffering, let her share as largely in the reward."[63]

Almira's birthday celebration did not last long. That morning, only four weeks after passage of the Black Law, deputy sheriff George Cady arrived at the school and presented Prudence and Almira with arrest warrants. The two sisters were accused of "instructing and teaching certain colored persons, who at the time so taught and instructed were not inhabitants of any town in this state."[64] The warrants also charged Prudence and Almira with "harboring and boarding certain colored persons" from out of state. The Crandall sisters were charged with teaching black women from other states without written permission from the selectmen of the town, as required by the new law. The deputy sheriff told them that he was "commanded forthwith" to arrest Prudence and Almira Crandall and bring them before attorney Rufus Adams, justice of the peace, to be "dealt with there on as the law doth require."[65]

Prudence Crandall had discussed this scenario with her family and staff and had prepared for this moment, yet it nonetheless came as a terrible shock. Her students were stunned at the sight of the sheriff arresting both Prudence and Almira and leading them away from their school. Prudence told her assistant Mariah Davis to go immediately to her father's house and tell him of the new developments.[66] The sheriff then escorted the sisters out the front door of the school to a waiting carriage and drove them to the house of Chauncey Bacon, where Bacon and Rufus Adams formally charged them with the crime of violating the Black Law.

Later that day, a messenger raced to Rev. May's home. May was told that a sheriff had arrested Prudence Crandall and her sister Almira, but the charges against Almira were dismissed—she was not yet twenty-one years old and was still a minor.[67] The messenger told May that Prudence Crandall remained in custody. May did not know the messenger, who likely was sent by Andrew Judson or Rufus Adams. The man told May that he or one of Crandall's friends should post her bail—$150—or else Prudence Crandall would spend the night in jail.

"There . . . (are) gentlemen enough in Canterbury whose bond for that amount would be as good or better than mine, and I should leave it for them to do Miss Crandall that favor," May told the messenger.[68] "But, are you not her friend?" the messenger asked. "Certainly," May replied. He said Miss Crandall did not need his help, and her accusers would be embarrassed by her unjust arrest.[69]

"But, sir, do you mean to allow her to be put into jail?" the man asked. "Most certainly," May replied, "if her persecutors are unwise enough to let such an outrage be committed." May wrote that the man "hurried back to tell Mr. Judson."[70]

Crandall's supporters had already investigated the arrangements for her stay at the Brooklyn jail. In response to a question from Samuel May, prison officials said that Crandall likely would stay in an unoccupied room that two years earlier held a notorious murderer, Oliver Watkins. Watkins had strangled his wife with a whipcord. He was convicted and sentenced to death by hanging. Local tavern owners had anticipated a huge crowd and brisk business on the day of Watkins's execution. They had ordered additional rum and spirits and hired an extra guard at the prison to monitor Watkins so he would not commit suicide.[71] The tavern owners persuaded the authorities to move Watkins to the debtor's room, where he was more easily monitored.

On the day of the hanging, August 2, 1831, wagons and carriages jammed all of the roads leading into Brooklyn, and an immense crowd gathered. Men filled the taverns. Historian Ellen Larned wrote that the execution was carried out "in stillness that seemed of the dead rather than that of the living."[72] The silence, however, quickly disappeared. "The vast throng present, the abundant supply of liquor and scarcity of food made the afternoon and following night a scene of confusion and disorder."[73]

The officials at the Brooklyn jail said that Prudence Crandall would stay in the debtor's room previously occupied by Oliver Watkins. May considered this good news. The notoriety of the Watkins execution was fresh in the minds of Windham County residents; May believed jailing Prudence Crandall in the same prison room where Watkins stayed "would add not a little to the public detestation of the Black Law."[74]

May gathered fresh linens from the Benson family, who lived a short distance away, and remade the bed at the jail. He brought an additional bed into the debtor's room so that Anna Benson—who did not want Crandall to spend the night in jail alone—could stay in the room with Crandall.[75] At two o'clock in the afternoon, another messenger told May that if he did not post Crandall's bail immediately, a sheriff would transport Crandall from Chauncey Bacon's house in Canterbury to the jail in Brooklyn. The opponents of the school suddenly realized that locking Prudence Crandall in the Brooklyn jail might result in sensational news stories casting Canterbury and the Black Law in an unfavorable light. May refused to pay Crandall's bail. Instead, he traveled with George Benson to the jail. When Crandall's carriage pulled up to the prison entrance, May and Benson greeted her. May spoke with her before the sheriff led her inside.[76]

"If now you hesitate, if you dread the gloomy place so much as to wish to be saved from it, I will give bonds for you even now," May told Crandall.[77] "Oh no," she replied. "I am only afraid they will not put me into jail . . . I am the more anxious that they should be exposed, if not caught in their own wicked devices."[78]

Sheriff Roger Coit slowly led Crandall down the walkway to the entrance of the jail. "He was ashamed to do it," May wrote.[79] Before Coit took Crandall through the door, he looked to see if someone might rush forward with the bail for Crandall's release. Coit whispered to two men standing nearby. The men walked over to May and made one last plea for Crandall's bail. "It would be a shame, an eternal disgrace to the state, to have her put into jail, into the very room that Watkins had last occupied," they told May.[80] "Certainly, gentlemen," May replied, "and you may prevent this."[81]

"We are not her friends . . ." the men said, "we don't want any more niggers coming among us. It is your place to stand by Miss Crandall and help her now. You and your abolition brethren have encouraged her to bring this nuisance into Canterbury, and it is mean (for) you to desert her now."[82]

May told the men he had not deserted Crandall. He candidly told them that Crandall's arrest and prosecution would help expose the infamous Black Law. May said the people of Connecticut would not "realize how bad, how wicked, how cruel a law it is, unless we suffer her persecutors to inflict upon her all the penalties it prescribes. . . . It is easy to foresee that Miss Crandall will be glorified, as much as her persecutors and our State will be disgraced, by the transactions of this day and this hour."[83]

The men cursed May, and Sheriff Coit led Crandall into the debtor's room where Oliver Watkins had spent his last night. As May and Benson walked from the jail to May's carriage to return home to Brooklyn, May noticed the sunset. "The sun had descended nearly to the horizon; the shadows of night were beginning to fall around us. . . . So soon as I had heard the bolts of her prison-door turned in the lock, and saw the key taken out, I bowed and said, 'The deed is done, completely done. It cannot be recalled. It has passed into the history of our nation and our age.'"[84]

After the tumult of the day, the night passed quietly. On Friday, George Benson posted the bond for Prudence, and she was set free on bail awaiting trial. As May had predicted, word of her imprisonment spread quickly. Newspapers throughout the country printed stories about the female schoolteacher who had spent a night in jail for the crime of teaching black women, including the *Liberator*, where guest editors Oliver Johnson and George Bourne continued to write and publish in William Lloyd Garrison's absence.

"Savage Barbarity! Miss Crandall Imprisoned!!! The persecutors of Miss Crandall have placed an indelible seal upon their infamy!" the *Liberator* screamed. "*They have* cast her into prison! Yes, into the *very cell occupied* by Watkins the Murderer!!"[85]

In response to the sensational news accounts, Andrew Judson received threatening letters from readers throughout the Northeast and as far away as Pennsylvania.[86] One person had a unique proposal. The man offered to "jail" Judson in a portable cage and display him for the curious of England

and France. The man promised "good food and no whipping or compulsion unless absolutely necessary."[87]

Crandall's opponents tried to counter the bad press with their own letters. They questioned the assertion that Crandall had spent the night in the same prison cell used by a murderer. "Some person has put in wide circulation the story that she was confined in the cell of Watkins the murderer," Andrew Judson and Rufus Adams wrote in a joint letter. "This is part of the same contrivance to 'get up more excitement.' She never was confined in the murderer's cell. She was lodged in the debtor's room, where every accommodation was provided, both for her and her friends, whose visits were constant."[88]

The complaining by Judson and Adams did little to counteract the story of Prudence Crandall's night in jail. Their criticism focused on the word "cell." They said Prudence did not spend the night in the "cell" where Watkins spent most of his days in jail. Their complaints were trivial and misleading by their own admission; they acknowledged that the debtor's room where Crandall stayed was the same room where Watkins had spent "the last days of his life . . . to receive the clergy and his friends."[89]

Days after Crandall's imprisonment, Samuel May received a letter from Arthur Tappan. Tappan may have read one of the many press accounts of Prudence Crandall's arrest and learned of May's defending Crandall and her school. While they had not kept in touch, Tappan and May knew each other from years before. Tappan's father worked as a silversmith in Northampton, Massachusetts, and later went into the dry goods business. In the spring of 1801, when Arthur was fourteen, his father sent Arthur to Boston for an apprenticeship with Sewall and Salisbury, importers and retailers in hardware and dry goods. Tappan stayed for two years and during that time lived with the family of Joseph May, Samuel's father. Samuel was very young—he was five years old when Tappan finished his apprenticeship—but he knew that Tappan had started his successful business career while living with May and his family.[90]

The paths of these two men had not crossed often since that time. When May received Tappan's letter, he recalled that he last saw Tappan ten years earlier in 1823.[91] May had followed Tappan's career and noted that they had significant "theological differences," most likely regarding Tappan's interest in the evangelical movement.[92] While May did not consider himself "personally acquainted" with Tappan in 1833, he had great respect for his generosity and his willingness to engage in the fight to end slavery in America.[93]

In his letter, Tappan thanked May for his courageous work on behalf of Crandall's "benevolent enterprise" and the right of colored people to obtain an education.[94] "This contest, in which you have been providentially called to engage, will be a serious, perhaps a violent one," Tappan wrote. "It may be prolonged and very expensive. Nevertheless, it ought to be persisted in to the last."[95]

Tappan knew that neither Crandall nor her supporters could afford the expense of a first-rate legal defense. The cause of equality in education, however, must be sustained, Tappan said. "Consider me your banker," Tappan told May. "Spare no necessary expense. Command the services of the ablest lawyers. See to it that this great case shall be thoroughly tried . . . I will cheerfully honor your drafts to enable you to defray that cost."[96] Tappan's latest act of generosity had a dramatic effect not only on May's state of mind that day—he was elated—but also on the quality of legal firepower that Prudence Crandall would have on her side. May moved immediately to retain "the three most distinguished members of the Connecticut Bar": William W. Ellsworth, Calvin Goddard, and Henry Strong.[97]

The good news from Arthur Tappan was tempered by a series of incidents that threatened to break the spirit of Crandall and the young women at her school. Crandall called the summer of 1833 the "weary, weary days."[98] The excitement of planning and launching the school had transformed into a seemingly endless string of obstacles and grinding opposition. The simple act of buying supplies from a local vendor constituted a violation of the Black Law. The harassment and vandalism that increased after the passage of the law continued. Students worried for their safety.

The court scheduled Prudence Crandall's trial for August. If convicted of violating the Black Law, Crandall knew that in a few weeks she might face the possibility of large fines that would close her school and destroy her financial future. In early July she came down with a fever. The *Liberator* attributed her sickness to her stay in prison, but more likely it was related to the stress of the enormous challenge she had undertaken and the responsibility she felt to her students and her family.[99] She did not recover quickly and rested for most of the month of July.

During this time, Crandall wrote a song for her students to sing. Crandall later recalled, "Four little colored girls dressed in white sang beautifully the following lines which I composed for them."[100]

Four little children here you see
In modest dress appear
Come listen to our song so sweet
And our complaints you'll hear

'Tis here we come to learn to read
And write and cipher too
But some in this enlightened Land
Declare 'twill never do

The morals of this favored town
Will be corrupted soon
Therefore they strive with all their might
To drive us to our homes

Some time when we have walked the street
Saluted we have been
By guns and drums and cow bells too
And horns of polished tin

With warnings threatened words severe
They visit us at times
And gladly would they send us off
To Afric's burning climes

Our teacher too they put in jail
Trust held by bars and locks
Did e're such persecution reign
Since Paul was in the stocks

But we forgive, forgive the men
That persecute us so
May God in mercy save their souls
From everlasting woe[101]

Throughout the summer, the *Liberator* published letters from Crandall's students. Crandall and her fellow teachers likely read and reviewed the letters prior to their delivery to the *Liberator*. The letters provide an important window into the life of the embattled school. On July 6, 1833, a student wrote of her appreciation for the opportunity to receive an education, but noted that prejudice born in selfishness and ignorance had overshadowed the "bright ray" of knowledge. The student had a pessimistic view of the school's future.

"From our land Justice seems to have taken her flight . . . Go tell the people that pride is coiling round their hearts . . . their tender hearts are growing cold and hardened, the path in which they walk is laid across human beings, and they are crushing them to the earth, beings like themselves, guilty of no other crime than wearing a complexion, 'not colored like their own.' If the unrighteous law which has lately been made in this state compels us to be separated, let us submit to it, my dear associates, with no other feelings towards those that so deal with us, than love and pity."[102]

Prudence Crandall and her students prepared for the intense challenges that loomed in the weeks and months ahead.

6 : Sanctuary Denied

The ongoing acts of vandalism against Prudence Crandall's school took a more serious turn in July 1833.

Almira Crandall managed the school as Prudence continued to recuperate from the sickness she suffered in the wake of her arrest. After a particularly long day, Almira sent the students to bed, paused to rest in the first-floor parlor room, and then went upstairs. Moments later a crash on the first floor resounded throughout the school. Almira rushed downstairs to investigate—an enormous impact had shattered the panes in the parlor window, and shards of broken glass covered the floor. Almira saw a rock in the middle of the floor "about the size of my hand and about an inch and a half in thickness."[1]

The students came downstairs to see what happened; they were frightened but relieved that no one was hurt. Later that night Almira heard a loud thud of a rock hitting the clapboard wall of the schoolhouse. The following morning, Almira checked the outside of the school and noticed stains and dents from eggs and rocks that had smashed against the front of the school.[2]

An anonymous author published a fresh attack on Prudence Crandall in the *Windham County Advertiser* in July. "In her reckless disregard of the rights and feelings of all her neighbors, in her obstinate adherence to her plan of defiance of the entreaties of her friends and of the laws of the land, in her attempts to excite public sympathy by ridiculously spending a night in prison without the smallest necessity of it, she has stepped out of the hallowed precincts of female propriety . . . With all her complaints of persecution, I suspect she is pleased with the sudden notoriety she has gained."[3] The writer claimed he did not live in Canterbury and had no other interest in the school; however, the writer's prose and point of view was consistent with that of Andrew Judson, the leader of the local colonization society.

"Let all things be done decently and in order," the writer said. "If such an institution is to be established, let it be done with ultimate reference to the removal of the pupils to Africa. Here, and here only, can they stand on the proud eminence of freedom and equality."[4] Oliver Johnson was sufficiently impressed with the irony of the author's assertion—true freedom and equality for blacks could exist only in Africa and not in the United States—that he reprinted the letter in its entirety in the *Liberator*.[5]

The vast majority of newspapers in Connecticut and elsewhere continued to express hostility toward Crandall and the abolitionists who supported her. The *Norwich Courier* called Crandall's actions "very objectionable, and no friend we have met with can furnish any justification."[6] The editors of the *Hartford Times* accused Crandall's supporters of "fraudulent misrepresentation" in their criticism of the Black Law and Crandall's arrest.[7] The *Times* took aim at "Tappan with his purse—Garrison with his insane projects—and zealots who are devoted to the welfare of Heathen abroad and Negroes and Indians at home."[8] Crandall and her abolitionist friends conspired to destroy the harmony of Canterbury, the *Times* said, "regardless of the feelings of those who happened to be white."[9] The *New Hampshire Patriot* described Crandall as a "fanatic old maid" who "knew what the law was but she wished to be considered a martyr."[10] The editors of the *Patriot* said Crandall was arrested "not exactly for teaching young negroes to read, but for *breaking the law*,"[11] and called her night in jail "a mere make-believe imprisonment."[12] The editors of the *New Haven Register* agreed with Crandall's opponents who said that town officials should be allowed to prohibit "a school of imported negroes . . . Should two or three mad persons have more power than the whole of the inhabitants of a town?"[13]

Samuel May wrote to Arthur Tappan to tell him of the new developments. He described the difficulties the school faced in the wake of Crandall's imprisonment, including the increased vandalism and hostile press coverage. Despite the success of publicizing Crandall's night in jail, May said "adversaries wielded several newspaper presses incessantly against Miss Crandall's school, and the others would not venture to defend it."[14] The articles "teemed with the grossest misrepresentations, and the vilest insinuations against Miss Crandall, her pupils and her patrons," and the newspapers refused to allow any space "to refute the slanders they were circulating."[15]

May knew that Crandall needed additional allies and resources to respond to Judson and his campaign to close the school. May sent his letter to Tappan and made plans to travel to New York City. Four days later, on the morning of Thursday, July 11, 1833, without warning, Arthur Tappan appeared at May's door in Brooklyn, Connecticut.[16]

"I never grasped a human hand with more joy or gratitude," May said.[17] Tappan left his pressing business matters in New York to see Crandall's school for a firsthand look at the challenges she faced. Tappan's visit came at a critical time. Prudence Crandall still had not regained her strength after months of fighting for the school's survival. May increasingly worried about the school's future in light of the passage of the Black Law and Crandall's pending trial. He also questioned his own effectiveness given that his abolitionist views had strained relations with his friends and parish. "I found myself becoming an object of general distrust," May wrote to Tappan, "and perceived that I was losing my hold upon the confidence of the few who had ventured to give me any support."[18] Once inside May's home, Tappan told May he needed to better understand how he could help Crandall's school.

"Your last letter implied that you were in so much trouble I thought it best to come and see," Tappan told May, "and consider with you what it will be advisable for us to do."[19] May suggested that the drumbeat of attacks in the press contributed significantly to ongoing opposition in the community. The publisher of one of the local papers, who was a friend of May, told him that he could not possibly print an article in defense of Crandall's school—it would result in the destruction of his readership and relations with advertisers.[20] After listening to May, Tappan called for a carriage and set off to Canterbury to visit the school. He made the six-mile journey to the school without May; Tappan wanted to see Crandall's school and its students on his own.

Prudence Crandall had met Arthur Tappan in New York City in February and subsequently had boasted to her neighbors about his support for her school. At the time she had no idea that her decision to educate young black women would place her in the center of a wrenching controversy leading to her arrest and imprisonment. When Tappan appeared at her door in July, she expressed surprise, disbelief, and gratitude. Tappan was as deeply moved, however, when he toured the school and experienced firsthand what Crandall had accomplished in the face of great adversity: the schoolhouse was filled to capacity with bright and eager young women receiving their lessons. Crandall had succeeded in establishing a thriving, ongoing school for black women. He listened carefully as Crandall spoke about the opposition to her school, her pending criminal trial, the ongoing vandalism and harassment, and the articles in the press that condemned the school.[21] He stayed at the school for nearly three hours before returning to May's home in Brooklyn.

"I believe I now fully understand 'the bad predicament' of which you wrote to me . . . It is even worse than I supposed," Tappan told May.[22] He told May that the fate of Crandall's school could well influence the cause of the entire black population of the United States.[23]

"You must start a newspaper as soon as possible, that you may disabuse the public mind of the misrepresentations and falsehoods with which it has been filled," Tappan said. "Get all the subscribers you can, and I will pay all the expenses you may incur more than the income you receive from subscribers and advertising patrons."[24] May wasted no time in accepting the offer. May told Tappan of a newspaper that had recently gone out of business, with offices and press equipment, in Brooklyn, Connecticut. "We must have it," Tappan said. "Let us go immediately and secure it."[25]

The printing office was a short distance from May's house, so the two men walked to the building, located the man who controlled the dormant press, and settled on a one-year lease of the premises and equipment.[26] On the walk back, May and Tappan talked about the need for immediate emancipation of the slaves and "the great conflict for liberty."[27] They agreed that the fight for liberty included the vigorous defense of Crandall's school.

Shortly thereafter the stagecoach arrived to take Arthur Tappan back to New York City. May and Tappan exchanged commitments of support and mutual farewells. As the coach pulled away, May realized he had agreed to publish a yet-unnamed newspaper that would tell the truth about Crandall's school, attack the unconstitutional Black Law, and refute scurrilous commentary from other newspapers. During the next year the expenses of the newspaper totaled more than six hundred dollars, a significant sum in 1833. Arthur Tappan paid all of it.[28]

Tappan's unexpected visit cheered Prudence Crandall and Samuel May.

When May awoke on Friday, July 12, however, he realized much work lay ahead. "A night's rest brought me to my senses, and I clearly saw that I must have some other help than even Mr. Tappan's pecuniary generosity could give me," May said.[29] At the time May published a religious paper, the *Christian Monitor*, served as pastor of the Unitarian Church in Brooklyn, and taught at Crandall's school. Publishing and editing a weekly political newspaper in addition to his other responsibilities "was wholly beyond my power," May said.[30] May recently had read a thoughtful, well-written article in the *Emancipator*, reprinted from Benjamin Lundy's *The Genius of Universal Emancipation*, criticizing Connecticut's Black Law. Charles C. Burleigh wrote the article and lived in Plainfield, Connecticut, a short carriage ride from Brooklyn. May decided to go to Plainfield and find Burleigh.[31]

May arrived at the Burleigh family farm later that same day. The dry, sunny weather made it a perfect day for haying, and Charles and his brothers were all in the fields. Charles's mother told May to come back another time, but May persisted. "My business with him is more important than haying," May said.[32]

Charles Burleigh did not impress May at first. Burleigh came in from the fields in his ragged farm clothes. He had a scruffy beard. Twenty-two years old, Burleigh taught in the local district school and studied law while helping his parents tend to their farm. As May and Burleigh talked about the antislavery movement, however, May heard the voice of the writer who wrote the eloquent article in the *Emancipator*. May trusted his instincts and immediately offered the job of newspaper editor to Charles. When May promised to help find a person to take Burleigh's place at the family farm, Charles accepted.[33] Burleigh began his new career in publishing the very next Monday, July 15, 1833.

In order to counter those who claimed that advocates of immediate emancipation favored breaking up the United States, May named the newspaper the *Unionist*. "It was soon acknowledged by the public that the young editor wielded a powerful weapon," May said.[34] Charles Calistus Burleigh had more than farming in his bloodlines. Burleigh's grandmother on his father's side, the former Lydia Bradford, was a direct descendant of William Bradford, who came to America in 1620 on the Mayflower. William Bradford became the second governor of the Plymouth Colony in 1621 and began the American tradition of Thanksgiving with a New England feast of friendship between the Pilgrims and the Wampanoag Indians.[35] Charles's father, Rinaldo Burleigh, overcame the childhood loss of an arm and graduated from Yale in 1803. He followed his mentor, Timothy Dwight, the eighth president of Yale and leader of the Federalist Party in Connecticut, into the profession of teaching until blindness ended his education career in 1827.[36] Rinaldo joined the abolitionist movement and served as a deacon in the Plainfield Congregational Church for forty-five years.

May and Charles Burleigh taught themselves how to operate the printing press and agreed to publish the newspaper every Thursday. They worked quickly and efficiently. On Thursday, July 25—just thirteen days after May met Burleigh on the farm in Plainfield—the first issue of the *Unionist* appeared.[37] May contributed extensively to the first two issues; afterward, Charles Burleigh wrote and edited the paper.

During this time, Prudence Crandall's school attracted many members of the clergy who wished to preach to her students and support her fight for equality. In addition to Samuel May, ministers from nearby churches stopped by to pray or teach the Gospel to her students. From as far away as Pawtucket, Rhode Island, evangelical ministers such as Reverend Ray Potter came to the school.[38] On one occasion when Rev. Potter preached to the students, vandals interrupted the service and "assailed the house with volleys of rotten eggs and other missiles."[39]

Potter, a friend and supporter of William Lloyd Garrison, later became a notorious figure in the antislavery movement. In the course of his ministerial duties in 1837, Potter met Abigail Bagley, an unmarried member of the Pawtucket Female Anti-Slavery Society, and engaged her initially in Bible study and later in a romantic relationship. When Bagley became pregnant, Potter, who was married, admitted paternity.[40] Convicted of adultery, Potter served six months in jail and lost his career in the ministry. He later wrote a best-selling "confessional" booklet and embarked on a successful career in business.[41]

Critics of the abolition movement pointed to the scandal as evidence of the moral deficiency of abolitionists. Some questioned the propriety of women working closely with men on issues such as temperance and abolition.[42] This issue was not new and followed Prudence Crandall during the years she ran her school for black women. Her opponents often insinuated a romantic involvement between Crandall and Garrison or equated her activism with the disregard of female sensibility and the proper role of women. As the anonymous writer in the *Windham County Advertiser* said, "In her obstinate adherence to her plan . . . she has stepped out of the hallowed precincts of female propriety."

Other than Samuel May, Rev. Levi Kneeland visited Crandall's school more often than any other minister. His charismatic preaching had attracted Crandall to religious revivals and stimulated an activist approach to her spiritual beliefs. As Crandall's minister at the Packerville Baptist Church in Plainfield, Kneeland invited Crandall and her students to attend his church whenever they wished.[43]

Crandall and her students regularly made the trip—a twenty-minute wagon ride—to Kneeland's church during the summer of 1833. Pardon Crandall drove one of the two wagons filled with Crandall's students. Daniel Packer, the mill owner whose family created Packerville and supported the Baptist church, drove the other. Packer had warned Crandall about the challenges of creating a school for black women, but he supported her effort to provide religious instruction to the young women.

Following a service at the church on a Sunday in July, Packer gathered enough students to fill his wagon and set off on the return trip to Canterbury. Pardon Crandall assembled the remaining girls and left for Canterbury about ten minutes later. After traveling for several minutes, Packer approached the Quinebaug River. The road led directly into a shallow stretch of the river; Packer usually slowed down to allow the horse to get its footing as it passed through the water. On this afternoon, before the horses entered the water, Packer noticed a group of young men on the other side of the river. They shouted taunts and threats. Packer instructed the young women to get out of the wagon and wait while he proceeded to drive across the Quinebaug River to confront the men. As Packer got to the midway point, the young men rushed into the water. Packer jumped off of the wagon to challenge them, but they ignored him and unhitched the horse from the wagon. They turned the wagon on its side and then completely over into the water and fled as Pardon Crandall appeared with his wagon. Pardon drove his wagon with the other students through the Quinebaug without incident and dropped off the students at the school. Pardon returned to the Quinebaug with his son Hezekiah, and they pulled Packer's wagon out of the river. Packer then returned to

Plainfield while Pardon took his daughter Prudence and the remaining girls back to Canterbury.[44]

Shortly thereafter, Daniel Packer decided to leave Plainfield on an extended trip to Saratoga and Niagara Falls. He left his son, Daniel Packer Jr., in charge of the family's affairs at the mill and the Packerville Baptist Church. Daniel let Crandall know that neither she nor her students could attend services at the church while his father was away. The influence of the Packer family—they built the church—was so significant that Rev. Kneeland's opinion does not appear to have played a role in the decision.[45]

Crandall considered taking her students to the Canterbury Congregational Church. Located across the street from her school, it made for a much easier trip, but some of Crandall's fiercest opponents—including Andrew Judson—worshipped there. On Saturday, July 6, Crandall asked Samuel Hough, the factory owner who helped finance the purchase of the school, to relay a message to two deacons of the church, Dr. Andrew Harris and Asahel Bacon. Following the custom where families purchased seats or entire pews as a way of supporting the church, Crandall offered to "purchase seats sufficient for my scholars."[46] As an alternative, Crandall asked Hough for permission to have her students sit in the gallery or "any part or portion of the meeting house you might see fit for us to occupy."[47]

When Crandall's students attended Packerville Baptist Church, they occupied "the back pews in the gallery near the door."[48] Blacks regularly attended church services in many New England churches—they did not have to ask permission—and sat in segregated portions of the church, usually in the rear of the balcony on narrow and straight-backed bench seating referred to as the "slave gallery."[49] Crandall knew, however, that given the animosity toward her school it made sense to ask permission in order to avoid another controversy.

After two weeks, Crandall had not received a reply from the deacons of the church. She sought out Sam Hough, who told her he spoke with deacons Harris and Bacon, and neither objected. On Sunday, July 21, 1833, with Prudence still not feeling well, Almira Crandall walked the students over to the Congregational Church for the morning service. They entered the church and took seats where they could find them, including in some of the pews on the main floor. The following Friday, a messenger delivered a notice to Prudence Crandall from a church committee consisting of Solomon Payne, Dr. Andrew Harris, and Isaac Knight.

"When the Committee visited you last February stating their objections to your school, they understood from you, by your voluntary suggestions, that you should never desire and never would put your colored scholars into the meeting house," Payne and the others wrote. "It now appears that you have departed from this voluntary declaration and put your colored scholars into pews even occupied by the white females of the Parrish."[50] The committee further claimed that Crandall assured them that religious instruction and services would take place at the schoolhouse, and "the citizens of Canterbury need have no anxiety on that account." They said Crandall assured them her students would not attend services at the church. They ended their letter by asking Crandall "by whose license you have thus taken possession of that part of the meeting house?"[51]

Frustrated with yet another controversy, and one she had tried to avoid, Crandall wrote a terse reply on Monday, July 29, 1833. Regarding the question of whose authority Crandall had relied on for entry to the church, she replied that she asked Samuel Hough to raise the issue with Dr. Andrew Harris and Asahel Bacon, and Hough had done so. "Dr. Harris, in answer, said we might occupy the seat in the gallery appropriated to colored persons," Crandall wrote. "Mr. Hough then remarked that the seat would not be sufficient to seat the scholars. Deacon Bacon then replied that we might take the next pews until we had enough to be seated."[52]

Crandall admitted that in February she had said, "The scholars that come here shall not trouble you on the Sabbath." She wrote that she changed her mind because the Congregational Church was so convenient to her school. "Upon mature consideration, as regular preaching here was not readily obtained, I considered that I had done entirely wrong in depriving my scholars from attending religious worship in this village. These are my reasons for asking the privilege of entering your church; and all the license I have is given above."[53] She did not receive a reply, but when Prudence walked across the street with her students the next Sunday, August 4, the deacons barred them from entering the church.[54]

Whether a majority of the parishioners of the Canterbury Congregational Church wished to exclude Crandall and her students from their church is unknown. Some in the congregation, particularly Andrew Judson and the town leaders, did not wish to pray with Crandall during the anxious time leading up to her trial and the test of the Black Law. What is known is that the refusal of the church deacons to allow Crandall's students to attend services led to a backlash in public opinion. Many believed that churches should admit those who wished to worship on Sunday morning, regardless of color. After receiving complaints about Crandall's exclusion, Judson and the other church officials simply denied that they had refused entry to Crandall and her students. A letter to the *Windham County Advertiser* asserted that no one turned the students away and stories to the contrary were "wholly false."[55] In the next issue of the *Unionist*, Charles Burleigh expressed "surprise at a declaration so unqualified."[56] Burleigh reprinted the July correspondence from the church committee to Prudence Crandall and their expectation that Crandall would never bring her "colored scholars into the meeting house."[57] Burleigh pointed out that church officials had indeed turned Crandall and her students away when they attempted to enter the church.[58] Burleigh said that Judson's curious denial proved that Crandall's opponents paid no mind to the facts and their own actions.

As Crandall continued her fight, another woman of independence became interested in Crandall's cause. Many throughout the United States knew Lydia Maria Child as the successful author of novels and the *American Frugal Housewife*, a popular domestic advice book. Living in the Boston area, she met William Lloyd Garrison and learned of Crandall through the antislavery work of her husband, David Lee Child. Garrison "got hold of the strings of my conscience, and pulled me into Reforms," Child wrote. "Old dreams vanished, old associates departed, and all things became new."[59] Child also had a connection with one of Prudence Crandall's strongest supporters, Samuel May—he was her husband David's college classmate and friend.

While at home in Massachusetts during the first half of 1833, Child researched and wrote an extensive work concerning the history of slavery and its destructive results in the United States. Child published *An Appeal in Favor of That Class of Americans Called Africans* in August 1833. She analyzed and rejected the idea of colonization and agreed with those who said it resulted in banishing free blacks and increasing the value of slaves.[60]

Child's book on slavery went to press just before Crandall's trial began in August. "The attempt to establish a school for African girls at Canterbury, Connecticut, has made too much noise to need a detailed account in this volume," Child wrote. "Had the Pope himself attempted to establish his supremacy over that commonwealth, he could hardly have been repelled with more determined and angry resistance."[61] The argument used to defend the Black Law—that the influx of black women from other states would cause lawlessness and moral decay—was a racist argument used to deny education and opportunity to black families, Child said.

"I have often heard it said that there was a disproportionate number of crimes committed by the colored people . . . the same thing is true of the first generation of Irish emigrants; but we universally attribute it to their ignorance, and agree that the only remedy is to give their children as good an education as possible," Child wrote.[62] "And what will so effectually elevate their character and condition as knowledge? I beseech you, my countrymen, think of these things wisely. . . ."[63]

Child did not believe Crandall's opponents were different from most citizens in Massachusetts or any other New England state. "Alas, while we carry on our lips that religion which teaches us to 'love our neighbor as ourselves,' how little do we cherish its blessed influence within our hearts," Child said.[64] "Thanks to our soil and climate, and the early exertions of the Quakers, the *form* of slavery does not exist among us; but the very *spirit* of the hateful and mischievous thing is here in all its strength."[65] If someone had proposed a school for black women elsewhere in New England, Child said, "a similar spirit would probably have been manifested."[66]

Child dedicated her *Appeal* to "the Rev. S. J. May, of Brooklyn, Connecticut. This volume is most respectfully inscribed, as a mark of gratitude, for his earnest and disinterested efforts in an unpopular but most righteous cause."[67] Charles Burleigh reviewed Child's book in the *Unionist* to ensure that those in Canterbury and the surrounding towns knew of the references to Crandall's school. Burleigh said if "every friend and every enemy of our cause" read Child's book, even some of Crandall's opponents might change their minds and "enlist under the banner of justice."[68]

During the previous year, Lydia Maria Child's husband, David, wrote a series of letters to Edward S. Abdy, a British philanthropist and fellow at Cambridge University. Abdy supported the antislavery cause in England, and Child hoped to interest him in the anti-slavery efforts in the United States. Abdy not only took an interest but also vowed to travel to America to visit Prudence Crandall's school.

Abdy arrived in New York and met William Lloyd Garrison just as Garrison was preparing to leave for England. They discussed antislavery societies in England and the need to discredit colonization.[69] Garrison told Abdy about those who wanted to capture him and send him south, and also about Andrew Judson's efforts to serve him with a lawsuit.[70] Abdy described Garrison as "a man who had already made some noise in the country, and is destined, if he live, to fill a niche in its history."[71]

While in Boston, Abdy met Lydia Maria Child and read her book on slavery. He credited her with being one of the first women in the United States to speak out publicly in favor of emancipation.[72] "Her devotion to an unpopular cause would alienate some of her friends," Abdy wrote. "These considerations would not, however, have the slightest effect in altering the course of conduct prescribed to her by a sense of duty, as she was as little likely to abandon any object from the fear of censure, as to pursue it from the love of praise."[73]

At the end of July, Charles Burleigh continued to rebut attacks in the local press in each issue of the *Unionist*. Almira Crandall and William Burleigh, a new teacher at the school and Charles's brother, met the daily responsibilities of running Crandall's school. In England, William Lloyd Garrison continued his efforts to thwart colonization, and in New York City, Arthur Tappan tended to his business. Prudence Crandall's attorneys furiously prepared her legal defense; her trial would begin in a matter of days.

A student at Crandall's school detailed the crisis atmosphere in a letter published in the *Liberator*. The local church did not allow the black students to worship. Vandals continued to cause damage to the school. Merchants refused to sell goods to Miss Crandall under penalty of the Black Law. Doctors refused to provide care at the school. Men jeered at the students when they walked outside. Crandall's students—the young black women who had traveled to Crandall's school to obtain an education and pursue a dream of opportunity—understood that lawyers, town officials, and a good portion of the general public seemed to hate them and wanted to send them home.

"We as a body, my dear school-mates, are subject to many trials and struggles, and we all know to what they are attributable—it is the prejudice the whites have against us that causes us to labor under so many disadvantages." The student wrote that Crandall persuaded her scholars "not to indulge in angry feelings towards our enemies—with unceasing and untiring earnestness has she plead with us to forgive them."[74]

"It is very necessary that we all have the principle of forgiveness instilled into our hearts," the student wrote. "We should always be careful that a spirit of retaliation does not get a seat in our affections, for how very unpleasant it is to feel envious towards our fellow creatures . . . If anyone has wronged us, let us in the spirit of meekness obey that injunction of our dear saviour—'Bless them that curse you, do good to them that hate you, and pray for them that despitefully use you and persecute you.'"[75]

At the beginning of August, British abolitionist Edward S. Abdy traveled from Boston to Providence. The forty-two-mile trip by stagecoach, including stops, took about seven hours, and he arrived at six in the evening. The next day he visited the Friend's School that Prudence Crandall had attended.

"On the 5th of August, I left Providence by the stage for Brooklyn in Connecticut, on my way to Canterbury, where a lady of the name of Crandall—a name that had been heard in every hamlet and house throughout the Union—had set up a school for colored girls," Abdy wrote. "My object, in thus going out of my road, was to see what could have caused so much ire to the liberal minds of republican America."[76]

On his trip through the countryside, Abdy noticed many farms in disrepair and families struggling to survive. The houses and barns were roughly constructed, the children were "shabbily clad," and the soil seemed poor and rocky. Abdy sat between the stagecoach driver and another passenger and asked the driver for his opinion of Miss Crandall's school. "I cannot see why a black skin should be a bar to anyone's rising in the world, or what crime there can be in trying to elevate any portion of society by education," the driver said. "It is prejudice alone that has made the distinction, and if a white man will not enter my coach because I have admitted, and always will admit, a colored person into it, all I can say is, he must find some other conveyance."[77] The other passenger agreed. Abdy concluded that laborers in the countryside exhibited less prejudice toward blacks than merchants or shopkeepers in the town center. "The humble tillers of the ground have, in this respect, more real dignity of character than the purse-proud merchant."[78]

When the coach arrived in Brooklyn, Abdy met Samuel May. After breakfast, May took Abdy by wagon to Crandall's school in Canterbury. Abdy noticed the broken window in the parlor. "The window was left in the same state as it was in after the outrage, and the stone, which was as broad as my fist though not quite so thick, was put into my hands. . . . Had it struck any of the females—there was not a man in the house—the blow might have inflicted a very serious injury."[79]

Abdy spoke at length with Crandall and learned that local shops and tradesmen refused to provide her with goods or services; she traveled hours to Norwich or Providence to purchase groceries and supplies for the school. Crandall still suffered from the lingering effects of her fever, and Abdy noted, "She was at the time in a weak state of health."[80] Nevertheless, Crandall described in detail the history of the school, the opposition she faced, and her arrest. She showed Abdy the letter she received from the local Congregational church, objecting to her black students sitting in the pews at the church, and also showed him a copy of her response. Abdy observed some of the classes at her school and met her students.

"If I might judge of what I saw, both of this lady and of her establishment during the three or four hours I remained there, never was there a person less deserving of such treatment," Abdy wrote. "As for her pupils, it would be no easy matter to explain to a European, how any man of common sense could fancy the tranquility of a country village could be disturbed and the 'rights of its inhabitants' could, by any possible combination of untoward circumstances, be invaded by nineteen young women."[81] Abdy said the persecution of Crandall by her neighbors for educating black women—a meritorious act—was "the most striking instance of intolerance and bigotry" he had witnessed.[82]

May and Abdy returned to Brooklyn where they joined with neighbors, young and old, at May's house. Abdy felt "as if I had been surrounded by the friends of my youth." He spoke for some time with eighty-year-old George Benson, who had worked with Moses Brown earlier in his life and called himself an "uncompromising abolitionist." They noticed that the women at May's house were interested in "a young man, whose voice, accompanied by a guitar he held in his hand, had greater attractions for his fair audience than a philosophical discussion on the aristocracy of the skin."[83]

The following day, May took Abdy on a tour of a local farm. The farmhouse was kept in a "neat and comfortable state," according to Abdy, with long-backed, rush-bottomed chairs, maple tables with the leaves down, a clock ticking against the wall, a gun hanging on the crossbeam near the ceiling, and a "cozy armchair for the old folks in the chimney corner."[84] On matters of race, the farmers said they did not object to Crandall's school. On the ride back to May's house, Abdy reflected on his meeting with Prudence Crandall and the people he had met, both black and white, in Brooklyn and Canterbury. "A new era was commencing for no inconsiderable portion of its population," Abdy wrote, "and the success which awaits the noble efforts made in their behalf will be associated in the memory of a grateful race with the humble but honored name of a schoolmistress in the neighborhood."[85]

The next day, Friday, August 9, 1833, Abdy took the stagecoach from Brooklyn to Hartford. The enlightened opinions that Abdy recently had heard were contradicted by the passengers of that day. All knew of the Prudence Crandall controversy, and all joined in condemning her. One passenger said that Crandall followed the orders of agitators and fanatics because they paid her debts. Another said the vandalism at the school was actually a case of fraud; the passenger claimed Crandall's supporters caused the damage themselves and blamed their opponents in order to embarrass Andrew Judson and other town officials. A soldier from Pittsburgh said he "never heard so much about the blacks" as he did during his short stay in Brooklyn.

Abdy told his fellow passengers the controversy was "much ado about nothing," given that young white and black schoolchildren often sat in the same classroom at the public district schools—as they did in Canterbury and many other towns.[86] "If the carpenter's and mason's child escape contamination in the public schools, the lawyer need not fear for his daughter's gentility and purity," Abdy said.[87] The other passengers strongly disagreed. For the first time Abdy experienced the hostility directed toward Crandall and the local support for "the Judsonian law for the suppression of knowledge."[88]

. Prudence Crandall, April 1834.

2. Slave purchase flyer,
Charleston, South Carolina.

CASH!

All persons that have **SLAVES** to dispose of, will do
well by giving me a call, as I will give the

HIGHEST PRICE FOR

Men, Women, & CHILDREN.

Any person that wishes to sell, will call at Hill's tavern, or at Shannon Hill for me, and any information they want will be promptly attended to.

Thomas Griggs.

Charlestown, May 7, 1835.

PRINTED AT THE FREE PRESS OFFICE, CHARLESTOWN.

THE PARTING "Buy us too."

THE LASH.

3. Slave traders and auctioneers were not
prohibited from separating husband from
wife or children from parents.

4. Slaves often were brutally punished;
no consequence ensued to a slave owner
who injured or killed a slave.

5. Hezekiah Carpenter House, Prudence Crandall's birthplace, in Hope Valley, Rhode Island.

6. Hezekiah Crandall, brother of Prudence.

7. Esther Carpenter Crandall, mother of Prudence Crandall.

8. Prudence Crandall's school in Canterbury, Connecticut, site of Prudence Crandall Museum.

9. *Canterbury, Connecticut, in the 1830s.* The Canterbury Congregational Church is in the foreground; Crandall's school is on the far left.

10. Unitarian Church of Brooklyn, Connecticut—Samuel Joseph May's church.

11. Canterbury Congregational Church, the location of the town meetings regarding Crandall's school.

12. Packerville Baptist Church, Plainfield, Connecticut, where Crandall and her students worshipped.

13. William Lloyd Garrison in the 1850s.

14. Helen Benson Garrison, wife of William Lloyd Garrison.

15. Arnold Buffum, an abolitionist and ally of Crandall and Garrison.

16. Samuel Joseph May, a minister, teacher at Prudence Crandall's school, and devoted friend to Crandall and Garrison.

17. Charles C. Burleigh, editor of the *Unionist*. He favored immediate emancipation, equal rights for women, and repeal of the death penalty.

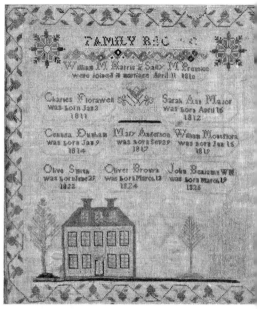

18. Harris family sampler, which states, "Sarah . . . was April 16, 1812." Sarah Harris was Prudence Crandall's firs black student.

(*left*)
19. William H. Burleigh, a teac at Crandall's sc He was a poet, journalist, and abolitionist.

(*right*)
20. Arthur Tapp a wealthy merc and financial supporter of abolitionism ar Prudence Cran school.

7 : **On Trial**

Using Arthur Tappan's financial resources, Samuel May hired three of the best attorneys in Connecticut to defend Prudence Crandall: William Ellsworth, Calvin Goddard, and Henry Strong. Crandall's attorneys expected to persuade the judge and jury that the Black Law violated the Constitution. Samuel May knew, however, that if they lost at the trial court level, they could appeal to the state supreme court, and if necessary, to the U.S. Supreme Court for a definitive ruling on the rights and citizenship of black men and women in America.

The Crandall case would require all of her attorneys to search the Constitution of the United States for direction and clarity regarding citizenship and human rights for blacks. Their mission was unlike that of any other legal team to date in the history of the young nation. For William W. Ellsworth, Crandall's lead attorney, the question of fairness and equality for the less powerful was not a case of first impression. As a congressman in 1830, he had argued against legislation sanctioning the removal of Indian tribes and in favor of the rights of American Indians. He said that American Indians "have the right of territory and self government, and that these have ever been accorded to them by the United States."[1] Ellsworth said the removal scheme was a thinly veiled attempt by certain states to abrogate well-established treaties and steal the Indians' land. "Sir, I declare there is no right in us to take it or their government from them. Power may do it, but the God in heaven will not sanction it. . . . We shall not stand justified before the world in taking any step which shall lead to oppression."[2]

William Ellsworth's family had a very direct connection to the roots of American law. Ellsworth's father, Oliver, represented Connecticut in the U.S. Senate, served as the third chief justice of the U.S. Supreme Court, nominated by President George Washington, and helped draft the Constitution of the United States.[3] William Ellsworth followed in his father's substantial legal and political footsteps. He graduated from Yale in 1810 and began practicing law in 1813 in Hartford with Thomas S. Williams, who later became chief justice of the Connecticut Supreme Court. That same year, Ellsworth married Emily Webster, the eldest daughter of Noah Webster, creator of the famous dictionary. At the time of the Crandall trial, Ellsworth served in Congress—then a part-time job—while teaching law at Trinity College and managing a busy law practice. He was fifty-three. Ellsworth later served as governor of Connecticut, judge of the superior court, and justice of the state supreme court.[4]

Calvin Goddard, Prudence Crandall's second attorney, studied law with his cocounsel's father, Oliver Ellsworth, after graduating from Dartmouth in 1786. Goddard taught at the Plainfield Academy and began practicing law in 1790. He served as speaker of the house in the state legislature, as state's attorney for New London County, three years as a judge of the superior court, and as a representative to Congress. In addition to his law practice, he had recently completed a series of terms as mayor of Norwich. Goddard brought substantial legal experience to Crandall's defense team; he was sixty-five years old.[5]

Crandall's third attorney had experience in education and overseeing an academy. After graduating from Yale in 1806, Henry Strong ran a school for young women in Norwich for two years; he knew something about Prudence Crandall's work.[6] Thereafter, he studied law with Judge Charles Chauncey in New Haven and began his law practice in 1810 when he was twenty-two years old. Strong lived in Norwich and later served in the state senate.[7]

A fourth attorney volunteered his services to help Prudence Crandall's legal team. Lafayette S. Foster had studied law in the office of Calvin Goddard and later opened his own office in Hampton.[8] Born in Franklin, Connecticut, Foster was twenty-six years old at the time of Crandall's trial. He later won election to the General Assembly of Connecticut, where he served as speaker of the house, and to the U.S. Senate beginning in 1855, where he served as president pro tempore. After President Abraham Lincoln's assassination in 1865, Foster became vice president of the United

States and continued to serve in the Senate.[9] Foster provided a critical vote against the impeachment of President Andrew Johnson in 1868.[10]

Ellsworth, Goddard, and Strong prepared to argue the first civil rights case in American history. Working together as a team for the first time, Crandall's attorneys did not plan to claim that Crandall was innocent as to the alleged violations of the Black Law. Instead, they intended to argue that her black students possessed all the rights and privileges afforded citizens of the United States under the Constitution. They contended that the Black Law violated those fundamental rights and was unconstitutional.

The trial did not begin as planned. On the appointed date, Thursday, August 22, 1833, Judge Joseph Eaton of Plainfield presided at the County Court House in Brooklyn.[11] Attorneys Ellsworth and Strong represented Prudence Crandall. The state's attorney for Windham County, Chauncey F. Cleveland, however, was absent. A sheriff delivered a message to Judge Eaton stating that Cleveland could not attend because of illness. Judge Eaton appointed attorney Ebenezer Stoddard of Woodstock, the state's lieutenant governor, to prosecute the case. Stoddard pleaded illness. The combination of the controversial nature of the case, the large turnout of spectators, and the interest of the press may have increased the odds of prosecutorial sickness. Judge Eaton then asked Jonathan A. Welch to serve as the state's attorney in the Crandall case. Welch had practiced law for twenty years in Windham County.[12] Despite the fact that Welch said he too was fighting sickness, Welch agreed to serve as temporary chief prosecutor.[13]

The court appointed Andrew Judson of Canterbury and Ichabod Bulkley of Ashford as assistant prosecutors.[14] Since Welch had no time to prepare or study the case, he deferred to Judson, who had recently finished his term as state's attorney and as Crandall's chief opponent knew every detail of the case. Ichabod Bulkley, a respected attorney who served as judge of probate in Ashford, assisted in research for the prosecution.[15] Bulkley had graduated from Yale and earlier in his career had worked with Crandall's lead attorney, William Ellsworth.[16] He later served in the state senate. With the team of prosecutors finally assembled, Judge Eaton told the parties the trial would start the next day.[17]

Henry Strong turned forty-five years old on Friday, August 23, but he had no time to celebrate. Together with William Ellsworth, Strong reported to the Brooklyn Courthouse to argue Crandall's case. Calvin Goddard did not participate in courtroom questioning or argument. There is no record of Lafayette Foster assisting with Crandall's case in the courtroom; he most likely helped his former employer Goddard with research.

In the small and familiar legal community of eastern Connecticut, Judge Joseph Eaton had crossed paths with the attorneys for both the defense and the prosecution. Thirty years earlier he had studied law with Calvin Goddard. More recently, Eaton had won an appointment as president of the Windham County Bank with the support of Andrew Judson, who served on the bank's board of directors. Joseph Eaton graduated from Brown University in 1795 and began the practice of law in 1800.[18] He served as a judge of the county court for many years, as probate judge from 1829 to 1845, and as a representative in the state legislature.[19]

The first order of business in the Crandall case was for Eaton and the attorneys to select a jury. The defense objected to one potential juror on the grounds that he signed petitions calling for the closure of the school, took an active role in the campaign against Prudence Crandall, and publicly advocated for passage of the Black Law. Judge Eaton agreed and dismissed the person.[20] Similarly, the defense objected to another potential juror, a sitting state legislator who had voted in favor of the Black Law. Eaton disagreed and allowed the legislator to serve on the jury. In Connecticut, legislators voted to appoint and reappoint judges, and Eaton may have made this seemingly contradictory decision in deference to the legislature. Eaton had a potential conflict of his own, however, that may have influenced his refusal to bar the legislator from serving on the jury. Eaton served as a state representative at the same time he presided as judge. (Connecticut did not constitutionally prohibit legislators from simultaneously serving in the executive or judicial branches until 1958.) As a state representative, Eaton served on the committee that had drafted and recommended the Black Law. Judge Eaton had voted for and spoken in favor of the Black Law on the floor of the House.[21] The motion by attorneys Ellsworth and Strong to dismiss the legislator from the jury pool was likely an indirect attack on Judge Eaton's own conflict and partiality. Before the trial proceeded, the legislator withdrew from jury duty because of illness.[22] Judge Eaton, however, never was challenged directly by Crandall's attorneys and continued to preside over the case.

An overflow crowd traveled to Brooklyn to watch the Crandall trial at the Brooklyn Courthouse, a square, federal-style building located in the center of town at the crossroads of two turnpikes leading to Canterbury, Windham, Hartford, and Providence. The courtroom was located on the second floor; the judge sat in the center of the back wall on a raised desk, and the court clerk and sheriff sat nearby at separate tables. Prudence Crandall and her attorneys sat opposite the prosecutors and within the line of sight of the jurors. The gallery—rows of seats behind the attorneys facing the front of the courtroom—filled the rest of the second floor.[23] Spectators took every seat in the gallery. Samuel May, the Benson family, Prudence Crandall's staff, and some of her students were present to support her.

As the trial began, the judge reviewed the facts of the case. The prosecution charged Crandall with violating two counts of the Black Law. They alleged that she taught "colored persons, not inhabitants of this State" without permission from the town and that she harbored and boarded out-of-state colored persons, while aiding and assisting in their education, without permission from the town. The judge told the jury that Crandall pleaded "not guilty."

The prosecution called its first witness, Asahel Bacon, a Canterbury town official. Andrew Judson asked Bacon about a visit he and Ebenezer Sanger made to Prudence Crandall's school in June and what Crandall had told him about the students at her school.

"She said she had four who were from New York and one from Hartford," Bacon said. "She called them in and introduced them. Theodosia Degrass, Ann Elizabeth Wilder, and Catharine Ann Weldon."[24] Bacon could not remember the specific day in June that he and Sanger had visited the school, but thought it was the day after the girls had arrived from New York. Ebenezer Sanger, another town official, took the stand and said he had heard the conversation between Mr. Bacon and Miss Crandall and confirmed what Bacon stated.

Judson called Sheriff George Cady. The previous Friday, Cady had traveled to the schoolhouse and served the out-of-state black students with subpoenas compelling them to testify at the trial. Cady recalled that Prudence Crandall had questioned the necessity of forcing her students to testify. "Miss Crandall said that she did not see that there was any need of witnesses at all, for she should confess that she had broken the law," Cady said.[25]

Prudence Crandall never testified at her trial. She knew prosecutors might ask her to implicate others in potential violations of the Black Law—those in the community who sold her supplies, helped at the school, and otherwise "aided and assisted" her. Crandall did not want to risk answering questions that might jeopardize her family and supporters. The prosecution could not compel Crandall to testify. As a consequence, however, the prosecution moved to call her students to the stand to help prove their case.

Crandall struggled throughout the school controversy to shield her students from abuse. Crandall had paid a fine when the town charged Ann Hammond with vagrancy rather than subject Hammond to legal action. Her opponents now had the opportunity to question and intimidate her students in a public trial. Crandall instructed her attorneys to fight as hard as they could to protect the young women.

Andrew Judson called Ann Peterson, a student he believed lived out of state, to the stand. William Ellsworth objected. Ellsworth said the Fifth Amendment of the Constitution protected Peterson; the court could not compel her to testify when she might implicate herself in a violation of the law. Prosecutor Welch responded that the recently approved Black Law considered any black student from another state to "be an admissible witness in all prosecutions . . . and may be compelled to give testimony."[26] Judson added that he did not believe his questions would implicate Peterson in any wrongdoing.

Ellsworth said the legislature had no power to compel a witness to answer a question that might implicate that witness in wrongdoing; the legislature could not take away Fifth Amendment rights by statute. He said Peterson's mere act of applying to the school, entering as a student, or paying tuition might be considered "aiding and assisting" the school.[27] Both the U.S. Constitution and the Connecticut Constitution protected Peterson against incriminating herself, Ellsworth said. As Judson and Ellsworth argued back and forth, Judge Eaton ended the debate and ruled that Peterson must answer the prosecution's questions.[28]

Before Judson could ask the first question, Ellsworth rose and once more addressed the court. He told the judge that he had instructed Peterson not to answer any questions regarding the school. "It is now my duty to repeat this advice," Ellsworth said. Ellsworth stood in open defiance of the judge and courtroom procedure—not common tactics for this experienced and esteemed attorney. Ellsworth said he did not intend to embarrass the court, but needed to remind the witness that the court could not command her to testify against herself.[29] Judson ignored Ellsworth and began questioning Peterson.

"Has Miss Crandall kept a school for colored Misses not inhabitants of the State?" Judson asked. "Will you say whether the defendant has or has not instructed any person of color other than yourself since the 10th of June last? With whom do you board? Has or has not Miss Crandall boarded and instructed colored persons not inhabitants of the State?"[30] Peterson refused to answer each question on the ground that she might incriminate herself.

The prosecution excused Peterson but reserved the right to request that the judge hold her in contempt and send her to jail. Judson called two more students, Catharine Ann Weldon and Ann Eliza Hammond. Ellsworth objected and Judge Eaton again overruled him. Judson asked similar questions and both students refused to answer. Judson dismissed them but, as with Peterson, reserved the right to move that the court hold them in contempt. The prosecutors huddled in response to their inability to elicit testimony from any of the out-of-state students. Welch and Judson theorized that if they could subpoena one of Prudence Crandall's students who resided in Connecticut, the student could not raise a Fifth Amendment claim since the Black Law did not prohibit the education of black students who lived in Connecticut. They dispatched a sheriff to Crandall's Canterbury school with a new subpoena.

Judson called Jacob C. Gould to the stand. Gould served as a constable from the fifth ward of Providence, Rhode Island. Judson asked if he knew Ann Eliza Hammond. "The daughter of Thomas Hammond, who died in 1826," Gould replied. "Her mother now lives in Providence—the father at his death was worth from $1,500 to $2,000 in real estate."[31] Gould said he had known Ann Eliza since she was a small child and also knew that she lived in Providence with her mother.

The next witness was Prudence Crandall's minister, Levi Kneeland. Judson asked Kneeland what he knew of the school. Kneeland said he had seen some of Crandall's students at his church during the summer. He told Judson he had no connection to her school.

"Did you advise Miss Crandall in relation to her school?" Judson asked. Kneeland refused to answer. "Did you see any of the students at Miss

Crandall's school?" Kneeland again refused to answer. "Did you visit Miss Crandall's school after the 10th of June last? Have you eaten at Miss Crandall's school since the 10th of June last?" Kneeland said he would not answer the questions.[32]

Judson and Welch moved for contempt and commitment to prison. Judge Eaton told Kneeland that he must answer the questions. Kneeland again refused and the judge ordered his arrest. The sheriff arrested the minister of the Packerville Baptist Church and took him across the street to the Brooklyn Jail.[33]

When the court came back to order, the prosecution called the housekeeper for Prudence Crandall's school as its next witness. Eliza Parkis, a black woman whom Crandall employed to wash clothes and help with other chores, said she saw Ann Eliza Hammond in Providence and at the school in Canterbury. Parkis said that a student from New York, Theodosia Degrass, boarded at the school. When asked whether she had witnessed Crandall teaching classes at the school, Parkis said she never saw any of the girls in class at the school.[34]

Dr. Roland Green, a physician who lived in Canterbury, testified that on occasion he took some of the sick students to his own house. Green said that while he heard Crandall talk about the students in general, he did not hear her discuss where they lived or whether they were from out of state.[35] As Judson dismissed Dr. Green, the trial came to a halt as the sheriff entered the courtroom with Rev. Kneeland. The minister told the judge that he meant no disrespect to the court when he had declined to answer questions earlier in the day. Kneeland—who said that the prosecutors had assured him his testimony would not be used against him—now wished to answer the prosecution's questions. Judge Eaton accepted Kneeland's offer and rescinded the order of contempt.[36]

Kneeland told Judson that he had visited the school on a number of occasions and had prayed with some of the students. As to whether he knew of any out-of-state students, he thought that some lived in other states, perhaps Rhode Island or New York, but was not sure. Kneeland had heard the students recite lessons but did not know where they lived.[37] Judson dismissed Kneeland after gaining virtually no beneficial testimony as a result of the immunity bargain.

The prosecution then called Albert Hinckley, a young abolitionist who acknowledged that he had visited Crandall's house several times in

July. When pressed about what he had seen at the school, Hinckley said that he had called on Crandall as a friend and did not talk with her about the school. He told the court he had tea with Crandall and other young women on one occasion, but he could not say whether the women in the courtroom were the same women he had seen at Crandall's house.[38]

At this point, another sheriff entered the courtroom with Eliza Glasko, a student from Crandall's school and a resident of Griswold, Connecticut.[39] Andrew Judson called Glasko to the stand; attorney Ellsworth objected on the same Fifth Amendment basis. Judge Eaton overruled his objection, and Judson began asking Glasko about the school. Glasko refused to answer any of the questions.

Andrew Judson knew that various witnesses had provided testimony in support of the prosecution's case. Constable Gould had positively identified Ann Eliza Hammond as a resident of Providence, Rhode Island. Other witnesses said that they understood Prudence Crandall operated a school. But prosecutors Judson and Welch also knew that despite what they regarded as obvious—Prudence Crandall taught and boarded black students from other states at her school—no one had said it with certainty and specificity. The Black Law statute specifically prohibited a person from establishing a school for out-of-state black students, instructing any such students, or boarding any such students for the purpose of their instruction without the consent in advance of the local town officials. The law was enforceable against "each and every person who shall knowingly do any act forbidden as aforesaid, or shall be aiding or assisting as therein." Not a single witness said they had seen Prudence Crandall teach Ann Eliza Hammond or any other out-of-state black women at Crandall's school.

When Judson and Welch took a hard line against Rev. Kneeland's refusal to testify, their strategy succeeded to a degree. Kneeland had ended his silence after a trip to the Brooklyn Jail. His testimony, however, proved useless. Judson and Welch had so far refrained from asking Judge Eaton to hold the female students in contempt. Judson likely recalled the backlash in the press that resulted when Prudence Crandall was arrested and spent a night in jail. Judson and Welch, however, needed a witness to confirm the simple fact that Prudence Crandall taught black students from other states at her school. Judson moved to hold Eliza Glasko in contempt of court and asked the court to commit her to prison. Judge Eaton granted the motion and ordered the clerk to draft the writ.[40]

Judson then called Prudence Crandall's brother Hezekiah Crandall to testify. Hezekiah said he had heard that his sister ran a school for colored girls, but he had never witnessed any classes. He thought he recognized Ann Eliza Hammond and Ann Peterson but had not heard his sister speak about the school "for some time."[41] A local wagon driver, George Roberts, said he had driven Ann Eliza Hammond to Crandall's school about five months earlier and thought he heard girls reciting their lessons inside the school. He said he had heard secondhand that Hammond lived in Providence, but he did not recognize any of the students in the courtroom and could not remember having seen any of them at the school.[42]

When Prudence Crandall's attorneys planned their strategy for the trial, they expected the prosecution to succeed in presenting the facts necessary to prove a violation of the Black Law. Samuel May had hired Calvin Goddard in part with the expectation that Crandall would lose at the trial court level; Goddard's task was to provide expertise in positioning the case for appeal and assisting in arguments before the state supreme court. As the trial progressed, however, the competitive spirit of Ellsworth and Strong intensified. They had not made their reputations from conceding at any level, and they did not intend to assist the prosecution in proving the basic facts of the case. Ellsworth and Strong knew that the prosecution had faltered. Denying Andrew Judson the ability to question Prudence Crandall had removed the most direct way for the prosecution to prove its case. The strategy of instructing the students not to testify so as to avoid self-incrimination—even to the point of defying the judge—had blocked the prosecution from obtaining critical testimony. Ellsworth and Strong sensed that, despite all odds, an acquittal was within their grasp.

Judson and Welch knew they had not proved their case with certainty. Rather than begin closing arguments, they desperately surveyed the gallery for an additional witness who might help erase any doubts about whether Crandall was violating the Black Law. Judson saw Mary Benson, a friend of Crandall's and one of the daughters of the Benson family of Brooklyn, and called her to the stand.

Benson said she had visited the school on a number of occasions but had never stayed for very long. When asked about Ann Eliza Hammond, Benson said she recognized her as one of the students she had seen at the school. Benson said that Hammond lived in Providence. Benson recognized another student in the courtroom—Ann Weldon—and said that she lived in New York. Judson asked Benson if she had witnessed any classes or teaching at the school. Benson remembered that about five weeks earlier she had watched Miss Crandall teaching the students geography and arithmetic, including some of the out-of-state students who were present in the courtroom.[43]

It had taken the entire day and the recollection of the very last witness, but Judson finally had obtained the crucial testimony he needed. Mary Benson had identified black students from other states and said that she had seen Prudence Crandall teaching them at her school. Mary meant no harm to Prudence Crandall, but she knew she had to speak the truth and had no constitutional basis on which to refuse to answer. Judson's calling Mary Benson to testify surprised Crandall's attorneys; they did not have an opportunity to prepare Benson regarding her testimony as they had with the other friendly witnesses. For Judson and Welch, Benson's testimony established that Prudence Crandall had violated the Black Law. The prosecution rested their case.

The defense called no witnesses, and the lawyers on both sides prepared to deliver their closing arguments. Ellsworth noticed a sheriff leading Eliza Glasko by the arm and escorting her out of the courtroom; the clerk had finished drafting the writ committing her to prison for contempt. Ellsworth sprang up, blocked the sheriff's path, and asked Judge Eaton to reconvene the trial to allow Glasko to testify.[44] Until this moment, none of Crandall's students had submitted to questioning from Judson or Welch. Ellsworth knew that after Mary Benson's testimony it did not matter whether Glasko identified the other students or confirmed that Crandall had taught out-of-state students. Benson's testimony had provided enough evidence to prove a violation of the Black Law.

Judge Eaton called the court back into session. Ellsworth told the judge that he had advised Miss Glasko and the other students not to speak because of "an impervious sense of professional duty."[45] He now advised Glasko to testify fully and completely. While Ellsworth earlier had defied Judge Eaton, the judge and prosecutors likely did not want this young student to spend the night in jail and create another sensational story for the press. At least two reporters were in the courtroom—a correspondent for the *Connecticut Courant* and Charles Burleigh for the *Unionist*. Judge Eaton agreed to hear Eliza Glasko's testimony.

Glasko said she attended Miss Crandall's school. She recognized the other girls in the courtroom—one lived in Providence and the others resided in New York. Glasko confirmed the identity of the out-of-state students and said that Crandall and her assistants taught the students at the school.[46]

"The ordinary branches were taught there by Miss Crandall, reading, writing, grammar, geography," Glasko said. "The school was usually opened and closed with prayer—the scriptures were read and explained, daily—some portions were committed to memory by the pupils, and considered a part of their education."[47] Andrew Judson concluded his questioning.

After a short break Judge Eaton called the court back to order, and Judson began his closing argument for the prosecution. He recounted the charges against Crandall, the provisions of the Black Law, and the testimony he said supported her conviction. Judson also anticipated William Ellsworth's arguments regarding the constitutionality of the Black Law.

The Black Law did not conflict with the constitutional requirement that "the citizens of each state shall be entitled to all privileges and immunities of citizens in the several states," Judson said, because blacks were not citizens. Connecticut permitted only "free white males" to vote in elections, Judson noted, and federal laws regarding immigration allowed only white persons to become naturalized citizens. He also stressed that the Black Law did not uniformly prevent blacks from attending school in Connecticut.

"The sole intention and provision of the law was that colored persons, from other jurisdictions, should not be intruded into any town in this state without written permission from the selectmen and civil authority of the town in which they proposed to reside."[48] Judson said the Black Law simply required a licensing process. The state required tanners and surveyors to apply for a license before they practiced their trade, Judson said. A tavern owner could not sell alcoholic beverages without first obtaining a permit.

Judson then employed some of the inflammatory arguments that had proved effective at town meetings and in the legislature. If blacks from other states could freely attend Connecticut's schools, "the southern states might emancipate their slaves and send them all to Connecticut instead of Liberia," Judson said. "The influx of that species of population might be so great as to be overwhelming."[49] After Judge Eaton warned Judson to refrain from speculation unrelated to the case, Judson told the jury he favored emancipation, but not if emancipation threatened "destruction to our constitutions and desolating our land."[50] In conclusion, Judson reminded the jury that the proof of Crandall's guilt "was abundant, conclusive."[51] If the jury found that Crandall taught or boarded any of the out-of-state black students at her school, he said, they must find her guilty.

William Ellsworth rose and approached the jury. "In order to convict my client you must find on your oaths that she has committed a crime," Ellsworth said. "You may find that she has violated an act of the state legislature, but if you also find her protected by a higher power, it will be your duty to acquit."[52] Ellsworth said the Constitution represented the highest power in the land. "Beyond that, no legislature can go, and if the jury finds the law not to stand well with the Constitution, they must say so."[53] Ellsworth disagreed with Judson's claim that citizenship depended on the color of a person's skin.

"Is it so that a person born on our soil is not a citizen of our land? In the days of Revolution, these men fought side by side with our fathers, and shed their blood for this country, which was their country—the country to which they owed indefeasible allegiance." Ellsworth noted that black veterans of the Revolutionary War received pensions for their service to their country. He then read the opening lines of the Declaration of Independence: "We hold these truths to be self-evident, that *all men are created equal*, that they are endowed by their creator with certain *unalienable rights*, that among these are life, liberty and the pursuit of happiness." Ellsworth said that if the court agreed with the prosecution's argument, the Declaration of Independence should say "except black men" after every clause.

Ellsworth said the power the legislature exercised over schools in the past—power regarding funding for public schools—did not imply a new right to tell prospective students of any color which schools they could or could not attend. If the legislature had the power to prohibit out-of-state blacks from coming to Connecticut for an education, what could prevent the legislature from requiring that all children go to a Presbyterian school or a Baptist or Methodist school? "Might not the legislature say, we do not like Roman Catholics, and we will therefore have no school where Catholics instruct?"[54] Ellsworth called the idea "an absurdity."[55]

The prosecution's claim that the Black Law did not exclude or prohibit blacks from obtaining an education was a "mere parade of liberality," Ellsworth said. "The selectmen of Canterbury would sooner shed their blood than grant Miss Crandall permission to keep this school. The power of a license is a power to deny, and we are to hold our most sacred rights and privileges at the pleasure of the selectmen—they can grant or they can prohibit."[56]

The general policy of the Black Law had a connection with the evils of slavery, Ellsworth said, but he told the court he would leave that line of argument for another day.[57] "The law when it says that no person shall keep a school for the instruction of blacks from abroad, says in effect, that no foreign person shall come here and be taught," Ellsworth said. "This law would extinguish the light of knowledge, would degrade those who are now degraded, and depress those who are now depressed. It said to the naked, go unclothed, and to the hungry, go unfed."[58]

Ellsworth thanked the jury for their attention. He trusted that Judge Eaton would find the Black Law unconstitutional and instruct the jurors accordingly; however, he told the jury that they ultimately would decide the constitutionality of the law and the fate of Prudence Crandall. "My appeal is to *the people*, and to *the people* I leave my client."[59]

Ellsworth's arguments had a visible impact on those in the courtroom. Henry Strong acknowledged this as he approached the jury to conclude the arguments for the defense. With apologies to the jury he briefly discussed the subject of "the liberties of the people." Strong said Crandall had done nothing wrong or unprincipled. He noted that even those who favored colonization agreed that blacks should be educated.

"If they were carried out of the country in ignorance, was it not carrying them away that they might destroy themselves? Unless education accompanied them, all was in vain," Strong told the jury. Strong asked the jury to consider the black students they saw in the courtroom. "Were they not worthy of being instructed?"[60]

"This law does not prevent colored persons from coming in this State. They may come and be idle, and welcome—they may come for any earthly purpose except education," Strong said. "We place our foot on the black, and hold him down in the dust, and then complain that he does not grow to the perfect stature of a man."[61] Strong reminded the jury that they could strike down the Black Law as conflicting with the constitution. "It was no reflection on the character of our state, that under excitement, it had passed an unconstitutional law—other states had done the same."[62]

Regarding the issue of citizenship, Strong noted that General Andrew Jackson, in a speech in New Orleans, addressed blacks as "fellow citizens." "Did he mean to insult them?" Strong asked. "No, he meant to recognize them as citizens, and the law so recognized them. They could purchase and hold real estate, could gain a settlement, and could, in fact, do what citizens could, and what aliens could not."[63]

Strong asked the jury to consider education a fundamental right and the basis of liberty. The Constitution required that blacks from other states receive the same opportunity to attend a school as those who lived in Connecticut. Strong thanked the jury and asked them to strike down the Black Law "which owed its creation to an excited state of being."[64] The defense concluded their arguments.

The prosecution had the last word, and Jonathon Welch summed up the state's case. He began by telling the jury he "regretted the duty that had devolved upon him." He said his state of health prevented him from doing justice to the proceeding. Welch acknowledged the "eloquence and ingenuity" of Crandall's lawyers but cautioned their attempt to divert "the mind of the jury from the real issue."[65]

Welch said the jury should consider the rights of the state as well as the rights of Crandall's students. If the jury declared the Black Law unconstitutional, jurors would substitute their judgment for that of the legislature and governor. An acquittal of Crandall would sacrifice "the rights of the state beyond remedy by doing so," Welch said. "Their verdict against the state was final." Welch argued that if the jury had any doubts about Crandall's guilt, they should convict Crandall; Crandall could appeal a conviction. "The case could be carried to another tribunal where she could have perfect justice, and where her rights would not be at all prejudiced by a conviction here," Welch said. "It was no hardship to her, and a contrary course might do an irremediable wrong to the state."[66] Welch's line of argument was unique if not clearly wrong: he asked the jury to *convict* Crandall rather than acquit if they had any reasonable doubt as to her guilt.

Welch recounted the obstacles the defense created to prevent the prosecution from obtaining the testimony it needed to prove the basic facts of the case. "They thought they had thrown a barrier around their client by closing the mouths of witnesses," Welch said. "It was the object of the gentlemen to go out of court in triumph for want of proof to convict, but the grating doors of a certain building, though it did not unstop deaf ears, did open dumb mouths. The witnesses then spoke, notwithstanding the gentlemen had hoped to apply to them the gag law. Their efforts had proved ineffectual."[67]

Turning to the issue of constitutionality, Welch produced a copy of *Webster's Dictionary*—created by the father of Ellsworth's wife—and read the definition of *citizen*. "A person, native or naturalized, who has the privilege of exercising the elective franchise, or the qualifications which enable him to vote for rulers, and to purchase and hold real estate."[68] Welch noted that Connecticut prohibited blacks from voting, and Massachusetts and Rhode Island prohibited marriage between blacks and whites. No one challenged the laws as unconstitutional. The only rational conclusion one could draw from such laws was that blacks were not citizens, Welch said. While Welch agreed that education was a fundamental right, what about marriage? he asked. Was that not a fundamental right? "The right of selecting the partner of one's joys and sorrows was, however, a right no less dear, no less sacred, than the right of selecting those whom we will have to educate our children," Welch said. "If our law was unconstitutional it was clear that all these laws . . . were also unconstitutional."[69] Welch predicted the prosecution would secure a conviction and compared the arguments of Ellsworth and Strong to the "quivering step of a retreating army."[70] Welch returned to his seat while the judge reviewed his instructions for the jury.

A reporter for the *Connecticut Courant* left the courtroom before the judge instructed the jury. "It was the almost universal opinion that the jury . . . never would convict Miss Crandall," the reporter wrote.[71] "The current was turning and setting with great force in her favor—Miss Crandall appeared at the bar of the court very interesting, and her pupils were inferior to no others, in their conduct, language and appearance."[72] Henry Benson had a similar reaction to the trial and praised the arguments of attorneys Ellsworth and Strong. "It is said that had they been pleading for the lives of their own children they could not have been more solemn and impressive."[73]

Judge Eaton told the jury they alone would decide whether the prosecution met its burden of proof as to whether Prudence Crandall had violated the Black Law. Regarding the constitutionality of the law, Judge Eaton said, "The opinion of the court is that the law *is* constitutional and obligatory on the people of this state." The judge also told the jury, "It is gratifying to the court, gentlemen, that its opinion is not final—that it can be revised by a higher tribunal, and corrected if erroneous."[74] Samuel May observed that the judge upheld the constitutionality of the Black Law "somewhat timidly."[75] Judge Eaton reminded the jury that they could ignore his finding; the jury had the power "to decide both the law and the fact."[76]

The jury deliberated for a few hours and returned unable to render a verdict. Judge Eaton sent them back to the jury room for further discussion, and they returned still unable to agree. After Judge Eaton ordered them to return to their deliberations for a third time, the jurors reassembled in the courtroom and the foreman told the judge they were deadlocked with "no probability that they should ever agree."[77] The twelve male jurors voted seven to five for conviction.[78] Judge Eaton discharged the jury; the lack of a unanimous verdict acted as a continuance of the case to the next term of the county court, scheduled for December.

"Should they continue their prosecution she will have another trial in December next," Henry Benson wrote, "but it is said it would be an utter impossibility to get a jury that would agree."[79] If a jury did agree on a verdict, Benson predicted, "it would be in her favor."[80] Benson gave credit to Charles Burleigh's defense of Crandall's school in the *Unionist*. "The *Unionist* . . . is doing much good and it is astonishing how rapidly public opinion is changing in favor of the school."[81]

Prudence Crandall and her sister Almira resumed teaching their students at the schoolhouse. Crandall and her supporters supposed they had at least a three-month reprieve from legal consequences. The opponents of the school, however, demonstrated their bitterness through new acts of vandalism.

"The latest measure which we have heard of their adopting, is the filling of Miss Crandall's well with manure from the barnyard, and then refusing to give her water from their own wells," Charles Burleigh wrote in the *Unionist*.[82] The vandals succeeded in rendering Crandall's water undrinkable. A second well in the basement of her school ran dry in the summer.

Despite her pleas, neighbors such as Richard Fenner refused permission for Crandall to draw water from their wells. As a last resort, Crandall hauled barrels of water by wagon from her father's farm to the school.[83]

At the beginning of the following week, Samuel May traveled with his family from Brooklyn to Boston, to spend a few weeks visiting friends in Massachusetts, including David and Lydia Maria Child. Sarah Harris and her friend Mariah Davis planned their weddings, scheduled for later in the fall. At the end of August, William Lloyd Garrison concluded his trip to England. While in England, Garrison witnessed the passage of a bill in Parliament that ended slavery in the British West Indies and marched in the funeral parade for William Wilberforce, a longtime British abolitionist.[84] He stalked the spokesman for the American Colonization Society, Elliot Cresson, who was also in England, and repeatedly challenged him to a public debate. Cresson refused. Garrison succeeded in helping to turn British public opinion against colonization, but he failed to raise funds for the abolitionist movement in America. Garrison returned to the United States with no money at all; he borrowed the funds necessary for his passage on the *Hannibal* and sailed for six weeks before arriving in New York City.[85] On his return to America, Garrison did not receive a triumphant welcome.

8 : Judge Daggett's Decision

As the long days of New England summer stretched into September, Maria Stewart carefully considered her future. For three years she had led a life filled with controversy. She had spoken out in public about politics, religion, equality among the races and sexes, and the evils of slavery and discrimination. She had addressed female societies and mixed crowds of men and women in halls and churches. In her speeches before black audiences in Boston, she had encouraged listeners to fight against slavery and discrimination, teach the young, follow the Bible, and become positive role models for others. Stewart had inspired women such as Sarah Harris and Prudence Crandall. As a trailblazer for the rights of both blacks and women, however, she also had offended some. "Little did I think," Stewart said at a meeting of black women, "that any of the professed followers of Christ would have frowned upon me . . . I am a strong advocate for the cause of God and for the cause of freedom. I am not your enemy, but a friend both to you and your children."[1]

Stewart grew weary of the animosity she faced within her own community. One commentator later observed, "For black men, whose place in the lecture halls Stewart briefly but no less effectively usurped, her aggressive rhetorical questions were a direct assault on their authority, their manhood, and their sense of a woman's place. . . . however, Stewart's presence was no less of an affront to some of Boston's most intellectually ambitious black women."[2] In September of 1833, Maria Stewart resolved to crusade no more and announced plans to move to New York City. She wanted a productive life, focusing on children and religion and out of the spotlight of public debate. Before she ended her time as a public figure in Boston, however, she planned one final and well-publicized address.

Stewart arranged to give her farewell speech at the African Meeting House on Belknap Street. David Walker, Maria's political and spiritual mentor, spoke at meetings at the African Meeting House. Stewart likely married her husband there, and schoolchildren learned how to read and write in the community room. William Lloyd Garrison and other opponents of slavery met with black leaders in the basement of the African Meeting House in January 1832, and they created the first antislavery society that endorsed immediate emancipation. Maria Stewart gave her farewell address in this special building on Saturday, September 21, 1833.

Stewart's supporters crowded the room that evening, the *Liberator* reported. She spoke of the importance of education and the need for black men and women to realize their potential. "It is not the color of the skin that makes the man or woman, but the principle formed in the soul. Brilliant wit will shine, come from whence it will, and genius and talent will not hide the brightness of its luster."[3] Stewart recalled that when she first spoke out, few in Boston's white community shared her ideas "except Mr. Garrison, and his friend Mr. Knapp." Garrison "observed that female influence was powerful."[4]

Stewart initially championed the rights of blacks; now she spoke as strongly in favor of the rights of women. "What if I am a woman, is not the God of ancient times the God of these modern days? Did he not raise up Deborah to be a mother, and a judge in Israel? Did not queen Esther save the lives of the Jews? . . . Women of refinement in all ages, more or less, have had a voice in moral, religious and political subjects."[5] Stewart spoke briefly about her personal hardships but did not provide specifics. She did not mention her childhood, the loss of her parents, or how she had moved from place to place barely earning enough to survive. Stewart did not tell the story of how when her husband died white men cheated her out of his estate and left her with nothing. She did say, "For several years my heart was in continual sorrow."[6]

Stewart surprised some in the audience when she recommended that the black community not participate in political activities. "It is high time to drop political discussions, and when our day of deliverance comes, God will provide a way for us to escape, and fight his own battles."[7] Participation in politics would sow "the seed of discord," Stewart said, "and strengthen the cord of prejudice."[8] Increased racial tensions in New York City and elsewhere reached a flash point less than a month after her speech;

race riots and violence erupted in many cities across America. "A spirit of animosity is already risen, and unless it is quenched, a fire will burst forth and devour us, and our young will be slain by the sword."[9]

In conclusion, Stewart told her audience she planned to leave Boston, perhaps never to return. "Farewell," she said, "a few short years from now, we shall meet in those upper regions where parting will be no more. There we shall sing and shout."[10] Just as David Walker did not end his *Appeal* on a hopeful note—his frustration and anger guided the final pages—Maria Stewart could not control her sorrow as she finished her speech. "Thus far has my life been almost a life of complete disappointment," she said. "God has tried me as by fire. Well was I aware that if I contended boldly for his cause, I must suffer. . . . I can now forgive my enemies, bless those who have hated me, and cheerfully pray for those who have despitefully used and persecuted me."[11] Not long after her speech, she packed her few belongings and traveled to New York City.

The prospect of waiting three months for a retrial of Prudence Crandall frustrated Andrew Judson and the opponents of the school. Judson believed the prosecution had met their burden of proof at the trial in August, yet five of the twelve jurors had refused to vote for conviction. Judson did not know whether those jurors truly believed the law was unconstitutional or sympathized personally with Prudence Crandall. Judson considered filing new charges against Crandall rather than waiting for the continuation of the first trial. A new trial with a stronger judge—someone who would not equivocate regarding the constitutionality of the law—might provide a better opportunity to win a conviction. In a new trial, Judson would need less time to establish the facts, and he could focus on making Crandall a less sympathetic defendant. Each day the school operated constituted a continuing violation of the law. Nothing prevented Judson from initiating a new action against Prudence Crandall.

The sheriff knocked on the schoolhouse door on Thursday, September 26, 1833, and served Prudence Crandall with a new writ. Judson charged Crandall with the same violations of the Black Law, and the court set the date for trial one week later on Thursday, October 3.[12] Richard Fenner and William Lester, both friends of Andrew Judson and strong opponents of the school, immediately paid the bond for Crandall to avoid news stories about her going to jail.[13] The arrest caught Crandall's supporters by surprise. Samuel May had commitments that kept him in Boston throughout the next week. William Ellsworth, who so effectively had led Crandall's defense, had other legal engagements that prevented him from representing her on such short notice. The prosecution, however, never stopped working on the Crandall case.

During the month of September, Judson had sought out those who could help tear down the benevolent image of Prudence Crandall. One of his friends agreed to testify about Crandall's explanations for her initial trip to Boston. Richard Fenner, a local merchant, signed a statement on September 11, 1833, stating that Crandall had called on him at the beginning of the year to ask for a letter of introduction to his friends in Boston. "She voluntarily told me that she was going to Boston to visit the infant schools and purchase an infant school apparatus," Fenner wrote. "This she did in such a manner as to preclude any belief that she had any other business."[14] He said Crandall had not disclosed any other reason for her trip to Boston and never told him she intended to meet with William Lloyd Garrison to discuss teaching only black women at her school. Judson used Fenner's statement to bolster the argument he made in letters to local newspapers—that Crandall deliberately took advantage of Fenner by soliciting his help while failing to tell him the truth about her plans for the school.

The prosecution attempted to undermine Crandall's credibility on another key point—the story of Sarah Harris's request to enroll at Crandall's school. The question of whether the request came from Sarah or whether Prudence Crandall asked Sarah to attend her school as a student may have seemed insignificant.[15] In the well-known history of the school, however, the soul-searching moment for Prudence Crandall had come when Sarah Harris had asked Crandall for permission to enroll in her school. After some deliberation, Crandall had agreed. Crandall had not sought out controversy or a leadership role in the abolitionist cause; she simply had responded to the request of a young girl who wanted an education. A new witness challenged this version of the school's history. Mary Barber and Sarah Harris both were servants in the household of Jedediah Shephard during the fall of 1832. In a statement, Barber claimed that Sarah Harris told her it was Crandall who invited Harris to "come to her school and become a scholar with her white scholars."[16] Barber claimed that Harris gave up her plans to get married in order to accept Crandall's offer. Barber said it was also Crandall who suggested to Harris that she should become a teacher. "She further added during the same conversation, that she should never have thought of going if Miss Crandall had not *proposed* it to her," Barber wrote. "She felt very grateful to Miss Crandall, for she should not have thought of such a thing, if had it not been for her invitation."[17]

Technically, Mary Barber's statement added nothing to the prosecution's legal case. The testimony of Mary Benson and Eliza Glasko in the first trial had established that Prudence Crandall taught and harbored blacks students from other states at her school, and the prosecution could obtain similar testimony in a new trial. Barber's statement had nothing to do with proving a violation of the Black Law. Judson planned, however, to use Mary Barber's words to damage Crandall's credibility. Sarah Harris's admission to Crandall's school did not come about through Crandall's altruism in response to Harris's unexpected request, Judson maintained, but rather through a calculated plan of Crandall's own making. Judson asserted that Crandall did not tell the truth about the beginnings of her school. The effect of this revelation, combined with Richard Fenner's statement that Crandall did not tell the truth about her trip to Boston, might help change the way a jury viewed Crandall and her school.

Judson faced numerous problems regarding Barber's statement. First, the two parties to the conversation in question—Prudence Crandall and Sarah Harris—disagreed with Barber's version. In addition, it appeared that Judson and the prosecution clumsily influenced Barber's statement or perhaps drafted it themselves. Barber twice repeated that Sarah "would never have thought" of applying if Crandall had not proposed it. Barber underlined the word "proposed" to make sure the point was not lost. Crandall's friends not only knew that Sarah Harris had initiated the conversation, but also that Crandall had ignored her initial request. Crandall had delayed giving Harris an answer to the point where Harris had made a second request. If Crandall had intended to solicit a black student for her school, she could have asked Mariah Davis, who worked at the school and had informally sat in on classes.

Barber also implied that in addition to plotting Sarah's admission, Crandall had helped to undermine Sarah Harris's marriage plans; this also would reflect poorly on Crandall in the court of public opinion. Barber said that because of Crandall's offer, Harris "had given up" her engagement. Sarah never broke off her engagement and continued to plan her wedding. This claim tended to undermine Barber's entire statement;

if Barber truly had discussed these issues with Harris, she would have known that Harris looked forward to her wedding. Despite the contradictions in Barber's story, however, the prosecution promoted her statement and claimed that Prudence Crandall did not tell the truth.[18]

Judson worked to publicize the statements of Mary Barber and Richard Fenner in the local and national press. He wrote to the antiabolitionist *New York Commercial Advertiser* and asked publisher William L. Stone to publish an attack on Crandall. "Should you deem it advisable to frame an article in addition to what good you have already done, we furnish you the foregoing materials."[19] Judson added, "By this you will see that she meant to deceive the people."[20] The *Commercial Advertiser* published two articles that attacked Crandall and her credibility, and the *New York Spectator* published a similar attack.[21]

The articles claimed that Prudence Crandall "was merely the instrument of Arnold Buffum and William Lloyd Garrison" and that she profited significantly from their scheme. "She had then contracted for twenty colored pupils, at one hundred dollars per annum, one half payable in advance, and that she could save half to herself," William Stone wrote in the *Commercial Advertiser*.[22] "Her duty and interest were happily combined."[23] The article implied that Arthur Tappan had guaranteed tuition payment for twenty students—a pledge of two thousand dollars for one year—in the same way he assisted in "the establishment of an abolition paper" in Brooklyn, Connecticut.[24] Tappan, who increasingly worried that his abolitionist activities were undermining his business interests, called the allegation "utterly destitute of truth."[25] Crandall certainly would have welcomed a commitment by Tappan or anyone else to pay the tuition of her students. No evidence exists, however, that anyone guaranteed tuition payment for all or some of Crandall's students. Crandall allowed the students who could pay only a portion of the tuition to make up the difference by working at the school. Simeon S. Jocelyn noted that Harriet Lanson of New Haven attended Crandall's school only because she provided "domestic assistance" at the school, "on account of which her expenses of board were defrayed."[26] For the rest of his life Arthur Tappan proudly recalled his association with Prudence Crandall's school but never claimed to have subsidized student tuition.

The editors at the *Commercial Advertiser* and the *Spectator* also accused Crandall of "unfair dealing" in abruptly closing her original school, and they claimed she desired "to bring herself into notice" and promote inter-racial marriage.[27] Stone offered as evidence Crandall's well-publicized statement that "Moses married a colored woman."[28] Andrew Judson's persistent campaign to plant stories in the press and turn public opinion against Prudence Crandall's school won significant support in the New York media.

On Wednesday, the day before the commencement of Crandall's second trial, William Lloyd Garrison arrived in New York City. While in England, he had succeeded in attacking colonization as a fraudulent means to end slavery. He did not anticipate, however, that supporters of colonization would seek revenge upon his return to the United States. As he disembarked from the *Hannibal*, the New York newspapers, which as a group strongly supported colonization, whipped up animosity against him and attacked "the notorious Garrison" as disloyal to the nation.[29]

Among the many speeches Garrison delivered in England, one was widely reported and reprinted by the supporters of colonization in the United States. On July 13, 1833, Garrison spoke at Exeter Hall in London to an overflow crowd. In addition to denouncing slavery and colonization, Garrison said the United States failed to live up to its ideals and principles; he criticized the founding fathers for allowing slavery. "Who or what were the framers of the American government, that they should dare confirm and authorize such highhanded villainy—such a flagrant robbery of the inalienable rights of man . . . It was not valid then—it is not valid now."[30] Garrison said America "shamelessly plays the tyrant" and hypo-critically promotes liberty and freedom while engaging in slavery.[31] He directed a series of "accusations" against the United States that drew an enthusiastic response from the British crowd. "I accuse her of stealing the liberties of two million of the creatures of God, and withholding the just recompense of their labor," Garrison said, "of tearing the husband from his wife, the mother from her babe, and children from their parents, and of perpetrating upon the poor and needy every species of outrage and oppression."[32] A well-known British abolitionist joined Garrison at the rally. Daniel O'Connell also criticized the United States and said Americans who were proud of their liberty yet tolerated slavery were "the vilest of hypocrites—the greatest of liars."[33]

The audience at the Exeter Hall speech included colonization support-ers who monitored Garrison's speeches.[34] They sent letters to newspapers in the United States that sensationalized Garrison's "attack on America," calling Garrison a dangerous fanatic who "abused and maligned" his country while on foreign soil.[35] Years later, Garrison's friend and guest editor of the *Liberator*, Oliver Johnson, wrote that while the language Garrison used at Exeter Hall was severe, "It was not possible to deny its truth."[36] Garrison's opponents, however, had no interest in a debate on the merits of slavery.

On his return from England, the *New York Commercial Advertiser* joined numerous newspapers in attacking Garrison for his Exeter speech.[37] "We hope, most sincerely, that not a hair of Mr. Garrison's head will ever be injured by personal violence; but he will do well to consider that his course of conduct in England has kindled a spirit of hostility towards him at home, which cannot be easily allayed. He will act wisely never to attempt addressing a public meeting in this country again."[38]

As the New York press increased their attacks on Garrison, Lewis and Arthur Tappan scheduled a meeting to form the New York City Anti-Slavery Society on October 2, 1833. When supporters of colonization caught wind of the plan and alerted the press, a flurry of late-edition newspapers and flyers circulated the news throughout the city. The *New York Courier and Enquirer* announced the time and place of the meeting and asked, "Are we tamely to look on, and see this most dangerous species of fanaticism extending itself through society? . . . Or shall we, by promptly and fearlessly crushing this many-headed Hydra in the bud, expose the weakness as well as the folly, madness, and mischief of these bold and dangerous men?"[39] Handbills asked "all persons from the South" to attend the Clinton Hall meeting.[40]

At the appointed hour for the antislavery meeting, a large and unruly mob gathered outside Clinton Hall—it was closed and locked. The crowd did not know that the owners of the hall had withdrawn permission for the meeting; it had been moved without public announcement to the Chatham Street Chapel. The mob marched on to Tammany Hall, the city's political center and headquarters, while the abolitionist leaders met and officially constituted the New York City Anti-Slavery Society. The members elected Arthur Tappan president of the Society, and his brother Lewis was named one of ten officers. As the antislavery meeting ended, the attendees exited through a rear door of the chapel. "They had just adjourned," reported the *Journal of Commerce*, "when the din of the invading army, as it approached from Tammany Hall, fell upon their ears; and before the audience was fairly out of the chapel, the flood poured in through the gates as if they would take it by storm. But lo! They were too late."[41]

Garrison stayed away from the meeting as a matter of personal safety. The press had encouraged the mobs to crush the "many headed Hydra" of the abolitionist movement, and an eyewitness who observed those at the Chatham Street Chapel reported that the "shouting, screaming, and cursing for Tappan and Garrison defy all belief."[42] One person who joined the crowd at the chapel said, "If I had my will, or if I could catch him, Garrison should be packed up in a box with air-holes, marked 'this side up,' and so shipped to Georgia."[43] The hostility toward Garrison and his antislavery supporters was so strong that the crowd continued to search the chapel well into the night and did not leave until police arrived and ordered everyone to go home.[44] The *Commercial Advertiser* speculated that if the mob had captured Garrison, "Many grave and respectable citizens, who under other circumstances would have been the last to participate in any disorderly popular proceedings, would at least have assented to his decoration in a coat of tar and feathers."[45]

On Thursday morning, October 3, 1833, the superior court for Windham County at the Brooklyn Courthouse came to order. Prudence Crandall's second trial proceeded with unusual speed, commencing just one week after her arrest. The prosecution had prepared and developed new evidence throughout September, while Crandall's attorneys thought they had a three-month reprieve following the continuance of the first trial. Andrew Judson and State's Attorney Chauncey Cleveland, who had recovered from his sickness, prosecuted the case against Crandall. Henry Strong and Calvin Goddard led the defense.

Since the parties did not dispute the facts and evidence of the case, the attorneys on both sides expected the new judge to have a significant impact on the outcome. A judge who instructed the jury that the Black Law was unconstitutional would almost certainly secure an acquittal for Crandall. In the alternative, a judge who upheld the constitutionality of the law would have to provide a strong and persuasive charge to the jurors in order to avoid another hung jury.

Judge David Daggett was assigned to preside over the second Crandall trial. Daggett had a long and distinguished career as a judge, attorney, educator, and politician. Throughout his career, he consistently opposed the extension of rights and privileges to the disenfranchised. One commentator referred to him as "the arch conservative Federalist judge."[46]

A political fixture in Connecticut for decades, Daggett showed promise at an early age. He left home to attend Yale when he was sixteen and went straight into the junior class, graduating with high honors at eighteen. For many years after his graduation he was known as "the presiding genius" of Yale's Graduate Club.[47] Daggett developed a thriving law practice in New Haven and helped create the Yale School of Law.[48]

In politics, the Federalist Party won Daggett's loyalty; he served in numerous political posts and elective offices, including U.S. senator.[49] "For many years," a legal colleague wrote, "no man in the state had so much political influence, an influence amounting so nearly to a political control of the state."[50] Daggett used his political influence to advance his legal career. Six years after his nomination to the superior court in 1826, he secured an appointment to the highest-ranking judicial position in the state—chief justice of the state supreme court.[51]

While serving as a superior court judge, Daggett was elected mayor of New Haven in 1828. He had his portrait painted by Nathaniel Jocelyn—brother of Simeon Jocelyn—four years before the failure of Simeon's proposed college for black men.[52] Daggett, however, did not hold the same opinions as the Jocelyn brothers regarding abolition and equality. Daggett was a founding member of the New Haven Auxiliary Colonization Society and wrote a summary of their first meeting on October 10, 1819. Regarding black men and women, Daggett wrote, "It is universally known and admitted that the condition of this unhappy people cannot be essentially ameliorated, so long as they continue in our country."[53] Blacks held in slavery never could expect an education, Daggett wrote, and free blacks should expect wretchedness and depression. "That the people of color thus situated should become useful and worthy members of the community or aspire to the condition of free men, will not be expected by any acquainted with the springs of human action."[54]

When Simeon S. Jocelyn proposed an academy for black men in New Haven in 1831, David Daggett led a committee of twelve individuals opposed to the school and helped draft two resolutions for a town vote. The first resolution called the school "destructive" and asked citizens to "resist the establishment of the proposed College in this place, by every lawful means."[55] The second resolution opposed immediate emancipation.

"Sentiments favorable to the immediate emancipation of slaves in disregard of the civil institutions of the States in which they belong . . . (are) unwarrantable and dangerous interference with the internal concerns of other States, and ought to be discouraged."[56] In the wake of the bloodshed of Nat Turner's slave rebellion, the townspeople overwhelmingly approved Daggett's resolutions by a vote of seven hundred to four.[57] Daggett succeeded in blocking Simeon S. Jocelyn's plan for a college for black men.

In a pamphlet titled *Count the Cost: An Address to the People of Connecticut*, Daggett opposed allowing all adults to vote. "The streets resound with the clamour that men are deprived of the invaluable privilege of choosing their rulers," Daggett wrote.[58] Daggett said it made no sense to allow "one who exhausts his earnings in a grog shop" or "women of full age and unmarried" to help choose the state's leaders.[59] Daggett maintained that only "*worthy* members of society" who owned land should have the privilege of voting.[60] "No nation which universal suffrage hath been allowed, hath remained free and happy," Daggett said.[61]

Religion was not central to Daggett's life until April 1832, seventeen months before the second Crandall trial. The evangelical awakening that occurred throughout New England interested Daggett, and he attended a continuous four-day religious revival in New Haven. "Seriously moved" by the experience, he "resolved, by the divine help, to serve and love, and trust the Saviour of sinners."[62] Thereafter he often quoted the Bible and said he studied it more than any other book.

David Daggett and his wife, Ann, had nineteen children, including a son named Oliver Ellsworth Daggett in honor of William Ellsworth's well-known father. They lived on Elm Street in New Haven in a large stone home with a garden "full of delightful fruits and flowers."[63] The Crandall trial in October 1833 was one of Daggett's last significant cases as he neared the mandatory judicial retirement age of seventy.

The trial commenced with Andrew Judson calling a number of Prudence Crandall's students to testify. They admitted that they lived out of state and received instruction at Crandall's school. Other witnesses testified that Crandall taught and boarded black students from Rhode Island, Pennsylvania, and New York, in violation of the Black Law.[64] Two Canterbury selectmen, Asahel Bacon and Ebenezer Sanger, testified that Crandall told them the names of her students and the various states where they lived. Prosecutor Andrew Judson also raised questions about Prudence Crandall's candor; he introduced the testimony of Mary Barber concerning Sarah Harris and Richard Fenner's testimony regarding Crandall's trip to Boston to show that Crandall repeatedly had failed to tell truth.

No one doubted the prosecution would establish the facts necessary to prove a violation of the Black Law. Even Charles Burleigh, the editor of the *Unionist*, did not find the evidentiary stage of the trial very engaging. Unlike his coverage of the first trial where he provided pages of detailed information about the testimony of each witness, in the second trial he summed up the testimony of all the witnesses in one sentence: "Several witnesses were examined, the facts necessary to conviction were proved and nothing remained but to establish the constitutionality of the law."[65]

All four attorneys then gave closing statements. Andrew Judson repeated most of the arguments he had made in the first trial; however, he delivered them in a sharper and more passionate manner. "There are indeed a few individuals in New England, who would prefer to see the Constitution torn into a thousand atoms, rather than live under it, so long as it tolerates slavery," Judson told the jury, referencing William Lloyd Garrison. He noted that Crandall's attorneys cited the Declaration of Independence for the proposition that blacks are entitled to citizenship. "It does say that '*all men are created equal*,'" Judson said. "But who does not know that on the 4th of July 1776, every Colony or State tolerated slavery—they had laws to hold their slaves in bondage. Still more, perhaps every signer of that declaration was himself a slaveholder, and that declaration did not dissolve those bonds."[66]

"There ever has been in this country, a marked difference between the black and the white men," Judson said. "There is still that difference, and it is impossible to do it away. Those who claim to be the exclusive philanthropists of the day will tell you this is prejudice. I give it no such name . . . It is national pride and national honor which mark this distinction . . . It was a nation of white men who formed and have administered our government, and every American should indulge that pride and honor which is falsely called prejudice, and teach it to his children. Nothing else will preserve the American name or the American character. Who of you would like to see the glory of this nation stripped away, and given to another race of men?"[67] The best way to help the slaves and free blacks, Judson said, is to send them back to Africa.

"Instead of aiding in this mighty work of preservation—of saving our own country, and redeeming Africa, there is a class of men, even in New England, who would prefer to have the slaves loosed from their chains and brought to Connecticut in such manner as to overwhelm our own inhabitants."[68] Judson suggested that Prudence Crandall's school for black women did not come about by accident, but rather was part of a larger plan for immediate emancipation. "The present is a scheme, cunningly devised, to destroy the rich inheritance left by your fathers. The professed object is to educate the blacks, but the real object is to make the people yield their assent by degrees to this universal amalgamation of the two races, and have the African race placed on the footing of perfect equality with the Americans."[69]

Judson told the jury that if they ruled the Black Law unconstitutional, abolitionists would propose schools for blacks in every town across the state. In a very few years, Judson said, "the evil will be spread over the state." The Black Law protects the entire state, Judson said. "Public policy demands it. The existence of the state requires its faithful execution. Its resistance is only for the purpose of sowing the seeds of disquiet at the South, and let it not be said, that a jury in Windham County commenced the work of dissolving the Union."[70] Judson's fiery appeal to the juror's fears of racial conflict appeared to move the jury in a manner similar to the way William Ellsworth's argument visibly had influenced the jury in the first trial.

Henry Strong touched on many of Ellsworth's arguments from the first trial. He said the Constitution provided blacks with the same privileges and immunities as any other Connecticut citizen, and the legislature could not deny the fundamental right of education to black students. After Goddard and Cleveland made brief remarks, the jurors awaited instructions from Judge Daggett and expected to begin deliberations that afternoon. Instead, Daggett announced that he needed additional time to draft his charge to the jury. He recessed the court until the following morning.

At ten o'clock the next day, spectators filled every space in the Brooklyn courthouse. "Many persons stood unable to obtain seats, all listening with profound attention," the *Unionist* reported.[71] Judge Daggett recited the charges against Prudence Crandall. He noted "it has scarcely been denied" that Crandall taught and boarded colored persons from other states at her school. Daggett said if the jurors determined that Crandall violated the Black Law, they must also determine the constitutionality of the law. He said it was his responsibility to provide the jury with direction as to the law. Daggett then spoke for well over an hour, briefly discussing the facts of the case and providing an extended explanation as to the constitutionality of the law.[72] Observers remembered Prudence Crandall's second trial less for the testimony of the witnesses or the arguments of counsel and more for the dramatic and pivotal role of Judge Daggett and his strong advocacy for the Black Law.

In rendering a verdict, Daggett instructed the jury to dismiss any consideration of the issue of slavery—it was not pertinent to the case. In addition, he told them that the advantages of education also had nothing to do with their deliberations. Daggett said the jury must consider the clause in the Constitution that stated, "The citizens of each state shall be entitled to all privileges and immunities of citizens in the several states." The constitutionality of the Black Law turned on whether the black students at Crandall's school were citizens. Daggett wasted no time answering that question. "The persons contemplated in this act are not citizens within the obvious meaning of that section of the constitution," Daggett said.[73]

"Are slaves citizens?" Daggett asked. "We know that slavery is recognized in the constitution; and it is the duty of this court to take that constitution as it is, for we have sworn to support it."[74] After significant discussion, he concluded that the framers of the Constitution did not consider slaves citizens.[75] "Are Indians citizens?" Daggett asked. "Who among us ever saw one of them performing military duty or exercising with the white men the privilege of the elective franchise, or holding an office?"[76] Daggett said that Indians, "literally natives of our soil," did not enjoy the rights of citizenship.

"Are free blacks citizens?" Daggett asked. Just because free blacks could own property or sail vessels under the American flag did not make them citizens. Daggett cited Chancellor James Kent, a respected legal authority who many considered "the most eminent personage in the annals of American jurisprudence."[77] "In most of the United States, there is a distinction in respect to political privileges, between free white persons and free coloured persons of *African* blood," Daggett said, quoting Chancellor Kent. "In no part of the country do the latter, in point of fact, participate equally with the whites in the exercise of civil and political rights."[78] Daggett cited a number of cases and statutes from various states that Kent had assembled in his legal commentaries regarding the prohibition of inter-racial marriage. While Kent's commentaries did not specifically address the question of citizenship for free blacks, Judge Daggett told the jury that Kent's legal analysis "determines this question, by fair implication."[79]

"To my mind, it would be a perversion of terms, and the well known rule of construction, to say that slaves, free blacks, or *Indians*, were citizens, within the meaning of that term, as used in the constitution," Daggett said. "God forbid that I should add to the degradation of this race of men; but I am bound, by my duty, to say they are not citizens."[80]

Daggett told the jurors he had "thus shown you that this law is not contrary to the 2nd section of the 4th article of the Constitution of the United States." He then argued that the legislature had the power to regulate schools and enforce the prohibitions and requirements of the Black Law. "This law does not prohibit schools. It places them under the care of the civil authority."[81] Daggett said the law did not violate either the United States Constitution or the Connecticut Constitution.

Finally, Daggett warned the jury not to consider "the popularity or unpopularity of this or any other law."[82] Just as citizens might not appreciate certain taxation laws, Daggett said they must still "submit to them, and carry them into full effect, as good citizens" and obey them "as long as they exist."[83] Daggett instructed the jury to return a verdict in accordance with the law. "I have done my duty, and you will do yours."[84]

The jurors rose and proceeded to the jury room to begin deliberations. No one in the courtroom had witnessed a similar charge to a jury. Judge Daggett spoke longer than all of the attorneys for the prosecution and the defense in their closing statements, combined. After only twenty minutes the jury returned to the courtroom. The foreman pronounced Prudence Crandall guilty as charged. The press cited Judge Daggett's speech as the decisive factor in the verdict for the prosecution. Andrew Judson took additional comfort, however, in the knowledge that his closing argument and the new testimony, striking at Crandall's credibility, likely played some role in Crandall's conviction.

The attorneys for Prudence Crandall filed a motion to overturn the jury verdict; Daggett denied the motion. Daggett ordered Crandall to pay a fine of one hundred dollars, as well as court costs. Her attorneys filed an appeal of the ruling to the state supreme court claiming the jury had erred by upholding the law's constitutionality. Both sides wanted a swift resolution to the appeal; however, the next session of the state supreme court was scheduled for July of 1834, a full nine months away.

One week after the conclusion of Crandall's trial, William Lloyd Garrison slipped out of New York City and returned to Boston. Even at home, he faced the threats of colonization supporters. A handbill distributed throughout Boston reported that Garrison, the "Negro Champion," had returned from his "disgraceful mission" to England, where he had sought British support to end slavery and deprive "the southern section of our happy union the only means of obtaining a livelihood." Garrison had "slandered the Americans to the utmost of his power" and embraced Daniel O'Connell, who said, "The blackest corner in Hell's bottomless pit *ought to be, and would be, the future destination of the Americans!*" The flyer included a call to capture and assault Garrison. "He is now in your power—do not let him escape you, but go this evening, armed with plenty of tar and feathers, and administer him justice at his abode at No. 9, Merchants' Hall, Congress Street."[85]

The handbill succeeded in turning out an angry crowd at the offices of the *Liberator*, which also served as Garrison's living quarters. The "dense mob, breathing threatenings which foreboded a storm" did not invade Garrison's office, and Garrison was not harmed.[86] The hostile reaction to his homecoming, however, prompted Garrison to respond in the next *Liberator*. The charge that he had slandered his country while in England was false, Garrison said. He simply had made the same points about slavery that he already had made for years in the United States. "I did not hesitate there—I have not hesitated here—I shall hesitate nowhere, to brand this country as hypocritical and tyrannical in its treatment of the people of color, whether bond or free."[87]

An editorial in a Connecticut-based newspaper, the *Christian Secretary*, criticized "the 'firebrand' handbill tossed up in Boston calling upon the enemies of William Lloyd Garrison to mob, tar and feather him" and "the barbarity practiced toward Miss Crandall in Canterbury, defiling her well and then forbidding her to use other wells, and assaulting her apartments and breaking her windows with rotten eggs in time of public worship." The *Christian Secretary* warned that increased mob violence against those who advocated equality indicated "an approaching crisis in the country."[88]

Garrison wrote in the *Liberator* that his adversaries should not delude themselves "with the notion that any abolitionist will abandon the holy cause which he has espoused in consequence of any threats or acts of personal violence." He said death threats would not deter his campaign for emancipation and equal rights. "I feel no uneasiness either in regard to my fate or to the success of the cause of abolition," he wrote in November 1833. "Slavery must speedily be abolished: the blow that shall sever the chains of the slaves may shake the nation to its center—may momentarily disturb the pillars of the Union—but it shall redeem the character, extend the influence, establish the security, and increase the prosperity of our great republic."[89]

9 : **Romantic Revolutionaries**

Newspapers throughout the United States and across the Atlantic in England reported on the progress of Prudence Crandall's October trial.[1] Fear of "amalgamation of the races" and the rights of free blacks—the subtexts of Crandall's trial—made for sensational reading. One man took a personal interest.

Calvin Philleo, minister of the First Baptist Church in Pawtucket, Rhode Island, read about Crandall's school for black women.[2] The relationship between the antislavery movement and religion interested Philleo; the temperance movement and revivalism had helped fill his evangelical church with members. In just three months in 1829, Philleo baptized more than seventy new parishioners at the First Baptist Church.[3] At a time when ministers of well-established churches avoided the divisive issue of slavery, others, including Philleo and fellow Pawtucket minister Ray Potter, saw the potential for both virtue and increasing church membership. One extra detail in the Crandall story, however, caught Philleo's attention. Prudence Crandall, the persecuted headmistress of the school for black women, was not married.

A sudden family tragedy recently had created turmoil in Calvin Philleo's life and threatened his personal and financial security. Born on July 4, 1787, on his father's farm near the town of Dover, New York, Calvin had experienced adversity early on in his life—during his childhood he helped his parents with the desperate chores of survival. "I can hardly describe the poverty and baldness of the life I saw at his house," one relative wrote. "A rude log hut, earthen floor, a life entirely barren of any refinement."[4] The Philleos lived hand to mouth. Over time, his father Enoch created apple and peach orchards and grew other crops.[5]

Calvin's father was "a good talker" and enjoyed bantering with his wife about religion and her Baptist faith.[6]

Enoch Philleo served in the Continental Army and fought in a number of battles against the British; he survived the terrible winter of 1778 with George Washington's army at Valley Forge.[7] Calvin remembered his father telling stories about the war with his brother-in-law William Bradshaw, who sided with the British against the Americans. After the war, Bradshaw bragged about Great Britain providing him with three hundred acres of land in Nova Scotia. "Often have I heard them tell their war stories together," Calvin Philleo wrote. "He (Bradshaw) was well paid for his treachery while my father received only worthless Continental money."[8]

As a young man, Calvin Philleo yearned for a more prosperous life and apprenticed with a blacksmith; however, Calvin soon gave up the blacksmith trade to pursue the ministry. He shared his father's gift of speech and his mother's Baptist faith. Calvin preached for a time in Amenia, New York, and was ordained in 1816.[9]

Philleo impressed parishioners with his "vivid imagination and remarkable descriptive powers, which he used to great advantage."[10] Philleo married Elizabeth Wheeler; they had three children—Emeline, Elizabeth, and Calvin.[11] As his family grew, so did Calvin's career in the ministry. A congregation in Suffield, Connecticut, called him to their church in 1824, where he was "emphatically a revival preacher, eccentric, impulsive, and enthusiastic."[12]

Calvin Philleo barnstormed throughout New England during the Second Great Awakening. "He was a remarkable man and his power over audiences was almost unequaled," Calvin's daughter Emeline remembered. "In his person was combined the minister and the choir. He possessed a voice remarkable for clearness and sweetness, with an ear so true he seldom erred in the pitch."[13] Based on his reputation for expanding the congregation in Suffield, the First Baptist Church in Pawtucket, Rhode Island, called him to their church in 1830. Emeline and her sister took care of the children in the vestry during the church services.[14]

Calvin and his wife Elizabeth worked as a team, and they each had important responsibilities within the church and their family. Calvin could not travel and build his reputation as a revival minister without his wife caring for their children and managing church business. Philleo succeeded in expanding the congregation. After two years in Pawtucket, however, the world Calvin and his wife created changed dramatically. In December of 1831, a sudden illness struck Elizabeth; she died the day after Christmas. Suddenly Calvin was a widower with three children; his two young daughters were unmarried and his son was nine years old.

The family of a single parent with young children could quickly face financial ruin—William Lloyd Garrison knew this bleak reality firsthand. Philleo knew this as well; at one time Calvin Philleo may have believed that marriage should flow from love and not economic partnership alone. In his new circumstance he believed that relationships prospered as well if not better when guided by the head as opposed to the heart.

In the midst of her October trial, Prudence Crandall answered a knock at the door of her schoolhouse—it was Calvin Philleo. He introduced himself as a friend of the colored people.[15] She invited him into the school, and they spoke briefly before he promised to call again. That was their first meeting. Thereafter he saw her with some frequency either at the school or the Packerville Baptist Church, where he preached at the invitation of Rev. Kneeland. Philleo, who was sixteen years older than Crandall, did not impress Crandall's friends. They questioned his motives and repeated unflattering stories passed on by Philleo's critics in Pawtucket.

Only nine months had passed since William Lloyd Garrison and Prudence Crandall had met in Boston to outline a strategy for her school for black women. Since that time Garrison had traveled throughout the Northeast to many cities and towns promoting immediate emancipation and had taken his fight against colonization across the Atlantic Ocean. While he faithfully chronicled the progress and challenges of Crandall's school in the pages of the *Liberator*, he never traveled to Canterbury to actually visit the school. That finally changed during the last week of October 1833.

Garrison arrived by stagecoach and found her school "in the full tide of successful experiment and worth a trip across the Atlantic to visit."[16] He saw "the stone which was thrown into the window by some unknown republican of Canterbury," various shards of broken glass from shattered windowpanes, and a window curtain stained by a volley of rotten eggs.[17] More important, Garrison finally saw the school in action; students were learning their lessons assisted by devoted teachers such as William Burleigh, Prudence, and Almira. To see the realization of Crandall's efforts—a true working school for young black women—and to know it existed in part because of his work with Crandall and his advocacy in the *Liberator* was deeply moving for Garrison.

While walking outside, Garrison caught a glimpse of Crandall's neighbor across the street. Writing about his visit to Canterbury in the *Liberator*, Garrison said he saw "a moral non-descript, though physically a human being, named A—T— J."[18] The "moral non-descript," also known as Andrew T. Judson, was delighted to see Garrison in northeastern Connecticut. Having narrowly missed Garrison on a previous visit, Judson wasted no time. He sent the local sheriff to the Benson home that night, Sunday, October 27, with libel writs in hand. Garrison wrote about the encounter in the *Liberator*.

"Just before midnight, on Sabbath evening last, in Brooklyn, Connecticut, the Deputy Sheriff of Windham County, in behalf of those . . . highminded patriots, those practical Christians, Andrew T. Judson, Rufus Adams, Solomon Paine, Capt. Richard Fenner, Doctor Harris, presented me with five indictments . . . in relation to Miss Crandall's *nigger school* in Canterbury."[19] A local newspaper, the *Brooklyn Advertiser*, speculated that the "Canterbury heroine" would enjoy standing together with Garrison in a courthouse, defending themselves and their "holy cause."[20]

For months some opponents of the school had been whispering about a romance between Crandall and Garrison, and the story in the *Brooklyn Advertiser* fanned those rumors. Crandall's detractors said she established her school for black women not because of moral or religious beliefs but because of her romantic relationship with Garrison—she had created the school at his request.[21] Some could not accept the idea of an independent woman who made decisions on her own. Others sought to discredit Crandall and portray her school as a part of a campaign by foreign abolitionists. As her family and supporters well knew, Crandall made her own decisions, and while she and Garrison shared a deep respect for each other and a commitment to equality in the face of severe persecution, there is no evidence of romance between them.

The passage of time and the trip to England had made Garrison less fearful of the libel lawsuit; it paled in comparison to the rumored kidnapping and trip to a southern state that some had predicted. Once the sheriff had served Garrison, the matter seemed less important to Andrew Judson as well. The moment Judson had fervently awaited—the specter of Garrison standing trial in Windham County—lost its urgency in the wake of the Black Law trials.

Garrison hardly referenced the lawsuit when writing to friends. Shortly after leaving Brooklyn, he wrote to George Benson, "My mind is crowded with pleasing remembrances of my late visit to Canterbury and Brooklyn. . . . I am more and more impressed with the importance of 'working whilst the day lasts.' If 'we all do fade as a leaf'—if we are 'as the sparks that fly upwards'—if the billows of time are swiftly removing the sandy foundation of our life—what we intend to do for the captive, and for our country, and for the subjugation of a hostile world, must be done quickly."[22]

On his return to Boston, Garrison realized the *Liberator's* declining subscription and advertising revenue did not cover his printing and postage expenses. Writing to thank a friend who had sent him a gift of sixty dollars, Garrison conceded he faced significant challenges. "During my absence to England, there seems to have been little interest taken in the *Liberator* on the part of subscribers, and our subscription list is gradually diminishing instead of growing larger."[23] Garrison attributed the decline to competition; a number of other abolitionist newspapers now competed for subscribers, including the *Emancipator*, a new antislavery newspaper created with Arthur Tappan's help and based in New York City. Garrison also acknowledged, "We have printed beyond our means—that is, we have published larger quantities of circulars, addresses, tracts, books, etc., for gratuitous distribution—and our reward has been not in money, but in an increase of the friends of justice, humanity, and equal rights."[24] As Garrison devoted more time to improving the finances of the *Liberator*, a new project captured his imagination.

After assisting many local antislavery societies in cities and towns throughout New England, Garrison wanted to form a larger, national antislavery society. On Tuesday, October 29, 1833, the directors of antislavery societies in New York, Boston, Philadelphia, and Providence issued a call for a convention in Philadelphia in December to form the new society. "Here is the warrant for our national meeting," Garrison wrote to George Benson on November 2. "Show it among the genuine friends of our cause as extensively as possible, and urge them to be fully represented in the Convention."[25] One of those excited by the idea was Benson's neighbor, Samuel May. May, however, had serious concerns about the timing of the event. The exaggerated accounts of Garrison's Exeter Hall speech in England—claiming that Garrison expressed hatred for America—still energized slavery's sympathizers and those who opposed immediate emancipation. The overall effect "lashed into fury all the proslavery-colonization-pseudo patriotism throughout the land," May said. "The storm had burst upon us in the mobs at New York, and whether it would ever subside until it had overwhelmed us, was a question which many answered in tones of fearful foreboding."[26]

Calvin Philleo continued to call on Prudence Crandall in November 1833. Sarah Harris and her brother Charles both prepared for their respective weddings. At the end of November, Garrison wrote once more to his friend George Benson. "What news from Canterbury? I long to get there once more—but more particularly under the hospitable roof of your father." Garrison clarified his intentions: "I confess, in addition to the other delightful attractions which are there found, the soft blue eyes and pleasant countenance of Miss Ellen are by no means impotent or unattractive."[27] Garrison erred slightly in his matter of the heart. In an amusing mistake from George Benson's point of view, Garrison had misheard the name of his sister, *Helen* Benson. George made sure Helen learned of Garrison's interest in "Ellen."

After months of planning, Sarah Harris and her fiancé, George Fayerweather, and Sarah's brother Charles and his bride-to-be, Ann Mariah Davis, held a double wedding at the Westminster Congregational Church in Canterbury, on November 28, 1833.[28] The wedding held great meaning for Prudence Crandall. Mariah Davis worked at her school. Crandall had met Sarah Harris through Mariah. The three women shared stories of their future plans and traded copies of the *Liberator*. Sarah had been the first black student at Crandall's school, precipitating all that had occurred in the past year. Prudence and all of the staff and students of the school attended the double wedding.[29] Afterward, Sarah and her husband, a blacksmith from Kingston, Rhode Island, lived in Canterbury and later moved to Rhode Island. Charles Harris and Mariah lived in Canterbury near Crandall, and Mariah and Charles worked at the school.

Attendees from throughout the Northeast made their way to the Anti-Slavery Convention in Philadelphia, including William Lloyd Garrison, David Child, Arnold Buffum, Isaac Knapp, George Bourne, Rev. Peter Williams, Benjamin Lundy, Simeon S. Jocelyn, George W. Benson, and

Rev. Ray Potter. Garrison noted that some traveled by foot through northeastern Connecticut. The poet John G. Whittier, whom Garrison earlier recruited to join the abolitionist movement, hoped to attend. "I long to go to Philadelphia," Whittier wrote to Garrison. "But the expenses of the journey will, I fear, be too much for me; as thee know, our farming business does not put much cash in our pockets . . . Can thee not find time for a visit to Haverhill before thee go on to Philadelphia?"[30] With financial help from a local abolitionist, Whittier joined his friends on the journey to Philadelphia.

Samuel May traveled by stagecoach and boat to New York City. There he met others on their way to the convention, including Garrison. "There was a large company on the steamer that took us from New York to Elizabethtown, and again from Bordentown to Philadelphia. There was much earnest talking by other parties besides our own," May wrote.[31] One passenger strongly disagreed with the goals of the abolitionists, and first May and then Garrison engaged him in a friendly debate as others gathered to listen. Garrison said slaves should have the same freedoms and opportunities as white men. After a lengthy discussion the man said he appreciated the "frank and temperate" explanation. He noted, however, that abolitionists such as William Lloyd Garrison caused great damage to the cause with reckless and "hair-brained" arguments. May said, "Allow me, sir, to introduce you to Mr. Garrison." May later wrote, "I need not describe, you can easily imagine, the incredulous surprise with which this announcement was received."[32]

When the delegates arrived in Philadelphia, they learned that their meetings would take place during the day since city officials could not assure their safety at night. May noted that articles in the local press described the delegates as "fanatics, amalgamationists, disorganizers, disturbers of the peace, and dangerous enemies of the country."[33] On Wednesday, December 4, 1833, the convention began at Adelphi Hall; police officers guarded the entrance at the order of the mayor. "These incidents helped us to realize how we and the cause we had espoused were regarded in that city of brotherly love and Quakers," May wrote.[34] Delegates received a meager lunch—baskets of crackers and pitchers of cold water in keeping with the wishes of those who supported the temperance movement.

Samuel May joined John G. Whittier, Simeon S. Jocelyn, William Lloyd Garrison, and seven others to formulate a Declaration of Principles for the new American Anti-Slavery Society.[35] The committee assigned May, Garrison, and Whittier the job of drafting the document, and on Wednesday evening the three men met at the home of James McCrummel, a successful black dentist whose home provided a sanctuary for escaped slaves on the Underground Railroad.[36] Garrison wrote the first draft.

"We left him about ten o'clock, agreeing to come to him again next morning at eight," May recalled. "On our return at the appointed hour we found him, with shutters closed and lamps burning, just writing the last paragraph of his admirable draft."[37] Garrison's work included an entire page condemning colonization. May proposed deleting all but the first paragraph of the colonization attack. May said colonization would not long survive, "and it was not worthwhile for us to perpetuate the memory of it, in this Declaration of the Rights of Man, which will live a perpetual, impressive protest against every form of oppression."[38] Garrison initially disagreed, but when the committee sided with May, Garrison acquiesced. "Brethren, it is your report, not mine," Garrison said.[39]

When the full convention reconvened on Thursday, various speakers referenced the attacks in the press on William Lloyd Garrison. "Some men, Mr. President, are frightened at a name," Lewis Tappan said. "There is good evidence to believe that many professed friends of abolition would have been here, had they not been afraid that the name of William Lloyd Garrison would be inserted prominently in our proceedings. Sir, I am ashamed of such friends. We ought to place that honored name in the forefront of our ranks."[40] Tappan recalled Garrison's work with Benjamin Lundy in Baltimore and his willingness to go to jail for the cause of emancipation.

"Who that is familiar with the history of Mr. Garrison does not remember the determination expressed in the first number of his paper—the *Liberator*—to sustain it as long as he could live on bread and water?"[41] Tappan reminded the convention delegates how Garrison's opponents had attacked his patriotism in an effort to discredit the abolitionist movement. "Look at his course during his recent mission to England. He has been accused of slandering his country. Sir, he has vindicated the American name. He has not slandered it. He has told the whole truth, and put hypocrites and doughfaces to open shame . . . Sir, we should throw the shield of our protection and esteem around Mr. Garrison. His life is exposed at this moment."[42]

Tappan referred to an incident earlier in the day. The son of a slave-holder had appeared at the entrance of Adelphi Hall and asked for Garrison. When security officers refused to admit him, he acknowledged he wanted "to wash his hands in Garrison's blood."[43] Others joined Tappan's call for Garrison's protection, including Robert Purvis, who earlier in the year almost went off a cliff with Garrison while transporting him by carriage.

At the end of the day, Samuel May presented the Declaration to the delegates. Lucretia Mott, a former schoolteacher and ardent abolitionist, suggested a few changes. Mott later found humor in the dynamics of the situation—a woman in a room full of men recommending changes to a document that the men had compared to the Magna Carta.[44] "When our friends felt that they were planting themselves on the truths of Divine Revelation, and on the Declaration of Independence, as an Everlasting Rock," Mott wrote, "it seemed to me, as I heard it read, that the climax would be better to transpose the sentence, and place the Declaration of Independence first, and the truths of Divine Revelation last, as the Everlasting Rock."[45] Mott recalled that one of the younger delegates turned to look for the woman who knew the meaning of the word "transpose."

The delegates accepted Lucretia Mott's suggestions; earlier she had contributed significantly to the convention in another important way. When local Philadelphia officials refused to lend their support to the convention, some members of the convention suggested that the delegates postpone it and adjourn. Mott disagreed and addressed the delegates. "Right principles are stronger than great names," she said. "If our principles are right, why should we be cowards? Why should we wait for those who never have had the courage to maintain the inalienable rights of the slave?"[46] Her remarks rallied the delegates, and the convention continued.

Despite Lucretia Mott's contributions, the convention officers did not allow the women who attended to vote as delegates or sign the Declaration that created the American Anti-Slavery Society. William Lloyd Garrison offered a motion on the final day of the convention that stated, "The cause of Abolition eminently deserves the countenance and support of American women."[47] Another motion expressed "thanks to their female friends for the deep interest they have manifested in the anti-slavery cause during the long and fatiguing sessions."[48] Despite the irony of denying women the same status as men at a convention concerning equality, Lucretia Mott regarded the proceedings as a step forward.

"Although we were not recognized as a part of the convention by signing the document, yet every courtesy was shown to us, every encouragement given to speak, or to make suggestions of alteration," Mott said. "I do not think it occurred to any one of us at that time, that there would be a propriety in our signing the document. It was with difficulty . . . that I ventured to express what had been near to my heart for many years, for I knew we were there by sufferance, but when I rose, such was the readiness with which the freedom to speak was granted, that it inspired me with a little more boldness to speak on other subjects."[49]

Delegates talked about Prudence Crandall's school at the Philadelphia convention. On the motion of Simeon S. Jocelyn, the delegates resolved "that the fountains of knowledge, like those of salvation, should be open to every creature, and that we regard those laws and prejudices which prevent or restrict the education of the people of color, bond or free, as pre-eminently cruel and impious, and disgraceful to a Christian state or nation. . . ."[50] John Prentice of Providence and William Goodell of New York City moved "that this Convention highly approve of the philanthropic efforts of Miss Prudence Crandall, of Canterbury, Connecticut, in her labors to instruct our colored sisters; and while we deeply sympathize with her in view of the persecutions she has endured in the prosecution of her pious purposes, we pledge ourselves to afford her our continued countenance and assistance."[51] The motion passed unanimously.

On Friday the convention delegates ratified the Declaration drafted by Garrison—all sixty-two members from ten states signed the document.[52] Lucretia Mott remembered that a deeply religious spirit pervaded the day. "The last hours of the convention were especially impressive," she said. "I had never before, nor have I ever since, witnessed anything fully equal to it."[53] Comparisons to the Magna Carta notwithstanding, the words and sentiments in the Declaration moved all of the delegates.

"More than fifty-seven years have elapsed since a band of patriots convened in this place to devise measures for the deliverance of this country," Garrison wrote. "The cornerstone upon which they founded the Temple of Freedom was broadly this—'that all men are created equal; that they are endowed by their Creator with certain inalienable rights; that among these are life, liberty, and the pursuit of happiness.' . . . We have met together for the achievement of an enterprise without which that of our fathers is incomplete; and which, for its magnitude, solemnity, and probable results upon the destiny of the world, as far transcends theirs as moral truth does physical force."[54] Emancipation must occur immediately, Garrison said, with no compensation to the slaveholders.[55] Slavery, or "man-stealing" as George Bourne said, constituted a criminal enterprise full of danger for the future of America and "must be broken up."[56]

"These are our views and principles—these are our designs and measures," Garrison concluded. "With entire confidence in the overruling justice of God, we plant ourselves upon the Declaration of our Independence and the truths of Divine Revelation, as upon the Everlasting Rock . . . Under the guidance and by the help of Almighty God, we will do all . . . to secure to the colored population of the United States all the rights and privileges which belong to them as men and as Americans—come what may to our persons, our interests, or our reputations."[57]

Those who attended the antislavery convention took a daring stand at a time when the idea of immediate emancipation provoked violence. "If I ever boast of anything it is this—that I was a member of the Convention that instituted the American Anti-Slavery Society," wrote Rev. Samuel May. "I cannot describe the holy enthusiasm which lighted up every face as we gathered around the table on which the Declaration lay, to put our names to that sacred instrument. It seemed to me . . . as if everyone felt that he was about to offer himself a living sacrifice in the cause of freedom, and to do it cheerfully. There are moments when heart touches heart, and souls flow into one another. That was such a moment."[58]

As 1833 drew to a close, Crandall's supporters and opponents looked forward to the state supreme court appeal in 1834. The long period of time between the end of the second trial and the time when Crandall's conviction would be heard on appeal—in the summer of 1834—allowed a sustained period of normality for the school. While still not accepted by the general community, Crandall's school was less a controversial novelty and more a real, ongoing place of learning for young black women. Crandall and her staff no longer felt besieged, and May wrote that her school was "in a flourishing condition."[59]

When May returned from the convention in Philadelphia, his optimism for Crandall's school returned. "Nothing that has ever happened in our country has operated so effectually, as the establishment of this little school, to bring the condition and the claims of our colored population before the public."[60] May said the school provided a crucial model in the struggle for equality; he anticipated the school's legal challenge would lead to a definitive and positive ruling from the U.S. Supreme Court. May predicted that Americans "will gratefully remember the establishment of the Canterbury School, as a leading event in the history of their deliverance."[61]

Crandall's opponents did not remain silent. An unsigned letter appeared in the *Windham County Advertiser* on December 19, 1833, claiming that Crandall had greatly increased the number of scholars at her school so as to "increase the grievances and insults of our citizens." The letter contained a veiled threat. "We have great reason to believe that a determination has been formed to BREAK UP the negro school in Canterbury by some means or other in less than two months . . . and we have no hesitation in saying that few towns in this or any other state would have shown so much forbearance towards such an establishment, as have the people of Canterbury."[62] The threatening letter concerned Crandall and her supporters given the recent violence against abolitionists in New York City and Boston.

■ Her name was Helen—Helen Eliza Benson—and this was now well known to William Lloyd Garrison. On January 18, 1834, he summoned the courage to tell her he cared for her. In a letter to Helen, Garrison wrote at length about the weather and described "when the bees are among the flowers, and the birds are on the wing."[63] He noted the obvious differences between the seasons and how the onset of cold weather caused "the trees to decline into 'the sear and yellow leaf.'"[64] Then he finally wrote, "Do you wish to know, Helen, what is a strong token of my esteem for a friend? It is an epistle." As a way of indicating his feelings toward her, he claimed he did not enjoy writing letters and did so only when very serious about the person to whom he was writing. This was not true; Garrison wrote hundreds of letters to all sorts of acquaintances. He told Helen he apologized if his request for her friendship seemed too forward. "In order to obtain your forgiveness, must I promise never to trespass again, in like manner? Indeed, I cannot. Pray, make some other condition."[65]

Garrison asked Helen to consider creating a female antislavery society in Providence; he made a similar request of Harriet Minot and her friends. Garrison also asked Helen about Prudence Crandall. "I have heard nothing recently from Brooklyn or Canterbury," Garrison wrote. "If you have information that may prove interesting to me, do communicate it."[66] In closing he told her, "I am an hour older than when I commenced this rambling epistle, but it has been spent in writing to one so highly deserving of the respect of your friend and well-wisher."[67] Garrison likely spent more than an hour laboring over his first love letter to Helen. Flattered and excited when she received it, Helen waited almost a month before sending a carefully crafted reply.

On Tuesday, January 28, 1834, a mutual friend of Mariah and Charles Harris traveled from Norwich to Canterbury. Mariah and Charles both worked at Prudence Crandall's school. One of Crandall's students, Maria Robinson, saw Frederick Olney, a black man, step out of a stagecoach at about 10:30 in the morning. He carried a few bundles into the school and noticed that the clock on the mantle in a room downstairs had stopped. Olney mentioned this to Prudence Crandall as he asked her about Charles and Mariah. Crandall replied that she had not noticed anything wrong with the clock and told Olney he could find Charles and Mariah in the kitchen. Olney visited with his friends and then wrote a letter to a relative who lived in New York. Olney stayed for lunch and continued to talk with Charles and Mariah in the kitchen. When Amy Fenner came downstairs to join a reading class, she saw Olney working on the clock but also saw smoke coming from another direction. She told Olney to turn around. He rushed toward the smoke in the corner of the room and put his ear to the floor. He told Amy he heard a fire roaring.[68]

The cry of "fire" echoed throughout the schoolhouse, and frightened students and staff ran to get outside. Once out, Charles Harris and Frederick Olney looked for the source of the fire. Olney saw small flames shooting out between two clapboards at the northeast corner of the house. Harris rushed to where the tools were stored and came back with an axe, and Olney chipped away at the clapboards. Prudence Crandall quickly brought a tub of water, and Olney poured it on the flames and into the hole he had opened with the axe. Charles Harris rang the school bell and sounded a general alarm in the neighborhood. Shopkeeper Richard Fenner arrived and saw smoke coming from the outside corner of the house. He helped Harris and Olney. Others carried water inside the house, where they pried loose floorboards and wallboards and poured water into the smoldering areas. By the time town selectman Ebenezer Sanger arrived, "The house was wet, and people were at work about it, cutting up floors." After extinguishing the fire, Prudence and her neighbors assessed the damage and tried to determine how the fire had started.[69]

Without the efforts of Frederick Olney the fire might have had tragic consequences. Olney and Charles Harris responded quickly and helped limit the damage. Even though the students ran out in a panic, no one suffered any injuries. Crandall's supporters raised questions about the cryptic comment that had appeared in the previous month's *Windham County Advertiser*: "A determination has been formed to BREAK UP the negro school in Canterbury by some means or other in less than two months."

The *Unionist* reported the news of the fire on Thursday, February 6, 1834, and William Lloyd Garrison wrote in the *Liberator* that the fire was likely "the work of an incendiary."[70] Garrison cited the threat published in the *Windham County Advertiser* and noted the paper's connection with Andrew Judson. The fire occurred "a short time since the *Advertiser*— a worthless and illiterate print (the pliant tool of Andrew T. Judson)— intimated that effectual measures would be taken to break up Miss Crandall's school."[71] Garrison told Helen Benson he hoped for Crandall's sake that no one deliberately set the fire. "I trust that the firing of her house will yet prove to have been accidental."[72]

After a brief investigation, State's Attorney Chauncey Cleveland concluded that the fire at Crandall's school occurred "feloniously, voluntarily, willfully, maliciously and with force."[73] Cleveland prepared writs and sent the sheriffs on their way. The man Cleveland charged with setting fire to Crandall's house was—Frederick Olney. Two sheriffs arrested Olney in a barbershop in Norwich. He pleaded "not guilty."

Accusing Frederick Olney of setting the fire shifted attention away from the opponents of the school to Crandall's own supporters. Andrew Judson and Crandall's opponents suggested that Olney and Crandall had conspired to set the fire to elicit sympathy for the school and cast suspicion on Crandall's critics. Charles Burleigh wrote in the *Unionist*, "Col. Judson and his coadjutors have been permitted to indulge their suspicions to the utmost, and to subject a perfectly innocent man to the mortification and expense of a criminal prosecution because he happened to be on the *inside* of Miss Crandall's house on the day of the fire."[74] Chauncey

Cleveland found a perfect defendant in Olney—he was black, was a friend of Crandall and her school, and did not live in Windham County; a local jury would know nothing of his nature and character. In addition, Olney served as the Norwich agent for the *Liberator*; he was linked to both Crandall and Garrison. Olney's trial was set for Friday, March 7, 1834, at the Brooklyn Courthouse.

The prosecution claimed that Frederick Olney had deliberately slipped a lighted paper or match between the baseboard and floor inside the northeast room on the first floor. Town selectman Ebenezer Sanger, local merchant Richard Fenner, Chauncey Bacon, and Solomon Payne all testified they believed the fire started inside the school. Three of Crandall's students—Maria Robinson, Amy Fenner, and Henrietta Bolt—recounted seeing Olney inside the house talking with Charles and Mariah Harris, writing a letter, and working on the clock.[75]

On cross-examination, the defense established that witnesses had monitored all of Olney's actions during his time in the school. No evidence linked Olney to the fire. One of the prosecution's witnesses, Ralph Hutchinson, an examiner for an insurance company, contradicted those who said the fire started inside the school. Hutchinson acknowledged the fire could have started outside on the northeast corner of the house.[76]

The judge continued the trial to Saturday. Helen Benson's home, which was a short walk from the courthouse, "was then thronged with colored pupils from Miss Crandall's school, who were summoned as witnesses at Mr. Olney's trial, and who had no other place in Brooklyn 'where to lay their heads.'"[77] Prudence Crandall later wrote that the Benson family's hospitality toward Crandall's students "was an honor to humanity."[78]

On Saturday the defense put on its case. After final arguments, the jury began deliberations at six o'clock in the evening. They almost immediately returned to the courtroom. "The Jury on their oath do say that the said Frederick Olney is *not guilty* of the crime charged against him," the foreman reported.[79] The verdict was unanimous. "The jury would probably have given their verdict without leaving their seats, if they had previously chosen a foreman," Charles Burleigh wrote in the *Unionist*.[80] Burleigh said that a number of rotten and waterlogged clapboards and interior timbers likely prevented the fire from spreading and destroying the school.

It rained for most of the day on Saturday, but after Frederick Olney's acquittal, Helen Benson noted the clouds scattered and the skies cleared.[81]

The Benson home had served as the headquarters for Olney's defense during the trial, and Olney walked there to celebrate with his friends and supporters.[82] Helen Benson told Garrison that she never did feel anxious for Olney during the trial "for I thought a Divine Providence would overrule and not permit the innocent to suffer for the guilty."[83] The work of Samuel May and the ideas expressed in previous months by Charles Burleigh at the *Unionist* may have helped the jury look beyond Olney's race.

In the aftermath of the "not guilty" verdict, the *Unionist* called for Andrew Judson and Chauncey Cleveland to "look diligently among those on the *outside* of the house for the real incendiary."[84] Prudence Crandall asked the publisher of the *Windham County Advertiser* to provide an explanation of the letter that predicted an effort to "BREAK UP" the school. The publisher refused. The *Unionist* noted, "Col. Judson and his fellow laborers against the school have done all in their power to excite the most virulent and reckless hostility to it. . . . They must wonder if those who have thrown stones and rotten eggs and filth, with impunity if not with applause, should be emboldened to apply even the slow match."[85] Charles Burleigh speculated that Crandall's opponents and the state's attorney "are in league to protect the real culprit, unless they now set about in earnest to find him."[86] The origin of the fire at Prudence Crandall's schoolhouse, however, remained a mystery. Chauncey Cleveland did not pursue the case.

William Lloyd Garrison attended Olney's trial at the Brooklyn Courthouse. He planned to quickly return to Boston where his schedule was "so crowded and crushed by my home duties, and so pinched for time."[87] In truth, Garrison visited Brooklyn as much to see Helen Benson as to witness the trial. A few weeks earlier Helen finally replied to Garrison's January letter. She told him about the fire and how those in Canterbury had "wickedly" charged Frederick Olney with the crime. She reported that Prudence Crandall's "peace and quiet [has] again been disturbed, and the little respite she enjoyed from persecution and which her friends hailed as the harbinger of happier days [has] been sadly broken in upon, and her cheering prospects put to flight by the dark designs of her enemies."[88] Helen wrote that she doubted she could maintain a correspondence with Garrison given his great "talents and attainments" and begged off Garrison's suggestion that she organize a female antislavery society in Providence. She did suggest that Garrison come to Brooklyn in March and stay with her family during Olney's trial. Prudence Crandall called the Benson home "Friendship Valley," as the Bensons provided a sanctuary for Crandall and her students. "Do you think it worthy of the title?" Helen asked Garrison.

Prudence Crandall's name came up often in the correspondence between Garrison and Helen Benson. While in Providence visiting her brother George, Helen described her home as "that little spot of earth which P. Crandall in the fullness of a grateful heart denominates the asylum of the oppressed."[89] Helen knew of Garrison's high regard for Prudence Crandall—she was unlike any woman Garrison or Helen had met. She had also heard and dismissed the rumors about Garrison and Crandall. As a postscript to her letter, the last thought Helen wrote for Garrison to consider was the news that Prudence Crandall had accepted a marriage proposal. She was engaged to a Baptist minister named Calvin Philleo.[90]

Without wasting any time, Garrison wrote back to Helen. His great happiness at receiving her letter poured out in his reply. "With all sincerity I say, I am delighted," he wrote. "I love its frankness. . . . I love its contemplative spirit: it is exactly in unison with my own."[91] Garrison thanked her for the invitation to stay with her family. "How great are my own obligations to your father and mother—to your brothers and sisters—and to you—for your united friendship, hospitality and aid!"[92] He did note that he had little time to spare and would have to come and go "like an arrow."

The news of Prudence Crandall's engagement did not elicit a reaction from Garrison. Instead, he rhapsodized over "the persecuted, the dauntless, the heroic Prudence Crandall!" He commented on her "severe trials" and hoped that "ecstatic joys shall be hers hereafter! She has my sympathy, my admiration, my prayers."[93] Garrison then referred to his earlier confusion about Helen's name—George Benson had wasted no time in passing on the story of Garrison's error to his family. "I shall ascertain your name by and by! I used to call you Ellen, but you rectified the error. Now I perceive by your signature that you have a middle name."[94]

On the same day he wrote Helen, Garrison also wrote to his close friend Samuel May. Garrison's mood in that correspondence differed significantly. "How is it that I accomplish so little?" he asked. "I toil much, and produce little. I am dissatisfied with almost everything that I perform."[95] Garrison said he looked forward to visiting Brooklyn, but other matters weighed on his mind. "Great as is my desire to see you—impatient as I am to be sheltered once more under the hospitable roof of my venerated friend and benefactor George Benson—strongly as I wish to see the noble Christian heroine, Prudence Crandall and her interesting pupils—still I am surrounded with obligations and duties at home . . . my constant presence is so much needed here."[96] Garrison referred to the ongoing challenge to keep the *Liberator* solvent. In addition, the writs Andrew Judson had succeeded in serving upon Garrison required that he stand trial in March. Garrison asked May for financial help to post bail and postpone his trial. "To obtain [bail], I must rely upon the kindness of those on the spot who are friendly to the cause of justice and humanity," Garrison wrote.[97]

Instead of coming and going like "an arrow," Garrison stayed with the Benson family for nearly a week. During that time, William Lloyd and Helen drove a carriage to Canterbury to visit Prudence Crandall prior to the Olney trial. "During our pleasant ride to Canterbury, I wished to disclose some of my feelings to you, but my tongue was tied," Garrison later told Helen.[98] On Friday, Garrison watched the prosecution put on its case against Olney, but he left early on Saturday morning for Providence, traveling with Samuel May and his wife, Lucretia, while Olney's defense attorneys argued their case. When the stagecoach stopped at a tavern, a man asked Garrison what he thought of the "nigger school" in Canterbury.[99] Garrison, who noticed the man was drunk, replied that he supported the school and interracial marriage. Lucretia May joined in and said she preferred a virtuous and sober colored man to an intemperate white man. The man at the tavern asked no more questions.[100]

When Garrison arrived in Providence, he visited Helen's brother George and her sister Mary and met with Moses Brown. Before the day was over, Garrison boarded a stagecoach and returned home to Boston exhausted, but not too tired to write Helen. "You have got possession of my heart," Garrison wrote. He referred to a gift she gave him, a small round box with "Liberty is the Watchword" inscribed on one side and "William Lloyd Garrison" on the other. "Have you anything to give me *in the shape of a heart?*" he asked. "Just examine carefully, if agreeable, and let me know hereafter."[101] At the end of his letter, he remembered the Olney case. "I feel extremely anxious to learn the result of Mr. Olney's trial. Will you write soon?"[102] Garrison said Olney's arrest occurred because of his color and proximity to the fire. "As he was taken up simply for being *in*

Miss Crandall's house at the time of the fire, suppose we have Andrew T. Judson arrested," Garrison told Helen, "as he lives in the dwelling next to her own."[103]

A few days later Garrison wrote to a black friend in Pittsburg about the efforts to end slavery in America. "The chains of every bondman will soon fall to the earth. . . . Anti-slavery societies are multiplying all over our land. This is the way to reform . . . and to overthrow iniquity and oppression."[104] Garrison's campaign to help Crandall's school continued while abolitionist allies began spreading the message of immediate emancipation across the country.

10 : **Race Riots**

The widening gap between rich and poor in the 1830s plunged a growing number of Americans into poverty. Wages for common workers remained stagnant, while agricultural prices rose 51 percent between 1829 and 1836.[1] Bank profits soared.[2] Theodore Dwight Weld noted that if the gap was not "speedily bridged, by bringing education within reach of the poor, it will widen into an impassable gulf, and our free institutions, our national character, our bright visions of the future, our glory and joy, will go down with it."[3] Weld said America needed a middle class created through education and opportunity.[4] "There is no benevolence in pointing a starving man to a leaf suspended in the air," Weld wrote, "unless you give him wings to fly to it."[5]

Arthur Tappan met Theodore Dwight Weld through his brother Lewis. In 1831 evangelical minister Charles Finney persuaded Lewis Tappan to send his two sons to the Oneida Academy, "a manual labor" school in western New York.[6] Weld taught and mentored Tappan's sons at the Oneida school.[7] The manual labor concept combined religious and academic instruction with physical labor—all students learned farming and trade skills. The mixture of work in the fields and lessons in the classroom narrowed "the distance between the learned and the laboring classes," Weld said.[8]

Opposition to slavery came naturally to Theodore Dwight Weld. The son and grandson of Congregational ministers, Weld was born in a colonial farmhouse in Hampton, Connecticut, on November 23, 1803. The church where Theodore's father preached, the Hampton Congregation Church, counted state senator Philip Pearl as one of its parishioners. Pearl's daughter Hannah attended Prudence Crandall's school when it served only white girls, and he drafted the legislative report that supported Andrew Judson's Black Law. Years later, with Theodore Dwight Weld's assistance, Pearl reconsidered his role in the passage of the Black Law and the persecution of Prudence Crandall. Weld was familiar with Prudence Crandall's school for black women—Canterbury was adjacent to Weld's hometown of Hampton. When Weld worked to establish a school for black women in Cincinnati in 1834, he referred to Prudence Crandall's school as a benchmark.

The Tappan brothers endorsed and actively promoted the concept of manual labor schools as a means of bridging the gap between rich and poor. They offered Weld the opportunity of leading a speaking tour into the southern and western states to promote abolition, temperance, and the manual labor school concept; Weld immediately accepted. Arthur Tappan also asked Weld to select a western site for a national theological seminary based on the "manual labor" philosophy.[9]

Weld narrowed his search for a site for a national theological seminary after a visit to the Lane Seminary in Cincinnati, Ohio. Rev. Franklin Vail, Lane Seminary's financial agent, offered Weld the guarantee of a professorship if Weld recommended the Lane site to Arthur Tappan.[10] Weld did recommend Lane based on the location and grounds of the school, but refused the professorship or any other compensation. Weld chose to enroll as a student and quickly became one of Lane's most influential and respected students.

Arthur Tappan agreed to underwrite Lane Seminary as a national model and persuaded evangelical minister Lyman Beecher to leave New England and serve as its president.[11] Tappan knew that Beecher strongly opposed slavery but did not realize that Beecher supported colonization.[12] When Weld proposed a series of debates regarding slavery and immediate emancipation, Weld invited Beecher and the faculty to participate. Beecher initially accepted the offer, but a number of faculty members objected. The faculty feared that debating slavery would invite criticism from the local community—no school in the country had sponsored debates on the issue of slavery—and they persuaded Beecher to reject the invitation and ask that Weld cancel the slavery debates.[13]

Weld resolved to go forward. On February 1, 1834, Weld and the students announced they would debate two questions: whether slaveholding states should immediately abolish slavery and whether colonization deserved the support of the Christian public.[14] The forum began on Tuesday evening, February 4, and continued in the school chapel during eighteen consecutive evenings. "There were eighteen speakers, eight of them were born and had always lived in slave states," Weld wrote. "The average age of the speakers was twenty-four years."[15]

William Allan of Alabama, "born, bred and educated in the midst of slavery," called for immediate emancipation, which he defined as "gradual emancipation, immediately begun."[16] Former slave James Bradley—the first black student at Lane—described how slave traders had kidnapped him in Africa when he was three years old and brought him by ship to Charleston, South Carolina.[17] James said his owner regularly beat him. "My master often knocked me down when I was young. Once, when I was a boy, about nine years old, he struck me so hard that I fell down and lost my senses. I remained thus some time, and when I came to myself, he told me he thought he had killed me."[18] James Thome descended from a prosperous Kentucky family that owned many slaves. "Though I am at this moment the heir to a slave inheritance . . . I am bold to denounce the whole system as an outrage, a complication of crimes and wrongs, and cruelties that make angels weep."[19]

At the conclusion of the debate, Weld presented his case for immediate emancipation. "Slavery, with its robbery of body and soul from birth to death . . . its baptisms of blood and its damning horrors to the eternity of the spirit—slavery, in this land of liberty and light . . . its days are numbered and well-nigh finished."[20] After nine evenings of debate and discussion, the students of Lane Seminary voted to support immediate emancipation.

For the next nine evenings the students debated whether colonization violated Christian ideals. Lyman Beecher dispatched his daughter Catherine to urge support for colonization. Catherine repeated her father's belief that supporters of abolition and colonization should work together. Huntington Lyman, a student from Louisiana, disagreed and said the leaders of colonization did not intend to end slavery. "We are astonished at the result of our own investigation. . . . We have been deceived by a specious exterior."[21] When the colonization debate ended, all of the students except one agreed that colonization did not deserve Christian support.[22]

Despite the volatility of the slavery issue, no acrimony among the students emerged. "When the debate commenced, I had fears that there might be some unpleasant excitement, particularly as slaveholders, and prospective heirs to slave property, were to participate in it," wrote student Henry Brewster Stanton. "But the kindest feelings prevailed. . . . Immediate emancipation is not only right and practicable, but is expedient."23

The Lane Debates received national attention. The students condemned slavery without condemning southerners in general. They avoided the unforgiving language that Garrison often employed in the *Liberator*. Theodore Weld downplayed his own role and relied on a diverse group of students to make the case against slavery and colonization.

Immediately following the debates, students at Lane organized an antislavery society. Weld, Augustus Wattles, and other students created a school out of three rooms; the students raised hundreds of dollars to outfit a library and rent space for classes. "Everything goes on here as we could wish," Wattles wrote in the *Emancipator*. "Our colored brethren are animated with hope. . . . Frequently, in passing their homes, old women will stop me, and ask if I think they are too old to learn. On receiving for answer, 'you are never too old to learn,' they brighten up, and commonly add, 'we have been slaves and never seen such times as these.'"24

Cincinnati's black community embraced the school; students filled the rooms to capacity each day. "We have formed a large and efficient organization for elevating the colored people of Cincinnati," Weld wrote to Arthur Tappan. "We believe that faith without works is dead."25

In addition to day and evening schools, Weld—inspired by Prudence Crandall's example—helped organize a school for black women. Weld told Lewis Tappan that he had a difficult time finding the right leader for the female school. "We know of no female, except Miss Crandall, who has the resolution and self-denial enough to engage in the enterprise."26 Weld said that Charlotte Lathrop of Norwich, Connecticut, who was teaching at a seminary near Cincinnati, had agreed to lead the female school. "These poor brethren and sisters MUST BE HELPED," Weld wrote. "Brother Tappan, do say something about them to our dear sisters in your city."27 Arthur Tappan sent Weld one thousand dollars and paid the expenses of four female teachers to travel from New York to Cincinnati and teach at the school.28

Weld immersed himself in the black community in Cincinnati. Many of those he met were former slaves who had purchased their freedom. "I found one man who had just finished paying for his wife and five children," Weld wrote. "Another woman . . . had recently paid the last installment of the purchase . . . for her husband. She had purchased him by taking in washing, and working late at night, after going out and performing as help at hard work. But I cannot tell half, and must stop . . . I was forced to stop from sheer heartache and agony."[29]

Lane students James Thome and Henry B. Stanton attended the first anniversary meeting of the American Anti-Slavery Society in May 1834 in New York City. They joined with the other delegates to support a new resolution that praised the efforts of Prudence Crandall. "Every measure for the thorough and proper education of colored females is a blow aimed directly at slavery," the delegates resolved. "This subject has been placed in the strongest light by the experiment of Miss Prudence Crandall. It was not because she had dared to teach colored females grammar and geography, nor indeed because she had taught them music and drawing, that the majesty of the State interfered with her humble and self-denying labors; but it was because she dared to teach them as if they were white—to treat them with the same delicacy and respect which an instructress is expected to extend to young ladies in good society. . . . We rejoice to see that public favor is beginning to smile upon that amiable philanthropist."[30]

The successful outreach to the black community by the students at Lane Seminary provoked outcry among some in the white community of Cincinnati. When classes resumed that fall, Lyman Beecher, anticipating controversy, left the seminary to travel east. The executive committee threatened Weld with expulsion unless he and the other students ended their work in the black community. Weld and fifty-three students signed a petition refusing to obey the school's ultimatum.

A nearby school opened its doors to the Lane Rebels. Weld and a majority of the students left Lane and enrolled in a school that had nearly closed its doors because of a lack of funds—Oberlin College. With a boost in enrollment and the financial help of Arthur Tappan—who shifted his support away from Lane—Oberlin grew and prospered. The former Lane students continued their work in the black community of Cincinnati.[31]

The work of Weld and the students had another lasting effect. Lyman Beecher's daughter Harriet attended most of the debates and heard Theodore Weld and his colleagues discuss the outrages of slavery. Weld later wrote a book, *American Slavery As It Is*, and Harriet Beecher Stowe cited Weld's book and what she had learned at the Lane Debates as inspirations for her landmark, antislavery novel that influenced the nation, *Uncle Tom's Cabin*.[32]

A few weeks after the Lane Debates, William Lloyd Garrison suggested to the members of the New England Anti-Slavery Society that they commission an oil painting of Prudence Crandall. The members agreed, and Garrison selected "one of our most distinguished artists" to paint Crandall's portrait.[33] Francis Alexander had studied at Alexander Robertson's Academy of Fine Arts in New York City and painted portraits of well-known political leaders and authors, including Daniel Webster, Henry Wadsworth Longfellow, and Charles Dickens. After traveling to Italy in 1831 to study and paint, he had returned to Boston and in 1834 accepted the offer to paint Prudence Crandall's portrait. Francis Alexander knew all about northeastern Connecticut and Canterbury—he was born in the nearby town of Killingly in 1800 and had spent his childhood on the family farm.[34] The idea of a portrait surprised Crandall, but she agreed to travel to Boston for the necessary sittings.

Prudence Crandall faced a critical personal decision. While she had accepted Calvin Philleo's proposal of marriage, during his time away she began to doubt the wisdom of her engagement. Knowing that the Benson family had extensive contacts in Rhode Island where Rev. Philleo preached, Crandall approached Helen Benson. "She then questioned me so closely as to what I heard, that I was obliged to tell her," Benson told Garrison. "I felt rather a weight off my mind by doing so though I do not think anything I said made the least difference to her."[35]

Helen Benson had heard many unflattering stories about Calvin Philleo's efforts to find a wife. Philleo once had called on a woman who owned a clothing store with the intention of asking her to marry him; he had proposed marriage upon meeting her for the first time. Philleo offended both the woman and her husband. On another occasion, Philleo had placed an advertisement in the newspaper encouraging women to contact him directly regarding marriage—a practice many regarded as scandalous. Benson also had learned that a woman recently had broken off an engagement with Philleo after she heard about his unorthodox pursuit of women.[36]

Helen Benson supposed Crandall would discount any negative comments. "Love, you know, 'heightens every virtue,' and I found in her estimation he was almost a perfect being."[37] After listening to Benson's

stories, Crandall said she "could at any moment withdraw her affections" toward Philleo.[38] Both Helen Benson and William Lloyd Garrison
thought Philleo's pursuit of Crandall had more to do with opportunism
than love. Garrison later told Benson, "You did well to deal frankly with
Miss C. in relation to her contemplated marriage."[39]

Rival ministers in Rhode Island criticized Philleo. Those from conventional, nonrevivalist churches viewed him with hostility and envy as he
succeeded in stealing away parishioners from their churches. Jacob Frieze,
a Universalist minister in Pawtucket, bitterly noted that Philleo had "succeeded in converting to his faith, some twenty or thirty persons, women
and children, exclusively."[40] Frieze said Philleo deliberately targeted
women and children and browbeat them into converting to his church.
Frieze asked the mothers and fathers of his congregation to "bar your
doors against the foul monster, that under the garb of sanctity, would invade your peaceful abode, and spread terror and dismay among the children of your love."[41] Frieze claimed that Philleo had said God enjoyed
wrapping a cord around the necks of sinners, pulling them within his
grasp, and dropping them into "endless Hell."[42] Philleo replied with a
blunt rebuke and warned Frieze of the "foretaste in this world of the Hell
which awaits him in the world to come."[43]

The attraction of the city and the need to sit for her portrait convinced
Crandall to catch the early morning stagecoach on Tuesday, April 1, 1834,
from Canterbury to Boston. She arrived late that afternoon and to the
delight of Garrison delivered a letter from Helen Benson. The next day,
Garrison met Crandall and escorted her to Francis Alexander's studio in
the Columbian Hall at the corner of Milk and Oliver Streets.

Alexander positioned Crandall in front of a window nearly covered by
heavy, dark red drapery; a narrow sliver of the outdoors showed through
on the right-hand side. Crandall wore a dark blue dress with a sheer silk
scarf trimmed in satin and fringe. Her chestnut hair was pulled back ex-
posing her ears on both sides. The facial expression that Alexander captured is serious but not solemn; Crandall's eyes are bright and there is a
slight hint of a smile. In her hands she clutched a leather-bound book to
convey her ability as a teacher and educated woman. Prudence wore no
rings, necklaces, or jewelry that might link her to family or a broader social
world. She displayed no personal items or effects. While her facial expression and posture conveyed confidence, Alexander also captured a solitary

quality to Crandall's demeanor. "I am happy to say that the artist has been very successful in taking the portrait of Miss Crandall, but the story of her persecution will outlive the canvas," Garrison wrote to Helen Benson.[44]

Francis Alexander's fees ranged from thirty to fifty dollars—a substantial sum for the time, and Garrison asked members of various antislavery societies to contribute toward Crandall's portrait. The person who contributed the most was not a member of the New England Anti-Slavery Society or one of Garrison's friends in Boston, but a black clothing dealer who lived in Philadelphia and had a keen interest in education. John Bowers contributed twenty-five dollars. He served as president of the first National Convention of the People of Color, held in Philadelphia in June 1831.[45]

Crandall sat for her portrait during the day and became the center of attention at abolitionist parties and gatherings each evening. The Boston abolitionists honored her as a true heroine of the antislavery cause, and she met throngs of supporters at every dinner and event. Crandall originally planned to leave Boston on Saturday, April 5, but with so many invitations she relented and prolonged her stay in Boston through Monday, April 7.

Garrison knew "there are hundreds yearning to see her, who cannot get an opportunity." The outpouring of admiration for Crandall concerned Garrison to an extent. "One thing she must guard against," he told Helen Benson, "namely, being exalted in her mind by the abundant panegyric of her friends."[46] While he told Benson that Crandall "must be careful lest she be 'exalted above measure,'" Garrison also conceded that "these remarks are strictly applicable to me as to her."[47]

During their days and evenings together in Boston, Garrison and Crandall discussed her pending marriage to Calvin Philleo. The questions she wished to ask Philleo regarding Helen Benson's stories remained unanswered. Crandall's friends disapproved of her engagement, and even her family was not enthusiastic. When Crandall told her mother she planned to marry Philleo, Esther gave a strange reply. "Prudy, I dreamed of thee last night. I dreamed thee walked the street with a toad in a glass pitcher."[48] The concern of her family and friends, combined with Philleo's absence, pushed her toward a decision. Crandall told Garrison she would break off her engagement to Philleo. On Monday, the day Crandall left Boston for Canterbury, Garrison told Helen he was "happy to inform you that

Prudence has wholly given up Mr. Philleo."[49] Garrison also said Crandall did not know about their recent engagement and supposed that Crandall would ask Helen about their relationship on her return to Canterbury. "Pray let me into the secret of her inquiries," Garrison wrote.[50]

Crandall returned to Canterbury energized by the outpouring of support she had received in Boston. She traveled to Brooklyn on Wednesday, April 9, to see the Benson family. "How happy she looked and how kindly she spoke of you as she greeted me," Helen Benson wrote to Garrison. "She was exceedingly gratified with the attention you paid her and her heart seemed almost too full for utterance."[51] Benson told Garrison that Crandall had "so many things to say of you, and about you, that I almost fancied I had caught a glimpse of you myself."[52] Crandall told Benson that her engagement with Calvin Philleo was over, "done with."[53] She did leave the door open a crack, Benson thought. "I have not a single proof of the numerous reports that are alleged against him," Prudence told Helen.[54] If and when Philleo did return to Canterbury, Crandall planned to confront him with the stories she had heard. After Crandall finished relaying her news regarding Calvin Philleo, Helen told Crandall of her engagement to Garrison. "She knows all," Benson later wrote to Garrison.[55]

As voters prepared to go to the polls to elect the Connecticut General Assembly in April 1834, State Representative Andrew T. Judson reflected on his previous term. He had initiated the petition drive that resulted in the passage of the Black Law. When Prudence Crandall had violated the Black Law, Judson had led the prosecution. No other person in Connecticut was more fiercely opposed to Crandall's school for black women. Judson had many reasons for his opposition, including the fact that she had located her school across from his house, but he also knew his constituents opposed her school. Judson began planning for his next term as the state representative from Canterbury.

When the votes were counted, Andrew T. Judson lost his bid for reelection. His defeat stunned his supporters and caused jubilation in the ranks of abolitionists. "The news of the infamous Judson's political overthrow has reached our city, as well as the complete regeneration of Connecticut, and excited universal joy," Garrison wrote to Helen Benson. "Let us now cherish the hope that the black laws of the State will be repealed by the new Legislature. Cheers for Miss Crandall!"[56] Crandall's allies saw Judson's defeat as a sign that public opinion had turned their way, that the tactics of Judson and his supporters had offended the people of Connecticut. The election of 1834, however, took place in the midst of a banking crisis in the United States and turned into a referendum on the policies of President Andrew Jackson, a Democrat, and the terrible state of the economy. Andrew Judson was affiliated with President Jackson and the Democrats. When Judson lost the April election, there were some who had voted against him because of his stand against Prudence Crandall, but others had voted against Judson and all the Democratic candidates because of President Jackson's policies and the banking crisis.[57]

Garrison continued to celebrate Judson's defeat in the pages of the *Liberator*. "How contemptible and yet deplorable is the condition of that wretched and guilty man—scorned and detested he is," Garrison wrote. "Twelve months ago this discarded and crestfallen nondescript towered high in his pride of place and exalted himself above all that is called good. His evil power was potent and his arrogance insufferable. Behold the change!"[58] In the same article, Garrison praised Prudence Crandall. If Garrison believed that Crandall had received too many compliments while in Boston, he did not show any restraint in his own description of her. "She stands upon a pinnacle of honor higher than the pyramids, and is receiving enthusiastic plaudits of millions," Garrison said. "Her fame is rising and brightening like the sun going up from beneath a cloudy horizon to an ethereal zenith."[59]

Throughout April and May, Prudence Crandall waited in vain for Calvin Philleo to return. "It seems to me that Mr. Philio is somewhat tardy in coming to Canterbury," Garrison wrote (Garrison often misspelled Philleo's last name as "Phillio" or "Philio").[60] Prudence told Helen that she expected Calvin any day. On Saturday, May 31, Philleo finally returned. He arrived by boat in Norwich and took the stagecoach to Canterbury. Dr. Roland Green of Canterbury met Philleo while traveling on the same boat and learned of his intention to marry Prudence Crandall. Green "took a very great dislike to him" and thought that Philleo was "very disagreeable."[61] Green's son reported to Helen Benson that his father was very sorry about Crandall's plans to marry Philleo.

When Philleo and Crandall met again in Canterbury, Crandall asked him directly about the stories she had heard, and he answered her frankly.[62] It was true, Calvin said, that once he had placed an advertisement in a newspaper seeking a wife. He confirmed that he had met a woman at a clothing shop, introduced himself, and offered to marry her the next time they met. He added that when he had learned the woman was married, he told her he would not call on her again. Calvin also admitted that he previously had been engaged to a woman who broke it off when she heard the various stories about him. He had done nothing wrong, he told Crandall. As a widower with young children he simply had to do everything he could to find a suitable mate.

One week later, Crandall visited Helen Benson in Brooklyn. She told Helen her engagement to Philleo was on again. Helen reminded Prudence of the troubling stories. Crandall recounted the stories, together with Philleo's answers, and much to Benson's dismay Crandall said she was satisfied with his explanations.

"He could make Prudence believe black was white if he chose," Benson wrote to Garrison. "Love is blind, blind to all faults and failings in the image it adores."[63] Philleo wanted to marry as soon as possible, Crandall told Benson. Crandall said she was willing to give up her school for her marriage. Helen immediately wrote to Garrison with the news and told him Philleo was a "much meeker looking man" than she expected.[64]

"I am troubled in spirit lest our dear friend Prudence marry ill," Garrison replied. "The step she is about to take will seal her earthly destiny, either for good or evil. Let her seriously weigh the consequences. Is not the thought of being indissolubly allied to a worthless person insupportable?"[65] Garrison doubted that Crandall could continue teaching if she had to support both Philleo's travels and the demands of her school. "I think if Prudence marries him, she will act wisely in giving up her school," Garrison said. "I have read your sketch of Mr. Philleo's visit to Brooklyn with considerable care, and feel as much perplexed in relation to the real character of the man. If he is an innocent man, he is certainly an injured man; and he had better be both than a bad man. Let us hope for the best."[66]

In a letter to Garrison, Crandall praised Philleo's character and told Garrison that Philleo wanted to expand the school to as many as one hundred students. Garrison expressed his dismay to Helen's brother, George Benson. "She had better take advantage of her marriage, and move off with flying colors, especially as the Legislature of Connecticut—to its everlasting disgrace—has adjourned, without repealing the odious law against her school."[67]

On Friday, June 20, 1834, just two weeks after he had referred to Calvin Philleo as a "worthless person," Garrison met Philleo for the first time. Prudence had sent Philleo to Boston to meet Garrison in person. Calvin arrived on Friday and stayed through Monday; Garrison was pleasantly surprised by their meeting and cautiously optimistic for Crandall. "He certainly appears to be a good man, and I sincerely hope that 'he is a man more sinned against than sinning.'"[68]

On Independence Day 1834, Rev. Ray Potter and the Pawtucket Anti-Slavery Society invited William Lloyd Garrison to address a gathering in Pawtucket and remind listeners of Jefferson's declaration that "all men are created equal." Abolitionists held similar rallies in halls and churches throughout New England. At an Independence Day sermon at the Second Congregational Church in Norwich, Connecticut, Rev. James T. Dickinson called slavery "a system of oppression, and therefore is regarded by the Bible as sin."[69] The Bible prohibited "oppression and injustice in *every form*, and surely it condemns injustice so flagrant," Dickinson said, "and whatever it condemns as wrong, it requires should be *immediately* repented of."[70]

Before receiving the offer to speak in Pawtucket, Garrison's friend and future brother-in-law, George Benson, asked him to speak on the Fourth of July in Providence, Rhode Island. Garrison declined. "There is too much prejudice against me in Providence for me to encounter it successfully at present," Garrison told Benson. "Although our cause is certainly advancing with a mighty stride, yet the opposition still to be encountered is truly formidable. . . . The Lord God of hosts is our strength and shield . . . he will put our faith and courage to a severe test."[71]

In New York City, the black community traditionally celebrated the Fourth of July as "Emancipation Day," with parades, music, and hearty consumption of rum and hard cider. Black religious leaders considered the presence of alcoholic beverages and drunkenness "scandalous and disheartening."[72] In 1834 black ministers, including Peter Williams and Theodore Wright, worked with Lewis Tappan to create a more serious and sober Independence Day "Service of Commemoration" at the Chatham Street Chapel (part of the Second Free Presbyterian Church). Tappan and the ministers agreed that choirs from black and white churches would sing hymns together, and black and white parishioners would sit together in the main sanctuary of the chapel.

When the service proceeded, shouts erupted from the pews. Newspaper editorials had encouraged those opposed to abolition to go to the Chatham Street Chapel and disrupt the program. William Leete Stone, publisher of the *New York Commercial Advertiser*, wrote that "friends of the UNION and of the SOUTH" should attend the meeting, and James Watson Webb of the *New York Courier and Enquirer* alerted readers to the fanatics who promoted "the doctrines of abolition and amalgamation."[73] Rev. Samuel H. Cox, minister of the Presbyterian Laight Street Church, pleaded for order in the sanctuary of the chapel. The disrupters shouted "treason" and threw prayer books. Security men from the mayor's office arrived to prevent further disorder.[74] The *Courier and Enquirer* denied responsibility and blamed those who organized the event. "However much we may regret such irregularities as those at Chatham Street Chapel, it must be borne in mind that it is the Tappanists who produce them."[75]

Three days later, on July 7, blacks gathered at the Chatham Street Chapel to mark the seventh anniversary of the end of slavery in New York State; the legislature had abolished slavery seven years earlier on Independence Day 1827. Some members of the New York Sacred Music Society erroneously thought they had booked the chapel for the same evening and pointedly asked the black men and women to leave. The situation deteriorated quickly into physical pushing and shoving followed by "considerable violence on both sides, and . . . broken heads and benches."[76] Later that evening an angry crowd formed outside the home of Lewis Tappan on Rose Street. Susan Tappan and her children heard the mob calling for her husband. Lewis Tappan had traveled to the Chatham Street Chapel to inspect the damage and was not at home. In the ensuing excitement, some in the crowd threw rocks at Tappan's home and broke most of the first-floor windows. When Tappan returned home, the crowd did not assault or injure him; a group of security men had arrived to keep the peace.[77]

The *Courier and Enquirer* called the incident a "Negro Riot" and predicted more "disgraceful negro outrages" in the city until "Arthur Tappan and his troop of incendiaries shall be put down by the strong arm of the law."[78] The *Courier* claimed an infuriated mob of blacks had beaten and bludgeoned innocent white citizens. "How much longer are we to submit? In the name of the country, in the name of heaven, how much more are we to bear from Arthur Tappan's mad impertinence?"[79] James Watson Webb published the *Courier and Enquirer*. One media observer described Webb as a "wealthy, hot-headed young aristocrat" whose "mercurial, impulsive temperament . . . was always the principal drawback" to the newspaper.[80] He physically assaulted rival publishers. "The sword, the pistol, the walking-cane and the fist were all handier if not mightier weapons than the pen to him."[81] Webb saw no moral problem with slavery and supported an aggressive version of colonization that included the deportation of all blacks, free and slave, whether they wanted to leave the country or not.[82] He called abolitionists unpatriotic and traitors to their country. Webb understood the economic value in exploiting racial prejudice. Fear spawned rumors, anger, and a thirst for news that resulted in greater sales of his newspaper. Race baiting increased profits.

In this tense and poisonous atmosphere, Webb and the editors of most newspapers in New York City chose to fan the flames of violence. "These abolitionists and amalgamators should know the ground on which they stand," Webb wrote. "When they openly and publicly promulgate doctrines which outrage public feelings, they have no right to demand protection from the people they thus insult."[83] Webb's words resonated with many white laborers who struggled in hard times. The idea that freed slaves might compete with whites in labor markets disturbed many citizens.[84]

Not all of the newspapers in New York incited whites to assault blacks and abolitionists.[85] The *New York Evening Post* disagreed with the "very inflammatory language" of the *Courier* and other morning papers, and it said that while both sides were at fault for the disturbance at the chapel, it was "more especially on the side of the whites."[86] The moderate opinions of the *Evening Post*, however, did not represent the majority view in the press.

Reports of interracial violence circulated throughout the city, increasing tensions. False rumors that Rev. Peter Williams, the black minister of the St. Philips African Episcopal Church, had performed a wedding between a black man and a white woman stirred anger and outrage.[87] The newspapers warned of another abolitionist meeting scheduled for the Chatham Street Chapel on Wednesday, July 9. In an editorial under the headline, "The Fanatics," the *Courier and Enquirer* said, "There is to be another meeting tonight at the Chatham Street Chapel . . . If the blacks continue to allow themselves to be made the tools of a few blind zealots, the consequences to them will be most serious."[88] The *Courier* was mistaken—no abolitionist group had scheduled a meeting. The story succeeded, however, in motivating an angry crowd to assemble at the chapel only to find it dark and locked. Rather than disperse, the crowd broke into the chapel and held a meeting of their own, denouncing abolitionists and whipping up fear of black and white conflict.[89]

After the impromptu meeting, the crowd marched to the Bowery Theatre, where four days earlier the press had reported that the British stage manager, George Farren, had insulted America and made "disrespectful expressions towards the American people."[90] A butcher allegedly overheard Farren say to a companion, "Damn the Yankees; they are a damn set of jackasses and fit to be gulled."[91] Hundreds of rioters poured into the theater demanding that Farren surrender so he could be hanged. The rioters vandalized the theater until a large contingent of security men arrived.[92]

The leaders of the mob decided that if they could not get their hands on Farren, they should end the evening by hanging a famous abolitionist. Shouts rang out, "Away to Arthur Tappan's!"[93] As they ran to Arthur Tappan's home, they passed Lewis Tappan's vandalized house on Rose Street. Warned about the likelihood of riots and mindful of his family's close escape on Wednesday, Lewis Tappan and his family had decided to spend the night in Harlem, on the other side of the city. The mob, led by a man on a white horse, decided to "finish off" Lewis Tappan's house. The attackers battered down the front door and ran through the house. No security men interfered. Men threw plates and glassware out the windows. They dragged furniture, bedding, and clothing into the middle of the street, where they created a bonfire. The flames lit up the street so that the crowd could see the other modest houses and structures nearby, including a Quaker meetinghouse across from Tappan's home.[94]

A messenger alerted Arthur Tappan that a crowd had returned to destroy his brother's house. Tappan dressed in a disguise and walked to Rose Street. He stood on the edges of the crowd—having no idea that the mob intended to find and kill him—and observed young laborers and members of ethnic gangs looting his brother's house. He also noticed that not all in the crowd were young thugs; a number of local merchants and "even a deacon or two" assisted in the destruction.[95] Simeon S. Jocelyn joined Tappan and together they proceeded to the mayor's office to plead for police intervention. Mayor Cornelius Lawrence, a Tammany Hall Democrat, finally agreed to send police to Rose Street. On returning to his brother's house, Arthur Tappan watched the mob continue to ransack Lewis's home. The police ordered Arthur Tappan to leave. "I shall not be able to protect him if it is known that he is here," an officer said.[96] A fire alarm sounded on account of the bonfire, and as firemen and more officers arrived, the crowd finally dispersed.

On Thursday, July 10, Lewis Tappan and his wife returned to Rose Street to assess the damage and sort through what remained of their belongings. Lewis Tappan wrote to Theodore Dwight Weld that the "mob-like temper exhibited by several of our newspapers" had whipped up rioters who had destroyed his home. "Brother, pray for us," Tappan told Weld. "If we fall here at our posts don't desert the anti-slavery cause."[97] The *Courier and Enquirer* published a story about the events of the previous night and claimed the only damage to Tappan's house was a single broken window, and that otherwise protesters had demonstrated peacefully outside.[98] Lewis Tappan did not repair his house for the entire summer so that the public could see what actually had occurred. He wanted the destruction to serve as a "silent Anti-Slavery preacher to the crowds who will flock to see it."[99]

After a week of intermittent violence and rioting, the New York City police found it increasingly difficult to maintain law and order. Rumors circulated that a mob planned to burn down the Chatham Street Chapel. The owners of the chapel published a notice in the *Commercial Advertiser* stating that "no meeting on the subject of slavery shall be hereafter held in the building."[100] Nonetheless, gang members assembled at the locked chapel that evening, but left shortly thereafter without damaging the building.

Thursday night, gang members and vigilantes gathered to attack Arthur Tappan's store. The future of Tappan's business and the jobs of his employees depended on preserving the inventory of his store and warehouse on Pearl Street. Tappan decided to personally stand guard with his employees; Simeon S. Jocelyn joined Tappan inside the store. They prepared for a shooting war—Tappan and his employees armed themselves with rifles and pistols. When a crowd formed outside, Tappan's men warned that armed guards would shoot and kill anyone who attacked the store. Men threw rocks through the front windows, breaking nearly every pane of glass. Tappan told his employees not to shoot unless someone entered the store. More rocks battered the front façade of the building. Tappan gauged the intensity of the attack and moved his employees into position near the windows. "During all this time Mr. Tappan was as firm as a man could be," Jocelyn later wrote. "He moved about quietly and coolly, giving directions, animating his friends by his bearing and words."[101] After a tense standoff, the crowd dispersed but most did not go home. They set their sights on other targets.

Black Presbyterian minister and journalist Samuel Cornish, one of Prudence Crandall's sponsors, recently had accompanied Arthur Tappan to church, where the two men sat together in the Tappan family pew. Dr. Samuel Cox, the white minister of the Presbyterian Church on Laight Street, did not object, but many in the congregation disapproved of a black man sitting with white parishioners. In his next sermon Cox spoke about the sinfulness of racial discrimination. He reminded his congregation that Jesus had a darker, Syrian complexion.[102] James Watson Webb at the *Courier and Enquirer* denounced Cox for suggesting that "the Saviour of mankind was a negro."[103] A local merchant read the *Courier*'s story and attacked Rev. Cox. "He's against slavery, and the South, and the Union! And, would you believe it, he called my Saviour a nigger! God damn him!"[104] A commentator noted that the remark highlighted the "queer mixture of religion, profanity, patriotism, and bigotry" that infused the hostility toward the abolitionists.[105]

Later that Thursday night, a crowd gathered outside Cox's Laight Street Church. Gang leaders called out a prearranged signal, and rocks, bricks, and other debris rained down on the church. As the mob threw stones through the church windows, a contingent of police thundered down the street on horseback and startled the crowd; the assault ceased. The vandals regrouped and raced to another destination—Cox's house on Charlton Street. With the destruction of Lewis Tappan's home the previous evening fresh in his mind, Cox earlier had barricaded the front entrance of his home, packed up his belongings, and left the city by steamboat with his family.[106]

When the mob arrived at Cox's house, they pounded on the barricaded front door until it splintered and gave way. Men looted rooms on the first floor and smashed all of the windows. The crowd moved down the street toward Broadway, where they pulled shuttered street carts and wagons into the middle of the street to block traffic and entry by the police.[107] The crowd pried loose paving stones and planks from a picket fence for use as weapons. When the violence ended that night, vandals had severely damaged more than a dozen buildings.[108] The next morning Samuel Cox returned to view the destruction at his house and church. A group of young men recognized Cox and threw rocks at him until he ducked into the nearby home of a parishioner.[109]

Average citizens and merchants now feared for their own property and safety. The riots—initially rooted in racial tension—tapped into broader class and financial stresses and frustration. Gangs plotted to attack not only blacks and abolitionists but also the financial institutions and banks on Wall Street.[110] The mayor ordered citizens to remain in their homes and refrain from violence. He criticized the abolitionists but also said, "Their conduct affords no justification for popular commotion."[111] The newspaper editors who had helped to whip up public sentiment against the abolitionists now decried the consequences and accepted no responsibility. "The press is of little avail in stemming the torrent of popular fury when it is once excited," wrote William Leete Stone, editor of the *Commercial Advertiser.* "We can now appeal only to the strong arm of the law, and even that, unless more vigorously extended than it has hitherto been, will prove inadequate to our protection. Day after day we are compelled to become the chroniclers of our city's disgrace."[112] On Friday, Mayor Lawrence declared a state of emergency and called up the militia.

Major General Jacob Morton, who had joined the state militia in 1786 and was seventy-two years old, commanded the city militia. He issued an order activating three hundred members of the Twenty-seventh Regiment at two o'clock on Friday afternoon; they assembled at the city arsenal shortly thereafter.[113] After an initial flurry of orders, however, no troops materialized on the street. Expecting hand-to-hand combat, Colonel Linus W. Stevens drilled his men at the arsenal in the use of the bayonet as well as how to load and reload rifles. City officials arrived later in the afternoon and ordered the regiment to leave the arsenal and proceed to city hall, but Colonel Stevens refused. The soldiers had muskets, but they had no bullets or powder cartridges. Stevens said they would not leave without bullets and cartridges.[114]

The employees maintained their armed vigil at Arthur Tappan's store and secured the broken doors and windows. A fresh contingent of policemen assembled to help protect the store. As afternoon turned to dusk, gangs took over the streets of New York. They targeted Arthur Tappan's

store together with the homes of prominent black leaders, including ministers and merchants, black churches, and the homes of black families in
the Five Points neighborhood. Gang members told the white families of
Five Points—a mixed neighborhood of impoverished blacks and white
immigrants—to place candles in the windows of their homes as a sign for
the gangs to spare the homes from destruction.[115]

Rumors of the attacks circulated throughout the city. Black merchants
Thomas Downing, who owned the popular restaurant Downing's Oys-
ter House at the corner of Broad and Wall Streets, and Hester Lane,
who ran her own interior decorating business, appealed to Mayor Lawrence for help in keeping the peace in their neighborhoods.[116] Lawrence
ignored their requests. The troops who gathered early Friday afternoon to
help secure the city still remained at the arsenal on Friday evening. After
Colonel Stevens's troops finally acquired bullets and powder cartridges,
they received orders to stand guard at the mayor's office.

On Friday night, rioters directed their first attacks against the homes
of black families. "The houses and quarters of the colored people were
stoned, and in some cases demolished, and the negroes, as they made
their appearance, were assaulted, tossed, and beaten, until they could
make their escape and reach a place of safety."[117] The *Commercial Advertiser* reported that "the vengeance of the mob appeared to be directed entirely against the blacks; whenever a colored person appeared, it was a signal of combat, fight and riot."[118] Most white families in the Five Points
neighborhood had candles in their windows. "The streets in the neighborhood of the Five Points presented a brilliant appearance" because of all
the candlelight, the *Commercial Advertiser* noted.[119] The mob inflicted the
greatest amount of damage on black-owned homes and businesses along
Orange, Centre, and Leonard Streets, the heart of the black neighborhood
in Five Points. They destroyed the African American Mutual Relief Hall
on Orange Street and broke all the windows of the African Baptist Church
on Anthony Street.[120]

In the wake of Thursday's riots, Arthur Tappan received new death
threats, and his friend Simeon S. Jocelyn persuaded him to spend the day
in Poughkeepsie.[121] On Friday, a mob attacked his store and overwhelmed
the twenty policemen outside the building. Rioters launched paving
stones against the front of the building and smashed all of the second-
floor windows. Armed guards inside the store once again prevented the

crowd from entering and causing additional damage. One of the store's defenders told the crowd to batter down the doors if they dared; the store was "full of armed men who were ready to blow their brains out the moment the door gave way."[122] The police returned with greater numbers and after a standoff the crowd drifted away.

Much further north near Canal Street and closer to the Hudson River, a crowd of three or four hundred fought their way into Samuel Cox's church, where they smashed the remaining windows with rocks and bricks.[123] Six blocks north on Spring Street another mob formed outside of Rev. Henry Ludlow's Presbyterian church. The mob chained together carts, ladders, wagons, and wheelbarrows to block incoming police and cavalry on both sides of Spring Street. Rioters then kicked down the doors to the church and broke windows, carried away furniture, pews, and altars, and ripped apart carpets. At ten o'clock someone rang the church bell. Word of the attack reached Colonel Linus Stevens, who was on his way to Arthur Tappan's store. Stevens turned the Twenty-seventh Regiment of the National Guard around and marched northwest toward Spring Street. As the troops reached the intersection of Spring and Sullivan Streets, the barricades constructed by the mob succeeded in halting Colonel Stevens's regiment. Rioters on the rooftops of buildings on both sides of the street hurled rocks, bricks, and paving stones down on the troops.[124] The rocks and missiles seriously wounded a number of men.[125] General Prosper M. Wetmore, who accompanied Colonel Stevens, noticed that in the darkness one could see "the shower of sparks struck out by the stones glancing on the bayonets and barrels of the muskets."[126] The troops waited for the order to shoot into the crowd, but Colonel Stevens insisted that they hold their fire.

A local political leader stood on the barricades and exhorted the mob to continue their destruction of the church.[127] Unbeknownst to Colonel Stevens, city aldermen who had accompanied the troops had struck a deal with the mob leaders for an end to the rioting in exchange for a retreat by Stevens.[128] Stevens refused to withdraw. He told the aldermen his orders required that he disperse the crowd, and he could "not retire until that was done."[129] Instead, he ordered his two divisions to break through the barricades. His troops crashed through the wall of carts and wagons and swept through the opening; they arrested the leader who had addressed the mob.[130] Stevens ordered the divisions to march through the center of the street, divide the crowd in half, and then turn and disperse them by leading with their bayonets.[131] The tactic worked. At the intersection of Spring Street and Varick Street, the crowd fled in four directions. Colonel Stevens had restored order without firing a shot, but the mob had succeeded in destroying the Spring Street Church.

Five blocks north of city hall, on Centre Street, thousands of rioters surrounded St. Philips Episcopal Church.[132] Rev. Peter Williams, another of Prudence Crandall's sponsors, watched helplessly as the mob pulled down the altar and smashed vases and windows, including the heavy and valuable stained-glass windows. They dragged pews, wooden furniture, and carpets into the street and tossed them onto a bonfire.[133] The congregation of St. Philips had recently purchased a magnificent pipe organ at the cost of one thousand dollars. The rioters ripped the pipes off the wall and destroyed the keyboard console.[134] For more than two hours rioters vandalized and destroyed as much of the church they could, and no authorities intervened. "It is next to impossible to describe the scene," an eyewitness wrote. "Hundreds of infuriated devils were shouting, hollowing and busily employed in tearing out the doors and windows, the interior of the church, and whatever they could lay their hands on, and throwing it in the street."[135] The *Commercial Advertiser* described the "fiend-like destruction" of St. Philips Church as "one of the most disgraceful scenes we have ever witnessed."[136] At the end of the long night, the exhausted Twenty-seventh Regiment arrived at Centre Street to disperse the crowd.

On Saturday, July 12, 1834, the rioting in New York City finally came to an end. Estimates of the number of those who participated in the riots ran as high as twenty thousand. The police arrested more than one hundred and fifty persons. "It cannot be disguised, however, that the mob were complete masters of the city," the *Commercial Advertiser* noted, "and the city government was overawed, and for the time, at an end."[137] James Watson Webb at the *Courier and Enquirer* blamed the abolitionists. "We trust the immediate abolitionists and amalgamators will see in the proceedings of the last few days, sufficient proof that the people of New York, have determined to prevent the propagation amongst them of their wicked and absurd doctrines, much less to permit the practice of them." Webb refused to apologize for encouraging the rioters to attack the abolitionists and blacks. "If we have been instrumental in producing this desirable state of public feeling, we take pride in it."[138]

Other newspapers such as the *New York Star* called for an end to the riots. "We are no longer a country of laws . . . we shall be all anarchy and confusion."[139] The *Journal of Commerce* said riots undermined fundamental freedoms. "Has it come to this, that in free America, men cannot express their opinions, because the whole community almost, holds to opposite opinions? Or admitting that no sentiments may be uttered but such as the majority approve; are *an infuriated mob* to act as censors of the pulpit and the press? Are they to do it, not by tearing down arguments, but by demolishing churches and dwellings—by turning the city into a scene of anarchy and confusion—in short, by acting like devils incarnate in the shape of men? God forbid. Sooner will we fight the battles of the Revolution over again."[140]

The riots caused a national sensation, and violence surfaced in other communities. In Norwich, Connecticut, on July 9, a mob gathered outside Rev. Dickinson's Presbyterian church while an abolitionist from Boston spoke. The crowd pushed their way into the church, captured the speaker, and dragged him outside. They did not damage the church or further assault the speaker, but they ordered him to leave town and threatened to cover him in tar and feathers.[141]

In Newark, New Jersey, on Friday, July 10, a crowd attacked the Fourth Presbyterian Church. The previous evening Rev. William R. Weeks allegedly had permitted a black man to enter the main floor of the church sanctuary and stand with him for a moment in the pulpit. This infuriated some in the community who had followed the news of the riots in New York City. The next day a large mob entered the church during a service, forcibly removed Rev. Weeks from the pulpit, and took him to the municipal jail. They threatened the jailor until he locked up Rev. Weeks; the crowd returned to the church and smashed all the windows, destroyed the altar, and pulled the pews out of the church and into the street. They destroyed the interior of the church.[142] On Saturday another crowd in Newark attacked and damaged a barbershop owned by a black man.

The news of the violence directed toward black ministers and their churches devastated Prudence Crandall. Rioters attacked the ministers who had helped her and destroyed many of the black churches she had visited when she traveled to New York City in February of 1833. The mob violence dealt a severe blow to the resources of black ministers throughout New York City and to Crandall's allies Arthur and Lewis Tappan. The rioting in New York did not change Prudence Crandall's firm stance to continue her school for black women. The vandalism against her school, however, took a strange turn. Someone slit the throat of a cat and hung it by the neck on the entrance gate to the school.[143]

William Lloyd Garrison followed the news as he arrived in Providence on Saturday, July 12. He tried to describe to Helen Benson the "tide of emotions" that crashed over him "respecting the riotous proceedings of the mob against our abolition brethren in that city."[144] Garrison bitterly noted that in New York and elsewhere many thousands "calling themselves honorable and high-minded men—patriots—*Christians* even" openly applauded the violent and racist mobs.[145] "We who venture to remonstrate against the utter debasement and cruel oppression of a large portion of our countrymen, are branded by the daily press as outlaws, and declared to be unworthy of the least protection from the murderous designs of a lawless mob!"[146] The "country is in an awful condition," Garrison told Samuel May. "We shall be called, my brother, to pass through many perils."[147]

The mob violence had a chilling effect on even the bravest of abolitionists. Arthur Tappan and John Ranking printed a handbill under the authority of the American Anti-Slavery Society that stated, "We disclaim any desire to promote or encourage intermarriages between white and colored persons." They also denied any intention of asking Congress to abolish slavery, which they said would transcend Congress's constitutional powers.[148] In addition, Tappan vowed to refrain from appearing in the company of blacks where social custom required the separation of the races.[149] As he recalled many years later, sharing his pew with Samuel Cornish was "the only overt act of mine in the way of amalgamation, that I remember."[150]

After a mob destroyed his church in Newark, Rev. William R. Weeks issued a statement. "I am no advocate for the amalgamation of colors," Weeks said. "I believe that God, in making men of different colors, has sufficiently indicated the duty to us of keeping them separate, and of allowing no intermarriages between them."[151]

At St. Philips Episcopal Church in New York, Rev. Peter Williams cancelled services scheduled for Sunday, July 13. Rioters had destroyed the church. The white Episcopal Bishop for New York City, Benjamin T. Onderdonk, urged Williams to resign from the American Anti-Slavery Society and to renounce all abolitionist activity. "My advice, therefore is, give up at once," Bishop Onderdonk wrote. "Let it be seen that which-soever side right may be, St. Philip's Church will be found on the Christian side of meekness, order, and self-sacrifice. . . . You will be no losers by it, for the God of peace will be to you also a God of all consolation."[152] Williams reluctantly heeded the Bishop's advice. He wrote a letter to the people of New York, published in the *New York Spectator*, renouncing his membership in the American Anti-Slavery Society. Williams went further and made peace with the Colonization Society.

"Whenever any man of color, after having carefully considered the subject, has thought it best to emigrate to Africa," Williams wrote, "I have not opposed him, but have felt it my duty to aid him, in all my power, on his way."[153] The *Spectator* provided a friendly forum for the letters of Bishop Onderdonk and Rev. Williams. The editor of the *Spectator*, William Leete Stone, supported colonization and despised abolitionists. Stone took "unfettered pleasure" in publishing Rev. Peter Williams's withdrawal of his connection with the Anti-Slavery Society.[154] If the abolitionists had briefly gained ground through moral persuasion and argument, the blunt force of rioters had turned that gain into retreat.

11 : **Appeal for Equality**

As Prudence Crandall's allies in New York City suffered and retreated in the face of violence, she lost an important ally in the press. One year earlier Samuel May and Arthur Tappan had secured a local printing press in Brooklyn and commenced publication of the *Unionist*. In July 1834 the lease of the facilities expired. In addition, the editor of the *Unionist*, Charles Burleigh, wished to be free of the weekly obligations required in editing the *Unionist*; he was increasingly involved in the abolitionist movement in Boston. May asked William Lloyd Garrison for help and advice.

"A young man, such as you need at Brooklyn to take charge of the *Unionist*, cannot be easily found," Garrison said. "I shall be sorry—very sorry to see the *Unionist* go down—for many reasons, but especially on account of its unwavering adherence to our most unpopular cause, and its advocacy of the Canterbury school. It will be a fresh scandal to Connecticut to let such a paper die."[1] Crandall and her allies lost their only ally in the local media just as they braced for a pivotal showdown—the appeal of Crandall's conviction to the Connecticut State Supreme Court.

Prudence Crandall and her supporters prepared for the July appeal to the Connecticut Supreme Court, where they hoped to overturn the jury's verdict. They did not intend to downplay the issue of race or apologize for Crandall's work on behalf of black women. They planned to assert that the rights of citizenship and the protections of the Constitution applied to all free black men and women.

Samuel May expected the appeal to lead to a historic showdown in the United States Supreme Court. The appeal from the trial of October 1833 did not involve the testimony of witnesses and the drama of cross-examination. Instead, prosecutors and Crandall's defense attorneys made their respective arguments to four justices of the Connecticut Supreme Court: Associate Justices Thomas S. Williams, Clark Bissell, Samuel Church, and Chief Justice David Daggett. Crandall's attorneys had the burden of convincing the justices that the lower court had erred in upholding the constitutionality of the Black Law. The panel of justices faced challenges, however, in approaching the case in an objective and impartial manner. Two of the four justices had glaring conflicts of interest that went unaddressed.

The most obvious conflict involved Chief Justice David Daggett. Justices on the state supreme court in the 1830s often performed double duty: they served the county courts and decided cases at the trial level, and then they heard appeals from county court cases at the state supreme court level. It was unusual, however, for a justice to hear an appeal as to whether his own decision as a trial judge was correct. A fifth state supreme court justice, John T. Peters, could have taken Daggett's place, but Daggett invoked his authority as chief justice to hear the appeal of the *Crandall* case. Daggett's presence had a chilling effect on the ability of the other justices to frankly discuss and debate Daggett's rulings.

Associate Justice Thomas S. Williams had two unique connections to the attorneys involved in the Prudence Crandall case. He became a judge in 1829 after he had defeated Andrew T. Judson in a state senate vote for a judicial appointment. This connection with Judson created no appreciable conflict. In 1812, however, Williams married Delia Ellsworth, the daughter of the famous Connecticut judge and political leader Oliver Ellsworth. His wife Delia was the sister of attorney William W. Ellsworth—Prudence Crandall's lead attorney—making Justice Williams the brother-in-law of attorney Ellsworth. No one seemed to think that his sitting in judgment of a case argued by his brother-in-law presented a conflict. In addition, Williams had worked with Ellsworth as partners in Williams's law office after Ellsworth had graduated from Yale. Justice Williams later wrote in his private diary, "I do much need wisdom to guide me in affairs so important to my fellow men. I would desire with Solomon, 'give to thy servant an understanding heart to judge this people, that I may discern between good and bad.'"[2]

The other two justices had no direct connection to the Crandall case. Clark Bissell did not begin life with the advantages of his fellow justices. When he entered college in 1802, "It is doubtful if a poorer young man ever pursued the course at Yale."[3] Bissell graduated in 1806 with a debt of four hundred dollars and paid it off by tutoring young students while he studied law with Roger Sherman in New Haven.[4] Sherman, a legendary Connecticut lawyer and leader, had signed the Declaration of Independence and helped draft the U.S. Constitution. Sherman once gave a friendly jab to David Daggett. While arguing a case, Sherman could not find a particular legal reference, and opposing attorney Daggett offered his glasses. "Take my spectacles," Daggett said pointedly. "No, thank you," Sherman replied. "No truth was ever discovered with *your* spectacles."[5]

Bissell left Sherman's office to start his own law practice in Norwalk in 1809. He won an appointment to both the county court and the state supreme court in 1829.[6] Years later, in 1848, Bissell won election as governor of Connecticut.

The fourth justice who considered the Crandall appeal, Samuel Church, had barely served two years on the state supreme court. Church obtained an appointment to justice of the peace in Litchfield County in 1818 "and thought not of aspiring to a higher place."[7] He soon changed his mind and found himself in competition with David Daggett. While serving as both state's attorney and state senator in 1826, his fellow senators nominated Church to fill a vacancy on the state supreme sourt. The Connecticut House of Representatives approved a different candidate for the same judicial vacancy: David Daggett. In a pitched political battle between Church and Daggett, Daggett defeated Church and became chief justice.[8] Church waited another six years before he won a judicial appointment; he then joined his former rival Daggett on the state supreme court in 1832.

The four justices gathered at the courthouse in the center of Brooklyn, Connecticut, on Tuesday, July 22, 1834. Spectators filled the courtroom to capacity expecting to hear historic arguments. William W. Ellsworth and Calvin Goddard argued for Prudence Crandall. Prosecutors Andrew T. Judson and Chauncey F. Cleveland defended the lower court's verdict for the state.

"May it please the Court," Ellsworth said. He described the Black Law. "The defense of Miss Crandall will be rested upon the unconstitutionality of this statute law of Connecticut." Crandall's students were "*citizens* of their respective states," Ellsworth said, and "as *citizens*, the constitution of the United States secures to them the right of residing in Connecticut, and pursuing the acquisition of knowledge."[9] Ellsworth noted that Article

Four, Section Two of the Constitution protected citizens of one state who traveled to another state from discrimination; they were entitled to receive all of the "privileges and immunities" of that state.[10]

Ellsworth noted that the Black Law distinguished citizenship solely on the basis of color. "A distinction founded in color, in fundamental rights, is novel, inconvenient and impracticable. . . . Our republican fathers put forth as the groundwork of all just government—the Declaration of Independence. There, we read, 'we hold these truths to be self-evident, that all men are endowed by their creator with certain unalienable rights, that among these are life, liberty and the pursuit of happiness.' These pupils are human beings, born in these states, and owe the same obligation to the state and the state's governments, as white citizens."[11]

Ellsworth reminded the justices that blacks fought for the United States in the Revolutionary War and received the same military pensions as white soldiers. "They had a country and had bled for it," Ellsworth said. "Here the free man of color may take his position, and upon the immutable principles of justice and truth demand his political rights from that government which he is bound to aid and defend . . . To talk then of a class of nondescript people among us, under these circumstances, to make a new classification, of half citizen and half alien, is equally against reason, justice, and policy."[12]

Nothing in the Constitution supported a distinction based on race, Ellsworth said. The fact that blacks could not vote in Connecticut—a point stressed by the prosecution—did not prove they lacked citizenship. Blacks *were* permitted to vote in Maine, Massachusetts, Vermont, New Hampshire, New York, New Jersey, Pennsylvania, and five other states. "Once property was a necessary qualification in Connecticut," Ellsworth said. "Were none but persons of property citizens? No female can vote, nor any minor, but are they not citizens?"[13]

Ellsworth then directly challenged Chief Justice Daggett. During the previous trial, Daggett said that "education is a fundamental privilege, but this (Black) Law does not prohibit schools."[14] Daggett told the jury the Black Law did not violate this "fundamental privilege" because blacks did not enjoy the same rights as whites. Ellsworth disagreed on legal and moral grounds. "Need I tell this honorable Court, that we owe a debt to the colored population of this country, which we can never pay—no *never*—unless we can call back oceans of tears, and all the groans and agonies of the middle passage, and the thousands . . . of human beings whom we have sent . . . undone to eternity."[15] The discriminatory terms of the Black Law conflicted with the Constitution, Ellsworth said. "As well might the legislature, in order to raise up a more beautiful or vigorous generation of citizens, prohibit the harboring or entertaining of any citizen from the other states who was not six feet high, or had not a well proportioned body, or black eyes, or a clear skin. . . . If the power claimed does exist, then I say the legislature has power to *regulate* every white student at Yale College, being citizens of other states, out of our borders, as *aliens*. The question is not one of color, but of power, to be exercised at the pleasure of the legislature. . . . *This is a repeal of the constitution*."[16]

Ellsworth argued that parents of black children had every right to send their children to schools such as Crandall's. "Education is the first and fundamental pillar on which our free institutions rest, and it is the last privilege we will give up," Ellsworth said. "And here let me add, that the restrictions of this law are exceedingly onerous and distressing to the parents of these pupils. Shut out as these children are virtually from the schools of white persons, they have retired to a place by themselves, in deference to the prevailing prejudice against them—here they have sought out a virtuous and competent teacher to instruct them in the common branches of education, spelling, reading, arithmetic, geography, and the like . . . And who, *who* will rise up to oppose this effort? Let our opponents act openly."[17]

Crandall's opponents wanted to prevent her from teaching black women "under the pretense that educating them will fill our state with a vicious and pauper population," Ellsworth said. "It is a most wanton and uncalled for attack upon our colored population, it opens wounds not easily healed, it exasperates to madness many who live among us, it strengthens the unreasonable prejudice already pervading the community against blacks, and, in short, it rivets the chains of grinding bondage, and makes our state an ally in the unholy cause of slavery itself."[18] The justices, attorneys, and spectators in the courtroom were aware of the recent riots in New York City and the violence in other cities. Ellsworth alluded to those disturbing events and the prospect for additional violence in his concluding statements.

"Slavery is a volcano, the fires of which cannot be quenched, nor its ravages controlled. We already feel its convulsions, and if we sit idly gazing upon its flames, as they rise higher and higher, our happy republic will be buried in ruin, beneath its overwhelming energies."[19] Ellsworth returned to the defendant's table and took his seat next to Calvin Goddard. On the other side of the courtroom, Andrew T. Judson rose and approached the bench.

"It shall be my humble effort to maintain that the law in question is constitutional and the magnitude of the question will assure to me a patient hearing," Judson began. "Although this question may be one of vital importance to the town of Canterbury, yet that interest is by no means confined to that town. . . . It is a question in which every town in this state, and every state in this Union, has an equal interest. Let the decision be against this law—let those principles so ingeniously urged by my worthy opponent be once established by the judiciary, the consequences will inevitably destroy the government itself, and this American nation— this nation of white men, may be taken from us, and given to the African race! In this question is involved the honor of the state—the dignity of its people—and the preservation of its name."[20]

Judson argued that the Black Law did not violate Article Four of the U.S. Constitution regarding the protection of rights of citizens from other states. "Suppose the corporation of Yale College should, by solemn vote, prohibit students from South Carolina, would any constitutional question arise on that prohibition, or could they claim admission as a matter of right under the constitution? The answer is obvious. The corporation has that right of exclusion, and so has the state. Should the trustees of the Plainfield Academy pass an order that in the future, no student from the state of Rhode Island should be admitted, is that a violation of the constitution of the United States? Surely not."[21] Except for David Daggett, Judson's line of argument did not resonate with the justices; the hypothetical examples he cited appeared to violate the constitutional rights of students from South Carolina and Rhode Island. Judson moved on to the issue of free blacks and citizenship.

"What was the intention of those who framed the constitution?" Judson asked. "Did they mean to place persons of color on the footing of equality with themselves, and did they mean to make them citizens? In answering this question, it matters little what may be the opinion of a few madmen or enthusiasts now, but what was the intention of the people of the United States at the time when the constitution was adopted."[22]

Judson concluded that the founding fathers granted citizenship to whites only.

Neither Indians nor blacks enjoyed citizenship, Judson said. "Surely the Indian stands far above the African. This was the Indian's home, it was once his soil, but it has passed into other hands. It is now the white man's country, and the white man is an American citizen."[23] Judson invoked the writings of Chancellor James Kent, who "emphatically told us, that there ever has been, and still is, this distinction of color."[24]

"So we may say with equal propriety, and equal force in this case, that the 'privileges and immunities' of education shall be subject to such restraints as the government may justly prescribe for the general good of the whole," Judson argued. "Who will not say that the whole system of education does not rest with the states? May we not, under this wise decision, preserve our constitutions—our pauper laws—our police laws, and our school laws? Yes, we may exclude from our state a bad population . . ."[25]

"There is an additional argument," Judson said, "founded in patriotism and love of country. Are we now called upon to adopt such construction of the constitution, as shall surrender the country purchased by the blood of our fathers, up to another race of men? Then I would appeal to this Court—to every American citizen, and say that America is ours—it belongs to a race of white men, the descendents of those who first redeemed the wilderness. The American name and character have been handed down to this generation, and it is our duty to preserve that character, and perpetuate that name. Let not the determination of this case aid those who are plotting the destruction of our constitution. It rests with the Court to say, whether the country shall be preserved or lost, and I leave it to them to decide."[26]

State's Attorney Chauncey F. Cleveland, Judson's partner in the prosecution of Crandall, spoke without prepared remarks or notes. "May it please your honors, the legislature has passed an act in these words . . ." Cleveland recounted the provisions of the Black Law. He disagreed with Ellsworth's interpretation of the Constitution regarding discrimination based on race. "I admire his candor," Cleveland said of Ellsworth. "He has the sympathies of all. The Court cannot be called upon to act on their sympathies—they have nothing to do with the hardship of the case. I address four judges who are white men. No black man can take the seat occupied by your honors. In a moral view, there is no difference as to the color of the skin, but to carry out the assertion of the gentleman will destroy a nation of free white Americans. Sound policy required those who have gone before us to make a distinction between these races—there ever has been, and there ever will be a distinction."[27]

"Need I go further? Need I occupy more time?" Cleveland asked. "The framers of the constitution made a distinction in color, and the entire argument on the other side was to show that there was no difference—no difference in this respect. . . . We have been asked to define what 'colored persons' are—perhaps I ought to tell. I refer the gentleman to his client to find out what 'little misses of color' are."[28]

"The Court will excuse me for not referring to the authorities. Need I go over the ground so ably occupied by my associate counsel? Need I refer to Kent, and to the various acts of Congress? If I am right in the views I have taken, the constitution of the United States and the laws of Congress make a distinction in color. The legislature of this state certainly has a right to do the same. The legislature must possess the power to regulate the inhabitants of the state, and by the law in question nothing else is proposed to be done."[29]

"Black men are sold to eternal servitude, to slavery for life in this country," Cleveland told the justices. "A white man cannot be a slave. The foundation of the distinction is color."[30] After invoking the institution of slavery as a supporting argument for the validity of Connecticut's Black Law, Cleveland discussed "Prudy Crandall and her school," arguing that it operated in violation of the wishes of the community and the Black Law. Following a brief discourse, punctuated a few more times with—"need I go further?"—Cleveland ended his argument, and the prosecution brought their case to a close. One attorney remained. Calvin Goddard made the final argument for Prudence Crandall.

Goddard had celebrated his sixty-sixth birthday five days earlier on July 17. He reflected on his many years dedicated to law and politics, including his experience early in his legal career working on behalf of black veterans of the Revolutionary War. As he addressed the justices, he discussed the significance of his argument for his client and his country.

"The questions involved in the decision of this case are of immense magnitude," Goddard began. "It is indeed singular, that occasion has never arisen since the existence of our constitution, in which the question whether the free, native inhabitants of the United States were citizens and entitled to the privileges of citizens, and been judicially decided. The circumstance that no such question has arisen is, to my mind, high evidence that their rights to the privileges of citizenship are unquestionable, for numerous occasions have arisen in which those privileges have been exercised."[31]

"We come to claim for them the privileges secured to us all," Goddard said. "We come on behalf of those, and the children of those who on the 4th of July, 1776, united in the self-evident truths then proclaimed to the world, 'that all men are created equal—that they are endowed by their creator with certain unalienable rights—that among these are life, liberty, and the pursuit of happiness.' We come on behalf of those and the children of those who fought and shed their blood with our fathers to secure these blessings—we come to ask to pursue that happiness for which they fought, and to enjoy that life and liberty which they then secured . . . We come to claim for those born free within the United States of America, the protection of the . . . Constitution of the United States."[32]

After the Revolutionary War, citizens who fought for the United States were rewarded with payment by the government, Goddard noted. He quoted James Madison, who in 1783 reported to Congress that "another class of creditors is that illustrious and patriotic band of fellow citizens, whose blood and bravery defended the liberties of their country."[33]

"And who were 'that illustrious and patriotic band' of our fellow citizens," Goddard asked, "whose toils and cares and calamities were to be rewarded? Were none of them colored? In looking at this subject recently in my office, I could not but recur to a list of applicants for pensions, under the act of 1818, when I was clothed with authority to examine the qualifications of applicants, and found within the little circle of my residence nineteen colored persons whose claims were well founded and successful. I cannot refrain from mentioning one aged black man, Primus Babcock, who proudly presented to me an honorable discharge from service during the war, dated at the close of it, wholly in the handwriting of George Washington. Was not Primus a citizen? An 'illustrious' citizen?"[34]

"If, as we believe, it has been shown that the colored children, for the instruction of whom Miss Crandall has been prosecuted, are citizens of the state where they reside, and of course, 'entitled to all the privileges and immunities of citizens in the several states,' it remains to be considered whether the statute law of this state infringes any of their rights,"

Goddard said.[35] "The statute prohibits their being instructed—it takes away from them the privilege of being taught to read and write—it deprives them of all opportunity to acquire that knowledge and those habits which may render them good citizens, useful to each other and their native country."[36]

"It was the intention of those who framed the law to put down the school," Goddard said, "and if their intention had been expressed in a few words, it would have been entitled, 'an act to prohibit Miss Crandall from setting up at Canterbury a school for colored citizens coming from other states—to prohibit her instructing them, boarding or harboring them, and to authorize those persons who come into the state for such purpose to be sent back. . . .' To my mind it is absurd to talk of securing personal privileges and immunities, and yet have them depend on the will of others, or limit, embarrass, and control their enjoyment in such manner as to render them valueless."[37] Goddard concluded by summarizing the argument that the Black Law violated the Constitution.

"The rights of a free government—of conscience—of education and religion, are . . . secured to all by this constitution; and why not to Miss Crandall the right to follow the dictates of her conscience in devoting her time to the instruction, boarding, and educating human beings abandoned by others, and teaching them to pursue happiness?" Goddard said.[38] "We trust that this honorable Court will wipe away this stain upon our statute book, by declaring this law utterly void, because it is opposed to the Constitution of the United States, the supreme law of the land."[39]

Goddard returned to his seat, concluding the arguments in *Crandall v. State of Connecticut*. Spectators congratulated the attorneys. Counsel on both sides knew they might meet again in a final appeal to the Supreme Court in Washington, D.C.

Justices Daggett, Williams, Bissell, and Church began their deliberations and considered the issue of Daggett's finding and charge to the jury that blacks were not citizens. Not surprisingly, Daggett argued forcefully as to the correctness of his charge. Justice Bissell recorded in his notes, however, that the other three justices thought the Black Law violated the Constitution.[40] Justice Williams later wrote, "I did not then doubt, nor since have doubted, that our respected friend was wrong in his charge to the jury."[41]

The justices deliberated for the next four days. Despite the inclination of Williams, Bissell, and Church to overturn the Black Law, they did not wish to embarrass their "respected friend," Chief Justice Daggett. Justice Williams reviewed the record and informed the other justices that he had discovered a potential technical defect. The Black Law prohibited teaching black students from other states unless the town officials first consented in writing to such teaching at a school. If the complaint against Prudence Crandall did not allege that the school operated without the consent of town officials, the justices could argue the complaint failed to allege a violation of the Black Law. Williams and the other judges saw a means to dispose of the case without ruling on the substantive issues. One commentator later wrote, "The court could not brave the storm of unpopularity by deciding in her favor and could not go on record as declaring an unconstitutional law as constitutional."[42]

The justices agreed to overturn the jury's verdict convicting Prudence Crandall of violating the Black Law on the grounds of a technicality: the prosecution had neglected to assert in its complaint against Crandall that she failed to secure a "license" from town officials for her school. "The omission is a fatal defect," Justice Williams wrote in the court's decision.[43] On Monday, July 28, 1834, the Connecticut State Supreme Court officially released its decision in *Crandall v. State of Connecticut*. Three of the four justices voted to reverse the lower court's verdict. Justices Bissell and Church joined Williams's opinion. In a brief separate opinion, Chief Justice Daggett said the flaw in the complaint did not require the court to dismiss the case.[44]

A review of the court records reveals that the technicality Justice Williams cited is speculative at best. Williams acknowledged that the complaint charged Crandall with setting up a school for persons of color who were not inhabitants of the state, for the purpose of their instruction and education.[45] Williams said the prosecution failed to allege that Crandall set up her school without first securing a "license" from the town.[46] The word "license," however, did not appear in the Black Law statute. In order to teach black students from other states lawfully, the statute required "the consent, in writing, first obtained of a majority of the civil authority, and also of the selectmen of the town in which such school, academy, or literary institution is situated." In fact, the complaint specifically charged that Crandall had committed "all which acts and doings" (regarding the setting up of the school and the instructing and boarding of the colored students from other states) "without the consent in writing first obtained of a majority of the civil authority and also of the Selectmen of the Town of Canterbury."[47] The certification to the court of the complaint against Crandall by Justice of the Peace Rufus Adams also said that Crandall "set up, in said Canterbury, for the instruction and education of colored persons, not residents of this state," a school "without the consent in writing first here and obtained of the civil authority and also of the selectmen of said town of Canterbury . . ."[48] Both the complaint against Crandall and the certification to the court tracked the language of the Black Law and stated that local authorities did not consent to the establishment of the school. Though no one challenged the justices at the time, it appears in hindsight that they stretched to find, if not invented, a technical defect in order to avoid overruling Justice Daggett and deciding the substantive issues.[49]

The inconclusive decision by the court came at a high price for both Prudence Crandall and the prosecution. The court reversed Crandall's conviction but did not overturn the Black Law. Since the court had avoided the substance of the case, there was no issue for either side to appeal to the U.S. Supreme Court. The *Hartford Review* summed up the ruling: "The present decision of the Court places Miss Prudy back whence she started and the proceedings must commence de novo."[50]

Both sides had spent more than a year on the case and many hundreds of dollars in legal fees and court costs—a fortune for the time. Their investment consisted of much more than dollars; the trials created stress and upheaval for Prudence Crandall, her students and supporters, and also the prosecution and those opposed to the school. All parties suffered from the debilitating war of words in the press, and neither side relished the prospect of beginning all over again, with an arrest of Crandall, another parade of witnesses, and a significant new investment of time and money.

Despite the unsatisfactory outcome, William Lloyd Garrison and Samuel May agreed that the arguments made by Crandall's attorneys deserved wide distribution. "A trial so important as Miss Crandall's— involving such momentous consequences to a large portion of our countrymen—implicating so deeply the character of this great nation— ought not to go unpublished," Garrison wrote to Samuel May.[51] Garrison decided to publish the arguments before he knew the final outcome of the case. He praised the work of Ellsworth but told May, "I fear he will not be able to redeem the reputation of Connecticut."[52]

The *Crandall* case drew the attention of Chancellor James Kent, the renowned legal commentator cited by Andrew Judson and David Daggett. When Kent revised his *Commentaries on American Law*, he specifically discussed *Crandall* and Daggett's contention that free blacks lacked citizenship. Kent disagreed and sided with the arguments of Ellsworth and Goddard.

"Blacks, whether born free or in bondage, if born under the jurisdiction and allegiance of the United States, are natives, and not aliens," Kent wrote. "The privilege of voting, and the legal capacity for office, are not essential to the character of a citizen, for women are citizens without either; and free people of color may enjoy the one, and may acquire, and hold, and devise, and transmit, by hereditary descent, real and personal estates."[53] Kent's comment on the *Crandall* case did not appear until 1848 and had no bearing on Crandall's school or appeal.

While absorbing the Court's decision and the news of recent violence against blacks and abolitionists, William Lloyd Garrison planned for his wedding. He made many of the logistical decisions himself in consultation with Samuel May and informed his fiancée after the fact. "If Providence permit, and it be agreeable to Helen, I propose to make the following arrangements," he told May. "On Monday morning, September 1st, I shall start from Boston in a barouche [a formal horse-drawn carriage], accompanied by my Aunt and friend Knapp, and go to Providence that day. On Tuesday, I shall endeavor to reach Brooklyn in the afternoon. On Wednesday, arrangements may be made for the wedding. On Thursday morning, you will be called upon to tie the nuptial knot, and make Helen and myself no more twain, but one. As soon as the ceremony is over, we shall take our departure with all decent dispatch, and calculate to reach Worcester on Thursday evening."[54]

Garrison also took on the task of selecting an apartment and investigated a number of cottages in the Roxbury section of Boston. "I have been looking at them," he wrote to Helen, "but they are much in demand." He had stayed in one of the cottages the previous winter and told Helen that "it has recently been enlarged and materially improved." The water from the well came directly into the kitchen, and Garrison told her she would not have to go outside to fetch water. "This will doubtless be an agreeable piece of information to you."[55]

Garrison's enthusiasm for making decisions on his own carried over into household purchases. "Today I have been round to some of our furniture stores, in order to make a selection of such articles as we shall need," he told Helen.[56] He told her his friends would ensure his choices were "tasteful and judicious." Garrison informed Helen that their apartment would contain a room for his friend Isaac Knapp, Knapp's sister Abigail, and another room for a servant girl. "I am advised by my married friends not to get any mattresses to put under the feather beds," Garrison said, "first, as they are somewhat expensive, and secondly, as straw beds answer the purpose equally well. What do you say?"[57]

The courtship of Prudence Crandall resumed in earnest with Calvin Philleo's return to Canterbury. Crandall forgave Philleo for his extended absence, and her friends began to moderate their opinions of Philleo. When two Baptist ministers visited Samuel May in July, May asked them if they knew Philleo. Both ministers praised Philleo's character but conceded he was "very eccentric, as everybody knows."[58]

In August 1834, the future of Prudence Crandall's school remained clouded. The reversal of her conviction allowed her to continue teaching for the time being. She knew, however, that at any moment a sheriff might once again knock at the door with a new writ and arrest her for a third time. The greatest endeavor of her life might still end in failure.

During this time of turmoil, Crandall decided to place her trust in Calvin Philleo. She agreed to move forward with the marriage. Crandall did not record any detailed thoughts about this momentous decision. It is impossible to know whether the stress of the school controversy played a significant role, whether it weakened Crandall's ability to resist Philleo's seemingly opportunistic advances, or if it convinced her she needed a partner to help survive the increasing adversity. What is certain is that without the well-publicized news of the school controversy, Philleo never would have heard of or pursued Prudence Crandall. In that context, the school controversy was directly responsible for her marriage to Philleo.

Philleo, unlike Garrison, had no interest in the formalities of a wedding ceremony. He was clear in his intent—he simply wanted to marry as soon as possible. If Prudence desired anything other than a justice of the peace reading the vows, she would have to manage the details herself.

In Roxbury, Garrison settled into the modest apartment he called "Freedom's Cottage." The furniture arrived, and Helen sent along boxes of her belongings. The cottage was located three miles from the center of Boston and near the omnibus line that carried passengers into the city every thirty minutes.[59] At the beginning of August, Garrison wrote to Helen and described how forty thousand people recently had gathered on the Boston Common to watch Charles Durant of New York create an unimaginable spectacle.

"We had one of those extraordinary exhibitions which even startle not merely a city, but a far-spread community, and call forth a great multitude of anxious observers," Garrison said. "Mr. Durant made a grand ascension in his balloon from our beautiful Common . . . At six o'clock, the intrepid aeronaut stepped into his car—the cords that bound him to the earth were cut—and up he rode heavenward, waving his hat and the Star-Spangled Banner most gracefully, amid the roar of cannon and the acclamations of the people."[60] A breeze carried Durant past Boston Harbor out over the ocean, where he narrowly escaped drowning. After his rescue he pledged to return to Boston for another flight in three weeks. "Shall I beseech him to wait until after our wedding, that you may get a view of the ascension?" Garrison asked. "Perhaps if you will consent to go up with him—and several ladies in this city have had the courage to offer to go up—he will consent to postpone his flight. I saw two men riding sublimely in a balloon over the great city of London—it was the finest sight I ever saw."[61]

Garrison and Benson set their wedding date for September 4, 1834. "Time seems to be almost as anxious as ourselves to see us united in the holy bands of wedlock,"[62] Garrison wrote to Helen. "My dear friend Rev. May keeps count very accurately. He will soon put a stop to our correspondence, by making us two *one*."[63]

While walking near his home in Roxbury on Thursday morning, August 14, Garrison saw a surprising sight—Prudence Crandall and Calvin Philleo, arm in arm. "Is it possible that the deed has been done, that the twain have become one, that the Gordian knot has been tied . . . that the maiden has been transformed into a wife, and the widower into a husband?" Garrison wrote to Helen.[64] After Crandall and Garrison exchanged embarrassed greetings, she told Garrison that she and Calvin had married two days earlier in Brooklyn, Connecticut.

"So, my dear," Garrison wrote to Helen, "they have got the start of us by almost a month!"[65] He could not resist a quotation from John Wol-cot's *The Works of Peter Pindar*: "O Matrimony, thou art like to Jerimiah's figs: the good were very good—the bad too sour to give the pigs." He told Helen he did not necessarily apply that sentiment to Calvin and Pru-dence's marriage.[66] Joy, peace, and prosperity be with them, Garrison wrote.

Prudence told Garrison the story of her recent wedding. She had planned a small but meaningful ceremony at her school in the presence of her students and staff. She wanted her minister, Levi Kneeland, to per-form the ceremony; however, Kneeland was confined to his bed with a severe illness. Prudence then approached Otis Whiton, the minister of the Canterbury Congregational Church, who agreed and posted the marriage bans at his church. On her wedding day, Whiton sent Crandall a short note telling her that "under existing circumstances" he could not perform the ceremony. Crandall later learned that someone—no doubt one of the opponents of her school—wrote to Whiton and requested that he not per-form Crandall's wedding, and included a significant donation.[67]

Whiton's withdrawal left Crandall and Philleo stranded at the altar for lack of a minister.[68] Calvin persuaded Prudence to search immediately for another minister to show her adversaries they could not spoil her wedding. Prudence and Calvin bid farewell to their students and friends and set off as a traveling wedding party of two. They drove a wagon from Canterbury to Brooklyn and presented themselves to Rev. George J. Tillotson, the minister of the Brooklyn Congregational Church. They described what had happened in Canterbury and their desire to be married that day. Since Crandall had published the wedding bans at the Canterbury Congrega-tional Church, Tillotson saw no reason to delay. He performed the brief ceremony and pronounced Calvin and Prudence man and wife.

Crandall most likely did not tell Garrison why she had failed to ask her friend and defender Rev. Samuel May to officiate at her wedding. While May was an obvious choice, she originally had wanted her own minister, Levi Kneeland, to perform the ceremony. When illness prevented Knee-land from administering the vows, geography may have played a role in her next choice—she walked across the street to the Canterbury Con-gregational Church. Perhaps most important, Crandall knew that May shared Helen Benson's reservations about her marriage to Philleo. Despite their close friendship, Crandall did not want to ask May to officiate if he doubted the wisdom of her marriage.

Newspapers throughout New England published the news of Crandall's wedding. As Garrison could appreciate, however, even this joyful occasion became fodder for those who wanted to embarrass Crandall. One newspaper story erroneously reported that Crandall's marriage had ended quickly in divorce. "It was very cruel on the part of the *Daily Advertiser*, this morning, to divorce this lady from her lawful husband so soon after the nuptials," the editors of the *New York Spectator* wrote. "Miss Prudence Crandall was married, beyond all reasonable doubt, on Tuesday morning last, at Brooklyn, Connecticut."[69] The *Spectator* editors noted that newspapers in New London and Norwich accurately reported her marriage, while "the editors of the *Daily* were hoaxed" by someone.[70] The editors of the *Brattleboro Messenger* reported Crandall's wedding and added their own racist commentary: "Miss Prudence Crandall, with more prudence than she has heretofore displayed, has consented to become a Madame, having joined in wedlock to Rev. Calvin Philleo . . . We hope she may now find sufficient attractions in her own offspring without recourse to caressing of youthful woolly heads and chubby lips."[71]

Crandall told Garrison how immediately after their wedding, Calvin Philleo wrote to the Selectmen of Canterbury and offered to move the school to a more remote part of the town.[72] The Philleos received no response. Prudence said she and Calvin quickly left Brooklyn for Boston because she expected Judson to serve her with new writs for her arrest.[73] For the time being she was safely away from the sheriffs of Windham County.

As Garrison considered Prudence's remarkable story, he had difficulty accepting that she was no longer Prudence Crandall, but Prudence Crandall Philleo. "I could not congratulate them upon their union," Garrison admitted to Helen, "but I could, and did, wish them much happiness."[74] Much had changed for Crandall and Garrison in the nearly two years of their association. Crandall knew that Garrison and Helen Benson planned a September wedding. While she and Garrison had forged an extraordinary partnership that produced against all odds a real school for black women, the future of the school was uncertain at best.

The trip by the newly wed Philleos to Boston was not only for the purpose of visiting Garrison and escaping the reach of Judson. The Philleos also visited Emeline Goodwin, Calvin's daughter from his first marriage. Prudence and Emeline met for the first time and began a long and close friendship. Emeline, at twenty-two years old, was only seven years younger than Prudence. She lived with her husband, John Marston Goodwin, a cashier at the People's Bank of Roxbury; he later served as superintendent of Massachusetts General Hospital.[75] Emeline had a son, eight-and-a-half-month-old John Marston Goodwin Jr. Prudence and Calvin stayed with Emeline and her family for several days.

Garrison invited Prudence and Calvin to visit him at Freedom's Cottage on Friday. When the Philleos saw Garrison's apartment, Prudence told Garrison he had made a wise choice and said Helen would enjoy her new home very much. On Sunday, Garrison accompanied Calvin and Prudence to a black church where Calvin preached at the afternoon and evening services. "Both sermons were very good, and apparently very sincere," Garrison wrote to Helen. "I am more and more puzzled to determine accurately his real character. He may be an eccentric man—a covetous man—and occasionally, an erring man in trivial matters, but I cannot think he is habitually a bad man."[76]

Prudence and Calvin Philleo planned to return to Canterbury by stagecoach on Monday, August 18. Garrison asked Prudence to deliver a letter to Helen, but at the last minute Prudence changed her plans. Just prior to her wedding day, Prudence had received a visitor from Philadelphia at her school, Lydia White.[77] After reflecting on her discussions with White, and perhaps additional conversations with Garrison, Prudence decided to travel with Calvin from Boston to Philadelphia. The trip concerned the future of her school. Garrison wrote an addendum to his letter to Helen mentioning that the Philleos would not return immediately to Canterbury and sent the letter by standard mail.[78]

Lydia White had attended the abolitionist convention in Philadelphia that established the American Anti-Slavery Society, and she had helped to create the Philadelphia Female Anti-Slavery Society.[79] She was also an entrepreneur; she opened a "free produce store," selling clothing, groceries, and other items made or harvested without slave labor. Some of her friends, including activists Lucretia Mott and Sydney Ann Lewis, also ran similar "free labor" stores for a time, but Lydia White kept her business going for sixteen years.[80] Demand for her "free-labor" goods increased to the point that White expanded her retail business into mail-order sales,

County Courthouse, Brooklyn, Connecticut, the location of the three Crandall trials.

Chauncey Cleveland ordered the arrest and prosecution of Prudence Crandall for violation of Connecticut's "Black Law."

23. Andrew T. Judson, initially a supporter of Crandall, became her chief antagonist and prosecutor after the admission of the black student Sarah Harris.

(*above left*)
24. Calvin Goddard, attorney for Prudence Crandall, served as mayor of Norwich, Connecticut, U.S. congressman, judge of th superior court, and speaker of the state hou of representatives.

(*above right*)
25. William W. Ellsworth, Prudence Cranda lead attorney, served as U.S. congressman, governor of Connecticut, and justice of the state supreme court.

(*left*)
26. Henry Strong, attorney for Prudence Crandall, served in the state senate.

Thomas S. Williams was a justice of the Connecticut Supreme Court at the time of *Crandall v. State.*

28. David Daggett was chief justice of the Connecticut Supreme Court at the time of *Crandall v. State.*

Samuel Church was a justice of the Connecticut Supreme Court at the time *Crandall v. State.*

30. Clark Bissell was a justice of the Connecticut Supreme Court at the time of *Crandall v. State.*

COLORED SCHOLARS EXCLUDED FROM SCHOOLS.

"If the *free* colored people were generally taught to read, it might be an induce
ment to them to remain in this country. WE WOULD OFFER THEM NO
SUCH INDUCEMENT."—*Rev. Mr. Converse, a colonizationist, formerly of N
H. now editor of the Southern Religious Telegraph.*

In those parts of the country where the persecuting spirit of colonization has
been colonized, such exclusion has ceased.

31. Engraving inspired by Crandall's school and the refusal of the Canterbury Congregational
Church to admit Crandall's students.

SCHOOL FOR COLORED GIRLS

COLORED SCHOOLS BROKEN UP, IN THE FREE STATES.

When schools have been established for colored scholars, the law-makers and the
mob have combined to destroy them;—as at Canterbury, Ct., at Canaan, N. H.
Aug. 10, 1835, at Zanesville and Brown Co., Ohio, in 1836.

32. Engraving based in part on the fire at Prudence Crandall's school.

Lydia Maria Child, an author and litionist, and a supporter of Crandall Garrison.

34. Theodore Dwight Weld, the leader of the Lane Debates on slavery at the Lane Seminary in Cincinnati, Ohio.

Crandall homestead in Troy Grove, Illinois.

36. U.S. Senator Charles Sumner. Sumner argued the first school desegregation case in 1849.

37. Dred Scott attempted to secure his freedom from slavery in *Dred Scott v. Sandford.*

38. As chief justice of the U.S. Supreme Court, Roger Taney cited *Crandall v. State* to support his decision in *Dred Scott.*

39. Advertisement for reprints of Taney's *Dred Scott* decision.

William Lloyd Garrison and his sons Wendell, Francis, William Lloyd II, George. Garrison sent this photo to Prudence Crandall.

The Fifty-fifth Massachusetts Volunteer Negro Regiment. The white officers ...utenant George Garrison and Prudence Crandall's step-grandson, Captain Frank ...odwin, led the black troops.

42. Sarah Harris Fayerweather. On the reverse, Crandall's niece Rena Keith Clisby wrote, "the colored girl . . . that caused all the trouble."

43. Prudence Crandall in Elk Falls, Kansas.

earning significant revenue from clients as far away as Indiana, Ohio, and Vermont.[81]

Lydia White's success as a black businesswoman who fought for equality made her a perfect role model for Crandall's students. She was a longtime friend of William Lloyd Garrison. "She is almost the first female pioneer in the anti-slavery cause in this country," Garrison wrote, "and by her efforts to sustain a free labor goods store—efforts which will never be fully appreciated on earth—she deserves to take a high rank in the annals of female philanthropy."[82]

White told Crandall and her students the story of her "free-labor" store and her involvement in the abolitionist community of Philadelphia. White's description of her allies in Philadelphia sounded similar to the supportive abolitionist network that Prudence had experienced in Boston. With all of the uncertainly in Canterbury, Crandall began to contemplate a future in Philadelphia.

When Prudence Crandall first explored the idea of creating a school for black women in January 1832, she sought out William Lloyd Garrison for his advice and help. Now she wanted to explore a new idea—to move her school from Canterbury to Philadelphia. She may have first considered this while speaking with Lydia White in Canterbury, or later while spending time with Garrison at Freedom's Cottage. During the Philleos' time in Boston with Garrison, Lydia White's friend Joshua Coffin paid a visit to Garrison. Coffin, an abolitionist from Philadelphia, knew that White had recently visited Prudence's school. Coffin's visit may have prompted Prudence to share with Garrison her idea of moving her school to Philadelphia.[83]

Garrison gave no hint in his letter to Helen Benson about Prudence possibly moving her school to Philadelphia. He did mention two of his friends from Philadelphia, Joshua Coffin and Lydia White, and noted that White recently had visited the Canterbury school. Garrison told Helen that Prudence and Calvin "may be detained by the way unexpectedly." He provided no further details. If Prudence Crandall Philleo had discussed moving her school to Philadelphia with Garrison and swore him to secrecy—as she had done after their first conversation in 1832—Garrison did not break that confidence, not even with his future wife.

When Prudence Philleo left Boston, she traveled to Philadelphia to meet with James Forten, one of the named sponsors of her school and a friend of Garrison, and Lucretia Mott, an activist and friend of both Garrison and Lydia White. Philleo needed their advice concerning the creation of a school for black children in Philadelphia. She wanted to extricate herself from the vandalism, the daily assaults in the press, the constant fear of arrest, and the uncertainty of the Black Law. If this new idea seemed feasible, Prudence Philleo would close her school in Canterbury, leave the State of Connecticut, and move with Calvin to Philadelphia.[84]

12 : The End of the Beginning

William Penn had envisioned Philadelphia as a "city of brotherly love." When Prudence and Calvin Philleo arrived in Philadelphia in late August 1834, they found a city torn apart by deadly interracial violence that had occurred just days earlier. One of the incidents that sparked three nights of rioting involved the family of James Forten, the black businessman Prudence and Calvin planned to visit.

James Forten and his wife Charlotte had raised a large family. They had five daughters and four sons; eight children survived into adulthood. Forten's successful sail manufacturing business employed many local laborers without a color barrier. Forten had expanded his workforce of both black and white employees.[1]

On the evening of Saturday, August 9, the Forten's eighth child, sixteen-year-old Thomas, walked home after running an errand. A gang of about fifty white men armed with wooden clubs intercepted him and blocked his path. After a momentary standoff, a young man swung his club and knocked Thomas to the ground. Initially stunned, Thomas sprang up and ran. A white neighbor and friend of James Forten who witnessed the attack intervened and stopped the men from chasing Thomas, but not before the gang leader told the others they would reconvene Monday evening "to attack the niggers."[2]

When the gang came back on Monday, a contingent of police officers met them. The officers captured and arrested seven men, while the others fled. The gang members threatened to return and kill James Forten, who called on the mayor's office for police protection. Based on the new threats, the mayor agreed to send a horse patrol to stand guard; some of Forten's white friends also came to his defense.[3] An Irishman named Hogan stopped by to protect

Forten's home. "Whoever would enter at this door to injure you or your family," Hogan said to James Forten, "must pass over my dead body."[4]

Tensions had increased in Philadelphia in the aftermath of the riots in New York City. As in New York, perceived economic competition between poor white laborers and free blacks fueled anger and resentment among whites. Three days after a gang assaulted Thomas Forten, violence erupted at the "Flying Horses" carousel, an amusement park that attracted both black and white children and their families. A gang of white youths attacked blacks at random and vandalized the carousel and surrounding buildings.[5] Police responded, and a bloody battle ensued with hundreds of people involved. "Many prisoners were taken and committed," a local newspaper reported. "A large number of the police were wounded. It was a very fierce and wicked affair."[6]

The mayor of Philadelphia, John Swift, had learned from the failure of New York's city government during the July riots. He took a more proactive role and agreed to James Forten's requests for police protection. When rioting erupted throughout the city on Wednesday and Thursday nights, Swift left city hall and personally led the police force into the troubled neighborhoods.[7] The courage displayed by the mayor and the city police, however, did not bring about a quick end to the violence.

Philadelphia's gang leaders also had learned from the New York City riots. They planned their attacks carefully and targeted black neighborhoods, churches, and meetinghouses. They purposefully waited until after eleven o'clock at night on Wednesday—when most of the police and city watchmen had retired for the night—before they initiated their assaults.[8] The gangs then attacked the homes of black families, broke down doors, smashed furniture and other belongings, and dragged black residents into the street where they beat them severely. After the residents had fled, thieves quickly moved in and plundered the homes. Rioters destroyed dozens of apartments, halls, and businesses that served the black community.[9]

The following evening, gangs engaged in "brutal assaults upon the defenseless and sleeping, murdering and maiming the aged and infirm, and robbing the poor and industrious negro of his toil-won earnings."[10] When the night ended—the final night of rioting—police arrested about twenty gang members. Hundreds of homeless black families sought shelter in abandoned buildings and open fields.[11]

While Mayor Swift reacted more decisively than the mayor of New York, a reporter for the *Philadelphia Enquirer* noted that the police did not intervene in most black neighborhoods.[12] The editors of *Niles' Weekly Register* worried that racial violence would spread and worsen. "Does it not appear that the character of our people has suffered a considerable change for the worse? If so—what is the cause? We fear that the moral sense of right and wrong has been rendered less sensitive than it was . . . The blacks have suffered cruelly, and submitted with much patience—but if they had resisted, or should retaliate—what then?"[13]

James Forten recounted these stories to the Philleos. Prudence and Calvin saw the physical evidence of the rioting—destroyed homes, broken glass, splintered wood, displaced paving stones and bricks—all around them in the streets. The racial prejudice that sparked the violence alarmed Forten.[14] He opposed colonization and helped lead the local antislavery movement. His wife Charlotte and his daughters Margaretta, Sarah Louisa, and Harriet all supported the Philadelphia Female Anti-Slavery Society. While Forten knew that many whites regarded these causes as controversial, he had not expected gangs to assault his son and threaten his own life.

Despite the riots, Prudence Philleo pressed ahead with her plan to assess opening a school for black children in Philadelphia. Charlotte Forten invited Prudence to meet members of the Philadelphia Female Anti-Slavery Society, including Esther Moore, the president of the society, and Lucretia Mott, the corresponding secretary.[15] Moore, a longtime abolitionist and wife of a Quaker physician, had attended the abolitionist convention the previous December that had created the American Anti-Slavery Society.[16] Lucretia Mott attended and influenced the same convention and also served as a Quaker minister and a leader in the women's rights movement. All three women shared Quaker roots and appreciated bold ideas. Prudence Philleo's plan for a school in Philadelphia excited both Esther and Lucretia.

Prudence Philleo explained the uncertainty of operating a school for black women in the shadow of Connecticut's Black Law.[17] She wanted to continue her school in a new location and told Mott she might move to New York or Philadelphia.[18] Black schools already existed in Philadelphia. Free blacks had organized a school in 1804, and an African Episcopalian church had opened a school for blacks at about the same time.[19] By 1822, sixteen schools for blacks existed in Philadelphia, and black teachers managed eleven of the schools.[20]

Both Lucretia Mott and Esther Moore had explored the idea of creating a new school for black children. "Our female society had appointed a committee to look out for a suitable teacher and try to get up such a school before we had heard of her intention of coming," Lucretia wrote to a friend.[21] They told Prudence that, after spending many days visiting all of the schools in Philadelphia, their committee had concluded that the city needed a new school for black children.[22] Esther encouraged Prudence Philleo to create such a school in Philadelphia.[23]

Philleo decided to spend an entire week in Philadelphia; Mott and Moore took her through the black neighborhoods, where they visited many families.[24] Four dollars per quarter for each student was the tuition Philleo calculated she needed to meet her expenses.[25] After the three women spent a few days recruiting, they received commitments from about fifty students and their families.[26] With the help of her new friends, Philleo laid the groundwork for the launch of a new school in Philadelphia. They next sought the endorsement of the local abolitionist community.

The president of the Pennsylvania Abolition Society did not embrace Crandall's proposal. Dr. Joseph Parrish, a white, fifty-five-year-old Quaker who had practiced medicine in Philadelphia for twenty-nine years, worried about an adverse reaction in light of the recent violence.[27] Parrish actively lobbied others in the abolitionist community to discourage Prudence Philleo from opening a school in Philadelphia. Lucretia Mott wrote, "There was so much opposition to the attempt by a few of our *prudent* abolitionists . . ."[28] Parrish speculated that violence might accompany the general elections scheduled for October, and racist gangs might use the opportunity to target black and abolitionist communities, especially if the well-known Prudence Crandall moved to Philadelphia and created a new controversy. Lucretia Mott understood Parrish's appeal for caution to a point, but she also knew that if abolitionists always heeded the concern for caution, no antislavery societies ever would have formed.

After spending a busy week exploring the potential for opening a new school, Prudence and Calvin Philleo prepared to return to Canterbury. Prudence reluctantly decided to postpone but not give up on the creation of a new school in Philadelphia. Lucretia Mott and Esther Moore viewed the decision as a temporary setback, a delay in Prudence's relocation to Philadelphia. They prepared to move forward with plans for the school after the October elections. "She will wait till after our elections are past," Lucretia Mott wrote, "when if nothing unfavorable occurs she contemplates moving here."[29] Mott told another person that Prudence and her husband would move to Philadelphia—"they will all remove here"—after the fall election.[30]

While the Philleos were in Philadelphia, Edward Abdy, the English traveler who had observed the school the previous year, returned to Canterbury on Tuesday, August 26, 1834. Almira Crandall had left the school for the day to run errands, leaving William Burleigh in charge. Burleigh told Abdy how Almira did a remarkable job of running the school when her sister Prudence traveled or was called away. Almira "never shrunk from the task she undertook," Burleigh said, "and though but twenty years of age, had remained firmly at her post, alone, and surrounded by enemies against whom even her life could hardly be considered safe."[31]

Abdy noticed about twenty students at the school. "On the table were lying Baxter's Bible and Cruden's Concordance, beautifully bound . . . They had been brought over from Scotland by Mr. Charles Stuart."[32] Stuart campaigned for emancipation in England, the West Indies, and the United States. He had recently traveled throughout Great Britain, where newspapers followed the story of Crandall's persecution.[33] When Stuart met Crandall in Canterbury, he brought gifts from British school children and antislavery societies, including a two-volume Bible inscribed to Crandall "by the Ladies of Edinburgh as a mark of the respect with which they regard the Christian courage of her conduct toward their colored Sisters in the United States."[34]

Abdy asked Burleigh about "a stone, twice as large as that I saw the year before," on the mantel of one of the rooms.[35] Someone had smashed out one of the windows with the stone. "The weight of it must have been at least two pounds. There were ten panes of glass completely destroyed by a long pole, which had been left on the premises, and which I saw," Abdy wrote in his journal.

Burleigh told Abdy about the legal costs Prudence Philleo had incurred in her trials, including the appeal to the state supreme court in July. Her expenses totaled about six hundred dollars, a small fortune in 1834. "Legal eloquence is by no means cheap," Abdy noted, "not that it is scarce, but that the seller too often puts his own price upon it. Mr. Ellsworth, of Hartford, the counsel for the defendant, charged $200 for the last pleadings."[36] Abdy said the high cost of good legal representation punished Prudence Philleo and her supporters. "Cheap law may encourage litigation, but dear law is undoubtedly a premium upon persecution."[37]

Abdy noted that the local doctors had failed Prudence almost completely. Burleigh told Abdy that Dr. Andrew Harris lived nearby but ignored the needs of the school. "When called upon to render medical assistance to one of the pupils who was suffering severe pain, he flatly refused to cross the road, and declared that he looked upon the request as a personal insult," Burleigh told Abdy. "No other medical advice was to be had within three miles!"[38]

Community hostility remained a daily challenge. Burleigh described how vandals loosened or cut the harnesses that attached horses to the wagons or carriages of visitors to help the horse escape or to cause a potentially fatal accident. One seven-year-old student who had traveled from England with her aunt to visit the school was shocked at the "unnatural conduct she had witnessed in a Christian people towards their fellow-men."[39]

Abdy listened to what he regarded as a tale of survival; the school continued to operate and black women still received an education despite ongoing hostility. Compared to the previous year, however, the mood at the school seemed less hopeful. "The lapse of a year had not produced either a relaxation of persecution, or an advance towards a truce, on the part of the oppressor," Abdy concluded. "The same dark and fanatical spirit still cast his baneful shadow over a village that one would have expected from its secluded and beautiful situation to be the abode of charity and good neighborhood.[40]

When Prudence and Calvin arrived back in Canterbury, they learned that their friend and supporter, Rev. Levi Kneeland, had died. Kneeland helped spur a religious awakening and conversion in the local area and in Prudence Crandall. He had baptized Crandall and later welcomed her students into his church. He had refused to help prosecutors when called as a witness during her first trial. He likely had a role in promoting the relationship between Calvin Philleo and Prudence Crandall through his invitations to Calvin to preach at his church. As the first minister of the new Packerville Baptist Church, Kneeland had built the congregation from nothing into a membership of more than three hundred. He was thirty-one years old.

Prudence and Calvin received another jolt of bad news. Two weeks earlier in Boston, Prudence had told Garrison she feared Andrew Judson would send the sheriff to arrest her again. Her suspicions were nearly correct. A sheriff had arrived at the door of her school, writs in hand, while Prudence and Calvin were away. This time, however, the sheriff had served her assistant teacher, William Burleigh. The sheriff had placed Burleigh under arrest, and court officials scheduled his trial for December. Newspapers throughout the North and South reported the latest news about Crandall's school. Under the headline, "Prudence Crandall's Lieutenant Captured," the *Baltimore Gazette and Daily Advertiser* detailed Burleigh's arrest and offered the hope that the prosecutor would "frame his indictment technically enough this time to bring this dark colored impudence to the punishment it deserves."[41]

Burleigh's arrest occurred a few days before Edward Abdy visited the school; Abdy speculated that Crandall's opponents meant to discourage future students and staff from associating with the school.[42] His arrest also marked a new strategy by the school's opponents. The prosecution could pursue a verdict against Burleigh—upholding the Black Law and closing the school—without the sensational and unpopular consequence of arresting and prosecuting a woman.

News of Burleigh's arrest made its way to William Lloyd Garrison, who wrote to Helen Benson, "The Canterbury crew, it seems, are still implacable." Andrew Judson would forever prosecute Prudence Crandall's school at the Brooklyn Courthouse, Garrison said. "Mr. Burleigh is now their victim—no, not exactly their victim, for though he is prosecuted, they have not yet triumphed over him."[43]

Garrison also told Helen that he planned to visit Philadelphia to see Lydia White. "I am really anxious that you should see that beautiful city, and become acquainted with those dear friends, and therefore desire to seize the first convenient opportunity to make them a visit."[44] He mentioned the recent "dreadful assaults upon some of the colored inhabitants of Philadelphia" and suggested that Helen read the unfortunate details in the latest edition of the *Liberator*. "It is somewhat difficult to decide who are most hated, or who are most in jeopardy, abolitionists or black people. . . . The cause which we espouse must surely obtain the victory, even though we may be defeated."[45]

William Lloyd Garrison and Helen Benson felt the stress and anxiety of a couple with only eleven days left until their wedding. The directness of Garrison's thoughts in his letters to Helen did not always put her mind at ease. Freedom's Cottage, the new home that Helen had not seen, had its deficiencies, Garrison told her. "It is not to be expected that a residence here will be so agreeable in the winter as in summer, and hence I wish it were the spring, instead of the fall of the year."[46] He told her, however, not to worry. "It is well that human happiness does not depend essentially upon external objects either of earth or sky. Some of the happiest days of my life were spent in a prison."[47]

In his last letter to Helen before their wedding, Garrison said, "I am everywhere branded as a madman, a fanatic, and a traitor—yet you bestow upon me your sweet love. . . . I am doomed, by my devotion to a cause which is full of benevolence and sublimity, to receive an inadequate re-muneration for my labors—so far as paltry dust is concerned—yet you do not withhold from me your sweet love!"[48] William Lloyd Garrison and Helen Benson knew theirs would be a strong union bound together by shared beliefs and love. "Our joy will spring from fountains of affec-tion within us," Garrison said, "which, mingling together, will make our stream of life pure and tranquil."[49]

The wedding took place at the Benson family home, "Friendship Val-ley," in Brooklyn, Connecticut. Helen and William Lloyd agreed to ban wine from the reception and to emphasize simplicity. "I object to wine, because it is impure and intoxicating, and I wish to brand it as a poi-son," Garrison said. "As to the cake, I will not be strenuous for its ban-ishment."[50] It wasn't so much the cake that Garrison wanted to avoid as the appearance of excess, "the rich and showy kind, which is commonly resorted to on similar occasions." Garrison knew that supporters and de-tractors would repeat stories of his wedding ceremony. "How we were married, will of course be widely told, especially among the colored popu-lation. It is for us, therefore, to avoid extravagance on the one hand, and eccentricity on the other."[51]

Garrison had no immediate family members as guests at the wedding. His father had disappeared when he was a boy, his mother and two sis-ters had died, and he did not know the whereabouts of his brother James.

Garrison invited his partner at the *Liberator*, Isaac Knapp, Isaac's sister Abigail Knapp, and Charlotte Lloyd Newell, Garrison's aunt, to travel with him from Boston for the wedding. Helen's parents and all of her siblings except her older brother George attended her wedding. Many friends attended as well, including the sister of George's business partner, Eliza Chace, one of Helen's closest friends.

The wedding began at eight in the morning on Thursday, September 4, 1834. The stagecoach schedule dictated the early wedding time. The Garrisons needed to leave early for Worcester, Massachusetts, where Lloyd and Helen planned to spend the night before going on to Boston and Freedom's Cottage in Roxbury. Isaac Knapp and his sister also had an early stagecoach ride to Providence. The beautiful Benson home and the warm atmosphere of family and close friends provided for a memorable, if brief, wedding ceremony.

"Less than an hour transpired from the assembling to the dispersing of the company—from the tying of the sacred knot to our departure from the valley," Garrison noted.[52] Rev. Samuel May performed the ceremony and was nearly overcome with emotion during the reading of the vows. "The dear minister's heart was deeply affected," Garrison said, "and almost too full for clear, unembarrassed utterance."[53]

Prudence and Calvin Philleo did not attend the Garrison wedding—it is unclear as to whether they were invited. In any case, Prudence wished Helen and William Lloyd much happiness and continued her work at the school. Town officials still had not responded to Calvin's offer to move the school. The December trial of William Burleigh was months away. The general elections in Philadelphia would take place in October; if no violence occurred, the Philleos might move to Philadelphia. The future of the Canterbury school remained very much unresolved.

On Tuesday, September 9, Prudence Crandall's first black student, Sarah Harris Fayerweather, gave birth to her first child. Sarah had moved with her husband, George, to Kingston, Rhode Island, and stayed involved with abolitionist activities. Sarah named the baby girl Prudence Crandall Fayerweather.[54]

That same Tuesday night, Prudence and Calvin Philleo, Almira Crandall, William Burleigh, and the students finished their work and went to sleep at the school. Albert Hinckley, a twenty-three-year-old abolitionist from Plainfield who often helped out at the school, also slept at the school that evening.[55] Outside, undetected, a gang of men assembled at midnight. Previously, vandals had acted alone when they threw eggs or rocks at the school. On this night many men worked together. They brought iron bars and large wooden clubs. They silently positioned themselves in front of and under the five main windows of the school. All at once they violently attacked each of the windows with the bars and clubs. For a few minutes the quiet of the night was shattered with the loud smashing of glass and crashing of weapons against the wooden frames of the windows. Shards of glass flew everywhere inside the school. Broken pieces of wooden frames splintered on the floors of the rooms. Two female students were sleeping in one of the rooms at the time of the attack; broken glass covered their beds, but miraculously neither girl was cut or hurt.[56]

Chaos erupted inside the school. Prudence and Almira led the crying girls to the rear of the school—carefully so as not to be cut by the broken glass scattered on the floor—to guard against a possible invasion of the school. Calvin and William rushed outside but heard and saw nothing. The gang of men slipped away into the night and disappeared.

Ordinarily, if a fire or loud commotion in the town center occurred in the middle of the night, friends and neighbors would come out to investigate and give assistance. On this night no alarm was sounded. No neighbors left their homes to investigate or see if anyone was hurt.[57]

At twelve-thirty in the morning, Calvin Philleo and Albert Hinckley walked across the street to Andrew Judson's house. Philleo had never met Andrew Judson. He wanted to inform Judson of the attack on the school and request a response by the town. When Judson answered the door, Hinckley—whom Judson had called as a witness in Prudence Crandall's first trial—introduced Judson to Calvin Philleo. They shook hands, but Judson did not invite Calvin inside.

"I should be happy, sir, to see you for a few moments," Philleo said.

"I do not want to see you, sir," replied Judson, "any more than I now see you." Judson said good night and shut the door.[58]

No one in the school fell asleep again that night. With all the main windows smashed, the breezes and small noises of the early morning hours flowed through the school. The students sobbed with fear, huddled together with Prudence and Almira, while Calvin, William, and Albert kept watch, waiting for the men to return and finish off the school.

The next morning, Calvin, Prudence, and their friends carefully inspected the building. Prudence sent William Burleigh to Brooklyn to fetch Samuel May so that he could help decide what to do. The damage and destruction shocked May. The downstairs rooms were uninhabitable. He had never seen Prudence as stunned and unsettled as she was that morning. May described the students as "terror stricken" and afraid to spend another night in the school.[59] Calvin, Prudence, and May discussed whether the school should continue. They could repair the windows, but they agreed that their enemies would likely destroy them again.[60] The violence against the school had dramatically escalated. What would occur during the next attack?

Prudence and Calvin Philleo had already lost their desire to operate the school at its controversial location. They remained interested in moving to Philadelphia and were awaiting the October elections to see whether the rioting and unrest continued. They also had offered to relocate their school elsewhere within the town. This violent and most extensive attack on the school, which mirrored the disturbing antiabolitionist violence occurring elsewhere, convinced the Philleos and Rev. May to close the school. The magnitude of the decision, however, and what it meant in light of all of the excruciating effort and perseverance of the past two years, had an immediate and crushing impact on Prudence Crandall Philleo.

Prudence Philleo could not summon the strength to tell her students that the school was finished. Students and staff met in one of the few rooms free from shards of glass and gathered around Samuel May. Prudence asked May to tell the girls of the school's fate; she did not join May and the students—she could not bear to hear the announcement. May said Prudence Philleo could not continue operating the school and risk further attacks that might harm the young women and staff. He told the students that the school would close immediately and that the staff would ensure that each girl safely returned home.

"Twenty harmless, well-behaved girls, whose only offence against the peace of the community was that they had come together there to obtain useful knowledge and moral culture, were to be told that they had better go away, because the house in which they dwelt would not be protected by the guardians of the town," Samuel May bitterly noted.[61] "The words almost blistered my lips. I felt ashamed of Canterbury, ashamed of Connecticut, ashamed of my country, ashamed of my color."[62] No one from the town offered to investigate the attack or help bring those who had damaged the school to justice.[63]

Calvin Philleo asked William Burleigh and Albert Hinckley to remain at the school for the next few days to keep it secured. Within three or four days most of the girls left Canterbury to return to their families. Parents interested in sending their daughters to the school continued to write to Prudence; they had not heard the news of the attack and the school's closure. A girl from a black family in Boston arrived in Canterbury only to be told that the school had closed.

Less than a week had passed since William Lloyd Garrison's wedding when he heard the news of the assault on Crandall's school. "The ruffians of Canterbury have been again at their dirty work, and Miss Crandall's school is broken up," Garrison wrote to Samuel May. "I do not wonder that you felt so mortified and indignant in addressing the persecuted scholars, and telling them that they had better return home."[64] Garrison agreed that continuing the school in the face of such violence and persecution made no sense. "Why attempt to reason with beasts?"[65]

More than thirty black women attended Prudence Crandall's school during its existence between April 1833 and September 1834. At least eleven came from New York, with others from Connecticut, Pennsylvania, Rhode Island, and Massachusetts.[66] Harriet Lanson, a student from New Haven, "never uttered, to my knowledge, one unkind word towards the people of Canterbury," Simon S. Jocelyn wrote.[67] A year after Crandall's school had closed, Lanson, who was nineteen, died in New Haven of tuberculosis.[68] Sarah Harris's younger sister Mary also attended Crandall's school. After the school had closed, Mary married a teacher from Massachusetts and moved to New Orleans, where she taught school.[69] Most other students returned home to communities where they had little opportunity for an education.

On Saturday, September 20, 1834, British traveler Edward Abdy returned for his third and final visit to the Canterbury school. He had read press accounts of the attack and wanted to view the damage personally. When he arrived, Calvin and Prudence described to him in great detail what had happened. He saw the broken windows and the rooms covered with shattered glass. Abdy sought out town officials to ask why no investigation of the crimes committed against Prudence Philleo had commenced. Not able to find Andrew Judson, Abdy spoke with Asahel Bacon.[70]

"Mr. Bacon told me that no proceedings had been instituted for the detection and prosecution of the offenders, and he had no reason to suppose that there would be any," Abdy wrote in his journal. Bacon noted that Prudence Crandall had opened her school for black women with no warning, and townspeople "had been justly indignant with the mistress for introducing a class of people whom they did not wish to see among them."[71] Crandall had not listened to those who had counseled her to give up her school, Bacon said. Abdy replied that Crandall had the right to challenge the Black Law and provide an education to black students. "Every one in a free country has a right to act as he pleases," Abdy stated, providing he does not injure other persons or property.[72]

Before leaving Canterbury, Edward Abdy asked Prudence Philleo what she expected to do in the future. She told Abdy she would sell the school and pay off her debts. She also told him she might move to England. England offered "asylum from persecution," Philleo said.[73] She would leave Canterbury and never see Andrew Judson and her tormentors again. Abdy thought of the Puritans who had fled England for America to escape persecution.

As Abdy boarded the stagecoach for Hartford, he considered the fate of Prudence Crandall's school. The riots in New York, Philadelphia, and elsewhere may have encouraged those who attacked her school, but the unfortunate outcome in Canterbury was not inevitable. Any number of changed circumstances might have prevented the violent end. If the town officials and Andrew Judson had approved moving the school to another part of town—a proposal that Samuel May made at the outset and Calvin Philleo renewed at the end—the controversy likely would have ended. If the white leaders of the abolitionist community in Philadelphia had welcomed Prudence Philleo and her school, she and Calvin could have announced their move and preempted the night of violence in Canterbury. Perhaps most important, the Connecticut Supreme Court could have settled the issue of the legitimacy of the school. Asahel Bacon underscored this point in his conversation with Edward Abdy. He made excuses for the violent attack by noting that Crandall's school violated the Black Law. If Justices Thomas S. Williams, Clark Bissell, and Samuel Church had voted to strike down the Black Law as unconstitutional—the outcome they privately supported—they would have affirmed the legality and constitutionality of Prudence Crandall's school. Their ruling would not have reversed the prejudice toward Crandall's black students, but it would have removed all doubt as to who was legally right and who was wrong, and it might have given pause to those who attacked the school in September. In addition, the ruling would have established black citizenship in America, a decision eventually validated by history if not by the U.S. Supreme Court of the day.[74]

The *Hartford Daily Courant* called the court's 1834 decision a masterful example of judicial restraint. Fifty-two years later, in 1886, the *Courant* recalled that in the *Crandall* case, Connecticut's justices "in a cowardly manner dodged the constitutional question, which from that day to this has never been decided."[75] The newspaper concluded that the legislature's passage of the Black Law and the failure of the court to strike it down resulted in mob rule that closed Crandall's school. It "encouraged the persecutors to resort to the more open acts of violence and outrage which resulted in breaking up the school and driving Miss Crandall away."[76]

Calvin Philleo offered a reward of fifty dollars for information leading to the arrest of those who attacked the school and published the notice in the *Liberator*.[77] He also said he had decided to sell the Canterbury schoolhouse because of the Black Law and vandalism—"the property and perhaps the lives of those connected with the school are insecure."[78] In the same issue of the *Liberator*, one of Prudence Philleo's students published a letter describing the final days of the school and the night of the attack. "A band of cruel men" created "a tremendous noise" in the middle of the night, the student wrote, and the damage caused by the attack "rendered our dwelling almost untenantable."[79] The student wrote that William Burleigh had called the students together so they could hear from Rev. Samuel May.

"He, with feelings of apparent deep regret, told us we had better go to our homes," the student wrote. "With regret I prepared to leave that pleasant, yet persecuted dwelling, and also my dear school-mates, in whose society I had spent so many hours . . . My teacher was ever kind," the student wrote about Burleigh. "With him I saw religion, not merely adopted as an empty form, but a living, all-pervading principle of action. He lived like those who seek a better country . . ."[80]

Andrew Judson withdrew the charges against William Burleigh and Crandall's school for violation of the Black Law since the school had ceased to exist. The libel action against William Lloyd Garrison that Judson once so enthusiastically had pursued now languished for lack of prosecution. On December 27, 1834, a representative for Judson offered unilaterally to withdraw the five counts of libel against Garrison. Garrison happily accepted the offer, ending the matter.[81] "I am truly glad that my Canterbury persecutors have withdrawn their suits against me; for law-business is anything but agreeable, and victory in it generally results in ruin," Garrison said.[82]

The Philleos rented the schoolhouse for a time to William Kinne, a friend of Prudence, and in November they sold it to James Aspinwall for two thousand dollars, the price Crandall had paid for it in 1831. As Prudence and Calvin considered their future, they took notice of the October elections in Philadelphia. Rioting broke out once more, first between partisans of different political parties and then in a black neighborhood where a fight between blacks and whites left one black man dead and ten arrested.[83] The white abolitionist leaders of Philadelphia would not invite Prudence and Calvin Philleo and their school to the city of brotherly love.

"Thus ended the generous, disinterested, philanthropic, Christian enterprise of Prudence Crandall," Rev. Samuel May wrote.[84] Crandall's legacy in the ongoing fight for equality, however, continued. "Prudence Crandall did more for the cause of freedom by her persistence in the 'Higher Law' doctrine of eternal right than the most eloquent anti-slavery lecturer could have accomplished in molding public sentiment of the whole north," Laura Smith Haviland wrote.[85] For Prudence Crandall and her allies, the years ahead would bring new challenges and tragedies.

13 : Family Trials and Tragedies

One of Prudence Crandall's students, Julia Williams, refused to let go of her dream of obtaining an education.[1] Originally from Charleston, South Carolina, Julia's family lived in Boston and knew William Lloyd Garrison. After Crandall's school closed, Julia traveled to Canaan, New Hampshire.

Two months before the final attack on Crandall's school, friends of Prudence Crandall and William Lloyd Garrison successfully petitioned the New Hampshire legislature to grant a charter for a school. Inspired by Crandall, the trustees agreed that the school "should be open to all pupils without distinction of color."[2] The supporters of Noyes Academy, named for local farmer and Revolutionary War veteran Samuel Noyes, included David Lee Child of Boston; Rev. Samuel H. Cox, the minister of the Laight Street Presbyterian Church of New York; and attorney Samuel Sewall of Boston.

Julia Williams enrolled at Noyes Academy. She joined twenty-eight white men, fourteen black men, and by the end of October 1834, twenty women scholars.[3] At Noyes, Julia met Henry Highland Garnet, another black student. Henry's family had escaped from slavery in Maryland in 1824 when he was nine years old. Julia and Henry later married in Troy, New York, in 1848. Both led activist lives; Julia taught black children in Boston and Jamaica and attended numerous antislavery conventions; Henry became a prominent black minister and abolitionist, and he published a new edition of David Walker's *Appeal* with a biographical sketch of Walker based on information Garnet had obtained from a conversation with Walker's widow.[4] Garnet wrote that "there is not much hope of redemption without the shedding of blood."[5]

Garnet's time at Noyes Academy helped him understand the depth of the racism that existed in the North; for Julia Williams, Noyes repeated her experience at Prudence Crandall's school in Canterbury. The townspeople in Canaan did not react well to the newly integrated school. They held a town meeting and resolved that blacks must not mix "with our own free white population."[6] They opposed equality for blacks "for the purpose of having Black Presidents, Black Governors, Black Representatives, (and) Black Judges . . ."[7] The Noyes trustees responded by asking, "What greater punishment can there be, what greater degradation, than to deprive the soul of its proper sustenance, the knowledge of divine and human things?"[8]

At dawn on Monday, August 10, 1835, men led teams of oxen and wagons filled with chains to Noyes Academy. The men tore down a fence that surrounded the school. Other men attached chains to the school building and the teams of oxen and attempted to pull the building off its foundation and onto wooden runners. The first few attempts succeeded only in breaking the chains and tiring the animals. After doubling and redoubling the chains, they succeeded in pulling the school building onto the runners, and "ninety-five yoke of cattle" dragged the building into the street, where they left it until the next day.[9] On Tuesday, the men returned with larger cables and pulled the building down the road to the town common.

Henry Highland Garnet and two of his black classmates, Thomas S. Sidney and Alexander Crummell, retreated to a local boarding house. Garnet obtained a shotgun and barricaded himself and his friends in his room. When someone rode past the boardinghouse and fired a single shot, Garnet returned fire with a shotgun blast.[10] The shot injured no one, and the black students quickly left Canaan. The *Boston Daily Atlas* compared Noyes Academy to Prudence Crandall's school and condemned any attempt to introduce "a more free and intimate intercourse between the white and black population."[11]

Two years after Noyes Academy closed, Henry Highland Garnet returned to Canaan to speak at the Congregational Church. Many townspeople, including some who had opposed the school, apologized to Garnet.[12] In 1839 the abandoned building—a shuttered reminder of Canaan's stand against equal rights for blacks—burned to the ground.

The years immediately following the closure of Prudence Crandall's Canterbury school were not kind to the Crandall family. Prudence and Calvin Philleo moved to Boonville, New York, in 1835. Calvin's younger brother, Bonaparte, a doctor, lived there and helped lead local temperance and antislavery efforts.[13] The economy in Boonville, a remote town thirty miles north of Utica, depended on farming and the sale of timber to the town's sole sawmill. Prudence did not enjoy the social and economic isolation of Boonville. She missed her family.

Prudence's brother Reuben managed a thriving medical practice in Peekskill, New York. While Reuben was never an ardent abolitionist, he developed an interest in the antislavery movement. He read the *Emancipator*, a New York antislavery newspaper edited by Joshua Leavitt and Theodore Dwight Weld and acquired a modest collection of abolitionist literature.

In 1835 one of Reuben Crandall's patients moved to Washington, D.C., and asked him to come along to care for his ailing wife. Reuben reluctantly agreed, intending to provide medical care for the man's wife, lecture on botany, and continue his work in the medical profession. He packed his personal items, medical books, and abolitionist literature in a trunk and set off for Washington, D.C. Once in Washington, a colleague, Henry King, noticed and borrowed a copy of the *Emancipator*. That particular issue criticized the American Colonization Society and praised immediate emancipation.

After King had discarded the paper, a proslavery man delivered the newspaper and information regarding its owner, Reuben Crandall, to the local federal prosecutor. After searching Rueben's home and belongings, the prosecutor charged Reuben Crandall with possessing materials likely to stir up revolution, hatred, and violence in the United States and arrested him on August 11, 1835.[14] A mob assembled outside the jail where Crandall was held and threatened to kill him. "A menacing assemblage surrounded the city prison bent upon administering 'Lynch Law' upon . . . a brother of Miss Prudence Crandall of Connecticut," the *Baltimore Patriot* reported.[15] Instead of storming the prison, the crowd looted and burned local tenements that housed black families.[16]

The prosecutor did not have a good case, Reuben wrote to his father Pardon from jail. The charges were absurd, Reuben said, and the prosecutor seemed bent only on sensationalism for the sake of publicity. "The people are distrustful of his honesty of motive. But what is more than all, he has acknowledged to some of his confidential friends that there is no evidence against me that can convict," Crandall said. The court set

Reuben's bail at the astronomical sum of five thousand dollars. "I am the same as dead to the world, as far as my usefulness is concerned."[17] Reuben did not tell his father that the prosecutor had discussed seeking the death penalty.

Federal prosecutor Frank Key brought the case against Reuben Crandall. Better remembered as Francis Scott Key, he began his law practice in partnership with Roger Taney, who later became chief justice of the U.S. Supreme Court and presided over the *Dred Scott* case. Key and Taney remained close friends; Taney married Key's sister, Anne. Key was best known for writing the words to "The Star Spangled Banner."

A founding member of the American Colonization Society, Frank Key wrote, "Any scheme of emancipation without colonization . . . (is) productive of nothing but evil."[18] Key said that even colonization "must be carried on with the consent of the slave owners."[19] Key owned slaves throughout his life. "I am still a slaveholder, and could not, without the greatest inhumanity, be otherwise," Key wrote. "I own, for instance, an old slave, who has done no work for me for years. I pay his board and other expenses, and cannot believe that I sin in doing so."[20]

Key knew that Reuben Crandall was the brother of Prudence Crandall, the famous headmistress of a school for black women, and he understood that prosecuting Crandall's brother would attract significant coverage in the press. Key planned to use the trial as a means to defend colonization and attack those who advocated immediate emancipation. The case did not proceed as Key expected.

Reuben languished in jail for eight months while awaiting trial. When the trial finally began in April 1836, a surprise character witness defended Crandall. Prudence Crandall's chief antagonist, Congressman and soon-to-be Federal District Court Judge Andrew T. Judson, testified on Reuben's behalf.

"I have known Dr. Crandall from his early boyhood," Judson testified. "I am a Representative from the district in which he was born. His father lives in the town where I live, in my immediate neighborhood. He studied with my family physician, Dr. Harris; and I have been acquainted with his reputation. No young man stood better in society. . . . I have always known Dr. Crandall as peaceable a citizen as any in the state."[21] Judson said he wanted to help Reuben Crandall because he believed Reuben had urged his sister Prudence to give up her school.

"Dr. Crandall is the brother of Prudence Crandall," Judson continued. "In the winter of 1833, Prudence Crandall, having kept a school for young ladies, immediately changed it, at the instigation of Garrison and others, to a colored school. It was the object of Tappan and Garrison to get colored children from the South and educate them and send them back. I had received a petition, being then a representative, for the legislature to interfere and suppress it by law. I had been to New York, and was going home in the steamboat, when I saw Dr. Crandall. I told him the difficulty we had had with his sister. He said he was going to break up the school. He said he didn't know as he could, because Prudence was a very obstinate girl; but he had another sister, younger, then engaged in it, that he could at all events get her away. . . . I always understood he used his whole influence to break up the school as much as any other individual, and appeared to be as zealous to effect that object."[22]

Congressman Judson described Crandall's school in a manner calculated to appeal to the fears of a southern-leaning jury. Judson said the abolitionists intended to "get colored children from the South and educate them and send them back." Having prosecuted Crandall and catalogued the various home states of the black girls at the school—none of whom were from the South—Judson knew his characterization of the school was false. He also knew that the perception of a threat to the South would enhance the jury's sympathy for Reuben's alleged efforts to close the school. Judson downplayed his own role and neglected to point out that he had personally led the opposition to the school.

Reuben Crandall's attorney, Richard Coxe, told the jury that the trial was a dangerous infringement on personal liberty and speech. Coxe said the newspapers Crandall possessed contained nothing threatening or seditious, and he noted that Patrick Henry and Thomas Jefferson had expressed similar thoughts regarding slavery.[23] After a short deliberation, the jury found Reuben Crandall "not guilty." Newspaper articles credited Andrew Judson's testimony with distinguishing Reuben from his sister, Prudence Crandall.[24] "A member of Congress testified that he (Reuben) went to Connecticut," reported the *Alexandria Gazette*, "and was active in breaking up and suppressing the school for blacks established under the care of his sister, Prudence Crandall."[25]

While the verdict was a victory for Reuben Crandall, eight months in prison had sapped him of his strength and spirit. He had contracted tuberculosis. For the next year and a half he fought the disease, finally traveling south to Jamaica to seek a warmer and more healing climate. Reuben died in Jamaica, on January 17, 1838, eleven days after his thirty-second birthday. William Goodell, an abolitionist who lived in New York City and was born in Pomfret, Connecticut, wrote that while Francis Scott Key failed to convict Reuben Crandall, he nevertheless imposed a death sentence. "Thus was a worthy citizen of a free state incarcerated and, in effect, murdered, though adjudged innocent . . . for no fault but having come under some suspicion of having disseminated publications hostile to slavery and the Colonization Society!"[26]

News of Reuben's death devastated Prudence Crandall and her family. Prudence must have reflected on the prosecutor's zeal in pursuing what amounted to a show trial against Reuben. Frank Key's eagerness to prosecute Reuben undoubtedly was linked to the fact that Reuben was the brother of the infamous Prudence Crandall. This must have made Reuben's death—related to the sickness he had acquired in prison—especially hard and troubling for Prudence, and it came in the middle of the worst year for the Crandall family.[27]

After Prudence's school closed, Almira Crandall met John W. Rand, whose father lived in New Salem, Massachusetts. John worked for a time in Boston at the Hamilton Bank as a teller.[28] They married in July 1835, in Boston, and moved to New York City, where John worked as a teacher. "She seems to have been fortunate in marriage," William Lloyd Garrison said after they visited him in Boston. "Mr. Rand is quite a pleasant, genteel and handsome looking man, and is doing very well as a school teacher."[29] Almira and John Rand rented a room at a school for girls run by Ann T. Green. The school was located about ten blocks south of Rev. Samuel Cox's Presbyterian Church on Laight Street.

"This morning I have a leisure hour, and that time or part of it, I intend to spend in talking to you," Almira wrote to Prudence in late August after she and John had arrived in New York. "I wish now, sis, when you are at liberty, take a trip down and see us. We have a nice room which Mr. Rand has fitted nicely, and I can assure you I am as happy as need be."[30]

The newspapers in New York City had reported Reuben Crandall's arrest, and Almira asked Prudence if she had heard from their brother. "I tremble for him," Almira told Prudence. "I fear his life will be sacrificed. Do you know anything respecting him? Do you know whether he is suffering and thinking he is forgotten by his friends? . . . If he is engaged in the anti-slavery cause, I think he will sacrifice his life before he will give up one iota of his principles. Our folks, mother in particular, are much disturbed about him."[31]

Two years later, in July of 1837, both Almira and Reuben were together at the Crandall home in Canterbury. "I am at home, sick with a pulmonic affliction which threatens my life," Reuben wrote to Prudence. "My health is so feeble that I could not finish this yesterday and I am still feeble today. I have much fever, chills and cough."[32] Reuben had more disturbing news for Prudence.

"You will be surprised when I tell you that sister Almira is on her death bed, to all human appearances, and destined to tarry but a few months at farthest, perhaps only for a few days," he wrote. "If you should think of coming home, you must make all possible haste if you wish to see our sister alive. . . . John Rand will be here ten or twelve days of his vacation. He has been up several times since sister has been here."[33]

Reuben explained that Almira first became ill in January, recovered somewhat, and suffered a relapse. Mary Burleigh, the sister of Charles and William Burleigh, moved into the Crandall home to serve as Almira's nurse and companion. The main trouble was Almira's lungs, Reuben said. "Her suffering is extreme beyond your imagination." John Rand built a special bed on rockers that allowed his wife to sway back and forth and seemed to relieve her pain.

Prudence wrote that she could not travel from Boonville to Canterbury. Almira dictated a brief letter to Prudence; Reuben recorded her words. "Tell my dear sister I would have answered her letter to me if I had the strength," Almira said. "Tell her I want her to forgive me all the trouble I ever caused her, and that I can freely forgive her everything. I do trust and believe the Lord will truly forgive us both."[34] Twenty-four-year-old Almira Crandall Rand died on August 18, 1837. "Death sends his withering blight," Reuben wrote. Shortly thereafter, Reuben left for Jamaica.

Within five months, the two youngest children of Pardon and Esther Crandall had died. Pardon resolved to leave Canterbury and take his wife west to Illinois. He wrote to Prudence in 1838 that he wanted to go deep into the wilderness and find asylum, a "hiding place from the turmoils and contentions of this world . . . a place to lay my weary and decrepit bones."[35] Pardon told Prudence that her mother Esther was "often in floods of tears." The neighborhood in Canterbury had suffered many deaths from sickness, Pardon said. Esther wrote in the same letter that she and Pardon planned to go on a long journey to Illinois later in the year. Esther did not look forward to the prospect of leaving Canterbury for parts unknown: "I am so nervous I can scarcely hold the pen in my hand."[36]

Prudence's older brother Hezekiah also was not well. Pardon said he was "raising some blood."[37] Pardon and Esther helped take care of Hezekiah's wife, Clarissa—she was pregnant with her sixth child. Hezekiah kept working at his farm and cotton mill, where he made twine and cotton batting for quilts and mattresses, and slowly regained his health.

Pardon persisted in his idea of moving to the Midwest. He bought 640 acres in La Salle County, Illinois, at $1.25 per acre. Pardon traveled to Illinois to investigate his land while Esther stayed in Canterbury. After surveying his future homestead, Pardon cleared the land, plotted a site for a log cabin, supervised its construction, and helped dig a well— backbreaking work for a man of sixty. In the process of clearing a wet, forested area, Pardon became sick with malaria. The mosquito-borne illness was commonplace in Illinois and other midwestern and southern states in the 1800s.[38] He suffered from fever, aching bones, and general weakness. After gathering his strength, he made the long journey back to Canterbury. When he arrived home, his wife Esther knew he was very sick.

On Monday, July 9, 1838, Hezekiah's wife, Clarissa, gave birth to a healthy girl. Pardon Crandall's condition, however, worsened. On Friday, July 20, Pardon died. On Saturday, Clarissa died unexpectedly, most likely because of infection. Hezekiah named the baby girl Clarissa to honor his wife.

The rapid series of tragedies must have had a numbing effect on Prudence Crandall. The violent end of her school was followed by the near destruction of her family. She lost her father, her younger sister and brother, and her sister-in-law, all while she remained apart and isolated from her family. The concern of her friends about Calvin's fitness as a husband seemed prophetic. In marrying Calvin, she had given up her independence but had not gained a protector or even a partner. The decision to sell the schoolhouse in Canterbury was technically Calvin's to make; as Prudence's husband he assumed the legal role of controller of assets, real estate, and contracts. The dramatic change she experienced from playing a central role in a national controversy to subordinating her vision of the future to that of Calvin Philleo must have been bewildering and debilitating. She struggled to take care of Calvin's children, Elizabeth and young Calvin, while managing the primitive farm in Boonville with Calvin away most of the time. Prudence was angered to learn that on one of Calvin's many trips he had stopped in Canterbury and asked her father for money.[39] She feared for her mother Esther's welfare, as well as for her brother Hezekiah, who now had to raise his children on his own.

Prudence convinced Calvin to sell the farm in Boonville and return to Canterbury. Calvin preached for a time at the Packerville Baptist Church. Prudence did not return to teaching or seek public attention of any kind. When Calvin's daughter Elizabeth became ill in 1841, Calvin's brother, Dr. Bonaparte Philleo, cared for her at his home in Herkimer County, New York. Elizabeth died in September. Calvin—away on a preaching tour—did not learn of his daughter's death in time to attend her funeral. Prudence traveled to Little Falls, New York, for the service.

Calvin Philleo increasingly suffered from deteriorating physical and mental health, which affected his personality and behavior. He suffered epileptic seizures and on one occasion convulsed headlong into a fireplace, burning the left side of his face and permanently losing sight in his left eye. Thereafter, he wore an eye patch and became irritable and abusive toward Prudence and his son. To escape his father's wrath, young Calvin left home to sail on merchant ships. In 1842, Prudence Philleo decided on a similar course and resolved to leave her husband. Married eight, mostly unhappy, years, Prudence could no longer endure Calvin's unpredictable and hostile behavior. She moved to the vacant Crandall family homestead in Illinois, taking along Hezekiah's thirteen-year-old son, Obediah. Calvin remained in Canterbury and later returned to Boonville, New York, to stay with relatives.

As Prudence traveled to La Salle County, she passed through Chicago and was recognized by the press. "Mrs. Philleo, formerly Miss Prudence Crandall, extensively known as the victim . . . for teaching a school of colored girls," reported the *Chicago Citizen*, "passed through this city a few days since on her way to Troy Grove."[40] Prudence and her nephew planted crops and fixed up the log house that Pardon had built. By the fall, they harvested fifty acres of wheat, cut a large amount of hay, and raised sheep and cattle. Hezekiah warned her not to tell Calvin about the cows or horses, "as he will be out and claim the whole lot."[41] Prudence also taught students in her home during the day. "She was hardly settled there before her house was filled with school children," a neighbor wrote.[42]

Ten years after the violent end of Prudence Crandall's school, the Windham County Anti-Slavery Society commemorated Crandall's heroism with a rally on the Canterbury town common on July 4, 1844.[43] Once again, controversy stirred. The minister of the Congregational Church warned his parishioners to stay away from the rally of abolitionists. Andrew Judson drafted a petition requesting that the town fathers prohibit the demonstration. This time, however, the efforts by Judson and other "ancient and honorable aristocracy of that so notorious town" did not succeed.[44] "Carriages of every description" filled the streets at the four corners of the town center, and hundreds gathered under an elm tree to hear Charles Burleigh speak. A band played patriotic instrumentals, and a chorus sang a popular civil rights song of the time, "Get Off the Track."[45] Written in 1844 the song was likely one of the first to use the imagery of riding the newly constructed railroads. "Get out of the way! Every station! Clear the track of Emancipation!"[46]

Unsuccessful in preventing the rally, Andrew Judson attempted to disrupt the gathering. "I was told that the Honorable United States Judge gave to a boy twenty-five cents, and told him to buy some powder with it to fire off nearby the assembly," Charles Burleigh wrote. "The boy was rude enough to obey the order, but the disturbance did not last long, for his guardian interposed after the first fire and stopped his sport so that the judge's 25 cent plot 'flashed in the pan.'"[47] Burleigh declared the Independence Day celebration of Prudence Crandall's school a success. "The enemies who had done so much to defeat it were chagrined and mortified by the result of that meeting."[48]

In October of 1844, Calvin Philleo returned for a visit to his former parish in Pawtucket, Rhode Island, and preached to the congregation. More than one thousand parishioners turned out to hear him. A sentimental and sad journey for Philleo, he remembered his first wife who had died while they raised their young children and shared in the responsibilities of running the church. "My dear child, I came into this place last week—I found a warm and friendly reception among all the people,"

Calvin wrote to his son. "I called at our old place where we once were together as a family. Oh how solemn the place where your dear mother breathed her last . . . I went to the grave to weep and pray."[49]

Prudence's mother Esther traveled to Illinois to join her daughter in the early 1840s and brought Hezekiah's young daughter Clarissa. Obediah, still a very young man, managed the farm. After Esther had settled into her new home where she could take care of Clarissa and Obediah, Prudence traveled back East to attempt a reunion with Calvin after he had pleaded for her help.

Calvin Philleo's behavior had become so unpredictable that his children, Emeline and young Calvin, successfully petitioned the probate court in Canterbury to appoint a conservator to manage his affairs. The court determined that "said Calvin Philleo is now an insane person, and by reason thereof is wholly incompetent to manage said estate and is unable to take care of himself."[50] Prudence heeded his pleas and joined him in Canterbury. Their reunion was not successful, and they moved to Providence where Prudence taught classes in phonotypy, an experimental form of reading that relied on phonetic symbols.[51] Phonotypy featured a unique alphabet of both roman letters as well as new shapes and symbols, all designed with the intention of eliminating inconsistencies in spelling and creating a more accessible and consistent form of English.

Calvin returned to his abusive ways. Emeline wrote to young Calvin that when one of Prudence's friends sought to visit her in Providence, the landlady said Prudence had left for Boston. "Mother had been obliged to give up her house as the only way of getting rid of father," Emeline wrote. "This woman spoke of father with the greatest dislike and said his abuse of mother was beyond conception."[52]

While in Boston in May of 1846, and without Calvin, Prudence again tried teaching phonotypy. She held classes in the basement room of the African Meeting House. "I view this reform as a great leveler," Prudence wrote, "by which the coalition of the human family is to be morally and intellectually raised."[53] Despite help from William Lloyd Garrison, who dutifully printed a letter from Prudence promoting her classes in the *Liberator*, neither phonotypy nor Prudence's classes grew sufficiently in popularity.[54]

Prudence returned to Illinois and began a commitment to life in frontier America, working the land year to year to make ends meet and spending time with her mother and Crandall relatives. She was in name Prudence Philleo, but in every other respect she lived as Prudence Crandall, making her own decisions and earning her own keep. She ran a school for local boys and girls and taught academic subjects along with manners, religion, and thrift. "Money was scarce and part of the tuition was paid in food and supplies that each farmer could spare," a relative remembered.[55] Prudence's only luxury was a small collection of books that grew over time. Calvin had discouraged Prudence from reading or possessing books. That encouraged her to accumulate as many books and periodicals as she could afford. Books and newspapers always provided Prudence with knowledge and a glimpse of a wider and better world.

■ The years following the end of Prudence Crandall's Canterbury school were a time of challenge and ideological combat for William Lloyd Garrison. Friction developed between abolitionists, particularly between the leaders of the New England Anti-Slavery Society founded by Garrison and the New York-based American Anti-Slavery Society promoted by Arthur Tappan. Garrison took a harder line in defending immediate emancipation than did Arthur Tappan; the two men increasingly were at odds regarding the tone and direction of the abolitionist movement. Supporting a movement led by a revolutionary who inspired rioting—purposefully or not—no longer appealed to Arthur Tappan. Abolishing slavery remained Tappan's goal, but he did not want to undermine commerce and personal safety.

To celebrate the first anniversary of the Boston Female Anti-Slavery Society on October 14, 1835, the members invited George Thompson—an Englishman and hero in the abolitionist community—to give a speech. His addresses electrified the supporters of immediate emancipation. "America must witness another revolution, and the second will be far more illustrious in its results than the first," Thompson wrote. "The second will be a moral revolution. A struggle for higher, holier, more catholic, more patriotic principles."[56] Thompson had his admirers, but he had more enemies because of his strong opposition to the American Colonization Society. "It is our duty to regard the ACS as the hateful bantling of a fiend-like prejudice," Thompson said.[57] Supporters of colonization saw Thompson as a threat to the union between northern and southern states.

A conservative Boston newspaper, the *Commercial Gazette*, encouraged citizens to turn out in force at the Boston Female Anti-Slavery Society meeting and oppose Thompson and abolitionism. "This resistance will not come from a *rabble*, but from men of property and standing . . . who are determined, let the consequences be what they may, to put a stop to the impudent, bullying conduct of the foreign vagrant, Thompson, and his associates in mischief," the editors of the *Gazette* wrote.[58] The *Gazette* advised the women who had invited Thompson to stay away from the event for their own safety. The leaders of the Female Anti-Slavery Society rescheduled their anniversary meeting for Wednesday, October 21, 1835, at their own offices on Washington Street and next door to Garrison's office for the *Liberator* and cancelled George Thompson's speech. That did not stop local merchants from meeting with the editor of the *Commercial Gazette*, James Homer, to discuss ways of disrupting the Anti-Slavery Society's anniversary meeting. They asked Homer to print "an inflammatory handbill in relation to the meeting . . . something that would wake up the populace."[59] Homer quickly drafted a flyer designed to bring a crowd into the downtown area, complete with an offer of a monetary prize.

"That infamous foreign scoundrel THOMPSON, will hold forth *this afternoon*, at the *Liberator* Office, No. 48 Washington Street. The present is a fair opportunity for the friends of the Union to *snake Thompson out!* It will be a contest between the Abolitionists and the friends of the Union. A purse of $100 has been raised by a number of patriotic citizens to reward the individual who shall first lay violent hands on Thompson, so that he may be brought to the tar-kettle before dark. Friends of the Union, be vigilant!"[60]

The merchants ordered five hundred copies to distribute throughout the city to insurance offices, business and commercial districts, boarding-houses, hotels and taverns, and the tradesmen and mechanics in the North End.[61] James Homer later wrote that businessmen disapproved of women taking a stand on the issue of slavery. "Women ought to be engaged in some better business than that of stirring up strife between the South and the North on this matter of slavery," the merchants allegedly told Homer. "They ought to be at home, attending to their domestic concerns, instead of sowing the seeds of political discord in the anti-slavery rooms."[62] More likely, however, the merchants wanted to entice a large crowd downtown for the same reasons that tavern owners ordered more liquor in advance of a public execution.

James Homer rushed the printing of the flyer in order to have it on the street early that afternoon.[63] Members of the Female Anti-Slavery Society noticed that many shops stayed open well into the evening. "Certain well known merchants did not go home to dine, so anxious were they to lose nothing of the expected scene."[64]

By late afternoon between six and ten thousand men filled the streets leading to Washington Street. Several men tore down and smashed the sign that identified the office for the Female Anti-Slavery Society. Unbeknownst to the crowd, the Anti-Slavery Society had substituted William Lloyd Garrison for the featured speaker, George Thompson. As Garrison conversed with the twenty or so women in attendance for the meeting, the mob surged into the building. Protesters quickly filled the two flights of stairs and the hallway leading to the meeting room. They shouted insults and threats; Garrison quickly decided he would not speak. He exited the room escorted by Charles Burleigh and made his way into the adjoining offices of his newspaper, the *Liberator*. Burleigh, the former editor of the *Unionist* and a friend of Garrison, locked the door once they were inside the *Liberator* offices.

The mob chanted George Thompson's name. The size and manner of the crowd attracted the attention of city authorities; Mayor Theodore Lyman arrived with a police escort and announced that Thompson had cancelled his appearance and left the City of Boston. After a brief lull, word spread that abolitionist William Lloyd Garrison was inside. "Lynch him," one protester shouted. "We must have Garrison! Out with him!"[65] Leaders of the mob demanded that Garrison surrender. The situation deteriorated and threats of violence increased. Samuel Sewall raced through the building looking for an escape route for Garrison. Sewall, an attorney and abolitionist, had been a friend of Garrison ever since he and his cousin Samuel May had first met Garrison in 1830 at Julien Hall in Boston.[66] One of the trustees of Noyes Academy, Sewall had helped to finance the *Liberator* during its many lean times. He looked out a back window on the second floor and saw a possible way out.

"I found a shed with a box on it, to which Garrison might reach by letting himself out of the window. I then went and found Garrison in the upper story of the building. He seemed more agitated than I had ever seen him."[67] The protesters searching for Garrison reached the locked office doors of the *Liberator*. As they pounded on a paneled door, Charles Burleigh opened the door, stepped out into the hallway and confronted the men directly. He relocked the door of the *Liberator* offices behind him to protect Garrison. Burleigh had a full black beard, long shoulder-length hair, and eccentric clothes; some said he resembled a stocky version of the painted images of Jesus Christ. His unusual appearance may have helped him on this day. Drawing on his powers of persuasion, he successfully engaged the men in debate and delayed them from entering the *Liberator* offices.[68]

While Burleigh distracted the protesters, Garrison climbed out the second-floor window holding onto the windowsill with his fingers—and let go. He landed on the roof of a shed one story below. Garrison, uninjured, slid off the roof onto the street where he saw a large crowd. As some in the crowd immediately recognized him, he dashed into a carpenter's shop. He thought he might come out on the other side of the building and escape into an alleyway, but there was no such passageway. The mob chased after him, but when they tried to enter the shop, the door remained bolted. The carpenters defended Garrison; they locked the door and told him to take shelter in a corner of the upstairs room. After a few minutes, the mob battered down the door and poured into the shop. They made their way upstairs, where they quickly found Garrison barricaded behind wooden boards. Garrison did not resist; they dragged him to an open window where the crowd outside could see him. For an instant the protesters considered tossing him out the window and killing him on the spot. "Three or four of the rioters, uttering a yell, furiously dragged me to the window, with the intention of hurling me from that height to the ground," Garrison said. "One of them relented and said, 'don't let us kill him outright.' So they drew me back, and coiled a rope about my body."[69]

His captors tied a rope around his waist, while those below put a ladder to the window. They forced Garrison to climb down—facing the crowd—into the excited mob. As Garrison reached the ground, two large, burly men attached themselves to him on either side and shouted to the others as they led him through the crowd, "He shan't be hurt, don't hurt him, he is an American!"[70] Garrison did not know the men, Daniel and Aaron Cooley; they ran a Boston delivery company. Their decision to protect Garrison was remarkable in that they strongly opposed abolition.

The Cooleys' ability to protect Garrison, however, was limited. "I saw the crowd pouring out from Wilson's Lane into State Street with a deal of clamor and shouting, and heard the exulting cry, 'They've got him—they've got him,'" Charles Burleigh said. "And so, sure enough, they had. The tide set toward the south door of City Hall, and in a few minutes I saw Garrison between two men who held him and led him along, while the throng pressed on every side, as if eager to devour him alive."[71] As the crowd surged around him, some assaulted him. He lost his hat and his coat, and the rest of his clothes were ripped and torn apart. Garrison and his unlikely bodyguards slowly made their way to the steps of city hall. Men rushed toward the main door to block Garrison's entrance, but Daniel and Aaron Cooley pushed through the crowd. "This was only effected by the use of great physical strength," noted Mayor Lyman. "For a moment, the conflict was dubious," Garrison said, "but my sturdy supporters carried me safely up to the Mayor's room."[72] As the crowd outside continued to grow, Mayor Lyman decided he could not guarantee Garrison's safety. Lyman hatched a plan to secretly slip Garrison out of city hall by carriage and take him to the city jail for his own protection.

A decoy carriage arrived at the north door of city hall, where security men lined up on either side to attract attention. When the mob surrounded the entrance and engaged the security men to block Garrison's escape, another carriage appeared at the south door, where constables rushed Garrison into the coach. The decoy did not fool everyone. Some rioters attempted to surround the second carriage. The mob briefly succeeded in rocking the coach so that it tilted up on one side, but the driver repeatedly lashed the horses until the carriage broke free and sped away. Garrison watched as another group of rioters rushed "like a whirlwind upon the frail vehicle in which I sat, and endeavor[ed] to drag me out of it. . . . They were, however, vigorously repulsed by the police—a constable sprang in by my side—the doors were closed—and the driver, lustily using his whip upon the bodies of his horses and the heads of the rioters, happily made an opening through the crowd and drove at a tremendous speed for Leverett Street."[73]

There was one final obstacle: a few hundred protesters had gathered at the jail to have one more go at Garrison. Police officers formed a line of protection around the carriage as it arrived and created a pathway leading from the coach into the jail. In minutes, they had Garrison inside the Leverett Street Jail and locked in a cell to protect him from an out-of-control mob.

While secure, the Leverett Street Jail was "badly situated, badly constructed, and very obnoxious to the residents . . . the scene of a great deal of human woe and wretchedness, guilt and despair."[74] Garrison spent one night there but memorialized his stay. "William Lloyd Garrison was put into this cell on Wednesday afternoon, Oct. 21, 1835, to save him from the violence of a 'respectable and influential' mob, who sought to destroy him for preaching the abominable and dangerous doctrine, that all men are created equal," Garrison wrote on his jail cell wall. "Confine me as a prisoner—but bind me not as a slave."[75] When the authorities released Garrison the next day, they encouraged him to leave the city. Garrison's wife, Helen, met him at the jail, and the police escorted the couple to Canton, where they boarded a train for Providence. The authorities searched all of the passenger cars for troublemakers before the Garrisons boarded the train.[76]

The Boston riot and near death of his friend Garrison outraged George Thompson, and he wrote a lengthy letter that was published in various newspapers, including the *Liberator*. Thompson recalled the violence that had closed Prudence Crandall's school and Noyes Academy. "A mob in Boston! The birthplace of the revolution—the Cradle of Liberty! A mob in Washington Street, Boston, to put down *free discussion*," Thompson wrote. "Call to judgment the barbarians of Baltimore, and Philadelphia, and New York . . . Gather again the scattered schools of Canterbury and Canaan . . . rend the veil of legal enactments by which the beams of light divine are hidden from millions who are left to grope their way through darkness . . . Go, shed your 'patriotic' tears over the infamy of your country."[77]

Garrison recuperated at the Benson family home in Brooklyn, Connecticut. "My life was almost miraculously saved," Garrison wrote.[78] He thanked those who had courageously helped him in the face of a near fatal predicament. "My obligations to you for your manifold kindnesses exceed, I fear, human ability to repay," he told Samuel Sewall.[79] "Has my lost hat yet been found?" he joked to Isaac Knapp.[80]

Throughout the 1830s and 1840s, Garrison continued to take risks with his safety. Three thousand abolitionist supporters cheered Garrison on May 17, 1838, when he spoke at Pennsylvania Hall in Philadelphia, a facility constructed specifically to host abolitionist events. At the conclusion of his remarks a mob broke into the hall and attempted to shut down the rally. Maria Chapman, Lucretia Mott, Angelina Grimke Weld, and

Abby Kelley all made antislavery remarks despite threats from the protestors, and the rally concluded as planned. The next day, however, the mob returned and burned the empty hall to the ground.

The violence against abolitionists took a significant toll. In July 1837 a mob in Cincinnati destroyed the office of abolitionist and philanthropist James Birney and threw a printing press into the Ohio River. In November, rioters in Alton, Illinois, killed Elijah P. Lovejoy, the publisher of the *St. Louis Observer* and a promoter of immediate emancipation. "Patriotism, politics, commerce, social influence, churchly ties, all united in condemning not the menacing slave power but the northern resistant to its despotism," wrote Rev. Lucius C. Matlock. "The lamb and not the wolf was guilty of disturbance."[81]

In 1842 Garrison again sought to redefine the goals of the abolitionist movement by thrusting forward the issue of "disunion." "I am for repeal of the union between the north and the south—alias, between Liberty and Slavery," Garrison wrote in March to a New York minister.[82] A few days later he told his friend George W. Benson that the principles and pursuits of the North and South had irretrievably diverged, and preserving the Union protected and affirmed the cause of slavery. "We must dissolve all connection with those murderers . . . of liberty, and traffickers in human flesh," Garrison said.[83] In April he publicly announced his support for the repeal of the Union in the *Liberator*, and on May 6, 1842, he launched an attack on the U.S. Constitution.[84]

In an editorial in the *Liberator*, Garrison wrote that if the Constitution sanctioned slavery, it was "a covenant with death and an agreement with hell."[85] Garrison alarmed some of his supporters, who feared that his provocative comments undermined the abolitionist movement. A writer for the *New York Tribune* who was sympathetic to Garrison said he was "like a man who has been in the habit of screaming himself hoarse to make the deaf hear" and who can "no longer pitch his voice on a key agreeable to common ears."[86] Garrison's friend and ally Lydia Maria Child briefly disavowed Garrison's stand. She expected the defenders of slavery to seize on Garrison's words as evidence of the anti-American nature of the abolitionist movement. The New York press proved Child correct; the publisher of the *New York Courier and Enquirer*, James Watson Webb, called Garrison's campaign for disunion "treasonable, revolutionary and dangerous."[87] Child later said that while she agreed with Garrison's sentiments,

"If precisely the same ideas had been worded a little differently, they could not have been made such effectual use of by our enemies."[88]

Garrison did not view his criticism of the Constitution and call for breaking up the Union as sensationalism for its own sake. He wanted to counter the threats of secession made by leaders in South Carolina and other proslavery states that had surfaced as early as the 1820s.[89] Garrison viewed the secession threats as negotiating tactics designed to leverage the growth of slavery and believed the best response was to answer in kind. He noted that John Quincy Adams's petition to dismantle the Union "resulted in frightening the boastful South almost out of her wits."[90]

Garrison found himself embroiled in another controversy concerning civil rights—the fight for equal rights for women. "As our object is *universal* emancipation—to redeem woman as well as man from a servile to an equal condition—we shall go for the rights of woman to their utmost extent," Garrison wrote.[91] His strong stand in favor of women's rights alienated other leaders of the abolitionist movement, including Arthur and Lewis Tappan. While attending the Anti-Slavery World Convention in London in June 1840, Garrison refused to take his seat as a delegate after convention officers declined to seat women delegates from the United States. When officials ordered the women to sit in the balcony, Garrison decided to give up his status as a delegate and join the women. Dignitaries made their way to the balcony to pay respect to Garrison, Lucretia Mott, and others who joined in the protest. Garrison wrote that "the rejection of the American female delegation by the London Convention" succeeded in doing more "to bring up for consideration of Europe the rights of women, than could have been accomplished in any other manner."[92]

14 : Dred Scott and the Winds of Change

During the years that Prudence Crandall and William Lloyd Garrison worked together to create her Canterbury school in the early 1830s, Garrison visited her school on only a handful of occasions—primarily because of the warrants for his arrest. In the summer of 1840—six years after the school had closed and Andrew Judson had withdrawn the libel charges—Garrison once again decided to see the house that had served as Prudence Crandall's school. He left Boston by train with his wife Helen. In 1834 the only way from Boston to Brooklyn, Connecticut, was a bumpy, daylong stagecoach ride that departed in total darkness at three in the morning and arrived in the evening. In 1840 the quick, morning train ride from Boston to Connecticut was a "pleasant jaunt" on "a straight path, leveling the hills and exalting the valleys, and using steam power."[1]

Garrison's friend and collaborator Oliver Johnson accompanied the Garrisons. They arrived in the town center and walked around the former schoolhouse that had created so much controversy. Crandall had left Connecticut; she had sold the house soon after the school closed in 1834 and moved to Boonville, New York. Across the street from the school to the east stood the Congregational Church, site of the town meetings where Samuel May and Arnold Buffum had argued on Crandall's behalf. On the other corner was the home of Andrew T. Judson. A man sat on the front porch—it was Judson—watching Garrison and Johnson. "We saw that unhappy and guilty man sitting at his front-door," Garrison wrote.[2] The two former opponents looked at each other from across the road but did not speak.

During the controversy surrounding Prudence Crandall's school, Andrew Judson lost his bid for reelection to the state legislature in 1834. The next year he won a seat in Congress. Garrison wrote a letter to Congressman Judson in 1836 and enclosed a petition signed by forty-six residents of Brooklyn, Connecticut, asking Judson to end slavery in the District of Columbia.[3] Judson did not agree and did not respond. When Garrison saw Judson at his home in 1840, Judson was a judge for the U.S. District Court of Connecticut; President Andrew Jackson had appointed him to the bench on June 28, 1836.[4]

Judson stayed involved in the local community and served as president of the Windham County Temperance Society. A report issued by the temperance society in 1838, written by Judson, attacked tavern owners who supplied alcohol to inebriates. Judson questioned the propriety of serving drunkards and allowing them, "under its influence, to go away and insult the innocent—to destroy his property—to depredate upon his rights—to break up his dwelling—or fire his habitation."[5] The same question in a different context might have been asked of Judson and the opponents of Prudence Crandall's school. "It is a sound principle," Judson wrote, "that every man in community, should so use his own, as not to injure his neighbor."[6]

If Garrison had cared to walk across the street, he and Judson might have had an engaging conversation about a recent court case involving Judge Judson. In late 1839 and early 1840, Judson presided over the most famous case of his judicial career. His ruling stunned his supporters and detractors, as well as President Martin Van Buren. The legal essence of the case involved criminal law, shipping, and the right to certain goods. The goods in question, however, were human cargo—slaves—according to the crew of the ship.

On June 28, 1839, a sleek schooner left the port of Havana, bound for Puerto Principe, Cuba, and its many sugarcane plantations. The two-mast vessel, originally named *Friendship* when it was built six years earlier in Baltimore, was light, unarmed, and built for speed and maneuverability. The cargo consisted of fifty-three blacks recently kidnapped from Africa. Spanish law prohibited the importation of slaves into Cuba, but slave traders routinely bribed officials and reclassified the blacks as Ladinos, or Cuban-born slaves. The Africans broke free from their chains on July 1, 1839, killed the captain, and took control of the schooner—the *Amistad*—and forced the crew to sail toward Africa. José Ruiz and Pedro Montez sailed east during the day but tricked the Africans and turned north and west at night. They made their way up the East Coast of the United States and sailed into a harbor near Montauk, New York. When the Africans tried to enlist the Montauk sailors to sail their ship back to Africa, some-one alerted the U.S. Navy. The warship USS *Washington*, commanded by Lieutenant Thomas R. Gedney, intercepted the *Amistad* and towed it to the port of New London, Connecticut.

Judge Andrew Judson convened a special session of the Federal District Court for Connecticut on board the *Washington* in New London. Crew members Ruiz and Montez claimed they were legally transporting slaves under Cuban law when the slaves took over the ship and murdered the captain. The court did not hear the Africans' side of the story because no one could understand or translate their language.[7]

Newspapers in Connecticut and New York sensationalized the story of the mysterious slave ship commanded by blacks. Lewis Tappan read about their arrest and joined with Joshua Leavitt, the editor of the *Emancipator*, and Simeon S. Jocelyn, to raise funds for a legal defense. Tappan traveled to the New Haven County Jail on September 6, 1839, to meet with the Africans and realized that he needed to find someone who could under-stand their language.

Tappan recruited professor and linguist Joshua Willard Gibbs of Yale University. Gibbs correctly guessed they were from Sierra Leone and spoke Mende.[8] Unfortunately, Gibbs could not speak Mende. Gibbs and the Amistad Committee hit on an ingenious strategy; Gibbs consulted his books and learned how to count to ten in Mende and then patrolled the busy docks of the New York harbor calling out the numbers to see if any of the sailors understood. Using this approach Gibbs met John Ferry and James Covey, who provided detailed descriptions of the Africans' ordeal.[9]

Two judges presided over the criminal trial in the U.S. Circuit Court: Andrew Judson, who shifted over from his district court post, and Smith Thompson, a U.S. Supreme Court Justice. Thompson's legal and political background informed his views in the *Amistad* matter. He served as chief justice of the New York Supreme Court for four years until his friend, President James Monroe, appointed him secretary of the Navy in 1818. Five years later, Monroe elevated Thompson to the U.S. Supreme Court.[10] While serving on the high Court, Thompson ran for governor of New York in 1829 and lost to Martin Van Buren.[11] During the 1830s, Thomp-son opposed the "strong presidency" philosophy of President Andrew

Jackson, including the idea that executive branch officers could ignore duties imposed by Congress. Thompson's political views likely played a role in his view of the *Amistad* case. One commentator described Justice Thompson as a "bitter political enemy" of both Presidents Jackson and Van Buren.[12]

Federal prosecutor William Holabird proceeded with the trial of the Africans for murder and piracy. The attorneys for the Africans, Theodore Sedgwick of New York and Roger Sherman Baldwin of New Haven, argued that the court had no jurisdiction over their clients. After the prosecution and defense concluded their arguments, Justice Thompson read the decision from the bench.

"My feelings are personally as abhorrent to the system of slavery as those of any man here, but I must on my oath, pronounce what the laws are on the subject."[13] Thompson ruled that the court had no jurisdiction over the defendants for criminal wrongdoing. "If the offense of murder has been committed on board a foreign vessel, with a foreign crew, and with foreign papers, this is not an offence against the United States. It is an offence against the country to which the vessel belonged."[14]

Thompson's ruling that the court had no criminal law jurisdiction over the defendants—a victory for the defense attorneys—was tempered by his refusal to set the defendants free. "The court does not undertake to say that these Africans have no right to their freedom, but leave that matter in litigation to the District Court, subject to appeal."[15] Justice Thompson referred the question—of whether the Africans were slaves—to District Court Judge Andrew Judson.

Hundreds of spectators crowded into the Federal District Court of New Haven on Tuesday, January 7, 1840, for a trial that lasted five days. Prosecutor Holabird argued that the *Amistad* transported slaves under Spanish authority, and accordingly the slaves belonged to Ruiz and Montez. President Martin Van Buren provided Holabird with specific orders regarding the *Amistad* case. The *Amistad* case mattered greatly to Van Buren. A New York Democrat, Van Buren served as President Andrew Jackson's vice president during Jackson's second term and was elected president in 1836. Shortly after taking office, however, an economic calamity known as the panic of 1837—caused by rampant real estate speculation and overextension of credit—brought ruin to the nation's economy. Van Buren's popularity suffered; by the fall of 1839, he rightly was concerned about his chances for reelection in 1840. Van Buren worried in particular about his ability to win southern votes as a New Yorker and aggressively cultivated support in the slave-holding states. Van Buren described himself as an "inflexible and uncompromising opponent" of abolishing slavery in the District of Columbia.[16] As to slavery in general, Van Buren said he would "resist the slightest interference with it in the states where it exists."[17]

The *Amistad* case presented a chance for President Van Buren to show the southern states that he not only respected slavery in the United States, but also supported the slave-owning and trading rights of other countries. He instructed federal prosecutors to ensure the return of the *Amistad* and its cargo of slaves to the Spanish crew. Van Buren ordered his secretary of state and attorney general to help influence the outcome of the *Amistad* case. Secretary of State John Forsyth communicated regularly with prosecutor Holabird and told him he must "take care that no proceeding . . . places the vessel, cargo, or slaves beyond the control of the Federal Executive."[18] The attorney general, Felix Grundy of Tennessee, claimed that the crew of the *Amistad* possessed documents that proved the ship's passengers were slaves. At various times the secretary of state and attorney general recommended the immediate removal of the Africans to Cuba without trial; they argued that U.S. courts had no jurisdiction over a matter governed by Spanish law.[19]

Van Buren believed Judson quickly would rule in their favor. Judson was no abolitionist; he had helped lead the fight against Prudence Crandall's school for black women. In addition, Judson was a fellow Democrat. Judson and Van Buren shared common political loyalties, and Judson knew that Van Buren and the Democrats faced a tough fight in 1840. A favorable resolution of the *Amistad* case—one that reassured southern states—would help Van Buren win reelection.

President Van Buren ordered the USS *Grampus*, a twelve-cannon schooner designed to battle pirate ships, to sail to the port of New Haven and stand ready to seize the slaves and deliver them to Cuba and Spanish control. The abolitionists feared that Van Buren would seize the Africans and send them back to Cuba before the conclusion of the trial, and they requested that Connecticut Governor William W. Ellsworth—the former lead counsel for Prudence Crandall—provide protection and security for the Africans.[20] Ellsworth, who as governor had continued his law practice, could not help his abolitionist friends; he was involved in the *Amis-*

tad case as legal counsel for Captain Henry Green. Green had met the Africans who went ashore at Montauk and filed a claim for the *Amistad* and its contents.

William Ellsworth and Andrew Judson found themselves together once again in a high-profile legal case. In the six years that had elapsed since the final *Crandall* case, their respective careers had flourished— Judson as a congressman and federal judge, and Ellsworth as an attorney and two-term governor. Ellsworth argued to Judge Judson that Lieutenant Gedney had no right to the salvage value of the *Amistad*. If his action warranted the award of the salvage value of the vessel, the money should go to the U.S. government and not Gedney personally, Ellsworth said. Captain Green had tried to assist the Africans and had the better claim to the ship, Ellsworth argued.[21]

In the weeks leading up to the trial, Lewis Tappan and the lawyers for the Africans had discovered important new evidence. William Lloyd Garrison met Richard R. Madden—the British Commissioner of the Anglo-Spanish Board in Havana—while Madden was in Boston to assist in an investigation of the U.S. Consul in Havana.[22] Madden prosecuted the illegal slave trade in Cuba. Garrison relayed to Lewis Tappan that Madden "has in his possession a large amount of valuable information" that could help the Africans.[23]

Madden testified at the Amistad trial regarding the documents the prosecution had introduced to prove the prisoners were slaves and said the documents were obvious forgeries.[24] In addition, Madden said the prisoners were not Ladinos but rather illegally kidnapped Africans, and Spanish and British law required that the court set them free.[25] Prosecutor Holabird objected to Madden's testimony, but Judson overruled the objection.

As the trial progressed, the Africans told their story of how slave traders had captured them in Sierra Leone at gunpoint and led them onto a slave ship bound for Havana. "We were chained—hand and feet together," Joseph Cinque told the court. "We were beaten."[26] The slave traders packed five hundred Africans onto the slave ship *Tecora*; the trip to Havana lasted two months. The crew did not take enough water for the captives, and one-third of the Africans died on the journey.[27] Once in Cuba, the slave traders forged documents that gave the Africans new Spanish names—Sengbe Pieh became Joseph Cinque—and forced the

Africans onto the *Amistad*. The court heard the story of the bloody uprising and takeover of the ship and the unintentional landing in New York.

The *Amistad* case brought together many different and sometimes feuding factions of the antislavery movement. Lewis and Arthur Tappan worked together with William Lloyd Garrison. Those who favored immediate emancipation and supporters of a gradual end to slavery joined forces to advocate for the release of the Africans. Ministers of numerous denominations worked for the Africans' freedom. Even colonizationists— including those who opposed emancipation—joined with abolitionists in advocating the Africans' return to Africa.[28]

After reviewing all the evidence and testimony, Judge Andrew Judson read his decision to the crowd assembled in the New Haven courthouse on Monday, January 13, 1840. Judson identified two main issues. First, the court had to decide how to dispose of the *Amistad*. Second, Judson said the court would resolve the fate of the Africans.

As to the first question, Judson rejected William Ellsworth's salvage claims on behalf of Captain Henry Green. "This claim is rested upon the idea that they had taken possession of the vessel," Judson said. "The facts proved will not sustain this claim."[29] Judson may have taken some satisfaction in denying the claim argued by Ellsworth, his former legal rival, but Judson's reasoning was sound. Captain Green never set foot on the *Amistad* and never took possession of the ship or its contents.[30] Judson did not, however, reward Navy Lieutenant Thomas Gedney with ownership of the ship and its contents. "The decree will be, that the schooner and her effects be delivered up to the Spanish government, upon the payment, at a reasonable rate, for the services in saving this property from entire loss."[31] Judson ruled that the "reasonable rate" awarded to Gedney would be one-third of the appraised value of the ship and its goods.

As to the fate of the Africans, Judson had considered the claims of the Spanish government and Ruiz and Montez. Even if the Africans were slaves, the Spanish government had no title to them and no legal claim, Judson said. As to Ruiz and Montez, "they have furnished no proof of payment, they have shown no bill of sale, no witness has sworn that he was present when these negroes were sold."[32] Judson concluded that the slave traders had kidnapped the Africans and forced them to leave their country against their will. Judson pledged by his ruling "to return to the land of their nativity all such Africans as may have been brought from thence wrongfully."[33] If the Africans wished to return to Sierra Leone, Judson said, the laws of the United States provided the means to send them home and "bid them God Speed."[34]

Judson's ruling shocked President Van Buren and his administration. The USS *Grampus*, which had stood ready to whisk the Mende away and deliver them back to Cuba and slavery, sailed away from New Haven without the Africans in tow. Van Buren instructed prosecutor Holabird to file an immediate appeal to the U.S. Circuit Court. On April 29, 1840, Justice Smith Thompson, the former gubernatorial opponent of Van Buren, upheld Judge Andrew Judson's ruling. Holabird then filed an appeal of Thompson's decision with the U.S. Supreme Court. Unfortunately for the Africans who remained in custody, the Supreme Court did not decide the appeal until March 9, 1841, nearly one year later. Former President John Quincy Adams argued the Mende's case before the Supreme Court. When Justice Joseph Story wrote the opinion for the Court, he upheld Thompson's circuit court opinion and Andrew Judson's district court ruling. The Africans won their freedom.[35]

The Supreme Court ratified the most significant judicial opinion of Andrew Judson's career as a judge. Judson shocked observers by ignoring the wishes of the president of the United States and the supporters of slavery. Those who had expected party loyalty from Judson did not know his political history. Judson had moved from the Federalist Party, to the Toleration Party, to the Jackson Party that became the new Democratic Party. As a judge, Judson found his new constituency in the judiciary, and here he had succeeded in working closely with and winning the support of Supreme Court Justice Smith Thompson, a political opponent of President Van Buren.

Judson also knew that public opinion had shifted since his opposition to Prudence Crandall and her school for black women. Shortly after his appointment to the district court, Judson wrote a brief autobiography of his life and achievements.[36] He discussed his years of service in the state legislature and as state's attorney for Windham County. Judson made no mention of his success in passing the Black Law that helped close Prudence Crandall's school and prohibited the teaching of blacks from other states. Times had changed in Connecticut; in 1838 the legislature repealed the Black Law. Judson had learned during the War of 1812 that public opinion could shift quickly and destroy political careers. Judson may have made his surprising decision in the *Amistad* case based on a changed political landscape. Other factors, however, likely moved Judson.

The story of the Mende people and the account of their kidnapping unfolded unexpectedly in Judson's courtroom; he listened carefully to Cinque and his desire to return to Africa. Both the law and the facts favored the Mende. Finally, setting the Africans free to return home to Sierra Leone was colonization in action. Since Judson had long supported colonization and continued to serve as president of the Windham County Colonization Society, returning the Mende to Africa must have appealed greatly to him. Regardless of his reasons or motivations, Judson's unexpected ruling won the respect of those who opposed slavery and the gratitude of the Mende.

The Mende lived for a time in Farmington, Connecticut, and attended lectures and gatherings where they described their ordeal and raised money for their return trip to Africa. On November 27, 1841, the thirty-five remaining Mende boarded the ship *Gentlemen* and sailed for Africa. In January 1842 they reached Sierra Leone and found their country transformed and decimated by slave wars. Slave traders had enlisted different chiefdoms of Mende into war against each other for the capture of slaves. In a short time, Sengbe Pieh and the other former *Amistad* captives disappeared into the country's violent interior and were never conclusively heard from again.

Andrew Judson's *Amistad* ruling did not presage a change in Judson's views toward emancipation or the abolitionists. In September 1850, Congress passed the Fugitive Slave Act, which required all states, including free, nonslaveholding states, to return any escaped slave to his or her owner. In an early and controversial test case, Judson upheld the return of an escaped slave. The *Washington Union* praised Judson for enforcing the controversial law and resisting the arguments of the abolitionists. The *Union* called Judson a "clear-headed, competent, and independent officer . . . Such judges as he are invaluable in these times of turmoil and agitation."[37]

Andrew Judson died in 1853 at his home in Canterbury, after a forty-year career in public service that began in 1813. Judson's death did not erase his notoriety in the minds of Prudence Crandall's supporters—they neither forgot nor forgave Judson. When Samuel May wrote a comprehensive book about the Fugitive Slave Law in 1861, twenty-seven years after Prudence Crandall's school had closed and eight years after Judson had died, May pointedly noted that Judson was "notorious for being the leader of the mob which broke up Miss Crandall's school for colored girls in Canterbury, Connecticut."[38]

Working with Prudence Crandall and William Lloyd Garrison forever changed Samuel May. Beginning in Brooklyn, Connecticut, May's home provided a reliable stop on the Underground Railroad. "When I was living in the eastern part of Connecticut, I had fugitives addressed to my care," May recalled.[39] "Fugitives came to me from Maryland, Virginia, Kentucky, Tennessee, and Louisiana. After I came to reside in Syracuse I had much to do as a station-keeper or conductor on the Underground Railroad."[40] In the years following the end of Crandall's school, May immersed himself in antislavery activity. May's efforts reached a flash point in August 1835 at an antislavery rally at the Freewill Baptist Church in Haverhill, Massachusetts.

"I had spoke about fifteen minutes, when the most hideous outcries, yells, from a crowd of men who had surrounded the house startled us, and then came heavy missiles against the doors and blinds of the windows," May said.[41] May ordered everyone to remain calm. As May walked out of the church, a young woman seized his arm and led him through the hostile crowd, shielding him from attack. May thanked the "brave young lady who would not leave me to go through the mob alone."[42] May's courageous protector was Harriet Minot, William Lloyd Garrison's young friend and correspondent.[43] As May escaped, he noticed "a posse of men more savage than the rest, dragging a cannon, which they intended to explode against the building and at the same time tear away the stairs."[44]

May's dedication to the antislavery cause took a toll on his ministry, and he resigned from the Unitarian Church in Brooklyn, Connecticut, in 1835, after fourteen years as pastor. May subsequently served as minister of the Second Church of Christ in South Scituate, Massachusetts, and later joined Horace Mann's education reform movement as principal of the state normal school in Lexington, Massachusetts. He ended his career in the ministry as pastor of the Unitarian Church of the Messiah in Syracuse, New York, where he preached for twenty-two years.

The activism May had displayed during the Prudence Crandall controversy continued throughout his life. He noticed malnourished and neglected boys working on the Erie Canal. The young men, many of them still children, were housed in primitive shacks and received no education or health care. When May spoke with the boys, he realized that many were orphans who had no protectors or advocates. May alerted other ministers to the plight of the "canal boys" and took their fight to the New York State Legislature. The legislators knew nothing of the canal boys, but they knew the commercial developers of the Erie Canal and the significant resources they commanded. The developers successfully blocked all reform except to punish any canal boys who became delinquents. For May, the only benefit from his unsuccessful campaign was that "it became more difficult for the public to wholly forget the claims of an unfortunate class."[45]

May also took an interest in the local Native American population at the nearby Onondaga Indian Reservation.[46] A reporter noted that the "reservation, most of which is very good land, is quite near a large city, and that if [the Indians] could be cleared away . . . there would be a lot of chances of land grabbing through the ordinary methods of the strong and crafty."[47] May saw extreme poverty at the reservation. Children did not have enough to eat, and adults barely survived through farming and hunting. No schools existed. May returned to the legislature in Albany. This time lawmakers responded favorably and passed *An Act to Provide for the Education of the Children of the Indians of the Onondaga Reservation*. The legislature appropriated funds to create a school on the reservation and specifically noted, "The school provided for by virtue of this act shall be subject to the visitation and inspection of Samuel J. May."[48]

While some abolitionists did not embrace women's rights—they thought the issue distracted from the goal of ending slavery—the men who worked directly with Prudence Crandall all championed equality for women. Samuel May encouraged his congregation to support women's rights.[49] "The Creator intended them to stand on an entire equality with men in their domestic, social, legal, and political relations," May said.[50] "If the people have the right of self-government, then I am unable to see why a half of the people have a right to govern the whole."[51]

In his support for women's rights, Charles Burleigh went further than either Samuel May or William Lloyd Garrison by suggesting that men share in childcare duties and help prepare meals and wash clothes.[52] Charles Burleigh had assisted Garrison after Crandall's school closed and later served as the primary speaker at the Free Congregational Society of Florence, Massachusetts.[53] He was an early advocate of abolishing the death penalty, an idea many considered more radical than immediate emancipation.[54] Burleigh pledged not to cut his shoulder-length hair until emancipation. He kept a full beard "covering his face and breast, so that you could see little more than his nose and eyes above the top vest bottom."[55]

Charles's brother William Burleigh ended his teaching career when Crandall's school closed and began a career in journalism. William traveled to Pittsburgh in 1837 and became the editor of the *Christian Witness and Temperance Banner*. In 1841 Burleigh published a book of poems and honored his friend and coworker Almira Crandall with the poem "Almira." During Prudence Crandall's many travels, Almira Crandall and William Burleigh had managed the school and faced the hostility of the community.

"They tell me thou art dying, though when I saw thee last, life's crimson glow brightened thy cheek," Burleigh wrote. "Alas, sweet friend, thy cheek is faded, and thy eye is dim . . . Thy coming step was music, and thy voice bade the desponding soul again rejoice. Thine was the power, sweet friend, to cure the smart of sorrow's wounds . . . Death is strong, and terrible in his strength—for earth thou art not long."[56] At the end of the poem Burleigh noted, "The preceding stanzas were written a few days before the death of Almira C. Rand—better known as Almira Crandall. . . . The hopes of her friends proved delusive, and the grave received, in the morning of her days, all that earth could claim of one so lovely."[57]

William Burleigh traveled throughout the country and spoke at antislavery and temperance conventions. In April of 1842, he met Charles Dickens during one of Dickens's tours of the United States and "enjoyed a short but pleasant intimacy during the stay of the distinguished novelist."[58] Burleigh's happy memory of his meeting with Charles Dickens differed from Dickens's own recollection.

"My friend the New Englander, of whom I wrote last night, is perhaps the most intolerable bore on this vast continent," Dickens wrote on the steamboat *Messenger*, traveling from Pittsburgh to Cincinnati. Dickens compared Burleigh's voice to the buzzing of a gigantic bee. "He drones, and snuffles, and writes poems, and talks small philosophy and metaphysics, and never *will* be quiet, under any circumstances. He is going to a great temperance convention in Cincinnati, along with a doctor . . .

I dodge them about the boat. Whenever I appear on deck, I see them bearing down upon me—and fly."[59]

■ In the fall of 1833, at the same time Prudence Crandall suffered a legal defeat at the hands of Judge Daggett, Dr. John Emerson received an appointment for the U.S. Army and reported for duty at Fort Armstrong in Rock Island, Illinois. Before leaving Missouri for Fort Armstrong, Emerson purchased a slave. Emerson had no idea that his purchase of a black man named Dred Scott would lead to one of the most notorious decisions by the U.S. Supreme Court. The Court's ruling would cite Prudence Crandall's case and David Daggett's opinion and help plunge the United States into the Civil War.

After Dr. Emerson died in 1843, Dred Scott sued for his freedom claiming that his residence in Illinois and Wisconsin, where slavery was prohibited, terminated his status as a slave. The case moved slowly through the courts for ten years, culminating in an appeal to the U.S. Supreme Court. On March 6, 1857, Chief Justice Roger B. Taney of Maryland delivered the opinion.[60]

For many years Congress sought to avoid a breakup of the United States along the lines of slave and free states. In 1820, Representative Henry Clay of Kentucky and Senator Jesse Thomas of Illinois negotiated the "Missouri Compromise," allowing Missouri to join the Union as a slave state and Maine to join as a free state.[61] Other attempts to resolve tensions between the slave and free states included the Compromise of 1850, which addressed western territories acquired through war with Mexico. Senator Henry Clay, then seventy years old, joined Senator Stephen Douglas of Illinois to pass legislation that admitted California as a free state and allowed the new western territories to decide whether to permit slavery. Congress passed the Fugitive Slave Act of 1850, requiring the return of escaped slaves, in an additional attempt to mollify the slave states.[62]

The era of compromise began to break down with the passage of the Kansas-Nebraska Act in 1854, allowing the voters of those two territories to decide whether to embrace slavery. Opposing factions set up rival territorial governments within Kansas. Gunfights erupted and lives were lost. On May 21, 1856, pro- and antislavery forces fought a pitched battle in the antislavery stronghold of Lawrence. Violence escalated to the point where observers called the territory "bleeding Kansas."[63] Slavery supporters held a referendum in 1855 that resulted in a proslavery victory amid allegations of fraud. In a speech made shortly after the passage of the Kansas-Nebraska Act in 1854, Abraham Lincoln said the act threatened the nation.

"It is an aggravation, rather, of the only one thing which ever endangers the Union," Lincoln said. "Is it not probable that the contest will come to blows, and bloodshed? Could there be a more apt invention to bring about collision and violence on the slavery question, than this Nebraska project?"[64]

Senator Charles Sumner of Massachusetts opposed further compromise. "It is the rape of a virgin territory, compelling it to the hateful embrace of slavery," Sumner told the Senate.[65] Two days later, Congressman Preston Brooks of South Carolina confronted Sumner in his capitol office and severely beat him with a gold-topped cane; Sumner collapsed on the floor gravely injured, bleeding from the head.[66]

In this explosive atmosphere, Chief Justice Taney and the Supreme Court considered the *Dred Scott* case. The makeup and politics of the Court had changed significantly since 1834, when the Court could have considered an appeal of the Connecticut Supreme Court's ruling in *Crandall*. In 1834 the U.S. Supreme Court consisted of seven justices. A majority came from northern states: Massachusetts, Ohio, Pennsylvania, and New York. Chief Justice John Marshall of Virginia was in the twilight of a remarkable career as chief justice, and he abhorred slavery. Marshall was not, however, an abolitionist. Historian Albert Jeremiah Beveridge observed that Marshall "regretted the existence of slavery, feared the results of it, [and] saw no way of getting rid of it."[67]

The Marshall Court never had the opportunity to consider Prudence Crandall's case. For procedural reasons, the Court likely would have avoided ruling on the controversial issue of black citizenship. During the Court's January 1835 term, the Court consisted of six out of seven justices, and Marshall stated that as a result of the vacancy, "constitutional cases will not be taken up."[68] The Court, however, did not strictly adhere to this guideline during its 1835 term and decided some cases on constitutional grounds.[69] If the Marshall Court—with a majority of northern state justices who opposed slavery—had heard the *Crandall* appeal and reached the merits of the case, a ruling that free blacks possessed some or all of the rights of citizens would have been stunning but not impossible.

When Chief Justice Marshall died in July 1835, President Andrew Jackson filled Marshall's vacancy with Roger Taney of Maryland. In 1837 Congress increased the size of the Court from seven to nine justices. Unlike the Marshall Court of 1834, the Taney Court in 1857 consisted of a majority of five justices from southern states. Of the four justices from northern states, two, Robert Grier of Pennsylvania and Samuel Nelson of New York, did not strongly oppose slavery. The justices initially favored ruling that Missouri law controlled Dred Scott's fate; they favored upholding the decisions of the Missouri Supreme Court and the U.S. Circuit Court and avoiding altogether the questions of whether Congress had the power to regulate slavery or whether a free black was a citizen. This holding would have been consistent with a nearly identical case, *Strader v. Graham*, decided by the Taney Court in 1850. "Every state has an undoubted right to determine the status, or domestic and social condition of the persons domiciled within its territory," Taney wrote in *Strader*. "There is nothing in the Constitution of the United States that can in any degree control the law of Kentucky upon this subject. . . . It was exclusively in the power of Kentucky to determine for itself whether their employment in another state should or should not make them free on their return."[70]

Increased tensions regarding slavery prompted the justices to reconsider their decision to dispose of the *Dred Scott* case on jurisdictional grounds. Chief Justice Taney and a majority of the Court made the politically charged decision to abandon the precedent in *Strader* and settle once and for all America's slavery dilemma—in favor of slavery. Taney ruled that Congress had no power to prohibit slavery in any territory or state. The Missouri Compromise, which prohibited slavery in certain areas, was unconstitutional according to Taney. He also said slaves and free blacks were not U.S. citizens.

Taney cited *Crandall v. State* to support his conclusion. "Chief Justice Daggett, before whom the case was tried, held that persons of that description were not citizens of a State, within the meaning of the word citizen in the Constitution of the United States," Taney wrote, "and were not therefore entitled to the privileges and immunities of citizens in other States."[71] Taney acknowledged that the Connecticut Supreme Court did not specifically affirm Judge Daggett's opinion and dismissed the case on a technical issue. Taney said *Crandall* was important, however, because "we expect to find the laws of that state as lenient and favorable to the subject race as those of any other State in the Union." If Connecticut did not see fit to elevate blacks to the status of citizens, Taney argued, "we shall hardly find them elevated to a higher rank anywhere else."[72]

At the time of the first Crandall trial in 1833, the *Baltimore Gazette and Daily Advertiser* wrote, "If the people of Connecticut are so incensed at the establishment of a public school among themselves for the instruction of blacks . . . we take it for granted that they are willing to show all charity to the prejudices of the Southern people in similar matters."[73] After the *Dred Scott* decision, newspapers in the South once again reminded their northern neighbors of Connecticut's Black Law and the *Crandall* case. The *Macon Weekly Telegraph* published an editorial titled "The Abolitionists Confronted with One of Their Own Decisions" and asserted that "the Supreme Court has decided no new point in the *Dred Scott* case," but rather followed Judge Daggett's ruling regarding Prudence Crandall.[74] The *Telegraph* editors wrote that "good old Puritan Connecticut, the home of a vigorous race of white men and the land of pumpkin pie," did not treat blacks as citizens.[75]

Two of Prudence Crandall's attorneys, Calvin Goddard and Henry Strong, did not live to see the *Dred Scott* decision and the citation of the *Crandall* case. Lead prosecutor Andrew Judson also died before the ruling in *Dred Scott*. History does not record what the other attorney for the state, Chauncey Cleveland, and Crandall's lead defense attorney, William W. Ellsworth, thought about the controversial decision. In 1857 Ellsworth served as a justice of the Connecticut Supreme Court, and Chauncey Cleveland practiced law after having served as a state legislator, congressman, and governor. Cleveland's views concerning blacks and slavery had evolved significantly following the *Crandall* case. Cleveland had joined the antislavery Republican Party; in 1860 he supported the nomination of Abraham Lincoln.

The *Hartford Daily Courant* gently criticized the *Dred Scott* decision. The *Courant* took issue with Taney's misleading citation of *Crandall v. State*. "Judge Daggett may have been right or wrong in that opinion. Our Supreme Court have never approved, and never in express words, disapproved his opinion."[76] Taney ruled too broadly, the *Courant* said. The

Courant contrasted Taney's opinion with Judge Thomas Williams's technical reversal in *Crandall*, which avoided the constitutional question of black citizenship. The *Courant* said Taney and the Court similarly should have found a way to avoid the divisive question. What the *Courant* and the public did not know until a letter discussing the *Crandall* judicial deliberations was published in 1886, was that all of the Connecticut justices except David Daggett favored ruling that free blacks *were* American citizens—the central issue of the *Crandall* case.[77]

The Connecticut legislature passed a resolution on July 4, 1857, condemning the *Dred Scott* decision. The resolution said that the founding fathers meant to "establish a government giving equal political rights to all" and that slavery "was at war with the principles upon which our government is founded." The legislators resolved that the justices in *Dred Scott* had "volunteered opinions which are not law" and "promulgated such opinions for partisan purposes, and thereby have lowered the dignity of said court and diminished the respect heretofore awarded to its decisions."[78]

The *Dred Scott* case provided one clear outcome. The era of legislative compromise designed to preserve both the Union and slavery was over. Chief Justice Taney—a defender of slavery and the old South—had unwittingly accelerated the forces that would destroy both slavery and the old South. "Slavery and free institutions cannot exist in contact for a long time," Edward Downing Barber said in 1834. "The one, must sooner or later, destroy the other."[79]

When Justice Taney wrote about the *Crandall* case and the Black Law in 1857, he failed to reveal a key fact. The Connecticut legislature had repealed the law in 1838. At that time legislators had recited many of the arguments put forth in 1833 by Prudence Crandall's attorneys. One of the prime sponsors of the original legislation, Senator Philip Pearl—who had recommended approval of the Black Law in 1833 and whose daughter had attended Prudence Crandall's original school for girls—had reconsidered his actions after a long conversation with Theodore Dwight Weld. Pearl said that his support for the Black Law had resulted from "my prejudices against that poor persecuted class of people."[80] Pearl prepared a petition to repeal the law on the grounds of injustice and unconstitutionality. "I could weep tears of blood for the part I took in that matter," Pearl said. "I now regard that law as utterly abominable."[81]

Repealing the Black Law in 1838 did not mean that Connecticut legislators favored racial equality and the sentiments later expressed in the 1857 resolution concerning the *Dred Scott* decision. In 1839, one year after the repeal of the Black Law, mill owner Asa Cutler of Killingly, who had sympathized with Prudence Crandall, submitted petitions calling for the repeal of all laws that discriminated on the basis of race.[82] Legislative leaders referred the petitions to a special committee.[83] State Senator Alvin Brown, the committee's chairman, recommended rejection of the petitions; his report said that "nothing can be more absurd, dangerous and impracticable than to attempt to establish political equality, among two races, with such marked distinctions, where no social equality exists."[84] The committee tabled Brown's findings and rejected the petitions.[85]

Abolitionists slowly moved public opinion in Massachusetts. William Cooper Nell—who as a fifteen-year-old witnessed the founding of the Massachusetts Anti-Slavery Society—led a campaign in 1840 to desegregate public schools. The effort culminated in the first desegregation court case in the United States, *Roberts v. the City of Boston*, which was decided in 1849. Attorney Charles Sumner, the future U.S. senator, argued, "There is nothing in these laws establishing any exclusive or separate school for any particular class, whether rich or poor, whether Catholic or Protestant, whether black or white."[86] The Massachusetts Supreme Court unanimously ruled against desegregation; however, in 1855 the Massachusetts legislature passed legislation overturning the *Roberts* case and desegregating all public schools in Massachusetts.[87] The *New York Herald* warned, "The North is to be Africanized. . . . God save the Commonwealth of Massachusetts!"[88]

Prudence Crandall Philleo continued to teach after she moved to Illinois. The Philleo Academy, a school she ran out of her home in Troy Grove in the 1850s, served the sons and daughters of her neighbors. She taught math, English, science, and world history in exchange for modest tuition that in hard times was a barter of goods and services. The income from the school supplemented the earnings from crops and livestock on Crandall's farm. The children of her brother Hezekiah—Obediah, Clarissa, and Reuben—joined Prudence in Illinois and helped run the farm.

Prudence and her husband, Calvin Philleo, lived apart for years at a time. Calvin suffered severe mood swings and often lashed out at those closest to him. Upon Calvin's request, Prudence allowed him to stay at her

Illinois farmhouse, but they led separate lives. She tolerated his eccentricities, and Calvin abided a house full of Crandalls. When he preached his caustic and unsettling sermons at local churches, the congregations rarely asked him to return.

The tragic deaths of Prudence's brother, sister, and father had prompted Prudence to investigate spiritualism. The movement had gained significant popularity in the United States and Europe as hundreds of intermediaries and clairvoyants promoted their abilities to hold séances and communicate—for a price—with friends and relatives who had passed away. A number of Crandall's friends and other abolitionists pursued spiritualism as a supplement to organized religion.[89] In 1857 William Lloyd Garrison and Susan B. Anthony exchanged correspondence discussing their mutual interest in spiritualism.[90] Garrison remained involved in spiritualism for the rest of his life; he said believing in spiritualism was no more or less irrational than believing in the claims of organized religion. Lydia Maria Child participated in a séance and concluded, "It cannot be trusted, and it is well that it cannot. We should become mere passive machines if spirits told us just what to do and what to believe."[91]

John Brown hated spiritualism.[92] As a strong Calvinist, Brown had no use for "knocking spirits" that made noises at parlor séances. Brown also had no use for the pacifism of William Lloyd Garrison.[93] Brown believed his life was preordained for the violent overthrow of slavery.

In October 1859, Brown traveled with twenty-one men to Harper's Ferry, Virginia, to seize weapons at the federal arsenal, take hostages, and flee as local slaves rallied to their support.[94] Brown previously had led violent attacks against supporters of slavery in Kansas and had traveled east to raise money for the war against slavery. Brown did not disguise his impatience with Garrison and others who opposed his call for the violent overthrow of slavery. The "milk and water principles" of the abolitionists accomplished nothing, Brown said.[95] "These men are all talk. What is needed is action—action!"[96]

At Harper's Ferry, Brown and a group of volunteers who supported his vision of the violent overthrow of slavery easily captured and took command of the government arsenal and rounded up prisoners from nearby farms. Instead of loading the weapons into their wagons and fleeing with the hostages, however, Brown decided to remain at the arsenal to await a divinely ordained slave revolt. The revolt never materialized, and U.S.

Army Lieutenant Colonel Robert E. Lee took command of a contingent of Marines, showered the arsenal with rifle fire, and captured Brown. Sixteen men were killed, including ten of Brown's contingent and two of his sons.

Newspapers rushed the story of Harper's Ferry into print throughout the United States. The raid's purpose—to spark a massive slave uprising—outraged and horrified many throughout the country. William Lloyd Garrison said Brown's attack was "misguided, wild, and apparently insane."[97] Garrison balanced his criticism of Brown's violent attack by remembering David Walker, who had asked blacks to take up arms against slavery. "Our views of war and bloodshed, even in the best of causes, are too well known to need repeating here," Garrison wrote, "but let no one who glories in the Revolutionary struggle of 1776 deny the right of the slaves to imitate the example of our fathers."[98]

Two weeks after Brown's capture, Wendell Phillips, a prominent Boston abolitionist, endorsed Brown's attack. "I think the lesson of the hour is insurrection," Phillips told an audience in Brooklyn, New York. "Insurrection of thought always precedes the insurrection of arms. The last twenty years have been an insurrection of thought. We seem to be entering on a new phase of this great American struggle."[99] Many in the South agreed with William Hand Browne: "The attempt itself might have been considered merely the deed of a few fanatical desperadoes, but for the universal uproar of enthusiastic approbation that burst out at the North. . . . The South could not be blamed for supposing that the North had passed from the stage of political antagonism to that of furious personal hate."[100] Nine days after the raid the editors of the *Richmond Enquirer* wrote, "The Harper's Ferry invasion has advanced the cause of Disunion more than any other event that has happened since the formation of the Government . . . it has revived with tenfold strength the desires of a Southern Confederacy."[101] William Lloyd Garrison questioned his own long-standing repudiation of violence: "If the doctrine of non-resistance ought to be spurned for oppressed white men, it is equally to be spurned for oppressed black men. Weapons of death for all, or for none, who are struggling to be free."[102]

Brown's attack on Harper's Ferry weighed heavily on the abolitionist movement and the campaign for president in 1860. In an appeal to western states, the proslavery Democratic Party nominated Illinois Senator

Stephen Douglas after fifty-nine ballots. Douglas defended slavery and championed legislative compromise, but southern delegates did not view Douglas as strong enough in his support of the South and walked out of the convention.

The antislavery Republican Party nominated an unknown one-term congressman from Illinois, Abraham Lincoln, who was personally opposed to slavery but did not support emancipation, immediate or otherwise. "Wrong as we think slavery is, we can yet afford to let it alone where it is, because that much is due to the necessity arising from its actual presence in the nation . . ."[103] The *Charleston Mercury* called Lincoln "a vulgar mobocrat and a Southern hater . . . possessed only of his inveterate hatred of slavery and his openly avowed predilections of negro equality."[104]

While many in the South viewed Lincoln as the greatest threat to slavery, abolitionists in the North did not believe he sufficiently supported their cause. Wendell Phillips called Lincoln a "pawn on the political chessboard."[105] Lewis Tappan said Lincoln was another in a long line of undistinguished candidates eager to appease the proslavery states. Tappan supported New York abolitionist Gerrit Smith for president under the banner of the Radical Abolition Party.[106] William Lloyd Garrison had no use for the Radical Abolition Party—"what a farce is the nomination of Gerrit Smith for the Presidency"—but Garrison remained skeptical of Lincoln.[107]

Other abolitionists had a more optimistic view of Lincoln. Lydia Maria Child regarded Lincoln as an "honest, independent man, and sincerely a friend to freedom."[108] Twenty-eight-year-old John Sella Martin, an escaped slave and minister of the First Independent Baptist Church in Boston, strongly supported Lincoln for president.[109] Prudence Crandall lived among many Lincoln supporters in Illinois; while there is no record of her opinion of Lincoln, in 1860 Lincoln won LaSalle County by nearly one thousand votes.[110]

On November 6, 1860, Lincoln won all the northern states and California, Oregon, Iowa, and Indiana. He beat Stephen Douglas in their mutual home state of Illinois. Many in the South refused to accept Lincoln's victory. Congressman William W. Boyce told the South Carolina General Assembly, "The way to create revolution is to start it. . . . The only thing left for us to do as soon as we receive authentic intelligence of the election of Lincoln and Hamlin, is for South Carolina, in the quickest manner and by the most direct means, to withdraw from the Union. To submit to Lincoln's election is to consent to death."[111] An editorial writer for the *Southern Confederacy*, a newspaper in Atlanta, Georgia, said, "Let the consequences be what they may—whether the Potomac is crimsoned in human gore, and Pennsylvania Avenue is paved ten fathoms deep with mangled bodies . . . The South, the loyal South, the constitutional South, will never submit to such humiliation and degradation as the inauguration of Abraham Lincoln."[112]

Lincoln waited four long months for his inauguration on March 4, 1861, and refrained from saying anything that might offend the southern states. On December 20, 1860, South Carolina held a secession convention and voted unanimously to break away from the United States. In January, five states—Mississippi, Florida, Alabama, Georgia, and Louisiana— all voted for secession. On February 1, 1861, Texas joined the others. In all, seven states voted to leave the Union prior to Lincoln's inauguration.

Supreme Court Chief Justice Roger B. Taney administered the oath of the presidency to Abraham Lincoln on March 4, 1861. The ceremony took place in front of the unfinished Capitol building that lacked the center dome. The nearby Washington Monument—also under construction— was only one-third of its intended height. Many wondered if the young nation would survive to see a finished capital city. In his address, Lincoln wasted no time in speaking specifically to those who wanted to break up the United States.

"In your hands, my dissatisfied fellow-countrymen, and not in mine, is the momentous issue of civil war," Lincoln said. "The government will not assail you. You can have no conflict without being yourselves the aggressors. You have no oath registered in heaven to destroy the government, while I shall have the most solemn one to 'preserve, protect, and defend it.'"[113]

Alexander Stephens, Jefferson Davis's vice president, replied to Lincoln's address and summarized the essence of the new Confederacy: "Its cornerstone rests upon the great truth that the negro is not equal to the white man; that slavery, subordination to the superior race, is his natural and moral condition."[114] Jefferson Davis said the South would repel an "organized system of hostile measures against the rights of the owners of slaves."[115]

Thirty-nine days after Lincoln's inauguration, on April 12, 1861, Confederate Army cannons opened fire on Union troops barricaded in Fort Sumter, in Charleston, South Carolina. After enduring continuous shelling throughout the day that caused most of the fort's interior wooden structures to catch fire, the Union troops surrendered Fort Sumter to the Confederates. The Civil War to end slavery and preserve the Union had begun.

15 : The Civil War

Shortly before the end of the 1850s, Prudence Crandall Philleo had moved from her farm in Troy Grove to a home in the newly developed town of Mendota, Illinois, where two Illinois railroad lines intersected.[1] Prudence moved there to be closer to the shops, churches, and transportation and also to get away from her erratic husband. In April 1861, however, life in Mendota and America changed dramatically.

After the attack on Fort Sumter, war fever gripped the country. Communities in Illinois and other northern and western states held spontaneous Union rallies. Prudence watched as the sons of her neighbors gathered at the local music hall to hear the details of the fall of Fort Sumter. The news "created the most intense feeling, and without distinction of party our citizens came together with cheeks burning with shame that our national flag had been insulted."[2] Nearly one hundred Mendota recruits gathered at the train depot to leave for Springfield on April 19, 1861.

"People came flocking into town from all the surrounding country and villages, with flags flying, to see the soldiers start off for the war," one young Mendota recruit recalled. "The streets were crowded with people who came to bid us the last goodbye. Flags were unfurled and speeches made in honor of our departure."[3]

Eastern Connecticut men held a massive rally at the Windham County Courthouse in Brooklyn on April 22, 1861. Former Governor Chauncey F. Cleveland presided; he had prosecuted Prudence Crandall in the same courthouse twenty-eight years earlier. After numerous fiery speeches, more than sixty men volunteered for the army. William H. Chandler of Thompson offered a donation of five hundred dollars for the war effort, and others quickly followed. Those gathered pledged to "expend their last dollar and exhaust the last drop of their blood ere they would submit to a disruption of the Nation."[4]

The Civil War tested William Lloyd Garrison, who, on pacifist grounds, did not want his sons to participate. The sons of many abolitionists, however, did join the army. While neither Prudence Crandall Philleo nor her brother Hezekiah had sons who could serve in the war, many Crandall relatives volunteered for duty.

George Washington Crandall of Pennsylvania enlisted in the army. George and Prudence Crandall shared the same great-great grandfather. When the war began in 1861, George was thirty-four years old; he and his wife, Mary, had four children. George rose to the rank of captain of the newly formed Company C of the One Hundred and Fifty-first Pennsylvania Volunteers and proceeded to the battlefields of Virginia.[5]

Emeline Philleo Goodwin, Prudence's stepdaughter, closely followed the war. She had raised two daughters and two sons—LeBaron and Frank—while living in Massachusetts. When her husband died in 1845, Emeline sent seven-year-old LeBaron to Illinois to live with Prudence Crandall Philleo.[6] LeBaron helped with the chores of the farm, learned lessons of finance and responsibility—Prudence and LeBaron had bought two horses together—and received a basic education from Prudence.[7] Emeline and Prudence feared for the lives of LeBaron and Frank when both young men marched off to war.

Most but not all of the Crandall relatives fought on the side of the Union. Henry E. Crandall had grown up in Palmyra, New York, near Rochester and Lake Ontario; he was related to both George Washington Crandall and Prudence Philleo. In his teens, Henry had learned the printing trade. Because of the poor economy in upstate New York, in 1853 he joined his brother in Tennessee and secured a job at the *Memphis Appeal*. When the Civil War began in 1861, Henry Crandall did not immediately volunteer for service, but as the war intensified he joined a Confederate cavalry company in 1862 to fight with the First Division of General Joseph Wheeler's Cavalry Corps.[8] He was twenty-nine. While traveling from Tennessee to Georgia, a Union soldier shot Henry's horse out from under him, but Henry was not injured.[9]

In Alfred, New York, about one hundred miles south of Palmyra where Henry Crandall was born, lived another offshoot of the Crandall family. Alonzo Crandall was twenty-four years old when he enlisted in the Union army. His regiment, the One Hundred and Thirty-sixth New York Volunteer Infantry, known as the "ironclads," received orders to march to Virginia; Alonzo Crandall first saw action at Chancellorsville.[10]

The young men who had answered Lincoln's call included the sons of Charles Ames, the orphan boy raised by Andrew T. Judson in Canterbury during the 1820s. Charles Ames was forty-nine years old at the start of the Civil War; he had moved from Elba, New York, to Republic, Ohio, in 1843. Charles and his wife Alvira raised a large family of nine children; all survived into adulthood.[11] His two oldest sons, twenty-three-year-old Andrew Judson Ames and twenty-one-year-old Henry Ames both enlisted in the Union army. At the height of the Battle of Chancellorsville in 1863, a Confederate bullet slammed into Andrew Judson Ames's leg. He was carried off the battlefield alive, received medical attention, and survived.

With the support of his congregation in Syracuse, Rev. Samuel May traveled south to visit the Army of the Potomac, bringing supplies and care packages prepared by his parishioners. Thirty years earlier in a sermon at the Unitarian Church in Brooklyn, Connecticut, May had told an astonished congregation that if the slaveholders did not renounce slavery the result would "eventually throw us into civil war."[12] May opposed violence and war in the same manner as William Lloyd Garrison; in the first days of the Civil War, May said, "I cannot find it in my heart to urge men to enlist."[13] After visiting hundreds of wounded soldiers, May wrote, "Nothing but slavery seems to me so bad as war."[14]

May traveled to Washington, D.C., to visit soldiers wounded at the battle of Yorktown. "The most touching thing was the patience and fortitude I everywhere witnessed," May wrote.[15] When he returned to Syracuse, May ministered to the soldiers' families, prepared boxes of supplies for the troops, and assisted with "constant, unwearied, but, it would appear, most exhausting activity."[16]

During the spring of 1862, Prudence Philleo contacted her friends in the American Anti-Slavery Society and Charles Whipple, who worked for Garrison at the *Liberator*, to ask how she could help. Whipple requested that she distribute antislavery literature to soldiers and civilians and sent her a box of pamphlets written by Lydia Maria Child.[17] Prudence filled the shops of Mendota, Illinois, with Child's pamphlet.

"The box and its contents arrived safely on Thursday the 7th [of May], and since that time I have been busily engaged in distribution," Prudence wrote to Whipple. "You said, 'send them broadcast and give them to soldiers.' This I am endeavoring to do."[18] Prudence received a positive response. "In all my reading, I have never happened on anything that so plainly contradicts the assertions of the enemies of emancipation as this little work," one grateful recipient wrote to Prudence, "and I have taken the greatest pleasure in reading it."[19] Whipple told Garrison, "Your old friend, Prudence Crandall Philleo, is still active in Anti-Slavery work."[20]

By the end of 1861, Garrison began to lose patience with the slow pace of the war and President Lincoln's willingness to negotiate a long-term phaseout of slavery with the four slave states that remained loyal to the Union—Delaware, Maryland, Kentucky, and Missouri. For some time Lincoln promoted the idea of purchasing the freedom of slaves as part of a "plan of gradual emancipation" that would extend through 1881.[21] "Mr. Lincoln is so infatuated as to shape his course of policy in accordance with their wishes, and is thus unwittingly helping to prolong the war, and to render the result more and more doubtful," Garrison wrote. "If he *is* 6 feet 4 inches high, he is only a dwarf in mind."[22] After the border state congressmen rejected Lincoln's offer of compromise, Lincoln resolved to free the slaves unconditionally.

Northern governors frustrated with the lack of decisive Union victories and the failure of Lincoln to end slavery announced plans for a conference in Altoona, Pennsylvania, to call for emancipation.[23] At a White House meeting, bank presidents told Lincoln they feared the Union could not survive. Lincoln recalled the meteor shower of 1833 and described the panic he had experienced when he saw the stars falling in great numbers. "But looking back of them in the heavens I saw all the grand old constellations with which I was so well acquainted, fixed and true in their places. Gentlemen, the world did not come to an end then, nor will the Union now."[24]

Lincoln wanted to announce a plan for emancipation in conjunction with a significant military victory.[25] On September 17, 1862, the Battle of Antietam, near Sharpsburg, Maryland, left twenty-three thousand Union and Confederate soldiers killed, wounded, or missing; it was the bloodiest single day of the Civil War.[26] Despite the unprecedented casualties, the press nonetheless regarded Antietam as a Union triumph. On September 22, 1862, Lincoln issued the Emancipation Proclamation, to take effect on

January 1, 1863. "All persons held as slaves within any State or designated part of a State, the people whereof shall then be in rebellion against the United States, shall be then, thenceforward, and forever free."[27]

In New York City, the abolitionists held an "Emancipation Jubilee" at the Cooper Union Hall. Lewis Tappan, seventy-five years old, reminded the audience of the years of abolitionist struggle and held up a letter from John Quincy Adams, dated March 9, 1841, which contained the news that the U.S. Supreme Court had upheld Judge Andrew Judson's ruling to free the *Amistad* "slaves."[28] Rev. Henry Highland Garnet read President Lincoln's proclamation and called Lincoln "an advancing and progressive man . . . the man of our choice and hope."[29]

While the Emancipation Proclamation was "a matter for great rejoicing" for William Lloyd Garrison, he noted that it applied only in Confederate states and did not end slavery in the border states that remained loyal to the Union.[30] Lincoln said he lacked the power to end slavery in states that had not waged war on the United States. Lincoln's explanation did not convince Garrison. "What was wanted, what is still needed," Garrison said, "is a proclamation, distinctly announcing the total abolition of slavery."[31]

William Lloyd Garrison had three sons old enough to serve in the army: George, William, and Wendell. William and Wendell opposed war as a matter of principle and refused to enlist. George, however, was inclined to answer the call because of a change in army procedure. The Emancipation Proclamation permitted blacks to join the army, and in January 1863, the army created regiments specifically for black soldiers. The army, however, did not permit black enlisted men to serve as officers. Black leaders such as Henry Highland Garnet, Robert Purvis, and Frederick Douglass criticized the ban on black officers but nonetheless helped recruit black volunteers. Black men enlisted in overwhelming numbers, and George Garrison considered joining the Massachusetts Fifty-fifth Volunteer Negro Regiment as an officer.

William Lloyd Garrison did not want George to enlist. Garrison believed that black troops would face the fiercest fighting and that George, as the son of a radical abolitionist and as a white officer overseeing black troops, would serve at tremendous risk.[32] Garrison's instincts were well founded. At the battle of Poison Springs, Arkansas, the sight of black troops inspired Confederate outrage. "Many wounded men belonging to the First Kansas Colored Volunteers fell into the hands of the enemy," a soldier recalled, "and I have the most positive assurances from eye-witnesses that they were murdered on the spot."[33]

Garrison tried to dissuade George from enlisting by reminding him of the troops "wounded, maimed or killed in the course of such a long campaign."[34] As a last ditch effort, Garrison asked George to think of his mother. "It makes me tremble in regard to the effect that may be produced upon the health and happiness of your mother, should any serious, especially a fatal, accident befall you," Garrison said. "Her affection for you is intense, her anxiety beyond expression."[35] Despite his father's pleadings, George Thompson Garrison enlisted in the United States Army as a second lieutenant with the Fifty-fifth Massachusetts Volunteer Negro Regiment.

There was a steady, hard rain the day George Garrison left Boston Harbor for South Carolina. Plans called for his regiment to bid farewell in a ceremonial parade past Boston Common. William Lloyd Garrison stood near the common to say good-bye to his son until he learned at the last minute of the parade's cancellation. Garrison rushed to Boston Harbor. "I followed you . . . all the way down to the vessel, hoping to speak to you," Garrison later wrote to George, "but I found myself on the wrong side, and the throng was so great and the marching so continuous that I could not press my way through."[36] Garrison stood on the wharf by the troop ship for more than an hour in the pouring rain, hoping to see his son and shout farewell. The troops had already boarded the ship, and there was no chance for parting words or a wave good-bye. "I miss you by my side at the table, and at the printing office, and cannot get reconciled to the separation," Garrison wrote to his son. "Yet I have nothing but praise to give you that you have been faithful to your highest convictions . . . God bless you, my boy!"[37]

Joining George Garrison on the rainy march to the troop ship was Frank Goodwin, Prudence Crandall Philleo's step-grandson. He had enlisted for his second tour of duty, this time as a captain for the black troops of the Fifty-fifth. Frank Goodwin served side by side with George Garrison as the Fifty-fifth Regiment began two years of fighting in North and South Carolina.

Alonzo Crandall and Henry Ames fought at perhaps the most important battle of the Civil War and a decisive turning point for the Union—

Gettysburg. General Lee prepared to gamble the fate of his army and the Confederacy on a daring strike above the Mason-Dixon Line. More than fifty thousand Union and Confederate troops had been killed or wounded when the three-day battle ended on July 3, 1863, and corpses filled the streets and fields of Gettysburg. A bullet nicked the face of Alonzo Crandall; listed as wounded, Alonzo continued to fight with his regiment.[38] Union troops stopped the Confederate advance and nearly destroyed Lee's army. Gettysburg ended the Confederacy's dream of a decisive northern victory and shattered the myth of General Lee's invincible army.

The black soldiers of the Massachusetts Fifty-fifth Regiment constructed entrenchments at Folly Island, South Carolina, during the summer and fall of 1863. Lieutenant George Garrison and Captain Frank Goodwin supervised the men. During an inspection of the company's laundry facility in February 1864, Garrison encountered a familiar black woman ironing clothes—Harriet Tubman. "She no sooner saw me than she recognized me at once, and instantly threw her arms around me, and gave me quite an affectionate embrace . . ."[39] Tubman knew George Garrison from her many stays at William Lloyd Garrison's house. Tubman told Garrison about her travels to Canada where she had visited her brother and her recent return to South Carolina to assist the Union troops as a spy, nurse, laundress, and cook.[40]

Inspired by the Emancipation Proclamation and the story of black regiments, Robert Forten left London, England, to return to the United States to enlist in the U.S. Army. Robert was the son of James Forten, the black sailmaker from Philadelphia and a sponsor of Prudence Crandall's school. Robert Forten had left the United States to escape discrimination. Upon hearing of the recruitment of black troops into the U.S. Army, Forten reconsidered his self-imposed exile. "Come, rally round the stars and stripes, now emblems of our hope," Forten wrote in a letter to the *Liberator*, "the negro's arm shall be the charm that gives it life again."[41]

Forten, who was fifty years old, joined Pennsylvania's Forty-third Regiment of the U.S. Colored Troops on March 2, 1864, and received the rank of private.[42] Recognized as a leader who could recruit other enlistees, the army promoted Forten to sergeant major and sent him to Maryland. Shortly after his arrival in Maryland, he contracted typhoid and returned to Philadelphia. Robert Forten died on April 25, 1864. Sixteen U.S. Army troops escorted his coffin and fired three volleys at his grave site. For the very first time, a black man in Philadelphia was buried with military honors.[43]

Henry E. Crandall of Tennessee, fighting for the Confederacy, engaged in defensive battles as Union troops pushed deeper into the South. As part of the southern forces commanded by General Joseph E. Johnston, Crandall and his fellow soldiers fought to stop the progress of Union soldiers led by General William Tecumseh Sherman. Henry Ames's Sixty-sixth was one of the Union regiments under Sherman's command, as was Alonzo Crandall's One Hundred and Thirty-sixth of New York.[44] In June of 1864 the troops of Johnston and Sherman clashed near Kenesaw Mountain, Georgia. Henry Ames and the rest of the Ohio Sixty-sixth engaged Henry Crandall and the Confederates in a battle that lasted the entire day. More than five hundred northern soldiers were killed or wounded. Ohio's Sixty-sixth suffered a loss of five killed and twenty-three wounded.[45] One of the wounded was Henry Ames—he was shot on June 16 and evacuated to a Union-occupied hospital in Chattanooga. The twenty-four-year-old second son of Charles Ames died on June 21, 1864.

As the commander of the Union's Army of the Potomac, General McClellan had failed to aggressively prosecute the war and relinquished his command under pressure from Lincoln at the end of 1862. After returning home to New Jersey, McClellan decided to run for president against Lincoln. Ironically, McClellan criticized Lincoln for the slow progress of the war—regarded by many as the fault of McClellan—and vowed to "exhaust all resources of statesmanship . . . to secure such peace, reestablish the Union, and guarantee for the future the Constitutional rights of every state."[46] McClellan's promise to pursue "statesmanship" and negotiation rather than war was interpreted by many in the South as a pledge to abandon the cause of emancipation. High casualties and the failure to win the war threatened Lincoln's reelection. On September 2, however, after cutting off the last key rail line and highway to Atlanta, Sherman's army, including Alonzo Crandall, captured Atlanta. The frustrations of the previous months melted away as anxious northerners burst into wild celebration. The *Richmond Examiner* predicted "the disaster at Atlanta" would save the party of Lincoln and "diffuse gloom over the South."[47]

For the first time in his life, William Lloyd Garrison plunged into party politics—on behalf of Abraham Lincoln. He broke with abolitionist friends, including Wendell Phillips, who never had trusted Lincoln and worried about Lincoln's approach to postwar issues such as reconstruction and citizenship for blacks.[48] While Garrison sympathized with Phillips's concerns, he thought Phillips missed a larger point. "A thousand incidental errors and blunders are easily to be borne with on the part of him who, at one blow, severed the chains of three million three hundred thousand slaves."[49] In the first political endorsement ever published in the *Liberator*, Garrison backed Abraham Lincoln for a second term as president. Garrison also recommended that abolitionists not run a third-party candidate who might divide the antislavery vote to the benefit of General McClellan.

In June 1864, Garrison traveled to Baltimore to witness the unanimous nomination of Lincoln for president and Andrew Johnson for vice president. He also visited the jail where thirty-four years earlier he had spent nearly two months for a libel conviction regarding Francis Todd and the issue of slavery. Much to Garrison's disappointment, the city had replaced the old jail with a modern facility; Garrison's jail cell with the words he wrote on the wall was long gone.

President Lincoln invited Garrison to travel from Baltimore to Washington, D.C., for a reception at the White House on Thursday, June 9, 1864. Lincoln's advisers did admirable advance work concerning Garrison's activities in Baltimore; Lincoln knew of Garrison's visit to the site of the old jail and joked with Garrison about the jail's demolition. "Then, you could not get out of prison," Lincoln told Garrison, "now you cannot get in."[50] To Garrison's surprise, Lincoln invited him back to the White House on the following day for a private meeting. After Garrison's first meeting with Lincoln, Garrison met with Secretary of War Edwin Stanton and then toured the Capitol, where Massachusetts Senator Charles Sumner escorted him onto the floor of the Senate. Senators crowded around him—they wanted to meet the infamous lion of the abolitionist movement. At the end of this remarkable day, Garrison realized he did not have a hotel room at a time when all the hotels were full. The junior senator from Massachusetts, Henry Wilson, took Garrison to dinner and used his influence to secure a room for Garrison at the Washington House, a renowned hotel in a prime spot on Pennsylvania Avenue. Much had changed from the time when Garrison's unpopular views made him a reviled political outcast.

President Lincoln received Garrison for the second time at the White House on Friday, June 10, 1864. The two engaged in frank conversation for an hour. Lincoln knew that Garrison, with his longtime advocacy for an immediate end to slavery and equal rights for blacks, had helped to prepare the country for emancipation. He also knew that Garrison's endorsement in the presidential election would help prevent the abolitionist vote from straying to a divisive third-party candidate.

Lincoln told Garrison of his strong commitment to a constitutional amendment banning all slavery and promised to secure passage after the 1864 election. "There is no mistake about it in regard to Mr. Lincoln's desire to do all that he can see it right and possible for him to do to uproot slavery, and give fair play to the emancipated," Garrison wrote to Helen the next day. "I was much pleased with his spirit, and the familiar and candid way in which he unbosomed himself."[51]

While Garrison enjoyed his remarkable status as a dignitary worthy of a private audience with the president, only blocks away a former protégé and colleague struggled for survival. Maria W. Stewart had forsaken her trailblazing role of antislavery crusader and contributor to the *Liberator* more than thirty years earlier. She kept apprised of efforts to enhance the rights of black men and women and stayed involved when she could afford it; she had attended the Women's Anti-Slavery Convention of 1837 in New York.[52] In addition, she had remained committed to educating black men and women. Stewart had moved from Boston to New York, where she taught at the No. 2 Primary School for Colored Girls for many years.[53] She later taught on Long Island until 1852, when she lost her job and moved to Baltimore.

Throughout her life, Stewart barely earned enough to survive. In Baltimore, she found work as a teacher and earned far less than she had expected. "I found myself teaching every branch for fifty cents per month, until informed by another teacher that no writing was taught for less than one dollar per month. . . . I never could get along like some people, and was always struggling to keep my head above water; but I could never get money enough to carry me home."[54]

At the beginning of the Civil War, the threat of violence and Confederate influence in the neutral state of Maryland prompted Stewart to move again. Her friends told her that Washington, D.C. "had become a perfect paradise for the colored people since President Lincoln had taken his seat."[55] She took letters of introduction to a minister's family in Washington and then organized prayer meetings for Rev. C. H. Hall at the Epiphany Church on Nineteenth Street. With financial support from Rev. Hall, Stewart established a school that taught children from the Epiphany Church.[56]

Epiphany served mostly white parishioners—Jefferson Davis and his wife had attended the church before he left Washington to become president of the Confederacy—but it attracted a growing number of black members who worshipped at satellite locations.[57] When Stewart suggested the consolidation of meeting sites for the sake of simplicity and convenience, she met resistance from other women in the congregation. "One of the ladies of the Epiphany, and I do not know how many more, were highly incensed, and went straight to Dr. Hall and told him I wanted all the praise and credit for getting up the work, and cast my name out as evil all over the city," Stewart wrote.[58] Hall surprised Stewart and sided with the women who had complained about her. Hall withdrew his support for Stewart's school.

"No tongue can portray my agony of mind," Stewart wrote. "I did not know what I should do, or how I should get along."[59] A friend of Stewart's noted, "There was a quiet sadness and melancholy of expression which, to a close observer, denoted a life of sorrow and disappointment."[60] After seeking advice from Rev. Henry Highland Garnet, the former Noyes Academy student and minister of the Fifteenth Street Presbyterian Church in Washington, she continued teaching and relied on the tuition paid by her remaining students to meet her expenses. With the support of a few key friends, her school survived as she struggled to pay her bills and grow her school.

As the presidential election neared, William Burleigh joined Garrison and other abolitionists who enthusiastically backed Abraham Lincoln. Burleigh campaigned extensively for Lincoln in New Jersey, McClellan's home state, and in New York. "I cannot do less than my utmost to secure the reelection of Mr. Lincoln," Burleigh wrote. "I cannot shirk the responsibility of the hour."[61] He addressed a crowd of three thousand in Patterson and spoke for nearly two hours in Passaic. As the campaign drew to a close, Burleigh ignored his exhaustion and pressed on to Brooklyn, New York, for a huge outdoor rally. "The crisis of the country is so solemn, and the themes demanding discussion are so inspiring, that standing before a large and eager audience I am very apt to forget everything relating to myself."[62]

On Tuesday, November 8, 1864, voters throughout the non-Confederate states went to the polls to elect either Abraham Lincoln or General George McClellan as president. Before the fall of Atlanta, many pundits had believed that McClellan would easily defeat Lincoln. Lincoln feared he would not carry New York and Pennsylvania, key electoral states, and wondered if the critical absentee soldier vote would break in favor of the former general. There was a decisive result when all the votes were counted. Among the Union troops, Lincoln had defeated the general who commanded the Army of the Potomac, winning a staggering 80 percent of the soldier vote. In the Electoral College, McClellan won only New Jersey, Delaware, and Kentucky. In the congressional elections, Lincoln's Republican/Union Party secured a two-thirds majority.[63]

Ralph Waldo Emerson wrote to a friend, "I give you joy of the election. Seldom in history was so much staked on a popular vote. I suppose never in history."[64]

On January 21, 1865, Congress passed the Thirteenth Amendment to the U.S. Constitution banning slavery in all states. Arthur Tappan never had expected to see emancipation in his lifetime. "It was like looking up there, to see where heaven is—it seemed so far off, but it was there."[65] The previous year, the amendment had passed the Senate with a two-thirds vote, but had failed to pass in the House by the same required margin. On this day, after much arm-twisting by Lincoln and attempts by opponents to delay the vote, the measure passed the House 119 to 56. As the success and magnitude of the vote became apparent to the packed gallery, journalists scrambled to capture the moment.

"The tumult of joy that broke out was vast, thundering, and uncontrollable," wrote a reporter for the *New York Tribune*. "Representatives and Auditors on the floor, soldiers and spectators in the gallery, Senators and Supreme Court Judges, women and pages, gave way to the excitement of the most august and important event in American legislation and American history since the Declaration of Independence."[66]

William Lloyd Garrison suggested to friends that it was time to close down the antislavery societies. He had struggled to write, edit and print a new issue of the *Liberator*—a labor of love always near financial collapse—every week since 1831. In March 1865, Garrison wrote, "We have concluded to discontinue the *Liberator* at the close of the present year . . . This is not the occasion for us to say all that such a conclusion naturally suggests. Let it be deferred till the time is at hand."[67] His friend Oliver Johnson, who had helped edit the *Liberator*, proposed merging it with the *National Anti-Slavery Standard*. Garrison said no; he had decided his newspaper would cease publication altogether corresponding with his own retirement. Garrison wanted to spend more time with his wife, Helen, who had suffered a debilitating stroke in 1863.

President Lincoln joined Union troops as they marched to the Confederate capital of Richmond. On Sunday, April 2, 1865, Lincoln wired Secretary of War Edwin Stanton that General Ulysses S. Grant had captured the city of Petersburg, Virginia, and twelve thousand southern troops had surrendered.[68] A soldier from Massachusetts made note of the events in his diary: "April 3rd: Marched with brigade through Petersburg, band playing and colors flying. President Lincoln rode through a street where the brigade had halted, and was received everywhere with shouts of joy."[69]

Lincoln greeted the black soldiers of the Fifth Massachusetts Cavalry and Lieutenant Daniel H. Chamberlain, a commanding officer for the Fifth. "His face, his figure, his attitudes, his words, form the most remarkable picture in my memory, and will while memory lasts," Chamberlain wrote. "I spoke to him of the country's gratitude for his great deliverance of the slaves. His sad face beamed for a moment with happiness as he answered in exact substance, and very nearly in words: 'I have been only an instrument. The logic and moral power of Garrison, and the anti-slavery people of the country, and the army, have done all.'"[70]

As the end of the war appeared in sight, William Burleigh's son, Private LeMoyne Burleigh, was fighting Confederate troops in northern Virginia. As part of a small scouting party for the First Volunteer Calvary of New York, Burleigh was awakened on the morning of April 3, 1865 by shouts and rifle fire. He attempted to untie his horse and flee, but was grabbed from behind by a rebel soldier. In an instant the Confederates surrounded Burleigh—one pointed a pistol at his head.[71] He surrendered.

Burleigh and another Union soldier were taken prisoner and sent by stagecoach to Lexington, Virginia. In Lexington, they were held with other Union prisoners and told they would be sent to Andersonville, the notorious Confederate prison in Georgia. Burleigh spent the night inside the deserted Zollman's General Store on the edge of Buffalo Creek. At midnight, Burleigh and the other prisoners threw off their blankets and overpowered the tired southerners who were guarding the doors. They seized rifles and commandeered a ferry that crossed Buffalo Creek.[72] After dodging Confederate search parties and hiding in farmhouses and barns, they arrived at a U.S. Army encampment in Lynchburg and received a hero's welcome. Burleigh received a promotion from private to second lieutenant.[73]

After the fall of Atlanta, Union troops captured Henry Crandall and sent him to a prison camp in Alton, Illinois. Alton was about 280 miles away from Mendota, where Prudence Crandall lived—a distant relative whom Henry did not know. At the end of the war, Henry Crandall returned to Tennessee and resumed his career as a printer at the *Memphis Appeal*.[74] Alonzo Crandall also survived the war and marched with Sherman's victorious troops when they paraded through Washington, D.C., for the Grand Review celebration on May 24, 1865. Captain Frank Goodwin of the Fifty-fifth Massachusetts Regiment, Prudence's step-grandson, lived to see the end of the war and traveled home to Boston.[75] LeMoyne Burleigh returned to New York, where he wrote for New York City newspapers and later published and edited the *Northampton Free Press*.[76] Andrew Judson Ames, despite the permanent injury to his leg, traveled west and lived a long and productive life. When Andrew Ames's father, Charles Ames, died thirty-two years later in Ohio, the family gave Andrew Judson special recognition in Charles's obituary. "Charles lived with Andrew T. Judson from the time he was ten years of age until he was eighteen," the *Tiffin Daily Tribune* reported. "There is a certificate of good moral character now in the hands of the family given by this eminent jurist, Judge Judson, in 1830, highly commending our subject for his good behavior and moral character during his stay with this family."[77]

Traveling by train and boat from Boston, William Lloyd Garrison arrived in New York City on April 7, 1865. The Lincoln administration invited Garrison to sail to Charleston, South Carolina, to join other dignitaries for the raising of the American flag at Fort Sumter. In a letter to Helen, Garrison noted, "Intelligence is this moment received—though it is not official—that Gen. Lee has surrendered with the remainder of his shattered army. If this be so, the rebellion is indeed crushed, and slavery along with it."[78] The steamship *Arago* left New York on April 8 carrying Garrison, George Thompson, Henry Ward Beecher, Senator Henry Wilson of Massachusetts, and many other dignitaries. George Thompson recalled that thirty years earlier, "I was denounced by a slaveholding President for preaching the doctrine of Universal Liberty. Today, I am the guest of an antislavery President, on board a United States government vessel . . . to see a flag raised which is not only the symbol of Union, but of freedom."[79]

The flag-raising ceremony occurred at noon on Friday, April 14, 1865. In the early morning hours, steamboats filled with guests and onlookers surrounded Fort Sumter. Recently emancipated slaves filled the three-tiered ship *Planter*.[80] The breeze of the morning created white caps on the water and carried smoke across the horizon as soldiers fired cannons in celebration. After Garrison's ship had arrived at Fort Sumter, he climbed the fifty steps to the top of the wall of the battered fort. The program began with a prayer, and Major-General Robert Anderson, who had commanded Fort Sumter in 1861, brought forth the tattered American flag that had flown over the fort at the time of its surrender. "The enthusiasm was immense," Garrison said.[81] That evening, Garrison and George Thompson attended a reception at the Charleston Hotel. When asked to address the dignitaries, Garrison scarcely could believe he was rising to speak his mind in the grand southern town of Charleston. "I have never been her enemy, nor the enemy of the South," Garrison said. "I came here to witness the unfurling of a flag under which every human being is to be recognized as entitled to his freedom."[82]

The following day, Garrison, George Thompson, and Henry Ward Beecher rode by carriage to a small cemetery across the street from St. Philips Church in Charleston. They saw the grave of Senator John Calhoun, the ardent defender of slavery. "One of the most impressive scenes I have witnessed was William Lloyd Garrison standing at the grave of John C. Calhoun," wrote Rev. Alfred P. Putnam. "The reformer laid his hand upon the monument before him and said impressively, 'Down into a deeper grave than this, slavery has gone, and for it there is no resurrection.'"[83]

The following morning, three thousand people, including many freed slaves, crowded into Zion's Presbyterian Church on Calhoun Street in Charleston. "Just before ten o'clock, the surging and cheering of the vast throng announced the arrival of Mr. Garrison," one of the attendees wrote.

"Not content with deafening shouts, they pressed towards their illustrious friend, and bore him on their shoulders to the speaker's stand."[84] A freed slave, Samuel Dickerson, stood at the podium with his two young daughters and addressed Garrison.

"I welcome you here among us, the long, steadfast friend of the poor, downtrodden slave," Dickerson said. "These children were robbed from me, and I stood desolate. . . . I lost a dear wife, and after her death that little one, who is the counterpart of her mother's countenance, was taken from me. . . . You have restored them to me. . . . Sir, we welcome and look upon you as our saviour. We thank you for what you have done for us."[85]

"My dear friend," Garrison said, "I have no language to express the feelings of my heart on listening to your kind and strengthening words . . . I never expected to look you in the face, never supposed you would hear of anything I might do in your behalf. I knew only one thing—all that I wanted to know—that you were a grievously oppressed people; and that, on every consideration of justice, humanity, and right, you were entitled to immediate and unconditional freedom."[86]

The greatest outpouring of affection at the Zion Church came for a man who did not speak and could not attend. "The enthusiasm . . . at the first mention by one of the speakers of the name Abraham Lincoln, was such as to defy description," Rev. Putnam wrote. "It was intense, wild, and almost fearful. The vast crowd cheered and waved their handkerchiefs, some screaming for joy, and others raising their hands and clasping them in gratitude to God, and hundreds weeping the tears they could not repress, as they thought of their great friend and benefactor."[87]

Garrison and other dignitaries set off on April 15 aboard the steamer *Arago* and headed south to Savannah on their way to Florida. When the ship docked in Beaufort, an emergency telegram arrived for Senator Wilson. The previous evening at the Ford Theatre in Washington, D.C., an assassin had shot President Lincoln at close range; he had lingered overnight and died earlier that day. Henry Ward Beecher was with Senator Wilson as he read the telegram. "Good God! The President is killed!" Wilson said.[88]

The *Arago* immediately left the port of Savannah and headed north. "We knew nothing but this," Beecher wrote, "that the President had been assassinated. All the rest was reserved for our coming into the harbor."[89] On reaching New York City, Garrison learned that Lincoln's assassination had not resulted in the collapse of the government or the Union. When word of Lincoln's assassination reached the family of Arthur Tappan in New Haven, one of his children said, a great "calamity has come upon us." Tappan replied, "God will overrule it for the good of our country. He has our country in hand, and will bring it out all right." [90]

16 : Reunions and Farewells

After living in Mendota for the war years, in 1865 Prudence and Calvin Philleo moved to a 140-acre farm near Cordova, Illinois.[1] In Cordova, Calvin enjoyed the peace and quiet he had long desired. The open farmland on the banks of the Mississippi River created an idyllic setting, and for a time Calvin was kind to Prudence and his daughter Emeline. During a thunderstorm, a reporter who passed through the area described the "perfect beauty" of the Philleo farm and recalled how he had walked into the farmhouse looking for the famous Prudence Crandall.

"The house seems deserted . . . there are books, pictures, photographs of familiar faces, Garrison, Phillips, Emma Hardinge, and others less noted."[2] The author described seeing an engraved copy of the portrait of Prudence Crandall, painted in Boston in the 1830s, and many books and newspapers. He met Prudence's eighty-four-year-old mother, Esther, but Prudence was away.[3]

The books and newspapers the reporter noticed likely included the *Liberator*. In the closing months of 1865, William Lloyd Garrison prepared to cease publication of the newspaper that had helped sustain a younger Prudence Crandall. Garrison had published the *Liberator* continuously for thirty-five years, never missing a weekly edition. His dedication came at considerable financial sacrifice for his wife and children. "It leaves me without a farthing laid up for my family," he wrote to a friend.[4] Yet, as the end of the year neared, he began to have second thoughts. "It will be, on many accounts, hard for me to discontinue its publication," Garrison wrote in October. "What I shall do after that time, I do not yet know."[5]

Garrison did not have the luxury of reflection during the last months of publication. As a result of declining subscription revenue, he was forced to embark on a lecture tour to raise money to cover the final expenses of the *Liberator*. Garrison arranged the engagements himself with little attention to fees, expenses, and scheduling.

"I know not what to ask, for the receipts will only cover the expense of the hall, advertising, etc.," Garrison wrote to Helen. "The whole thing is a muddle and a failure."⁶ He told Helen that his engagement in Erie, Pennsylvania, "will prove another flash in the pan . . . Lecturing is not to my taste."⁷ Despite many poorly planned and attended lectures, Garrison succeeded in raising money—he grossed approximately $1400 with expenses of about $200—enough to meet the final costs of publishing the *Liberator*. On Saturday, December 9, 1865, Garrison arrived home in Boston and celebrated his sixtieth birthday.

"It is a period of life that I once regarded as aged, and even venerable; but what is aged and venerable seems, now, considerably beyond me," Garrison wrote to his friend Samuel May. "Where is the magic line that perceptibly indicates we have parted with infancy, boyhood, manhood, and become positively aged? In spirit, certainly, I still feel very young; nevertheless, I must cherish no delusion about my state. I am sixty years old."⁸ Rev. May—always a faithful friend and concerned about the welfare of Garrison and his family—had bought a life and health insurance policy for Garrison in October when he had learned that Garrison planned to go on a grueling speaking tour. The policy provided for Garrison's family if anything happened to him. Upon his return to Boston, Garrison insisted on taking over the payments.⁹

Because of the need to fundraise for the *Liberator*, Garrison did not edit many of the last issues of his newspaper. Charles Whipple oversaw the publication of the *Liberator* while Garrison was away. On Monday, December 11, Garrison returned to the offices of the *Liberator* to write and edit the final three issues of his newspaper. Two weeks later—with only one issue of the *Liberator* left to publish—he told his friend Oliver Johnson that his life's occupation had ended. Lydia Maria Child credited the *Liberator* with preparing the country for emancipation. "We early abolitionists, you know, dreamed of great miracles to be wrought from moral influence," Child wrote in the final issue of the *Liberator*. "Would Northern sentiment have been in any readiness to meet the grand emergency had it not been for truths previously scattered and broadcast through the land by the warnings, exhortations and rebukes of the early abolitionists?"¹⁰

Just days after the publication of the last issue of the *Liberator*, Garrison's oldest daughter, Fanny, married Henry Villard, publisher of the *Nation*, at the Garrison family home on January 3, 1866. A wedding cake baked by Sarah Harris Fayerweather, Prudence Crandall's first black student, arrived by special delivery from Rhode Island. Sarah had stayed in touch with the Garrisons. She and her husband George had lived in New London, Connecticut, from the 1840s through 1855 when they moved to Kingston, Rhode Island. During her years in Kingston, Sarah had worked with various abolitionist leaders and activists, including Frederick Douglass and Wendell Phillips.

The wedding cake delivered in 1866 was part of a tradition of gifts and long-lasting fruitcakes that Sarah sent to the Garrisons each year. "We received a beautiful cake from you," Helen Garrison wrote to Sarah in 1863. "The sight of it daily reminds me how kind and thoughtful you always are, and how greatly indebted we are for your nice gift. I have not cut it yet . . . I must make it last a year, for my particular anti-slavery friends. The one you brought a year ago lasted nearly a year, and grew nicer every day."[11]

Sarah Harris Fayerweather also had maintained her subscription to the *Liberator*. She told Garrison how she had enjoyed reading the news of his travels to Fort Sumter for the flag-raising ceremony. "My joy is full, and when I think of your being at Charleston, S.C., having those very slaves for whom you have toiled a persecuted lifetime bowing down at your feet," she wrote to Garrison, "I can say that it is Glory enough for our Century." Sarah knew that some had criticized Garrison for his decision to cease publishing the *Liberator*, and she carefully mourned the end of his newspaper. "I miss the *Liberator* very much," Sarah told Garrison. "It was a welcome visitor but as its need is passed I should not regret its loss."[12]

Sarah also kept in touch with Prudence Philleo. Sarah told Prudence of the death of her husband George Fayerweather in 1869. Prudence wrote back to express her sorrow and convey news of her life in Illinois. "We are very comfortably and very happily situated," Prudence told Sarah. "I am now 65 years old and I joy and rejoice to see this day. I thank God that Garrison has lived to see the shackles fall from the slave."[13] Prudence also hoped to reunite with her former student. "You do not know how much I thank you for your kind remembrance, and how much my cup of joy would run over if I could see [you] face to face if it was but one hour."[14]

In the spring of 1869, Prudence received a letter from a Connecticut woman she did not know. Ellen Douglas Larned had tracked down Prudence Philleo's address and told her she was writing a history of northeastern Connecticut; she wanted to know more about Prudence's school in Canterbury. Larned was the first woman admitted to the Connecticut Historical Society and had compiled various genealogies and historical sketches of families and events in Connecticut. When Philleo did not respond, Larned sent a second request.

"Dear Stranger," Prudence replied, "at my earliest possible convenience after the reception of your second letter I give you a reply."[15] In her precise, cursive handwriting, Prudence Philleo told the story of her school and how she had admitted Sarah Harris as a student. Philleo recalled reading the *Liberator* and how it had convinced her that slavery must end through immediate emancipation. She described her night in the Brooklyn Jail and her trials for violation of the Black Law. Prudence also enclosed the letter her father Pardon had delivered to the Connecticut legislature and an article that summarized the history of the school.

As soon as Larned received Prudence's reply, she sent another letter with additional questions. More than a month passed before Prudence responded, and she apologized for the delay. "On Monday last while washing, I laid down my spectacles somewhere and have not been able to find them since," Prudence wrote. "I am now writing with an old pair with only one glass, and I am obliged to keep the other eye shut in order to see at all."[16] Larned wanted to know where Prudence was born and asked about the academic performance of her black students.

"It is my opinion that the colored scholars under my care made as good, if not better progress than the same number of whites taken from the same positions in life," Prudence responded. "W.H. Burleigh taught in my school for some time. I would refer you to him for any information you may wish."[17] At the beginning of 1870, Larned sent Prudence a draft of her history of the Canterbury school, and Prudence made certain corrections. "When your book is ready, send me a copy together with the price if you please, and I will send you back the amount," Prudence wrote.[18] "I hope you are an advocate of the Woman Suffrage Question."[19] Prudence exchanged more letters with Larned; ten years elapsed before Larned published the story of Prudence Crandall's school in 1880.

Larned took Philleo's advice and contacted William Burleigh to learn more about the school. Burleigh told her about the classroom subjects and routines, the contribution that Prudence's sister Almira made to the school, and the opposition they encountered.[20] Much had changed for Burleigh since the days of his youth teaching at Prudence Crandall's school. In the span of two years a rapid series of tragedies had rocked his personal life.[21] Early in 1863, his father died. In May of the same year Burleigh lost his wife of twenty-eight years. In 1865 his oldest daughter died; she left a husband, a five-year-old daughter, and a three-year-old son. Eighteen days later, Burleigh's son, William Henry, studying medicine in Brooklyn, New York, died from a sudden illness. He was twenty-two.

"This mystery of suffering must have some kindly meaning, and though I cannot feel it, and my soul rebels, I stay my faith on the certainty that God is good, and does not willingly afflict the children of men," Burleigh wrote. "It is a difficult matter for me to drag myself from the solitude of my chamber."[22]

Celia Burr, a journalist, literary editor, and teacher, helped end Burleigh's sadness. They had met briefly in Syracuse when Burleigh had visited Rev. Samuel May. They married and lived in New York City.

In the summer of 1870, Burleigh spent a number of days at Gerrit Smith's home in Peterboro, New York. Smith, a controversial abolitionist who had supported John Brown, was now an elder of the faded abolitionist movement.[23] At a picnic at Smith's home, Burleigh unexpectedly met up with Samuel May. They discussed Prudence Crandall's school, the election of Abraham Lincoln, and the end of slavery. "Mr. Burleigh referred to it many times as one of the delightful episodes of the summer," Celia wrote.[24]

At the end of the summer of 1870, Celia noted that William's poor health prevented him from writing, and he "gave himself up to the enjoyment of the beautiful world around him."[25] William Burleigh died on March 18, 1871. There were many formal tributes, but it was a black student—one of his own students at Prudence Crandall's school—who had best memorialized him in a sentence in 1834. "He lived like those who seek a better country."[26]

After his wife Lucretia died in 1865, Samuel May continued as pastor of the Church of the Messiah in Syracuse. Two years later, after he turned seventy, he preached a long sermon to his parish. May recounted a trip he took as a young man into Virginia where he saw slavery for the first time and resolved to help bring about its end. He recalled listening to William

Lloyd Garrison speak in Boston in 1830; Garrison's speech gave "direction and character to my course as a citizen and minister."[27] May then told his congregation he intended to step down. "I am now an old man, unable to labor as I would and as I once could . . . Now therefore, as I have long intended to do if I should live to be seventy, I tender to you, trustees and members of this church, my resignation."[28]

In the spring of 1871, May planned to visit Garrison and other friends in New England, but illness kept him home in Syracuse. May recovered but had a relapse in June. Cornell University President Andrew White visited him at his home in July and found May resting in bed. "If I die, I may have a clearer vision, but I cannot have a surer faith," May said.[29] A large oil painting of a woman—the original portrait of Prudence Crandall painted in 1834—hung over May's bed. Crandall had given the painting to May for all of his efforts on her behalf. May always displayed it where he would see it each day.[30]

That night at ten o'clock, Samuel Joseph May died. When the new minister of May's church announced May's passing to the congregation the next day, the service came to a halt as parishioners openly grieved. Word spread through the neighborhoods in Syracuse, and black citizens put on mourning badges as they had after Abraham Lincoln's death.[31] "A zealot, he had none of the zealot's bitterness," the editors of the *Syracuse Daily Standard* said. "A reformer, he had not the reformer's caustic tongue; a theologian of pronounced views, he had none of the theologian's regard for sect." The *Daily Standard* noted that May fought for causes not supported by popular opinion and lived to see "the triumph of nearly all the principles for which he contended."[32]

Garrison summoned the strength to travel to Syracuse. "Farewell—at the longest a brief farewell—friend of liberty, of temperance, of peace, of universal brotherhood, of equal rights for the whole human race," Garrison said. "Farewell . . . most loving and most loved of men."[33]

"I had the sad news of the death of our dear old friend Samuel J. May," Prudence Philleo wrote to Sarah Fayerweather. "He was one of the best persons I ever knew, and he has gone to that heaven where soul responds to soul, and love and affection never dies."[34] Prudence noted that of all the memorials to May she had read, Garrison's "was the only one that said anything in relation to the active part Rev. May had taken in the female suffrage question. Bless his dear old soul."[35]

Prudence took care of both Calvin and her mother Esther, who were in poor health. Esther Crandall died on February 13, 1872. Calvin increasingly spent his time indoors reading in the study and eating simple meals of bread, milk, cornbread, and apples.[36] In addition to the black eye patch he wore dating back to his headfirst fall into a fireplace, Calvin often wore a long dressing gown of "bright, large, fringed calico, flapping about his legs in the wind."[37] At dinnertime, Calvin kept everyone waiting while he offered lengthy blessings that focused on divine but severe punishment for sinners.[38]

In the spring of 1872, Prudence expanded her herd of cattle and dairy cows and planted a variety of crops.[39] "The rye crop is good, corn very good, buckwheat filling nicely, my team excellent, my plow-boy not to beat," Prudence wrote. In 1873 Prudence's niece, Clarissa Crandall Keith, and her three young children, Lucy, Willie, and Rena, arrived at Prudence's farm after Clarissa's husband had deserted her to prospect for gold. "Here my mother came with her three children . . . while father was prospecting in the mines of Colorado," Rena later wrote. "Mother was a rather helpless woman and so asked Aunt to take us in. This she did without a question though she was seventy at this time, with a sick husband to care for. I remember we had to carry wood and water up an outdoor stairway."[40]

Later that year Calvin suffered a paralyzing stroke; he died on January 5, 1874.[41] "I was in the house when he died," Rena Keith Clisby remembered. "I still maintain that Aunt's relations with her husband were not particularly unpleasant." Rena said Calvin and Prudence shared an appreciation for what they had endured together. "It was only that she wanted to be free to teach and to lecture. Her's was a free spirit."[42]

Three years before Calvin died, Prudence wrote a poem titled "A Lover's Wish." "I wish I had a lover, to smooth life's thorny way . . . I'd never more be sad, to be loved and to be loving."[43] Prudence showed Calvin more compassion than he might have expected or deserved in the last years of his life. After his death she remained close to his children; they greatly appreciated her love and support. LeBaron Goodwin, Prudence's step-grandchild who had lived with Prudence before joining the Army, moved back to Illinois in 1875 in order to help Prudence. He brought his wife and two young daughters and lived next door to her farm.

Helen Garrison's niece, Anna Benson Percy, came to live with the Garrisons at their home in Boston in June of 1875. Anna provided care for

Helen Garrison, whose condition from an earlier stroke had worsened. In January 1876, the health of the Garrisons took a turn for the worse. Both William Lloyd and Helen suffered terrible colds. Their doctor suspected they had pneumonia. Toward the end of the month, Helen lost consciousness. On Tuesday, January 25th, family members gathered by her bedside with William Lloyd—still very sick—resting in a chair next to her. At ten o'clock that morning, Helen Benson Garrison died. The grief of her children was tempered by the knowledge that she was finally free from the paralysis she had endured for twelve years. "Although we could not help weeping, we could not but rejoice and be thankful for her great release from suffering and pain," her son Frank wrote.[44]

William Lloyd Garrison did not see things the same way. He always saw Helen as his vital, loving wife, even in her diminished state. Her mind was sound. When he traveled extensively in the 1860s and 1870s, he wrote to her almost daily. Through his letters he shared his experiences with her, and she replied with news about their family. Helen's death was an end to the life she had created for Lloyd and their children. As she told him in a letter written near the end of her life, "My happiness is in seeing others made to feel that they are appreciated, and to add my mite to their enjoyment . . . But I need nothing so much as your dear smiling face to cheer and enliven my few remaining days."[45]

The family held a private funeral in their home. Samuel May's sister, Abigail May Alcott, remembered Helen and her sisters. "I can never forget the early impression the sweet Benson sisters at Brooklyn made upon me . . . those charming days at Brooklyn are hallowed to my memory as among the happiest of my girlhood. It was a lovely circle of peace, goodwill, and godliness."[46]

Garrison wrote his own memorial to Helen. In a thirty-page tribute he expressed his grief at her loss and remembered their first meeting. "If it was not 'love at first sight' on my part, it was something very like it—a magnetic influence being exerted which became irresistible."[47] Garrison devoted three pages of Helen Garrison's memorial booklet to Prudence Crandall. He described how the Benson family had helped and supported Prudence and then wrote at length about the controversy regarding her school. "Her case is without a parallel," Garrison wrote, "and the new generation which has since come upon the stage will read the facts pertaining to it as though they related to some occurrence in a remote age and among a semi-civilized people."[48] Crandall had stood firm while "assailed in the most violent and opprobrious manner."[49] Garrison ended his praise for Prudence Crandall by noting, "After the lapse of forty-three years, she is still living to bless God for the marvelous deliverance which has since been wrought in behalf of that class so long 'peeled, meted out, and trodden under foot.'"[50]

After Prudence Crandall's older brother, Hezekiah, lost his third wife, Patience, to disease in 1876, Prudence invited him to visit her in Illinois. She suggested that he move permanently to Illinois. With the help of his grandchildren, who settled his affairs in Connecticut, Hezekiah traveled west to join his sister.[51]

The 1876 centennial celebrations planned for the summer intrigued Prudence. She wanted to travel to Boston for the anniversary of the Revolutionary War. She remembered her dreamlike visit in 1834 when the abolitionist community celebrated her courage and leadership. She also wanted to attend the Centennial Exposition in Philadelphia. Rena Keith Clisby remembered that Prudence wanted "to see the progress our nation had made in one hundred years."[52] Unfortunately, as Rena recalled, "her means would not permit such a journey."[53]

By June, William Lloyd Garrison felt well enough to travel. He too wanted to celebrate the nation's founding and made his way to Philadelphia with his son Frank to visit the Centennial Exhibition. The exhibition—an urban fair on a scale the country had never before witnessed—featured gigantic displays of modern technology and architecture, steam engines and machinery, and new wonders for the household, including typewriters, mechanical calculators, and Alexander Graham Bell's telephone. Everywhere Garrison saw tributes to the Founding Fathers and the Constitution. The crowds and strenuous activity proved too much for Garrison, along with what he deemed a whitewash of history. He retreated to Boston and wrote a column for the *Independent* titled "Centennial Reflections." Garrison said Americans should resist the temptation to "burn incense to the memories of the famous dead" and should portray the country's history of slavery honestly. Garrison reminded readers that George Washington, Thomas Jefferson, and Patrick Henry all owned slaves and did little or nothing to protest the institution of slavery. "The melancholy fact is that the nation has never repented of its great transgression," Garrison wrote.[54]

Three days after his column appeared, Garrison received a letter from his son Wendell, who did not appreciate his father's harsh tone. Garrison thanked Wendell for his opinion but explained why he needed to "induce sober reflection" into what was otherwise a circus of "gush and glorification." He sharpened his words in a manner reminiscent of the *Liberator* and the inflammatory speeches of George Thompson. "This nation has been the guiltiest of all the nations of the earth since its independence of Great Britain," Garrison wrote to Wendell. "Too long have 'our Revolutionary Fathers' been held up as the noblest of patriots and the truest friends of liberty. They were too cowardly and too selfish to adhere to the principles they laid down. . . . I trust no child of mine will ever fail to recognize their exceeding blameworthiness, or consider a reference to it ill-timed when they are presented for the admiration of the world."[55]

William Lloyd and Wendell were increasingly at odds during this time. Wendell's choice of occupation—journalist and editor at the *Nation*—created the potential for friction between father and son. The *Nation* was not the *Liberator*. In 1874 the *Nation* had refused to condemn vigilante activity carried out by the Ku Klux Klan. Wendell had defended his magazine's stance by inferring that illegal violence and intimidation by southern whites provided balance to the corrupt Reconstruction governments run by blacks.[56] Wendell's work at the *Nation* placed him in the ranks of moderates who supported an end to the policies of Reconstruction, a return to local governmental control in the South, and the Democratic Party's presidential candidate in 1876.[57] For William Lloyd Garrison, this agenda was nothing less than a national disaster and a reversal of the Civil War.

Garrison's fears about the direction of the country were confirmed in the aftermath of the presidential election of 1876. The Republican presidential candidate—Rutherford Hayes—won the election, but only through a disputed process. Supporters of Democrat Samuel J. Tilden believed he had won the popular vote; the margin was so close that the House of Representatives had to determine the outcome. The House—with a majority of Democrats—surprisingly voted to install Republican Hayes as president, leading to speculation about a deal between Hayes and the Southern Democrats. After his inauguration, Republican Hayes did exactly what the Democratic presidential candidate had promised to do, "namely, withdraw the Federal troops—and thus leave the poor colored people of the South, and also all the loyal white Republicans, without any protection."[58] The Republicans sold their soul to retain the presidency, Garrison said, ending the federal government's pledge to guarantee equality for the former slaves. Violence escalated against blacks in the South, and many former slaves migrated to northern and western states.

The year 1876 was a fateful one for Prudence Crandall. Her brother Hezekiah joined her in Illinois. Her inability to travel to the centennial celebrations and witness the sensational changes in science and technology left her wanting. When two parishioners of the Baptist Church in Cordova, Illinois, took a trip to Kansas and returned with stories of favorable opportunities for farming and business, Crandall took notice. They told her about progressive political and social policies in Kansas. When a man approached Crandall and her brother and offered to trade a 160-acre farm in Kansas for Prudence's house in Illinois, Crandall impulsively agreed to swap for the Kansas property, sight unseen.[59]

Prudence Crandall had succeeded in transforming her father's ill-fated homestead in Illinois into various properties that sustained members of the Crandall family. She recently had moved from her farm in Cordova to a house in town, where her quality of life was good. Despite her success, Crandall apparently longed for new challenges. Her surprising decision to leave the security of Illinois for an unseen prairie farm, however, was in keeping with a certain Crandall tradition. Her father had left the comfort of the Rhode Island town created by his in-laws in order to create a new life in Canterbury. Her brother Hezekiah had left the family farm to gamble on the creation of a cotton factory. Prudence's own life was marked by many unconventional choices and the well-known story of her school for black women.

In spring of 1877, Prudence, Hezekiah, Clarissa, and Clarissa's children Lucy, Willie, and Rena packed their belongings and headed west. "What a venture," Rena remembered. "We went by train across the state of Missouri to southeastern Kansas, to the town of Elk Falls, going the last 35 miles by stage, carrying the six of us with all our baggage. The roads were new and rough, and many times we swayed perilously, while grandfather shouted, 'We're gone!'"[60]

They reached the small, isolated Kansas town of Elk Falls, where they hired a wagon to carry them to their farm. After traveling a mile they finally reached their destination. Clarissa and Prudence made beds for everyone on the floor of the farmhouse. "The house was poor and small,"

Rena wrote. "The farm of 160 acres was only half in cultivation, with poor soil at that."[61]

Rena believed that her Aunt Prudence had lost money on the property swap and observed that others had tried to take advantage of Prudence. "She never pressed those who owed her," Rena wrote. "She hired a man to build a stone wall fence around the farm, paying him $500 *before* it was finished—it was never finished!"[62]

Of necessity, they all pitched in—including seventy-three-year-old Prudence and seventy-seven-year-old Hezekiah—to try to make the farm productive. Prudence bought an ox team to plow the fields for corn and sorghum. They planted a garden with pumpkins, potatoes, turnips, and greens and bought a few chickens and cows. "Our living was the plainest," Rena said. Prudence's niece Esther worried that Prudence and her brother Hezekiah would not have enough food. "Esther fears we shall starve here in Kansas," Prudence wrote to Esther's sister Huldah. "Do assure her there is no sort of danger as yet."[63]

The primitive and challenging conditions did not overwhelm Prudence, and the Crandall kin lived on cornbread, potatoes, molasses, and milk, Rena remembered. "I never remember being hungry."[64] The harvest that fall included a large quantity of corn, sorghum—which yielded eighteen gallons of sweet syrup—garden vegetables, and three wagon loads of peaches from two hundred peach trees. "We have had no grasshoppers except the native hopper, and they have done no harm," Prudence wrote.[65] In 1874 grasshoppers and locusts had devastated the crops in Kansas. No infestations occurred in 1877. With much hard work, Prudence and her relatives survived through the summer and fall. Prudence exaggerated for the benefit of Hezekiah's children back East when she wrote to her niece Huldah, "I never spent a more pleasant summer than this has been in all the seventy-four years of my life."[66]

Prudence continued to write to Sarah Harris Fayerweather. After moving to Illinois, Prudence often invited Sarah to travel west for a visit. "You do not know how much I value every word you write," Prudence told Sarah. "I have not a friend on earth I would be more rejoiced to see than yourself."[67] They shared scarce information about the black students who had attended Prudence's school. Prudence learned that Amy Fenner "is now Mrs. Parker if I remember the name."[68] Ann Hammond had traveled to England. Prudence hoped to see Sarah again. "I do want you to come out here very much indeed."[69]

Sarah celebrated her sixty-sixth birthday on April 16, 1878. Despite occasional bouts of poor health, Sarah felt well enough to make the long journey to visit to her teacher and friend. The trip from Rhode Island to Elk Falls, Kansas—half the distance across the United States—took a few days by train. Sarah packed her clothes and personal items and boarded the train for the longest journey of her life. She looked out the passenger car window as the steam train rolled from Rhode Island into Connecticut along the Long Island Sound, through the urban center of New York City into the countryside of New Jersey and Pennsylvania. The landscape continued to change as she passed through occasional rolling hills and plenty of flat, lush farmland in Ohio, Indiana, and Missouri. From Missouri, the train brought Sarah into southeastern Kansas and her final stop by rail, in Independence, Kansas. A line running east and west through Elk Falls was under construction and scheduled to open in 1879.[70] Sarah collected her baggage at the depot in Independence and boarded a stagecoach for the thirty-mile trek to Elk Falls. After riding a few hours on rough roads, she made one last transfer. As Prudence and her relatives had done one year before, Sarah hired a wagon to drive the final mile from Elk Falls to Prudence's farm.

Rena Keith was nine years old when Sarah arrived at the front door and greeted Prudence. "She was quite a fine looking woman with regular features, and with white hair with deep waves," Rena wrote. "There was much animated talk between them."[71] Prudence told Rena that Sarah had been the first "colored girl who applied for admission to her school in Canterbury."[72]

Sarah Harris Fayerweather and Prudence Crandall had a joyful reunion. These two remarkable women—united after so much time—shared many days of reflection surrounded by a prairie landscape of open fields, low orchards of fruit trees, and occasional rocky hills. Prudence was gratified to learn that two of Sarah's children, young Sarah and George, had become teachers.[73]

In their days together and years apart, Sarah and Prudence shared times of profound upheaval and growth. Much had changed in their personal lives and much more had changed in their country. Just nineteen years earlier, "Bloody Kansas" was a dangerous battleground in a prelude to the Civil War. Now Kansas exemplified America's rapid expansion and development westward.

Young Rena, who now had to share her aunt with a guest from the East Coast, grew impatient as Sarah stayed for two weeks. So much time had elapsed by Rena's estimation that she speculated, "Aunt would have been glad to have her visit someone else!"[74] But Prudence had waited years to catch up with her former student, the person who more than anyone else had changed her life, and Sarah had traveled a great distance to see her friend. They had lost many of their friends and relatives—Samuel and Lucretia May, Pardon, Esther, Almira and Reuben Crandall, and William Burleigh—as well as their own husbands. Prudence and Sarah had lived to see each other once again; they did not hurry their time together.

When Sarah returned to Rhode Island, she had a reoccurrence of a health problem she had experienced earlier in her life—an acute swelling in her neck. This time the illness intensified, and she lost the ability to speak. Sarah Harris Fayerweather died on November 16, 1878. Prudence wrote to one of her daughters, Mary Fayerweather, and told Mary how sorry she was to hear of her mother's passing and offered her love to all of Sarah's children.[75]

Before the decade ended, abolitionists bade farewell to other friends and allies. Simon S. Jocelyn, who had attempted to create a school for black men in New Haven and later had assisted Arthur Tappan, Prudence Crandall, and William Lloyd Garrison, died on August 17, 1879. At Jocelyn's funeral, black and white ministers including Henry Ward Beecher celebrated his life.[76] In Florence, Massachusetts, Charles C. Burleigh, William's brother, served as the resident speaker of the Free Congregational Society of Florence. Few of his friends in Florence, however, knew that as a young man he had worked with Samuel May and Prudence Crandall, edited the *Unionist*, and helped to save William Lloyd Garrison's life during riots in Boston. Burleigh's appearance had not changed since his younger days except that his long black hair had turned gray. He still had a full beard that touched his chest and shoulder-length hair that curled in ringlets.[77] Years earlier he had pledged not to cut his hair or shave his beard until slavery had ended. After the Civil War and the end of slavery, however, Burleigh could not bear to change his appearance.

On Thursday, June 13, 1878, Charles rushed down the street to mail a letter at the train depot just as a train approached. When he attempted to cross the tracks just ahead of the train, he slipped and fell on the rails. The train struck Burleigh and killed him instantly.[78] Charles was five months short of his sixty-eighth birthday. His ailing friend William Lloyd Garrison, who spent an increasing amount of time attending funerals and writing memorials for his friends, recovered well enough to travel to Florence for Charles's funeral on Sunday, June 16.[79] "He traveled many thousands of miles," Garrison said, "addressed hundreds of thousands of hearers, cheerfully encountering every hardship, serenely confronting mobocratic violence, shrinking from no peril."[80]

In October 1878, Garrison journeyed to the town of his birth, Newburyport, Massachusetts. Sixty years earlier as a boy of twelve, he had begun his career in journalism as an apprentice at the *Newburyport Herald*. The humble beginnings as a "printer's devil," boiling the inky liquid that coated the press, quickly had led to setting type and then to writing and editing the newspaper. His time at the *Herald* had allowed for the creation of the *Liberator* and everything that followed.

The publisher and editors of the *Herald* invited Garrison to return to the newspaper that gave him his first job. When he walked into the *Herald's* office on State Street, the employees greeted him with applause. Those who had worked at the *Herald* with Garrison in the 1820s were long gone; the *Herald* employees viewed the white-haired abolitionist as a living historical character. The editor of the *Herald* gave Garrison a tour; steam-powered presses had replaced the primitive hand presses and buckets of boiled ink. Printers, however, still set the type by hand, and Garrison gamely put his skills to the test. With a surprising speed that impressed the men in the *Herald's* print room, he quickly set into type three of his own poems. "I did not squabble a line," Garrison said proudly, "and on taking a proof of what I had set, there was not a single error."[81]

On October 14, 1878, the New England Franklin Club, a local association of publishing houses and newspapers, held a dinner in Boston in honor of Garrison's sixtieth anniversary in journalism. The son of *Herald* publisher Ephraim W. Allen spoke and "described in glowing phrase the apprentice boy who had lived in his father's house and won the affection of the whole family."[82] Garrison appreciated the irony of receiving accolades from representatives of the very newspapers that had attacked him when he launched the *Liberator* in 1831. One person at the dinner admitted he helped print the inflammatory flyer in 1835 that had offered a one hundred dollar reward to the first person who attacked George Thompson, which led to the riot that nearly killed Garrison.[83] When Garrison spoke, he did not ignore those who had opposed his antislavery efforts.

"However we may have differed in opinion, in regard to the modus operandi in seeking the abolition of slavery, I am quite sure of one thing at this hour," Garrison said, "and that is one of thankfulness to God that chattel slavery no longer curses our land. . . . By speaking the truth and applying it boldly to the conscience of the people, there is no need of despairing the final result. . . . Every craft is honorable if it is useful, but the printing craft is that which takes hold of the mind and intellect and soul. It is the power to move the world, and it is moving it. . . . As long as we have a free press, free speech, free inquiry, and free schools, we shall never go down."[84]

In the weeks and months thereafter, Garrison's health worsened. He rested in bed with a painful sore throat. Garrison said that at his age the "outward man" encountered inevitable deterioration.[85]

Despite his poor health, Garrison spoke out against new forms of prejudice and injustice. When the California legislature and the U.S. Congress passed legislation permitting discrimination against Chinese immigrants, Garrison wrote letters criticizing the policies. Senator James G. Blaine of Maine, who led a movement to close America's borders to the Chinese, particularly offended Garrison. "The reasons advanced by Mr. Blaine in opposition to the Chinese were unworthy of his head and heart, and therefore unworthy of the least consideration," Garrison wrote to the *New York Tribune* in February 1879.[86] When Garrison condemned the persecution of the Chinese immigrants, he received "some hot denunciations from California, as I used to from the South for my anti-slavery articles."[87] Once more Garrison threw himself into the fray against a new rising tide of prejudice. "It is essentially the old anti-slavery issue in another form," Garrison said, "whether one portion of mankind may rightfully claim superiority over another on account of birth, descent, or nativity, or for any other reason, and deny to them those rights and interests which pertain to our common humanity."[88]

At the beginning of March 1879, Garrison wrote to Prudence Crandall. He told her that he had only recently discovered her "locality and post office address." He sent her a copy of the *Memorial* he had written for Helen, which included his lengthy tribute to Prudence, together with newspaper clippings of some of his columns and a personal letter. That led to a warm exchange of letters. Prudence wrote back, "As Samuel J. May would say, 'My dear Garrison.' I thank God that you still live, and have the ability to hold up the standard of justice as in former days."[89] She told him that she always looked for his articles and letters in the newspapers and knew he would advocate "something good for humanity." She asked about Helen's brother George Benson and told Garrison of the death of Sarah Harris Fayerweather. Prudence described the favorable climate in Kansas and life at her home. "In a frame under glass I have a group of dear friends, I mean their pictures," she joked, "and among them is Benjamin Lundy, Wendell Phillips, and your noble self. I would cut the picture of your dear Helen from the book you sent, were it not for injuring the book so sadly."[90] She said surveyors had plotted the path of a new rail line to Elk Falls, "so we shall be connected by rail to the large cities again as we were at Cordova. Yours for justice and truth, Prudence."[91]

Garrison continued the correspondence. "I warmly reciprocate your congratulations on having been permitted to live to see the marvelous changes that have taken place in public sentiment and in the condition of the colored people generally," Garrison wrote.[92] He told Crandall how she had met the "trials and outrages" of her opponents in Canterbury "so nobly in the true martyr spirit" and that her efforts had secured "to you everlasting historical fame."[93] Garrison said that George Benson lived not far from her in Lawrence, Kansas, but was "greatly broken in health." He discussed his grandchildren and sent photographs, including a picture of Helen. Crandall told Garrison how she had cried "tears of joy" when she read his memorial to Helen—"I think that there are but few more perfect unions this side of the Eternal World."[94] She said she would not mingle the photograph of Helen with her other pictures "for it would be too much like allowing my unholy hands to touch you."[95] Prudence reflected on those who recently had passed away, including Charles Burleigh and George Thompson. Then she told Garrison she was ready for a new adventure.

"I saw in some paper that a company of colored persons are about to make a settlement in the Indian Territory west of Kansas," Prudence wrote. "I almost wish I could go with them. My health is very good and if I should continue to enjoy the same till they get settled, I am sure that

I shall visit them sometime. Indians often camp in a grove on the stream called the Wild Cat, in sight of our door."[96]

During the time that Garrison and Crandall exchanged letters, a daughter of New England returned to Boston. She had come to secure a small military pension that was owed to her on behalf of her deceased husband, who had served in the War of 1812. While in Boston, she inquired about William Lloyd Garrison and learned that he lived in Roxbury. On Friday, April 4, 1879, she took a tram to his neighborhood, walked to his house, and knocked on the door. When he opened the door, to his great surprise and delight, William Lloyd Garrison looked upon Maria W. Stewart.

"It is seldom, indeed, that two persons, after a separation of forty-six years, are permitted to see each other again in the flesh," Garrison said.[97] They talked about their lives during the past five decades. Stewart knew of Garrison's work as publisher of the *Liberator* and his leadership in the antislavery movement. Garrison, however, knew nothing of what had happened to Maria Stewart. He told her he had entirely lost sight of her and did not know where she had gone or even whether she was still alive. Stewart told him of her experiences teaching in New York City, her move to Baltimore, and her many years in Washington, D.C., teaching Sunday school and working at the Freedmen's Hospital. At various times she had lived in poverty but told him she never had abandoned her faith in God, her belief in the benefit of education, and her desire to encourage those around her to fulfill their potential.

Garrison and Stewart discussed the progress they had witnessed that seemed almost impossible in 1833—the growth and success of the abolitionist movement, emancipation, and the increasing interest in equal rights for women. Stewart had advocated for all of those causes. Garrison acknowledged that the fight for equality for blacks was far from over. "I feel sure that a just God will yet fully vindicate their cause and pour his retribution upon their cruel persecutors," he told Stewart, reaching back in time for the spirit of David Walker.[98] He recounted Maria's first appearance at the office of the *Liberator*, manuscripts in hand. "I was impressed by your intelligence and excellence of character," Garrison said.[99] They talked about her essays and her speeches and how she had blazed a trail in Boston that no woman—black or white—had ever pursued.

After their unexpected and happy reunion, Garrison wrote Stewart a note. "The sight of you at once carried me back in memory to the very commencement of the anti-slavery movement in this city," he said. "You . . . were in the flush and promise of a ripening womanhood, with a graceful form and a pleasing countenance."[100] Garrison praised her commitment to the advancement of women and blacks. "Your whole adult life has been devoted to the noble task of educating and elevating your people, sympathizing with them in their affliction, and assisting them in their needs," he wrote. "You are still animated with the spirit of your earlier life and striving to do what in you lies to succor the outcast, reclaim the wanderer, and lift up the fallen. . . . Cherishing the same respect for you that I had at the beginning, I remain your friend and well-wisher, William Lloyd Garrison."[101]

At long last, Maria Stewart received good financial news. As a result of legislation passed by Congress in 1878, Maria qualified for her husband's military pension. The afternoon she spent with Garrison influenced her decision to use the first payments she received to reprint and expand her pamphlet of speeches and essays that Garrison had published in the 1830s.[102] In August 1879, an advertisement appeared in the *People's Advocate*, a black newspaper in Washington, D.C., promoting *Meditations*, by Mrs. Maria W. Stewart: "A new and enlarged edition, containing the devout and fervid meditations of the author, her lectures delivered before New York and Boston audiences, and an interesting account of her sufferings during the war."[103]

Prudence Crandall finished what would be her last letter to William Lloyd Garrison on April 20, 1879. She put it aside and did not send it right away; she intended to add a few lines. Prudence had no idea that William Lloyd was dying. The cold he had contracted at the beginning of the year had turned into walking pneumonia. "My throat had been so sore and inflamed as to make any attempt to swallow even liquids very painful," Garrison told his daughter Fanny.[104] He pushed himself to travel to the state capital when the Massachusetts legislature considered a bill that would allow women to vote for members of school committees and boards of education, and he spoke in favor of the measure. Garrison left before the Senate voted for final passage because of fatigue.[105]

Perhaps in part as a result of his correspondence with Prudence Crandall, Garrison took a strong interest in the plight of blacks migrating from the south to the western states and to Kansas in particular. In a letter to the *Boston Journal*, Garrison asked readers to help blacks "fleeing from insupportable wrong and outrage . . . in quest of freedom and safety."[106] He urged readers to send donations to a minister who helped former slaves travel "forward to free Kansas."[107] At the request of Robert Morris, the black attorney who had argued the first school desegregation case in Boston in 1848, Garrison issued a public statement. Garrison said if the United States failed to honor the promises of emancipation, "The battle of liberty and equal rights is to be fought over again . . . Let the rallying cry be heard from the Atlantic to the Pacific coast, 'Liberty and equal rights for each, for all, and forever . . .'"[108]

One week later, Frank Garrison helped his frail father board a train for New York City. In a last-ditch effort to find successful medical treatment, his daughter Fanny had convinced her father to consult with Dr. Leonard Weber, a professor at the New York Post Graduate Medical School and president of St. Mark's Hospital. Weber initially gave a favorable prognosis and predicted steady recovery. By May 10, however, Garrison could no longer get out of bed.

Prudence Crandall finally put her letter to Garrison in the mail on May 10. She sent it to Boston where it was forwarded to New York City. Garrison could barely sit up and read his mail when Prudence's letter arrived. She wrote about her young niece Rena Keith and asked if Garrison had any information concerning a particular lecture given by Wendell Phillips. She discussed the exodus of blacks from the southern states and told Garrison, "The colored people from the South are by scores coming into Kansas—but I heard of none near us—but quite a number have been sent to Topeka."[109] She told Garrison that his grandchildren and "the coming generation 'will rise up and call you blessed.'" Prudence closed her letter with a special wish for her dear friend. "'May the dove of peace rest upon you' is the prayer of your admiring friend, Prudence C. Philleo."[110] It was one of the very last letters Garrison read.[111]

On Friday, May 23, Garrison spoke of "going home" and seeing his mother. At one point he asked if he was in England. Garrison told Dr. Weber he wanted "to finish it up!"[112] That night his children gathered around him and sang his favorite hymns. Garrison fell silent but tapped his hand in time with the music. With his family at his bedside, William Lloyd Garrison died on Saturday, May 24, 1879. Lydia Maria Child wrote, "In the very city where he had been dragged to prison to save his life from a mob, and where his effigy had been hung on a gallows before his own door, the flags were placed at half-mast to announce his decease."[113]

Garrison's funeral on May 28, 1879, was one of the last great reunions of the abolitionists of the 1830s and 1840s. The pallbearers included Wendell Phillips, Theodore Dwight Weld, Rev. Samuel May Jr.—the cousin of Samuel Joseph May—and a number of those who had worked with Garrison at the *Liberator*. They included Charles Mitchell, a black man who had served in the Fifty-fifth Massachusetts Volunteer Colored Regiment with George Garrison, and Samuel Sewall, the attorney who had helped finance the *Liberator*.

Theodore Dwight Weld's voice filled with emotion as he recalled how Garrison risked his life for the principle of equality. Weld spoke of "the power of a single soul, *alone*, of a single soul touched with sacred fire . . . the indomitable will, the conscience that never shrinks, and always points to duty."[114] Garrison spoke out when others refused to see the evil of slavery, Weld said. "No wonder he used words that sounded hard to those very soft and shrinking people who loved smooth things, and to those who sympathized with slavery. . . . No wonder the slaveholders put a price upon his head . . . He had struck the very heart of the monster."[115]

Rev. Samuel Johnson observed that in the years following the Civil War, historians had credited political strategies and military victories with ending slavery. This ignored the essential work of "the great abolition movement, which for more than thirty years rocked the foundation of church and state," he said. Garrison had helped lead the movement by opposing colonization and fighting for equal rights and immediate emancipation. "The soul of the people was lifted by that steadfast pressure of an eternal principle," Johnson said.[116]

Garrison's death gave Frederick Douglass pause. Garrison and Douglass had been friends and rival publishers who sometimes had disagreed about the substance and strategy of the abolitionist movement. At a memorial service for Garrison in Washington, D.C., Douglass did not ignore their differences. "Speaking for myself, I must frankly say I have sometimes thought him uncharitable to those who differed from him," Douglass said. "Honest himself, he could not always see how men could differ from him and still be honest."[117]

In attacking slavery and prejudice, however, Douglass said Garrison had been necessarily severe. "He moved not with the tide, but against it. He rose not by the power of the Church or the State, but in bold, inflexible and defiant opposition to the mighty power of both. It was the glory of this man that he could stand alone with the truth, and calmly await the result."[118]

Douglass said that in the years since the Civil War the United States had not kept faith with emancipation and the constitutional amendments guaranteeing equality. A spirit of evil had been revived. "The lessons he taught fifty years ago from his garret in Boston are only yet half learned by the nation."[119] Douglass noted that even in the last weeks of Garrison's life, he had called attention to increased hostility toward blacks and discrimination against Chinese immigrants. "With him it was not race or color but humanity," Douglass said.[120] "In this second battle for liberty and nation we shall sorely miss the mind and voice of William Lloyd Garrison."[121]

Prudence Crandall witnessed a remarkable transformation of the western United States during her years in Elks Falls, Kansas. The transcontinental railroad—completed in 1869—spawned rapid development. Settlers increasingly fenced and farmed the open plains. "How many changes we have passed through," Crandall wrote.[1]

At the beginning of the 1870s, buffalo filled the grasslands of Kansas and other western states. Scouts reported herds fifty miles wide. When herds forced the trains to slow or stop, the railroads waged war against the animals. Hunters killed tens of millions of buffalo in the great slaughter of the 1870s.[2] Tourists were encouraged to join in the killing. The *London Times* advertised a holiday hunt in Kansas where British citizens could "shoot from the window of a railway carriage on the Union Pacific."[3] The son of Czar Alexander II of Russia, Grand Duke Alexis, traveled to Kansas to join in gunning down the buffalo.[4] By the end of the decade the animal was nearly extinct.

"After the buffalo and the Indian disappeared, after the hunters were gone, the pioneers came," Kansas commentator Sheridan Ploughe wrote in 1917. "It is but a half century from bison to shorthorn, from the untamed herds on the plains to the silos of modern farming."[5] Ploughe celebrated displacing "the tenants of the soil of a thousand years" to make way for settlers and domesticated livestock.[6]

The railroad extension into Elk Falls had increased opportunity and commerce. "There is a nice hotel built at the depot where four trains a day stop to take meals," Prudence wrote to her grandniece. "It is quite surprising to see the amount of cattle that are passed through here on the trains together with every kind of freight you can mention."[7] Local dairy farmers increased the size of their herds to sell milk and cheese to other cities and towns. A gristmill produced flour for statewide markets. Local congregations built two new churches, and the state constructed a school in nearby Howard.[8] "Our little city gains finely," Prudence said.[9] The railroad also created new hazards. In July 1880, when a few of Prudence's cattle crossed the new tracks, a speeding freight train struck and killed one of Prudence's prized oxen.[10]

Prudence's niece Clarissa and her children moved out of Crandall's home to a farm a few miles down the road in 1879. "We moved away from Aunt's and lived by ourselves, not far away," Rena Keith Clisby remembered, "near enough that we could go to see her at least once a week. We knew what awaited us on arrival—a warm welcome, with a 'pop up little dears,' as she told us to sit on her high couch bed."[11]

Clarissa married a stonemason, thirty-six-year-old "John" Hannant, the same man who had convinced Prudence Crandall to trade her property in Cordova, Illinois, for his farm in Elk Falls, sight unseen, and took five hundred dollars from her as payment to build a stone fence that he never completed.[12] In his dealings with Prudence he had heard her on more than one occasion remark that "everything I have shall go to Clarissa on my death."[13] Rena Keith Clisby thought Hannant had married her mother for her inheritance.

A visit by Clarissa's children on Sunday provided the highlight of the week for Prudence and Hezekiah. "Rena is coming soon to make a scrapbook of stories that she has been reading for a long time in the *Windham County Transcript*," Prudence wrote to a grandniece. "She has read them with great interest ever since we have been in Kansas."[14] Rena had most likely read old stories describing the school controversy. In addition to copies of the *Windham County Transcript*, Prudence subscribed to the *New York Tribune*, the *Boston Transcript*, and a spiritualist journal printed weekly in Boston, the *Banner of Light*.[15] "I enjoyed the séances and the testimonies of those who saw and talked with their loved ones on the 'other side,'" Rena wrote. "No doubt, Aunt (Prudence) was psychic."[16]

Maria W. Stewart published her collection of essays and speeches, *Meditations*, in August 1879. She enjoyed her new financial security for a brief time—she became ill toward the end of the year. Stewart, seventy-six years old, died in December. Rev. Alexander Crummell, a former student at Noyes Academy, presided at her funeral at St. Luke's Episcopal Church in Washington, D.C., on December 17, 1879.

"She was, in the early 1830s, in a real sense alone in unexplored territory," historian Marilyn Richardson wrote, "a woman placed by God—as she saw it—on an ethical and societal frontier. . . . Orphan, widow, solitary visionary, a woman who could claim to have 'traveled a good bit in my day,' she was both an independent and an isolated figure in the world."[17] The *People's Advocate* wrote, "Very few know of the remarkable career of this woman whose life has just drawn to a close. For half a century she was engaged in the work of elevating her race by lectures, teaching and various missionary and benevolent labors."[18]

The town of Canterbury and the views of its citizens had changed significantly in the fifty years following the closure of Crandall's school. In 1880 the *Windham County Transcript* wrote a story about the fiftieth wedding anniversary of a local black couple. Thomas Lathrop and his wife had married in 1830 in Canterbury just prior to the launch of Prudence's school. They received the "ill treatment put more or less largely upon every colored person in the town."[19] At a celebration at the Canterbury Westminster Congregational Church on November 25, 1880, friends honored the Lathrops with poems, hymns, and a collection that produced ninety dollars in gold for their golden anniversary.[20]

At the end of the celebration, attendees recalled the Prudence Crandall controversy. One white man admitted that opponents of the school had asked him to "be one of the number who should burn the house of Miss Crandall."[21] The man did not name the person who had made the request and said he had refused the invitation. Prudence Crandall never learned of the man's story; his confession, however, appeared to confirm what Crandall and her supporters had believed in 1834—that officials arrested Frederick Olney as a ploy to divert suspicion away from the true arsonists.

In 1880 Ellen Larned published the second volume of the history of Windham County, including the story of Prudence Crandall's school. Larned's book came at a time of renewed interest in Crandall. In response to Larned's account and Samuel May's book written eleven years earlier, a Providence attorney wrote an essay about Crandall's school that he presented to the Rhode Island Historical Society on December 28, 1880.

"The story of Prudence Crandall and her school has been told by

Samuel J. May from the standpoint of the abolitionists," Abraham Payne wrote. "It has been told by Miss Larned in her *History of Windham County* with judicial impartiality. If I venture to tell it again it is not because I expect to add anything to the eloquent dissertation of Mr. May or the careful narrative of Miss Larned, but because there are some features of the case about which no man living knows anything but myself."[22]

Payne, a Canterbury native who was fifteen years old when Prudence Crandall admitted Sarah Harris as a student, revealed little new information in his essay. He did, however, represent those who had opposed slavery but did not support equality for blacks. As to the violence that closed Crandall's school, Payne said, "We must remember that all government, in the last resort, must depend upon force, and that lynch law and other forms of lawless force will always appear when legal means are ineffectual to protect people in what they suppose to be their rights."[23]

Prudence and her brother Hezekiah turned seventy-seven and eighty in 1880, and they struggled with the physical labor their farm required. Their yield of peaches declined. "Last year they were killed with the frost, and why they do not bear this year I do not know," Prudence said.[24] To earn extra income, Prudence rented some of her land and expanded her small herd of dairy cows from nine to eleven. "We shall make butter as we did last winter; it will pay for milking in the winter and will bring cash."[25]

Kansas experienced an especially harsh winter from 1880 to 1881. A three-day ice storm in February preceded a severe blizzard that made it nearly impossible to travel. Livestock died in the fields from exposure and lack of food; farmers could not get through the deep snow with hay. "No such winter was ever known before in Kansas," a minister wrote.[26] On Friday, March 11, 1881, after awakening early and feeding the animals as he did each morning, Hezekiah Crandall came in for breakfast but could not eat. He told Prudence he needed to lie down, and she noticed he was trembling. Thinking he might have malaria, Prudence gave him quinine water, to no effect. On Saturday morning, despite having a bad cough and fever, Hezekiah got dressed and fed the animals. When he came back inside, he nearly fainted, and Prudence helped him into bed. His condition worsened. When friends visited, Hezekiah asked them to sing the hymns that William Lloyd Garrison's children had sung when Garrison lay dying.[27]

On March 22, 1881, Hezekiah "passed to the higher life," Prudence wrote. He "possessed a kind and forgiving spirit . . . A family moved in with us a few days before brother was taken sick, otherwise I should have been alone."[28] Rena Keith Clisby remembered Hezekiah's funeral. "I saw Aunt cry over him. The schools and stores of the town closed on the day he was buried. The song 'Sweet By and Bye' was sung at his funeral. Aunt must have been lonely after his death for she was all alone in the house on the hill."[29] Prudence, the last surviving Crandall in her immediate family, wrote, "I am the last leaf upon the tree."[30]

Prudence Crandall found her way back into the classroom. School officials in the nearby town of Howard invited her to speak on a number of occasions.[31] The school included both black and white students; one black female student rode into town on horseback each day. The experience stimulated Prudence to dream of creating an integrated school for black and white students. "I have great hopes yet—may I live to see it—[for] a college built on my farm for all classes and colors, particularly the children of the colored wanderers," she wrote in 1882. "I want professorships of the highest order."[32]

Despite her desire to take on new challenges, Prudence could no longer manage her farm. "She found it hard to hire anyone to work for her," a friend remembered, "so she advertised for a young man to run the place."[33] In 1882 she met Abraham C. Williams and invited him to live at her farm.[34] Prudence enjoyed Abraham's company so much that she adopted him as her son. Soon thereafter, Prudence's niece Clarissa returned to live with her aunt after leaving her second husband.

Prudence Crandall continued to fight for women's rights. She spoke for an hour at the Elk Falls July Fourth celebration of 1884, speaking in favor of equal rights for women and the fundamental freedoms of the United States.[35] The following year she spoke at an Independence Day rally in Winfield, Kansas, and again promoted the issue of women's rights.

In the summer of 1884, Mariana T. Folsom traveled to Kansas and interviewed Crandall for an article in the *Woman's Journal*. Folsom toured extensively throughout the United States and led a seven-month campaign for suffrage in Texas in 1885.[36] "I want to vote because when men and women work together they build homes, schools and safeguards for the good of society," Folsom said, "and men working alone build armies, navies, saloons and dens of vice and perpetuate the same with their ballots."[37]

"I am glad you have come," Crandall told Folsom.[38] Folsom said she never had dreamed of shaking hands with the "heroine" Prudence Crandall. "Prudence Crandall today is as vigorous an advocate of woman suffrage and temperance as of anti-slavery in the olden time," Folsom wrote.[39] Folsom wrote that Crandall had started an annual temperance festival at her farmhouse in 1881 and moved it to the grounds of the local school as it grew in popularity. "An adopted son lives with her in a home whose walls are pictured with the faces of heroic souls. Not an old but a heroic woman, hers is one of the spirits that keep their youth."[40]

Newspaper articles about Folsom's trip to Elk Falls inspired others to visit Crandall. Another traveler found Crandall "as bright, fresh, original, and pronounced in her views and her personality as perhaps any woman in the land," and "thoroughly-going liberal" in all matters.[41] "It would pay anyone going West who wants to see a unique character—an old abolitionist and Quakeress who has . . . no other complaint than that in her little Western village she can't get books and papers enough for her soul to feed on—to call on her."[42]

Children continued to energize Prudence Crandall. Her grandniece complimented Prudence on her poems and writings. "Anyone having as large self-esteem as I have likes to be appreciated," Prudence wrote. "I thank you for your opinion that some of my compositions are worthy of a place in your scrapbook."[43] Another girl, Emma McClearn, lived in Elk Falls and befriended Prudence Crandall. "She had many books and I was in heaven because there were few books in town," McClearn remembered.[44] "She made her room into a very pleasant place, with slip covers of bright-colored goods, but only a few patronized her. She would pick out books for me to read and I haunted the place—it was an education for me. . . . She was much interested in spiritualism, and conducted séances at her home."[45]

Rena Keith Clisby said that Aunt Prudence dressed in an "eccentric" way. "Her dresses were always made from the same black cotton material, made in one piece hanging full from the shoulder with a narrow string belt which tied . . . She wore a white ruche [lace] at her neck. Her style never changed. I have often heard her say, 'stand still and you will see the same styles return after a course of years.'"[46] Prudence made some of her clothes but appreciated receiving store-bought items in the mail from her relatives back East. "I think of you every day when I put that nice bonnet on my head," she wrote to her grandniece Josephine, "and that splendid brown apron I wear every forenoon—it is the most valuable apron I ever had. I have cut one just like it for the afternoon."[47]

"I can see her now, a little bent old lady dressed in Quaker grey," Emma McClearn later wrote. "She did wear bloomers, not as we know them, but more like slacks that came to the ankle, over which was a short, very full skirt that came a little below her knees, a long flowing Quaker cape, and a Shaker bonnet . . . Always a fine snowy kerchief about her neck. She also carried a heavy cane. Her hair one seldom saw, but it was grey."[48]

Crandall's appearance intimidated some. "I was very bitter with the children who pointed her out and were afraid of her," McClearn wrote.[49] Crandall's activism and antislavery past made her controversial to some in the small town of Elk Falls. Local ministers did not appreciate her interest in spiritualism, and her call for women's rights dismayed others. "You could imagine a small town of very bigoted and illiterate people who could not understand one like her," McClearn said.[50] Crandall had a more favorable opinion of her adopted town and state. "I like this part of Kansas very much indeed," Crandall said. "There seems to be a thought in the hearts of the people for the best interests of humanity."[51]

In the years following William Lloyd Garrison's death, his sons Wendell and Francis began work on a four-volume biography, *William Lloyd Garrison, 1805–1879: The Story of His Life Told by His Children*. The project relied on the vast collection of letters, pamphlets, and papers that Garrison had kept from the 1820s onward and the hundreds of issues of the *Liberator*. The Century Company published the first two volumes in 1885 and promoted the biography in the *Century Magazine*, a general interest magazine that had a broad national readership.

In September 1885, Wendell Garrison published an article in *Century Magazine* entitled "Connecticut in the Middle Ages," chronicling the story of Prudence Crandall's school in Canterbury.[52] The story, told in part through the letters between Crandall and Garrison, promoted Garrison's biography. The article focused, however, on the dramatic and short history of Prudence Crandall's school.

A new generation of Americans read about Crandall's fight for equality. The article detailed her stand against powerful opponents, her arrest and night in jail, and her work with Garrison and Samuel Joseph May. Wendell Garrison noted that Crandall "is still living, in the full vigor of her faculties, at Elk Falls, Kansas."[53]

After reading the article, author Anna Campbell Palmer (who used the pen name "Mrs. George Archibald") wrote to Crandall.[54] "What strange happenings," Palmer wrote. "To think of the village magistrates assembling at town meetings to gravely discuss the question of allowing a colored school to exist within their gates. To think of a special act of the legislature making the same illegal. . . . Can it be that we are only forty years away from such savage and illiberal conduct?"[55] Two weeks later Palmer received a reply from Crandall. "Dear stranger friend, your kind letter was duly received, for which I thank you. Many strangers have written me since the September magazine came out, as well as old friends who had lost my whereabouts."[56]

Professor Andrew Atchison, who founded the Freedmen's Academy of Kansas to teach children of former slaves in 1880, asked his students to contact Prudence Crandall and learn about her school.[57] Atchison praised Crandall's efforts to achieve equality through education. "Poverty and ignorance make poor citizens . . . it is more esteemed to aid the poor than to honor the rich," Atchison said.[58]

Professor James H. Canfield, who taught history at the University of Kansas, also wanted to help the newly freed slaves and knew the story of Prudence Crandall's school.[59] Canfield located Crandall and sent his students to Elk Falls to interview her. In the *Topeka Daily Capital* of October 18, 1885, Canfield described his impression of Crandall as "keen-eyed, quick in her movements with some reserve when speaking of herself and her past, but with exceptional conversational powers, full of energy and zealous in all good works."[60]

"I am earnestly engaged in the temperance cause, women's rights question and indeed every reform for the good of the human race," Crandall told Canfield. "I feel like one alone in the world, but I have great hopes of the future good I may do before I die in the way of schools for the poor and needy, and shall do what I can to have my farm made useful in that way."[61] Crandall was eighty-two years old. Canfield observed, "How natural it is that such a woman with such a history, and with the old fire still in her veins should be spending her declining years in this tempest-born-freedom-loving state!"[62]

Crandall's hopes for her future were tempered by the fact that she could barely survive on the income from her farm. The articles concerning Prudence Crandall caught the attention of John S. Smith, who was offended by the idea of courageous Prudence Crandall struggling to survive on a prairie farm in her old age.

John S. Smith lived in Plainfield, Connecticut, served in town government, and supported the temperance movement.[63] Smith was so taken by Crandall's story that he traveled from Connecticut to Kansas in the fall of 1885 to meet her; they had a mutual friend who lived nearby and occasionally visited her in Elk Falls.[64] Smith suggested that the State of Connecticut should compensate her for the loss of her school. Crandall had mixed feelings about the idea. "I shall never plead poverty," she told Smith, "for with industry and the economy that I daily practice I have enough to lay me honorably in the grave."[65]

Despite her protests, the economies of farm life no longer worked in her favor. Crandall could not depend on the extra money she had earned in the past by raising and selling a few livestock; she could not compete with the new large-scale ranches that drove down prices.[66] "Beef is very low and pork too," Crandall wrote. "But I think with care . . . I shall never be in want for bread."[67] When Smith visited her, Crandall asked him for a loan of seventy dollars so she could fence part of her land; she needed to protect her farmland from the itinerant ranchers who used her land and paid no rent.[68] Prudence slowly warmed to the prospect of receiving compensation so that she could own "a horse and buggy to take me where I wish to go, and not walk or be dependent on some good friend."[69] She also told Smith that she wanted to visit her friends and former students back East.[70] Crandall agreed to work with Smith on an appeal for fair compensation.

"My plea will be for justice," Crandall said. "When a state has falsely imprisoned an innocent citizen and passed unconstitutional laws by which they are harassed and property destroyed, it is right they should compensate the abused. I wish to make no exorbitant demands—I would willingly leave the amount of compensation to their own honor and I would be content."[71]

Crandall expected that she would need "smart lawyers" similar to the attorneys who had defended her against the Black Law. "I could do it myself if I was there," she told Smith. "I cannot pay a big price to someone to speak for me . . . If you say go ahead, then I will write a petition and send it to you for inspection and if it is not all right, correct it and send it back and I will copy, sign and return."[72]

John Smith contacted George Shepard Burleigh, a prolific poet and author and the last surviving son of Rinaldo Burleigh of Plainfield. George had supported the antislavery movement and helped his brother William edit the *Charter Oak* newspaper in Hartford during the 1840s. George knew that Prudence Crandall had greatly influenced the lives of his brothers William and Charles; he gladly volunteered to help.

Smith asked Burleigh to draft Crandall's petition to the legislature. "It will be remembered that she stands in the Records of the Court as a convicted criminal for the offense of teaching colored girls to read," Burleigh wrote. "We respectfully suggest that you make a fair appropriation in her behalf, which shall at once relieve her from any anxiety for the future, and from the official stigma that rests upon her name, and purge our own record from its last remaining stain in connection with the colored race."[73]

Smith sought help from local leaders to solicit signatures for Crandall's petition. The greatest activity came in the Town of Canterbury, where Samuel Coit, the son of Sheriff Roger Coit, who had escorted Prudence Crandall to jail, personally lobbied the legislature. Thomas G. Clarke, Canterbury's state representative and a relative of Andrew Judson, led Canterbury's petition effort on behalf of Crandall and quickly gathered 112 signatures.

Clarke presented the petition to the legislature in Hartford on Wednesday, January 20, 1886. The *Hartford Daily Courant* supported the "late and inadequate reparation for the wrongs" done to Crandall.[74] The *New Haven News* noted Crandall's heroism and concluded that in her old age, "she certainly ought to find help" from the state that "once passed a statute for her suppression."[75] The story of Crandall's pension campaign circulated in newspapers throughout the country.[76]

At the Appropriations Committee hearing in February, Representative Clarke asked for prompt and generous action. The minister of the Asylum Hill Congregational Church in Hartford, Rev. Joseph H. Twichell, recommended that the state pay a "generous annual pension to her for the rest of her life."[77] Samuel Coit gave similar testimony, as did Henry Taintor, an attorney from Hartford and a cousin of William Ellsworth.[78] State Supreme Court Justice Elisha Carpenter, who lived in Windham County and had studied law with Jonathan Welch, who had prosecuted Prudence Crandall, also testified in favor of the petition. Despite the request of Crandall's supporters for swift relief for Prudence Crandall, the legislators scheduled another hearing for Tuesday, February 16, 1886.

John Smith wrote to Crandall and asked if she could recall the specific monetary loss she had suffered because of the closure of her school. "To tell the amount of loss occasioned by the destruction of my prospects in life," Crandall wrote, "that I might not only sustain myself in independence from the labor of others, but be enabled to do some good to the world of mankind besides, is a question difficult to solve."[79]

At the second hearing, Hartford attorney Elisha Johnson led the testimony in favor of Crandall. He read a portion of a letter Crandall had written to Samuel Coit, thanking those who had testified on her behalf and agreeing with those who had suggested that a yearly pension would be better than a large lump-sum payment. "Any sum, however small, that the state may see fit to appropriate, will be thankfully received," Crandall wrote.[80] Representative Thomas Clarke said that Crandall lived on a small prairie farm with a young man as her only assistant and barely earned an income.[81] Clarke estimated Crandall's monetary loss because of the violent closure of her school at one thousand dollars. Stephen A. Hubbard, the managing editor of the *Hartford Daily Courant*, testified next. Hubbard had no problem mixing his advocacy with his avocation. In the *Courant's* article concerning Crandall's hearing, published on the following day, Hubbard inserted a good portion of his own testimony. Crandall had succeeded in establishing a profitable school that could have grown and prospered through the years but for the passage of the Black Law, Hubbard said. He compared her original school to Miss Porter's School in Farmington.[82]

"Who could tell what might have been the measure of Miss Crandall's success if she had been allowed to go on fifty years ago with what might have been her life work," Hubbard told the legislators. "Instead of a pittance of three or four hundred dollars a year, if real justice could be done, her old place in Canterbury might be purchased, an income provided sufficient to secure her kindly care, and she be allowed and invited to spend her last days among the New England hills where she was born, instead of on a lonesome farm in the far west."[83]

Hubbard's suggestion that Crandall might return home to Canterbury struck a positive chord with a number of observers. Crandall's hardship moved one reader in particular; he contacted Hubbard and said he would purchase the former schoolhouse in Canterbury and allow Crandall to live there for the rest of her life. Hubbard was delighted—what a triumphant end to Crandall's story, especially when combined with legislative approval of a yearly pension. Hubbard had no idea, however, whether Prudence Crandall wanted to move back to Connecticut.

Crandall did not want charity, despite her financial difficulties. As a result, Hubbard decided not to tell her about the private offer to purchase the school. Hubbard wrote to Crandall and told her about the progress of her petition and the two hearings at the state capital. He also asked her if she had ever entertained the thought of moving back to Connecticut to live in the former schoolhouse. He did not reveal that someone had offered to purchase her former home for her use—Hartford citizen Samuel Clemens, better known as Mark Twain.

A biographer wrote that as 1885 ended and 1886 began, "At no time in his life were Mark Twain's fortunes and prospects brighter; he had a beautiful family and . . . great prosperity."[84] Twain had just published *The Adventures of Huckleberry Finn* to tremendous acclaim and sales. Twain had launched his own publishing company and had a runaway hit with former President Ulysses S. Grant's *Memoirs*. Helping a courageous woman who had risked all to teach black women appealed to Twain; the gesture offered deliverance for her and in a literal sense brought her story back to the point of its beginning, with an honorable conclusion.

Crandall responded to Hubbard's curious question and told him that she preferred the climate of Kansas. "You ask if I would like to go back under suitable circumstances to my old home?" Crandall wrote. "Home is like heaven, it is where we find content[ment]. I think I would rather not. I am very happy in my little pioneer box house of three rooms, situated on the side of a hill about one mile west of the little city of Elk Falls, of which I have a fine view."[85] She thanked Hubbard for his support before the Appropriations Committee and said she hoped that the legislature would grant her some small financial relief.[86]

Crandall's reply meant that Hubbard would not have the fairy-tale ending to Crandall's story that he wanted. Returning from Kansas to Connecticut to live once again in the Canterbury schoolhouse would have made a great news story, with no less than Mark Twain as the white knight. Hubbard soon learned, however, of a more fundamental problem. During the first week of March, the legislators on the Appropriations Committee voted against recommending Prudence Crandall's petition to the full General Assembly, effectively killing her request for relief. The news stunned Hubbard, John Smith, and Crandall's other supporters.

Some legislators had decided that the Town of Canterbury, and not the state, had caused Crandall's woes, and therefore the state owed her nothing. Others opposed rewarding Crandall for violating the Black Law in 1833, even though the law had been proved unjust and was repealed. Still other lawmakers wanted to dismiss her petition on the theory that any valid claim regarding a wrong committed in 1834 had long since expired under the statute of limitations. Some simply preferred to bury the controversies of the abolitionist days and avoid conceding the state's complicity in a notorious wrong, in legislative and judicial weakness on a grand scale.

The clerk of the Connecticut Supreme Court spoke out in favor of Prudence Crandall's petition. John Hooker rebutted the argument that Crandall did not deserve compensation because she had broken the law. Hooker reviewed the notes of the justices who had considered Crandall's state supreme court case and noted that in their letters and memos, the majority of the justices had considered free blacks citizens and the Black Law unconstitutional.[87] Hooker wrote a letter to the *Hartford Daily Courant* and concluded, "The law which Prudence Crandall disobeyed was not merely wicked in its object, but an unconstitutional one, and one therefore which it was in every point of view commendable for her to disregard."[88]

The minister of the Unitarian Church on Pratt Street in Hartford, John C. Kimball, preached a sermon supporting Crandall's petition and defended her against those who claimed her actions were too adversarial and defiant. Kimball praised her fighting spirit and strong convictions in favor of equality. "When God lays an axe at the root of a tree of wrong which he means to have cut down," Kimball said, "he is very apt to make its edge not of lead or putty, but of hardened steel."[89]

On Friday, March 5, Stephen Hubbard blasted the legislators in the *Daily Courant*. He called on them to overturn the ill-considered verdict of the Appropriations Committee, and he rejected the idea that the state did not play a role in the demise of Crandall's school. "The members of the general assembly of 1833 did not personally participate in the midnight assault with clubs and stones upon Miss Crandall's defenseless house, but they were like Saul of Tarsus; they held the garments of and furnished ammunition to those who did the stoning," Hubbard wrote. "This is a simple fact of history."[90] The *Courant* quoted U.S. Vice President Henry Wilson, who wrote that the destruction of Crandall's school was not the fault of a few. "The town and its church, the county and its court, the State and its legislature, all joined in this dark business and contributed to this sad result."[91]

Every major newspaper in the country was reporting on the attempt to bring relief to Prudence Crandall, Hubbard said. "In no small sense, the eyes of the nation are turned on Connecticut to know what she shall do for Prudence Crandall. . . . To plead the statute of limitations in such a case, or to avoid doing justice on any pretext whatever, is beneath the dignity of the state, and is to neglect a golden opportunity to wipe out a foul blot on its record."[92] Hubbard recommended that the legislature provide her with a yearly pension of no less than five hundred dollars per year, "not grudgingly or as if it were a gratuity, but as part payment of a just debt."[93]

Other newspapers joined the *Courant* in condemning the legislature's failure to approve Crandall's petition. The *Waterbury American* called the committee vote "a surprise and humiliation."[94] The *Providence Journal* wrote, "The present legislature, instead of pleading the statute of limitations, ought to be figuring up the interest due to Prudence."[95] "The legislature will do well and wisely to reverse the decision of its committee," the *New Haven Palladium* said.[96] The *Boston Journal* said the refusal to grant Crandall's petition "would bring fresh dishonor to the state."[97] Connecticut should apologize to Crandall, the *Springfield Republican* wrote, and approve reasonable compensation. "Let us hope there will be no further exhibition of meanness in this matter."[98] The *Worcester Spy* suggested that, in addition to a liberal pension, the state should erect a monument to Crandall "in honor of her goodness and constancy, and as a warning for all time against the vices of bigotry and prejudice."[99] Other editorials supporting Crandall's petition appeared in the *New York Sun*, the *Boston Advertiser*, the *Philadelphia Press*, the *Troy Times*, and many others. The *Windham County Transcript* wrote, "The members of the assembly of 1886 should covet the honor of extending justice, at last, to the venerable and historic woman."[100]

Isabella Mitchell, daughter of Sarah Harris Fayerweather, wrote to offer Crandall support and sent pictures of her siblings. "How much I

Gristmill at Elk Falls, Kansas, late nineteenth century.

PRUDENCE CRANDALL'S HOME, ELK FALLS, KAN.

Newspaper reporter's sketch of Prudence
ndall's farmhouse, Elk Falls, Kansas.

46. The Elk Falls business district at the time
that Prudence Crandall lived in Kansas.

Prudence Crandall

47. When this engraving of Prudence Crandall, based on Francis Alexander's 1834 painting, appeared in "Connecticut in the Middle Ages," *Century Magazine*, in October 1885, it renewed national interest in Crandall's life story.

Stephen A. Hubbard, the managing editor
he *Hartford Courant*.

49. Ellen Larned, a historian who
corresponded with Prudence Crandall.

State Representative Thomas G. Clarke of
nterbury, Connecticut.

51. Samuel Coit, son of the sheriff who led
Crandall into the Brooklyn jail.

87 UNION SQR., N. Y

52. Samuel Clemens, a.k.a. Mark Twain. Twain supported Crandall's quest for a pension and hoped she would return to Connecticut. He sent this photo to her from Hartford, Connecticut, on April 22, 1886.

Rena and Lucy Keith, nieces of Prudence Crandall, as they appeared in 1924. During the ...s through the 1880s, they lived with Crandall in Illinois and Kansas.

...Prudence Crandall in 1882 in Elk Falls, ...sas, wearing clothes she made.

55. Prudence Crandall is buried next to her brother Hezekiah in the Elk Falls Cemetery.

56. The Civil War reunion of 1913, marking the fiftieth anniversary of the Battle of Gettysburg
all the speeches at the reunion, no one celebrated emancipation as an achievement of the v

57. Ku Klux Klan march in Washington, D.C., 1926. Between 1900 and 1925,
there were 1,585 murders by lynching of black citizens in the United States.

he constitutional scholar Howard Jay
ham. Recruited by Thurgood Marshall to
st in *Brown v. Board of Education*, Graham
that *Crandall v. State* provided the
esis" of the Fourteenth Amendment.

59. Thurgood Marshall, the lead counsel for
the NAACP's Legal Defense Fund in *Brown v.
Board of Education*.

The United States Supreme Court on December 14, 1953. Front row: Felix Frankfurter, Hugo
:k, Chief Justice Earl Warren, Stanley Reed, and William O. Douglas. Back row: Tom Clark,
ert H. Jackson, Harold Burton, and Sherman Minton.

61. Remains of a stone wall near where Prudence Crandall's farmhouse stood in Elk Falls, Kansas; the farmhouse was destroyed by a tornado in 1916.

thank you for that beautiful group of photographs," Prudence wrote to Isabella. "How glad your dear mother would have been to have known that if I never could have the pleasure of seeing her dear children, that in my old age those beautiful pictures would be sent to me."[101] Prudence told Isabella that, if her petition succeeded, she would try to visit the families of her former students.

A black soldier stationed on the West Coast read about Prudence Crandall. In a letter to a black newspaper, he suggested that "colored men contribute a fund to aid the old lady who had always been so firm a friend to the negro."[102] The newspaper collected pennies, nickels, and dimes and sent $38.75 to Crandall. The editors of the newspaper "received a hearty letter of thanks from the venerable abolitionist."[103]

The *Courant* continued to lead the fight for Crandall, regularly commenting on the action or inaction of the legislature and reprinting supportive comments from other newspapers. The *Courant* published a letter from Ellen Larned, who said a pension of four or five hundred dollars would be "a trifle for the state, but it would be much to her . . . It is an act not merely of justice but of kindness and courtesy."[104]

Legislative leaders felt the heat of public opinion. In a session of the Connecticut House of Representatives on Thursday, March 11, 1886, the chairman of the Appropriations Committee, Charles E. Searls of Thompson, moved to recommit his committee's adverse recommendation regarding Crandall's petition. This technical procedure nullified his committee's unfavorable report. At the same time, legislators agreed to draft a new resolution in favor of a pension for Prudence Crandall. The *New Haven Register* said the willingness of the legislature to take a fresh look at Crandall's petition "paid a very handsome tribute to the influence of the state press."[105]

The *Kansas City Journal* sent a reporter two hundred miles to Elk Falls to hear "from her own lips the story of her wrongs."[106] The reporter described Crandall's house on the outskirts of Elk Falls as a plain box with only a few rooms. A small shed stood behind the house. Once inside Crandall's home the reporter noticed a primitive couch and a roughly made desk covered on top with thick brown paper. Numerous books filled shelves in a corner of the room and newspapers covered a small table. A wood stove in the main room kept the house warm. Crandall's clothes were neat but worn and faded, and the reporter said her home "bore a poverty stricken appearance."[107] The reporter concluded Crandall "is hopeful and cheery and strives to make the best of things. . . . She is always ready to help the suffering, care for the sick and cheer the sorrowing, and whenever any of the few colored people in Elk Falls are ill or in need she flies to their succor."[108]

Stephen Hubbard had suggested a modest annual pension for Prudence Crandall of no less than five hundred dollars. The new legislative resolution proposed a pension of four hundred dollars; this most likely was a small way that some members of the Appropriations Committee registered their displeasure with the *Courant*. If any lingering resentment in the legislature existed, however, it vanished when the House voted with only one dissenting vote to approve Crandall's resolution on March 31, 1886.[109] Attorney James Hovey of Norwich cast the sole "no" vote. Hovey had apprenticed with Chauncey Cleveland—who together with Andrew Judson had prosecuted Crandall—in the late 1830s.[110] The Connecticut State Senate scheduled a vote on the resolution for April 2.

Prudence Crandall thanked Ellen Larned for her letter of support in the *Courant*. "You do not know how much I have valued your womanly independence," Crandall wrote.[111] She reminded Larned that she still had not seen "your valuable *History of Windham County*."[112] Larned quickly sent both volumes to Crandall. A week later—after Crandall had received the books and was writing a letter to thank Larned—Crandall received a telegram. As a postscript, Crandall excitedly wrote to Larned, "From Hartford I received a telegraphic dispatch stating that the legislature had passed a bill in my favor . . ."[113]

"Our heroine still lives and can know and appreciate our acts on her behalf," State Senator John W. Marvin said during the Senate debate. "Recall the heroic struggle for usefulness in her early days so completely frustrated—the result of the legislation of her native state—and tell me if her wrongs should not be redressed . . . it is an act of right and justice."[114] The resolution passed the Senate unanimously and was signed by Governor Henry B. Harrison. The editors of the *Courant* immediately telegraphed the news to Prudence Crandall in Elk Falls.

"What an amount of obligation I am under to the press generally, and above all to those noble, progressive persons who got up the petition at the first to be presented to their state legislature," Crandall wrote to the *Courant*. "In 1833, when the law was passed by which my life prospects were destroyed, it was celebrated by ringing the bell hung in the steeple of the church, into which we were not allowed to enter, and by firing a cannon thirteen times . . . Today, when your telegram arrived, the only jubilant display I wished to make was to have a private nook where my tears of joy and gratitude could flow, unobserved, for the change that has been wrought in the views and feelings of the mass of people."[115]

"Now let the band play," the editors of the *New Haven Register* wrote. "Prudence Crandall Philleo is avenged."[116] Stephen Hubbard reminded his readers about the offer to purchase Crandall's former school for her use. "Now that the matter is over, we take the liberty to say that this kind and considerate offer was made by Samuel L. Clemens, 'Mark Twain.' He volunteered to lease the farm, and give her the free use of it for her life."[117] Hubbard noted that Crandall had chosen "perhaps a more dignified course" in remaining in Kansas, and he thanked Clemens for his "generous and public spirited offer."[118]

The revelation led to an exchange of letters between Prudence Crandall and Mark Twain. She told him she had no idea he had offered to help bring her back to Canterbury to live in her former home. "God bless your dear heart . . . It is a matter of great surprise that anyone could be so kind to an old woman like me . . ."[119] She told Twain she had enjoyed reading a borrowed copy of *Innocents Abroad* but had to return it before she had finished the book. She asked if he might send her a copy together with his photograph, which she would "place under glass with other dear friends."[120] Twain promptly replied and enclosed a signed photograph, but no book. She wrote back and told him how grateful she was for his help and thanked him for the photo.[121]

For Prudence Crandall, the pension campaign stirred memories of her school and thoughts of "what might have been." "Few, except some intimate friends, know the extent of her personal sacrifices since her work was rudely interrupted, and her young hopes crushed," the *Courant* noted. "Prudence Crandall may deservedly rank as one of the noblest examples of pure, brave, and high-minded New England womanhood."[122] For Stephen A. Hubbard, John S. Smith, Thomas G. Clarke, and the other "noble, progressive persons," it was a righteous cause brought to a successful conclusion.

At the start of the New Year, Helen M. Gougar traveled to Elk Falls to meet Crandall in January 1887. Gougar lived in Indiana and toured the country speaking in favor of temperance and equal rights for women.[123] In 1885 and 1886, Gougar pushed for women's rights in Kansas. She worked with the Kansas Equal Suffrage Association and other advocates, including Lucy Stone and Julia Ward Howe, and drafted legislation that allowed women to vote in municipal elections. After a tie vote in the Kansas State Senate had defeated the measure in 1885, Gougar campaigned extensively in 1886, drawing "large and enthusiastic crowds" throughout Kansas.[124] The effort paid off—Kansas Governor John A. Martin signed the bill into law on Valentine's Day 1887.[125]

Gougar interviewed Crandall for an article that appeared in the Chicago *Inter Ocean*. "Elk Falls is a small town situated on the Southern Kansas Railway in the north part of the state, justly noted for its broad prairies, beautiful sunsets, and progressive ideas," Gougar wrote.[126] Crandall told Gougar that her proudest moment was when she had stood firmly against those who wanted to close her school for black women. "Mrs. Philleo has been a woman of more than ordinary beauty of person in her time, and is still a woman of brilliant mind and a charming conversationalist. Her great desire is now to live to see the emancipation of her sex."[127] Gougar noted that the Connecticut legislature recently had granted Crandall an annual pension of four hundred dollars; she asked Crandall if the pension provided sufficient means to live comfortably.

"Oh dear, yes," Prudence replied. "I have a good farm just on the edge of town, and it is well stocked. I have all the reading matter I want, and all my faculties, except, as you see, I am a little deaf, and I am comfortable and happy. My whole family have preceded me to the home beyond, but I have an adopted son of whom I am very fond, and nieces living with me, so you see I have nothing of which to complain."[128]

A few months later, after a decade of living on her farm outside Elk Falls, Prudence decided to move into town. At eighty-three years old, she had decided to simplify her life. She bought a large house on Osage Street next to the Methodist Church near the center of Elk Falls. She could easily walk to the local shops. With her guaranteed pension, she bought the home for $850 in April. Her niece Clarissa moved with Prudence to the new house, and her adopted son, Abraham Williams, continued to manage and live on her farm.[129]

That spring, a reporter for the *Hartford Evening Post* bicycled across the country from Connecticut to San Francisco and then took a boat to

Portland, Oregon, where he ended his westward trek. In July he began his trip back to Connecticut, intending to visit Prudence Crandall and file stories with the *Evening Post* as he traveled.[130] Cycling wherever the roads permitted and otherwise riding the train, George Burton Thayer traveled east through Idaho, Utah, and Colorado. After reaching Emporia, Kansas, Thayer bicycled the ninety-mile trek to Elk Falls through open plains, patches of forest, and occasional farmhouses. When he reached Crandall's home in Elk Falls, Abraham Williams greeted him.

"Mrs. Philleo is at church," Williams said. Within an hour, Prudence appeared. "As she removed her bonnet, it showed a good growth of sandy gray hair, smoothed back with a common round comb, and cut straight around," Thayer noted, "the ends curling around in under and in front of her ears; of medium height, but somewhat bent and spare, and with blue eyes, and a face very wrinkled, and rather long; her chin quite prominent, and a solitary tooth on her upper jaw, the only one seen in her mouth."[131] Crandall offered him tea, apple pie, and an entire meal of ham, potatoes, bread, johnnycakes, and ginger snaps. "I am glad to see anyone from good old Connecticut," she told Thayer.[132]

After Thayer had finished eating, Crandall showed him the sitting room with the photographs of her abolitionist friends and the more recent photos of those who had helped her secure a pension. Thayer said the legislature should have approved a more generous pension, but Prudence disagreed. "O, I am so thankful for that," she said. "It is so much better than nothing."[133] Another visitor stopped by her house that evening, and Thayer watched as Crandall carefully led her new guest to the collection of photographs, describing each individual. "It is plain to be seen," Thayer wrote, "the sight of those faces does her a great amount of good."[134] Thayer noticed how Crandall craved and enjoyed conversation and could talk with authority on many different subjects; Crandall appreciated that Thayer was a good listener.

"My whole life has been one of opposition," Crandall told Thayer. "I never could find anyone near me to agree with me. Even my husband opposed me, more than anyone. He would not let me read the books that he himself read, but I did read them."[135] She told Thayer about her desire to read and learn as much as she could. "I read all sides," Crandall said, "and searched for the truth whether it was in science, religion, or humanity."[136] Thayer thought Crandall might have had second thoughts about her decision to stay in Kansas as opposed to returning to Connecticut. "I some-times think I would like to live somewhere else," Crandall said. "Here, in Elk Falls, there is nothing for my soul to feed upon. Nothing, unless it comes from abroad in the shape of books, newspapers, and so on."[137]

The issues and reforms that interested her occasionally caused her prob-lems, she said. She had a difficult relationship with local ministers. They feared her interest in spiritualism and women's rights would unsettle their congregations. She told Thayer of her support for the peace movement and the International Arbitration League. "I don't want to die yet," Cran-dall told Thayer. "I want to see some of these reforms consummated. I never had any children of my own to love, but I love every human being, and I want to do what I can for their good."[138]

Thayer spent what he described as two very pleasant days with Cran-dall, conversing on many topics and becoming fast friends. "Sometimes we would both commence speaking at the same instant. 'Go ahead,' she would say, or 'keep on, I have kept hold of that idea I had.'" While at Pru-dence's house, George Thayer wrote an article for the *Hartford Evening Post* that she copied to submit to her local newspaper. When he bid good-bye, Prudence said, "If the people of Connecticut only knew how happy I am, and how thankful I am to them, it would make them happy too."[139] Thayer wrote that Connecticut's small pension for Crandall provided the state with a narrow escape from disgrace. "What a shame had this good woman, this great mind, gone to another world without having even that slight justice done."[140]

As Prudence had expected, living in the town of Elk Falls provided more convenience than life on her nearby farm; this was increasingly im-portant, as it became difficult for her to get around in 1888. Clarissa helped keep up the household, and Abraham Williams checked on Prudence and Clarissa whenever he came into town. Prudence finally had the money to travel east to see friends in Connecticut and elsewhere, but she no longer had the strength for such a journey. In April 1888 she wrote her will; she left her farm to Abraham and her home in town to Clarissa.[141]

Toward the end of her life, Crandall befriended a traveling Congrega-tional minister, Charles Luther McKesson. McKesson was born in Iowa and graduated from the University of Nebraska. He shared with Crandall a restless and questioning nature. He traveled throughout Elk County preaching at different churches; Prudence invited him to use her home s a base for his travels. When her black friends dropped by for a visit, McKesson noted that she happily greeted the younger women as "my daughters."[142]

Local schools continued to receive visits from Prudence throughout 1888. She told the students about her own experiences and lectured on the need for peace throughout the world. During one visit she passed around a white flag made of cheesecloth and explained that the flag symbolized peace. On another occasion she recited one of her poems, modeled after the Civil War song "Battle Cry of Freedom," which began, "Rally round the white flag, rally once again."[143]

Crandall often discussed religion with Rev. McKesson. He knew that her parents had raised her as a Quaker and that she later became a Baptist, migrated toward Unitarian, and for many years had described herself as "an enthusiastic spiritualist."[144] Crandall did not believe that any one religion had a monopoly on truth or a sole connection to God. It made perfect sense that God had revealed himself to all nations and religions, she told McKesson. McKesson learned that local ministers did not welcome Crandall into their churches because of her beliefs.

"I am sorry for once in my life, that I am associated with the so-called Christian churches of Elk Falls," Rev. McKesson wrote. "My face burns with shame, my nerves tingle with the thought that such injustice should be perpetuated in the name of Christianity."[145] When a local minister suggested to McKesson that Crandall's interest in spiritualism and her doubt about the literal truth of the Bible proved she was not Christian, McKesson strongly disagreed. "She is a Christian, not by any theological test, but by the test that Christ gave—'He that doeth the will of my Father,'" McKesson said.[146]

In October and November of 1889, Americans read about a fast-spreading outbreak of influenza or "the grip." The epidemic began in Russia and swept across Europe. With modern rail and steamship transportation linking countries and continents, the disease spread quickly throughout the world. Reports of influenza outbreaks in the United States began on December 11, 1889, in New York City, and by the next week newspapers had reported cases in Buffalo, Baltimore, Detroit, Philadelphia, and Kansas City.[147] Most of those initially affected recovered within ten days, but as the epidemic spread from Europe into the United States, the strain became more potent and the death toll increased.[148] Seven hundred and fifty thousand people eventually died from the Russian Flu, the world's worst and most deadly influenza epidemic until the devastating Spanish Flu of 1918.[149]

In the fall of 1889, Prudence Crandall had a severe asthma attack.[150] She did not seek the help of a doctor and told Rev. McKesson that she believed "the mind has a great power on matter, and I think I can drive away the disease."[151] She accepted the help of a Christian Scientist friend, who told Prudence not to take any medicine. Prudence followed her friend's advice, and her condition improved.[152]

At the beginning of November, Prudence received a letter from the editor of the *Magazine of Poetry* in Buffalo, New York, offering to publish a number of her poems together with her portrait and biography.[153] "We have not arranged for the biographical sketch as yet, and would be glad to have you refer us to someone competent and willing to prepare it," Charles W. Moulton wrote to Crandall.[154] Crandall did not have the energy to respond. Her asthma subsided, but throughout the fall she suffered a debilitating cold. At the beginning of January, she had the Russian Flu.

"Her heart grew weak and her breathing was most difficult," Rena Keith Clisby wrote.[155] "She was ill only a short time."[156] Already weakened from asthma and her eighty-six years, Prudence Crandall succumbed to influenza and died on Monday, January 28, 1890, with her niece Clarissa by her side.[157] At the Baptist Church in Elk Falls where Prudence's funeral was held two days later, Clarissa arranged flowers and evergreens behind the casket and spelled out Prudence's name and the word "Hope." Rev. Charles L. McKesson conducted the service.

McKesson described Prudence Crandall's courage in admitting Sarah Harris to her school for young women. "Miss Crandall, beneath her modest Quaker garb, had a soul as heroic and determined as that of any Joan of Arc who ever in outward armor went forth into battle.... She said to me a few days ago, 'You may come in anytime and find me gone, and I want you to preach my funeral sermon,'" McKesson said. "I asked her what I should say. She said, 'Preach the truth.... Say to them that God is a spirit, I am a spirit, therefore I am a spiritualist and I think all Christians ought to be spiritualists.'"[158]

"Friends," McKesson said, "I only ask that when it comes ours to leave this world, we may be able to leave behind us as many kind acts, cheerful words and noble deeds, that we may be as well fitted to take the next step onward in this life eternal, as was this peer of the noblest hero or heroine of the nineteenth century, Prudence Crandall Philleo."[159]

During the height of the campaign for Crandall's Connecticut pension, the *Hartford Courant* published a brief reflection on Crandall's life.

"Prudence, in her frontier cabin on the Kansas prairie, thinks little of the toil and hardships and disappointments of her life, knows little perhaps of the good she has caused, and is thankful that she may still earn her living by the work of her hands. A life like that of Prudence Crandall is a notable object lesson, to show what one obscure young woman in an obscure country town can accomplish by devotion to a principle and to the cause of humanity. The influence of her work has been a potent force ever since."[160]

18 : **Prudence Crandall in the Twentieth Century**

Twenty-one years after Prudence Crandall's death, three Connecticut legislators sought to honor her with an official memorial.[1] In 1911 they introduced legislation to appropriate $1500 for the construction of a monument near the Packerville Baptist Church in Plainfield. The Appropriations Committee held the request over from one public hearing in February to another hearing in March.[2] The committee then balked at the amount requested and rejected the proposal.

On hearing of the reluctance of Connecticut lawmakers to honor Crandall, the Rhode Island legislature appropriated $150 for a Connecticut memorial, as did the leaders of Hopkinton, the Rhode Island town near Crandall's birthplace. With the prodding of Rhode Island officials, the Connecticut legislature finally approved a contribution of $300.[3] The legislature also voted to move the location of the memorial from Plainfield to Canterbury. The committee assigned to carry out the project, however, failed to agree on the design or message of the tribute to Crandall. In 1916 a reporter for the *Waterbury Herald* noted that four years had passed without any progress on the Crandall memorial. He speculated that despite the eighty-two years since the closure of her school, lingering resistance to her ideals continued.

"She was a fanatic to most of her neighbors when she opened that negro school," the reporter wrote. "She brooked the same intolerant spirit that in earlier times had sent 'witches' to the stake and Quakers to the whipping post. . . . Now, her enemies are forgotten except by their descendants, perhaps who in the light of history are by no means willing that their connection with her prosecution be widely known."[4] The memorial was never constructed.[5]

In the last quarter of the nineteenth century, states

created new barriers between the races, often referred to as "Jim Crow Laws." The laws imposed literacy tests and poll taxes to disenfranchise black voters and memorialized segregation throughout daily life, including transportation and the requirement that blacks refrain from sitting in train cars reserved for whites. The railroads crowded blacks into poorly maintained cars or portions of the baggage car. "The 'Jim Crow' cars are hitched close to the engine," one observer wrote. "Naturally this would cause them to catch more smoke and soot."[6]

Six months after Prudence Crandall's death, on July 10, 1890, the Louisiana Legislature passed a law that prohibited blacks from sitting in the same railway cars as whites. The Separate Car Law required railroads to provide "equal but separate accommodations for the white and colored races."[7] Outraged black leaders in New Orleans challenged the law.

In February 1892, Daniel Desdunes, who was one-eighth black, left New Orleans on a train bound for Alabama. He deliberately took a seat in a railway car reserved for whites and was arrested. The Louisiana Supreme Court dismissed his case, noting that the Commerce Clause of the Constitution prohibited hindering travel from one state to another.

Emboldened by their victory, black leaders arranged for a black man to once again sit in a coach reserved for whites, this time on a train traveling *within* state borders. Without the protection of the Commerce Clause, this case would focus on the constitutionality of Louisiana's "separate but equal" law. Thirty-year-old Homer Plessy bought a first-class ticket on the East Louisiana Railway for a trip from New Orleans to Covington, Louisiana, on June 9, 1892. He took a seat in a car reserved for whites and encountered no problems until he told the conductor he was one-eighth black.[8] When Plessy refused to move to the "colored" car, the police arrested him.[9] Both the trial court and the Louisiana Supreme Court ruled that the law requiring segregation in intrastate travel did not violate the Constitution.

Plessy appealed to the U.S. Supreme Court. Writing for a nearly unanimous Court on May 18, 1896, Justice Henry B. Brown upheld Louisiana's Separate Car Law in *Plessy v. Ferguson*. Justice Brown, who was born in Massachusetts, said that laws requiring the separation of the races "do not necessarily imply the inferiority of either race to the other" and did not violate the Constitution.[10] Brown said neither Congress nor the courts could "abolish distinctions based upon physical differences."[11]

Justice John Marshall Harlan filed the lone dissent. The son of a Kentucky politician, Harlan came from a family that had owned slaves.[12] Harlan rejected racism and segregation and argued that the Thirteenth and Fourteenth Amendments to the Constitution prohibited the discrimination inherent in "separate but equal" accommodations. "In view of the constitution, in the eye of the law, there is in this country no superior, dominant, ruling class of citizens," Harlan wrote. "There is no caste here. Our constitution is color-blind, and neither knows nor tolerates classes among citizens. In respect of civil rights, all citizens are equal before the law. . . . In my opinion, the judgment this day rendered will, in time, prove to be quite as pernicious as the decision made by this tribunal in the *Dred Scott* case."[13]

With the Supreme Court's endorsement of "separate but equal," hostility toward blacks was perpetrated not only by white supremacy vigilantes such as the Ku Klux Klan, but through laws passed by states and municipalities. Many southern and western states required segregation at virtually every facility and public gathering place where the races might mingle—parks, beaches, theaters, restaurants, hotels, restrooms, water fountains, and even hospitals, prisons, and cemeteries.

In 1895 the state superintendent of schools in Florida drafted a law that created official segregation in Florida's schools. William Sheats "revived in substance the law by which Connecticut sixty years ago convicted Prudence Crandall of the crime of admitting colored pupils into her private school."[14] The Florida law made it a crime to teach black and white students together in the same classroom; violations resulted in fines and imprisonment.[15] The *Charlotte Observer* made similar use of the Crandall story in 1912; the editors concluded that "prejudice against color is not confined to any particular part of the country . . . it is not altogether the wisest and best thing to attempt by arbitrary measures, even in Northern communities, to obliterate the color line in educational affairs."[16]

Newspapers in Georgia defended their school segregation laws by referencing Connecticut's opposition to Prudence Crandall's school in the 1830s. "We reproduce the [Crandall] account itself to illustrate the feeling of caste that once animated the people of Connecticut, who kept slaves so long as they were profitable, then sold them to the South, and then subsequently assisted to rob the Southern people of them," the editors of the *Macon Telegraph* wrote. The Connecticut legislature "may have scored a point in giving a pension to Prudence Crandall, and there may be people in Connecticut today quite willing that their children shall be educated with negroes, but all of this should have no weight in sanctioning defiance of a constitutional mandate of the State of Georgia or of opening the way to miscegenation."[17]

Northern states did not often memorialize segregation into law; however, rampant discrimination and de facto segregation occurred in employment, housing, and social activities. Despite the bravery of black troops during the Civil War, even veterans' organizations fell into patterns of discrimination. The largest association, the Grand Army of the Republic, faced increasing pressure from southern chapters to exclude black veterans, while in the north, blacks who applied for membership often were rejected without explanation.[18] Some white veterans noted the irony of Union veterans embracing their former Confederate opponents but not the black veterans who had fought to save the Union. Those who took offense at that paradox, however, did not necessarily consider black veterans as equals. "I would rather shake hands with the blackest nigger in the land than with a traitor," said California Commander Edward S. Salomon of the Grand Army of the Republic in 1887.[19]

The largest reunion of Civil War veterans occurred at the end of June 1913 in Gettysburg, Pennsylvania, corresponding with the fiftieth anniversary of that battle. More than fifty thousand Union and Confederate veterans pitched thousands of tents on three hundred acres of sprawling military encampment. The ceremonies lasted four days capped by President Woodrow Wilson's closing speech on July 4, 1913.

The Gettysburg reunion underscored reconciliation between the North and the South and also served as a stark reminder of the failed promise of equality between the races. Black veterans did not receive invitations to the ceremonies.[20] Incredibly, no speaker directly recognized or celebrated emancipation and the end of slavery as part of the legacy of the Civil War. Most echoed the sentiment of Pennsylvania Governor John K. Tenner, who said that time had healed all wounds between the Union and the Confederacy. "The bitterness is gone, past differences are settled, and hand in hand, the foes of other days stroll in soldierly companionship through the vales and over the hills of this great battlefield."[21] A Confederate veteran, John C. Scarborough of North Carolina, made the only direct reference to race.

"The negro knew what the war was for," Scarborough told the crowd. "They knew if the North succeeded that they would be free."[22] Scarborough said that slaves in North Carolina, however, had not responded to the call for freedom. Scarborough claimed the average slave "was as loyal to the South as he was to his master and his mistress."[23] Scarborough said whites needed to show the Negro "that we are his friends. . . . We owe it to the black men and the black women and the black children, to make them the best citizens the material will allow. . . . You need not treat him as an equal, but as a good citizen, and you stand in your place and have him stand in his place."[24]

The press lavished praise on the Gettysburg reunion. "There is now no difference between the North and the South except cold bread and hot biscuit," reported the *Hartford Courant*, quoting Vice President Thomas Riley Marshall.[25] "God bless us everyone, alike the Blue and the Gray, the Gray and the Blue," wrote the *Louisville Journal-Courier*. "Beholding, can we say happy is the nation that hath no history?"[26]

The black press did not share this view. The *Baltimore Afro-American Ledger* speculated that Lincoln's famous words at Gettysburg of a government "by the people" actually meant "only white people."[27] One historian called the 1913 event "a Jim Crow reunion, and white supremacy might be said to have been the silent, invisible master of ceremonies."[28] Alfred W. Nicholson, president of Bettis Academy, a school for black students in South Carolina, asked if "the Blue and the Gray can now march side by side in reunions, and a Confederate veteran can deliver an oration at Gettysburg, ought not the negro and the Southern white man, with calmness and without passion, look the past in the face and read the lesson it has for them both?"[29]

When abolitionist hero Harriet Tubman died on March 10, 1913, officials dedicated a bronze plaque to her memory in her hometown of Auburn, New York. While the plaque described her courage in leading slaves to freedom, those who drafted Tubman's quotation decided to put her words into minstrel show idiom: "I nebber run my train off de track and I nebber los' a passenger."[30] Tubman biographer Catherine Clinton wrote, "The use of dialect on the plaque was creative license, reflecting the way in which white projections and racist shadings shaped 'negro' achievements," and this overshadowed any attempt to convey Tubman's exact words.[31]

The issue of equality surfaced in the presidential campaign of 1912—equality for women, not blacks. In that election cycle, Theodore Roosevelt challenged incumbent President William H. Taft for the Republican nomination. When Taft emerged as the party's nominee, Roosevelt abandoned the Republican Party and formed the Progressive Party. Roosevelt's new party endorsed numerous labor and social reforms, including suffrage for women, but rejected civil rights for blacks. Officials at the Progressive Party convention refused to seat black delegates from the South.[32] After Democrat Woodrow Wilson won the three-way general election, he reintroduced segregation into federal civil service.[33] Wilson and his administration had given "segregation a tremendous impetus and . . . marked its systematic enforcement," a study concluded after the first six months of Wilson's presidency.[34]

The idea that blacks preferred segregation imposed on them by whites was a consistent theme expressed by white writers. "Birds of a feather flock together," said a white reporter about school segregation in 1919. Black parents wanted their children to have opportunity, he wrote, "but they feel that they get that chance most surely by staying in their own crowd." After observing the segregated, all-black Frederick Douglass Public School in Cincinnati, located in the same neighborhood as the former Lane Seminary, the writer concluded, "This community, while reaching up toward white standards, prefers racial seclusion. These people revere their own racial personality."[35]

Black writers, when given a voice, disagreed. "Experience has taught us that Jim Crow Schools mean poorly equipped and inefficient schools, and segregated districts are always undesirable and neglected districts," the editors of the *Chicago Enterprise* wrote. "How could the idea of our oneness as American citizens prevail if we insist on complete divergence socially and racially?"[36]

Prudence Crandall, William Lloyd Garrison, Maria Stewart, and David Walker all would have recognized America in the first half of the twentieth century. Racially motivated discrimination and violence continued, with slavery replaced by segregation and economic exploitation. The pervasive segregation in schools at the beginning of the twentieth century—with the inference that black children deserved less than their white counterparts—would have deeply offended Prudence Crandall.

During the 1930s and 1940s, black advocates for equality in education fought their battles primarily within the confines of *Plessy v. Ferguson* and sought better facilities and conditions in the "separate but equal" black schools. By the end of the 1940s and the beginning of the 1950s, attorneys for the National Association for the Advancement of Colored People (NAACP) had resolved to challenge and strike down segregation and the "separate but equal" doctrine.[37] The most famous civil rights case decided by the U.S. Supreme Court, the case that directly challenged *Plessy*, began in Kansas. The arguments of Prudence Crandall's attorneys, articulated more than a century earlier, played a role in that pivotal decision.

With help from President Franklin Roosevelt's New Deal programs, workers built the Sumner Elementary School in Topeka, Kansas, in 1936, in a modern art deco style. Named for Charles Sumner, the school honored the famous abolitionist senator from Massachusetts, who had delivered a blistering speech on the Senate floor in 1856 condemning the expansion of slavery into Kansas.[38] In 1849 Sumner had joined with black attorney Robert Morris to argue that segregated schools in Massachusetts violated "that fundamental right of all citizens, equality before the law." Segregation stigmatized blacks, Sumner said, and "widens their separation from the rest of the community, and postpones that great day of reconciliation."[39]

Oliver Brown took his seven-year-old daughter Linda to the Sumner Elementary School to register for the third grade in September 1950. Linda could walk six blocks to Sumner; she had to ride an hour on a bus to attend the all-black Monroe School. School officials at Sumner refused to register Linda Brown. Kansas state law required segregated elementary schools for black and white children, and because Linda was black, she could not attend the all-white school named for abolitionist Charles Sumner. Oliver Brown joined with other aggrieved parents and the NAACP, and they challenged the law in federal court on February 28, 1951. Because Oliver Brown's name was listed first alphabetically among all of the plaintiffs, the case became known as *Brown v. Board of Education*.

The U.S. District Court for Kansas reached a decision on August 3, 1951. Writing for a three-judge panel, Judge Walter Huxman held that Kansas's segregation law did not violate the Constitution or result in "substantial discrimination."[40] The "separate but equal" standard in *Plessy* had provided the basis for lawful segregation of the Kansas elementary schools, Huxman wrote.[41] The NAACP and its lead counsel, Thurgood

Marshall, appealed to the U.S. Supreme Court. The plaintiffs consolidated the case with four other lawsuits from South Carolina, Virginia, Washington, D.C., and Delaware involving similar challenges to school segregation laws.

Above the two entrances to the Supreme Court building in Washington, D.C., are the inscriptions "Equal Justice Under Law" and "Justice the Guardian of Liberty." Hundreds of people waited patiently in line on the marble steps of the nation's preeminent courthouse on the morning of Tuesday, December 9, 1952, hoping for a seat in the Court's gallery. By the time the nine justices of the Supreme Court took their seats, the courthouse had filled to capacity. American flags hung on either side of the row of justices. Chief Justice Frederick M. Vinson signaled the lead attorney for the appellants, Thurgood Marshall, to begin his argument.

"May it please the Court," Marshall began. "The specific provision of the South Carolina Code as set forth in our brief . . . reads as follows: 'it shall be unlawful for pupils of one race to attend the schools provided by boards of trustees for persons of another race.' The constitutional provision [of the South Carolina Constitution] is: 'Separate schools shall be provided for children of the white races,' and this is the significant language," Marshall told the justices, *"and no child of either race shall ever be permitted to attend a school provided for children of the other race.'* Those are the two provisions of the law of the State of South Carolina under attack in this particular case."[42]

In *Brown v. Board of Education*, Thurgood Marshall and the attorneys for the NAACP's Legal Defense Fund presented a new argument on behalf of black students in segregated schools. No longer would advocates for equal rights settle for marginal improvements in facilities. No longer would black children accept the exile of separate black schools. In *Brown*, Marshall urged rejection of *Plessy* and the "separate but equal" doctrine. The idea that states could impose segregation without interference from the courts was "the direct opposite of what the Fourteenth Amendment was passed for," Marshall told the justices, "and the direct opposite of the intent of the Fourteenth Amendment and the framers of it."[43]

Marshall and the NAACP's legal defense team cited two Supreme Court rulings that had removed the barriers of segregation from a law school at the University of Texas and a graduate program at the University of Oklahoma. In both cases, however, the Court did not need to overrule *Plessy* because the schools had offered no comparable "separate but equal" programs to blacks.[44] Marshall also made extensive use of studies of black schoolchildren. Thirty-two social scientists concluded that segregation resulted in "feelings of inferiority and a sense of personal humiliation" among black children.[45] Dr. David Krech, a social psychologist at Harvard University, said that "legal segregation hampers the mental, emotional, physical and financial development of colored children and aggravates the very prejudices from which it arises."[46] Segregation resulted in discrimination and stigmatization, Marshall said.

On Saturday, December 13, 1952, when the attorneys had concluded their arguments, the justices discussed their initial impressions. Justice William O. Douglas noted that only four of the nine justices favored overruling *Plessy* and striking down segregation as unconstitutional.[47] Chief Justice Vinson acknowledged both the "long continued acceptance of segregation" and the fact that the court could not "close our eyes to problems in various parts of the country."[48] Vinson questioned whether officials could enforce a ruling overturning *Plessy*.[49] Four other justices shared Vinson's concerns or, in the case of Justice Stanley Reed of Kentucky, firmly believed that the Constitution permitted segregation. A law clerk for Justice Robert Jackson wrote a memo recommending that the court uphold *Plessy* and segregation.

"In the long run it is the majority who will determine what the constitutional rights of the minority are," William Rehnquist wrote to Justice Jackson. "I realize that it is an unpopular and unhumanitarian position, for which I have been excoriated by 'liberal' colleagues, but I think *Plessy v. Ferguson* was right and should be re-affirmed." Nineteen years later President Richard M. Nixon appointed Rehnquist to the Supreme Court; in 1982 President Ronald Reagan elevated him to the position of Chief Justice.[50]

When it became clear during the Court's term that the justices could not resolve their differences, Justice Felix Frankfurter suggested that they delay their decision. Frankfurter wanted additional time to work toward a favorable and, ideally, unanimous decision. The social science testimony regarding the effects of segregation, while illuminating, did not provide a constitutional basis for overruling *Plessy*. The justices agreed to ask the parties in *Brown* to file additional briefs and specifically address the history of the Fourteenth Amendment and whether the amendment prohibited segregation in schools. The Court announced that the parties in *Brown* would reargue the case in the fall of 1953.

"We were all astonished," Jack Greenberg wrote, speaking for the attorneys at the NAACP Legal Defense Fund.[51] The Court's questions "shook us," wrote Robert Carter, another attorney for the Legal Defense Fund. "Where we had been 75 percent confident, we were now down to 50 or 55 percent confident" of overturning *Plessy* and segregation.[52]

The Fourteenth Amendment, passed by Congress in 1866 and ratified by the states in 1868, extended all rights of citizenship to former slaves and "all persons born or naturalized in the United States." Most important for the *Brown* case, the Fourteenth Amendment prohibited states from denying "to any person within its jurisdiction the equal protection of the laws" and "life, liberty or property, without due process of law." To help answer the question of whether the Fourteenth Amendment provided a constitutional basis for prohibiting segregation, Thurgood Marshall turned to a group of distinguished academics. He recruited black historian John Hope Franklin, a professor at Howard University and the author of *From Slavery to Freedom: A History of American Negroes*, a groundbreaking account of African American history in the United States. Franklin agreed to lead the critical task of researching the origins of the Fourteenth Amendment. Franklin recruited other scholars, including C. Vann Woodward of Yale, Rayford Logan of Howard University, Herbert Gutman of the University of Rochester, and Alfred Kelly of Wayne State. The historians immersed themselves in research and regularly convened at the Legal Defense Fund offices in New York City.

Thurgood Marshall also reached out to historian Howard Jay Graham. Graham's deafness prevented him from teaching at a university, and he served as the law librarian at the Los Angeles County Law Library. Graham had written many articles on the origins and meaning of the Fourteenth Amendment.[53] Two articles that Graham had written for the *Wisconsin University Law Review* in 1950 caught Marshall's attention—articles that focused on the antislavery origins of the Fourteenth Amendment.[54] According to Graham, the "genesis" of the Fourteenth Amendment came from the antislavery movement and the case of *Crandall v. State*. Prudence Crandall's attorneys, William Ellsworth and Calvin Goddard, had argued that blacks possessed the same rights as white citizens and enjoyed the same constitutional system of protection for those rights. "The importance of the Ellsworth-Goddard arguments can hardly be exaggerated," Graham wrote.[55]

Chief Justice Vinson retired for the night on September 7, 1953, with the weight of the *Brown* case and the future of equality in America on his shoulders. While sleeping during the early morning hours of the next day, Vinson suffered a heart attack and died.[56] President Dwight D. Eisenhower appointed California's Republican Governor Earl G. Warren to take his place, and the Court rescheduled the October arguments for *Brown v. Board of Education* for December. Prior to his election as governor, Warren had served as California's attorney general and state district attorney, but he had no prior experience as a judge in any court.[57] Earl Warren's first significant case as Chief Justice of the U.S. Supreme Court was *Brown v. Board of Education*.

Thurgood Marshall's team of historians continued to research the origins of the Fourteenth Amendment. Howard Jay Graham called the amendment the "reconsummation" of the antislavery movement.[58] The points raised by Ellsworth and Goddard in *Crandall* "convincingly stated the social and ethical case for equality of opportunity irrespective of race and gave strong impetus to a gradually emerging concept of American nationality and citizenship," Graham said. "They remain to this day among the most persuasive and prophetic, as well as the most neglected, of early constitutional arguments."[59]

The historians and attorneys working on *Brown v. Board of Education* did not neglect the abolitionists or Ellsworth and Goddard's arguments in *Crandall*. In the brief submitted to the Court, Thurgood Marshall's team discussed the formation of the American Anti-Slavery Society, the campaign for emancipation and equality, and the contributions of abolitionists such as William Lloyd Garrison, Lewis and Arthur Tappan, and Theodore Dwight Weld.[60] Marshall cited *Crandall v. State* and liberally incorporated passages from Graham's research in the brief for *Brown v. Board of Education*.

"The first comprehensive crystallization of antislavery constitutional theory occurred in 1834 in the arguments of W.W. Ellsworth and Calvin Goddard, two of the outstanding lawyers and statesmen of Connecticut, on the appeal of the conviction of Prudence Crandall," Marshall and his attorneys wrote in their brief to the Court. "The Ellsworth-Goddard argument is one of the classic statements of the social and ethical case for equality of opportunity irrespective of race. It gave immense impetus to the emerging concept of American nationality and citizenship. Fully reported and widely circulated as a tract, it soon became one of the fountainheads of antislavery constitutional theory."[61]

"The dependence of the lawyers upon the historians was much in evidence," John Hope Franklin recalled. "In discussing the views of members of Congress such as Thaddeus Stevens or Benjamin Butler, the legal staff appeared to be in awe: 'Let's hear what Vann has to say,' one of them would ask, while another might want to hear from Al Kelly, the great constitutional historian. . . . For me, and I suspect it was true for the other scholars, it was exhilarating."[62]

Alfred Kelly's research failed to produce persuasive evidence that the legislators who drafted the Fourteenth Amendment meant to eliminate segregation in education. He found the opposite—some legislators who had supported the amendment also had maintained that it would *not* prohibit segregated schools. One prominent historian invited by Marshall to assist in the *Brown* case declined to help for that very reason. Henry Steele Commager told the NAACP lawyers, "The framers of the amendment did not, as far as we know now, intend that it should be used to end segregation in schools. . . . I strongly urge that you consider dropping this particular argument as I think it tends to weaken your case."[63] Other researchers noted that the inconclusive legislative history of the Fourteenth Amendment did not mean that the Constitution sanctioned segregation. When the southern states had redrafted their state constitutions for readmission to the Union after the Civil War, none had sanctioned segregation or mentioned race in connection with the public school system.[64]

In the months prior to the reargument of *Brown*, Howard Jay Graham published a law review article intended as a public memo to the Supreme Court. In "The Fourteenth Amendment and School Segregation," Graham imagined Rip Van Winkle slumbering for eighty years after the passage of the amendment, awakening in the twentieth century, and expressing shock at racial segregation in schools and other aspects of daily life despite the "equal protection of the laws" secured by the amendment.[65] "Law, essentially, at best, is a rational, principled, sovereign rule and choice," Graham said. "Race discrimination, overt or covert, is a tacit, personal, irrational choice."[66]

Graham did not see an inconsistency between the existence of segregated schools after the adoption of the Fourteenth Amendment in 1868 and the use of the same amendment to strike down segregated schools in 1953. "Does it follow—dare it follow—we *today* are bound by that imperfect understanding of *equal protection* of the laws?" Graham asked. "Must we and our children, obliged to live in a world, and assume moral leadership in a world, only one-third of whose population is white, where racism daily is becoming more menacing and hateful, and a stain upon our national honor, must we accept that understanding? Must we enforce that understanding? For all time? . . . Did the generation that struck shackles from slaves, somehow shackle our minds?"[67]

Graham said the nature and quality of constitutional rights—and the application of the Fourteenth Amendment—can and must change over time. Horace Mann Bond, president of Lincoln University, noted that while compulsory public education was only a "developing concept" in the 1860s, it since had evolved into a fundamental civil right.[68] Bond's research supported the idea that rights could change or expand.

"We pounced on a phrase Jay Graham had dug up," Alfred Kelly recalled. "Constitutions are writ broad for ages yet unborn."[69] William Robert Ming, the first black law professor at the University of Chicago, argued in favor of Graham's interpretation of the Fourteenth Amendment. Ming agreed with Graham's conclusion that the abolitionist movement led to the adoption of the amendment in the spirit of racial equality and social advancement.[70] "This is the argument, essentially, that you will find incorporated in the historical portions of the NAACP brief as it went to the Court," Alfred Kelly said in a speech to historians in 1961, referring to Howard Jay Graham's reading of the Fourteenth Amendment. "This is the argument Marshall used in oral argument in answer to the questions from the justices."[71] The lack of legislative history linking the Fourteenth Amendment to the elimination of segregation had troubled Kelly. He initially did not embrace Graham's argument but later concluded that Graham's view "nevertheless contains an essential measure of historical truth."[72]

On Monday, December 7, 1953, the attorneys for the parties in *Brown v. Board of Education* gathered to reargue the case before the Supreme Court. One year had passed since the initial arguments. NAACP attorney Spottswood W. Robinson began by telling the justices that Congress had passed the Fourteenth Amendment to eliminate discrimination against blacks and strike down state laws informally known as the Black Codes. Robinson acknowledged, "We do not claim that every state in the Union understood the Fourteenth Amendment as abolishing segregation"; however, he said the Fourteenth Amendment operated "as a prohibition against the imposition of any racial classification in respect of civil rights."[73] Thurgood Marshall urged the Court to reject segregation. "We are convinced that the answer is that any segregation, which is for the purpose of setting up either class or caste legislation, is in and of itself a violation of the Fourteenth Amendment."[74]

Attorney John W. Davis argued on behalf of the school districts that sought to uphold segregation. Davis had argued many times before the Supreme Court. He had served as U.S. solicitor general for President Woodrow Wilson and was the Democratic nominee for president in 1924. Davis questioned whether integration would improve the quality of education for anyone.

"Would that make the children any happier?" Davis asked the justices. "Would they learn any more quickly? Would their lives be more serene?"[75] Davis noted that segregated schools had existed in Washington, D.C., prior to and after the ratification of the Fourteenth Amendment. Davis said that segregated schools provided equal education in the manner known and preferred by blacks and whites. "Shall it be thrown away on some fancied question of racial prestige?"[76]

Thurgood Marshall rebutted Davis the following day. "Mr. Davis said yesterday, the only thing the Negroes are trying to get is prestige. Exactly correct. Ever since the Emancipation Proclamation, the Negro has been trying to get . . . the same status as anybody else regardless of race."[77]

When the arguments by counsel in *Brown v. Board of Education* had concluded, Chief Justice Earl Warren gathered his fellow justices together for a conference. Warren announced that he strongly favored overturning *Plessy*. "I can't see how in this day and age we can set any group apart from the rest and say that they are not entitled to exactly the same treatment as all others. . . . I can't see how today we can justify segregation based solely on race."[78] While the justices took no formal vote, Justice William O. Douglas believed that a bare majority—five to four—favored ending segregation.[79]

Warren spent the next three months skillfully reaching out to the justices who were reluctant to overrule *Plessy*. Warren wanted a unanimous decision to overturn school segregation in order to inspire maximum public support. Warren's political experience proved invaluable; one by one, he assembled eight out of nine votes with only Justice Stanley Reed of Kentucky holding out. Warren lunched often with Reed during this period; Reed indicated that he planned to file a dissenting opinion.[80] Warren always concluded their discussions by stressing the need to "do the best thing for the country."[81]

On Monday, May 17, 1954, the Supreme Court announced their decision in *Brown v. Board of Education*. Chief Justice Warren read the opinion. After noting the challenge to the "separate but equal" holding of *Plessy* and discussing the importance of public education, Warren quickly came to the point. "Does segregation of children in public schools solely on the basis of race, even though the physical facilities and other 'tangible' factors may be equal, deprive the children of the minority group of equal educational opportunities?" he asked. "We believe that it does."[82]

Warren did not rely on the "inconclusive" legislative history of the Fourteenth Amendment; instead, he said, "We cannot turn the clock back to 1868" and noted that substantial changes in public education had occurred since the adoption of the amendment.[83] "These days, it is doubtful that any child may reasonably be expected to succeed in life if he is denied the opportunity of an education," Warren said. "Such an opportunity, where the state has undertaken to provide it, is a right which must be made available to all on equal terms."[84] Warren wrote that separating children solely by race contributed to the perception of inferiority of minority children and denied them equal opportunity. The Fourteenth Amendment of the Constitution guaranteed equal protection under the law and therefore prohibited segregation in public schools. The Court overruled *Plessy* and accepted the NAACP's interpretation of the Fourteenth Amendment.

"We conclude that in the field of public education the doctrine of 'separate but equal' has no place," Warren said. "Separate educational facilities are inherently unequal."[85] The Court's ruling was unanimous. Justice Reed's law clerk noticed tears on Reed's face as Warren finished reading the decision.[86]

One hundred and twenty years after the closure of Prudence Crandall's school and eighty-nine years after the end of the Civil War, the Supreme Court finally protected what Prudence Crandall had sought when she admitted Sarah Harris as a student in 1833 — to teach black students in the same classroom as white students.

When Prudence Crandall died in 1890, the editors of the *New Haven Register* wrote: "We of today are only too ready to denounce our fathers for their hostility to the Negro. And yet had we been living at that time, and surrounded by the environments and prejudices of that age we would probably have been no better than the fathers. They looked at matters as they had been taught to look at them; shared the feelings of the majority of men and women of the time and of many of those whose names will live forever in American history as among the best friends the young nation had in its early career. That we of today look at matters in an entirely different light is due to the determined stand of the Prudence Crandalls and the William Lloyd Garrisons, who were not satisfied to see what they believed to be wrong perpetuated forever. . . . We ought to be grateful to them for their noble, self-sacrificing efforts, and no one is more worthy of a large portion of that gratitude than she who has just been laid to rest in Kansas soil."[87]

■ "Human progress is neither automatic nor inevitable," Martin Luther King Jr. said in 1959. "Even a casual look at history reveals that no social advance rolls in on the wheels of inevitability. Every step toward the goal of justice requires sacrifice, suffering, and struggle; the tireless exertions and passionate concern of dedicated individuals."[88]

EPILOGUE

The abolitionists of this country were never a numerous class. Their power and influence were always greater than their numbers, for they had with them the invisible and infinite forces of the moral universe.
— FREDERICK DOUGLASS

I don't want any of you to fool yourselves, it's just begun, the fight has just begun.
— THURGOOD MARSHALL, speaking after the *Brown v. Board of Education* victory.

Brown itself stands as a living testament to the fact that we have a living Constitution. . . . Much of the language of the Constitution, particularly the provisions of the Bill of Rights and the Fourteenth Amendment, require interpretation. After two centuries of vast change, the original intent of the Founders is difficult to discern or is irrelevant. Indeed, there may be no evidence of intent. The Framers of the Constitution were wise enough to write broadly, using language that must be construed in light of changing conditions that could not be foreseen.
— LEWIS F. POWELL JR., U.S. Supreme Court Justice

Those who long to keep their faith in the upward and onward tendencies of the human race will be cheered by the fact that such wonderful revolutions in public sentiment were produced within the memory of one generation by the exercise of clear-sighted conscience and indomitable will.
— LYDIA MARIA CHILD

What seems unmistakable, but oddly enough, is rarely said in public settings nowadays, is that the nation, for all practice and intent, has turned its back upon the moral implications, if not yet the legal ramifications, of the *Brown* decision. The struggle being waged today, where there is any struggle being waged at all, is closer to the one that was addressed in 1896 in *Plessy v. Ferguson*, in which the court accepted segregated institutions for black people, stipulating only that they must be equal to those open to white people. The dual society, at least in public education, seems in general to be unquestioned.
— JONATHAN KOZOL

Who shall tell the story of those early abolitionists, and enable us to understand what it cost them to be true to their convictions? Who will portray the lives so heroic under persecution, the hardships so uncomplainingly borne, the mobs and violence and social ostracism, the heartsickness and almost despair that must have come to them again and again? It is not a pleasant thing . . . to be scorned, railed at, denounced as a fanatic and disturber of the peace . . .

— CELIA BURLEIGH, wife of William Burleigh

My father died in 1961, just seven years after *Brown*, so he didn't live long enough to know that *Brown* would become the foundation on which so much else would rest with respect to civil rights and human rights. I just have to believe that he knows, because it's comforting, but I still wish that he were here to see the changes.

— CHERYL BROWN HENDERSON, daughter of Oliver Brown

Langston Hughes called us to "make America again." In a sense, it is a call—is it not?—to recreate our habits, our institutions, and our hearts. . . . Work with what it means to claim both Jefferson *and* David Walker, Lincoln *and* Frederick Douglass, Whitman *and* Frances Ellen Watkins Harper. Allow Sojourner, Harriet Tubman, and Ida B. Wells-Barnett to open us up to a host of sister ancestors, like Angelina Grimke, Prudence Crandall, and Susan B. Anthony—who have not even appeared on your list of exemplary white Americans. . . . Enter and listen, teach and learn. Let there be new dreams, worthy of our new realities.

— VINCENT HARDING

The story of Prudence Crandall's life and legacy remains relevant to many challenges we face today. Crandall, William Lloyd Garrison, and their allies demonstrated that securing societal progress and enlightenment often requires great courage and perseverance; it is difficult yet essential. Their examples serve to remind us that those who fight for equality, and for tolerance and respect between those of different races and beliefs, fight for the fundamental values of America.

Prudence Crandall's schoolhouse in Canterbury, Connecticut, still stands today. The state purchased the property in 1969 and opened a museum in 1984.

NOTES

1. FIRE IN THE NIGHT SKY

1. Jean McMahon Humez, *Harriet Tubman, The Life and the Life Stories* (Madison: University of Wisconsin Press, 2003), 175–177.

2. Kate Clifford Larson, *Bound for the Promised Land: Harriet Tubman: Portrait of an American Hero* (New York: One World Books/Random House, 2004), 41. Tubman's name was Araminta Harriet Ross until she married John Tubman in the 1840s.

3. T. G. Onstot, *Pioneers of Menard and Mason Counties* (Peoria, Ill.: J. W. Franks and Sons, 1902), 25.

4. Walt Whitman, *Specimen Days and Collect* (Philadelphia: David McKay, 1883), 336; Donald W. Olson and Laurie G. Jasinski, "Abe Lincoln and the Leonoids," *Sky and Telescope Magazine* (November 1999): 34–35.

5. Garrett Putman Serviss, *Curiosities of the Sky: A Popular Presentation of the Great Riddles and Mysteries of Astronomy* (New York: Harper and Brothers, 1909), 186.

6. Joseph Bates, *The Autobiography of Elder Joseph Bates* (Battle Creek, Mich.: Steam Press, 1868), 239.

7. *Friends' Intelligencer*, November 24, 1877.

8. Bates, *The Autobiography of Elder Joseph Bates*, 241. The meteors were part of the Leonid stream of meteors seen each year in November. The showers occurred with the greatest intensity in 1799, 1833, and 1866.

9. Frederick Douglass, *My Bondage and My Freedom* (Auburn, N.Y.: Miller, Orton and Mulligan, 1855), 186.

10. Mark Littmann, *The Heavens on Fire: The Great Leonid Meteor Storms* (New York: Cambridge University Press, 1998), 8.

11. *Portland Evening Advertiser*, November 26, 1833.

12. *Richmond Enquirer*, November 19, 1833; Littman, *The Heavens on Fire*, 7.

13. Herbert Aptheker, *American Negro Slave Revolts* (New York: International Publishers Company, 1983), 296–297.

14. *Niles Weekly Register*, December 31, 1831. The state of Georgia offered five thousand dollars for the arrest and conviction of anyone circulating Garrison's *Liberator*.

15. *Report of the Arguments of Counsel in the Case of Prudence Crandall before the Supreme Court of Errors* (Boston: Garrison and Knapp, 1834), 22.

16. *Andrew T. Judson's Remarks to the Jury on the Trial of the Case, State v. P. Crandall, Superior Court, Oct. Term 1833, Windham County, Ct.* (Hartford, Conn.: John Russell, 1833), 22.

17. Ibid.

18. Ibid.

19. Richard Hildreth, *The White Slave, Another Picture of Slave Life in America*

(London: George Routledge, 1852), 144. Hildreth reported rather than editorialized; he sympathized with the abolitionist movement.

20. Prudence Crandall, letter to Simeon S. Jocelyn, April 17, 1833, Prudence Crandall Collection, Charles E. Shain Library, Connecticut College.

21. William Lloyd Garrison, *Helen Eliza Garrison, A Memorial* (Cambridge, Mass.: Riverside Press, 1876), 20.

22. Ibid.

23. The Fourteenth Amendment to the U.S. Constitution provides that all persons born in the United States are U.S. citizens; prohibits states from limiting the privileges or immunities of any citizen or denying life, liberty, or property without due process of law; and guarantees all citizens equal protection under the law. The Fifteenth Amendment guarantees the right of all citizens to vote, regardless of race.

24. Wendell Phillips Garrison, "Connecticut in the Middle Ages," *Century Magazine* 30, no. 5 (September 1885): 780. The article includes an extract of a letter from Crandall to Ellen Larned, May 15, 1869, where Crandall wrote that she was "taught from early childhood the sin of slavery."

25. George H. Moore, *Notes on the History of Slavery in Massachusetts* (New York: D. Appleton, 1866), 75.

26. Scott J. Hammond, Kevin R. Hardwick, and Howard Leslie Lubert, eds., *Classics of American Political and Constitutional Thought*, vol. 2, *Origins Through the Civil War* (Indianapolis: Hackett Publishing, 2007), 17, 18.

27. L. H. Butterfield, ed., *The Diary and Autobiography of John Adams*, vol. 1 (Cambridge, Mass.: Belknap Press of Harvard University Press, 1962), 257.

28. Robert Hume, *Christopher Columbus and the European Discovery of America* (Leominster, U.K.: Gracewing, 1992), 117.

29. Junius P. Rodriguez, *Slavery in the United States: A Social, Political, and Historical Encyclopedia*, vol. 2 (Santa Barbara, Calif.: ABC-CLIO, 2007), 450, 451.

30. John Adams to Robert Evans, June 8, 1819, *Selected Writings of John and John Quincy Adams*, ed. Adrienne Koch (New York: Knopf, 1946), 209–210.

31. George Washington to Robert Morris, April 12, 1786. *George Washington: A Collection*, ed. W. B. Allen (Indianapolis: Liberty Classics, 1989), 319.

32. Benjamin Franklin, *Writings*, ed. J. A. Leo Lemay (New York: Library of America, 1987), 1154.

33. William Jay, *The Life of John Jay: With Selections from His Correspondence and Miscellaneous Papers*, vol. 2 (New York: J. and J. Harper, 1833), 181–182.

34. Jonathan Elliot, ed., *The Debates of the Several State Conventions on the Adoption of the Federal Constitution, as Recommended by the General Convention at Philadelphia in 1787*, vol. 3 (Philadelphia: J. B. Lippincott, 1891), 590–591.

35. John R. Howe, Jr., "John Adams' Views of Slavery," *Journal of Negro History* 49, no. 3 (July 1964): 201; David McCullough, *John Adams* (New York: Simon and Schuster, 2001), 134.

36. Dumas Malone, *Jefferson the Virginian: Jefferson and His Time*, vol. 1 (Boston: Little, Brown, 1948), 266–267. Malone acknowledged the tortured path that Jefferson

had traveled regarding the rights of blacks and maintained that Jefferson's view was humane and realistic for his time. See generally, ibid., 264–269.

37. Ibid., 266; Thomas Jefferson, *Notes on the State of Virginia* (Boston: H. Sprague, 1802), 190.

38. Jefferson, *Notes*, 192.

39. Ibid.

40. Ibid., 198–199.

41. Merrill D. Peterson, ed., *Thomas Jefferson: Writings* (New York: Library of America, 1984), 289; Jefferson, *Notes*, 224.

42. Thomas Jefferson to James Heaton, May 20, 1826, *Thomas Jefferson: Writings*, ed. Merrill D. Peterson (New York: Library of America, 1984), 1516.

43. Peter P. Hinks, ed., *David Walker's Appeal to the Coloured Citizens of the World* (University Park: Pennsylvania State University Press, 2000), 78–79.

44. Ibid., 79.

45. United States Census Office, *Ninth Census of the United States, Statistics of Population* (Washington, D.C.: U.S. Government Printing Office, 1872), 4–6, tab. 1–8.

46. Alan D. Watson, *Wilmington, North Carolina, to 1861* (Jefferson, N.C.: McFarland, 2003), 31.

47. Clyde Wilson, ed., *The Papers of John C. Calhoun, 1835–1837*, vol. 8 (Columbia, S.C.: University of South Carolina Press, 1980), 389–390.

48. Frederick Augustus Ross, *Slavery Ordained of God* (Philadelphia: J. B. Lippincott, 1857), 99.

49. Ibid., 6.

50. "Address of W. M. Ballard Preston before the Virginia Agricultural Society," *The American Farmer* 10, no. 6 (December 1854): 171.

51. Alexandra A. Chan, *Slavery in the Age of Reason: Archaeology at a New England Farm* (Knoxville: University of Tennessee Press, 2007), 71–73; Jay Coughtry, *The Notorious Triangle: Rhode Island and the African Slave Trade, 1700–1807* (Philadelphia: Temple University Press, 1981), 6–7.

52. See generally, Thomas Norman DeWolf, *Inheriting the Trade: A Northern Family Confronts Its Legacy as the Largest Slave Trading Dynasty in U.S. History* (Cambridge, Mass.: Beacon Press, 2009).

53. Winslow C. Watson, ed., *Men and Times of the Revolution, or, Memoirs of Elkanah Watson* (New York: Dana, 1856), 58.

54. John Hope Franklin, *The Free Negro in North Carolina, 1790–1860* (Chapel Hill: University of North Carolina Press, 1943), 35.

55. Hinks, *David Walker's Appeal*, 19.

56. Sherman S. Griswold, *Historical Sketch of the Town of Hopkinton: From 1757 to 1876* (Hope Valley, R.I.: Wood River Advertiser Press, 1877), 58.

57. *Rhode Island: A Guide to the Smallest State* (Federal Writer's Project) (Cambridge, Mass.: Riverside Press, 1937), 357, discussing the history of Hopkinton. After Carpenter sold his mills in the 1820s, the village was renamed Hope Valley.

58. John Cortland Crandall, *Elder John Crandall of Rhode Island and His Descen-*

dants (New Woodstock, N.Y.: J. C. Crandall, 1949), 155; Rena Keith Clisby, *Canterbury Pilgrims* (n.p., 1947), 8, Prudence Crandall Collection, Charles E. Shain Library, Connecticut College.

59. Crandall, *Elder John Crandall*, 155, 306, 312. Hezekiah was born on September 22, 1800; Reuben was born on January 6, 1806; and Hannah Almira was born on June 27, 1813.

60. Susan Strane, *A Whole Souled Woman: Prudence Crandall and the Education of Black Women* (New York: W. W.W. W. Norton, 1990), 4.

61. Clisby, *Canterbury Pilgrims*, 9.

62. Ibid., 3.

63. Ibid., 11.

64. Ibid., 9–10. See also Griswold, *Historical Sketch of the Town of Hopkinton*, 58. Griswold wrote that Hezekiah Carpenter gave land in Carpenter's Mills (now Hope Valley) and Locustville, Rhode Island, to Pardon and Esther Crandall. Today Locustville is part of Hope Valley.

65. Clisby, *Canterbury Pilgrims*, 10.

66. Strane, *A Whole Souled Woman*, 5–6.

67. Marvis Olive Welch, *Prudence Crandall, A Biography* (Manchester, Conn.: Jason, 1983), 5; Clisby, *Canterbury Pilgrims*, 10.

68. "Black Hill," *The R.I. Schoolmaster* 7, no. 11 (November 1861), 322. An anonymous former student of the Black Hill School wrote an account of student life at the school in the 1820s.

69. Ibid., 324.

70. Ibid., 322.

71. Louis Ruchames, ed., *The Letters of William Lloyd Garrison: A House Dividing Against Itself, 1836–1840*, vol. 2 (Cambridge: Harvard University Press, 1971), 26 n. 16.

72. Kenneth Morgan, *Slavery and the British Empire: From Africa to America* (New York: Oxford University Press, 2007), 66.

73. John S. Schroeder, *Matthew Calbraith Perry: Antebellum Sailor and Diplomat* (Annapolis: Naval Institute Press, 2001), 9; Elaine Forman Crane, *A Dependent People: Newport, Rhode Island in the Revolutionary Era* (New York: Fordham University Press, 1992), 35–37. One of the most successful Newport slave importers was Godfrey Malbone, whose son, also named Godfrey, left Newport to live in Brooklyn, Connecticut, next to Canterbury. He brought between fifty and sixty slaves, who helped construct his Brooklyn farm and a small Episcopal church in the late 1700s. See James A. Rawley and Stephen D. Behrendt, *The Transatlantic Slave Trade: A History* (Lincoln: University of Nebraska Press, 2005), 313; and William Chauncey Fowler, *Local Law in Massachusetts and Connecticut: Historically Considered; and The Historical Status of the Negro, in Connecticut* (Albany, N.Y.: Joel Munsell, 1872), 122.

74. United States Census Office, *Ninth Census of the United States*, 17.

75. Ibid.

76. Ellen D. Larned, *History of Windham County, Connecticut*, vol. 2 (Worcester, Mass.: Charles Hamilton, 1880), 431.

77. Ibid., 432.

78. *Resolves and Private Laws of the State of Connecticut from the Year 1836 to the Year 1857*, vol. 4 (New Haven: Thomas J. Stafford, 1857), 1374. The Connecticut General Assembly passed a law in 1848 that incorporated the Rowland's Brook Reservoir Company, named Hezekiah Crandall as a shareholder, and referenced his mill and its products.

79. Larned, *History of Windham County*, 2:503.

80. Ibid., 433.

81. Samuel G. Goodrich, *A System of Universal Geography: Popular and Scientific, Comprising a Physical, Political, and Statistical Account of the World and Its Various Divisions* (Philadelphia: Key, Mielke and Biddle, 1832), 100. Goodrich recorded his impressions traveling from England through the United States, including daily life in New England.

82. Ibid., 100–101.

83. Ibid., 101.

84. Ibid.

85. Ibid.

86. Ibid.

87. Larned, *History of Windham County*, 2:423.

88. Ibid.

89. Linda Eisenmann, ed., *Historical Dictionary of Women's Education in the United States* (Westport, Conn.: Greenwood Press, 1998), 109.

90. Letter from Elisabeth Weeks (administrator at Moses Brown School, Providence, Rhode Island) to Helen Earle Sellers, October 28, 1948, Prudence Crandall Collection, Charles E. Shain Library, Connecticut College.

91. Edward Field, *State of Rhode Island and Providence Plantations at the End of the Century: A History*, vol. 2 (Boston: Mason, 1902), 116.

92. Rayner Wickersham Kelsey, *Centennial History of Moses Brown School, 1819–1919* (Providence, R.I.: Moses Brown School, 1919), 142.

93. Edward Everett Hale, *Lend a Hand*, vol. 10 (Boston: J. Stilman Smith, 1893), 49.

94. William J. Brown, *The Life of William Brown of Providence, Rhode Island: With Personal Recollections of Incidents in Rhode Island* (Durham, N.H.: University of New Hampshire Press, 2006), xxiii.

95. Rufus Matthew Jones, *Eli and Sybil Jones: Their Life and Work* (Philadelphia: Porter and Coates, 1889), 21.

96. Elizabeth C. Stevens, *Elizabeth Buffum Chace and Lillie Chace Wyman: A Century of Abolitionist, Suffragist, and Workers' Rights Activism* (Jefferson, N.C.: McFarland, 2003), 12. Elizabeth Buffum Chace was the daughter of Arnold Buffum, who assisted Prudence Crandall and her school. Elizabeth Buffum attended the Friend's School during the 1824–25 term; Prudence attended in the fall of 1825.

97. Ibid.

98. Field, *Providence Plantations*, 2:116.

99. Stevens, *Elizabeth Buffum Chace*, 12.

100. Jones, *Eli and Sybil Jones*, 21.

101. Ibid.

102. Kelsey, *Centennial History of Moses Brown School*, 142; Welch, *Prudence Crandall*, 8.

103. Kelsey, *Centennial History of Moses Brown School*, 146.

104. Ibid., 146–147.

105. Amory Dwight Mayo, "The American Common School in New England, from 1790 to 1840," in *Report of the Commissioner of Education*, ed. U.S. Office of Education (Washington, D.C.: U.S. Government Printing Office, 1896), 1583.

106. Ibid., 1582.

107. Janice Law Trecker, *Preachers, Rebels and Traders: Connecticut 1818 to 1865* (Chester, Conn.: Pequot Press, 1975), 5.

108. Mayo, "The American Common School in New England, from 1790 to 1840," 1583.

109. *Connecticut Common School Journal* 4, no. 13 (July 1, 1842), 141–142. In 1841 the Connecticut legislature continued to allow children fifteen years old and younger to work in factories, provided that they worked no more than ten hours per day and attended school for three months of the year. Rhode Island passed a similar law in 1840, and Massachusetts followed suit in 1866.

110. "Letter from Rev. Eliphalet Nott, D.D., Dated Jan. 1861," in *American Journal of Education*, vol. 13, ed. Henry Barnard (Hartford, Conn.: Henry Barnard, 1863), 132. Nott served as principal of the Plainfield Academy and president of Union College.

111. "Memoir of William A. Alcott," in *American Journal of Education*, vol. 12, ed. Henry Barnard (Hartford, Conn.: F. C. Brownell, 1858), 645–649, discussing conditions in district schools in Tolland County, Connecticut, in 1831.

112. Larned, *History of Windham County*, 2:477.

113. "Letter from Rev. Eliphalet Nott, D.D., Dated Jan. 1861," *American Journal of Education*, 133.

114. Mayo, "The American Common School in New England, from 1790 to 1840," 1582.

115. Helen Earle Sellers, unfinished draft of Prudence Crandall's biography written during the 1940s, chap. 1, page 1 (quoting Jehiel Chester Hart), Prudence Crandall Collection, Charles E. Shain Library, Connecticut College Collection.

116. "Letter from Rev. Eliphalet Nott, D.D., Dated Jan. 1861," *American Journal of Education*, 133.

117. Ibid.

118. Prudence Crandall to Ellen D. Larned, Mendota, Illinois, March 7, 1870, Ellen Douglas Larned Papers, Connecticut State Library, Hartford, Connecticut.

119. Welch, *Prudence Crandall*, 17.

120. Samuel May, "Miss Crandall's School," in *The Oasis*, ed. Lydia Maria Child (Boston: Benjamin C. Bacon, 1834), 180–181.

121. Welch, *Prudence Crandall*, 18.

122. Strane, *A Whole Souled Woman*, 8.

123. Theophilus Parsons, *Laws of Business for All the States and Territories of the Union and the Dominion of Canada* (Hartford, Conn.: S. S. Scranton, 1909), 37.

124. Strane, *A Whole Souled Woman*, 12.

125. Ibid., 13.

126. Garrison, "Connecticut in the Middle Ages," 780; Lamin O. Sanneh, *Abolitionists Abroad: American Blacks and the Making of Modern West Africa* (Cambridge, Mass.: Harvard University Press, 2001), 49–50.

127. Welch, *Prudence Crandall*, 9.

128. William E. Gienapp, "Abolitionism and the Nature of Antebellum Reform," in *Courage and Conscience, Black and White Abolitionists in Boston*, ed. Donald M. Jacobs (Bloomington: Indiana University Press, 1993), 27.

129. Paul G. Faler, *Mechanics and Manufacturers in the Early Industrial Revolution: Lynn, Massachusetts, 1780–1860* (Albany: State University of New York Press, 1981), 100–101.

130. William G. McLoughlin, ed., *The American Evangelicals, 1800–1900* (New York: Harper and Row, 1968), 4–5. The "Second Great Awakening" lasted from 1800 to 1835; see also Joseph Tracy, *The Great Awakening, A History of the Revival of Religion* (Boston: Charles Tappan, 1845), 1. The "First Great Awakening" occurred in the 1730s and 1740s.

131. McLoughlin, *The American Evangelicals*, 70.

132. Ibid.

133. Henry Mayer, *All on Fire: William Lloyd Garrison and the Abolition of Slavery* (New York: St. Martin's Press, 1998), 118.

134. McLoughlin, *The American Evangelicals*, 87.

135. Ronald Walters, *American Reformers, 1815–1860* (New York: Hill and Wang, 1978), 26.

136. Jacobs, *Courage and Conscience*, 26–27. In an article entitled "Abolitionism and the Nature of Antebellum Reform," William E. Gienapp said revivalists such as Charles G. Finney "made religion a major force for social reform. . . . [They] changed the whole emphasis of the religious experience by insisting that salvation was only the beginning. Having gained salvation, true Christians would undertake to perfect society by attacking sin wherever they found it. . . . Men and women deeply alienated from this emerging competitive, market-oriented society . . . all turned to humanitarian reform."

137. Robert Andrew Baker, *Relations between Northern and Southern Baptists* (New York: Arno Press, 1980), 40; Francis Butler Simkins, *A History of the South* (New York: Alfred A. Knopf, 1953), 165.

138. Larned, *History of Windham County, Connecticut*, vol. 2 (Worcester, Mass.: Charles Hamilton, 1880), 505. Daniel Packer acquired the Andrus Factory in 1818 and significantly improved and enlarged the dormant mill. The revitalized mill resulted in an expanded local community that became known as Packerville.

139. Henry S. Burrage, *Baptist Hymn Writers and Their Hymns* (Portland, Maine: Brown, Thurston, 1888), 307; see also A. H. Newman, *A History of Baptist Churches in*

the United States (New York: Christian Literature Company, 1894), 479. The Hamilton Literary and Theological Institute later became Colgate University.

140. Larned, *History of Windham County*, 2:506.

141. Burrage, *Baptist Hymn Writers and Their Hymns*, 307. Included is a brief biography of Levi Kneeland. See also Larned, *History of Windham County*, 2:506.

142. Welch, *Prudence Crandall*, 9; see David S. Heidler and Jeanne T. Heidler, *Daily Life in the Early American Republic, 1790–1820: Creating a New Nation* (Westport, Conn.: Greenwood Publishing, 2004), 123.

143. Welch, *Prudence Crandall*, 21.

144. Clisby, *Canterbury Pilgrims*, 15.

145. Ibid.

146. Larned, *History of Windham County*, 2:485.

147. Ibid., 481.

148. Ibid., 482.

2. LIBERATORS

1. William Lloyd Garrison to Maria W. Stewart, April 4, 1879, in *Maria W. Stewart, America's First Black Woman Political Writer: Essays and Speeches*, ed. Marilyn Richardson (Bloomington: Indiana University Press, 1987), 89.

2. Ibid.

3. Ibid., 8.

4. Ibid., 30.

5. *Liberator*, October 8, 1831; Richardson, *Maria W. Stewart*, 28.

6. Richardson, *Maria W. Stewart*, 11.

7. Ibid. American newspapers often had a separate ladies or "women's section" well into the twentieth century. The *Washington Post* was among the first to rename its women's department when it created the "Style Section" in 1969. See Paula Maurie Poindexter, Sharon Meraz, and Amy Schmitz Weiss, eds., *Women, Men, and News: Divided and Disconnected in the News Media Landscape* (New York: Routledge, 2008), 91.

8. Richardson, *Maria W. Stewart*, 29.

9. Ibid., 38.

10. Ibid., 3.

11. Ibid., 117.

12. Ibid.

13. Ibid., 117.

14. Ibid., 7, 123 n. 19.

15. Ibid., 92. Louise C. Hatton, supporting document for pension application of Maria W. Stewart, May 28, 1879, Washington, D.C.

16. Peter P. Hinks, ed., *David Walker's Appeal to the Colored Citizens of the World* (University Park: Pennsylvania State University Press, 2000), 12.

17. Richardson, *Maria W. Stewart*, 38.

18. Ibid., 48.

19. Ibid., 49.

20. Ibid., 53, 54. In "An Address Delivered before the African-American Female Intelligence Society of America," delivered in the spring of 1832, Stewart suggested that "our own color are our greatest opposers" and further offered that "a lady of high distinction among us, observed to me that I might never expect your homage."

21. William Lloyd Garrison to Simeon S. Jocelyn, May 30, 1831, in *The Letters of William Lloyd Garrison, I Will Be Heard! 1822–1835*, vol. 1, ed. Walter M. Merrill (Cambridge, Mass.: Harvard University Press, 1971), 119. Garrison said that after five months of publishing, the *Liberator* "gets along bravely" as a result of more than five hundred voluntary subscribers, most of whom were "colored individuals."

22. Ibid., 124. William Lloyd Garrison to Henry Benson, July 30, 1831. Garrison discussed his success with black subscribers and his desire to "put a copy of my Address to the Free People of Color into the hands of every colored man." Benson was the brother of Helen Benson, who would later marry Garrison, and served as an agent for the *Liberator*.

23. Henry Mayer, *All on Fire: William Lloyd Garrison and the Abolition of Slavery* (New York: St. Martin's Press, 1998), 134. "The *Liberator* could boast the names of forty-seven agents and several thousand subscribers enrolled in Brother Knapp's ledger by spring 1832."

24. *Vital Records of Norwich, 1659–1848*, vol. 2 (Hartford: Society of Colonial Wars in Connecticut, 1913), 654–655.

25. *The Plaindealer* 1, no. 14 (March 4, 1837): 213.

26. *Vital Records of Norwich*, 2:655.

27. Richardson, *Maria W. Stewart*, 44; *Liberator*, July 14, 1832.

28. Richardson, *Maria W. Stewart*, 45.

29. Ibid., 38. Richardson summarized the challenge and dilemma faced by Maria Stewart: "Convinced of a calling she could not refuse, Stewart was thrust into the public role of not only teacher—an acceptable position for a woman—but of prophet. . . . In order to obey God she had to act in contradiction to the secular identity to which she had once aspired, that of a traditionally refined and accomplished woman. . . . Her calling was not merely reformist, it was subversive, and she was the first to encounter its transformative character by its challenge to her own identity." Ibid., 26.

30. Susan Strane, *A Whole Souled Woman: Prudence Crandall and the Education of Black Women* (New York: W. W. Norton, 1990), 24.

31. Marvis Olive Welch, *Prudence Crandall: A Biography* (Manchester, Conn.: Jason, 1983), 23.

32. Bernard C. Steiner, "History of Slavery in Connecticut," in *Studies in Historical and Political Science, Labor, Slavery and Self-Government*, vol. 11, ed. Herbert B. Adams (Baltimore: John Hopkins Press, 1893), 415. Steiner wrote that Sarah Harris "took Garrison's '*Liberator*' and loaned it to Marcia (Mariah), who used frequently to show the paper to Miss Crandall"; see also Strane, *A Whole Souled Woman*, 24.

33. Carl R. Woodward, "A Profile in Dedication: Sarah Harris and the Fayerweather Family," *New England Galaxy* 25, no. 1 (Summer 1973): 5.

34. *A Statement of Facts Respecting the School for Colored Females, in Canterbury, Con-*

necticut, Together with a Report of the Late Trial of Miss Prudence Crandall (Brooklyn, Conn.: Advertiser Press, 1833), 5.

35. "Letter from Prudence Crandall," *Windham County Advertiser*, May 7, 1833. See Welch, *Prudence Crandall*, 51–53; see also William Jay, *An Inquiry into the Character and Tendency of the American Colonization and American Anti-Slavery Societies* (New York: Leavitt, Lord, 1835), 28. Jay was a noted abolitionist and wrote the constitution for the American Anti-Slavery Society. His father, John Jay, was one of the founding fathers who served as president of the Continental Congress.

36. Ibid.

37. Strane, *A Whole Souled Woman*, 25.

38. Samuel May, "Miss Crandall's School," in *The Oasis*, ed. Lydia Maria Child (Boston: Benjamin C. Bacon, 1834), 181. Samuel May wrote an essay for *The Oasis* detailing the beginnings of Prudence Crandall's school. It is a rare if not singular account written contemporaneously with the operation of the school by someone who worked at the school.

39. Prudence Crandall to William Lloyd Garrison, Canterbury, Connecticut, January 18, 1833, in Wendell Phillips Garrison, "Connecticut in the Middle Ages," *Century Magazine* 30, no. 5 (September 1885): 780.

40. *Liberator*, July 14, 1832; Truman Nelson, ed., *Documents of Upheaval: Selections from William Lloyd Garrison's The Liberator* (New York: Hill and Wang, 1966), 54.

41. Ibid.

42. Richardson, *Maria W. Stewart*, 43; *Liberator*, July 14, 1832.

43. Richardson, *Maria W. Stewart*, 44.

44. Ibid., 46, 48; *Liberator*, November 17, 1832. Richardson noted that Stewart quoted Thomas Grey's "Elegy Written in a Country Churchyard," published in 1751. Grey wrote, "Full many a flower is born to bloom unseen, and waste its sweetness on the desert air."

45. Crandall to Ellen Larned, May 15, 1869, in Garrison, "Connecticut in the Middle Ages," 780.

46. *A Statement of Facts Respecting the School for Colored Females, in Canterbury, Connecticut, Together with a Report of the Late Trial of Miss Prudence Crandall* (Brooklyn, Conn.: Advertiser Press, 1833), 5.

47. "Letter from Prudence Crandall," *Windham County Advertiser*, May 7, 1833. See Welch, *Prudence Crandall*, 51–53.

48. Hinks, *David Walker's Appeal*, 28.

49. Peter P. Hinks, *To Awaken My Afflicted Brethren: David Walker and the Problem of Antebellum Slave Resistance* (University Park: Pennsylvania State University Press, 1997), 151.

50. Ibid.

51. *Niles Register*, March 27, 1830; Hinks, *To Awaken My Afflicted Brethren*, 124.

52. *Richmond Enquirer*, January 28, 1830; Hinks, *To Awaken My Afflicted Brethren*, 124.

53. George M. Fredrickson, *The Black Image in the White Mind: The Debate on Afro-American Character and Destiny, 1817–1914* (Middletown, Conn.: Wesleyan University Press, 1987), 6–7.

54. Vincent B. Thompson, *Africans of the Diaspora: The Evolution of African Consciousness and Leadership in the Americas* (Trenton, N.J.: Africa World Press, 2000), 132.

55. Hinks, *David Walker's Appeal*, 70, 71–72.

56. Ibid., 34.

57. Child, *The Oasis*, 182.

58. Ibid.

59. Crandall to Ellen Larned, May 15, 1869, in Garrison, "Connecticut in the Middle Ages," 780. Crandall wrote: "I had a nice colored girl, now Mrs. Charles Harris, as help in my family, and her intended husband regularly received *The Liberator*. The girl took the paper from the office and loaned it to me. In that the condition of the colored people, both slaves and free, was truthfully portrayed, the double-dealing and manifest deception of the Colonization Society were faithfully exposed, and the question of Immediate Emancipation of the millions of slaves in the United States boldly advocated. Having been taught from an early childhood the sin of slavery, my sympathies were greatly aroused. . . . I allowed her [Sarah] to enter as one of my pupils." See also "Letter from Prudence Crandall," *Windham County Advertiser*, May 7, 1833. Crandall wrote: "Previous to any excitement concerning her [Sarah] there fell in my way several publications that contained many facts relative to the people of color of which I was entirely ignorant. My feelings began to awaken. I saw that the prejudice of whites against color was deep and inveterate."

60. Child, *The Oasis*, 182. Samuel May said that Crandall saw how blacks "are denied a participation in the privileges of which we boast, shut out from all our seminaries of learning, except it be those of the lowest grade, and in effect forbidden to aspire after knowledge or excellence." This was a point often made by Maria W. Stewart.

61. Richardson, *Maria W. Stewart*, 37.

62. Child, *The Oasis*, 181.

63. Woodward, "A Profile in Dedication: Sarah Harris," 5.

64. Child, *The Oasis*, 182. While teaching at Crandall's school, Samuel May wrote that Sarah Harris was "well known to many of Miss Crandall's pupils, having been their classmate in the district school." Carl R. Woodward has pointed out that Sarah's father purchased a farm in Canterbury in January 1832, making it unlikely that Sarah had attended the local district school. Woodward, "A Profile in Dedication: Sarah Harris," 5. Woodward notes, however, that William Harris's name appears on the Canterbury tax lists as early as 1821, raising the possibility that Samuel May's statement is correct. See also Janice Law Trecker, *Preachers, Rebels, and Traders: Connecticut 1818–1865* (Chester, Conn.: Pequot Press, 1975), 5, 30. Trecker noted that district and common schools in Connecticut often were characterized by neglect and poor facilities, and education usually was limited to learning letters, numbers, and moral sentiments such as "contentment is great gain" and "children, obey your parents."

Some district schools admitted both black and white students, such as the school in Canterbury; however, because students were responsible for certain school expenses, "only a fraction of the state's black children attended school."

65. Woodward, "A Profile in Dedication: Sarah Harris," 6.

66. Child, *The Oasis*, 182.

67. Strane, *A Whole Souled Woman*, 27.

68. Ibid.

69. *A Statement of Facts Respecting the School for Colored Females, in Canterbury, Connecticut, Together with a Report of the Late Trial of Miss Prudence Crandall* (Brooklyn, Conn.: Advertiser Press, 1833), 6.

70. Crandall to Larned, May 15, 1869, in Larned, *History of Windham County*, 2:491.

71. Ibid.

72. Ibid.

73. Ibid.

74. "Letter from Prudence Crandall," *Windham County Advertiser*, May 7, 1833. See Welch, *Prudence Crandall*, 51–53.

75. Garrison, "Connecticut in the Middle Ages," 780.

76. Ibid.

77. Ibid.

78. When Crandall presented her proposal to create a school for black women to Garrison, she had not yet met Samuel May, Charles or William Burleigh, or the other local abolitionists who would later help her. Crandall's opponents suggested that radical abolitionists had prevailed on Crandall to create a school for black women; however, no evidence has surfaced to support this theory. To the contrary, her later correspondence with Garrison makes it clear that she is proposing the idea to him. Crandall's opponents likely wanted to belittle her role and promote the idea that her school was created by outside agitators.

79. Garrison, "Connecticut in the Middle Ages," 780.

80. Wendell Phillips Garrison and Francis Jackson Garrison, *William Lloyd Garrison, 1805–1879: The Story of His Life Told by His Children*, vol. 1 (New York: Century, 1885), 17.

81. Ibid., 23.

82. Samuel Eliot Morison, *The Maritime History of Massachusetts, 1783–1860* (Boston: Houghton Mifflin, 1921), 191.

83. Wendell and Francis Garrison, *William Lloyd Garrison*, 1:24.

84. Ibid., 26–27.

85. Joshua Coffin and Joseph Bartlett, *A Sketch of the History of Newbury, Newburyport, and West Newbury, from 1635 to 1845* (Boston: Samuel G. Drake, 1845), 277.

86. Ibid., 276–277.

87. Mayer, *All on Fire*, 17–18.

88. Ibid., 18–19.

89. Wendell and Francis Garrison, *William Lloyd Garrison*, 1:28.

90. Ibid., 30–31.

91. Ibid., 34–35.

92. Mayer, *All on Fire*, 22–24.

93. William Nelson, *Notes toward a History of the American Newspaper*, vol. 1 (New York: Charles F. Heartman, 1918), 366.

94. Ibid.

95. Mayer, *All on Fire*, 27.

96. Wendell and Francis Garrison, *William Lloyd Garrison*, 1:59–60.

97. Mayer, *All on Fire*, 42.

98. Cushing was later elected to Congress and served four terms from 1835 to 1843. See John Livingston, *Portraits of Eminent Americans Now Living*, vol. 3 (New York: R. Craighead, 1853), 243.

99. Mayer, *All on Fire*, 49–50.

100. Ibid.

101. Garrison to the editor of the *Boston Courier*, February 8, 1827, in Merrill, *The Letters of William Lloyd Garrison*, 1:36.

102. Garrison to the editor of the *Boston Courier*, July 14, 1827, in Merrill, *The Letters of William Lloyd Garrison*, 1:50.

103. Wendell and Francis Garrison, *William Lloyd Garrison*, 1:105–106.

104. Ibid., 104.

105. Mayer, *All on Fire*, 59.

106. Ibid., 61.

107. Garrison to the editor of the *Boston Courier*, August 11, 1828, in Merrill, *The Letters of William Lloyd Garrison*, 1:64.

108. Garrison to Jacob Horton, June 27, 1829, in Merrill, *The Letters of William Lloyd Garrison*, 1:83.

109. Ibid.

110. Ibid. "I expect to get a journeyman's berth immediately after the 4th," Garrison wrote, "but, if I do not, I shall take the stage for Newburyport, and *dig on* at the case for Mr. Allen."

111. William Lloyd Garrison, *Selections from the Writings and Speeches of William Lloyd Garrison* (Boston: R. F. Wallcut, 1852), 53.

112. Ibid., 57.

113. Eric Robert Taylor, *If We Must Die: Shipboard Insurrections in the Era of the Atlantic Slave Trade* (Baton Rouge: Louisiana State University Press, 2006), 149.

114. Ibid., 150.

115. Thomas Earle, ed., *The Life, Travels, and Opinions of Benjamin Lundy* (Philadelphia: William D. Parrish, 1847), 29.

116. Taylor, *If We Must Die*, 150.

117. John W. Christie and Dwight L. Dumond, *George Bourne and the Book and Slavery Irreconcilable* (Baltimore: Historical Society of Delaware and the Presbyterian Historical Society, 1969), vii.

118. Ibid., 204. Bourne crusaded for immediate emancipation for blacks; however,

he was also a leader in the nativist movement that promoted discrimination against Catholics. See Jenny Franchot, *Roads to Rome: The Antebellum Protestant Encounter with Catholicism* (Berkeley: University of California Press, 1994), 109. Lyman Beecher and other Protestant ministers also criticized Catholic schools and their influence on children.

119. Elizabeth Heyrick, *Immediate, Not Gradual Abolition, or, An Inquiry into the Shortest, Safest, and Most Effectual Means of Getting Rid of West Indian Slavery* (London: Hatchard and Son, 1824), 20.

120. Ibid., 19. Dashes that were included as punctuation in the original quotation have been removed to assist in readability.

121. Lundy and Earle, *The Life, Travels, and Opinions of Benjamin Lundy*, 216.

122. *Liberator*, January 8, 1831. See Garrison to La Roy Sunderland, September 8, 1831, in Merrill, *The Letters of William Lloyd Garrison*, 1:129. Garrison wrote, "I do not justify the slaves in their rebellion: yet I do not condemn them . . . Of all men living, however, our slaves have the best reason to assert their rights by violent measures, inasmuch as they are more oppressed than others."

123. Mayer, *All on Fire*, 90–91.

124. Ibid., 92.

125. Garrison to Harriet Farnham Horton, May 12, 1830, in Merrill, *The Letters of William Lloyd Garrison*, 1:91.

126. Ibid.

127. Benjamin Lundy, "The Editor to the Public," *Genius of Universal Emancipation* 1 (April 1830).

128. Arthur Tappan to Benjamin Lundy, May 29, 1830, in Wendell and Francis Garrison, *William Lloyd Garrison*, 1:190.

129. Mayer, *All on Fire*, 93.

130. Wendell and Francis Garrison, *William Lloyd Garrison*, 1:172–173, reprinting an excerpt from the *Genius of Universal Emancipation*, March 5, 1830.

131. Ibid., 173.

132. Garrison to the editor of the *Newburyport Herald*, June 1, 1830, in Merrill, *The Letters of William Lloyd Garrison*, 1:101.

133. Wendell and Francis Garrison, *William Lloyd Garrison*, 1:211–212.

134. George B. Emerson, Samuel May, Thomas J. Mumford, eds., *Life of Samuel May*, or *Memoir of Samuel Joseph May* (Boston: Roberts Brothers, 1873), 140.

135. Ibid., 142.

136. Ibid.

137. Ibid., 69–70.

138. Ibid., 70–71.

139. Ibid., 144.

140. Ibid.

141. Ibid., 144–145.

142. Ibid., 145.

143. Garrison to Oliver Johnson, March 1, 1874, in *The Letters of William Lloyd*

arrison: To Rouse the Slumbering Land, 1868–1879, vol. 6, eds. Walter M. Merrill and *,ouis Ruchames (Cambridge, Mass.: Harvard University Press, 1981), 300.

144. Mayer, *All on Fire,* 103.

145. Ibid., 106.

146. Wendell and Francis Garrison, *William Lloyd Garrison,* 1:217.

147. Ibid., 199.

148. Nelson, *Documents of Upheaval,* 1–2.

149. *Liberator,* January 1, 1831.

150. Ibid.

151. Ibid.

152. Ibid.

153. Garrison to Henry E. Benson, July 30, 1831, in Merrill, *The Letters of William ,loyd Garrison,* 1:124.

3. EDUCATION FOR ALL

1. Wendell Phillips Garrison, "Connecticut in the Middle Ages," *Century Maga-ine* 30, no. 5 (September 1885): 780.

2. Ibid.

3. Abel Bowen, *Bowen's Picture of Boston, or the Citizen's and Stranger's Guide to the ,Metropolis of Massachusetts* (Boston: Henry Bowen, 1829), 206.

4. *Bay State Monthly,* vol. 2 (Boston: John N. McClintock, February 1885), 109.

5. Prudence Crandall to William Lloyd Garrison, January 29, 1833, in Wendell *'hillips Garrison and Francis Jackson Garrison, William Lloyd Garrison, 1805–1879: The ,tory of His Life Told by His Children,* vol. 1 (New York: Century, 1885), 316.

6. Wendell and Francis Garrison, *William Lloyd Garrison, 1805–1879,* 260.

7. Ibid.

8. Crandall to Garrison, February 12, 1833, in Wendell and Francis Garrison, *William Lloyd Garrison, 1805–1879,* 317.

9. Ibid.

10. Ibid.

11. Ibid. 317 n. 4, quoting letter from Henry Benson to Garrison.

12. Ibid., 317.

13. Ibid.

14. Ibid.

15. William Cooper Nell, *The Colored Patriots of the American Revolution, With ,Sketches of Several Distinguished Colored Persons: To Which Is Added a Brief Survey of ,he Condition and Prospects of Colored Americans* (Boston: Robert F. Wallcut, 1855), *,20–321.*

16. Lydia Maria Francis Child, *The Freedmen's Book* (Boston: Ticknor and Fields, .865), 110.

17. George W. Gore, Jr., *Negro Journalism: An Essay on the History and Present Con-,ditions of the Negro Press* (Greencastle, Ind.: DePauw University, 1922), 5.

18. Ibid.; see also Booker T. Washington, *The Story of the Negro: The Rise of the Race*

from Slavery, vol. 1 (New York: Doubleday, Page, 1909), 292. Cornish was familia with the work of David Walker, who was one of the contributors to *Freedom's Journa*

19. Enoch Hutchinson and Stephen Remington, eds., *The Baptist Memorial an Monthly Record*, vol. 8 (New York: Z. P. Hatch, 1849), 298. Rev. James Haybor served as pastor of the Abyssinian Baptist Church from 1831 to 1835. The church wa founded in 1809 with the help of Rev. Thomas Paul of Boston.

20. Wendell and Francis Garrison, "Postscript" to *William Lloyd Garrison*, xv. Rev George Bourne was "the first to broach the doctrine of immediatism in the Unite States."

21. *Liberator*, March 2, 1833.

22. Lewis Tappan, "The Life of Arthur Tappan," in *New Englander*, vol. 19, eds George P. Fisher, Timothy Dwight, and William Kingsley (New Haven: Stafford 1870), 713–714.

23. Lewis Tappan, *The Life of Arthur Tappan* (New York: Hurd and Houghton 1870), 269.

24. Prudence Crandall to Simeon S. Jocelyn, February 26, 1833, Prudence Crandal Collection, Charles E. Shain Library, Connecticut College; see "Abolition Letter Collected by Captain Arthur B. Spingarn," *Journal of Negro History* 18 (1933): 80–81

25. *Annual Book, City of New Haven, 1871–72* (New Haven: Tuttle, Morehouse an Taylor, 1872), 389. "Constituted by colored members in September, 1829. . . . Pas tors—Rev. Simeon S. Jocelyn, from 1829 to 1834."

26. Garrison to Simeon S. Jocelyn, May 30, 1831, in *The Letters of William Lloy Garrison: I Will Be Heard! 1822–1835*, vol. 1, ed. Walter M. Merrill (Cambridge, Mass. Harvard University Press, 1971), 120 (see editor's note at end of letter).

27. Garrison to Harriet Minot, May 1, 1833, in Merrill, *The Letters of William Lloy Garrison*, 1:226.

28. Garrison to George W. Benson, April 23, 1834, in Merrill, *The Letters of Willian Lloyd Garrison*, 1:327.

29. Prudence Crandall to Simeon S. Jocelyn, February 26, 1833, Prudence Crandal Collection, Charles E. Shain Library, Connecticut College.

30. Ibid.

31. Samuel May, "Miss Crandall's School," in *The Oasis*, ed. Lydia Maria Chil (Boston: Benjamin C. Bacon, 1834), 183.

32. Ibid.

33. A Friend of the Colonization Cause, "Negro School in Canterbury" (letter t the editor), *Norwich Republican*, April 6, 1833.

34. Susan Strane, *A Whole Souled Woman: Prudence Crandall and the Education o Black Women* (New York: W. W. Norton, 1990), 28.

35. Ellen D. Larned, *History of Windham County, Connecticut*, vol. 2 (Worcester Mass.: Charles Hamilton, 1880), 492.

36. William Jay, *An Inquiry into the Character and Tendency of the American Coloni zation and American Anti-Slavery Societies* (New York: Leavitt, Lord, 1835), 28.

37. Ibid.

38. *Windham County Advertiser*, May 7, 1833; see Marvis Olive Welch, *Prudence Crandall, A Biography* (Manchester, Conn.: Jason, 1983), 51–53.

39. *Windham County Advertiser*, May 7, 1833.

40. *A Statement of Facts Respecting the School for Colored Females, in Canterbury, Connecticut, Together with a Report of the Late Trial of Miss Prudence Crandall* (Brooklyn, Conn.: Advertiser Press, 1833), 7.

41. Ibid.

42. Prudence Crandall to Simeon S. Jocelyn, February 26, 1833, Prudence Crandall Collection, Charles E. Shain Library, Connecticut College.

43. Ibid.

44. *A Statement of Facts Respecting the School for Colored Females*, 7.

45. Prudence Crandall to Simeon S. Jocelyn, February 26, 1833, Prudence Crandall Collection, Charles E. Shain Library, Connecticut College.

46. Ibid.

47. Ibid.

48. Samuel May, *Some Recollections of Our Anti-Slavery Conflict* (Boston: Fields, Osgood, 1869), 42.

49. Samuel J. May, *Letters to Andrew T. Judson, Esq. and Others in Canterbury, Remonstrating with Them on Their Unjust and Unjustifiable Procedure Relative to Miss Crandall and Her School for Colored Females* (Brooklyn, Conn.: Advertiser Press, 1833), 5, quoting letter from Samuel J. May to Prudence Crandall, February 28, 1833, Samuel J. May Anti-Slavery Collection, Cornell University Library, Ithaca, New York.

50. Ibid.

51. May, *Some Recollections of Our Anti-Slavery Conflict*, 42.

52. Garrison to George W. Benson, March 8, 1833, in Merrill, *The Letters of William Lloyd Garrison*, 1:212.

53. Marilyn Richardson, ed., *Maria W. Stewart, America's First Black Woman Political Writer: Essays and Speeches* (Bloomington: Indiana University Press, 1987), 58–59; 64.

54. Ibid., 57, 58.

55. Dorothy Porter Wesley and Constance Porter Uzelac, eds., *William Cooper Nell: Selected Writings, 1832–1874* (Baltimore: Black Classic Press, 2002), 24.

56. *A Statement of Facts Respecting the School for Colored Females*, 7.

57. Ibid.

58. Ibid.

59. Ibid.

60. Ibid.

61. Ibid.

62. *Norwich Republican*, April 6, 1833; "Table Talk," *North American Magazine* 2, no. 7 (June 1833), 111.

63. *Windham County Advertiser*, May 7, 1833.

64. *A Statement of Facts Respecting the School for Colored Females*, 7.

65. *Liberator*, March 2, 1833.

66. Ibid. Other ministers from New York listed as references for the school in-

cluded Rev. Peter Williams, Rev. Theodore Raymond, Rev, Theodore Wright, and Rev. James Hayborn.

67. Martin R. Delaney, *The Condition, Elevation, Emigration, and Destiny of the Colored People of the United States* (Baltimore: Black Classic Press, 1993), 94–95.

68. Lydia Maria Child, *The Freedman's Book* (Boston: Ticknor and Fields, 1866), 102. Forten ran his profitable sail-making business for more than fifty years. He was sensitive to the issue of equality in education; his eight children were prohibited from attending the local white schools, and he paid tutors to educate them.

69. David E. Swift, *Black Prophets of Justice: Activist Clergy before the Civil War* (Baton Rouge: Louisiana State University Press, 1989), 174–175. Rev. Jehiel Beman was a leader in the temperance movement and the antislavery movement. He was the son of a slave and worked in Colchester in a shoe factory prior to becoming a minister. He helped found the Middletown Anti-Slavery Society in 1834 and was called to lead Boston's First African Methodist Episcopal Zion Church in 1838.

70. *Liberator*, March 2, 1833.

71. Ibid.

72. Douglas L. Stein, "The *Amistad* Judge: The Life and Trials of Andrew T. Judson, 1784–1853," *The Log of Mystic Seaport* 49, no. 4 (Spring 1998): 107–108.

73. Larned, *History of Windham County*, 2:298–299.

74. Ibid.

75. Andrew T. Judson, "A Short Sketch of My Own Life," Andrew T. Judson Papers, 2–3, G. W. Blunt White Library, Mystic Seaport, Mystic, Connecticut. The sixteen-page, handwritten autobiographical essay is not dated, but it ends with Judson's activities through July 1836.

76. Dwight Loomis and J. Gilbert Calhoun, *The Judicial and Civil History of Connecticut* (Boston: Boston History Company, 1895), 237–238. Gilbert typically tutored one or two students in the law per year up through 1810. Between 1810 and 1816, he taught nine or ten students per year.

77. Andrew T. Judson, "A Short Sketch of My Own Life," 3.

78. Ibid.

79. Ibid.

80. David Stephen Heidler and Jeanne T. Heidler, *The War of 1812* (Westport, Conn.: Greenwood Publishing, 2002), 40; see Larned, *History of Windham County*, 2:403–411. The war initially was unpopular in Windham County, as it was elsewhere in New England. Larned argued that over time the arrival from the South of large quantities of cotton for textile mills that would otherwise have gone to England, and the influx of troops traveling through the area, actually helped the local economy and "kept alive a pleasant excitement."

81. Heidler and Heidler, *The War of 1812*, 40.

82. Ibid., 40–41; see Donald R. Hickey, *The War of 1812: A Forgotten Conflict* (Urbana: University of Illinois Press, 1990), 257–259.

83. Hickey, *The War of 1812: A Forgotten Conflict*, 259.

84. Andrew T. Judson, "A Short Sketch of My Own Life," 5.

85. Alfred Thayer Mahan, *Sea Power in Its Relations to the War of 1812*, vol. 1 (Boston: Little, Brown, 1905), 259.

86. Andrew T. Judson, "A Short Sketch of My Own Life," 4.

87. Ibid., 7.

88. Doron S. Ben-Atar and Barbara B. Oberg, *Federalists Reconsidered* (Charlottesville: University of Virginia Press, 1998), 221. In a complicated recombination based on religious infighting, Episcopalians left the Federalist Party because of its alliance with Congregationalists and joined the Republicans to support the formation of the new Toleration Party.

89. Ibid.

90. Andrew T. Judson, "A Short Sketch of My Own Life," 9.

91. Ibid., 11.

92. *New York American*, May 19, 1832, reprinted in *American Railroad Journal and Advocate of Internal Improvements* 1 (January to July 1832): 346.

93. Andrew T. Judson, "A Short Sketch of My Own Life," 14.

94. "Obituary of Charles Ames," *Tiffin Daily Tribune*, Tiffin, Ohio, November 15, 1897, p. 8; Daughters of the American Revolution, *Lineage Book, National Society of the Daughters of the American Revolution* (Washington, D.C.: Daughters of the American Revolution, 1933), 80. William Ames, a descendent of Charles Ames, kindly provided additional details to the author. Charles Ames married Alvira Higley in 1837, about seven years after leaving Andrew Judson's home. Charles died in 1897 at age eighty-five, and his wife Alvira died in the same year at age eighty; his son Andrew Judson Ames died in 1906 at age sixty-eight.

95. A Friend of the Colonization Cause, "Negro School in Canterbury" (letter to the editor), *Norwich Republican*, April 6, 1833; Andrew T. Judson, "To the American Colonization Society" (letter to the editor), *Norwich Republican*, April 6, 1833.

96. George W. Benson to William Lloyd Garrison, Providence, Rhode Island, March 5, 1833, in the *Liberator*, March 9, 1833.

97. Ibid.

98. Ibid.

99. Ibid. See May, *Some Recollections of Our Antislavery Conflict*, 42.

100. Wendell and Francis Garrison, *William Lloyd Garrison*, 1:319.

101. May, *Some Recollections of Our Antislavery Conflict*, 42.

102. James Monroe to Ellen Larned, Oberlin, Ohio, October 18, 1897, Ellen Douglas Larned Papers, Connecticut State Library, Hartford, Connecticut. Monroe grew up in Canterbury and later taught in the Department of Political Science and Modern History at Oberlin College.

103. Ibid.

104. May, *Some Recollections of Our Antislavery Conflict*, 43.

105. Ibid.

106. Ibid.

107. Child, *The Oasis*, 185.

108. May, *Some Recollections of Our Antislavery Conflict*, 43.

109. Child, *The Oasis*, 185. May stated that Crandall maintained "it was no part of her plan to disoblige her neighbors; and therefore she assured me she would hold herself in readiness to remove, whenever her opposers would enable her so to do."

110. Samuel J. May, *Letters to Andrew T. Judson, Esq. and Others in Canterbury, Remonstrating with Them on Their Unjust and Unjustifiable Procedure Relative to Miss Crandall and Her School for Colored Females* (Brooklyn, Conn.: Advertiser Press, 1833), 7; see Strane, *A Whole Souled Woman*, 41.

111. Garrison to George W. Benson, March 8, 1833, in Merrill, *The Letters of William Lloyd Garrison*, 1:212.

112. Ibid.

113. George W. Benson to William Lloyd Garrison, Providence, Rhode Island, March 5, 1833, in the *Liberator*, March 9, 1833. George Benson's fingers were in such pain that he dictated his account of his trip to Canterbury to his brother Henry.

114. Garrison to George W. Benson, March 8, 1833, in Merrill, *The Letters of William Lloyd Garrison*, 1:212.

115. Ibid.

116. Ibid.

117. May, *Some Recollections of Our Antislavery Conflict*, 43.

118. Ibid.

119. Ibid.

120. Ibid., 43–44.

121. Ibid., 44; see Amy E. Orlomoski and A. Constance Sear, *Canterbury: The First 300 Years* (Charleston, S.C.: Arcadia Publishing, 2003), 34. The First Congregational Church stood for 158 years, from 1805 until a fire destroyed the historic meetinghouse on December 23, 1963; see also Andrew Jackson Hetrick, *A Historical Discourse Preached October 27, 1895 in the Meeting House on Canterbury Green in Recognition of Its Renovation* (Norwich, Conn.: Record Job Print, 1895), 11.

122. May, *Some Recollections of Our Antislavery Conflict*, 44.

123. Ibid.

124. Henry B. Benson to William Lloyd Garrison, Providence, Rhode Island, March 12, 1833, in the *Liberator*, March 16, 1833.

125. Andrew T. Judson, "To the American Colonization Society" (letter to the editor), *Norwich Republican*, April 6, 1833.

126. May, *Some Recollections of Our Antislavery Conflict*, 44.

127. *Liberator*, March 16, 1833.

128. Ibid.

129. May, *Some Recollections of Our Antislavery Conflict*, 45.

130. Henry B. Benson to William Lloyd Garrison, March 12, 1833, Providence, Rhode Island, in the *Liberator*, March 16, 1833.

131. Ibid.

132. Ibid. Henry Benson described the man who refuted Judson and the other critics of Crandall's school as "G.S. White, a tanner." It is likely that White was Rev.

George S. White, given the match of his name and the initials and the fact that his comments as reported by Benson stressed religious themes.

133. Larned, *History of Windham County*, 461; see the *Connecticut Mirror*, January 12, 1823 (regarding the *Putnam v. White* lawsuit). White claimed that Daniel Putnam made false claims about his war record in order to secure a pension from the government. Putnam said that White slandered him as revenge for Putnam's leaving the church and sued White for libel; Putnam won damages of three hundred dollars.

134. *Liberator*, March 16, 1833; see *Obituary Record of the Graduates of Yale University* (New Haven, Conn.: Yale University, June 1899), 643 (obituary of Andrew Judson White). George S. White and Judson had been close friends in prior years. After White left Trinity Church in Brooklyn and relocated to Canterbury in the early 1820s, he named his son who was born on May 19, 1824, Andrew Judson White. A. J. White later left the "narrowness and lack of opportunity" in Canterbury to go to Yale Medical School.

135. Ibid.

136. May, *Some Recollections of Our Antislavery Conflict*, 45.

137. Ibid.

138. Ibid.

139. *Liberator*, March 16, 1833.

140. Ibid.

141. Ibid.

142. May, *Some Recollections of Our Antislavery Conflict*, 46.

143. *Liberator*, March 16, 1833.

144. May, *Some Recollections of Our Antislavery Conflict*, 46.

145. *Liberator*, March 16, 1833.

146. Ibid.

4. A MOUNTAIN OF PREJUDICE

1. Andrew T. Judson, "To the American Colonization Society," *Norwich Republican*, April 6, 1833.

2. Ibid.

3. Ibid.

4. Ibid.

5. A Friend of the Colonization Cause, "Negro School in Canterbury" (letter to the editor), *Norwich Republican*, April 6, 1833.

6. Samuel J. May, *Letters to Andrew T. Judson, Esq. and Others in Canterbury, Remonstrating with Them on Their Unjust and Unjustifiable Procedure Relative to Miss Crandall and Her School for Colored Females* (Brooklyn, Conn.: Advertiser Press, 1833), 8.

7. Ibid.

8. Samuel Joseph May, *Some Recollections of Our Antislavery Conflict* (Boston: Fields, Osgood, 1869), 46.

9. Ibid., 47. The conversation between Judson and May was recollected many years

later by May and consequently reflects May's point of view. The opinions expressed by Judson as quoted by May, however, closely mirror Judson's views in his letters to the local press and later in his arguments in the Crandall trials.

10. Ibid., 47–48.

11. Ibid., 48–49.

12. Ibid., 49.

13. Ibid.

14. Ibid., 50.

15. Susan Strane, *A Whole Souled Woman: Prudence Crandall and the Education of Black Women* (New York: W. W. Norton, 1990), 53.

16. Ibid.

17. *Liberator*, March 16, 1833.

18. *Norwich Republican*, April 6, 1833.

19. "Table Talk," *North American Magazine* 2, no. 7 (June 1833): 109–110.

20. Ibid., 110.

21. Wendell Phillips Garrison and Francis Jackson Garrison, *William Lloyd Garrison, 1805–1879: The Story of His Life Told by His Children*, vol. 3 (New York: Century, 1889), 277.

22. Rebecca J. Winter, *The Night Cometh: Two Wealthy Evangelicals Face the Nation* (South Pasadena, Calif.: William Carey Library, 1977), 56.

23. Ibid.

24. Ibid.

25. Lewis Tappan, *The Life of Arthur Tappan* (New York: Hurd and Houghton, 1871), 128.

26. Ibid., 129.

27. Ibid.

28. Martha Elizabeth Hodes, *Sex, Love, Race: Crossing Boundaries in North American History* (New York: New York University Press, 1999), 194. "In 1833, the Tappans were the most visible and wealthy defectors from the colonizationists, and others followed suit throughout the 1830s. . . . As the anti-abolitionist David Meredith Reese said of the radical abolitionists, they were 'not the creed and practice of Jefferson, Franklin, Rush, and John Jay, of the *old* school, for those laboured for gradual abolition . . .'"

29. George W. Benson to William Lloyd Garrison, Providence, Rhode Island, March 30, 1833, Anti-Slavery Collection, Boston Public Library.

30. Bernard C. Steiner, "History of Slavery in Connecticut," in *Studies in Historical and Political Science, Labor, Slavery and Self-Government*, ed. Herbert B. Adams (Baltimore: John Hopkins Press, 1893), 418.

31. Ibid.

32. Ibid.

33. Ibid.

34. William Jay, *An Inquiry into the Character and Tendency of the American Colonization and American Anti-Slavery Societies* (New York: Leavitt, Lord, 1835), 31.

35. Samuel J. May, *Letters to Andrew T. Judson, Esq. and Others in Canterbury, Remonstrating with Them on Their Unjust and Unjustifiable Procedure Relative to Miss Crandall and Her School for Colored Females* (Brooklyn, Conn.: Advertiser Press, 1833), 23.

36. Ibid.

37. Ibid., 24.

38. Ibid.

39. Ibid.

40. Ibid.

41. Wendell and Francis Garrison, *William Lloyd Garrison*, 1:320.

42. Prudence Crandall to William Lloyd Garrison, March 19, 1833, in Strane, *A Whole Souled Woman*, 57.

43. May, *Letters to Andrew T. Judson, Esq. and Others in Canterbury*, 8.

44. Walter M. Merrill, ed., *The Letters of William Lloyd Garrison, I Will Be Heard! 1822–1835*, vol. 1 (Cambridge, Mass.: Harvard University Press, 1971), 229. The letter from Garrison was printed in the *Liberator*, May 23, 1833.

45. Prudence Crandall to Simeon S. Jocelyn, April 9, 1833, Prudence Crandall Collection, Charles E. Shain Library, Connecticut College.

46. Ibid.

47. *Students of Prudence Crandall, 1832–1833*, Prudence Crandall Museum, Canterbury, Connecticut. Coit had traded goods to Crandall in exchange for the tuition of his daughters when they attended her school.

48. Prudence Crandall to Simeon S. Jocelyn, April 9, 1833.

49. Ibid.; Strane, *A Whole Souled Woman*, 61; see Diana Ross McCain and Kazimiera Kozlowski, *African-American Students Who Attended Prudence Crandall's Female Boarding School in Canterbury, Connecticut, April 1, 1833–September 9, 1834*, Connecticut Historical Commission (2001), 17, Prudence Crandall Museum, Canterbury, Connecticut.

50. Prudence Crandall to Simeon S. Jocelyn, April 9, 1833.

51. Garrison to Harriet Minot, March 19, 1833, in Merrill, *The Letters of William Lloyd Garrison*, 1:215. Ms. Minot was one of three young ladies from Haverhill, Massachusetts, who called themselves the "Inquirers after Truth" and corresponded with Garrison.

52. Garrison to George Bourne, March 7, 1833, in Merrill, *The Letters of William Lloyd Garrison*, 1:211.

53. John W. Christie and Dwight L. Dumond, *George Bourne and the Book and Slavery Irreconcilable* (Baltimore: Historical Society of Delaware and the Presbyterian Historical Society, 1969), 83.

54. Ibid., 75. The authors claim that Garrison often appropriated Bourne's ideas and language without attribution in the *Liberator*. Garrison frequently recognized Bourne, including the following from March, 1833: "Mr. Bourne we consider one of the most extraordinary men of the age; for energy of purpose, he resembles Luther—for faithfulness, the apostle Paul—for courage, John Knox, and for zeal, the indefatigable Whitefield." Bourne preferred to write anonymously in the *Liberator*; he re-

quested no credit or acknowledgment for serving as guest editor and did not sign the editorials he wrote as guest editor.

55. Ibid., 96.

56. Garrison to Harriet Minot, March 19, 1833, in Merrill, *The Letters of William Lloyd Garrison*, 1:215.

57. Garrison to Harriet Minot, March 26, 1833, in Merrill, *The Letters of William Lloyd Garrison*, 1:215–216.

58. Wendell and Francis Garrison, *William Lloyd Garrison*, 1:330.

59. Ibid., 331.

60. Garrison to Stephen Foster, March 30, 1829, in Merrill, *The Letters of William Lloyd Garrison*, 1:81 n. 6. In the summer of 1828, while editing a newspaper in Bennington, Vermont, Garrison met Mary Cunningham, a young woman from Boston. Garrison wrote poetry for her benefit in the newspaper. While he did not identify her last name, he did write, "My bachelorship I throw aside, my haughtiness—my lofty bearing, sweet Mary! wilt thou be my bride?" The romance did not flourish.

61. Garrison to Harriet Minot, April 3, 1833, in Merrill, *The Letters of William Lloyd Garrison*, 1:216.

62. Ibid.

63. Garrison to Isaac Knapp, April 11, 1833, in Merrill, *The Letters of William Lloyd Garrison*, 1:221.

64. Garrison to Harriet Minot, April 9, 1833, in Merrill, *The Letters of William Lloyd Garrison*, 1:218.

65. Ibid., 219.

66. Garrison to Isaac Knapp, April 11, 1833, in Merrill, *The Letters of William Lloyd Garrison*, 1:221.

67. Garrison to Harriet Minot, April 9, 1833, in Merrill, *The Letters of William Lloyd Garrison*, 1:220.

68. Prudence Crandall to Simeon S. Jocelyn, April 9, 1833; see Garrison to Harriet Minot, April 9, 1833, in Merrill, *The Letters of William Lloyd Garrison*, 1:220 and Garrison to Isaac Knapp, April 11, 1833, in Merrill, *The Letters of William Lloyd Garrison*, 1:221.

69. Garrison to Isaac Knapp, April 11, 1833, in Merrill, *The Letters of William Lloyd Garrison*, 1:221.

70. Wendell Phillips Garrison, "Connecticut in the Middle Ages," *Century Magazine* 30, no. 5 (September 1885): 785. Henry Benson to Isaac Knapp, April 9, 1833.

71. Garrison to Isaac Knapp, April 11, 1833, in Merrill, *The Letters of William Lloyd Garrison*, 1:221.

72. Prudence Crandall to Simeon S. Jocelyn, April 9, 1833.

73. Garrison to Isaac Knapp, April 11, 1833, in Merrill, *The Letters of William Lloyd Garrison*, 1:221–222.

74. Prudence Crandall to Simeon S. Jocelyn, April 9, 1833.

75. Garrison to Isaac Knapp, April 11, 1833, in Merrill, *The Letters of William Lloyd Garrison*, 1:221–222.

76. Ibid.

77. Garrison to Harriet Minot, April 22, 1833, in Merrill, *The Letters of William Lloyd Garrison*, 1:233–234.

78. Garrison to Isaac Knapp, April 17, 1833, in Merrill, *The Letters of William Lloyd Garrison*, 1:222.

79. Garrison to Harriet Minot, April 22, 1833, in Merrill, *The Letters of William Lloyd Garrison*, 1:224.

80. Ibid.

81. Garrison, "Connecticut in the Middle Ages," 784.

82. Ibid.

83. May, *Some Recollections of Our Antislavery Conflict*, 50–51.

84. Prudence Crandall to Simeon S. Jocelyn, April 17, 1833, Prudence Crandall Collection, Charles E. Shain Library, Connecticut College.

85. Ibid.

86. May, *Some Recollections of Our Antislavery Conflict*, 51.

87. Prudence Crandall to Simeon S. Jocelyn, April 9, 1833.

88. Ibid.

89. Ibid.

90. Ibid.

91. *Liberator*, May 18, 1833.

92. May, *Some Recollections of Our Antislavery Conflict*, 51.

93. Ibid.

94. Ibid.

95. Ibid.

96. Almira Crandall to Henry Benson, April 30, 1833, in Garrison, "Connecticut in the Middle Ages," 786.

97. Wendell and Francis Garrison, *William Lloyd Garrison*, 1:343.

98. Ibid.

99. Garrison, "Connecticut in the Middle Ages," 785.

100. Garrison to Robert Purvis, April 30, 1833, in Merrill, *The Letters of William Lloyd Garrison*, 1:224.

101. Wendell and Francis Garrison, *William Lloyd Garrison*, 1:345.

102. Garrison to Harriet Minot, May 1, 1833, in Merrill, *The Letters of William Lloyd Garrison*, 1:226.

103. Wendell and Francis Garrison, *William Lloyd Garrison*, 1:345.

5. THE BLACK LAW

1. Prudence Crandall to Simeon Jocelyn, April 17, 1833, Prudence Crandall Collection, Charles E. Shain Library, Connecticut College.

2. Pardon Crandall to Andrew T. Judson and Chester Lyon, May 5, 1833, in Marvis Olive Welch, *Prudence Crandall: A Biography* (Manchester, Conn.: Jason, 1983), 50–51.

3. Ibid.

4. A. B. Lyon and G.W.A. Lyon, eds., *Lyon Memorial, Massachusetts Families, In-*

cluding Descendents of the Immigrants William Lyon of Roxbury, Peter Lyon of Dorchester, and George Lyon of Dorchester (Detroit: Wm. Graham Printing Company, 1905), 292.

5. Welch, *Prudence Crandall*, 50–51.

6. Ellen D. Larned, *History of Windham County, Connecticut*, vol. 2 (Worcester, Mass.: Charles Hamilton, 1880), 495.

7. Ibid.

8. Welch, *Prudence Crandall*, 50–51.

9. Ibid.

10. Diana Ross McCain and Kazimiera Kozlowski, *African-American Students Who Attended Prudence Crandall's Female Boarding School in Canterbury, Connecticut*, Connecticut Historical Commission (2001), 14–25, Prudence Crandall Museum, Canterbury, Connecticut. The authors note that primary source documentation exists for eighteen students; an additional eight students have been mentioned in various accounts. Samuel May, who taught at the school, counted twenty-two students at the end of the summer of 1833; see Samuel J. May, "Miss Crandall's School," in *The Oasis*, ed. Lydia Maria Child (Boston: Benjamin C. Bacon, 1834), 190.

11. Prudence Crandall to Simeon Jocelyn, April 17, 1833.

12. Leslie M. Harris, *In the Shadow of Slavery: African Americans in New York City, 1626–1863* (Chicago: University of Chicago Press, 2003), 186.

13. Ibid.

14. Ibid.; see Lewis Tappan, *The Life of Arthur Tappan* (New York: Hurd and Houghton, 1871), 162.

15. Samuel E. Cornish to the editors of the *New York Observer*, December 7, 1833, in *The Colonizationist and Journal of Freedom* (Boston: George W. Light, 1834), 306.

16. Elizabeth McHenry, *Forgotten Readers: Recovering the Lost History of African American Literary Societies* (Durham, N.C.: Duke University Press, 2002), 54, referencing "Phoenix Library—Donations," *Emancipator*, February 4, 1834.

17. See generally, Elizabeth McHenry, *Forgotten Readers*, and for a specific discussion of the importance of literary societies, see 79–83.

18. Larned, *History of Windham County*, 2:495.

19. Records of the Connecticut General Assembly, Boxes 17–18 (1833), Connecticut State Library, Hartford, Connecticut. Fifteen towns sent petitions to the legislature; the number of signatures on each petition is indicated in parentheses: Bethany (27), Brooklyn (118), Colchester (38), Hampton (57), Hebron (62), Killingly (20), Middletown (82), New London (33), Norwich (36), Plainfield (81), Stafford (41), Sterling (34), Thompson (28), Waterbury (43), and Windham (72).

20. Welch, *Prudence Crandall*, 50–51.

21. *A Statement of Facts Respecting the School for Colored Females, in Canterbury, Connecticut, Together with a Report of the Late Trial of Miss Prudence Crandall* (Brooklyn, Conn.: Advertiser Press, 1833), 10; Welch, *Prudence Crandall*, 55.

22. *A Statement of Facts Respecting the School for Colored Females*, 9.

23. Ibid.

24. Ibid.

25. Ibid., 9–10.

26. *Liberator*, May 18, 1833; see Truman Nelson, *Documents of Upheaval* (New York: Hill and Wang, 1966), 67.

27. *A Statement of Facts Respecting the School for Colored Females*, 10.

28. Ibid.

29. Philip Sheldon Foner, *History of the Labor Movement in the United States, from the Colonial Times to the Founding of the American Federation of Labor*, vol. 1 (New York: International Publishers Company, 1947), 118.

30. *A Statement of Facts Respecting the School for Colored Females*, 11.

31. Ibid.

32. Edmund Fuller, *Prudence Crandall: An Incident of Racism in Nineteenth-Century Connecticut* (Middletown, Conn.: Wesleyan University Press, 1971), 65.

33. Samuel Joseph May, *Some Recollections of Our Antislavery Conflict* (Boston: Fields, Osgood, 1869), 52.

34. Ibid.; see Welch, *Prudence Crandall*, 57–58, and Susan Strane, *A Whole Souled Woman, Prudence Crandall and the Education of Black Women* (New York: W. W. Norton, 1990), 76, discussing the immediate reaction in Canterbury to the passage of the law.

35. May, *Some Recollections of Our Antislavery Conflict*, 57.

36. Anonymous student to the *Liberator*, May 25, 1833, in the *Liberator*, June 22, 1833.

37. Ibid.

38. Ibid.

39. Garrison to the *Liberator*, May 23, 1833, in *The Letters of William Lloyd Garrison: I Will Be Heard! 1822–1835*, vol. 1, ed. Walter M. Merrill (Cambridge, Mass.: Harvard University Press, 1971), 228.

40. Ibid.

41. Ibid., 229.

42. Kenneth Morgan, *Slavery and the British Empire: From Africa to America* (New York: Oxford University Press, 2008), 62.

43. Garrison to unknown recipient, May 27, 1833, in Merrill, *The Letters of William Lloyd Garrison*, 1:234.

44. Garrison to Harriet Minot, April 3, 1833, in Merrill, *The Letters of William Lloyd Garrison*, 1:216.

45. *Emancipator*, June 22, 1833; see Welch, *Prudence Crandall*, 60–64, reprinting the letter in its entirety.

46. *Emancipator*, June 22, 1833.

47. *Connecticut Courant*, June 24, 1833.

48. Ibid.

49. Ibid.

50. Ibid.

51. William Jay, *An Inquiry into the Character and Tendency of the American Colonization and American Anti-Slavery Societies* (New York: Leavitt, Lord, 1835), 35–36.

52. Ibid.

53. Ibid.

54. Ibid.

55. Larned, *History of Windham County*, 2:496–497.

56. Ibid., 497.

57. Ibid.

58. May, *Some Recollections of Our Antislavery Conflict*, 53, detailing May and Benson's visit with Prudence Crandall.

59. Ibid., 53–54.

60. Ibid.

61. Ibid., 54.

62. Ibid.

63. Samuel May, "Miss Crandall's School," in *The Oasis*, ed. Lydia Maria Child (Boston: Benjamin C. Bacon, 1834), 190.

64. Writ of Arrest of Prudence Crandall, June 27, 1833, Connecticut State Library, Hartford, Connecticut; see Welch, *Prudence Crandall*, 67–68.

65. Welch, *Prudence Crandall*, 68.

66. Ibid. Welch refers to Mariah as Marcia; see Strane, *A Whole Souled Woman*, 24 n. 13. Strane notes that the name "Mariah" Davis is recorded at the time of her marriage to Charles Harris on November 28, 1833; the name "Marcia" "is probably a misreading of Prudence's handwriting in a letter to Ellen Larned on May 15, 1869.

67. Strane, *A Whole Souled Woman*, 80.

68. May, *Some Recollections of Our Antislavery Conflict*, 53. All of the quoted dialogue between May and the messenger is from May's account.

69. Ibid.

70. Ibid.

71. Larned, *History of Windham County*, 2:479. All of the details concerning Watkins contained in this paragraph are derived from Larned's account.

72. Ibid.

73. Ibid.

74. May, *Some Recollections of Our Antislavery Conflict*, 54.

75. Welch, *Prudence Crandall*, 70; Strane, *A Whole Souled Woman*, 82.

76. May, *Some Recollections of Our Antislavery Conflict*, 54–55; the details included in this paragraph are from May's first-person account.

77. Ibid., 55.

78. Ibid.

79. Ibid.

80. Ibid.

81. Ibid.

82. Ibid.

83. Ibid., 55–56.

84. Ibid., 56.

85. *Liberator*, July 6, 1833.

86. Miriam R. Small and Edwin W. Small, "Prudence Crandall: Champion of Negro Education," *New England Quarterly* 17, no. 4 (December 1944): 520–521.

87. Ibid., 521.

88. *Unionist*, August 8, 1833; see Fuller, *Prudence Crandall*, 73, discussing Judson's letter and the publication of letters by opponents of Prudence's school.

89. *Unionist*, August 8, 1833.

90. Tappan, *The Life of Arthur Tappan*, 13, 33–34.

91. Ibid., 155, quoting "A Tribute to the Memory of Arthur Tappan" by Samuel May.

92. Ibid.; see also 388. Tappan had "a firm belief in the evangelical faith" and "relied upon the mercy of God through the atoning sacrifice of the Saviour, discarding all thoughts of his good deeds as meriting reward in another life."

93. May, *Some Recollections of Our Antislavery Conflict*, 58.

94. Ibid.

95. Ibid.

96. Ibid.

97. Ibid., 59.

98. *Kansas City Journal*, March 28, 1886; See Strane, *A Whole Souled Woman*, 79.

99. *Liberator*, July 20, 1833.

100. Prudence Crandall to Ellen Larned, May 15, 1869, Connecticut State Library, Hartford, Connecticut.

101. Ibid.

102. *Liberator*, July 6, 1833.

6. SANCTUARY DENIED

1. Susan Strane, *A Whole Souled Woman: Prudence Crandall and the Education of Black Women* (New York: W. W. Norton, 1990), 90.

2. "Outrage on Outrage!" *Liberator*, July 20, 1833.

3. Miriam R. Small and Edwin W. Small, "Prudence Crandall, Champion of Negro Education," *New England Quarterly* 17, no. 4 (December 1944): 522. The letter from the *Windham County Advertiser* was reprinted in the July 20, 1833, issue of the *Liberator*.

4. Ibid.

5. Ibid.

6. *Norwich Courier*, July 24, 1833.

7. *Hartford Times*, August 5, 1833.

8. Ibid.

9. Ibid.

10. *New Hampshire Patriot*, July 29, 1833.

11. Ibid.

12. *New Hampshire Patriot*, August 5, 1833.

13. *Hartford Times*, July 22, 1833, reprinting an editorial from the *New Haven Register*.

14. Lewis Tappan, *The Life of Arthur Tappan* (New York: Hurd and Houghton, 1871), 156.

15. Ibid.

16. Samuel Joseph May, *Some Recollections of Our Antislavery Conflict* (Boston: Fields, Osgood, 1869), 64.

17. Tappan, *The Life of Arthur Tappan*, 156.

18. Ibid.

19. May, *Some Recollections of Our Antislavery Conflict*, 60.

20. Ibid.

21. Tappan, *The Life of Arthur Tappan*, 156; Samuel May, *Some Recollections of Our Antislavery Conflict*, 61.

22. Tappan, *The Life of Arthur Tappan*, 156.

23. May, *Some Recollections of Our Antislavery Conflict*, 61.

24. Ibid.

25. Tappan, *The Life of Arthur Tappan*, 156.

26. Ibid.

27. May, *Some Recollections of Our Antislavery Conflict*, 62.

28. Ibid.

29. Ibid.

30. Ibid., 63.

31. Ibid.

32. Ibid.

33. Ibid., 63–64.

34. Ibid., 64.

35. William Henry Burleigh and Celia Burleigh, *Poems by William H. Burleigh, with a Sketch of His Life by Celia Burleigh* (New York: Hurd and Houghton; Cambridge, Mass.: Riverside Press, 1871), vii; see Fanny Winchester Hotchkiss, *Winchester Notes* (New Haven, Conn.: Tuttle, Morehouse and Taylor, 1912), 167, regarding William Bradford. See also John Stetson Barry, *The History of Massachusetts, The Colonial Period*, vol. 1 (Boston: Phillips, Sampson, 1855), 103; and Marie Irish, *The Days We Celebrate* (Chicago: T. S. Denison, 1904), 96, regarding Bradford and Thanksgiving.

36. Charles Burleigh, *The Genealogy of the Burley or Burleigh Family of America* (Portland, Maine: Brown Thurston, 1880), 132–133; William and Celia Burleigh, *Poems by William H. Burleigh*, vii.

37. May, *Some Recollections of Our Antislavery Conflict*, 64.

38. Ellen D. Larned, *History of Windham County, Connecticut*, vol. 2 (Worcester, Mass.: Charles Hamilton, 1880), 500.

39. Ibid. Larned wrote, "Religious services in their own house were exposed to unseemly interruption, as when the Rev. Potter of Pawtucket was preaching, and a clamorous rabble assailed the house with volleys of rotten eggs and other missiles."

40. Deborah Bingham Van Broekhoven, *The Devotion of These Women: Rhode Island in the Antislavery Network* (Amherst: University of Massachusetts Press, 2002), 32–33.

41. See in general Ray Potter and Nicolas G. Potter, *Admonitions from the Depths*

f the Earth, or the Fall of Ray Potter (Pawtucket, R.I.: R. Sherman, 1838); Massena Goodrich, *Historical Sketch of the Town of Pawtucket* (Pawtucket, R.I.: Nickerson, Sibley, 1876), 105–106. Potter had significant success in manufacturing cardboard.

42. Van Broekhoven, *The Devotion of These Women*, 33. Van Broekhoven wrote that the Potter scandal "heightened suspicions that almost any involvement by women in anti-slavery work was 'promiscuous.'"

43. Marvis Olive Welch, *Prudence Crandall: A Biography* (Manchester, Conn.: Jason, 1983), 71.

44. Ibid., 72; all of the details in this paragraph are based on the account provided by Welch; see Susan Strane, *A Whole Souled Woman: Prudence Crandall and the Education of Black Women* (New York: W. W. Norton, 1990), 89 n. 17. Strane, who spoke with Welch about this incident, said an elderly member of the Packerville Baptist Church had told the story to Welch.

45. Esther Baldwin to Hannah Baldwin, July 28, 1833, Baldwin Collection, Connecticut Historical Society, Hartford; Strane, *A Whole Souled Woman*, 89.

46. Prudence Crandall to Solomon Payne, Andrew Harris, and Isaac Knight, July 29, 1833, reprinted in Welch, *Prudence Crandall*, 73.

47. Ibid.

48. Wendell Phillips Garrison and Francis Jackson Garrison, *William Lloyd Garrison, 1805–1879: The Story of His Life Told by His Children*, vol. 1 (New York: Century, 1885), 317 n. 1.

49. Katherine Greider, "Rediscovering a Relic of a Past Long Obscured," *New York Times*, February 26, 2006; Henry Collins Brown, ed., *Valentine's Manual of the City of New York, 1917–1918* (New York: Old Colony Press, 1917), 190, discussing All Saint's Church and the "slave gallery." Accessed on October 21, 2013, http://query.nytimes.com/gst/fullpage.html?res=F30B17FD345A0C758EDDAB0894DE404482.

50. Solomon Payne, Andrew Harris, and Isaac Knight to Prudence Crandall, July 26, 1833, Prudence Crandall Museum, Canterbury, Connecticut.

51. Ibid.

52. Prudence Crandall to Solomon Payne, Andrew Harris, and Isaac Knight, July 29, 1833, reprinted in Welch, *Prudence Crandall*, 73.

53. Ibid.

54. Ibid.

55. *Unionist*, August 29, 1833, reprinted in the *Connecticut Courant*, September 2, 1833 (quoting a source in a contemporaneous issue of the *Windham County Advertiser*).

56. Ibid.

57. Solomon Payne, Andrew Harris, and Isaac Knight to Prudence Crandall, July 26, 1833, Prudence Crandall Museum, Canterbury, Connecticut.

58. Ibid.

59. Carolyn L. Karcher, *The First Woman in the Republic: A Cultural Biography of Lydia Maria Child* (Durham, N.C.: Duke University Press, 1994), 175.

60. Lydia Maria Child, *An Appeal in Favor of That Class of Americans Called Afri-*

cans, ed. Carolyn L. Karcher (Amherst: University of Massachusetts Press, 1996), 94 Lydia Maria Francis Child published the first edition in 1833.

61. Ibid., 190.

62. Ibid., 125.

63. Ibid., 191.

64. Ibid.

65. Ibid., 186.

66. Ibid., 191.

67. Ibid., 3.

68. *Liberator*, December 14, 1833, reprinting the *Unionist*'s review of "Mrs. Child's Appeal."

69. Edward Strutt Abdy, *Journal of a Residence and Tour in the United States of North America: From April 1833 to October 1834*, vol. 1 (London: John Murray, 1835), 14.

70. Ibid., 14–15.

71. Ibid., 14.

72. Ibid., 155.

73. Ibid., 154.

74. *Liberator*, August 3, 1833.

75. Ibid.

76. Abdy, *Journal of a Residence and Tour in the United States*, 1:191–192.

77. Ibid., 195.

78. Ibid., 195–196.

79. Ibid., 200.

80. Ibid.

81. Ibid., 203.

82. Ibid., 196.

83. Ibid., 214.

84. Ibid., 214–215.

85. Ibid.

86. Ibid., 220.

87. Ibid., 221.

88. Ibid., 223–224.

7. ON TRIAL

1. *Speeches on the Passage of the Bill for the Removal of the Indians, Delivered in the Congress of the United States, April and May 1830* (Boston: Perkins and Marvin, 1830), 137. Ellsworth delivered his remarks before Congress on May 17, 1830.

2. Ibid., 138, 145.

3. Joseph C. Morton, *Shapers of the Great Debate at the Constitutional Convention of 1787: A Biographical Dictionary* (Westport, Conn.: Greenwood Publishing Group, 2006), 86; James H. Charleton, Robert G. Ferris, and Mary C. Ryan, eds., *Framers of the Constitution* (Washington, D.C.: National Archives and Records Administration, 1986), 142.

4. Dwight Loomis and Joseph Gilbert Calhoun, *The Judicial and Civil History of Connecticut* (Boston: Boston History Company, 1895), 463.

5. *The National Cyclopedia of American Biography, Being the History of the United States*, vol. 5 (New York: James T. White, 1894), 200. All facts in this paragraph concerning Goddard are from this source, except for the reference to Goddard teaching at Plainfield Academy; see R. H. Howard and Henry E. Crocker, eds., *A History of New England*, vol. 1 (Boston: Crocker, 1880), 391.

6. Franklin Bowditch Dexter, *Biographical Sketches of the Graduates of Yale College with Annals of the College History*, vol. 4 (New Haven: Yale University Press, 1912), 61.

7. Loomis and Calhoun, *The Judicial and Civil History of Connecticut*, 262.

8. Wendell Phillips Garrison, "Connecticut in the Middle Ages," *Century Magazine* 30, no. 5 (September 1885): 781; see Andrew Dickson White, *The Autobiography of Andrew Dickson White* (New York: Century, 1914), 163. White, who was president of Cornell University, described a conversation with Rev. May regarding Prudence Crandall many years after the Crandall controversy; White noted that "Mr. May had taken up her case earnestly, and, with the aid of Mr. Lafayette Foster, afterward president of the United States Senate, had fought it out until the enemies of Miss Crandall were beaten."

9. *Records and Papers of the New London County Historical Society, 1890–1894*, vol. 1 (New London, Conn.: Day, 1890), 27.

10. David Miller Dewitt, *The Impeachment and Trial of Andrew Johnson* (New York: Macmillan, 1903), 179.

11. Ellen D. Larned, *History of Windham County, Connecticut*, vol. 2 (Worcester, Mass.: Charles Hamilton, 1880), 473. The Courthouse was designed and built by Benjamin E. Palmer of Brooklyn, Connecticut, from 1819 to 1820.

12. Loomis and Calhoun, *The Judicial and Civil History of Connecticut*, 570.

13. *Connecticut Courant*, August 26, 1833.

14. Loomis and Calhoun, *The Judicial and Civil History of Connecticut*, 546. Ichabod Bulkley graduated from Yale in 1819. He was admitted to the bar in 1822 and practiced in Ashford after studying law with attorney David Bowles. In 1825 Bulkley took over the management from William Perkins of one of the first Aetna Insurance local agencies, in Ashford. Bulkley was judge of probate for several years "and was connected with the famous Crandall case." He died in 1838. See W. E. Robinson, R. W. Wright, George Northrop, and Jacob Story, eds., *A Catalogue of the Society of Brothers in Unity, Yale College, Founded 1768* (New Haven: Hitchcock and Stafford, 1841), 45; Henry Ross Gall and William George Jordan, *One Hundred Years of Fire Insurance: Being a History of the Aetna Insurance Company, Hartford, Connecticut 1819–1919* (Hartford: Aetna Insurance, 1919), 158.

15. Larned, *History of Windham County*, 2:523.

16. Franklin Bowditch Dexter, *Biographical Notices of Graduates of Yale College* (New Haven: Yale University, 1913), 46–47.

17. *Connecticut Courant*, August 26, 1833; see the *Unionist*, September 5, 1833, as reprinted in the *Connecticut Courant*, September 9, 1833.

18. Nathan Crosby, *Annual Obituary Notices of Eminent Persons Who Have Died in the United States for 1857* (Boston: Phillips, Sampson, 1858), 138.

19. Ibid.; see *Plainfield Bicentennial: A Souvenir Volume* (Norwich, Conn.: Bulletin Company, 1899), 92.

20. *Unionist*, August 29, 1833, as reprinted in the *Connecticut Courant*, September 2, 1833.

21. *Connecticut Courant*, August 26, 1833; see Edward Strutt Abdy, *Journal of a Residence and Tour in the United States of North America: From April 1833 to October 1834*, vol. 1 (London: John Murray, 1835), 205.

22. *Connecticut Courant*, August 26, 1833.

23. The former Brooklyn Courthouse still stands today but is no longer used as a court; it serves as the town hall and has been altered significantly on the interior through numerous renovations since it was built in 1820.

24. *Unionist*, August 29, 1833, as reprinted in the *Connecticut Courant*, September 2, 1833; see *A Statement of Facts Respecting the School for Colored Females, in Canterbury, Connecticut, Together with a Report of the Late Trial of Miss Prudence Crandall* (Brooklyn, Conn.: Advertiser Press, 1833), 13. There are at least three published reports of the trial. *A Statement of Facts* was published separately from the versions published by the *Unionist* or the *Connecticut Courant*. All three versions originate with the text provided by the *Unionist*. The *Connecticut Courant* simply reprinted the account in the *Unionist*, with attribution to the *Unionist*. The *Statement of Facts* published by the Advertiser Press, however, contains no attribution, even though it is mostly identical. There are editorial comments, however, critical of Prudence Crandall and her supporters. In addition, the Advertiser Press reprinted summaries of witness testimony—showing the case most favorable to the prosecution—and omitted a lengthy section outlining the arguments made by Crandall's counsel concerning the constitutionality of the Black Law.

25. *Unionist*, August 29, 1833, as reprinted in the *Connecticut Courant*, September 2, 1833. The details and quotations in successive paragraphs concerning the trial are from this account unless otherwise indicated.

26. Ibid.

27. *Connecticut Courant*, August 26, 1833.

28. *Unionist*, August 29, 1833, as reprinted in the *Connecticut Courant*, September 2, 1833; *A Statement of Facts Respecting the School for Colored Females*, 13–14.

29. *Unionist*, August 29, 1833, as reprinted in the *Connecticut Courant*, September 2, 1833.

30. Ibid.

31. Ibid.

32. Ibid.

33. Ibid.

34. Ibid.; *A Statement of Facts Respecting the School for Colored Females*, 14–15.

35. *Unionist*, August 29, 1833, as reprinted in the *Connecticut Courant*, September 2, 1833; *A Statement of Facts Respecting the School for Colored Females*, 15.

36. *Unionist*, August 29, 1833, as reprinted in the *Connecticut Courant*, September 2, 1833.

37. Ibid.

38. Ibid.

39. Diana Ross McCain and Kazimiera Kozlowski, *African-American Students Who Attended Prudence Crandall's Female Boarding School in Canterbury, Connecticut*, Connecticut Historical Commission (2001), 17, Prudence Crandall Museum, Canterbury, Connecticut.

40. *Unionist*, August 29, 1833, as reprinted in the *Connecticut Courant*, September 2, 1833; *A Statement of Facts Respecting the School for Colored Females*, 15.

41. *Unionist*, August 29, 1833, as reprinted in the *Connecticut Courant*, September 2, 1833.

42. Ibid.; *A Statement of Facts Respecting the School for Colored Females*, 16.

43. *A Statement of Facts Respecting the School for Colored Females*, 16.

44. Ibid. "The sheriff having served his process on Eliza Glasko was about committing her to prison, when Mr. Ellsworth interposed and stated to the court that rather than have the girl committed he should advise her to testify."

45. Ibid.

46. Ibid.

47. Ibid.

48. *Unionist*, August 29, 1833, as reprinted in the *Connecticut Courant*, September 2, 1833.

49. Ibid.

50. Ibid.

51. Ibid.

52. Ibid.

53. Ibid.

54. *Unionist*, September 5, 1833, as reprinted in the *Connecticut Courant*, September 9, 1833.

55. Ibid.

56. Ibid.

57. Ibid.

58. Ibid.

59. Ibid.

60. Ibid.

61. Ibid.

62. Ibid.

63. Ibid.

64. Ibid.

65. Ibid.

66. Ibid.

67. Ibid.

68. Noah Webster, *An American Dictionary of the English Language* (New York: S. Converse, 1830), 148.

69. *Unionist*, September 5, 1833, as reprinted in the *Connecticut Courant*, September 9, 1833.

70. Ibid.

71. *Connecticut Courant*, August 26, 1833.

72. Ibid.

73. Henry Benson to William Lloyd Garrison, Providence, Rhode Island, August 30, 1833, Anti-Slavery Collection, Boston Public Library.

74. *Connecticut Courant*, August 26, 1833.

75. May, *Some Recollections of Our Antislavery Conflict*, 68.

76. *New York Spectator*, August 29, 1833.

77. *Unionist*, September 5, 1833, as reprinted in the *Connecticut Courant*, September 9, 1833.

78. May, *Some Recollections of Our Antislavery Conflict*, 69.

79. Henry Benson to William Lloyd Garrison, Providence, Rhode Island, August 30, 1833, Anti-Slavery Collection, Boston Public Library.

80. Ibid.

81. Ibid.

82. *Unionist*, September 12, 1833, as reprinted in the *Liberator*, September 21, 1833.

83. Marvis Olive Welch, *Prudence Crandall: A Biography* (Manchester, Conn.: Jason, 1983), 84–85; Susan Strane, *A Whole Souled Woman: Prudence Crandall and the Education of Black Women* (New York: W. W. Norton, 1990), 112.

84. Wendell Phillips Garrison and Francis Jackson Garrison, *William Lloyd Garrison, 1805–1879: The Story of His Life Told by His Children*, vol. 1 (New York: Century, 1885), 379.

85. Ibid.

8. JUDGE DAGGETT'S DECISION

1. Marilyn Richardson, ed., *Maria W. Stewart, America's First Black Woman Political Writer: Essays and Speeches* (Bloomington: Indiana University Press, 1987), 52, speech before the African-American Female Intelligence Association, delivered in Boston in spring 1832.

2. Elizabeth McHenry, *Forgotten Readers: Recovering the Lost History of African American Literary Societies* (Durham, N.C.: Duke University Press, 2002), 71–72.

3. Richardson, *Maria W. Stewart*, 70.

4. Ibid., 66–67, quoting from Maria Stewart's "Farewell Address."

5. Ibid., 68.

6. Ibid.

7. Ibid., 72.

8. Ibid.

9. Ibid.

10. Ibid., 73.

11. Ibid., 73, 74.

12. *Unionist*, October 3, 1833, as reprinted in the *Connecticut Courant*, October 7, 1833.

13. Marvis Olive Welch, *Prudence Crandall: A Biography* (Jason, 1983), 84. Welch referred to William Lester as "Lister"; historian Ellen Larned referenced "William Lester" as the Canterbury citizen who had helped Andrew Judson circulate petitions against the school. See John Cortland Crandall, *Elder John Crandall of Rhode Island and His Descendants* (New Woodstock, N.Y.: J. C. Crandall, 1949), 309, referencing "William Lester."

14. Miriam R. Small and Edwin W. Small, "Prudence Crandall: Champion of Negro Education," *New England Quarterly* 17, no. 4 (December 1944): 512.

15. Prudence Crandall to Ellen Larned, Cordova, Illinois, May 15, 1869, Connecticut State Library, Hartford, Connecticut. Years later Crandall recalled conversations with Sarah: "In some of her calls I ascertained that she wished to attend my school and board at her father's house at some distance from the village."

16. Statement of Mary Barber, September 10, 1833, Prudence Crandall Museum, Canterbury, Connecticut. See also Small and Small, "Prudence Crandall: Champion of Negro Education," 509.

17. Statement of Mary Barber, September 10, 1833.

18. There was at least one other possible explanation for Barber's account. Sarah Harris could have told Barber that Crandall had asked her to enroll rather than admit that she had put such a question directly to Crandall. Under that scenario, Barber's statement technically would have been truthful, but not representative of what actually had happened. Such an explanation still would not resolve Barber's false claim that Harris had given up her plans for marriage as a result of her enrollment, which tended to undermine the veracity of Barber's entire statement.

19. *New York Commercial Advertiser*, September 16, 1833. In this issue, the *Advertiser* published an article attacking both Crandall and Arthur Tappan and included Andrew Judson's letter to the *Advertiser*, September 10, 1833.

20. Ibid.

21. Ibid.; *New York Commercial Advertiser*, August 21, 1833; *New York Spectator*, September 19, 1833.

22. *New York Commercial Advertiser*, September 16, 1833.

23. Ibid.

24. Ibid.; see the *New York Commercial Advertiser*, August 21, 1833.

25. *New York Commercial Advertiser*, September 16, 1833.

26. *Liberator*, April 9, 1836.

27. *New York Commercial Advertiser*, September 16, 1833; *New York Spectator*, September 19, 1833.

28. *New York Commercial Advertiser*, September 16, 1833.

29. Henry Mayer, *All on Fire: William Lloyd Garrison and the Abolition of Slavery* (New York: St. Martin's Press, 1998), 166.

30. Oliver Johnson, *William Lloyd Garrison and His Times, or Sketches of the Anti-*

Slavery Movement in America (Boston: Houghton, Mifflin, 1881), 132, quoting a letter Garrison had published in the *London Patriot*.

31. Ibid., 161, quoting Garrison's speech as reported in three successive issues of the *Liberator*, November 9, 16, and 23, 1833.

32. Wendell Phillips Garrison and Francis Jackson Garrison, *William Lloyd Garrison: The Story of His Life Told by His Children*, vol. 1 (New York: Century, 1885), 373.

33. Ibid., 377.

34. Ibid.

35. Ibid., 381.

36. Johnson, *William Lloyd Garrison and His Times*, 132.

37. Mayer, *All on Fire*, 167. Mayer cited numerous newspapers as having published timely attacks on Garrison, including the *New York Gazette*, October 2, 1833; *New York Courier and Enquirer*, October 2, 1833; *New York Standard*, October 2, 1833; and the *New York Evangelist*, October 5, 1833. See Albert Bushnell Hart and John Gould Curtis, eds., *American History Told by Contemporaries*, vol. 3 (New York: MacMillan, 1901), 604, reprinting the *New York Commercial Advertiser* article of October 2, 1833, concerning Garrison's return to New York, and including the referenced quotation.

38. Hart and Curtis, *American History Told by Contemporaries*, 3:604.

39. Wendell and Francis Garrison, *William Lloyd Garrison*, 1:381.

40. Ibid., 381–382.

41. Lewis Tappan, *The Life of Arthur Tappan* (New York: Hurd and Houghton, 1871), 174–175.

42. Wendell and Francis Garrison, *William Lloyd Garrison*, 1:384.

43. Ibid.

44. William Lloyd Garrison, *The Abolitionist, or Record of the New England Anti-Slavery Society* (Boston: Garrison and Knapp, 1833), 171.

45. Hart and Curtis, *American History Told by Contemporaries*, 3:604.

46. Arthur H. Saxon, *P.T. Barnum: The Legend and the Man* (New York: Columbia University Press, 1989), 43. P.T. Barnum was convicted of libel in a trial with Judge Daggett presiding; Barnum spent sixty days in jail. Barnum noted that "Daggett had charged the jury in such a manner that many intelligent men who were present remarked that he was the best lawyer that had plead in behalf of the state."

47. Macgrane Cox, "Chancellor Kent at Yale," *Yale Law Journal* 7, no. 5 (March 1908): 335 n. 2.

48. Dwight Loomis and Joseph Gilbert Calhoun, *The Judicial and Civil History of Connecticut* (Boston: Boston History Company, 1895), 265.

49. Ibid.

50. Ibid.

51. Ibid.

52. Ellen Strong Bartlett, "A Patriarch of American Portrait Painters, Nathaniel Jocelyn," *Connecticut Magazine* 7, no. 5 (February-March, 1903): 594.

53. David Daggett, "New Haven Auxiliary Colonization Society," *Religious Intelligencer* 4, no. 22 (October 30, 1819): 349.

54. Ibid.

55. *College for Coloured Youth: An Account of the New-Haven City Meeting and Resolutions: With Recommendations of the College, and Strictures upon the Doings of New Haven* (New York: Published by the Committee, 1831), 5, Rare Book and Manuscripts Library, Yale University. See Johnson, *William Lloyd Garrison and His Times*, 123.

56. Ibid.

57. Tappan, *The Life of Arthur Tappan*, 150.

58. David Daggett, *Count the Cost: An Address to the People of Connecticut* (Hartford: Hudson and Goodwin, 1804), 14, reprinted by the *Magazine of History* 20, no. 4 (1922): 14. Daggett originally distributed the speech under the name "Jonathon Steadfast," but he was identified by name as the author in the pamphlet and in the reprint.

59. Ibid., 14–15.

60. Ibid., 15.

61. Ibid., 16.

62. Rev. Edward J. Giddings, *Christian Rulers, or Religion and Men of Government* (New York: Bromfield, 1890), 152.

63. Ellen Strong Bartlett, "A Patriarch of American Portrait Painters, Nathaniel Jocelyn," *Connecticut Magazine* 7, no. 5 (February-March, 1903): 593.

64. *Unionist*, October 10, 1833, as reprinted in the *Connecticut Courant*, October 14, 1833. The following black students were cited by Judson and Cleveland as being from out of state and taught by Prudence Crandall at her school: "M. E. Carter, Sarah Hammond, A. E. Hammond, C. A. Weldon, Emila Wilson, Eliza Weldon, C. G. Marshal, Maria Robinson, and Elizabeth Henly." *Andrew T. Judson's Remarks to the Jury, on the Trial of the Case State v. P. Crandall, Superior Court, Oct. Term, 1833, Windham County, Ct.* (Hartford, Conn.: John Russell, 1833), 5.

65. Ibid.

66. *Andrew T. Judson's Remarks to the Jury, on the Trial of the Case State v. P. Crandall, Superior Court, Oct. Term, 1833, Windham County, Ct.* (Hartford, Conn.: John Russell, 1833), 21; see Paul Finkelman, *Abolitionists in Northern Courts: The Pamphlet Literature; Slavery, Race, and the American Legal System, 1700–1872*, vol. 3 (New York: Garland, 1988), 79.

67. Ibid. All of the words and phrases in italics appear as they were typeset in the booklet.

68. Ibid., 22.

69. Ibid.

70. Ibid., 23.

71. *Unionist*, October 10, 1833, as reprinted in the *Connecticut Courant*, October 14, 1833.

72. Ibid.

73. *Crandall v. State*, 10 Day 339, 344 (1834).

74. Ibid.

75. Ibid., 345.

76. Ibid.

77. Charles Wells Moulton, *The Library of Literary Criticism of English and American Authors*, vol. 5 (Buffalo, N.Y.: Moulton, 1902), 503. See John S. Hart, *A Manual of American Literature* (Philadelphia: Eldredge and Brother, 1876), 126.

78. *Crandall v. State*, 10 Day 339, 346 (1834).

79. Ibid.

80. Ibid., 347.

81. Ibid.

82. Ibid.

83. Ibid., 348.

84. Ibid.

85. Wendell and Francis Garrison, *William Lloyd Garrison*, 1:385–386; see the *Liberator*, October 12, 1833.

86. Ibid., 386.

87. Ibid., 387; see the *Liberator*, November 9, 1833.

88. Welch, *Prudence Crandall*, 85, quoting a *Christian Secretary* editorial entitled "Mobocracy and the Order of the Day."

89. Wendell and Francis Garrison, *William Lloyd Garrison*, 1:387; see the *Liberator*, November 9, 1833.

9. ROMANTIC REVOLUTIONARIES

1. *Bury and Norwich Post* (Suffolk, England), October 9, 1833 and December 4, 1833.

2. Mark Saunders Schantz, *Piety in Providence: Class Dimensions of Religious Experience in Antebellum Rhode Island* (Cornell University Press, 2000), 176.

3. Ibid.

4. D. H. Van Hoosear, *The Fillow, Philo and Philleo Genealogy: A Record of the Descendants of John Fillow, a Huguenot Refugee from France* (Albany, N.Y.: Joel Munsell's Sons, 1888), 49.

5. Ibid.

6. Ibid.

7. George O. Jones and Norman S. McVean, *History of Wood County, Wisconsin* (H. C. Cooper, Jr., 1923), 481; Van Hoosear, *The Fillow, Philo and Philleo Genealogy*, 49.

8. Van Hoosear, *The Fillow, Philo and Philleo Genealogy*, 50.

9. Thomas Baldwin, ed., *The American Baptist Magazine and Missionary Intelligencer*, vol. 1 (Boston: James Loring and Lincoln and Edmands, January 1817), 38.

10. *Celebration of the Two Hundred and Fiftieth Anniversary of the Settlement of Suffield, Connecticut* (Suffield, Conn.: Quarter Millennial General Executive Committee, 1921), 121.

11. Van Hoosear, *The Fillow, Philo and Philleo Genealogy*, 112–113.

12. *Celebration of the Two Hundred and Fiftieth Anniversary of the Settlement of Suffield, Connecticut*, 121.

13. Van Hoosear, *The Fillow, Philo and Philleo Genealogy*, 68.

14. Marion Leahy (librarian at the Pawtucket Public Library) to Helen Earle Sellers, July 28, 1948, quoting from a brochure entitled *On the Occasion of the Centennial Anniversary of the First Baptist Sunday School*, October 24, 1897, Prudence Crandall Collection, Charles E. Shain Library, Connecticut College.

15. Prudence Crandall Philleo to Emeline Philleo Whipple, inscribed on letter from Hezekiah Spencer Sheldon to Prudence C. Philleo, December 6, 1880, Sheldon Collection, Kent Memorial Library, Suffield, Connecticut. "The first time I ever saw your father, he came to visit my school as a friend of colored people," Prudence wrote.

16. Wendell Phillips Garrison and Francis Jackson Garrison, *William Lloyd Garrison: The Story of His Life Told by His Children*, vol. 1 (New York: Century, 1885), 390.

17. Ibid.

18. *Liberator*, November 2, 1833.

19. Ibid.

20. Susan Strane, *A Whole Souled Woman: Prudence Crandall and the Education of Black Women* (New York: W. W. Norton, 1990), 113.

21. Ibid. See Henry Mayer, *All on Fire: William Lloyd Garrison and the Abolition of Slavery* (New York: St. Martin's Press, 1998), 172–173, regarding the rumors of romance between Garrison and Crandall.

22. Garrison to George W. Benson, November 2, 1833, in *The Letters of William Lloyd Garrison: I Will Be Heard! 1822–1835*, vol. 1, ed. Walter M. Merrill (Cambridge, Mass.: Harvard University Press, 1971), 267. Merrill noted that Garrison had assembled a string of biblical allusions from Psalms 41:1, Isaiah 64:6, Job 5:7, and II Corinthians 4:17.

23. Garrison to John B. Vashon, November 5, 1833, in Merrill, *The Letters of William Lloyd Garrison*, 1:267–268.

24. Ibid., 268.

25. Garrison to George W. Benson, November 2, 1833, in Merrill, *The Letters of William Lloyd Garrison*, 1:266.

26. Samuel Joseph May, *Some Recollections of Our Antislavery Conflict* (Boston: Fields, Osgood, 1869), 80.

27. Garrison to George W. Benson, November 25, 1833, in Merrill, *The Letters of William Lloyd Garrison*, 1:272.

28. Carl R. Woodward, "A Profile in Dedication: Sarah Harris and the Fayerweather Family," *New England Galaxy* 25, no. 1 (Summer 1973), 6.

29. Strane, *A Whole Souled Woman*, 114.

30. John G. Whittier to Garrison, November 11, 1833, in Wendell and Francis Garrison, *William Lloyd Garrison*, 1:393–394.

31. May, *Some Recollections of Our Antislavery Conflict*, 81.

32. Ibid., 81–82.

33. Ibid., 83.

34. Ibid., 84.

35. Ibid., 85.

36. William J. Switala, *Underground Railroad in Pennsylvania* (Mechanicsburg, Penn.: Stackpole Books, 2001), 151.

37. May, *Some Recollections of Our Antislavery Conflict*, 86.

38. Ibid., 87.

39. Ibid.

40. Wendell and Francis Garrison, *William Lloyd Garrison*, 1:402.

41. Ibid., 403.

42. Ibid.

43. Ibid., 404 n. 1.

44. May, *Some Recollections of Our Antislavery Conflict*, 87. In describing the *Declaration*, Samuel May said, "It was as finished and powerful in expression as any part of that Magna Carta."

45. Anna Davis Hallowell, *James and Lucretia Mott: Life and Letters* (Boston: Houghton, Mifflin, 1884), 115.

46. Ibid., 116.

47. Wendell and Francis Garrison, *William Lloyd Garrison*, 1:413.

48. Ibid.

49. Hallowell, *James and Lucretia Mott: Life and Letters*, 114–115.

50. William Lloyd Garrison, *The Abolitionist, or the Record of the New England Anti-Slavery Society* (Boston: Garrison and Knapp, 1833), 184.

51. Ibid.

52. Ibid.,180.

53. Hallowell, *James and Lucretia Mott: Life and Letters*, 114.

54. Wendell and Francis Garrison, *William Lloyd Garrison*, 1:408.

55. Ibid., 411.

56. Ibid., 412.

57. Ibid.

58. May, *Some Recollections of Our Antislavery Conflict*, 89, 96.

59. Samuel May, "Miss Crandall's School," in *The Oasis*, ed. Lydia Maria Child (Boston: Benjamin C. Bacon, 1834), 190.

60. Ibid.

61. Ibid., 190–191.

62. *Windham County Advertiser*, December 18, 1833, as reprinted in the *Unionist*, March 13, 1834, New-York Historical Society. See also Mavis Olive Welch, *Prudence Crandall: A Biography* (Manchester, Conn.: Jason, 1983), 87.

63. Garrison to Helen E. Benson, January 18, 1834, in Merrill, *The Letters of William Lloyd Garrison*, 1:279.

64. Ibid.; Garrison quoted from Shakespeare's *Macbeth*, V, iii, 23.

65. Ibid., 280.

66. Ibid.

67. Ibid.

68. *Unionist*, March 13, 1834, New-York Historical Society. All of the details con-

cerning the fire come from the *Unionist*, which contains a lengthy article detailing the circumstances.

69. Ibid.

70. *Liberator*, February 8, 1834. Garrison referenced the February 6, 1834, news account in the *Unionist*.

71. Ibid.

72. Garrison to Helen E. Benson, February 18, 1834, in Merrill, *The Letters of William Lloyd Garrison*, 1:284.

73. *State v. Frederick Olney*, Windham County Court Records, 29 (1828–1838), 304, Connecticut State Library, Hartford.

74. *Unionist*, March 13, 1834, New-York Historical Society.

75. Ibid.

76. Ibid.

77. Wendell and Francis Garrison, *William Lloyd Garrison*, 1:424.

78. Ibid.

79. *State v. Frederick Olney*, 304.

80. *Unionist*, March 13, 1834, New-York Historical Society.

81. Helen Benson to William Lloyd Garrison, March 13, 1834, Fanny Garrison Villard Papers, Houghton Library, Harvard University. See also Welch, *Prudence Crandall*, 93.

82. Garrison to George Benson, May 31, 1834, in Merrill, *The Letters of William Lloyd Garrison*, 1:352.

83. Helen Benson to William Lloyd Garrison, March 13, 1834, Fanny Garrison Villard Papers, Houghton Library, Harvard University. See also Welch, *Prudence Crandall*, 93.

84. *Unionist*, March 13, 1834, New-York Historical Society.

85. Ibid.

86. Ibid.

87. Garrison to Henry E. Benson, February 26, 1834, in Merrill, *The Letters of William Lloyd Garrison*, 1:287.

88. Helen E. Benson to William Lloyd Garrison, February 11, 1834, Fanny Garrison Villard Papers, Houghton Library, Harvard University. See also Welch, *Prudence Crandall*, 91.

89. Ibid.

90. Ibid.

91. Garrison to Helen E. Benson, February 18, 1834, in Merrill, *The Letters of William Lloyd Garrison*, 1:283.

92. Ibid., 284.

93. Ibid.

94. Ibid.

95. Ibid., 285. Garrison to Samuel J. May, February 18, 1834.

96. Ibid., 286.

97. Ibid.

98. Ibid., 304. Garrison to Helen E. Benson, March 26, 1834.

99. Ibid., 289. Garrison to Helen E. Benson, March 8, 1834.

100. Ibid.

101. Ibid.

102. Ibid., 290.

103. Ibid., 296. Garrison to Helen E. Benson, March 19, 1834.

104. Ibid., 299, 300. Garrison to John B. Vashon, March 22, 1834.

10. RACE RIOTS

1. Robert Andrew Margo, *Wages and Labor Markets in the United States, 1820–1860* (Chicago: University of Chicago Press, 2000), 146–148; Howard Bodenhorn, *State Banking in Early America: A New Economic History* (New York: Oxford University Press, 2003), 289.

2. Bodenhorn, *State Banking in Early America*, 292–293.

3. Theodore D. Weld, *First Annual Report of the Society for Promoting Manual Labor in Literary Institutions* (New York: S. W. Benedict, 1833), 41.

4. For biographical information on Weld, see Robert H. Abzug, *Passionate Liberator: Theodore Dwight Weld and The Dilemma of Reform* (New York: Oxford University Press, 1980); Benjamin P. Thomas, *Theodore Weld: Crusader for Freedom* (New Brunswick, N.J.: Rutgers University Press, 1950); and Gilbert Hobbs Barnes, *The Antislavery Impulse, 1830–1844* (Washington, D.C.: American Historical Association, 1933).

5. Weld, *First Annual Report of the Society for Promoting Manual Labor in Literary Institutions*, 41.

6. Thomas, *Theodore Weld*, 24.

7. Bertram Wyatt-Brown, *Lewis Tappan and the Evangelical War against Slavery* (Cleveland, Ohio: Case Western Reserve University Press, 1969), 98.

8. Weld, *First Annual Report of the Society for Promoting Manual Labor in Literary Institutions*, 60.

9. Barnes, *The Antislavery Impulse*, 38–39.

10. Robert Davidson, *History of the Presbyterian Church in the State of Kentucky* (New York: Robert Carter, 1847), 331–332. Vail was originally from Bridgeport, Connecticut; see Thomas, *Theodore Weld*, 41–42.

11. Thomas, *Theodore Weld*, 43. Arthur Tappan committed $50,000 to support Beecher and the Lane Seminary on the condition that Beecher serve as president of the school.

12. Ibid., 70–71. See Paxton Hibben, *Henry Ward Beecher: An American Portrait* (New York: G. H. Doran, 1927), 48. "I am not apprized of the ground of controversy between the Colonizationists and the Abolitionists," Lyman Beecher said. "I am myself both, without perceiving in myself any inconsistency."

13. Thomas, *Theodore Weld*, 43.

14. *Debate at the Lane Seminary, Cincinnati; Speech of James A. Thome, of Kentucky, Delivered at the Annual Meeting of the American Anti-Slavery Society, May 6, 1834; Let-*

er of the Rev. Dr. Samuel H. Cox, Against the American Colonization Society (Boston: Garrison and Knapp, 1834), 3.

15. Theodore Weld, "Letter to James Hall, Editor," *The Western Messenger*, May 30, 1834.

16. Barnes, *The Antislavery Impulse*, 66.

17. James Bradley, "Brief Account of an Emancipated Slave," in *The Oasis*, ed. Lydia Maria Child (Boston: Benjamin C. Bacon, 1834), 107. James Bradley submitted this essay while attending Lane Seminary.

18. Ibid.

19. *Debate at the Lane Seminary, Cincinnati*, 7.

20. Theodore Dwight Weld to *Western Monthly Magazine*, May 20, 1834, in *Letters of Theodore Dwight Weld, Angelina Grimke Weld and Sarah Grimke, 1822–1844*, vol. 1, eds. Gilbert H. Barnes and Dwight L. Dumond (New York: D. Appleton-Century, 1934), 146.

21. Barnes, *The Antislavery Impulse*, 67–68.

22. Ibid., 68. The one vote in support of colonization was J.F.C. Finley, son of Robert S. Finley, one of the founders of colonization.

23. *Debate at the Lane Seminary, Cincinnati*, 5.

24. Thomas, *Theodore Weld*, 74.

25. Theodore Dwight Weld to Lewis Tappan, March 18, 1834, in Barnes and Dumond, *Letters of Theodore Dwight Weld, Angelina Grimke Weld and Sarah Grimke*, 1:133.

26. Ibid., 133–134.

27. Ibid., 135.

28. Barnes, *The Antislavery Impulse*, 69.

29. Barnes and Dumond, *Letters of Theodore Dwight Weld, Angelina Grimke Weld and Sarah Grimke*, 1:135.

30. *First Annual Report of the American Anti-Slavery Society, with the Speeches Delivered at the Anniversary Meeting, Held in Chatham Street Chapel, in the City of New York, on the Sixth of May, 1834* (New York: Dorr and Butterfield, 1834), 47–48.

31. Barnes, *The Antislavery Impulse*, 70–76; Thomas, *Theodore Weld*, 81–87.

32. Barnes, *The Antislavery Impulse*, 73; Joan D. Hedrick, *Harriet Beecher Stowe: A Life* (New York: Oxford University Press, 1994), 230–231. *Uncle Tom's Cabin* was first published eighteen years after the Lane debates, in 1852; see Theodore Dwight Weld, *Slavery as It Is: Testimony of a Thousand Witnesses* (New York: American Anti-Slavery Society, 1839).

33. Garrison to Helen E. Benson, March 25, 1834, in *The Letters of William Lloyd Garrison, I Will Be Heard! 1822–1835*, vol. 1, ed. Walter M. Merrill (Cambridge, Mass.: Harvard University Press, 1971), 302.

34. William Dunlop, *A History of the Rise and Progress of the Arts of Design in the United States*, vol. 3 (Boston: C. E. Goodspeed, 1918), 232–240. Dunlop reprinted an autobiographical letter written by Francis Alexander.

35. Helen Benson to William Lloyd Garrison, March 13, 1834, Fanny Garrison Villard Papers, Houghton Library, Harvard University.

36. Helen Benson to William Lloyd Garrison, June 16, 1834, Fanny Garrison Villard Papers, Houghton Library, Harvard University.

37. Helen Benson to William Lloyd Garrison, March 13, 1834, Fanny Garrison Villard Papers, Houghton Library, Harvard University.

38. Ibid.

39. Garrison to Helen E. Benson, March 19, 1834, in Merrill, *The Letters of William Lloyd Garrison*, 1:296.

40. Jacob Frieze, *Letter to Rev. Mr. Philleo: Dedicated to the People of Pawtucket* (Providence, R.I.: August 27, 1829); Teresa Anne Murphy, *Ten Hour's Labor: Religion, Reform, and Gender in Early New England* (Ithaca, N.Y.: Cornell University Press, 1992), 94.

41. Murphy, *Ten Hour's Labor*, 95.

42. Ibid.

43. Richard Eddy, *Universalism in America*, vol. 2 (Boston: Universalist Publishing House, 1886), 516. In a bibliography, Eddy cited and briefly described the reply of Philleo to Frieze.

44. Garrison to Helen E. Benson, April 12, 1834, in Merrill, *The Letters of William Lloyd Garrison*, 1:318.

45. Joseph Willson and Julie Winch, *The Elite of Our People: Joseph Willson's Sketches of Black Upper-class Life in Antebellum Philadelphia* (University Park: Pennsylvania State University Press, 2000), 133 n. 46.

46. Garrison to Helen E. Benson, April 5, 1834, in Merrill, *The Letters of William Lloyd Garrison*, 1:311.

47. Ibid.

48. Florence Crandall Huss to Helen Gilbert, March 23, 1948, Prudence Crandall Collection, Charles E. Shain Library, Connecticut College. Florence Crandall Huss was Prudence Crandall's niece, and she recalled a story told by Prudence's mother.

49. Letter to Helen E. Benson, April 7, 1834, in Merrill, *The Letters of William Lloyd Garrison*, 1:315.

50. Ibid., 318. Garrison to Helen E. Benson, April 12, 1834.

51. Helen Benson to William Lloyd Garrison, April 9, 1834, Fanny Garrison Villard Papers, Houghton Library, Harvard University.

52. Ibid.

53. Ibid.

54. Ibid.

55. Ibid.

56. Garrison to Helen Benson, April 12, 1834, in Merrill, *The Letters of William Lloyd Garrison*, 1:318.

57. For a detailed discussion of Andrew Jackson and his financial policies in 1834, see Sean Wilentz, *Andrew Jackson* (New York: Henry Holt, 2005), 104–113.

58. *Liberator*, April 19, 1834.

59. Ibid.

60. Garrison to Helen E. Benson, June 2, 1834, in Merrill, *The Letters of William Lloyd Garrison*, 1:357.

61. Helen E. Benson to William Lloyd Garrison, June 2, 1834, Fanny Garrison Villard Papers, Houghton Library, Harvard University. See Marvis Olive Welch, *Prudence Crandall: A Biography* (Manchester, Conn.: Jason, 1983) 100.

62. Helen E. Benson to William Lloyd Garrison, June 18, 1834, Fanny Garrison Villard Papers, Houghton Library, Harvard University. See Welch, *Prudence Crandall*, 102.

63. Helen E. Benson to William Lloyd Garrison, June 9, 1834, Fanny Garrison Villard Papers, Houghton Library, Harvard University. See Welch, *Prudence Crandall*, 100.

64. Helen E. Benson to William Lloyd Garrison, June 18, 1834, Fanny Garrison Villard Papers, Houghton Library, Harvard University.

65. Garrison to Helen E. Benson, June 6, 1834, in Merrill, *The Letters of William Lloyd Garrison*, 1:360.

66. Ibid., 361. Garrison to Helen E. Benson, June 14, 1834.

67. Ibid., 365. Garrison to George W. Benson, June 16, 1834.

68. Ibid., 370. Garrison to Helen E. Benson, June 21, 1834. Garrison paraphrased Shakespeare's *King Lear* (III, ii, 59–60), "I am a man more sinn'd against than sinning."

69. James T. Dickinson, *A Sermon, Delivered in the Second Congregational Church, Norwich, on the Fourth of July, 1834, at the Request of the Anti-Slavery Society of Norwich and Vicinity* (Norwich, Conn.: Anti-Slavery Society of Norwich, 1834), 4; Mitchell Snay, *Gospel of Disunion, Religion and Separatism in the Antebellum South* (New York: Cambridge University Press, 1993), 55.

70. Dickinson, *A Sermon*, 11, 34; Snay, *Gospel of Disunion*, 55.

71. Garrison to George W. Benson, June 16, 1834, in Merrill, *The Letters of William Lloyd Garrison*, 1:364–365.

72. Wyatt-Brown, *Lewis Tappan and the Evangelical War against Slavery*, 117.

73. *New York Commercial Advertiser*, July 4, 1834; *New York Courier and Enquirer*, July 4, 1834. See Jonathan Halperin Earle, *Jacksonian Antislavery and the Politics of Free Soil, 1824–1854* (Chapel Hill: University of North Carolina Press, 2004) 21.

74. Wyatt-Brown, *Lewis Tappan and the Evangelical War against Slavery*, 117.

75. *New York Courier and Enquirer*, July 7, 1834; see Lewis Tappan, *The Life of Arthur Tappan* (New York: Hurd and Houghton, 1871), 205.

76. Tyler Anbinder, *Five Points: The 19th-Century New York City Neighborhood That Invented Tap Dance, Stole Elections, and Became the World's Most Notorious Slum* (New York: Simon and Schuster, 2001), 10.

77. Wyatt-Brown, *Lewis Tappan and the Evangelical War against Slavery*, 117.

78. *New York Courier and Enquirer*, July 8, 1834; see Tappan, *The Life of Arthur Tappan*, 206.

79. Ibid.

80. Charles H. Levermore, "The Rise of Metropolitan Journalism," *American Historical Review* 4, no. 3 (April 1901): 453–454.

81. Ibid., 454.

82. Austin Sarat and Thomas R. Kearns, *Legal Rights: Historical and Philosophical Perspectives* (Ann Arbor: University of Michigan Press, 1997), 63.

83. *New York Courier and Enquirer*, July 11, 1834; William Jay, *Slavery in America: or, An Inquiry into the Character and Tendency of the American Colonization and the American Anti-Slavery Societies* (London: F. Westley and A. H. Davis, 1835), 107.

84. Wyatt-Brown, *Lewis Tappan and the Evangelical War against Slavery*, 116.

85. Tappan, *The Life of Arthur Tappan*, 207.

86. Ibid.

87. John H. Hewitt, *Protest and Progress: New York's First Black Episcopal Church Fights Racism* (New York: Garland, 2000), 41.

88. *New York Courier and Enquirer*, July 9, 1834; see Tappan, *The Life of Arthur Tappan*, 207.

89. *New York Commercial Advertiser*, July 10, 1834, as reprinted in *Niles National Register*, July 19, 1834.

90. Tappan, *The Life of Arthur Tappan*, 208; Rosemarie K. Bank, *Theatre Culture in America, 1825–1860* (New York: Cambridge University Press, 1997), 155–156.

91. Leonard L. Richards, *Gentlemen of Property and Standing: Anti-Abolition Mobs in Jacksonian America* (New York: Oxford University Press, 1970), 116; Don B. Wilmeth and C.W.E. Bigsby, *The Cambridge History of American Theatre: Beginnings to 1870*, vol. 1 (New York: Cambridge University Press, 1998), 361.

92. Tappan, *The Life of Arthur Tappan*, 208; Herbert Asbury, *All around the Town: Murder, Scandal, Riot and Mayhem in Old New York* (New York: Thunder's Mouth Press, 2003), 162–163.

93. Tappan, *The Life of Arthur Tappan*, 209; Asbury, *All around the Town*, 162–163.

94. Tappan, *The Life of Arthur Tappan*, 208–209. Lewis Tappan provided a detailed, eyewitness account of the damage to his house and the events leading up to the riots; see Wyatt-Brown, *Lewis Tappan and the Evangelical War against Slavery*, 117–118.

95. Wyatt-Brown, *Lewis Tappan and the Evangelical War against Slavery*, 118.

96. Tappan, *The Life of Arthur Tappan*, 209.

97. Lewis Tappan to Theodore Dwight Weld, July 10, 1834, in Barnes and Dumond, *Letters of Theodore Dwight Weld, Angelina Grimke Weld and Sarah Grimke*, 1:153, 155.

98. Wyatt-Brown, *Lewis Tappan and the Evangelical War against Slavery*, 118.

99. Lewis Tappan to Theodore Dwight Weld, July 10, 1834, in Barnes and Dumond, *Letters of Theodore Dwight Weld, Angelina Grimke Weld and Sarah Grimke*, 1:155.

100. Tappan, *The Life of Arthur Tappan*, 210–211.

101. Ibid., 222.

102. Henry Fowler, *The American Pulpit: Sketches, Biographical and Descriptive, of Living American Preachers, and of the Religious Movements and Distinctive Ideas Which They Represent* (New York: J. M. Fairchild, 1856), 374.

103. Ibid.

104. Ibid., 375.

105. Ibid.

106. Joel Tyler Headley, *The Great Riots of New York, 1712 to 1873* (New York: E. B. Treat, 1973), 88–89.

107. Ibid., 89.

108. Emmons Clark, *History of the Seventh Regiment of New York, 1806–1889* (New York: Seventh Regiment, 1890), 221.

109. Headley, *The Great Riots of New York*, 89.

110. Tappan, *The Life of Arthur Tappan*, 212.

111. *Journal of Commerce*, July 12, 1834, reprinting the proclamation of Mayor Cornelius W. Lawrence. See Tappan, *The Life of Arthur Tappan*, 213.

112. *New York Commercial Advertiser*, July 12, 1834, as reprinted in *Niles National Register*, July 19, 1834. In addition to editing the *Advertiser*, William Leete Stone served as secretary of the New York Colonization Society.

113. Tappan, *The Life of Arthur Tappan*, 212. See Clark, *History of the Seventh Regiment of New York*, 250–251, for a discussion of Major-General Jacob Morton.

114. Clark, *History of the Seventh Regiment of New York*, 222.

115. Paul A. Gilje, *The Road to Mobocracy: Popular Disorder in New York City, 1763–1834* (Chapel Hill: University of North Carolina Press, 1987), 166.

116. Graham Russell Hodges, *Root and Branch: African Americans in New York and East Jersey, 1613–1863* (Chapel Hill: University of North Carolina Press, 1999), 228. Regarding Hester Lane, see Edward Strutt Abdy, *Journal of a Residence and Tour in the United States of North America: From April, 1833, to October, 1834*, vol. 2 (London: J. Murray, 1835) 31–34. Lane purchased the freedom of at least eleven slaves. Regarding Thomas Downing, see Hewitt, *Protest and Progress*, 79–80. Downing was a parishioner of Rev. Peter Williams's African Episcopal Church.

117. Clark, *History of the Seventh Regiment of New York*, 221–222.

118. *New York Commercial Advertiser*, July 12, 1834, as reprinted in *Niles National Register*, July 19, 1834.

119. Ibid.

120. Anbinder, *Five Points*, 11–12.

121. Tappan, *The Life of Arthur Tappan*, 223.

122. Headley, *The Great Riots of New York*, 90.

123. *New York Commercial Advertiser*, July 12, 1834, as reprinted in *Niles National Register*, July 19, 1834.

124. Clark, *History of the Seventh Regiment of New York*, 222.

125. William Leete Stone, *History of New York City* (New York: Virtue and Yorston, 1872), 463. Stone was the editor of the *New York Commercial Advertiser* during the time of the 1834 riots.

126. Ibid.

127. Ibid., 464.

128. Ibid.

129. Ibid.

130. Ibid.

131. Ibid. See also Clark, *History of the Seventh Regiment of New York*, 222–223.

132. *New York Commercial Advertiser*, July 12, 1834, as reprinted in *Niles National Register*, July 19, 1834.

133. Hewitt, *Protest and Progress*, 41.

134. Ibid. But see the *New York Journal of Commerce*, July 15, 1834. The *Journal of Commerce*, which was fiercely antiabolitionist, claimed that "the damage reported to have been done to St. Philip's church was much exaggerated. The fence around it, and the steps were injured, but not the interior. The organ, reported as destroyed, was not touched." This statement is at odds with numerous other contemporary accounts that described interior destruction of the church and the burning of furniture in the street, including eyewitness reports published in the *New York Commercial Advertiser*.

135. *New York Commercial Advertiser*, July 12, 1834, as reprinted in *Niles National Register*, July 19, 1834.

136. Ibid.

137. *New York Commercial Advertiser*, July 12, 1834, as reprinted in *Niles National Register*, July 19, 1834.

138. *New York Courier and Enquirer*, July 14, 1834, as reprinted in the *New York Journal of Commerce*, July 15, 1834.

139. *New York Journal of Commerce*, July 12, 1834, quoting the *New York Star*.

140. *New York Journal of Commerce*, July 15, 1834.

141. *Niles National Register*, July 19, 1834.

142. Ibid. See William B. Sprague, *Annals of the American Pulpit: or Commemorative Notices of Distinguished American Clergy of Various Denominations*, vol. 4 (New York: Robert Carter and Brothers, 1858), 473–474, discussing the career of Rev. William Raymond Weeks, who was born in Brooklyn, Connecticut, in 1783.

143. Garrison to George W. Benson, July 10, 1834, in Merrill, *The Letters of William Lloyd Garrison*, 1:374.

144. Ibid., 375. Garrison to Helen E. Benson, July 15, 1834.

145. Ibid., 376.

146. Ibid., 375.

147. Ibid., 382. Garrison to Samuel May, July 23, 1834.

148. *Niles National Register*, July 19, 1834.

149. August Meier and Elliott Rudwick, *From Plantation to Ghetto* (New York: Hill and Wang, 1976), 137.

150. Tappan, *The Life of Arthur Tappan*, 201, quoting letter from Arthur Tappan to A. F. Stoddard, August 27, 1863.

151. *Niles National Register*, July 19, 1834.

152. *New York Spectator*, July 15, 1834; Milton C. Sernett, *African American Religious History: A Documentary Witness* (Durham, N.C.: Duke University Press, 1999), 212.

153. *New York Spectator*, July 15, 1834; see "Address of Rev. Peter Williams," *African Repository and Colonial Journal* 10, no. 6 (August 1834): 187.

154. Ibid.

11. APPEAL FOR EQUALITY

1. Garrison to Samuel J. May, July 23, 1834, in *The Letters of William Lloyd Garrison: I Will Be Heard! 1822–1835*, vol. 1, ed. Walter M. Merrill (Cambridge, Mass.: Harvard University Press, 1971), 381.

2. Rev. Isaac P. Langworthy, "Thomas Scott Williams," *Congregational Quarterly* 5, no. 1 (January 1863): 8.

3. Frederick Calvin Norton, *The Governors of Connecticut* (Hartford, Conn.: Connecticut Magazine Company, 1905), 210.

4. Ibid.

5. *Harper's Magazine*, April 1883, 806.

6. Norton, *The Governors of Connecticut*, 211.

7. Franklin Bowditch Dexter, *Biographical Sketches of the Graduates of Yale College with Annals of the College History, June 1792–September 1805*, vol. 5 (New York: Henry Holt, 1911), 567.

8. Leonard M. Daggett, "The Supreme Court of Connecticut," in *The Green Bag*, vol. 2, ed. Horace W. Fuller (Boston: Boston Book Company, 1890), 432.

9. *Report of the Arguments of Counsel in the Case of Prudence Crandall before the Supreme Court of Errors* (Boston: Garrison and Knapp, 1834), 5.

10. Ibid., 7–8.

11. Ibid., 6.

12. Ibid., 6–7.

13. Ibid., 10.

14. *Crandall v. State*, 10 Day 339, 347 (1834).

15. *Report of the Arguments of Counsel in the Case of Prudence Crandall*, 12.

16. Ibid., 13, 14.

17. Ibid., 12.

18. Ibid., 12, 15.

19. Ibid.

20. Ibid., 15–16.

21. Ibid., 17.

22. Ibid.

23. Ibid., 18.

24. Ibid.

25. Ibid., 22.

26. Ibid.

27. Ibid., 23.

28. Ibid.

29. Ibid., 23–24.

30. Ibid., 24.

31. Ibid.

32. Ibid.

33. Ibid., 29. See Gaillard Hunt, ed., *The Writings of James Madison: 1769–1783*, vol. 1 (New York: G. P. Putnam's Sons, 1900), 459.

34. *Report of the Arguments of Counsel in the Case of Prudence Crandall*, 29.

35. Ibid., 31.

36. Ibid.

37. Ibid., 32–33.

38. Ibid., 27.

39. Ibid., 34.

40. John Hooker to the editor, *Hartford Courant*, March 12, 1886. Hooker, a prominent Hartford attorney, abolitionist, husband of Isabella Beecher Hooker (youngest daughter of Dr. Lyman Beecher), and the official court reporter to the Connecticut Supreme Court from 1858 through 1894, stated that he had reviewed the notes made by Judge Clark Bissell. Hooker wrote, "It appears by minutes of the consultation taken by Judge Bissell, and found since his death among his papers, and which the writer has had an opportunity to examine, that the question of citizenship of free blacks was discussed at considerable length by the judges, and that, while Judge Daggett adhered to the opinion expressed by him in the court below, all the other judges either held or inclined to the opinion that they were citizens." Hooker was aware that the state supreme court had been asked by the legislature in 1865 to opine on the question of whether blacks were citizens of Connecticut and the United States. The court answered in the affirmative and in a note discussed the *Crandall* case and the inclination of three of four justices to rule in favor of black citizenship. See Supplement, 32 Conn. 365 (1865).

41. Ibid.

42. William H. Ferris, *The African Abroad or His Evolution in Western Civilization*, vol. 2 (New Haven, Conn.: Tuttle, Morehouse and Taylor Press, 1913), 724.

43. *Crandall v. State*, 10 Day 339, 369 (1834). Years later, John Hooker, who worked for the Connecticut State Supreme Court as its official reporter, said that generally Justice Williams "came to his conclusions by a single step, and with something like intuition, and looked about afterwards for his reasons, and this, less to satisfy his own mind than to convince his associates on the bench . . ." See Isaac P. Langworthy, "Thomas Scott Williams," *Congregational Quarterly* 5, no. 1 (January 1863): 6.

44. *Crandall v. State*, 10 Day 339, 372.

45. Ibid., 369.

46. Ibid. Justice Williams wrote, "This information charges, that this school was set up in Canterbury, for the purpose of educating these persons of colour, not inhabitants of the state, that they might be instructed and educated; but omits to state, that it was not licensed. This omission is a fatal defect."

47. Complaint of Nehemiah Ensworth against Prudence Crandall, September 25, 1833, Windham County Superior Court Files, January 1834–January 1835, Connecticut State Library, Box 211, Hartford, Connecticut.

48. Ibid. See also Judgment Binding Her (Prudence Crandall) Over to Superior Court, September 26, 1833, Connecticut State Library, Hartford, Connecticut.

49. The complaint did allege, as Justice Williams noted, that Crandall had harbored and boarded colored persons from other states for the purpose of attending and

eing taught at a school Crandall set up for the purpose of teaching colored students. The complaint further stated, "all which acts and doings of the said Prudence Crandall were done and committed without the consent in writing first obtained of a majority of the civil authority and also of the selectmen of said town of Canterbury . . ." Williams either deliberately ignored this language or did not read "all which acts and doings" to include the setting up of the school.

50. *Newport Mercury*, August 9, 1834, quoting the *Hartford Review*.

51. Garrison to Samuel May, July 28, 1834, in Merrill, *The Letters of William Lloyd Garrison*, 1:384.

52. Ibid.

53. James Kent, *Commentaries on American Law*, 6th ed., vol. 2 (New York: Alex S. Gould, 1848), 258 n. b.

54. Garrison to Samuel May, July 23, 1834, in Merrill, *The Letters of William Lloyd Garrison*, 1:382.

55. Garrison to Helen E. Benson, July 21, 1834, in Merrill, *The Letters of William Lloyd Garrison*, 1:379–380.

56. Ibid., 380.

57. Ibid.

58. Helen Benson to William Lloyd Garrison, July 19, 1834, Fanny Garrison Villard Papers, Houghton Library, Harvard University. See Marvis Olive Welch, *Prudence Crandall: A Biography* (Manchester, Conn.: Jason, 1983), 104–105.

59. Garrison to Helen E. Benson, July 21, 1834, in Merrill, *The Letters of William Lloyd Garrison*, 1:379. See also Henry C. Binford, "The First Suburbs: Residential Communities on the Boston Periphery, 1815–1860," in *The Suburb Reader*, eds. Becky M. Nicolaides and Andrew Wiese (New York: CRC Press, 2006), 86–87, discussing omnibuses as a significant step in mass transportation and the development of suburban communities.

60. Garrison to Helen E. Benson, August 4, 1834, in Merrill, *The Letters of William Lloyd Garrison*, 1:391.

61. Ibid.

62. Ibid., 390.

63. Ibid., 395. Garrison to Helen E. Benson, August 11, 1834.

64. Ibid., 398. Garrison to Helen E. Benson, August 18, 1834.

65. Ibid., 399.

66. Ibid.

67. Edward Strutt Abdy, *Journal of a Residence and Tour in the United States of North America: From April 1833 to October 1834*, vol. 3 (London: John Murray, 1835), 212–213; see Helen E. Benson to William Lloyd Garrison, August 13, 1834, Fanny Garrison Villard Papers, Houghton Library, Harvard University. See also Welch, *Prudence Crandall*, 105.

68. Abdy, *Journal of a Residence and Tour in the United States of North America*, 3:213. Abdy reported that Whiton's refusal to perform Crandall's wedding offended many in his church, and he soon regretted his decision. "He had bitterly repented his

conduct, I was told; the majority of his congregation having become displeased with him." On January 17, 1837, the church deacons dismissed Whiton.

69. *New York Spectator*, August 25, 1834.

70. Ibid.

71. *Brattleboro Messenger*, August 29, 1834.

72. Abdy, *Journal of a Residence and Tour in the United States*, 3:304.

73. Garrison to Helen E. Benson, August 18, 1834, in Merrill, *The Letters of William Lloyd Garrison*, 1:399.

74. Ibid.

75. *Proceedings of the American Society of Civil Engineers*, vol. 17 (New York: American Society of Civil Engineers, 1891), 267, obituary of John Marston Goodwin, son of John and Emeline Goodwin.

76. Garrison to Helen E. Benson, August 18, 1834, in Merrill, *The Letters of William Lloyd Garrison*, 1:399.

77. Ibid., 400.

78. Ibid., 399.

79. Jean Fagan Yellin and John C. Van Horne, eds., *The Abolitionist Sisterhood: Women's Political Culture in Antebellum America* (Ithaca, N.Y.: Cornell University Press, 1994), 278.

80. Ibid.; Peter Hinks, John McKivigan, and R. Owen Williams, eds., *Encyclopedia of Antislavery and Abolition*, vol. 1 (Westport, Conn.: Greenwood Publishing 2006), 267.

81. Julie Roy Jeffrey, *The Great Silent Army of Abolitionism: Ordinary Women in the Antislavery Movement* (Chapel Hill: University of North Carolina Press, 1998), 20.

82. Garrison to Helen E. Benson, August 18, 1834, in Merrill, *The Letters of William Lloyd Garrison*, 1:400–401.

83. Ibid., 399–400.

84. Lucretia Mott to Phebe Post Willis, September 13, 1834, in *Selected Letters of Lucretia Coffin Mott*, eds. Lucretia Mott and Beverly Wilson Palmer (Urbana: University of Illinois Press, 2002), 29. Mott wrote, ". . . a few weeks since Prudence Crandall [Phillio]—came here with the intention of giving up her school at Canterbury and opening up a day school for colored children in this city—we went round among them and soon had 50 scholars engaged @ $4 per quarter, but the Dr. and some others were apprehensive of the consequences and discouraged her coming for the present, she will wait till after our Elections are past—when if nothing unfavorable occurs she contemplates moving here—Our female society had appointed a committee to look out for a suitable teacher and try to get up such a school before we had heard of her intention of coming—We have devoted several days to visiting all the schools in the city and found such a one was much needed." The "Dr." in the letter was Dr. Joseph Parrish (1779–1840), who was the president of the Pennsylvania Society for Promoting the Abolition of Slavery and the Mott family doctor.

12. THE END OF THE BEGINNING

1. Julie Winch, *A Gentleman of Color: The Life of James Forten* (New York: Oxford University Press, 2002), 112–113.

2. Edward Strutt Abdy, *Journal of a Residence and Tour in the United States of North America: From April 1833 to October 1834*, vol. 3 (London: John Murray, 1835), 319–320.

3. Ibid., 321.

4. Ibid.

5. *Niles Weekly Register*, August 16, 1834; Winch, *A Gentleman of Color*, 289.

6. *Niles Weekly Register*, August 16, 1834.

7. *Pennsylvanian*, August 15, 1834; *Philadelphia Gazette*, August 15, 1834; both reprinted in *Niles Weekly Register*, August 23, 1834.

8. Ibid.

9. Ibid.

10. *Pennsylvanian*, August 16, 1834, as reprinted in *Niles Weekly Register*, August 23, 1834.

11. Ibid.

12. *Philadelphia Enquirer*, August 15, 1834, as reprinted in *Niles Weekly Register*, August 23, 1834.

13. *Niles Weekly Register*, August 23, 1834.

14. Winch, *A Gentleman of Color*, 290. By the end of 1834, Forten was "depressed . . . at the condition and prospects of his race."

15. Ira Vernon Brown, *Mary Grew: Abolitionist and Feminist, 1813–1896* (Selinsgrove, Pa.: Susquehanna University Press, 1991), 14, with regard to the officers of the Philadelphia Female Anti-Slavery Society; Otelia Cromwell, *Lucretia Mott* (Cambridge, Mass.: Harvard University Press, 1958), 53, as to Mott and Moore meeting Prudence Crandall.

16. Gerda Lerner, *The Grimke Sisters from South Carolina: Pioneers for Woman's Rights and Abolition* (New York: Oxford University Press, 1998), 91.

17. Lucretia Mott to James Miller McKim, September 25, 1834, in Cromwell, *Lucretia Mott*, 53.

18. Ibid.

19. Carter Goodwin Woodsen, *The Education of the Negro Prior to 1861* (New York: G. P. Putnam's Sons, 1915), 104.

20. Ibid.

21. Lucretia Mott to Phebe Post Willis, September 13, 1834, in Mott and Palmer, *Selected Letters of Lucretia Coffin Mott*, 29.

22. Ibid.

23. Lucretia Mott to James Miller McKim, September 25, 1834, in Cromwell, *Lucretia Mott*, 53.

24. Ibid.

25. Lucretia Mott to Phebe Post Willis, September 13, 1834, in Mott and Palmer, *Selected Letters of Lucretia Coffin Mott*, 29. The tuition of four dollars per quarter was

far less than the twenty-five dollars per quarter that Crandall charged at her school in Canterbury.

26. Ibid.

27. Ibid.

28. Lucretia Mott to James Miller McKim, September 25, 1834, in Cromwell, *Lucretia Mott*, 53.

29. Lucretia Mott to Phebe Post Willis, September 13, 1834, in Mott and Palmer, *Selected Letters of Lucretia Coffin Mott*, 29.

30. Lucretia Mott to James Miller McKim, September 25, 1834, in Cromwell, *Lucretia Mott*, 53.

31. Abdy, *Journal of a Residence and Tour in the United States*, 3:211.

32. Ibid., 209.

33. *London Standard*, October 4, 1833; *Bury and Norwich Post*, October 9, 1833 and December 4, 1833; *Royal Cornwall Gazette*, December 7, 1833.

34. Mavis Olive Welch, *Prudence Crandall: A Biography* (Manchester, Conn.: Jason, 1983), 97; see Abdy, *Journal of a Residence and Tour in the United States*, 3:209–210.

35. Ibid.

36. Ibid., 210.

37. Ibid.

38. Ibid.

39. Ibid., 213.

40. Ibid., 212.

41. *Baltimore Gazette and Daily Advertiser*, September 12, 1834, quoting the *New York Commercial Advertiser*.

42. Ibid., 208.

43. Garrison to Helen E. Benson, August 23, 1834, in *The Letters of William Lloyd Garrison, I Will Be Heard! 1822–1835*, vol. 1, ed. Walter M. Merrill (Cambridge, Mass.: Harvard University Press, 1971), 403–404.

44. Ibid., 403.

45. Ibid.

46. Ibid., 404.

47. Ibid.

48. Ibid., 408. Garrison to Helen E. Benson, August 29, 1834.

49. Ibid., 404. Garrison to Helen E. Benson, August 23, 1834.

50. Ibid., 370. Garrison to Helen E. Benson, June 21, 1834.

51. Ibid.

52. Ibid., 413. Garrison to George W. Benson, September 12, 1834.

53. Ibid.

54. Carl R. Woodward, "A Profile in Dedication: Sarah Harris and the Fayerweather Family," *New England Galaxy* 15, no. 1 (Summer 1973): 6; Susan Strane, *A Whole Souled Woman: Prudence Crandall and the Education of Black Women* (New York: W. W. Norton, 1990), 151.

55. Abdy, *Journal of a Residence and Tour in the United States*, 3:304. Hinckley often

stopped by the school; he had been called as a witness by the prosecution in the first Black Law trial. In May 1834 he attended the New England Anti-Slavery convention in Boston.

56. Ibid. Abdy's account of the September 9 attack is likely the most accurate in existence, as it was recorded by Abdy just days after the event. He viewed the damage at the school and spoke with both Prudence and Calvin Philleo, who gave him their firsthand accounts of what had occurred. There is no mention in Abdy's report of the front door having been battered down or men having entered the school, as later accounts occasionally would claim.

57. Ibid., 303–304.

58. Ibid. at 304.

59. Samuel Joseph May, *Some Recollections of Our Antislavery Conflict* (Boston: Fields, Osgood, 1869), 71.

60. Ibid.

61. Ibid.

62. Ibid.

63. Abdy, *Journal of a Residence and Tour in the United States*, 3:305.

64. Garrison to Samuel J. May, September 15, 1834, in Merrill, *The Letters of William Lloyd Garrison*, 1:415–416.

65. Ibid., 416.

66. See generally, Diana Ross McCain and Kazimiera Kozlowski, *African-American Students Who Attended Prudence Crandall's Female Boarding School in Canterbury, Connecticut, April 1, 1833–September 9, 1834*, Connecticut Historical Commission (2001), Prudence Crandall Museum, Canterbury, Connecticut.

67. *Liberator*, April 9, 1836.

68. McCain and Kozlowski, *African-American Students Who Attended Prudence Crandall's Female Boarding School*, 21.

69. Ibid., 19.

70. Abdy, *Journal of a Residence and Tour in the United States*, 307.

71. Ibid.

72. Ibid.

73. Ibid., 306.

74. See Jean Edward Smith, *John Marshall: Definer of a Nation* (New York: Henry Holt, 1996), 488–490. The U.S. Supreme Court consisted of seven justices in 1834. Four of the associate justices were from northern states: Massachusetts, Ohio, Pennsylvania, and New York; two were from the southern states of Maryland and Georgia. The chief justice, John Marshall, was from Virginia. By 1834, at the end of a remarkable tenure as chief justice, Marshall abhorred slavery. In the 1829 case of *Boyce v. Anderson*, which concerned whether a slave was a person or mere property for the purposes of a personal injury action regarding a slave, Justice Marshall wrote for the court that slaves were persons, not property.

75. *Hartford Daily Courant*, "Prudence Crandall," March 10, 1886.

76. Ibid., March 30, 1886.

77. *Liberator*, September 20, 1834; Strane, *A Whole Souled Woman*, 151.

78. *Liberator*, September 20, 1834.

79. Ibid.

80. Ibid.

81. Wendell Phillips Garrison and Francis Jackson Garrison, *William Lloyd Garrison, 1805–1879: The Story of His Life Told by His Children*, vol. 1 (New York: Century, 1885), 391–392.

82. Garrison to George Benson, January 12, 1835, in Merrill, *The Letters of William Lloyd Garrison*, 1:435.

83. Winch, *A Gentleman of Color*, 288; John Russell Young, ed., *Memorial History of the City of Philadelphia*, vol. 2 (New York: New York History Company and Winthrop Press, 1898), 213.

84. May, *Some Recollections of Our Antislavery Conflict*, 71.

85. Laura S. Haviland, *A Woman's Life-Work: Labors and Experiences of Laura S. Haviland* (Chicago: C. V. Waite, 1887), 515.

13. FAMILY TRIALS AND TRAGEDIES

1. Diana Ross McCain and Kazimiera Kozlowski, *African-American Students Who Attended Prudence Crandall's Female Boarding School in Canterbury, Connecticut*, Connecticut Historical Commission (2001), 24, Prudence Crandall Museum, Canterbury, Connecticut.

2. William Allen Wallace, *The History of Canaan, New Hampshire* (Concord, N.H.: Rumford Press, 1910), 255.

3. Ibid., 265–266. Mary Harris was hired to teach the female students.

4. David Walker and Henry Highland Garnet, *Walker's Appeal: With a Brief Sketch of His Life by Henry Highland Garnet* (New York: J. H. Tobitt, 1848).

5. Henry Highland Garnet and James McCune Smith, *A Memorial Discourse* (Philadelphia: Joseph M. Wilson, 1865), 49.

6. Wallace, *The History of Canaan, New Hampshire*, 259.

7. Ibid. In 1834 the townspeople of Canaan resolved that they would never support abolitionists "for the purpose of having Black Presidents . . ." On November 4, 2008, the voters of New Hampshire and the Town of Canaan (by a 1132 to 697 margin) helped elect Barack Obama, America's first black president.

8. Ibid., 261.

9. Ibid., 275.

10. Leon F. Litwack and August Meier, *Black Leaders of the Nineteenth Century* (Urbana: University of Illinois Press, 1991), 132.

11. *Connecticut Courant*, August 24, 1835, reprinting an editorial from the *Boston Daily Atlas*.

12. Wallace, *The History of Canaan, New Hampshire*, 292.

13. D. H. Van Hoosear, *The Fillo, Philo and Philleo Geneaology: A Record of the Descendants of John Fillow, a Huguenot Refugee from France* (Albany, N.Y.: Joel Munsell's Sons, 1888), 72.

14. *The Trial of Reuben Crandall, M.D., Charged with Publishing Seditious Libels by Circulating the Publications of the American Anti-Slavery Society, before the Circuit Court for the District of Columbia, Held at Washington, in April, 1836, Occupying the Court the Period of Ten Days* (New York: H. R. Piercy, 1836), 50–51.

15. *Gloucester Democrat*, August 18, 1835, quoting the *Baltimore Patriot*.

16. *New Hampshire Sentinel*, August 20, 1835, quoting the *National Intelligencer*.

17. Reuben Crandall to Pardon Crandall, January 29, 1836, in Marvis Olive Welch, *Prudence Crandall: A Biography* (Manchester, Conn.: Jason, 1983), 117.

18. Francis Scott Key, "Mr. Key's Address," in *African Repository and Colonial Journal* 4, no. 10 (December 1828): 300.

19. Ibid., 299.

20. Francis Scott Key to Rev. Benjamin Tappan, October 8, 1838, in George Combe, *Notes on the United States of North America, During a Phrenological Visit in 1838–40*, vol. 2 (Edinburgh: MacLachlan, Stewart, 1841), 384.

21. *The Trial of Reuben Crandall, M.D., Charged with Publishing Seditious Libels by Circulating the Publications of the American Anti-Slavery Society*, 34.

22. Ibid., 35.

23. Ibid., 58.

24. *Alexandria Gazette*, April 29, 1836, quoting the *National Intelligencer*.

25. Ibid.

26. William Goodell, *Slavery and Anti-Slavery: A History of the Great Struggle in Both Hemispheres, with a View of the Slavery Question in the United States* (New York: William Goodell, 1853), 438.

27. Reuben Crandall to Prudence Crandall, July 13, 1831, in Rena Keith Clisby, *Canterbury Pilgrims* (n.p., 1947), 14, Prudence Crandall Collection, Charles E. Shain Library, Connecticut College. Prudence Crandall was Rena Clisby's great-aunt. Clisby lived for a time with Prudence beginning in 1873, when Prudence lived in Cordova, Illinois.

28. *Stimpson's Boston Directory* (Boston: C. Stimpson, 1832), 17.

29. William Lloyd Garrison to Isaac Knapp, Brooklyn, Connecticut, August 19, 1836, Anti-Slavery Collection, Boston Public Library.

30. Almira Rand to Prudence Philleo, August 26, 1835, in Clisby, *Canterbury Pilgrims*, 28.

31. Ibid.

32. Ibid., 21. Reuben Crandall to Prudence Philleo, July 17, 1837.

33. Ibid., 22.

34. Ibid., 21.

35. Pardon Crandall to Prudence Philleo, February 23, 1838, in Welch, *Prudence Crandall*, 126.

36. Ibid.

37. Ibid.

38. Randall M. Packard, *The Making of a Tropical Disease: A Short History of Malaria* (Baltimore: John Hopkins University Press, 2007), 62–64.

39. Welch, *Prudence Crandall*, 126–127.

40. *Emancipator and Republican*, September 22, 1842, quoting the *Chicago Citizen*.

41. Hezekiah Crandall to Prudence Philleo, November 29, 1842, Prudence Crandall Collection, Charles E. Shain Library, Connecticut College.

42. *History of LaSalle County, Illinois*, vol. 2 (Chicago: Interstate Publishing Company, 1886), 628–630.

43. *Liberator*, July 19, 1844.

44. Ibid.

45. Ibid.

46. *Liberator*, April 19, 1844.

47. *Liberator*, July 19, 1844.

48. Ibid.

49. Calvin Philleo to son Calvin Wheeler Philleo, October 22, 1844, Prudence Crandall Collection, Charles E. Shain Library, Connecticut College.

50. Emeline Philleo Goodwin to Calvin Wheeler Philleo, February 24, 1847, in Welch, *Prudence Crandall*, 141.

51. See generally, *A Report upon Phonotypy*, American Academy of Arts and Sciences (Cambridge, Mass.: Metcalf, 1847), 10. The main idea of Phonotypy was that "each sound of the language should be represented by one and only one sign, and that each sign should constantly represent one sound."

52. Welch, *Prudence Crandall*, 135–136.

53. Prudence Crandall to William Lloyd Garrison, April 22, 1846, in the *Liberator*, May 1, 1846.

54. Ibid.

55. Mrs. Charles R. (Joy) McDougall to Rena Clisby, May 23, 1948, Prudence Crandall Collection, Charles E. Shain Library, Connecticut College.

56. George Thompson, *Letters and Addresses by George Thompson During His Mission in the United States* (Boston: Isaac Knapp, 1837), 107.

57. Ibid., 161.

58. *Commerical Gazette*, October 12, 1835; Wendell Phillips Garrison and Francis Jackson Garrison, *William Lloyd Garrison, 1805–1879: The Story of His Life Told by His Children*, vol. 2 (New York: Century, 1885), 6.

59. Ibid., 10. James Homer to George Rand, August 19, 1852.

60. Ibid., 9.

61. Ibid., 11.

62. Ibid., 10.

63. Ibid.

64. *Report of the Boston Female Anti-Slavery Society: With a Concise Statement of Events, Previous and Subsequent to the Annual Meeting of 1835* (Boston: Boston Female Anti-Slavery Society, 1836), 28.

65. Wendell and Francis Garrison, *William Lloyd Garrison*, 2:16.

66. Samuel Joseph May, *Some Recollections of Our Antislavery Conflict* (Boston: Fields, Osgood, 1869), 17–18.

67. Nina Moore Tiffany, *Samuel E. Sewall: A Memoir* (Boston: Houghton, Mifflin, 1898), 47.

68. Wendell and Francis Garrison, *William Lloyd Garrison*, 2:14.

69. Ibid., 20.

70. Ibid., 21.

71. Ibid., 22.

72. Ibid., 23.

73. Ibid., 26.

74. *New York Daily Times*, November 8, 1851.

75. Wendell and Francis Garrison, *William Lloyd Garrison*, 2:28.

76. Ibid., 29.

77. Thompson, *Letters and Addresses by George Thompson*, 110–111.

78. Garrison to George W. Benson, October 26, 1835, in *The Letters of William Lloyd Garrison: I Will Be Heard! 1822–1835*, vol. 1, ed. Walter M. Merrill (Boston: Harvard University Press, 1971), 543.

79. Ibid., 541. Garrison to Samuel E. Sewall, October 24, 1835.

80. Ibid., 545. Garrison to Isaac Knapp, October 26, 1835.

81. Oliver Johnson, *William Lloyd Garrison and His Times* (Boston: Houghton, Mifflin, 1881), xi.

82. Garrison to Abel Brown, March 18, 1842, in *The Letters of William Lloyd Garrison, No Union With Slaveholders, 1841–1849*, vol. 3, ed. Walter M. Merrill (Cambridge, Mass: Harvard University Press, 1973), 57.

83. Ibid., 62. Garrison to George W. Benson, March 22, 1842.

84. *Liberator*, April 22, 1842 and May 6, 1842.

85. *Liberator*, May 6, 1842.

86. Margaret Fuller, Judith Mattson Bean, and Joel Myerson, eds., *Margaret Fuller, Critic: Writings from the New York Tribune, 1844–1844* (New York: Columbia University Press, 2000), 132.

87. Carolyn L. Karcher, *The First Woman in the Republic: A Cultural Biography of Lydia Maria Child* (Durham, N.C.: Duke University Press, 1995), 285.

88. Ibid., 286.

89. Margaret L. Coit, *John C. Calhoun: American Portrait* (Boston: Houghton Mifflin, 1950), 230–231.

90. Garrison to Richard Webb, February 27, 1842, in Merrill, *The Letters of William Lloyd Garrison*, 3:53.

91. *Liberator*, December 15, 1837; see Wendell and Francis Garrison, *William Lloyd Garrison*, 2:204.

92. Garrison to Henry C. Wright, August 23, 1840, in *The Letters of William Lloyd Garrison: A House Dividing Against Itself, 1836–1840*, vol. 2, ed. Louis Ruchames (Cambridge, Mass.: Harvard University Press, 1971), 680.

14. DRED SCOTT AND THE WINDS OF CHANGE

1. Garrison to Nathaniel P. Rogers, September 4, 1840, in *The Letters of William Lloyd Garrison: A House Dividing Against Itself, 1836–1840*, vol. 2, ed. Louis Ruchames (Cambridge, Mass.: Harvard University Press, 1971), 692.

2. Ibid., 693.

3. Ibid., 71. Garrison to George W. Benson, April 10, 1836.

4. *Biographical Directory of the United States Congress, 1774–2005* (Washington, D.C.: United States Government Printing Office, 2005), 1357.

5. Andrew T. Judson, *Temperance Report, 1838* (Brooklyn, Conn.: Carter and Foster, 1838), 23.

6. Ibid.

7. Iyunolu Folayan Osagie, *The Amistad Revolt: Memory, Slavery, and the Politics of Identity in the United States and Sierra Leone* (Athens: University of Georgia Press, 2003), 7.

8. Ibid., 9.

9. Ibid.

10. Peleg Whitman Chandler, ed., *Law Reporter*, vol. 6 (Boston: Bradbury, Soden, 1844), 432.

11. Jean Edward Smith, *John Marshall: Definer of a Nation* (New York: Henry Holt, 1996), 470–471. Chief Justice Marshall was not pleased that Justice Thompson ran for governor while retaining his seat on the Court. During Marshall's tenure, justices increasingly recognized the need to demonstrate independence from politics and campaigns for elective office.

12. Timothy S. Huebner, *The Taney Court: Justices, Rulings, and Legacy* (Santa Barbara, Calif.: ABC-CLIO, 2003), 49.

13. Samuel Hazard, ed., *Hazard's United States Commercial and Statistical Register*, vol. 1 (Philadelphia: Wm. F. Geddes, 1840), 244, reprinting "Decision of Judge Thompson" from the *New York Commercial Advertiser*.

14. Ibid., 245.

15. Ibid.

16. Albert Bushnell Hart, ed., *The American Nation: A History*, vol. 16 (New York: Harper and Brothers, 1906), 296.

17. Ibid.

18. Joseph Wheelan, *Mr. Adams's Last Crusade: John Quincy Adams's Extraordinary Post-Presidential Life in Congress* (New York: PublicAffairs, 2009), 172.

19. John W. Barber, *A History of the Amistad Captives* (New Haven, Conn.: E. L. and J. W. Barber, 1840), 31–32.

20. William A. Owens, *Black Mutiny: Revolt on the Schooner Amistad* (New York: J. Day, 1953), 167.

21. Barber, *A History of the Amistad Captives*, 22.

22. Ruchames, *The Letters of William Lloyd Garrison*, 2:536 n. 2. Nicholas Trist was investigated for "failure to support the rights of American citizens, of subservience to Spanish officials, and of collaboration in the slave trade."

23. Ibid., 535. Garrison to Lewis Tappan, November 1, 1839.

24. Bertram Wyatt-Brown, *Lewis Tappan and the Evangelical War against Slavery* (Cleveland, Ohio: Press of Case Western Reserve University, 1969), 210.

25. Ibid.

26. *Testimony of Cinque, January 8, 1840, U.S. District Court, Connecticut*, Amistad Library, Mystic Seaport Museum of America and the Sea, Mystic, Connecticut.

27. Eric Robert Taylor, *If We Must Die: Shipboard Insurrections in the Era of the Atlantic Slave Trade* (Baton Rouge: Louisiana State University Press, 2006), 151.

28. *Thirty-Third Annual Report of the American Colonization Society, with the Proceedings of the Board of Directors, and of the Society at Its Annual Meeting on January 15, 1850* (Washington, D.C.: C. Alexander, 1850), 22.

29. "The Amistad Case," *African Repository and Colonial Journal* 16, no. 6 (March 15, 1840): 92.

30. *The Friend: A Literary and Religious Journal* 13, no. 19 (February 7, 1840): 144, reprinting an article from the *New Haven Palladium* detailing the decision of Judge Andrew Judson in the *Amistad* case. The *Friend* was a Quaker publication, edited by Robert Smith.

31. Ibid., 145.

32. Ibid., 147.

33. Ibid.

34. Ibid.

35. *United States v. The Amistad*, 40 U.S. 518, 597 (1841).

36. Andrew T. Judson, "A Short Sketch of My Own Life," Andrew T. Judson Papers, 1847, G. W. Blunt White Library, Mystic Seaport, Mystic, Connecticut.

37. Ibid.

38. Samuel J. May, *The Fugitive Slave Law and Its Victims* (New York: American Anti-Slavery Society, 1861), 13.

39. Samuel J. May, *Some Recollections of Our Anti-Slavery Conflict* (Boston: Fields, Osgood, 1869), 297.

40. Ibid.

41. Ibid., 152.

42. Ibid., 153.

43. Francis Henry Underwood, *John Greenleaf Whittier: A Biography* (Boston: James R. Osgood, 1884), 115. In 1844 Harriet Minot married Isaac Pitman; they lived in Providence and later in Somerville, Massachusetts. They frequently hosted authors and antislavery activists such as Garrison and Whittier. See *Twenty-Fifth Annual Report of the Trustees of the Public Library of the City of Somerville, Massachusetts for the Year 1897* (Somerville, Mass.: Somerville Journal Print, 1898), 59–60.

44. May, *Some Recollections of Our Anti-Slavery Conflict*, 153.

45. Samuel May, George B. Emerson, and Thomas J. Mumford, *Life of Samuel J. May, or Memoir of Samuel Joseph May* (Boston: Roberts Brothers, 1873), 188–189. The book has the former title on the cover and spine and the latter on the title page.

46. Ibid., 189–190.

47. "New York Indians: The Onondagas," *Friends' Intelligencer and Journal* 47, no 16 (April 26, 1890): 270.

48. *Laws of the State of New York, Passed at the Seventy-Seventh Session of the Legislature* (Albany: Gould, Banks, 1854), 358.

49. May, Emerson, and Mumford, *Life of Samuel J. May*, 190.

50. May, *Some Recollections of Our Anti-Slavery Conflict*, 245.

51. Samuel J. May, *The Rights and Condition of Women Considered, (Sermon) in the Church of the Messiah, November 8, 1846* (Syracuse, N.Y.: Stoddard and Babcock, 1846), 4, 5.

52. Dorothy Sterling, *Ahead of Her Time: Abby Kelley and the Politics of Antislavery* (New York: W. W. Norton, 1991), 266.

53. *History of the Free Congregational Society of Florence, Massachusetts, with Its Articles of Association and Bylaws* (Northampton: Wade Warner, 1882), 3–4. The society claimed to be one of the first religious entities organized "on a platform of entire freedom of thought and speech. . . . not so much for the 'worship of God' in any conventional sense, as for the instruction of man in everything that pertained to human welfare."

54. Charles Burleigh, *Thoughts on the Death Penalty* (Philadelphia: Merrihew and Thompson, 1847), 144.

55. C. B. Galbreath, "Anti-Slavery Movement in Columbia County," *Ohio Archaeological and Historical Quarterly*, vol. 30 (Columbus, Ohio: Ohio Archaeological and Historical Society, 1921), 390.

56. William Henry Burleigh, *Poems* (Philadelphia: J. Miller M'Kim, 1841), 140–141.

57. Ibid., 141.

58. William H. Burleigh and Celia Burleigh, *Poems by William H. Burleigh, with a Sketch of His Life by Celia Burleigh* (New York: Hurd and Houghton; Cambridge, Mass.: Riverside Press, 1871), vii.

59. Charles Dickens to John Forster, April 1–4, 1842, in *The Letters of Charles Dickens*, vol. 3, eds. Madeline House, Graham Storey, and Kathleen Tillotson (Oxford: Oxford University Press, 1974), 179.The doctor was most likely William Burleigh's friend Andrew McDonald. See William and Celia Burleigh, *Poems by William H. Burleigh*, vii n. 6.

60. Paul Finkelman, *Dred Scott v. Sandford: A Brief History with Documents* (Boston: Bedford Books, 1997), 3–4.

61. See generally, Robert Pierce Forbes, *The Missouri Compromise and Its Aftermath: Slavery and the Meaning of America* (Chapel Hill: University of North Carolina Press, 2007).

62. See generally, Holman Hamilton, *Prologue to Conflict: The Crisis and Compromise of 1850* (Lexington: University Press of Kentucky, 2005).

63. James A. Rawley, *Race and Politics: "Bleeding Kansas" and the Coming of the Civil War* (Lincoln: University of Nebraska Press, 1980), 129–134.

64. Mario Matthew Cuomo and Harold Holzer, eds., *Lincoln on Democracy* (New York: Fordham University Press, 2004), 74, 75. Lincoln delivered his speech against

the Kansas-Nebraska Act in Peoria, Illinois, on October 16, 1854, immediately following a speech at the same venue by Senator Stephen Douglas defending the legislation.

65. Charles Sumner, *The Works of Charles Sumner*, vol. 4 (Boston: Lee and Shepard, 1875), 140; Lewis Copeland, Lawrence W. Lamm, and Stephen J. McKenna, eds., *The World's Great Speeches* (Mineola, N.Y.: Dover Publications, 1999), 291.

66. James M. McPherson, *Battle Cry of Freedom: The Civil War Era* (New York: Oxford University Press, 1988), 149–152. Representative Brooks was related to Senator Andrew Butler of South Carolina, whom Sumner mocked and criticized in his speech. Brooks told Sumner that he had libeled his state and his cousin and then commenced beating him with a cane. After a long period of recovery, Sumner returned to the Senate three years later in 1859.

67. Albert Jeremiah Beveridge, *The Life of John Marshall*, vol. 4 (Boston: Houghton Mifflin, 1919), 479.

68. *Briscoe v. Commonwealth's Bank of Kentucky*, 34 U.S. 85 (1835). Justice Gabriel Duvall of Maryland resigned from the Court on January 12, 1835, further tipping the balance toward justices from Northern states, four to two.

69. See Paul Carrington, "The Supreme Court: The Problem of Minority Decisions," *ABA Journal* 44, no. 2 (February 1958): 138–139.

70. *Strader v. Graham*, 51 U.S. 82, 93–94 (1850).

71. *Scott v. Sandford*, 60 U.S. 393, 415 (1856).

72. Ibid.

73. *Baltimore Gazette and Daily Advertiser*, September 3, 1833.

74. *Macon Weekly Telegraph*, March 31, 1857.

75. Ibid.

76. *Hartford Daily Courant*, March 17, 1857.

77. *Hartford Courant*, March 12, 1886. The information contained in the letter of John Hooker, the official reporter for the Connecticut State Supreme Court, was also included in a footnote to a judicial opinion regarding the status of black citizenship requested by the state legislature in 1865, but does not appear to have been publicized in any meaningful way at the time. See Supplement, 32 Conn. 365 (1865).

78. Resolution by the General Assembly of the State of Connecticut, July 4, 1857, State Archives Record Group no. 005, folder 12.

79. Edward Downing Barber, *An Oration Delivered before the Addison County Anti-Slavery Society, on the Fourth of July, 1836* (Middlebury, Vt.: Knapp and Jewett Printers, 1836), 8.

80. Theodore Dwight Weld to Lewis Tappan, June 8, 1837, in *Letters of Theodore Dwight Weld, Angelina Grimke Weld and Sarah Grimke, 1822–1844*, vol. 1, eds. Gilbert H. Barnes and Dwight L. Dumond (New York: D. Appleton-Century, 1934), 397–398.

81. Ibid.

82. *Hartford Daily Courant*, May 4, 1839.

83. Ibid.

84. *Report of the Joint Select Committee to Whom Was Referred Sundry Petitions Rela-*

tive to the Subject of Slavery, Senator Alvin Brown, Chairman (Hartford, Conn.: Patriot Office Press, 1839), 7.

85. "Report and Resolutions Laid on the Table," *Hartford Daily Courant*, June 8, 1839.

86. Charles Sumner, "Argument Against the Constitutionality of Separate Colored Schools, before the Supreme Court of Massachusetts, in the Case of *Sarah C. Roberts v. the City of Boston*, December 4, 1849," in Charles Sumner, *Orations and Speeches*, vol. 2 (Boston: Ticknor, Reed and Fields, 1850), 346.

87. Stephen Kendrick and Paul Kendrick, *Sarah's Long Walk: The Free Blacks of Boston and How Their Struggle for Equality Changed America* (Boston: Beacon Press, 2004), 229.

88. *Liberator*, May 4, 1855, quoting the *New York Herald*.

89. See generally, Dawn C. Adiletta, "The Spirits of Reform: The Surprising Relationship between Spiritualism and Reform," *Hog River Journal* 7, no. 1 (Winter 2008–09): 40.

90. Garrison to Susan B. Anthony, June 19, 1857, in Merrill, *The Letters of William Lloyd Garrison*, 3:449.

91. Carolyn L. Karcher, *The First Woman in the Republic: A Cultural Biography of Lydia Maria Child* (Durham, N.C.: Duke University Press, 1994), 402–403.

92. David S. Reynolds, *John Brown, Abolitionist: The Man Who Killed Slavery, Sparked the Civil War, and Seeded Civil Rights* (New York: Vintage Books, 2006), 194.

93. Franklin Benjamin Sanborn, *The Life and Letters of John Brown: Liberator of Kansas, and Martyr of Virginia* (Boston: Roberts Brothers, 1891), 78.

94. James L. Abrahamson, *The Men of Secession and Civil War, 1859–1861* (Wilmington, Del.: Scholarly Resources, 2000), 3–5.

95. Sanborn, *The Life and Letters of John Brown*, 421.

96. Wendell Phillips Garrison and Francis Jackson Garrison, *William Lloyd Garrison, 1805–1879: The Story of His Life Told by His Children*, vol. 3 (New York: Century, 1889), 488.

97. *Liberator*, October 21, 1861.

98. Ibid.

99. Wendell Phillips, "Lesson of the Hour," in *Echoes of Harper's Ferry*, ed. James Redpath (Boston: Thayer and Eldridge, 1860), 43.

100. Oswald Garrison Villard, *John Brown, 1800–1859: A Biography Fifty Years After* (Boston: Houghton Mifflin, 1910), 475.

101. Ibid., 476.

102. Garrison to James Redpath, December 1, 1860, in *The Letters of William Lloyd Garrison: From Disunionism to the Brink of War, 1850–1860*, vol. 4, ed. Louis Ruchames (Cambridge, Mass.: Harvard University Press, 1975), 704.

103. Abraham Lincoln, Address at Cooper Union, New York, February 27, 1860, in Abraham Lincoln, John H. Clifford, and Marion M. Miller, *The Works of Abraham Lincoln: Speeches and Presidential Addresses, 1859–1865*, vol. 5 (New York: C. S. Hammond, 1907), 42.

104. *Charleston Mercury*, October 15, 1860. See McPherson, *Battle Cry of Freedom*, 228.

105. Wendell Phillips, *Speeches, Lectures and Letters* (Boston: James Redpath, 1863), 294.

106. Wyatt-Brown, *Lewis Tappan and the Evangelical War against Slavery*, 336. Smith and the Radical Abolition Party had no impact on Lincoln's electoral success in the northern states.

107. Garrison to Samuel J. May, September 28, 1860, in Ruchames, *The Letters of William Lloyd Garrison*, 4:694.

108. Karcher, *The First Woman in the Republic*, 438.

109. James Oliver Horton and Lois E. Horton, *Black Bostonians: Family Life and Community Struggle in the Antebellum North* (New York: Holmes and Meier, 1999), 51.

110. Susan Strane, *A Whole Souled Woman: Prudence Crandall and the Education of Black Women* (New York: W. W. Norton, 1990), 193; *History of La Salle County, Illinois*, vol. 1 (Chicago: Inter-State Publishing, 1886), 271.

111. Samuel Wylie Crawford, *Genesis of the Civil War: The Story of Sumter, 1860–1861* (New York: Charles L. Webster, 1887), 11.

112. Paul F. Boller, *Presidential Campaigns: From George Washington to George W. Bush* (New York: Oxford University Press, 2004), 102.

113. Abraham Lincoln, John G. Nicolay, and John Hay, *Complete Works of Abraham Lincoln*, vol. 4 (New York: Tandy-Thomas, 1894), 184.

114. Kenneth Milton Stampp, *The Causes of the Civil War* (New York: Simon and Schuster, 1991), 152–153.

115. Ibid., 153–155.

15. THE CIVIL WAR

1. Elmer Baldwin, *History of La Salle County, Illinois* (Chicago: Rand, McNally, 1877), 478–479.

2. *Mendota Reporter*, April 12, 1861; Marvis Olive Welch, *Prudence Crandall: A Biography* (Manchester, Conn.: Jason, 1983), 161.

3. Henry Harrison Eby, *Observations of an Illinois Boy in Battle, Camp and Prisons—1861 to 1865* (Mendota, Ill.: Henry H. Eby, 1910), 16.

4. Ellen Douglas Larned, *History of Windham County, Connecticut*, vol. 2 (Worcester, Mass.: Charles Hamilton, 1880), 583–584.

5. *Commemorative Biographical Record of Northeastern Pennsylvania Including the Counties of Susquehanna, Wayne, Pike and Monroe* (Chicago: J. H. Beers, 1900), 460–461, containing a detailed biography of George Washington Crandall and his Civil War experience.

6. D. H. Van Hoosear, *The Fillo, Philo and Philleo Genealogy: A Record of the Descendants of John Fillow, a Huguenot Refugee from France* (Albany, N.Y.: Joel Munsell's Sons, 1888), 194.

7. Susan Strane, *A Whole Souled Woman: Prudence Crandall and the Education of Black Women* (New York: W. W. Norton, 1990), 183.

8. John Cortland Crandall, *Elder John Crandall of Rhode Island and His Descendants* (New Woodstock, N.Y.: John Cortland Crandall, 1949), 355.

9. Ibid.

10. Ibid., 434.

11. Mary Coffin Johnson, *The Higleys and Their Ancestry: An Old Colonial Family* (New York: Grafton Press, 1892), 415.

12. Samuel J. May, *A Discourse on Slavery in the United States: Delivered in Brooklyn, July 3, 1831* (Boston: Garrison and Knapp, 1832), 24.

13. Ibid., 227.

14. Ibid., 229.

15. George B. Emerson, Samuel May, and Thomas J. Mumford, eds., *Life of Samuel May*, or *Memoir of Samuel Joseph May* (Boston: Roberts Brothers, 1873), 228.

16. Ibid., 230.

17. Carolyn L. Karcher, *The First Woman in the Republic: A Cultural Biography of Lydia Maria Child* (Durham, N.C.: Duke University Press, 1994), 429.

18. *Liberator*, May 23, 1862. Whipple had another connection to Prudence Crandall in addition to his work with William Lloyd Garrison at the *Liberator*; he was the husband of her daughter-in-law, the former Emeline Philleo Goodwin.

19. Ibid.

20. Ibid.

21. Abraham Lincoln to James A. McDougall, March 14, 1862, Rare Books and Special Collections, University of Rochester Library.

22. Garrison to Oliver Johnson, October 7, 1861, in *The Letters of William Lloyd Garrison: Let the Oppressed Go Free, 1861–1867*, vol. 5, ed. Walter M. Merrill (Cambridge, Mass.: Harvard University Press, 1979), 37.

23. Harold Holzer, Edna Greene Medford, and Frank J. Williams, *The Emancipation Proclamation: Three Views* (Baton Rouge: Louisiana State University Press, 2006), 67.

24. Walt Whitman, *Specimen Days and Collect* (Philadelphia: David McKay, 1883), 336; Donald W. Olson and Laurie G. Jasinski, "Abe Lincoln and the Leonoids," *Sky and Telescope Magazine* (November 1999), 34–35.

25. James M. McPherson, *Battle Cry of Freedom* (New York: Oxford University Press, 1988), 503–504.

26. Ibid., 540–541; Isaac C. Heysinger, *Antietam and the Maryland and Virginia Campaigns of 1862* (New York: Neale, 1912), 141.

27. Abraham Lincoln and Charles Washington Moores, ed., *Lincoln Addresses and Letters* (New York: American Book Company, 1914), 184.

28. Bertram Wyatt Brown, *Lewis Tappan and the Evangelical War against Slavery* (Cleveland, Ohio: The Press of Case Western Reserve University, 1969), 337.

29. Edna Greene Medford, Frank J. Williams, and Harold Holzer, *The Emancipation Proclamation: Three Views* (Baton Rouge: Louisiana State University Press, 2006), 22.

30. William Lloyd Garrison to Fanny Garrison, September 25, 1862, in Merrill, *The Letters of William Lloyd Garrison*, 5:114.

31. Brian McGinty, *Lincoln and the Court* (Cambridge, Mass.: Harvard University Press, 2008).

32. William Lloyd Garrison to George Thompson Garrison, June 11, 1863, in Merrill, *The Letters of William Lloyd Garrison*, 5:160.

33. David J. Eicher, *The Longest Night: A Military History of the Civil War* (New York: Simon and Schuster, 2001), 653.

34. William Lloyd Garrison to George Thompson Garrison, June 11, 1863, in Merrill, *The Letters of William Lloyd Garrison*, 5:160.

35. Ibid.

36. Ibid., 167. William Lloyd Garrison to George Thompson Garrison, August 6, 1863.

37. Ibid.

38. Civil War Newspaper Clipping Files, One Hundred Thirty-Sixth New York Infantry Regiment, New York State Military Museum, Saratoga Springs, New York; correspondence listing those killed, wounded, and missing at Gettysburg, July 5, 1863, and listing among the wounded "Alonzo Crandall, head, slight." The Bureau of Military Statistics compiled the clipping files during the Civil War, and most clips, including this one, do not name the publication source.

39. Kate Clifford Larson, *Bound for the Promised Land: Harriet Tubman: Portrait of an American Hero* (New York: Random House, 2004), 222.

40. Ibid.

41. *Liberator*, February 19, 1864; Julie Winch, *A Gentleman of Color: The Life of James Forten* (New York: Oxford University Press, 2002), 345.

42. Winch, *A Gentleman of Color*, 345.

43. Ibid., 346.

44. David T. Thackery, *A Light and Uncertain Hold: A History of the Sixty-Sixth Ohio Volunteer Infantry* (Kent, Ohio: Kent State University Press, 1999), 195.

45. Ibid., 198.

46. Stephen W. Sears, ed., *The Civil War Papers of George B. McClellan: Selected Correspondence, 1860–1865* (New York: Ticknor and Fields, 1989), 595.

47. James M. McPherson, *Battle Cry of Freedom* (New York: Oxford University Press, 1988), 775.

48. Henry Mayer, *All on Fire: William Lloyd Garrison and the Abolition of Slavery* (New York: St. Martin's Press, 1998), 566.

49. *Liberator*, March 18, 1864; Mayer, *All on Fire*, 564.

50. Garrison to Helen E. Garrison, June 9, 1864, in Merrill, *The Letters of William Lloyd Garrison*, 5:210.

51. Ibid., 212. Garrison to Helen E. Garrison, June 11, 1864.

52. Marilyn Richardson, ed., *Maria W. Stewart, America's First Black Woman Political Writer: Essays and Speeches* (Bloomington: Indiana University Press, 1987), 27.

53. David T. Valentine, *Manual of the Corporation of the City of New York for the Years 1844–45* (New York: J. F. Trow, 1844), 200.

54. Richardson, *Maria W. Stewart*, 99–100.

55. Ibid., 102.

56. Ibid., 104–106; H. W. Crew, *Centennial History of the City of Washington, D.C.* (Dayton, Ohio: United Brethren Publishing House, 1892), 544–545.

57. "Rev. Dr. Hall's Washington Pastorate," *New York Times*, September 16, 1895.

58. Richardson, *Maria W. Stewart*, 107.

59. Ibid.

60. Ibid., 91.

61. William Henry Burleigh and Celia Burleigh, *Poems by William H. Burleigh, with a Sketch of His Life by Celia Burleigh* (New York: Hurd and Houghton; Cambridge, Mass.: Riverside Press, 1871), xxvi.

62. Ibid.

63. Doris Kearns Goodwin, *Team of Rivals* (New York: Simon and Schuster, 2005), 665–666.

64. James Elliot Cabot, *A Memoir of Ralph Waldo Emerson*, vol. 2 (Boston: Houghton, Mifflin, 1888), 609.

65. Lewis Tappan, *The Life of Arthur Tappan* (New York: Hurd and Houghton, 1871), 376.

66. Albert Bushnell Hart, ed., *American History Told by Contemporaries*, vol. 4 (New York: MacMillan, 1901), 467.

67. *Liberator*, March 24, 1865.

68. W. J. Tenney, *The Military and Naval History of the Rebellion in the United States* (New York: D. Appleton, 1866), 692, quoting a telegraphic dispatch from President Lincoln to Secretary of War Edwin Stanton, April 2, 1865.

69. William Schouler, *Annual Report of the Adjutant General of the Commonwealth of Massachusetts for the Year Ending December 31, 1865* (Boston: Wright and Potter, 1866), 486.

70. Wendell Phillips Garrison and Francis Jackson Garrison, *William Lloyd Garrison, 1805–1879: The Story of His Life Told by His Children*, vol. 4 (New York: Century, 1889), 132 n. 1, quoting the *New York Tribune*, November 4, 1883. Chamberlain later settled in Charleston, South Carolina, where he became involved in politics and served as attorney general and governor.

71. William H. Beach, *The First New York (Lincoln) Cavalry, from April 19, 1861 to July 7, 1865* (New York: Lincoln Cavalry Association, 1902), 480–481.

72. Ibid., 482–483.

73. Charles Burleigh, *The Genealogy of the Burley or Burleigh Family of America* (Portland, Maine: B. Thurston, 1880), 142.

74. Crandall, *Elder John Crandall of Rhode Island and His Descendants*, 355.

75. Van Hoosear, *The Fillo, Philo and Philleo Genealogy*, 194. Captain Frank Goodwin was twenty years old when the war ended. He married Laura Amanda Hustings almost ten years later, on Janurary 28, 1875, but the marriage ended tragically. They

had a daughter on November 12, 1876; Laura died of complications two weeks later, and the baby girl, named Laura to honor her mother, died two years thereafter.

76. Burleigh, *The Genealogy of the Burley or Burleigh Family of America*, 142.

77. *Tiffin Daily Tribune* (Ohio), November 15, 1897. Regarding the details about Andrew Judson Ames's life after the Civil War, I am grateful and indebted to William Ames, a descendant of Charles and Andrew Judson Ames.

78. Garrison to Helen E. Garrison, April 7, 1865, in Merrill, *The Letters of William Lloyd Garrison*, 5:265. General Robert E. Lee officially surrendered to General Ulysses S. Grant on Sunday, April 9, at Appomattox; this note was likely added as a postscript to his letter of April 7.

79. Wendell and Francis Garrison, *William Lloyd Garrison*, 4:137 n. 1.

80. J. Clement French and Edward Cary, *The Trip of the Steamer Oceanus to Fort Sumter and Charleston S. C., April 14, 1865* (Brooklyn, N.Y.: The Union Steam Printing House, 1865), 43.

81. Garrison to Helen E. Garrison, April 15, 1865, in Merrill, *The Letters of William Lloyd Garrison*, 5:265.

82. Wendell and Francis Garrison, *William Lloyd Garrison*, 4:142–143.

83. Ibid., 144.

84. French and Cary, *The Trip of the Steamer Oceanus to Fort Sumter*, 96.

85. Ibid., 97–98.

86. Ibid., 98–99.

87. Ibid., 117.

88. Wendell and Francis Garrison, *William Lloyd Garrison*, 4:151.

89. Ibid.

90. Tappan, *The Life of Arthur Tappan*, 376.

16. REUNIONS AND FAREWELLS

1. *History of LaSalle County, Illinois*, vol. 2 (Chicago: Interstate Publishing Company, 1886), 628–630; Susan Strane, *A Whole Souled Woman: Prudence Crandall and the Education of Black Women* (New York: W. W. Norton, 1990), 194.

2. "Prudence Crandall and the West," June 25, 1867, in *Christian Register*, July 6, 1867; see also Ann Taves, *Fits, Trances, and Visions: Experiencing Religion and Explaining Experience from Wesley to James* (Princeton: Princeton University Press, 1999), 167. Emma Hardinge Britten was an early leader and historian of the spiritualist movement.

3. *Christian Register*, July 6, 1867.

4. Garrison to Elizabeth Pease Nichol, October 9, 1865, in *The Letters of William Lloyd Garrison, Let The Oppressed Go Free, 1861–1867*, vol. 5, ed. Walter M. Merrill (Cambridge, Mass.: Harvard University Press, 1979), 303.

5. Ibid., 302.

6. Ibid., 316. Garrison to Helen E. Garrison, November 2, 1865.

7. Ibid., 317.

8. Ibid., 357.

9. Ibid., 355.

10. Lydia Maria Child, "Through the Red Sea into the Wilderness," *Liberator*, December 29, 1865.

11. Helen E. Garrison to Sarah Fayerweather, June 5, 1863, University of Rhode Island Library, Special Collections, Fayerweather Family Papers.

12. Carl R. Woodward, "A Profile in Dedication, Sarah Harris and the Fayerweather Family," *New England Galaxy* 15, no. 1 (Summer 1973): 10.

13. Prudence Crandall Philleo to Sarah Fayerweather, December 2, 1869, University of Rhode Island Library, Special Collections, Fayerweather Family Papers.

14. Ibid.

15. Prudence Crandall Philleo to Ellen D. Larned, May 15, 1869, Connecticut State Library, Hartford, Connecticut.

16. Prudence Crandall Philleo to Ellen D. Larned, July 2, 1869, Connecticut Historical Society, Charles J. Hoadley and George Hoadley Autograph Collection, Hartford, Connecticut.

17. Ibid.

18. Prudence Crandall Philleo to Ellen D. Larned, March 7, 1870, Connecticut State Library, Hartford, Connecticut.

19. Ibid.

20. Ellen D. Larned, *History of Windham County, Connecticut* (Worcester, Mass.: Charles Hamilton, 1880), 499.

21. William Henry Burleigh and Celia Burleigh, *Poems by William H. Burleigh, with a Sketch of His Life by Celia Burleigh* (New York: Hurd and Houghton; Cambridge, Mass: Riverside Press, 1871), xx.

22. Ibid., xx–xxi.

23. David S. Reynolds, *John Brown, Abolitionist: The Man Who Killed Slavery, Sparked the Civil War, and Seeded Civil Rights* (New York: Random House, 2006), 254–255; Edward J. Renehan, Jr., *The Secret Six: The True Tale of the Men Who Conspired with John Brown* (Columbia, S.C.: University of South Carolina Press, 1997), 222–223.

24. William and Celia Burleigh, *Poems by William H. Burleigh*, xxxiii.

25. Ibid., xxxiii.

26. *Liberator*, September 20, 1834.

27. Samuel J. May, *A Brief Account of His Ministry, Given in a Discourse, Preached to the Church of the Messiah, in Syracuse, N.Y., September 15th, 1867* (Syracuse: Masters and Lee, 1867), 19.

28. Ibid., 42, 43–44.

29. George B. Emerson, Samuel May, and Thomas J. Mumford, eds., *Life of Samuel J. May*, or *Memoir of Samuel Joseph May* (Boston: Roberts Brothers, 1873), 292 n. 2.

30. Andrew Dickson White, *The Autobiography of Andrew Dickson White*, vol. 1 (New York: Century, 1905), 162.

31. Emerson, May, and Mumford, *Life of Samuel J. May*, 292–293.

32. *Syracuse Daily Standard*, July 3, 1871.

33. Rev. William Phillips Tilden, "Samuel May," *Religious Magazine and Monthly Review* 46, no. 2 (August 1831): 178.

34. Prudence Crandall Philleo to Sarah Fayerweather, July 26, 1871, University of Rhode Island Library, Special Collections, Fayerweather Family Papers.

35. Ibid.

36. Joy Constance McDougall to Rena Clisby, May 23, 1948, Prudence Crandall Collection, Charles E. Shain Library, Connecticut College. Joy, born April 16, 1889, was a great-grandniece of Prudence Crandall.

37. Ibid.

38. Jessica Huss Nashold to Helen Sellers, September 29, 1949, Prudence Crandall Collection, Charles E. Shain Library, Connecticut College. Nashold was Obediah Crandall's great-granddaughter.

39. Prudence Crandall Philleo to Esther Worsley, May 21 (and continued on June 7), 1875, Prudence Crandall Collection, Charles E. Shain Library, Connecticut College.

40. Rena Keith Clisby, *Canterbury Pilgrims* (n.p., 1947), 33, Prudence Crandall Collection, Charles E. Shain Library, Connecticut College.

41. Marvis Olive Welch, *Prudence Crandall: A Biography* (Manchester, Conn.: Jason, 1983), 178.

42. Rena Keith Clisby to Helen Earle Sellers, June 3, 1948, Prudence Crandall Collection, Charles E. Shain Library, Connecticut College.

43. Clisby, *Canterbury Pilgrims*, 36.

44. Henry Mayer, *All on Fire: William Lloyd Garrison and the Abolition of Slavery* (New York: St. Martin's Press, 1998), 621.

45. William Lloyd Garrison, *Helen Eliza Garrison: A Memorial* (Cambridge, Mass: Riverside Press, 1876), 33.

46. Ibid., 53.

47. Ibid., 18.

48. Ibid., 13.

49. Ibid., 14.

50. Ibid., 15.

51. Welch, *Prudence Crandall*, 180.

52. Clisby, *Canterbury Pilgrims*, 34.

53. Ibid.

54. Nicholas Guyatt, *Providence and the Invention of the United States, 1607–1876* (New York: Cambridge University Press, 2007), 323.

55. Garrison to Wendell Phillips Garrison, July 21, 1876, in *The Letters of William Lloyd Garrison: To Rouse the Slumbering Land, 1868–1879*, vol. 6, eds. Walter M. Merrill and Louis Ruchames (Cambridge, Mass.: Harvard University Press, 1981), 410–411.

56. Harriet Hyman Alonso, *Growing Up Abolitionist: The Story of the Garrison Children* (Amherst, Mass.: University of Massachusetts Press, 2002), 271.

57. Ibid., 272–273.

58. Garrison to William E. Chandler, January 21, 1878, in Merrill and Ruchames, *The Letters of William Lloyd Garrison*, 6:501–502.

59. Welch, *Prudence Crandall*, 180–181.

60. Clisby, *Canterbury Pilgrims*, 34.

61. Ibid.

62. Ibid.

63. Prudence Crandall Philleo to Huldah Webster, November 1, 1877, Prudence Crandall Collection, Charles E. Shain Library, Connecticut College.

64. Ibid.

65. Ibid.

66. Ibid.

67. Prudence Crandall Philleo to Sarah Fayerweather, July 26, 1871, University of Rhode Island Library, Special Collections, Fayerweather Family Papers.

68. Ibid.

69. Ibid.

70. Frank W. Blackmar, ed., *Kansas: A Cyclopedia of State History, Embracing Events, Institutions, Industries, Counties, Cities, Towns, Prominent Persons, Etc.*, vol. 2 (Chicago: Standard, 1912), 574.

71. Clisby, *Canterbury Pilgrims*, 34–35.

72. Ibid., 34.

73. Carl R. Woodward, "A Profile in Dedication: Sarah Harris and the Fayerweather Family," *New England Galaxy* 15, no. 1 (Summer 1973): 13.

74. Clisby, *Canterbury Pilgrims*, 34–35.

75. Prudence Crandall Philleo to Mary E. Fayerweather, March 23, 1879, University of Rhode Island Library, Special Collections, Fayerweather Family Papers.

76. *New York Times*, August 20, 1879.

77. Seth Hunt, "Charles C. Burleigh," in *The History of Florence, Massachusetts, Including a Complete Account of the Northampton Association of Education and Industry*, ed. Charles Arthur Sheffeld (Florence, Mass.: Charles Arthur Sheffeld, 1894), 211.

78. Ibid., 213.

79. Garrison to Fanny Garrison Villard, June 14, 1878, in Merrill and Ruchames, *The Letters of William Lloyd Garrison*, 6:521.

80. Wendell Phillips Garrison and Francis Jackson Garrison, *William Lloyd Garrison, 1805–1879: The Story of His Life Told by His Children*, vol. 4 (New York: Century, 1889), 289.

81. Ibid., 290.

82. Ibid.

83. Ibid., 292. George C. Rand said that as an apprentice, he helped to print and distribute the flyers. The George C. Rand and Avery Company later contracted with the publishing house of John P. Jewett to print the first edition of Harriet Beecher Stowe's *Uncle Tom's Cabin*.

84. Ibid., 291, 292.

85. Garrison to Fanny Garrison Villard, February 20, 1879, in Merrill and Ruchames, *The Letters of William Lloyd Garrison*, 6:561–562.

86. Garrison to the editor of the *New York Tribune*, February 15, 1879, in Merrill and Ruchames, *The Letters of William Lloyd Garrison*, 6:559.

87. Garrison to Fanny Garrison Villard, February 20, 1879, in Merrill and Ruchames, *The Letters of William Lloyd Garrison*, 6:559.

88. Garrison to A. J. Grover of Chicago, March 7, 1879, in Wendell and Francis Garrison, *William Lloyd Garrison*, 4:301. Grover was the chairman of the executive committee of the National Greenback and Labor Party of Illinois. See the *New York Times*, May 31, 1878.

89. Prudence Crandall Philleo to William Lloyd Garrison, March 20, 1879, in Welch, *Prudence Crandall*, 187.

90. Ibid.

91. Ibid., 188.

92. William Lloyd Garrison to Prudence Crandall (transcript of letter), Boston, March 25, 1879, Anti-Slavery Collection, Boston Public Library.

93. Ibid.

94. Prudence Crandall Philleo to William Lloyd Garrison, April 20, 1879, in Welch, *Prudence Crandall*, 187. Crandall would have read the references to her included in Garrison's memorial to Helen.

95. Ibid.

96. Ibid., 189.

97. William Lloyd Garrison to Maria W. Stewart, April 4, 1879, in *Maria W. Stewart, America's First Black Woman Political Writer: Essays and Speeches*, ed. Marilyn Richardson (Bloomington: Indiana University Press, 1987), 89.

98. Ibid., 90.

99. Ibid., 89.

100. Ibid.

101. Ibid., 90.

102. Ibid., 94; Alexander Crummell said that Stewart was encouraged "especially by William Lloyd Garrison" to republish her essays.

103. Ibid., 87.

104. Garrison to Fanny Garrison Villard, February 20, 1877, in Merrill and Ruchames, *The Letters of William Lloyd Garrison*, 6:561.

105. Ibid., 569–570. Garrison to Fanny Garrison Villard, March 19, 1879.

106. Ibid., 575. Garrison to the editor of the *Boston Journal*, April 17, 1879.

107. Ibid.

108. Ibid., 579–580. Garrison to Robert Morris, April 22, 1879.

109. Prudence Crandall Philleo to William Lloyd Garrison, April 20, 1879, in Welch, *Prudence Crandall*, 189.

110. Ibid.

111. Mayer, *All on Fire*, 624.

112. Wendell and Francis Garrison, *William Lloyd Garrison*, 4:305.

113. Carolyn L. Karcher, *The First Woman in the Republic: A Cultural Biography of Lydia Maria Child* (Durham, N.C.: Duke University Press, 1994), 600.

114. John Greenleaf Whittier and James Russell Lowell, eds., *Tributes to William Lloyd Garrison at the Funeral Services, May 28, 1879* (Boston: Houghton, Osgood, 1879), 29.

115. Ibid., 32.

116. Ibid., 23.

117. Frederick Douglass, "Speech at the Death of William Lloyd Garrison," June 2, 1879, 5, Frederick Douglass Papers, U.S. Library of Congress. Douglass spoke at the Garrison memorial meeting at the Fifteenth Street Presbyterian Church in Washington, D.C.

118. Ibid., 3.

119. Ibid., 5.

120. Ibid., 6.

121. Ibid., 6–7.

17. PURSUIT OF JUSTICE

1. Prudence Crandall to Huldah Webster, November 1, 1877, Prudence Crandall Collection, Charles E. Shain Library, Connecticut College.

2. Bruce E. Johansen, *The Native Peoples of North America: A History*, vol. 1 (New Brunswick, N.J.: Rutgers University Press, 2006), 251–252; Mari Sandoz, *The Buffalo Hunters: The Story of the Hide Men* (Lincoln: University of Nebraska Press, 1954), 35.

3. Evan S. Connell, *Son of the Morning Star: Custer and the Little Bighorn* (San Francisco: North Point Press, 1984), 136.

4. Joanna L. Stratton, *Pioneer Women: Voices from the Kansas Frontier* (New York: Simon and Schuster, 1982), 118.

5. Sheridan Ploughe, *History of Reno County, Kansas: Its People, Industries and Institutions*, vol. 1 (Indianapolis: B. F. Bowen, 1917), 64.

6. Ibid.

7. Prudence Crandall Philleo to grandniece Josephine Crandall, July 25 and 28, 1880, Prudence Crandall Collection, Charles E. Shain Library, Connecticut College.

8. Ibid.

9. Ibid.

10. Ibid.

11. Rena Keith Clisby, *Canterbury Pilgrims* (n.p., 1947), 35, Prudence Crandall Collection, Charles E. Shain Library, Connecticut College.

12. Rena Keith Clisby, "Personal Memoir of Rena Keith Clisby Written for Her Son Keith" (n.p., n.d.), describing her life, including her time in Elk Falls with her mother Clarissa, Kansas State Historical Society, Topeka, Kansas.

13. Ibid.

14. Prudence Crandall Philleo to grandniece Josephine Crandall, July 25 and 28, 1880.

15. Clisby, *Canterbury Pilgrims*, 34.

16. Ibid.

17. Marilyn Richardson, ed., *Maria W. Stewart, America's First Black Woman Political Writer: Essays and Speeches* (Bloomington: Indiana University Press, 1987), 24–26.

18. *People's Advocate*, February 28, 1880. Stewart was buried in Graceland Cemetery.

19. *Hartford Daily Courant*, December 21, 1880, reprinting an article from the *Windham County Transcript* by H. L. Read of Lisbon, Connecticut.

20. Ibid.

21. Ibid.

22. "Prudence Crandall and Her School: A Paper Read before the Rhode Island Historical Society, December 28, 1880, by Abraham Payne," in *Windham County Standard*, May 12, 1886.

23. Ibid.

24. Prudence Crandall Philleo to grandniece Josephine Crandall, July 25 and 28, 1880.

25. Ibid.

26. "In Other Perils—The Snow Blockade," *Presbyterian Monthly Record* 32, no. 4 (April 1881): 111.

27. Prudence Crandall Philleo to Esther and Huldah Crandall (Prudence's nieces and daughters of Hezekiah), April 12, 1881, Prudence Crandall Collection, Charles E. Shain Library, Connecticut College.

28. Prudence Crandall Philleo to the editor, May 25, 1881, in *Providence Morning Star*, June 6, 1881.

29. Clisby, *Canterbury Pilgrims*, 36.

30. *Providence Morning Star*, June 6, 1881.

31. Prudence Crandall Philleo to grandniece Josephine Crandall, July 25 and 28, 1880.

32. D. H. Van Hoosear, *The Fillo, Philo and Philleo Geneaology: A Record of the Descendants of John Fillow, a Huguenot Refugee from France* (Albany, N.Y.: Joel Munsell's Sons, 1888), 68.

33. Emma A. McClearn to Helen Earle Sellers, May 23, 1948, Prudence Crandall Collection, Charles E. Shain Library, Connecticut College.

34. Marvis Olive Welch, *Prudence Crandall: A Biography* (Manchester, Conn.: Jason, 1983), 198; Susan Strane, *A Whole Souled Woman: Prudence Crandall and the Education of Black Women* (New York: W. W. Norton, 1990), 212.

35. Welch, *Prudence Crandall*, 198; Strane, *A Whole Souled Woman*, 213–214.

36. Susan B. Anthony and Ida Husted Harper, eds., *The History of Woman Suffrage*, vol. 4 (Rochester, N.Y.: Susan B. Anthony, 1902), 416.

37. Benjamin O. Flower, ed., *The Arena*, vol. 11 (Boston: Arena Publishing, 1895), 361.

38. Mariana T. Folsom to the editor, *Woman's Journal*, September 2, 1884.

39. Ibid.

40. Ibid.

41. *Friends' Intelligencer*, December 25, 1886.

42. Ibid.

43. Prudence Crandall Philleo to grandniece Josephine Crandall, July 25 and 28, 1880.

44. Emma A. McClearn to Helen Earle Sellers, May 23, 1948.

45. Ibid.

46. Clisby, *Canterbury Pilgrims*, 34.

47. Prudence Crandall Philleo to grandniece Josephine Crandall, July 25 and 28, 1880.

48. Emma A. McClearn to Helen Earle Sellers, May 23, 1948.

49. Ibid.

50. Ibid.

51. Prudence Crandall Philleo to grandniece Josephine Crandall, July 25 and 28, 1880.

52. Wendell Phillips Garrison, "Connecticut in the Middle Ages," *Century Magazine* 30, no. 5 (September 1885): 780.

53. Ibid.

54. John W. Leonard, ed., *Who's Who in America, 1899–1900* (Chicago: A. N. Marquis, 1899), 544.

55. *Northern Christian Advocate* 47, no. 49 (December 8, 1887): 6.

56. Ibid.

57. Donald F. Nelson, *To the Stars: Over Rough Roads: The Life of Andrew Atchison, Teacher and Missionary* (Cambridge, Mass: TidePool Press, 2008), 32, 34. The school initially was named the Dunlap Academy and Mission School and was located in Dunlap, Kansas.

58. Ibid., 32.

59. Ibid., 35; *Graduate Magazine of the University of Kansas* 7, no. 7 (April 1909): 270. Canfield originally was from Ohio and later served as chancellor of the University of Nebraska and president of Ohio State University, before ending his career at Columbia University.

60. *Topeka Daily Capital*, October 18, 1885; see Welch, *Prudence Crandall*, 202.

61. Welch, *Prudence Crandall*, 202.

62. Ibid.

63. Richard M. Bayles, *History of Windham County, Connecticut* (New York: W. W. Preston, 1889), 1092.

64. See Prudence Crandall Philleo to John S. Smith, November 3, 1885 and January 30, 1886, Prudence Crandall Collection, Charles E. Shain Library, Connecticut College. Both letters make reference to "Artie," a person who visited Crandall. Crandall told Smith that Artie "is closely confined to his office. I presume you know more about his business than I do."

65. Prudence Crandall Philleo to John S. Smith, November 3, 1885.

66. Prudence Crandall Philleo to John S. Smith, December 2, 1885, Prudence Crandall Collection, Charles E. Shain Library, Connecticut College.

67. Ibid.

68. Prudence Crandall Philleo to John S. Smith, January 30, 1886.

69. Prudence Crandall Philleo to John S. Smith, December 2, 1885.

70. Prudence Crandall Philleo to John S. Smith, November 3, 1885.

71. Ibid.

72. Ibid.

73. Connecticut State Legislature, House Petition No. 48, January Session, 1886, Connecticut State Library, Hartford, Connecticut; see Welch, *Prudence Crandall*, 205.

74. "Prudence Crandall," *Hartford Daily Courant*, January 21, 1886.

75. "State Press," *Hartford Daily Courant*, January 25, 1886, reprinting article from the *New Haven News*.

76. *Boston Journal*, March 11, 1886; *Dallas Morning News*, April 3, 1886; *San Francisco Bulletin*, February 5, 1886; *Cincinnati Commercial Tribune*, January 31, 1886; *Kansas City Times*, June 11, 1886.

77. "Prudence Crandall: A Hearing on the Bill for Her Relief Yesterday," *Hartford Daily Courant*, February 4, 1886.

78. Ibid.; Dwight Loomis and Joseph Gilbert Calhoun, *The Judicial and Civil History of Connecticut* (Boston: Boston History Company, 1895), 318.

79. Prudence Crandall Philleo to John S. Smith, January 30, 1886.

80. Prudence Crandall Philleo to Samuel Coit, February 9, 1886, in the *Hartford Daily Courant*, February 17, 1886.

81. "Prudence Crandall," *Hartford Daily Courant*, February 17, 1886.

82. Ibid.

83. Ibid.

84. Albert Bigelow Paine, ed., *Mark Twain's Letters*, vol. 2 (New York: Harper and Brothers, 1917), 465.

85. Prudence Crandall Philleo to "Sir" (most likely Stephen A. Hubbard), February 22, 1886, in "The Case of Prudence Crandall," *Hartford Daily Courant*, March 5, 1886.

86. Ibid.

87. John Hooker to editor, March 11, 1886, in *Hartford Daily Courant*, March 12, 1886.

88. Ibid.

89. John C. Kimball, *Connecticut's Canterbury Tale: Its Heroine Prudence Crandall and Its Moral for Today* (Hartford: Plimpton Press, 1886), 14.

90. "The Case of Prudence Crandall," *Hartford Daily Courant*, March 5, 1886.

91. Ibid. See Henry Wilson, *History of the Rise and Fall of the Slave Power in America*, vol. 1 (Boston: James R. Osgood, 1875), 246–247.

92. *Hartford Daily Courant*, March 5, 1886.

93. Ibid.

94. "Prudence Crandall, Her Claims on the State, Opinions of the Press," *Hartford Daily Courant*, March 10, 1886.

95. "Current Comment," *Hartford Daily Courant*, March 8, 1886, quoting the *Providence Journal*.

96. *Hartford Daily Courant*, March 10, 1886.

97. Ibid.

98. Ibid.

99. "What Connecticut Should Do," *Worcester Spy*, reprinted in the *Hartford Daily Courant*, March 18, 1886.

100. "Prudence Crandall, More Press Comments," *Hartford Daily Courant*, March 12, 1886.

101. Prudence Crandall Philleo to Isabella Mitchell, March 14, 1866, University of Rhode Island Library, Special Collections, Fayerweather Family Papers.

102. *Kansas City Times*, June 11, 1886.

103. Ibid.

104. "Prudence Crandall Philleo," *Hartford Daily Courant*, March 30, 1886.

105. "It Was a Pull Altogether," *New Haven Register*, reprinted in "Prudence Crandall, The Law of Equity," *Hartford Daily Courant*, March 13, 1886.

106. *Kansas City Journal*, March 28, 1886.

107. Ibid.

108. Ibid.

109. "Legislative Notes," *Hartford Daily Courant*, April 1, 1886.

110. Duane Hamilton Hurd, ed., *History of New London County, Connecticut* (Philadelphia: J. W. Lewis, 1882), 54; "Obituary of James A. Hovey," 66 Conn. 603 (1895).

111. Prudence Crandall Philleo to Ellen Larned, March 21, 1886, Connecticut State Library, Hartford, Connecticut.

112. Ibid.

113. Prudence Crandall Philleo to Ellen Larned, April 1 through 2, 1886, Connecticut State Library, Hartford, Connecticut. True to her word, in addition to the thank-you note, Crandall enclosed fifty cents' worth of stamps as payment to Larned for the books.

114. *Hartford Daily Courant*, April 3, 1866; "Prudence Crandall," *Connecticut Magazine* 5, no. 7 (July 1899): 386.

115. "A Touching Letter from Prudence Crandall," *Hartford Daily Courant*, April 9, 1886.

116. *New Haven Register*, March 31, 1886.

117. "Prudence Crandall: The Liberal Offer of Mr. Clemens," *Hartford Daily Courant*, April 3, 1886.

118. Ibid.

119. Prudence Crandall Philleo to Mark Twain, April 14, 1886, Mark Twain Papers, Bancroft Library, University of California at Berkeley.

120. Ibid.

121. Prudence Crandall Philleo to Mark Twain, May 19, 1886, Mark Twain Papers, Bancroft Library, University of California at Berkeley.

122. "A Touching Letter from Prudence Crandall," *Hartford Daily Courant*, April 9, 1886. The article was unsigned, but it was most likely written by Stephen A. Hubbard, who had taken the greatest interest at the *Courant* in Prudence Crandall's case. Hub-

bard served continuously as managing editor of the *Courant* for twenty-three years, beginning in 1867. While editing the *Courant*, he served twice in the state legislature. Hubbard died of a heart attack fours years after Crandall's relief was approved, in 1890. He was sixty-three. See "Obituary: Stephen A. Hubbard," *Hartford Courant*, January 13, 1890; "Obituary: Stephen A. Hubbard," *New York Times*, January 12, 1890.

123. See generally, Renee Stowitzky, "Helen Gougar Biographical Essay" (2006), Women's Legal History Biography Project, Robert Crown Law Library, Stanford University.

124. Elizabeth Cady Stanton, Susan B. Anthony, Matilda Joslyn Gage, and Ida Husted Harper, eds., *History of Woman Suffrage: 1876–1885*, vol. 3 (Rochester, N.Y.: Susan B. Anthony, 1886), 709.

125. Micheal L. Goldberg, *An Army of Women: Gender and Politics in Gilded Age Kansas* (Baltimore: John Hopkins University Press, 1997), 86, 88; "Women with the Ballot: The Experiment in Progress in Kansas," *New York Times*, April 8, 1889; Noble Lovely Prentis, *A History of Kansas* (Winfield, Kans.: E. P. Greer, 1899), 177. Gouger obtained her law degree in 1895; she argued a case before the Indiana State Supreme Court contending that a woman's right to vote was required by the state constitution. The Court did not agree, but Gouger's arguments were vindicated years later. See *Gougar v. Timberlake*, 148 Ind. 38 (1897).

126. *Daily Inter Ocean* 15, no. 311 (January 29, 1887): 2.

127. Ibid.; see also "Prudence Crandall: The Woman Who Was Persecuted for Teaching Colored People," *Kansas City Star*, February 2, 1887. Gougar was a journalist; she owned and edited the *Our Herald* newspaper. In 1885 she sold the paper to a woman who merged *Our Herald* with the Chicago-based *Inter Ocean*.

128. *Daily Inter Ocean* 15, no. 311 (January 29, 1887): 2.

129. Welch, *Prudence Crandall*, 209.

130. See generally, George B. Thayer, *Pedal and Path, Across the Continent Awheel and Afoot* (Hartford: Evening Post Association, 1887).

131. Ibid., 211.

132. Ibid., 210–211.

133. Ibid., 212.

134. Ibid.

135. Ibid., 213.

136. Ibid.

137. Ibid.

138. Ibid.

139. Ibid., 214.

140. Ibid., 214–215.

141. Welch, *Prudence Crandall*, 209.

142. "Prudence Crandall Philleo, Funeral Address Delivered by the Rev. Chas. L. McKesson," *Moline Republican*, February 7, 1890.

143. Ibid.

144. *Moline Republican*, February 7, 1890.

145. Ibid.

146. Ibid.

147. Frank Gérard Clemow, *The Geography of Disease* (Cambridge, U.K.: University Press, 1903), 200.

148. *The Journal of the Kansas Medical Society* 18, no. 10 (October 1918): 250.

149. Geoffrey L. Zubay, *Agents of Bioterrorism: Pathogens and Their Weaponization* (New York: Columbia University Press, 2005), 80.

150. *Moline Republican*, February 7, 1890.

151. Ibid.

152. Ibid.

153. C. W. Moulton to Prudence Crandall Philleo, November 2, 1889, Kansas State Historical Society, Topeka, Kansas.

154. Ibid.

155. Clisby, *Canterbury Pilgrims*, 37.

156. Ibid.

157. "Obituary: Prudence Crandall," *New York Times*, January 30, 1890; "Prudence Crandall Philleo: Her Death from the Grip—How Her Pension Was Secured," *Hartford Courant*, January 29, 1890; *Moline Republican*, February 7, 1890.

158. Ibid.

159. Ibid.

160. "Prudence Crandall," *Hartford Daily Courant*, March 30, 1886.

18. PRUDENCE CRANDALL IN THE TWENTIETH CENTURY

1. *Bridgeport Herald*, November 26, 1911. The legislators were Thomas O. Elliott of Pomfret, Charles S. Hyde of Canterbury, and Caleb T. Bishop of Plainfield.

2. *Hartford Courant*, February 10, 1911.

3. *Hartford Courant*, August 9, 1911.

4. *Waterbury Herald*, February 20, 1916.

5. Many years later this oversight was addressed. Crandall was designated the Connecticut State Heroine in 1995. In 2008 a statue of Crandall and a black student was unveiled at the state capitol in Hartford, the result of a campaign by schoolchildren and State Representative Elizabeth Boukus.

6. Hannibal Gerald Duncan, *The Changing Race Relationship in the Border and Northern States* (Philadelphia: University of Pennsylvania Press, 1922), 57.

7. Alexander Tsesis, *We Shall Overcome: A History of Civil Rights and the Law* (New Haven, Conn.: Yale University Press, 2008), 126.

8. Ibid.

9. Evelyn L. Wilson, *Laws, Customs and Rights: Charles Hatfield and His Family: A Louisiana History* (Westminster, Md.: Willow Bend Books, 2008), 90.

10. *Plessy v. Ferguson*, 163 U.S. 537, 544 (1896).

11. Ibid., 551.

12. Loren P. Beth, *John Marshall Harlan: The Last Whig Justice* (Lexington: University Press of Kentucky, 1992), 11, 75.

13. *Plessy v. Ferguson*, 163 U.S. 537, 559 (1896).

14. "Sheats as an Educator," *Congregationalist*, September 19, 1895.

15. Ibid.; see also James M. McPherson, *The Abolitionist Legacy: From Reconstruction to the NAACP* (Princeton: Princeton University Press, 1975), 226.

16. *Charlotte Observer*, March 7, 1912.

17. *Macon Telegraph*, August 17, 1887.

18. Paul Alan Cimbala and Randall M. Miller, eds., *Union Soldiers and the Northern Home Front: Wartime Experiences, Postwar Adjustments* (New York: Fordham University Press, 2002), 446–447.

19. Ibid., 443.

20. David W. Blight, *Race and Reunion: The Civil War in American Memory* (Cambridge, Mass.: Harvard University Press, 2001), 9.

21. Lewis E. Beitler, ed., *Fiftieth Anniversary of the Battle of Gettysburg: Report of the Pennsylvania Commission* (Harrisburg: State of Pennsylvania, 1913), 102.

22. Ibid., 125.

23. Ibid.

24. Ibid., 125–126.

25. "Pickett's Charge is Re-enacted at Gettysburg," *Hartford Courant*, July 4, 1913.

26. Blight, *Race and Reunion*, 9.

27. Charles W. Mitchell, *Maryland Voices of the Civil War* (Baltimore: John Hopkins University Press, 2007), 474.

28. Blight, *Race and Reunion*, 9.

29. Alfred William Nicholson, *Brief Sketch of the Life and Labors of Rev. Alexander Bettis* (Trenton, S.C.: Alfred William Nicholson, 1913), 44.

30. Catherine Clinton, *Harriet Tubman: The Road to Freedom* (New York: Little, Brown, 2004), 216.

31. Ibid.

32. Eric Foner, *The Story of American Freedom* (New York: W. W. Norton, 1998), 186.

33. John Milton Cooper, Jr., *Reconsidering Woodrow Wilson: Progressivism, Internationalism, War, and Peace* (Baltimore: Johns Hopkins University Press, 2008), 108–111.

34. Arthur Stanley Link, *Wilson: The New Freedom* (Princeton: Princeton University Press, 1956), 247.

35. R. H. Leavell, "What Does the Negro Want: The Answer of the Douglass Public School," *Outlook* (August 20, 1919): 605, 606.

36. *The Crisis* 23, no. 3 (January 1922), 132.

37. Mark V. Tushnet, *Making Civil Rights Law: Thurgood Marshall and the Supreme Court, 1936–1961* (New York: Oxford University Press, 1994), 116–121.

38. Paul E. Wilson, *A Time to Lose: Representing Kansas in Brown v. Board of Education* (Lawrence: University Press of Kansas, 1995), 8.

39. Stephen Kendrick and Paul Kendrick, *Sarah's Long Walk: The Free Blacks of Boston and How Their Struggle for Equality Changed America* (Cambridge, Mass.: Beacon Press, 2004), 165, 166.

40. *Brown, et al. v. Board of Education of Topeka*, 98 F. Supp. 797, 798 (D. Kan. 1951).

41. Ibid.

42. Leon Friedman, ed., *Brown v. Board of Education: The Landmark Oral Argument before the Supreme Court* (New York: New Press, 2004), 36–37.

43. Ibid., 40.

44. *Sweatt v. Painter*, 339 U.S. 629 (1950); *McClaurin v. Oklahoma State Regents*, 339 U.S. 637 (1950).

45. Tushnet, *Making Civil Rights Law*, 172.

46. Juan Williams, *Thurgood Marshall: American Revolutionary* (New York: Times Books, 1998), 201.

47. Tushnet, *Making Civil Rights Law*, 187.

48. Ibid., 191.

49. James T. Patterson, *Brown v. Board of Education: A Civil Rights Milestone and Its Troubled Legacy* (New York: Oxford University Press, 2001), 55.

50. Mark V. Tushnet, *A Court Divided: The Rehnquist Court and the Future of Constitutional Law* (New York: W. W. Norton, 2005), 19.

51. Jack Greenberg, *Crusaders in the Courts* (New York: Basic Books, 1994), 177.

52. Ibid., 178.

53. Graham collaborated on his research in the 1940s with Jacobus tenBroek, professor of political science at the University of California at Berkeley.

54. Howard Jay Graham, "Early Antislavery Backgrounds of the Fourteenth Amendment, Part I, Genesis, 1833–1835," 1950 Wis. L. Rev. 479; Howard Jay Graham, "Early Antislavery Backgrounds of the Fourteenth Amendment, Part II, Systemization, 1835–1837," 1950 Wis. L. Rev. 610.

55. Howard Jay Graham, "The Early Antislavery Backgrounds of the Fourteenth Amendment," 1950 Wis. L. Rev. 479, 505.

56. Patterson, *Brown v. Board of Education: A Civil Rights Milestone and Its Troubled Legacy*, 57. Justice Frankfurter told his clerk, "This is the first indication I have ever had that there is a God."

57. Michal R. Belknap, *The Supreme Court under Earl Warren, 1953–1969* (Columbia, S.C.: University of South Carolina Press, 2005), 4, 6. Warren served as district attorney for Alameda County for fourteen years (1925–1939) and attorney general for California for four years (1938–1942).

58. Greenberg, *Crusaders in the Courts*, 186.

59. Howard Jay Graham, "The Early Antislavery Backgrounds of the Fourteenth Amendment," 1950 Wis. L. Rev. 479, 499.

60. *Brown, et al. v. Board of Education of Topeka*, Brief for Appellants in Nos. 1, 2, and 4, and for Respondents in No. 10 on Reargument, 205 (U.S. Supreme Court, October Term, 1953).

61. Ibid., 208–209.

62. John Hope Franklin, *Mirror to America: The Autobiography of John Hope Franklin* (New York: Hill and Wang, 2005), 157.

63. Greenberg, *Crusaders in the Courts*, 181.

64. Wayne J. Urban, *Black Scholar: Horace Mann Bond, 1904–1972* (Athens: University of Georgia Press, 1992), 172.

65. Howard Jay Graham, *Everyman's Constitution: Historical Essays on the Fourteenth Amendment, the "Conspiracy Theory," and American Constitutionalism* (Madison: State Historical Society of Wisconsin, 1968), 270–271, reprinting Graham's article "The Fourteenth Amendment and School Segregation," 3 Buffalo Law Review (Winter 1953), 1.

66. Graham, *Everyman's Constitution*, 585.

67. Ibid., 291–292.

68. Tushnet, *Making Civil Rights Law*, 199.

69. Mark Whitman, *Removing a Badge of Slavery: The Record of Brown v. Board of Education* (Princeton, N.J.: Markus Wiener Publishing, 1993), 227; reprinting "An Inside View of *Brown v. Board of Education*," an address by Alfred Kelly to the American Historical Association, Washington, D.C., December 28, 1961.

70. Tushnet, *Making Civil Rights Law*, 198.

71. Whitman, *Removing a Badge of Slavery*, 227. Alfred Kelly also gave credit to attorney John P. Frank, who assisted the NAACP in the *Brown* case—Kelly referred to "what I shall call the Graham-Frank theory of the amendment." Frank later represented Ernesto Miranda, resulting in the "Miranda rights" U.S. Supreme Court ruling.

72. Ibid.

73. Friedman, *Brown v. Board of Education: The Landmark Oral Argument*, 193.

74. Ibid., 203.

75. Friedman, *Brown v. Board of Education: The Landmark Oral Argument*, 215.

76. Ibid., 216.

77. Ibid., 236.

78. Whitman, *Removing a Badge of Slavery*, 280.

79. Ibid.

80. David Laurence Faigman, *Laboratory of Justice: The Supreme Court's 200-Year Struggle to Integrate Science and the Law* (New York: Times Books, Henry Holt, 2004), 195.

81. Patterson, *Brown v. Board of Education: A Civil Rights Milestone and Its Troubled Legacy*, 55.

82. *Brown v. Board of Education*, 347 U.S. 483, 493 (1954).

83. Ibid., 489, 492.

84. Ibid., 493.

85. Ibid., 495.

86. Mark Whitman, *Removing a Badge of Slavery*, 285; Patterson, *Brown v. Board of Education: A Civil Rights Milestone and Its Troubled Legacy*, 68.

87. *New Haven Register*, January 30, 1890.

88. Martin Luther King, Jr., "Address at the Thirty-Fourth Annual Convention of the National Bar Association, August 20, 1959," in *The Papers of Martin Luther King, Jr.*, vol. 5, ed. Clayborne Carson (Berkeley: University of California Press, 2005), 267.

EPILOGUE

Epilogue epigraphs: Frederick Douglass, "Speech on the Death of William Lloyd Garrison," June 2, 1879, 2, Frederick Douglass Papers, U.S. Library of Congress; Juan Williams, *Thurgood Marshall: American Revolutionary* (New York: Times Books, 1998), 229; Lewis F. Powell, Jr., "Stare Decisis and Judicial Restraint," *New York State Bar Journal* 62, no. 5 (July 1990): 18, 21; Lydia Maria Child, "William Lloyd Garrison," *Atlantic Monthly* 44 (August 1879): 237–238; Jonathan Kozol, *Savage Inequalities: Children in America's Schools* (New York: Crown Publishers, 1991), 3–4; William Henry Burleigh and Celia Burleigh, *Poems* (Boston: Riverside Press, 1871), x–xi; James Anderson and Dara N. Byrne, eds., *The Unfinished Agenda of Brown v. Board of Education* (Hoboken, N.J.: John Wiley and Sons, 2004), 168; Vincent Harding, "Toward a Darkly Radiant Vision of America's Truth: A Letter of Concern, An Invitation of Recreation," in *Community in America: The Challenge of Habits of the Heart*, ed. Charles H. Reynolds (Berkeley: University of California Press, 1988), 79–80.

ILLUSTRATION CREDITS

1 Prudence Crandall. Oil portrait by Francis Alexander, April 1834, #6953. Courtesy of the Division of Rare and Manuscript Collections, Cornell University Library.

2 Slave purchase flyer, Charleston, South Carolina, 1835. Library of Congress.

3 *The Parting*, Henry Louis Stephens, 1863. Library of Congress.

4 *The Lash*, Henry Louis Stephens, 1863. Library of Congress.

5 Hezekiah Carpenter House, Prudence Crandall's birthplace, in Hope Valley, Rhode Island. Photo by author.

6 Hezekiah Crandall, brother of Prudence. Collection of the Prudence Crandall Museum, Connecticut Department of Economic and Community Development, State of Connecticut.

7 Esther Carpenter Crandall, mother of Prudence Crandall. Collection of the Prudence Crandall Museum, Connecticut Department of Economic and Community Development, State of Connecticut.

8 Prudence Crandall's School in Canterbury, Connecticut. Collection of the Prudence Crandall Museum, Connecticut Department of Economic and Community Development, State of Connecticut. Photographer: Dennis Oparowski.

9 *Canterbury, Connecticut, in the 1830s*. From John Warner Barber, *Connecticut Historical Collections* (New Haven, Conn.: B. L. Hamlen, 1836), 423. Collection of the Prudence Crandall Museum, Connecticut Department of Economic and Community Development, State of Connecticut.

10 Unitarian Church of Brooklyn, Connecticut. Library of Congress.

11 Canterbury Congregational Church. Collection of the Prudence Crandall Museum, Connecticut Department of Economic and Community Development, State of Connecticut.

12 Packerville Baptist Church, Plainfield, Connecticut. Collection of the Prudence Crandall Museum, Connecticut Department of Economic and Community Development, State of Connecticut.

13 William Lloyd Garrison. Courtesy of the Metropolitan Museum of Art. Gift of I. N. Phelps Stokes, Edward S. Hawes, Alice Mary Hawes, and Marion Augusta Hawes, 1937 (37.14.37). Image © The Metropolitan Museum of Art.

14 Helen Benson Garrison. Collection of the Prudence Crandall Museum, Connecticut Department of Economic and Community Development, State of Connecticut.

15 Arnold Buffum. From Wendell Phillips Garrison and Francis Jackson Garrison, *William Lloyd Garrison, 1805–1879: The Story of His Life Told by His Children*, vol. 1 (New York: Century, 1885), 430.

16 Samuel Joseph May. From Wendell Phillips Garrison and Francis Jackson Garrison, *William Lloyd Garrison, 1805–1879: The Story of His Life Told by His Children*, vol. 1 (New York: Century, 1885), 466.

17 Charles C. Burleigh. From Wendell Phillips Garrison and Francis Jackson Garrison, *William Lloyd Garrison, 1805–1879: The Story of His Life Told by His Children*, vol. 3 (New York: Century, 1885), 226.

18 Harris family sampler. Courtesy of the Collection of Glee Krueger.

19 William H. Burleigh. From William H. Burleigh and Celia Burleigh, *Poems by William H. Burleigh with a Sketch of His Life by Celia Burleigh* (New York: Hurd and Houghton, 1871), frontispiece.

20 Arthur Tappan. From Wendell Phillips Garrison and Francis Jackson Garrison, *William Lloyd Garrison, 1805–1879: The Story of His Life Told by His Children*, vol. 1 (New York: Century, 1885), 190.

21 County Courthouse, Brooklyn, Connecticut (later converted to the Brooklyn Town Hall). Library of Congress.

22 Chauncey Cleveland. From Frederick Calvin Norton, *The Governors of Connecticut* (Hartford: Connecticut Magazine, 1905), 188. Courtesy of the Connecticut State Library, State Archives.

23 Andrew T. Judson. Collection of the Prudence Crandall Museum, Connecticut Department of Economic and Community Development.

24 Calvin Goddard. Courtesy of the City of Norwich, Connecticut.

25 William W. Ellsworth. From Frederick Calvin Norton, *The Governors of Connecticut* (Hartford: Connecticut Magazine, 1905), 182. Courtesy of the Connecticut State Library, State Archives.

26 Henry Strong. From Dwight Loomis and J. Gilbert Calhoun, *The Judicial and Civil History of Connecticut* (Boston: Boston History Company, 1895), 510.

27 Thomas S. Williams. From Dwight Loomis and J. Gilbert Calhoun, *The Judicial and Civil History of Connecticut* (Boston: Boston History Company, 1895), 36.

28 David Daggett. Oil portrait by Jared Bradley Flagg. Courtesy of the Yale Law School.

29 Samuel Church. Courtesy of the Connecticut State Library, State Archives.

30 Clark Bissell. Courtesy of the Connecticut State Library, State Archives.

31 *Colored Scholars Excluded from Schools.* From *American Anti-Slavery Almanac for 1839* 1, no. 4 (Boston: Isaac Knapp, 1839), 13.

32 *Colored Schools Broken Up in the Free States.* From *American Anti-Slavery Almanac for 1839* 1, no. 4 (Boston: Isaac Knapp, 1839), 15.

33 Lydia Maria Child. Engraving based on the 1826 oil portrait by Francis Alexander in the possession of the Medford, Massachusetts Historical Society. Library of Congress.

34 Theodore Dwight Weld. From Wendell Phillips Garrison and Francis Jackson Garrison, *William Lloyd Garrison, 1805–1879: The Story of His Life Told by His Children*, vol. 2 (New York: Century, 1885), 116.

35 Crandall homestead in Troy Grove, Illinois. Collection of the Prudence Crandall Museum, Connecticut Department of Economic and Community Development, State of Connecticut.

36 U.S. Senator Charles Sumner. From James E. McClees, *McClees' Gallery of Photographic Portraits of the Senators, Representatives and Delegates of the Thirty-Fifth Congress* (Washington, D.C.: McClees and Beck, 1859), 20. Library of Congress.

37 Dred Scott. From John G. Nicolay and John Hay, "Abraham Lincoln, a History: The Attack on Sumner and the Dred Scott Case," *Century Magazine* (June 1887), 208. Library of Congress.

38 U.S. Supreme Court Chief Justice Roger Taney. Library of Congress.

39 Advertisement for reprints of Taney's *Dred Scott* decision. *Harper's Weekly* 3, no. 134 (July 23, 1859): 479. Library of Congress.

40 William Lloyd Garrison and sons Wendell, Francis, William Lloyd II, and George. From Prudence Crandall's personal collection of photographs. Collection of the Prudence Crandall Museum, Connecticut Department of Economic and Community Development, State of Connecticut.

41 The Fifty-fifth Massachusetts Volunteer Negro Regiment. *Harper's Weekly* 9, no. 429 (March 18, 1865), 165. Library of Congress.

42 Sarah Harris Fayerweather. From Prudence Crandall's personal collection of photographs. Collection of the Prudence Crandall Museum, Connecticut Department of Economic and Community Development, State of Connecticut.

43 Prudence Crandall in Elk Falls. Collection of the Prudence Crandall Museum, Connecticut Department of Economic and Community Development, State of Connecticut.

44 Gristmill at Elk Falls, Kansas, late nineteenth century. Courtesy of the collection of Steven Fry.

45 Reporter's sketch of Prudence Crandall's farmhouse, Elk Falls, Kansas. *Kansas City Journal*, March 28, 1886.

46 The Elk Falls business district at the time Prudence Crandall lived in Kansas. Courtesy of the collection of Steven Fry.

47 Engraving of Prudence Crandall based on Francis Alexander's 1834 painting. From Wendell Phillips Garrison, "Connecticut in the Middle Ages," *Century Magazine* (October 1885), 781. The engraving also appeared in Wendell Phillips Garrison and Francis Jackson Garrison, *William Lloyd Garrison, 1805–1879: The Story of His Life Told by His Children*, vol. 1 (New York: Century, 1885), 316.

48 Stephen A. Hubbard. From Prudence Crandall's personal collection of photographs. Collection of the Prudence Crandall Museum, Connecticut Department of Economic and Community Development, State of Connecticut.

49 Ellen Larned. From Richard M. Bayles, *The History of Windham County, Connecticut* (New York: W. W. Preston, 1889), 714.

50 State Representative Thomas G. Clarke of Canterbury. From Prudence

Crandall's personal collection of photographs. Collection of the Prudence Crandall Museum, Connecticut Department of Economic and Community Development, State of Connecticut.

51 Samuel Coit. From Prudence Crandall's personal collection of photographs. Collection of the Prudence Crandall Museum, Connecticut Department of Economic and Community Development, State of Connecticut.

52 Samuel Clemens, a.k.a., Mark Twain. From Prudence Crandall's personal collection of photographs. Collection of the Prudence Crandall Museum, Connecticut Department of Economic and Community Development, State of Connecticut.

53 Rena and Lucy Keith, nieces of Prudence Crandall, as they appeared in 1924. Collection of the Prudence Crandall Museum, Connecticut Department of Economic and Community Development, State of Connecticut.

54 Prudence Crandall, Elk Falls. Photograph by William Haddock, 1882. Collection of the Prudence Crandall Museum, Connecticut Department of Economic and Community Development, State of Connecticut.

55 Prudence Crandall's headstone in the Elk Falls Cemetery. Collection of the Prudence Crandall Museum, Connecticut Department of Economic and Community Development, State of Connecticut.

56 The Civil War reunion of 1913, marking the fiftieth anniversary of the Battle of Gettysburg. Library of Congress.

57 Ku Klux Klan march in Washington, D.C., 1926. Library of Congress.

58 The constitutional scholar Howard Jay Graham. Courtesy of Donald Graham.

59 Thurgood Marshall, the lead counsel for the NAACP's Legal Defense Fund in *Brown v. Board of Education*. Library of Congress.

60 The United States Supreme Court on December 14, 1953. Collection of the Supreme Court of the United States.

61 Site near Prudence Crandall's Elk Falls homestead. Photo by author.

INDEX

ground and role in, 139–41, 143–45; prosecution case, 141–42; prosecution's preparations, 134–37, 139 *Crandall v. State of Connecticut (appeal to state supreme court)*: appeal procedure, 191–92; and *Brown v. Board of Education*, 339–40; decision and conclusion, 201–2; defense preparation and arguments, 191, 193–96, 198–200; justices of, 192–95, 196, 200–202, 400n40, 400n43, 400n46, 401n49; lack of definitive settlement on Black Law, 223; post-appeal debate, 202–3; prosecution arguments, 196–98
Crummell, Alexander, 227, 308–9
Cutler, Asa, 262

Daggett, David, 139–41, 143–45, 192, 193, 194–95, 200–201, 386n46
Danforth, Joshua N., 77
Davis, Ann Mariah, 25, 26, 130, 153, 376n66
Davis, John W., 343
Degrass, Theodosia, 120
Dickens, Charles, 256–57
Dickinson, James T., 178, 188
Douglas, Stephen, 257, 265
Douglas, William O., 338, 343
Douglass, Frederick, 2, 305–6, 346
Dred Scott case, 229, 257–62, 332
Dwight, Timothy, 103

Eaton, Joseph, 115, 116, 119, 120, 121, 123, 128–29
Elk Falls, Kansas, 236–37, 295, 301, 307–8, 310–13, 324
Ellsworth, Delia, 192
Ellsworth, Oliver, 113–14, 192
Ellsworth, William W.: on American Indian removal schemes, 113; and *Amistad* case, 249–50; as attorney for Crandall, 95, 115, 118–19, 121, 122, 123, 124, 383n44; background

of, 113–14; closing argument in first trial, 125–26, 128; and colonization movement, 249–50; *Crandall v. State* argument, 193–96, 197–98; inability to represent Crandall in second trial, 134; as justice of Connecticut Supreme Court, 260; long-term impact on Fourteenth Amendment, 339; marriage of, 114; power of equal opportunity argument, 340–41; relationship to T. S. Williams, 192
Emancipation Proclamation, 271–72
equality: for blacks, 3, 20, 24, 99, 132, 143, 195, 196, 227; Crandall's pursuit of, 4, 159; in education, 9–10, 16, 26, 29, 66, 87, 108, 127, 140, 167, 195, 335–36, 339–41, 343, 366n68; Garrison's life purpose to promote, 27, 36, 305; for women, 4, 25, 26, 244, 311, 335

Fayerweather, George, 153, 287
Fayerweather, Mary, 298
Fayerweather, Prudence Crandall, 219
Fayerweather, Sarah (née Harris), 219, 287, 296–98. *See also* Harris, Sarah (Mrs. G. Fayerweather)
female antislavery societies, 159–60, 208, 213, 237–42
Fenner, Amy, 160, 162, 296
Fenner, Richard, 51, 52–53, 130, 133, 134, 151, 160, 162
Finney, Charles G., 18, 167, 355n136
Folsom, Mariana T., 311–12
Forsyth, John, 249
Forten, Charlotte, 211, 213
Forten, James, 54, 209, 211, 213, 274, 366n68
Forten, Robert, 274–75
Foster, Lafayette S., 114–15, 116, 381n8
Frankfurter, Felix, 338
Franklin, John Hope, 339, 341
Freedom's Journal, 42, 47

Garnet Books

ABOUT THE AUTHOR

DONALD E. WILLIAMS JR. is president pro tempore of the Connecticut State Senate. He holds a J.D. from Washington and Lee University School of Law and a B.S. in journalism from Syracuse University.

ABOUT THE

DRIFTLESS CONNECTICUT SERIES

The Driftless Connecticut Series is a publication award program established in 2010 to recognize excellent books with a Connecticut focus or written by a Connecticut author. To be eligible, the book must have a Connecticut topic or setting or an author must have been born in Connecticut or have been a legal resident of Connecticut for at least three years.

The Driftless Connecticut Series is funded by the

BEATRICE FOX AUERBACH FOUNDATION FUND

at the Hartford Foundation for Public Giving.

For more information and a complete list of books in the Driftless Connecticut Series, please visit us online at http://www.wesleyan.edu/wespress/driftless.